The History of

The Black Watch

(Royal Highland Regiment) of Canada

Volume III: 1946–2022

The History of

The Black Watch

(Royal Highland Regiment) of Canada

Volume III: 1946–2022

Roman Johann Jarymowycz

Published for
The Royal Highlanders of Canada
by
McGill-Queen's University Press
Montreal & Kingston • London • Chicago

ISBN 978-0-2280-1710-3 (vol. 1, cloth)
ISBN 978-0-2280-1711-0 (vol. 1, ePDF)
ISBN 978-0-2280-1713-4 (vol. 2, cloth)
ISBN 978-0-2280-1714-1 (vol. 2, ePDF)
ISBN 978-0-2280-1716-5 (vol. 3, cloth)
ISBN 978-0-2280-1717-2 (vol. 3, ePDF)
ISBN 978-0-2280-1719-6 (set, cloth)
ISBN 978-0-2280-1720-2 (set, ePDF)

Legal deposit second quarter 2023
Bibliothèque nationale du Québec

Printed in Canada on acid-free paper

Funded by the Government of Canada   Financé par le gouvernement du Canada

Canada Council for the Arts   Conseil des arts du Canada

We acknowledge the support of the Canada Council for the Arts.

Nous remercions le Conseil des arts du Canada de son soutien.

Library and Archives Canada Cataloguing in Publication

Title: The history of the Black Watch (Royal Highland Regiment) of Canada / Roman Johann Jarymowycz.
Other titles: Black Watch (Royal Highland Regiment) of Canada
Names: Jarymowycz, Roman Johann, 1945–2017, author.
Description: Includes bibliographical references and indexes. | Contents: Volume III: 1946–2022.
Identifiers: Canadiana (print) 20220429960 | Canadiana (ebook) 20220429987 |
    ISBN 9780228017196 (set ; cloth) | ISBN 9780228017165 (v. 3 ; cloth) |
    ISBN 9780228017202 (set ; ePDF) | ISBN 9780228017172 (v. 3 ; ePDF)
Subjects: LCSH: Canada. Canadian Army. Black Watch (Royal Highland Regiment) of Canada—History.
Classification: LCC UA602.R6 J37 2023 | DDC 356/.10971—dc23

Book design by Mike Bechthold.

Unless otherwise noted, all images were sourced from the Black Watch Archives.

The Black Watch of Canada welcomes any updates, corrections, or additional contributions to this history. This and other supplementary material may be found at www.blackwatchcanada.com/history Please contact museum@blackwatchcanada.com with your submissions.

CONTENTS

LIST OF APPENDICES | *xiii*

PART V
THE BLACK WATCH OF CANADA AND THE COLD WAR – 1946–1992

CHAPTER 7
1946 –START OF THE COLD WAR | 3

A Single Battalion, Lieutenant Colonels IL Ibbotson, FM Mitchell, and VE Traversy: 1945–49 | 5

Black Watch Associations | 6

Lieutenant Colonel JW Knox and Lord Wavell's Visit – 1948 | 6

Visiting the Imperials in Berlin | 9

The Cold War and New Battalions | 10

Forming Highland Battalions for the Regular Force | 11

Lieutenant Colonel Richard (Dickie) Lewis Rutherford | 13

The 1st Canadian Highland Battalion, 1951 | 14

1 CHB Training with NATO | 16

Lieutenant Colonel H Hugh Alexander Parker OBE | 19

More Regular Battalions: 2 CHB, 1952 | 20

The Laird: Lieutenant Colonel RM Ross, OBE | 21

Conversion at Sea: Becoming The Black Watch – 1953 | 22

Burgeoning Battalions | 24

The Black Watch in Korea, 1953–1954 | 24

Battalion Routines | 26

Lieutenant Colonels Parker and Seamark: From a Pan-Canadian to a Maritime Battalion | 27

The Regiment Rising: Dress and Customs in Three Battalions | 30

Lieutenant Colonel William de Norban Watson DSO MC CD, 2 RHC | *32*

Rocky vs. Bucko | *35*

Lieutenant Colonel JME Clarkson MC CD, 1 RHC 1956 | *36*

Piping for the Queen and President | *37*

Lieutenant Colonel CHE Askwith CD | *37*

Gagetown Garrison Duties | *38*

Bastion of Military Boxing – Sergeant Les Mason, Canadian Champion | *39*

CHAPTER 8

THE THIRD BATTALION RHC IN A NEW ROLE AND "MILITIA" AGAIN | *41*

A New Role for the Reserves and an Old Name Resurrected | *41*

Lieutenant Colonel John Bourne ED CD, 1953–1955 | *42*

Root Root Root For the Home Team – The Regular Battalions | *43*

Royal Performance and Determined Training | *44*

The Blue Balmoral with the Red Hackle | *45*

Two Regimental Greats: Colonel Cantlie and Major General Ross | *46*

Lieutenant Colonel IR McDougall CD, 1955–1958 | *48*

Foreign Visits: Philadelphia RHC and USMC, 1956 | *49*

Memorial Service St Andrew and St Paul, 6 October 1957 | *50*

Lieutenant Colonel WA Wood CD, Claymores and Football: Philadelphia 1958 | *51*

Major Darcy McGovern in Philadelphia: Dirks n' Gavels | *53*

Joining and Serving the Regiment in Montreal – Pre Millennium | *54*

The Subalterns' Inquisition | *56*

The First Colonel of the Regiment: Brigadier KG Blackader CBE DSO MC ED CD | *58*

Brigadier A Hamilton Gault DSO ED CD 1882–1958 | *58*

Dinners and Clubs – 1958 | *59*

Storm Clouds on Horizon: Order-in-Council in 1959, National Survival | *60*

Lieutenant Colonel D'Arcy McGovern 1959–62 – the Last War-Time CO | *62*

How Recruit Company Nearly Started an Indian War | *63*

CHAPTER 9

THE BLACK WATCH IN GAGETOWN AND GERMANY | *65*

The Regular Battalions New Brunswick, New Home – Camp Gagetown 1958 | *65*

Good-bye Bucko; Lieutenant Colonel Askwith | *68*

The Golden Era: The Canadians in Europe | *69*

Lieutenant Colonel DS MacLennan, CO 1 RHC, 1959 | *70*

The Royal Highlanders in Deutschland, 1959–1965 | *73*

The Black Watch Military Band 1961 | *74*

Lieutenant Colonels Bill Leonard and Bill Teed – 1960–63 | *75*

Empire Hockey | *77*

Montreal: The Reunion Dinner | *78*

Preparing for the Royal Presentation of Colours | 79

The Regimental Centennial | 82

The Queen Mother, 8 June 1962 | 83

The Parade – Molson Stadium | 84

The Reunion Dinner, 17 November 1962 | 86

Hogmanay, 1963 and Foreign Visits | 88

Regimental Items: Old RSMs, New Colonels, 1963 | 90

CHAPTER 10

A NEW ARMY, A NEW MILITIA | 93

The Suttie Commission 1964 | 93

Lieutenant Colonel John Wemyss Sharp CD | 94

Lieutenant Colonel TE Price, 3 RHC 1965–67 | 94

Terrorism in Montreal: FLQ attacks on the City – 1963 | 97

The Queen Mother's Photograph: Pte Conway vs. RHQ | 98

The Exodus of Senior NCOs | 99

University COTC Contingents | 100

The Auld Battalions | 101

Mobile Command | 102

Regimental Traditions – The St Andrew's Ball | 103

Black Watch at Harvard: The Hasty Pudding Club Commemorate Robert Sherwood | 104

After the Centennial: Lieutenant Colonel JIB Macfarlane Takes Over 3 RHC 17 October 1967 | 105

Pipe Major William John (Willie) Hannah, 1967 | 106

The Black Watch Cadet Corps, 1967 | 106

Militia Fights for Survival 1968–69 | 107

CHAPTER 11

THE REGULAR BLACK WATCH – GLOBAL DEPLOYMENTS | 109

Lieutenant Colonel GH Sellar, 1 RHC 1963–1966 | 109

Mechanized Infantry – 1 RHC | 110

The Army Boxing Title; Shooting and Hockey Laurels | 111

Finnie Retires; 1 RHC Winter Training 1965–66 | 112

ACE Mobile Force – NATO in Norway 1966 | 113

Agent Orange | 114

A Wicked Assault on Pipers, 1966 | 115

4 CIBG in NATO: a Modern, Nuclear Army | 116

Lieutenant Colonel (Lieutenant General) DA McAlpine, Germany 1963–65: *Osae Waza* | 116

The Wakefield Sword | 118

Regimental Art: *Sanctuary Wood* then, Aphrodite | 119

Lieutenant Colonel HJ Harkes MC CD, 2 RHC 1966–1968 | 121

CWO Don Reekie: Archetypal Regimental Sergeant Major 1966–1970 | 122

Lieutenant Colonel WJ Newlands, CD 1 RHC 1966 | *123*

The Black Watch and the Canadian Centennial, 1967 | *124*

The Canadian Centennial Tattoo: Major (Colonel) IS Fraser ONS OMM CD | *124*

Braw Hard Workin' Hairy-legged Hielan' Men | *125*

Three Battalions together: The Royal Parade, 12 July 1967 | *127*

A Daunting Future: Unification and Integration | *128*

Centennial Losses: Blackader, Motzfeldt, Worthington | 130

1 RHC: Lieutenant Colonel Newlands CD to Lieutenant Colonel GS Morrison CD, 1968 | *130*

2 RHC: Lieutenant Colonel HJ Harkes MC CD to Lieutenant Colonel WB MacLeod CD, 1968 | *131*

Black Watch Depot – The Last Graduating Class 1968 | *132*

Colonel John G Bourne, New Colonel of the Regiment | *133*

The Minister of Defence Attends the Annual Reunion Dinner, 2 November 1968 | *133*

25th Anniversary of Verrières Ridge 1969 | *135*

1969 – Lance Sergeant Herman Good VC | *136*

A Pan-Canadian Regiment – Black Watch Demographics | *136*

"Drastic changes" – 19 September 1969 | *138*

Apocalypse Now: Announcement of Disbandment | *140*

A Most Melancholy Reunion Dinner, 8 November 1969 | *141*

Political Surprise: The St Andrew's Ball 1969 | *142*

The Final Year in Gagetown | *142*

Cyprus. 2 RHC, UN Duty, spring 1970 | *143*

CFB Gagetown: The Final Parade, 6 June 1970 | *145*

Montreal: Laying-Up The Colours, 14 June 1970 | *146*

Epilogue | *147*

CHAPTER 12

THE POST-APOCALYPSE BLACK WATCH – A REGIMENT OF ONE BATTALION | *149*

Old Soldiers – The Black Watch Veterans' Reunions | *149*

Soldiering On into the 1970s | *151*

Lieutenant Colonel SF Angus – October 1970 | *154*

Alone, Yet Not alone – RHC 1970–1975 | *155*

Captain Alexei Malashenko | *156*

FLQ Terrorists: "The October Crisis" 1970 | *156*

Regimental Duty 1970 | *159*

Summer Student Training Programme, 1969–72 | *160*

Sergeant Bill Carlisle | *160*

A Regimental Name and Historic Crosses, 1971 | *161*

Lieutenant Colonel LN Ferdon CD, 1972 | *161*

The Last Black Watch Serving General, 1965–2015 | *163*

Montreal Marches On ... | *164*

Training in 1973: Exercise *Black Hussar* | *165*

Presentation of The Queen's Colour, June 1974 | *165*
Lieutenant Colonel W Sewell CD, 1974–77 | *167*
Padres Stephen Hayes and WR Russell | *168*
Carpentry and Exotic Travel | *170*
Getting with the Times: Peace Keeping | *170*
Tradition vs. the Modern Army: the First BW Female Officer | *171*
Planning for the Future 1975–77 | *173*
Lieutenant Colonel GD Robertson CD PhD | *174*
The General Waters Trophy 1978–79 | *175*

CHAPTER 13
TO THE END OF THE COLD WAR | *179*

Lieutenant Colonel Harold Klepak CD PhD, 1980–83 | *179*
Highland Panzer-Grenadiers – the *Grizzly* AVGP | *182*
Highland Winter 1982 | *183*
Colonel WSM MacTier MC | *184*
Ex Quick Sword – TEWT Advance and Quick Attack, 16 April 1983 | *185*
Lieutenant Colonel John Charles Stothers CD | *185*
Captain DG Fraser MD | *186*
Recruiting and Retention | *187*
Overseas Visits | *188*
Lieutenant Colonel VG Chartier OMM CD | *189*
Black Watch Women, 1971–1987 | *191*
Black Watch – Gender-Free, 1987–1991 | *192*
Veterans on Parade: Refused | *193*
HM Queen Elizabeth, Colonel-in-Chief – The Last Great Parade | *194*
The Regimental Dinner | *196*
Church Service, Sunday 7 June 1987 | *197*
Awards: The Proven Cup | *198*
1987 – John Bourne Retires as Honorary Colonel | *198*
Lieutenant Colonel DF O'Connor CD 1989–1993 | *200*
The Purple Network | *203*
The Oka Crisis and Cinematic History 1990 | *202*
The Freedom of the City of Montreal, World Scottish Festival, 1992 | *204*
Relationships with District HQ and Succession | *206*

NOTES TO PART V | *209*

PART V – ILLUSTRATIONS | *233*

CHAPTER 14

ENDING THE CENTURY | 273

Lieutenant Colonel IM McCulloch CD, 1993–96: Bosnia and Archives | 273
His Militia Moment | 275
The 1993 Pipe Band Calamity | 276
Corporal Kieran Boyle and the Case of the Missing Pipes | 277
Black Watch Archives | 278
Black Watch in Bosnia, 1993 | 280
Colonel Tom Price | 283
Lieutenant Colonel GT Lusk CD, 1996–2000: At the Edge | 283
Black Watch Ordered Disbanded, August 1996 | 285
Rescinded | 286
With the Imperials in Ticonderoga, 1997 | 288
Gracious in Tough Times: The Reunion Dinner, 1 November 1997 | 289
Black Watch Veterans Recognized | 290
Khaki Pattern Tam Adopted | 290
Valcartier 1998 – Unit Viability Assessment, Tactical Evaluation | 290
Operation Recuperation: The Ice Storm 1998 | 291
Fort Drum – 1998 | 293
The Dubuc Trophy, February 1999 | 294
St Jean Baptiste Parade 24 June 1999 | 294
Lusk's Third Freedom: 11 September 1999 Verdun | 295

CHAPTER 15

THE HIGHLAND MILLENNIUM | 297

Lieutenant Colonel BD Bolton MMM CD, 2000–2003: The Piper as *Laird* | 297
Honorary Colonel Lieutenant General McAlpine, 2000 | 300
The Canadian Red Hackle Magazine, 2000 | 300
Queen Elizabeth, The Queen Mother, 4 August 1900 – 30 March 2002 | 301
Training for the Taliban via the Dubuc Trophy | 302
The Changing Pages of RHC history – Colonel John G Bourne CVO ED CD, 1918–2002 | 304
Lieutenant Colonel J Potter MC, 2003: *Desert Storm* dans *Montréal* | 305
The Piper Redux: Lieutenant Colonel BD Bolton MMM CD, 2003–2005 | 306
New Reserve Units: PSYOPS | 307
Backhanded Thanks … | 307
The Black Watch Pipes and Drums – Oldest in North America | 309
The Black Watch School of Piping and Drumming | 309
Black Watch Stalwarts – *Slainte deagh* | 310

Forming the Future: The Cadet Corps 1953–2013 | *312*

Lieutenant Colonel TEC MacKay CD, 2005–2009 | *314*

Adjutants at Work: Captains Radman and Farnham | *315*

Running the Regiment in Peace and War: *parades dangereux* | *316*

HRH Prince Charles Presents Colours to The Black Watch, 9–11 November 2009 | *319*

CHAPTER 16

REGIMENTAL BUSINESS | *323*

Associations of The Black Watch | *323*

A National Historic Site, Regimental Museum, et al | *325*

Anniversary Highland Dinners | *327*

The Honorary Colonel's Dining-In 2012: The American Ambassador | *328*

Atlantic Personae | *329*

Reunions at Home and France | *329*

Battalion Training and Competitions 2011 to 2013 | *330*

Chums with the 111th US Regiment | *332*

The March and Shoot Hat-Trick | *333*

CWO Mike Kelly MMM CD, the First Army Reserve Chief Warrant Officer | *335*

Major Mike Walker | *336*

CHAPTER 17

THE BLACK WATCH AT WAR AND BEYOND, 2002–2022 | *337*

Part 1: The Home Front | *337*

Part 2: Outside the Wire – Fire Fights and Air Strikes | *340*

Corporal JP Warren KIA, July 2006 | *342*

Staff Officers, Afghanistan | *343*

Colonels at the Front | *344*

Comrades in Arms: RHC and 3 SCOTS – *Ceud mìle fàilte* | *345*

Ladies From Hell – the nom de guerre made real | *348*

New Battle Honour "Afghanistan" – 9 May 2014 | *350*

Lieutenant Colonel Bruno Plourde CD – The Regular Reservist, 2009–2013 | *351*

The Regular Force Support Staff in the Millennium Watch | *353*

Honorary Colonel Lieutenant General Duncan McAlpine 1922–2010 | *354*

Farewell to a Wartime Padre: Captain, the Rev RR Topping, PhD | *355*

Millennium RSMs | *356*

Remembrance and Honour | *357*

Properly Dressed On Parade: The Regimental Uniform | *358*

Trooping The Colour, Fletcher's Field 2012 | *360*

Châteauguay – Two Hundred Year Battle Honour | *362*

Honouring Their Own: The Regimental Boards | *362*

Lieutenant Colonel Christopher Phare CD, 2013–2016 | *363*

HIGHLAND CODA | *365*

EPILOGUE, 2013–2022 | *367*

Lieutenant Colonel Christopher Phare, CD | *368*
Lieutenant Colonel Thomas MacKay, CD | *371*
OP LENTUS, 2017 | *373*
Lieutenant Colonel Bruno Plourde, CD | *375*
The Pipes and Drums 2018–19: Mons, Normandy, and Edinburgh | *377*
OP LASER | *379*
Lieutenant Colonel Francis Roy, CD – A New Decade, A New Challenge | *382*

NOTES TO PART VI | *385*

PART VI – ILLUSTRATIONS | *405*

APPENDICES | *463*
INDEX | *487*

APPENDICES

Appendix A – Black Watch Regimental Appointments 1950–2022 | *463*

Appendix B – The Black Watch Command List –1945–2022 | *465*

Appendix C – Regimental Bagpipe Tunes | *469*

Appendix D – Final Parade: Officers of The Black Watch (RHR) of Canada, Base Gagetown –1 April 1970 | *471*

Appendix E – 3 Scots, Affiliations and Cadet Corps | *473*

Appendix F – Dates for Regimental Parades, Memorials, Annual Meetings and Social Occasions | *475*

Appendix G – The Captain George Fraser Dinner | *477*

Appendix H – Presentation of New Colours Parade 2009 | *479*

Appendix I – 3 RHC Strength 1955–2014 – As per Annual Hist Reports | *481*

ROMAN JOHANN JARYMOWYCZ OMM, CD, PhD (1945–2017) was a decorated Canadian soldier–scholar, military historian, mentor and educator. An acclaimed expert on the historical evolution of the operational art, throughout his long career he was a prolific author of many well-received publications, among them, *Cavalry from Hoof to Track, The Royal Montreal Regiment: 1945–1989*, and *Tank Tactics from Normandy to Lorraine*, for which he received the United States Army History Foundation Award for distinguished writing and research. During his lifetime he was a frequent and passionate contributor to CBC documentaries helping Canadians understand their military history. An eminent graduate of Montreal's Loyola College and McGill University, the author often lectured at the Royal Military College of Canada. He ended his military career as the Dean of the Canadian Army's Militia Staff Course in Kingston, Ontario. A highly respected former commanding officer of the Royal Canadian Hussars in Montreal, he lived his regiment's motto: *Non nobis sed patriae* (not for ourselves, but for our country). It is indeed unfortunate that the author did not live to see the publication of this history which he considered his best work.

Part V

The Black Watch of Canada
and The Cold War
1946–1992

Chapter 7

1946 –Start of the Cold War

The Black Watch had begun the Second World War by showing considerable initiative, determined to do all the right things – especially lessons learned in battle by its Great War battalions. Unfortunately, they proved to be all the wrong things as far as Army Headquarters was concerned. Starting its own training battalion and creating the Provisional Officers Training School (POTS) was interpreted as the Regiment's attempt to go it alone. More efficient than the slow-moving and disorganized District HQ, it gave the Regiment a reputation for being "difficult" – a reputation that dogged it throughout the war. Their independent style and insistence on doing things "their way" was not appreciated as the apparel of pride, but seen as naked elitism. After a solid start in England, 1 RHC went through a rough patch. After Blackader, three Black Watch COs came and went. When Stuart Cantlie was brought back from a senior post at headquarters to lead the Regiment into Normandy, D Day was only six months away. Despite this, the appointments of Cantlie and a new RSM proved effective. The battalion that arrived in France in July 1944 was a splendid facsimile of its predecessors. Its first major battle, Operation *Atlantic,* was highlighted by a determined counterattack against the 1st *SS Leibstandarte Adolf Hitler* – simply the best panzer division in the Third Reich. That action not only saved the brigade from being overrun, but possibly the entire 2nd Canadian Division. Regrettably, this proved the pinnacle of Black Watch military success in Europe. The Regiment was virtually annihilated not once, but twice, atop Verrières Ridge in July and August, and then ground down by bitter, expensive victories during a harsh wet winter in the

Scheldt and Holland. Led by a succession of commanding officers (six in the period between July 1944 and April 1945), relations between the Regiment and its Brigadier continued to sour, forcing regimental headquarters in Montreal to take the unusual step of dispatching a delegation of Great War generals to Ottawa to seek answers. In short, the Second World War was less than the successful crusade envisioned by the Black Watch. Once again, the Regiment won international acclaim, but it was at a disastrous cost and with sour results. The debacle that was Verrières Ridge rocked The Black Watch community in Montreal and resulted in a Cabinet inquiry. Compelled to wrest acre and polder from Normandy to Holland and Germany, the Regiment was only too glad to see the end of this war. Unhappily, there was no *Hundred Days* to celebrate and no string of VCs to reward their sacrifice. It was a relieved Black Watch that returned to Bleury Street, anxious to put the painful memories of the Second World War behind it.

The city was covered in snow when they arrived home on 21 November 1945. The day turned into a greater blizzard as tons of shredded paper and ticker tape rained down on the parade as it marched along St. James to Craig Street and then into the great Drill Hall, where their families waited. They were led by Val Traversy, the youngest of the nine commanding officers, who had led the Regiment during the war. He was still in his twenties.[1] Directly the parade ended, Pipe Major E "Torchy" Peden approached the CO: "Permission to go home sir." "But of course Pipe Major!" replied Traversy, thinking Verdun. Peden hailed from Vancouver. He left Montreal and was never seen again; his kit was returned by mail.[2]

Still under the rule of Colonel Hutchison, the Black Watch found itself in what was dubbed "the atomic age." The colonel was looking forward to retirement. He had recently (16 June 1945) appointed two new commanders for the 2nd and 3rd (Reserve) Battalions of the Black Watch at a ceremony held on the McGill campus. Major WW Ogilvie, a manufacturer and recent veteran of Italy, replaced Lieutenant Colonel HA Johnston DSO MC, a prominent stockbroker, as CO 2nd Battalion RHC; Major DCA McEachran, also a stockbroker and past member of the 13th Bn CEF during the Great War, took over command of 3rd (Reserve) Bn RHC from Lieutenant Colonel WE Macfarlane MC and Bar. Macfarlane, who had been commissioned in the field after Ypres, completed the war surviving four wounds. He was an investment banker and, like Johnston, a senior organizer of successive Victory Loan campaigns. In theory, Hutchison had an embarrassment of riches with many qualified senior officers to choose from as the war ended, as most were decorated veterans. Yet, few were anxious to serve in the Reserve Army. The war took its toll; veterans were weary and, save for the gladness of a clan gathering, reserve camps and armoury training had little attraction. At the annual reunion dinner held 8 December 1945, the guests of honour were the eleven regimental officers who commanded field units during the war, only nine of whom could attend.

Colonel PP Hutchison then handed over command to Colonel Ivan Leonard Ibbotson, a stockbroker. His father had commanded the 5th Royal Scots at the turn of the century (1897–1901); his Regimental Sergeant Major was WO1 E Bleasdale. Ibbotson served the Regiment in both World Wars, most recently as second-in-command for 1 RHC in England. He had been appointed brigade major in 1941 and then returned to Canada in 1941 to perform senior staff appointments in NDHQ Ottawa, where he was promoted lieutenant colonel.

A Single Battalion, Lieutenant Colonels IL Ibbotson, FM Mitchell, and VE Traversy: 1945–49

During the immediate post-war period, the Reserve Army was reorganized by zealous bureaucrats. There was even a scheme to convert one of the Black Watch Reserve battalions into an anti-aircraft unit! The Regiment took pains to explain they were *Highland infantry* and would find it somewhat difficult to train two totally different types of formations. The Area Headquarters initially conceded, but followed up by disbanding regimental headquarters and reducing its two battalions, thus ending a very short period in command for the recently appointed battalion commanders. On 1 April 1946, the redesignated The Black Watch (RHR) of Canada, became a single battalion in the newly created 9th Infantry Brigade of the Reserve Army and subsequently commanded by a regimental officer, Brigadier James Buchanan Weir, who had served with 1 RHC and was then transferred to command the Cape Breton Highlanders during the war.

Lieutenant Colonel Ibbotson served for a year, retiring in March 1946. He was succeeded by Frank Mitchell, whose appointment was both a recognition and quiet statement to the CMHQ generals who had cut short his field command. He was supported by WO1 Ralph Diplock MBE, who wore a chest-full of medals that were mostly earned in Italy. Like his predecessor, Mitchell served twelve months, and it was left to Val Traversy, the last wartime CO of 1 RHC, to bring the Watch into what was eventually termed "the Cold War." The battalion was greatly reduced in strength. Traversy paraded thirty officers, a distinct change from the seventy who had worked for Paul Hutchison in the wartime armoury. His Regimental Sergeant Major was WO1 AF Turnbull DCM, who had taken over from Leitch in Europe in April 1945, and had now returned to help his old battlefield commander. At the 1947 regimental Church Parade, held in June, the Colours of the disbanded 2nd Battalion were carried one last time. Its Honorary Lieutenant Colonel, Major General Eric McCuaig, took the salute. The Reserve Battalion continued to parade twice weekly, actively recruiting from Verdun and Montreal. Exercises were held in farm areas around Montreal: Shawbridge, St-Bruno, St-Jérôme and Ste-Adèle. Ski exercises were held in winter. The Black Watch was the first unit in Eastern Canada to renew summer camp training[3]; two hundred went to Camp Farnham in July 1947. The following year, the camp was held at Valcartier, where it remained for the next decade.

Black Watch Associations

After the war, the attendance at Black Watch messes and clubs exploded. The Montreal armoury's messes were packed every evening with veterans. The Toronto Black Watch Association (TBWA) enjoyed a spectacular success that made it the equal of its Montreal cousin. The origins of the TBWA had always made it unique and proudly independent. It originated as an annex to the original association, an imperial outfit begun by Black Watch members who had retired to Canada. Exclusively British, it eventually morphed into the Toronto collegium, a stand-alone comrades' club that is mistakenly referred to as the "Toronto Branch" – it was not. The TBWA was incorporated on 26 December 1934, though its first meeting was in 1929.[4] By 1950, it boasted two clubs in downtown Toronto, overflowing with thirsty, demob'd soldiers, forever Highlanders and Black Watch, but living away from Montreal. It was a testament to the vast numbers recruited through Bleury Street. Initially, the Regiment was permitted two active battalions, but the 2nd RHC battalion was stood down in 1943; its cadre was sent to reinforce battalions in Italy, which was a particularly unfair and unnecessary decision by Ottawa.

After the Second World War, the rules changed: associate memberships were available to servicemen and their friends who wanted to access the clubhouses on Wellington and York Street in Toronto. Full acceptance came after 1953, with the return of the Korean battalion and European veterans from the 27th Infantry Brigade.

Lieutenant Colonel JW Knox and Lord Wavell's Visit – 1948

It was just like coming home, sir.

L/Corporal AW Pugh, recounting the visit to the
allied regiment in Berlin, 5 October 1950

The well-established traditions of the Regiment were dutifully maintained: the reunion dinner, the St Andrew's Ball, and the Burns' Supper. On 11 March 1949, a special dinner was held for the officers of the 42nd RHC Bn CEF thirty years after their return from the Great War. Colonel George Cantlie DSO presided. It was a wonderful evening, and ended with everyone playing the old battalion's favourite trench game, *Chase the Ace*: "To the delight of everyone, on this occasion, Major Walter Molson (who usually won) was finally eliminated by the Colonel himself."[5] With his greatcoat buttoned against the winter snowfall, a beaming Cantlie disappeared into the darkness of Bleury, his officers lining the great staircase bidding him goodnight.

Lieutenant Colonel James W Knox MBE ED CD, who had succeeded Val Traversy as CO in 1949, conducted a particularly festive reunion dinner on 4 November 1949. Lord Wavell, the Colonel of the Imperial Regiment, was the guest of honour. He had come to open the Memorial Museum, which was the Regiment's tribute to all who had served the Canadian Black Watch. "The history, the valour, the traditions of our Regiment and particularly the memory of our fallen soldiers were the sentiments in the minds of Colonel Paul P Hutchison and Lieutenant Colonel VE Traversy when, in 1949, they proposed the founding of our Regimental Museum and Archives."[6] This major post-war project was intended to organize and display the Regiment's considerable collection of war souvenirs and artifacts, which had been "scattered about the armoury but, for the most part, housed in display cabinets in the officers' mess where they were not readily available to the other ranks and their friends."[7] Major General Eric McCuaig DSO was head of the fundraising committee. The new rooms, designed by Mr Leslie Coppold ARCA, occupied what had once been the Quartermaster stores. The Field Marshal keenly examined each artifact. He was especially taken with the Great War section. Most of the day was spent with Brigadier Hamilton Gault and Sir Montagu Allan, the Honorary Colonel, who was then ninety years of age. When, on 1 December 1947, Her Majesty Queen Elizabeth was officially named Colonel-in-Chief of the Canadian Black Watch, the Regiment commemorated the occasion with an inscribed jewel case. This was accepted by Lord Wavell to be presented on the Regiment's behalf immediately following his stay in Montreal.

Besides Lord Wavell, another esteemed guest was Robert E Sherwood, the noted playwright and close advisor to President Roosevelt. Sherwood had served as a private in the 42nd Battalion CEF. When Lord Wavell met Robert Sherwood, he quoted without hesitation a line from one of his plays, to which the winner of four Pulitzer Prizes responded by quoting from the Field Marshal's *Other Men's Flowers*.[8] Wavell's visit was marked throughout the City by a series of receptions that included the McGill Convocation. The University bestowed upon him an honorary doctorate of letters. As the colourful hood was placed over on the Field Marshal's head, the regimental band and the pipes and drums broke into *Heilin' Laddie*. Wavell visited local military hospitals endeavouring to meet as many veterans as he could. He was robust and full of life. It was a complete shock to the Regiment to learn of his death the following May.

The new year proved a bleak period for the Regiment. A fire in the armoury broke out on 4 March 1950 and caused considerable damage to the second floor, particularly the Officers' Mess and its staircase. The great wooden plaques commemorating the CEF Battalions' Battle Honours were badly scorched and had to be replaced. Lamentably, the 1st Battalion Colours, all the pipe banners and many rare prints and paintings were completely destroyed.[9] One large painting, depicting 1 RHC attacking May-sur-Orne on 25 July 1944, had been presented by the Molson family. It was part of a series of commissions depicting actions by Montreal's fighting units in the war presented by the Molsons to each City regiment and squadron. Fortunately, the Museum was spared. Lieutenant Colonel Knox, supported by Lieutenant Colonel Traversy, directed the rescue and safe storage of regimental artifacts and records. The front of the building was in sorry shape; the occasion was made even more desolate as the regimental flag was lowered to half-mast in memory of Lord Wavell. Undaunted, rapid repairs were organized and the Regiment soon returned to its own home. A dance celebrating the event was held.

Montreal had changed from pre-war years but milk, bread and ice were still delivered by horse. Every soldier in the Black Watch grew up watching the *JJ Joubert* or *Borden* milk wagon, with its glassed front to shield the driver from blowing snow. His dutiful steed reminded some of a Highland soldier: dour and slightly shabby, plodding along through drifts, slush, and mud. The nag stopped at each door or stairway, waiting while the driver-milkman delivered clinking bottles. Most Canadian cities had four seasons; Montreal had five: 'Horse Manure Season'. It began around St Patrick's Day and was the time of year when a winter's worth of horse leavings cascaded downhill with the Spring Melt. The children were not allowed to play outside while it lasted! Meanwhile, the principal arteries were clogged with vehicles. Behemoth tram cars still rolled down Bleury, St Catherine and Sherbrooke Streets – their steel rails ready to trip the unwary, their iron wheels a clattering danger, their bells clanging as they passed the armoury gates, and their trolley poles giving off sparks as they crossed the main intersections.

During the repairs to the armoury, the Victoria Rifles, old friends of the Regiment, offered the use of their armoury for continued training. For the city regiments, the sergeants' and officers' messes were social centres. When soldiers and officers got together, discussions seldom dealt with tactics or modern doctrine. Nevertheless, time-honoured soldierly skills were keenly pursued. Sergeant Major Charles Foam, continuing a family tradition, helped the regimental rifle team win four major trophies at the Province of Quebec Rifle Association Matches in 1950. His brother Victor, also a famed marksman, led D Company up Verrières Ridge in July 1944. During the 1950 competitions, Charles Foam won the Transvaal Cup, tied for first place for the Governor General's Medal, and won (yet again) a place on the 1952 Bisley Team. At the matches, Sergeant A Parnell, who represented Canada on the Bisley Team on a number of occasions:

> ...displayed the type of sportsmanship for which we like to think the regiment is well known. In shooting for the Governor General's Bronze Medal, having tied with another competitor, [Parnell] withdrew from the competition since he won this medal several times before whereas his opponent had yet to win it for the first time.[10]

Visiting the Imperials in Berlin

There is no task so hard, so exacting, as that of a good infantry soldier.

General Sir Neil Ritchie KCB KBE DSO MC at the
Bleury Street Armoury, November 1950

Knox and Traversy trekked to Europe. They were invited to Balmoral for luncheon with the Queen and then hopped the Channel to visit the 1st Battalion of the allied regiment, commanded by Lieutenant Colonel BE Fergusson DSO, which was garrisoned in Berlin. There was a rousing dinner with speeches acknowledging, "The two regiments were married." The next day, they toured Berlin and exchanged parchment scrolls containing a challenge to a cricket game and a baseball match: "the idea was that at least one team knew the rules of each game." Colonel Knox then presented the *Fergusson-Knox Trophy*: "a remarkable piece of tin-plate and cutlery designed to contain an everlasting supply of liquor – an ingenious quick-release device via a rubber pipe attached to the bottom. The mechanics were simple – high pressure through gravity."[11] It was well tested.

In the fall, the Bleury Street armoury was finally refurbished. The battle honour plaques of the 13th, 42nd and 73rd Battalions were replaced. New additions included the display of two large wooden crosses, which had marked graves of the 13th at Vimy Ridge and Hill 70. To celebrate the Bleury resurrection, Knox decided to hold a gala regimental function – six hundred attended. This was followed by a most pleasant visit by General Sir Neil Ritchie (his first visit as Colonel of the Imperial Regiment) on his way to Washington where he was chairman of the British Joint Services Mission. During the Reunion Dinner, an American friend, Mr C Kennedy Allan from Philadelphia, presented the new museum with a splendid gift – a large painting depicting the Imperial 42nd Regiment at the Battle of Bushy Run in 1763 entitled, 'The Road to Pittsburgh'. The work commemorated the occasion when the Scots broke through French and Indian rearguards and relieved the besieged Fort Pitt (originally Fort Duquesne, later, Pittsburgh). The rescued American unit became the US 111th Infantry Regiment. They never forgot the Black Watch; the Philadelphia-based unit developed a strong proxy relationship with the Montreal Watch which continues into the millennium.[12]

The Cold War and New Battalions

With the end of the Second World War, the Russians, staunch allies against Nazi Germany, reverted to Bolshevik aims and styles. The Allied powers took over four occupation zones: American, British, French and Soviet; but a chill soon fell on their relations. The Soviets blocked access to their sector (officially the German Democratic Republic, but informally known as *East* Germany) effectively dividing the country and eventually the whole of Europe. Churchill declared dramatically: "An iron curtain has descended across the continent." It was a dark time, quashing the fervent hopes for a lasting peace after a long and costly war. Europe was transformed into an armed camp. The period became known as the "Cold War" and featured a grim line of defence drawn across Europe where great armies faced each other in menacing postures. The Allies simply never went home. Brigades and divisions rotated back and forth, and the army of occupation became the garrison for a new anti-Soviet military alliance named the *North Atlantic Treaty Organization* (NATO). The western powers, led by the USA, were active participants, including Canada, which contributed an infantry division with one brigade stationed in Central Europe and two earmarked in Canada.

Western concern was fostered by two realities: 1) By 1950, Russia had acquired a nuclear arsenal; and 2) had orchestrated a series of communist takeovers in previously 'pro-western' states. While this occurred throughout the globe, the situation was made more threatening in the Far East by the emergence of China as a revolutionary Marxist state. "The sleeping giant has awakened," Western newspapers announced. China's appearance as an anti-western state was accompanied by its instigation of Communist North Korea's policy of aggression. The former Japanese satellite was divided into north and south by US and Russian occupation troops. The Russians left in 1948. Tensions escalated. In June 1950, North Korean troops, equipped with Russian arms and supported by China, invaded South Korea, overran border troops and nearly destroyed the entire US-South Korean force on the peninsula. When the Soviet Union boycotted the United Nations Security Council, the United States seized the opportunity to pass a resolution authorizing military intervention. An American-led UN force under General Douglas MacArthur launched a bold counterattack and appeared about to vanquish the North Korean armies. UN troops reached the Yalu River, China's border, which prompted further escalation. Chinese Armies joined the fighting in October 1950 and rudely shoved UN forces back to the 38th parallel. Korea was the first hot confrontation of the Cold War.

The United Nations sanctioned a peacekeeping force comprising US, British, French, and Canadian troops to assist the South Korean government in re-establishing its border. Although sixteen nations joined the UN action, 88 percent of the troops were American. Canada sent the third largest contingent.[13] Less than six years after a long and costly war, unexpectedly, Canadian troops were again going into action. The fact that the Soviet Union was a staunch ally of Red China was a matter of great concern in Europe and in North America. There was a real possibility that Russian forces might enter a war fought near Soviet borders and engage American-led troops. This might spark conflict in Europe, perhaps even North America. The spectre of nuclear warfare dominated the Cold War Period. Jet bombers and intercontinental missiles became available as strategic weapons. Canadian citizens were suddenly very much on a front line from which no one was safe as vast oceans could no longer offer protection from European or Asian nuclear attack. Further, there remained painful memories of appeasement to Hitler in the 1930s.

Forming Highland Battalions for the Regular Force

I asked if I could join up. A smiling lieutenant was at the recruiting desk when the time came for me to put my name on that important dotted line. He was very pleasant and called me "mister" when I entered, but that salutation was dropped when I applied my signature to the paper [and] for the rest of my army life.

Corporal Bud Pauls[14]

The post-war Canadian Army was a much reduced force – a shadow of the half-million-man army that fought the Second World War. It consisted of one active brigade, grouping the 'original' Permanent Force infantry: a battalion each of The Royal Canadian Regiment (RCR), Princess Patricia's Canadian Light infantry (PPCLI) and the Royal 22e Régiment (R22eR). Its tasks were to defend Canada and to train the Reserves. However, by 1951, Canada committed two complete brigades to foreign deployments: the 25th Canadian Infantry Brigade deployed to Korea and, in April of the same year, a second brigade to the defence of Europe.[15] Minister of Defence Brooke Claxton announced, "a new formation, to be known as the 27th Canadian Infantry Brigade, will be recruited around the framework of some of our famous Militia units."[16]

This proved difficult: Korea was not a popular war. Cold War recruiting was stunted. Reserve units grouped aging Second World War veterans and very young inexperienced students. No regiment, not even the Montreal Black Watch, could raise a complete volunteer battalion. Despite the nuclear threat, garrison duty in Europe and UN 'Police' action in Korea had little cachet in a North America where there was plenty of work in a booming post-war economy.

As stated, two brigades were required: one in Germany (the 27th, in NATO) and a second destined for Korea (the 25th Brigade). The intention was to send the latter brigade to Europe as reinforcements and augmentees to 'top-up' the NATO brigade once the Korean War came to an end. However, there were legal implications. The CASF soldiers had signed on "for the duration" only and were thus ineligible for general service. Lieutenant General Guy Simonds, the new CGS, decided to use the Reserve Army to make up the 27th Brigade. The difficulty was that none of its units could provide sufficient soldiers prepared to form complete individual battalions for a proper overseas brigade. Simonds proposed an interim solution: composite infantry, rifle and Highland battalions from fifteen Reserve units. It was a bit of a smorgasbord. The men still bore the titles and badges of their parent regiments, making it difficult for the troops to develop a sense of loyalty to these ad-hoc battalions.

The initial three composite battalions were: 1st Canadian Highland Battalion (1 CHB); 1st Canadian Rifle Battalion and 1st Canadian Infantry Battalion, each of four rifle companies and a support company. Designated Reserve battalions were tasked to recruit and train a single company. The Black Watch immediately formed its company under Major Allan Paterson Boswell, who had been Knox's second-in-command. He was the manager of the Black Horse Brewery in Montreal (originally the Boswell family business) but recently bought by Dawes Brewery. An RMC and a BCS graduate who had served the Regiment in Europe and India during the war, Boswell saw action in Burma, where he commanded an infantry company on secondment to The Lincolnshire Regiment. His hurriedly assembled command was ready by 20 May and marched in the annual church parade where Brigadier Blackader presented Boswell a battle pennant to fly at his headquarters. "Our training was carried out in the armouries and the Greater Montreal areas with field training on Mount Royal, athletics at the YMCA and range [musketry] work at the Mount Bruno ranges ... the company strength was only 67, including just one officer – the Company Commander."[17]

They were a tough street-wise bunch, born and bred in Montreal and Verdun, most arriving with nicknames. They were augmented and embellished in the Highland Battalion by a caboodle of monikers from across Canada: *Hoodlum* MacLean (more commonly called *Hooch*) came from Cape Breton; Aloysius "Wish" Frampton from Newfoundland; Stan "Fender Bender" Bush; Harry "Stone Blind" Stonewall, "Beekie" Marshall and "Pull-Through" Hamilton (the *pull-through* was a rifle cleaning cord and brush).[18] The RQMS recalled one middle-aged soldier who could neither read nor write. He carried a folded paper with his signature inscribed and would copy it carefully when he was required to endorse documents. After receiving his equipment for Germany, he was ordered to sign. He balked, searching his pockets. The new supply tech grew impatient: "Private, I ordered you to sign for your kit!" The soldier replied angrily: "I can't. I left my name in my other pants!"

The company sergeant major was WO II Frost DCM. Before the company left Montreal, it was inspected twice on 11 June by General Sir Neil Ritchie and, towards the end of the month, by Major General ROG Morton, DOC of the Montreal garrison. They went off to become part of 1 CHB.

Lieutenant Colonel Richard (Dickie) Lewis Rutherford

He was wounded while leading his company in the final assault on the town.[19]

Before we consider the formation of the 1st Canadian Highland Battalion in May 1951, some account must be given of its Commanding Officer, Lieutenant Colonel Richard Rutherford OBE from the Queen's Own Camerons of Winnipeg. Colonel Rutherford was an experienced officer and would become the first post-war Black Watch commander in the Regular army. He was not unfamiliar with the Royal Highlanders. As a major in the Camerons, he was wounded while leading his company during the fighting for May-sur-Orne on Verrières Ridge in July 1944. The two battalions, the Black Watch and the Queen's Own Cameron Highlanders, had fought side by side during Operation *Spring*, and at one point formed a joint rear guard at the St-André/St-Martin crossroads. Rutherford was on a first-name basis with John Kemp, Ronnie Bennett and Phil Griffin. It was a curious situation – the Camerons were from Winnipeg, and originally organized by Stuart Cantlie's father, Lieutenant Colonel James A Cantlie, during the Great War. Oddly enough, Cantlie, raised in Winnipeg, now commanded the Montreal battalion that had been taken into battle in 1915 by his uncle, Colonel George Cantlie, DSO.

The Cameron battle, fought in the village of St-André, is often mistakenly cited as a Black Watch battle. The Camerons desperately hung on against repeated assaults from the 272nd German Infantry Division, supported by Kampfgruppen (battlegroups) from three panzer divisions: "During the three days following, the enemy launched several major counterattacks with heavy supporting fire, infantry and tanks, and the

Camerons' position was at all times subject to intense mortar and artillery fire from the exposed right flank." Rutherford was wounded, but soon returned to France and was immediately appointed second-in-command. The Camerons were then engaged in the battle over the sand dunes near the Bray Dunes, on the Channel coast, just east of Dunkirk. The area presented many difficult administrative problems: "Rutherford surmounted the difficulties of supplying the forward troops, by so organizing his echelons, that vital supplies of ammunition, rations and water reached them by means of carrying parties, where it was impossible to use vehicles."[20]

At the end of the Scheldt campaign, Rutherford was given command of his battalion and later, appointed Brigade Major, 6 Canadian Infantry Brigade. His sound tactical appreciations and administrative abilities won him the OBE: "The outstanding ability, devotion to duty, and superb courage of Lieutenant Colonel Rutherford throughout the campaign in North Western Europe has always been a source of inspiration to all who have worked with him."[21] The Black Watch would quickly concur.

The 1st Canadian Highland Battalion, 1951

> He was found guilty and sentenced to be executed.
>
> Discipline in the new Highland Battalion

The 1st Canadian Highland Battalion, under Rutherford's command, combined companies from five selected regiments. The Black Watch provided A Company; Toronto's 48th Highlanders formed B Company; Vancouver's Seaforth Highlanders raised C Company; and Victoria's Canadian Scottish provided D Company. The North Nova Scotia Highlanders completed the Support Company. It was a bit of a kaleidoscope in that each company wore their distinct regimental uniform, badge and tartan and "everyone signed on for three years."[22] The second-in-command was a westerner from the Calgary Highlanders, Major Mac Reid. Easterners were not overlooked. The padre was Norm Sharkey from the Stormont, Dundas and Glengarry Highlanders. RSM A Watson was followed within a year by a Black Watch legend-in-the-making, WOII Ron Finnie; the battalion pipe band was under Pipe Major Keith Lee, who came from the 48th Highlanders: "He had a big job on his hands – to take pipers from one coast to the other and transform us from a bunch of individuals into a team. He was an excellent man for the job, starting all of us back to the basics and having all of us play the same tunes the same way."[23]

The old Cameron motto, *Unite*, must have seemed particularly appropriate as the inaugural commanding officer set about moulding his sundry collection of men into a battle-ready battalion. They were as diverse in their origins as their tartans, mottos and customs; the prairie boys and Maritimers could not have been more different from the urbanite Montrealers and Torontonians. The gathering of the clans took place at Camp Valcartier in the summer of 1951.[24] Most of the officers and senior non-commissioned officers were veterans; the privates were generally young recruits with only basic training, given by their parent battalions. Private RD Cain, from the 48th Highlanders, recalled his first introduction to the army:

> Screaming NCOs and mass confusion ... Never did I suspect that man was born to run and not walk ... we were introduced to a Sergeant of the PPCLI [Sergeant John Henry Richardson who was to win a DCM in Korea]. A charming warm-hearted six foot four inch professional paratrooper with an absolute hostile attitude to anyone who remotely looked or even thought like a civilian. We soon found out that not only was the army now sending him teenage hoods, but our lot looked worse than anything he had seen in the past five years.[25]

They conducted extensive training on the ranges, becoming proficient in every weapon from rifle to 2" mortar. By September, the battalion was issued its shoulder patch that was a large thistle fixed on a shield in French gray with the word *Canada* at the top. 1 CHB was soon near its establishment of thirty-eight officers and 932 other ranks. It slowly evolved. The 48th Highlanders and the North Nova Scotia regiments proved best at recruiting and subsequently men from these units could be found in every company: "You learned something from those different locations but it was the North Novies who taught us how to handle the army – work hard, play hard and don't take life too seriously."[26] That fall they were inspected by HRH Princess Elizabeth and the Duke of Edinburgh on the historic Plains of Abraham and passed with flying colours.

Morale grew. Soon daring pranks occurred: six officers concocted a convoluted raid into the officers' mess of their rivals, the 1st Canadian Infantry Battalion, in order to steal their beloved mascot, a five-foot wooden Indian, the symbol of the Algonquin Regiment. They succeeded and then left the statue in Lieutenant Colonel Rutherford's quarters, dressed in the colonel's glengarry, belt, kilt and sporran. To their surprise, nothing was said next morning at breakfast; nothing happened throughout the day, until the late afternoon. A battalion parade was suddenly called. Tables were set up on the square, behind one sat the legal officers from the Judge Advocate's Branch, complete in formal black robes.

> Muffled drums could be heard in the distance, and in due course the 1st Cdn Inf Bn arrived, forming up facing the Highland battalion. Three of their officers joined the legal officer and charges of desertion to the enemy were read against the Indian. He was found guilty and

sentenced to be executed. The firing party detached itself from the Algonquin Company; the Indian was stripped of his kilt, shot with blanks, placed on a stretcher and marched away.[27]

The parade ended but all officers from both battalions were ordered into the Highland officers' mess. To their delight, they discovered there was an open bar! Halfway through the roaring party the adjutant gathered the infamous six culprits and advised: "You of course will be volunteering to pick up the tab for the evening." Highland justice!

1 CHB Training with NATO

der kanadischen Dudelsack-Kapelle[28]

... eventually peace was declared, but not before Peter "Moose" Malbeuf hung the young orderly officer onto a coat hook to keep him from getting injured.

Col AC Cameron, "The Heart and Soul of 1 RHC"[29]

That fall, the first contingents from 27th Brigade departed for Europe, leaving from Wolfe's Cove.[30] They reached Germany on 21 November 1951, greeted by General Eisenhower and Minister of National Defence Brooke Claxton. 1 CHB followed on 1 December and by the new year, the battalion was comfortably quartered in Chatham Barracks, Hanover – part of the British Army of the Rhine (BAOR). The Germans took the Russian threat most seriously, and the Canadians were quickly accepted by the civilian population who preferred them to British troops, although it took some time. There was some excessive exuberance in May right after spring manoeuvres in Lüneburg Heath. "No Canadian casualties but a few black eyes." However, three German policemen were roughed-up after about sixty to seventy Canadian soldiers gathered in front of a German *kneipe* (bar). The brigade immediately declared the reports were "exaggerated" and that the Germans should have summoned the Canadian provost (military police) instead of the German riot squad. "It was nothing but a little soldier's brawl as happens when soldiers are together with a little too much beer." Subsequent reports of their enthusiasm and performance in the field were better – and after the next manoeuvres, the NATO HQ pronounced the Canadians tops as soldiers. They were an intricate lot but despite a few donnybrooks, the German press noted that the Canadians were "the least disliked of Alien Troops in Germany. [They] would win a Popularity Poll hands down."[31] The Germans enjoyed *der kanadischen Dudelsack-Kapelle* once they got used to it. On the other hand, NATO comradery was often tested. On one occasion, the battalion marched into Waterlooplatz in Hanover for the Queen's birthday parade. It was the first time the whole battalion paraded in the kilt, the last consignment having just arrived by air from Scotland. The streets were lined with enthusiastic Germans and there were representatives from other NATO formations. As the battalion passed a halted US convoy: "heads, complete with cameras, appeared from everywhere as do porpoise from the sea, and as we passed by, one very American voice screamed out at a company commander, 'Hey bub, goin' steady with anyone?' Fortunately all ranks remembered they were not marching easy."[32] What occurred after the company was broken off is not recorded.

The 27th Brigade was equipped with a mix of British and American weapons. The soldier's rifle continued to be the .303 Lee Enfield. The Anti-Tank Platoon had increased clout to deal with superior Soviet tanks: US Army 3.5-inch rocket launchers to replace the woeful PIAT. The deadly British 17-pounder remained (for a while) towed by Oxford tracked carriers. In case of war, the brigade would have less than ten hours' warning time. 1 CHB was made ready to deploy on two hours' notice and able to operate without support for forty-eight hours. Fitness was emphasized and training was constant. They initially conducted a battalion exercise per week, as well as day-long route marches. Their first test was a three-day, 58-mile forced march from Hanover to Munsterlager. When the Highlanders heard that the two other battalions had barely straggled into Munsterlager, they smartened up, closed ranks, and crossed the finish line led by the pipes and drums, marching in good order. The sergeants' mess January 'Burns' Nite' was preceded by a 75-mile day-long movement exercise. The tired NCOs were cheered by the contents of "a gigantic bottle Colonel Fergusson had presented to the mess at Christmas when he arrived bearing the gift like a wee bairn in a shawl."[33]

The Highland battalion brought enthusiasm and its own élan to major exercises. The best sniper group in 27th Brigade was 1 CHB's sniper section, dubbed "Granger's Rangers" after their Sergeant, John Granger. Their legendary exploits included raiding an RAF base, marking ammunition dumps as *blown up* and terrifying young British airmen: "We Ruskies – you prisoners." In one corps-level exercise, their advance was fast enough to overrun the self-propelled gun batteries of the 1st Royal Horse Artillery. "It was the first time the Regt lost their guns either on an exercise or in war ... by God there was almost a fist-fight ... but eventually the umpires prevailed."[34] On yet another exercise, the battalion outdistanced their own corps reconnaissance squadron. Their German training areas included Putlos, Munsterlager, Bergen-Hohne, Soltau, Haltern and Sennelager. Putlos gave 1 CHB its first opportunity to "fire in" its weapons; Munsterlager and Bergen-Hohne were similarly used by Canadian artillery and armour; Soltau was employed by all brigade units for *dry training*. By far, the most comprehensive and flexible facility was the

Sennelager training centre – it had something for everyone. The manoeuvre area had been 'modernized' by Bismarck in the 19th century and later revamped by General Heinz Guderian during his development of *Blitzkrieg* tactics.

1 CHB eased into garrison life. The days began with the pipes and drums playing 'Johnny Cope'. However, tradition among Highland regiments allows pipers and drummers playing reveille to dress in attire of their own choosing "[which] resulted in such dress combinations as a piper wearing nothing but gym shoes, a black tie, a steel helmet and a whisk broom around his vitals."[35] This was quickly sorted out. Discipline was exactingly administered and the 1 CHB Regimental Sergeant Major, WOI RH Finnie, was a living legend. He was overtly stern, and fearsome, but devoted to his soldiers. The adjutant recalled:

> One day when I was going to the battalion lines with Mr Finnie he spotted a soldier, across the small parade square and yelled at him to come and join us. While the soldier was obeying the command Mr Finnie kept up a banter of "go around the parade square not on it, double, get your legs up etc." To the extent that all who heard the RSM, including myself, were convinced the soldier was in serious trouble. But not so. When the soldier joined us Mr Finnie advised him that Mrs Finnie would that day be visiting the soldier's wife in hospital and that arrangements were being made to look after their children until she was back on her feet. The soldier was then told to "carry on" but, as he moved off, he was again yelled at to, "double etc." – the RSM did not want to ruin the image for those who might be listening.[36]

In the two years of training and exercises, the battalion became a cohesive unit with a distinct *esprit de corps*. Nevertheless, "the companies from the [original] Militia units never lost their individual regimental identities, nor their individual spirit."[37] Soldiers from Black Watch Company won the piping and Highland dancing competitions 16 June 1952, under the direction of Lieutenant G Huggett. Back home, Verdun was glad to read that their own Pte Wilfrid Sullivan took top honours in the brigade track and field meet. All triumphs, battalion gossip and events were duly reported by the weekly newspaper, *The Kilt and Sporran*. The amalgam battalion experiment did create some concerns:

> The most basic problem of all was that the composite battalion idea had not really worked. For one thing, there was great difficulty building up any institutional focus or loyalty to the generic battalions. For another, when the first of the married men took leave for home in early 1953, it was found that three or four of the contributing militia regiments could not generate enough recruits to keep their companies up to strength. That cut to the heart of the whole philosophy of the composite regiments as they now existed. It made little

sense to perpetuate the Algonquins, Regina Rifles, and Seaforths in the Regular Army, for example, if vacancies in these companies had to be filled with surplus volunteers provided by the Carleton and Yorks, Queen's Own, or Black Watch.[38]

The first part of the adventure ended in November 1952. Brigadier JEC Pangman took over command of 27th Brigade from Brigadier Geoffrey Walsh. Major Boswell returned to Canada, being replaced by a veteran Black Watch officer, and POTS graduate, Major Duncan McAlpine, who would enjoy a most successful career. The new CO was Lieutenant Colonel H Hugh Alexander Parker OBE – "Harry" to his friends.

Lieutenant Colonel H Hugh Alexander Parker OBE

Parker was an ideal choice for a Highland battalion. He was born in Lockerbie, Scotland, graduated from Trinity College (University of Toronto), and worked for Confederation Life Insurance. When the Second World War began, Parker enlisted in the 48th Highlanders and was posted as a staff instructor to RMC, and later was appointed to the staff of the 4th Canadian Armoured Brigade. Parker left Europe with an OBE, awarded for his performance as deputy assistant adjutant and quartermaster-general in the brigade throughout the dash across France and Belgium:

> During this period, through the foresight, administrative ability and dogged endurance of this officer, no tank was without petrol or ammunition – no shortage of supplies or ordnance stores was ever apparent. He made night-long journeys over unfamiliar roads, through unmarked minefields and country uncleared of the enemy to knit together the fully extended and prolonged armoured column. Lieutenant Colonel Parker originated and organized the "Compo Commandos" – a body of maintenance personnel trained to fight their way forward to the tanks with their supplies and services.[39]

After a short term in command of 4 Canadian Armoured Division Training School, Lieutenant Colonel Parker assumed command of the Lake Superior Regiment (Motor) on 11 May 1944. "Near Sluis, in the Scheldt, commanding a task force of his own unit supported by a squadron of tanks, two troops of 25-pounder guns, six 4.2-inch mortars and eight .50 Brownings, so carefully was his fire plan devised and so energetically developed that a crossing by boats over an extensive body of water was made possible with very small losses."[40] As Parker assumed command of 1 CHB, he could not help but notice that prominent in his first official mail delivery were telegrams from Montreal, and an envelope from Brigadier Kenneth Blackader, bearing the inscription 'The Black Watch, Royal Highland Regiment'.

More Regular Battalions: 2 CHB, 1952

It was hoped that the regimental depot might be established in or near Montreal, which was the headquarters of the Black Watch for nearly a century. However, NDHQ, for various reasons, decided that for the present in any event the depot would have to be in the Maritimes.

Colonel Paul P Hutchison[41]

A year after 1 CHB had been formed, the government created three additional infantry units following what now seemed as a practicable system: the 2nd Canadian Infantry Battalion; the 2nd Canadian Rifle Battalion; and the 2nd Canadian Highland Battalion (2 CHB). As before, they were to reflect regional representation from across Canada. The Black Watch immediately raised a second rifle company for 2 CHB. They would replace the sub unit in the 1st Highland Battalion, scheduled to return from Germany.[42]

On 15 May 1952, the Second Battalion marshalled at Camp Aldershot, Nova Scotia, which was selected as a permanent training centre. Quarters were in the pinewoods beyond Kentville, Nova Scotia. It still consisted of wartime "H hut" structures heated by oil stoves; in winter, plastic sheets were fixed to the windows of sleeping quarters. Aldershot had prepared officers and men for service in the Boer War, both World Wars, as well as NATO and United Nations service. The Montreal Black Watch trained there early during the Second World War. The connection began in 1940 when the training centre produced reinforcements for 1 RHC, which was extremely unpopular in Montreal. It took instructor NCOs and recruits away from Bleury Street and put them "under control of strangers" – which constantly vexed Paul Hutchison. The very first Black Watch church parade held in Aldershot totalled sixteen hundred men. It was led by Kenneth Blackader on 13 August 1940, a week before the battalion journeyed to Halifax to embark for England. The parade square was not to see the RHC again until the Cold War, when it became (and to some retired soldiers, continues to be) "the old Home Station" – the Maritime equivalent of Bleury Street. The officer commanding The Black Watch Company (A Coy) this time was Major GA Donaldson, but he was not from Montreal.

The new battalion, as a Highland collective, included: as second-in-command, Major G McLean Logan, a Cape Breton Highlander; the adjutant was Captain Kitch Tracey, North Nova Scotia Highlanders; and the regimental sergeant major was WO1 Fred Blakeney MM BEM CD, from the West Nova Scotia Regiment. Sergeant Hal Young, Camerons of Ottawa, was the regimental quartermaster sergeant; the quartermaster was Lieutenant AW Gemmill, RCOC; and, as Pipe Major, WO Duncan Rankine CD, "a crusty old Scot who had been with the Royal Scots during the Second

World War. He was a very good pipe major and we learned a great deal from him."[43] Rankine had served with the 1st Battalion of the Royal Scots and had the bad luck to be captured in Hong Kong, Christmas 1941. He spent the rest of his war in a Japanese POW camp. He was a cool-headed, experienced leader – just what the new pipe band needed.

The Laird: Lieutenant Colonel RM Ross, OBE

His men followed him without the slightest hesitation.

Ross, MID citation

The commanding officer of 2 CHB was Lieutenant Colonel Richard Montgomery (Dick) Ross OBE, who was better known as 'The Laird'. Ross was one of those larger-than-life COs. He had served continuously in the Canadian Army overseas from June 1940 to 1945 and successfully held every key appointment from platoon commander to battalion commander. Ross had joined The Cameron Highlanders of Ottawa in 1933, and when war came, he promptly volunteered. The Camerons were appointed the machine-gun battalion for 3rd Canadian Infantry Division. His *curriculum vitae* included the Dieppe raid, 19 August 1942, where he proved cool and steady under fire and was recommended for a DSO. He was instead *Mentioned in Despatches* for leading an intrepid advance which proved to be the deepest penetration of the entire raid.

> At the very outset of the engagement while under continuous enemy fire ... [Ross] inspired the entire company. Later when it became necessary for plans to be changed and extremely hazardous work attempted, Major Ross's conduct was such that his men followed him without the slightest hesitation. He kept his company under perfect control and advanced some 2 miles inland from the beach, beating off all enemy opposition, and displayed tactical ability of a high order.[44]

He then successfully withdrew the company to the shore: "On the beach while waiting for the evacuation craft to come in, he organized the defensive position and the handling of the wounded, and his men were largely responsible for the successful withdrawal of a considerable part of the company."[45] The next time he landed in Normandy, Ross was the commanding officer of the Cameron Highlanders of Ottawa. By September 1945, he fought through France, Belgium and into Germany, much like his 1 CHB confrere Dickie Rutherford. At the end of the war, he was awarded the Order of the British Empire:

> Lt-Colonel Ross was the chief factor in maintaining the magnificent support to the infantry attacks...he was on several occasions placed in command of the divisional "Pepper-pots" composed of machine guns, mortars, anti-tank guns and light anti-aircraft guns, supporting infantry attacks. All the responsibilities which Lieutenant Colonel Ross has been called upon to assume have been discharged by him most efficiently, willingly and competently.[46]

The new Highland battalion grouped together in May 1952, at Camp Aldershot; all companies wore their own distinctive tartan. Ross was certainly up to the challenge. He was stern ("he wasn't a man given to wild expressions of charm") and immediately terrified all subalterns and most soldiers: "He glowered at me from behind the bushiest eyebrows I have ever seen."[47] Ross turned his group of novice and veteran soldiers, raised with different traditions as varied as the country they served, into an effective infantry battalion.[48] In June 1952, the Commonwealth celebrated the coronation of the new Queen, Elizabeth II. The 27th Brigade sent a contingent representing Canada to participate in the coronation parade: six soldiers from each of the fifteen different companies in the brigade. The A Company representative was a Black Watch 'original', Corporal Dave M Mulligan.[49] The coronation contingent was glad of a break from route marches and flies. That same summer General Sir Neil Methuen Ritchie, a desert warrior who led the 8th Army against Rommel during the Second World War, decided to settle in Canada on his retirement. He felt it necessary to tender his resignation as colonel of the regiment, a position he had held since 1950. Sir Neil was immediately welcomed by the RHC and invited to sit on their Advisory Board.

The battalion was scheduled for NATO duty in Germany, but instead, at Christmas 1952, the very new 2nd Canadian Highland Battalion was ordered to Korea – reassigned to replace 3 PPCLI. The advance party departed by air, arriving at Pusan via USAF *Globemaster*, where they were met by their Patricia opposite numbers. Meantime, the main body was entrained and sent west, to Camp Wainwright, for more training. New schedules were drawn up with plenty of range work. In summer, the flat featureless Wainwright plagued the men with clouds of black flies and torrential rains.[50]

Conversion at Sea: Becoming The Black Watch – 1953

Nemo Me Impune Lacessit[51]

Having both endured and profited from their "refresher training" in Camp Wainwright, the 2nd Highland Battalion entrained for the port of Seattle, Washington, there to embark for the far east as a unit in 25th Canadian Infantry Brigade, part of the Commonwealth Division.[52] They boarded the USNS *Marine Lynx*, a United States naval transport on 8 October 1953.[53] Before putting to sea, Lieutenant Colonel Ross ordered the battalion to stand by for an announcement on the public address system. Satisfied that all soldiers could hear him, Ross tore open a waxed-sealed envelope and read the contents: The 1st and 2nd CHB formally became The 1st and 2nd Battalions The Black Watch. The decision was explained in a letter from Lieutenant General Guy Simonds: "To make a choice from the many famous regiments represented in the 2nd Highland Battalion was no easy task. The fairest course was to fall back upon the well-established principle of regimental seniority. The Black Watch (Royal Highland Regiment) of Canada is the oldest Highland Regiment in the Canadian Army."[54]

Since formal approval could not be obtained until a cabinet defence committee meeting (scheduled on the night 2 RHC sailed), the redesignation became official when the battalion was at sea. Simonds assured Brigadier Ken Blackader, Chairman of The Black Watch Regimental Advisory Board, he would give him forty-eight hours warning to convene a meeting of the board "to state the case for using their regimental name for the two Highland battalions."[55] Lieutenant Colonel Ross had received a sealed package from Army HQ just before leaving Wainwright and a number of envelopes, one inside another. The sealed orders were accompanied by cartons of the necessary Black Watch trappings to be opened only on a receipt of a special code message from Simonds. The next mail from Canada contained a genial letter from Kenneth Blackader, the Honorary Colonel of the Regiment, welcoming the battalion into the Black Watch regimental family.

The ship sailed that afternoon; the men tried to avoid seasickness by sewing on new RHC badges and affixing the Red Hackles (kilts were not immediately available).[56] They expected to cruise to Korea at seventeen knots but the boilers broke down and speed was reduced: 1256 miles from Seattle, they were forced to put in to Whittier, Alaska for repairs. The jocks began calling the *Marine Lynx*, the *Sea Cow*. They continued through the North Pacific, braving rough seas. In the messes, or *ward rooms,* the officers were fortified by an ample supply of *Pink Gins* and *Horse's Necks*. There were some minor diversions: while on board the *Marine Lynx*, the 2nd Battalion was initiated into "The Mystic Order of the Golden Dragon – Ruler of the 180th Meridian" as voyagers to the Far East. There were minor theatrics and cabarets. The ship's canteen sold cigarettes at 9 cents a pack; chocolate bars cost more. The Pioneer Platoon all grew beards. On 15 October, the war diary chronicled: "The sun shined today for the first time since our journey started."[57] After logging nearly five thousand miles at sea, they reached Sasebo, Japan. After a short layover, 2 RHC landed at Inchon on 28 October, scarcely sixteen months after mobilization, and less than a month as a Black Watch battalion – most of it spent aboard ship.

Burgeoning Battalions

Everything suddenly went right. The existence of two Regular battalions on active service gave the Regiment a greater-than-normal élan, but it had pretty much emptied Bleury Street. It was time for the Black Watch to rebuild.

In the Maritimes, the First Battalion's year was dominated by sports, particularly hockey and boxing at local competitions.[58] However, it was the pipes and drums that first gave the 'Regular' Black Watch international recognition. They were selected to represent Canada in the renowned Royal Edinburgh Military Tattoo at Edinburgh Castle, and afterwards to take part in the British Military Tattoo in Copenhagen, Denmark. The Regiment despatched Scottish-born Captain JD Morton (from 2 RHC) and thirty-eight other ranks, including P/Major W Magennis (1 RHC), P/Major D Rankine (2 RHC) and D/Major M Phelan (2 RHC). They were assisted by the distinguished senior piper, P/Major R Hannah of 3 RHC. After additional rehearsal in Montreal, they left on the CPR steamer *Empress of France* and crossed a calm Atlantic. They often practised on deck, much to the delight of the passengers. In Edinburgh, The Black Watch (RHR) of Canada were combined with the 1st Gordons (Scotland) and the 8th Punjab Regiment (Pakistan) to form "The Commonwealth Pipes and Drums." Also present were pipers from Nepal (Gurkhas), Ireland, South Africa and New Zealand. The massed pipes and drums (dubbed "Scotland's Pride") included the Argyles, Seaforths, 1st and 2nd Bns Scots Guards, the Royal Scots Greys and the Highland Light Infantry. A British officer, Major David Murray was put in charge and he selected Captain Morton as his 2IC. Sergeant Don Roy, then a member of 1 RHC Pipe Band, recalls that P/Major Keith Lee deserved much of the credit: "He did an admirable job in preparing us for the Tattoo so that when we were there playing with the other bands, we were second to none of them."[59] The Black Watch's three-month tour took them to Denmark and later Germany, where they played for Canadian troops in Soest. They sailed back, never missing a parade on deck and landed in Montreal in mid-November; the Regulars took the night train to Kentville, tired and glad to be home.

The Black Watch in Korea, 1953–1954

In his distinctive jeep with the St Andrew's Cross flying from an aerial...

Lieutenant Colonel Ross in Korea, 1953

The Black Watch reached the front lines in December 1953 after a cease–fire had been arranged; the war settled into a routine of patrols and observation. The battalion deployed behind the 'No Pass Line', two kms from the Demarcation Line. They were welcomed with curiosity: "Say buddy, I thought we sent you out of here a few months ago. What are you doing back here?" (referring to the Imperial 1st Black Watch under Lieutenant Colonel David Rose). The record was soon put straight.[60]

The Canadian brigade was deployed north of the Imjin River as a covering force for 1 Commonwealth Division. The Bn also acquired 150 Korean Augmentation Troops assigned to the Commonwealth Divisions (KATCOMS for short) – thirty per company that were invaluable in support of operations. The companies received additional 30- and 50-calibre machine-guns. The main defence position (the *Kansas Line*) overlooked the Imjin River, but their initial deployment was a reinforced platoon along the forward *Wyoming Line* to provide early warning. The battalion was allotted a squadron of armour to assist it in breaking contact and withdrawing to the Imjin River in case of a Chinese attack. Their tour featured regular exercises and rehearsals sometimes punctuated by periods of increased tension. A patrol from D Company, avoiding mines, took a routine short cut – the route meandered back and forth across the Demarcation Line. When they stepped north of the line, they were taken prisoner by waiting Chinese soldiers and kept overnight.

Colonel Ross created a well–trained, supremely confident battalion in a remarkably short time. He often held short periods of drill supported by the pipes and drums playing on the gravel parade square. This was followed by briefings on Black Watch history and customs. Ross was an inspiring CO, always immaculately turned out, seen throughout the battalion area in his distinctive jeep with the St Andrew's Cross flying from an aerial. They were brigaded with The Queen's Own Rifles and worked through a bleak, rainy Yuletide, which combined tramping down muddy roads for divine services and sending out 4–man patrols "in hope of at least seeing some of the Chinese coming over into our area on Christmas Eve."[61] It was not exciting work, and their greatest annoyance was that the mail was invariably late. The battalion had memorable characters. Sergeant Major Cluie Louis MacLean was kidded for confusing the *VD list* and the *leave roster* in Korea. He sent those on the VD list on leave, and confined–to–barracks everyone entitled to go on leave. One of his favourite sayings was: "He was the kind of a guy the padre would like to punch in the mouth." Once, a company route–march was interrupted for pay parade. MacLean fell out the company by the side of the road and sorted out the soldiers alphabetically. He suddenly paused and shouted: Phillips! What the hell are you doing down here with the Ps? Get up there with the Fs where you belong!"[62] Contact with enemy consisted of long–range-sightings of personnel or equipment. In March 1954, they were inspected by Prime Minister Louis St Laurent. The occasion was made more exciting when two Canadian Military Policemen (MPs) were captured by the enemy while on normal patrol. They were later released after negotiations by the Joint Observer team, which included two lieutenants from the battalion and 2 RHC Intelligence Officer DS Paisley.

Five Black Watch soldiers died during the Korean campaign and remain buried in the Orient. Sergeant Gerry Steacy, who was the battalion sniper sergeant, recalls the first loss – Private Ralph Turnbull (C Company, 1 January 1954): "He was preparing for a night patrol when a Sten Gun [sub machine gun] accidentally went off, mortally wounding Turnbull." The second was Pte Clifford Laframboise (HQ Company, 15 February 1954) who was employed with the Unit Armourer: "They were neutralising a Chinese Burp Gun [sub machine gun] when it went off and wounded Laframboise. He was sent to Japan for medical treatment but when operated on, he passed away. He is buried in Japan."[63]

In May, the brigade commander, Brigadier Jean Victor Allard DSO conducted a spring inspection. Some thought the brigadier was very much like MacDonnell of the Great War – quite fond of the Black Watch. He made a point of visiting them. Ross and the brigadier enjoyed most cordial relations – a pleasant change from the previous war's experiences. Allard's aide was a future Black Watch colonel, Captain Harry Harkes: "We used to run up hills together in Korea, [he was] very competitive."[64] When Allard was absent in May 1954, Ross took over as acting brigade commander – unimaginable during the Mitchell, Ritchie vs. Megill era.

Battalion Routines

Sports remained an important part of battalion life. The RHC did well in brigade track and field meets, competing against the rival Queen's Own Rifles. Conducting regular sports events was always a challenge. The weather and the poor shape of the grounds often cancelled the meets. Nonetheless, the year passed remarkably quickly. USO shows entertained the troops – that, and the pipes and drums, who performed regular retreats. There were as well *Rest and Recreation* leaves in Japan. When summer finally arrived, it was rainy; streams became rushing torrents and roads washed away. The Black Watch continued to occupy observation posts and carefully log personnel sightings around the DMZ. At last, on 2 October 1954, 2 RHC was relieved of all security commitments and handed over to 1st Bn The Royal Irish Fusiliers. There was a brigade commander's farewell parade and inspection, and a last church parade on 24 October, but it was "the arrival of the Canadian customs team [that] made many of us realize that we haven't long to go."[65] On Tuesday, 2 November 1954, they boarded the USS *Marine Phoenix*. The Black Watch left Korea.

Lieutenant Colonels Parker and Seamark:
From a Pan-Canadian to a Maritime Battalion

As they passed I recognized half a dozen men whom I had known in my home town … It was at that moment that I made up my mind that I would serve with the Black Watch as long as they would have me.

AH Matheson[66]

When Lieutenant Colonel Harry Parker took command, he received warm welcomes from Colonels Cantlie and John Bourne. Parker responded: "We are proud to be members of that family and to inherit its great traditions. We will do our best to live up to them." However, his brave words were soon put to the test via a series of immigrations as the battalion, indeed both Regular units, began a gradual cultural transition. It was not going to be easy. Since the short-lived Korea deployment and the termination of the Germany tour, the soldiers considered a future life in Aldershot – a dot at the end of the Annapolis Valley. When Lieutenant Colonel WH Seamark CD, took over from Parker in November 1954, he inherited an inundation of resignation letters.

Bill Seamark originated in Brockville, Ontario. His task was quite different from the COs who led the Regular battalions into Asia and Europe. Prospects of exotic adventure had diminished, indeed, disappeared. Instead of foreign vistas and the excitement of meeting the enemy, the returning veterans faced the barracks in tranquil and very rural Nova Scotia. There was much grumbling. The original CHBs were a collective of regional companies from across Canada. Now, the prospect of being permanently based in the Maritimes, hundreds, perhaps thousands of miles from home, prompted soldiers to request transfers to other battalions or service branches. Many simply quit. By February 1954, 1 RHC's strength shrank to twenty-eight officers and 470 other ranks. The 1 RHC pipe band was destitute. The Pipe Major resigned: "after much discussion with his wife and family, decided he had better remain a civilian after the Germany tour…most of our pipers who are qualified to be pipe sergeants or a pipe major are not too interested in joining the Active Force." The band was short fourteen pipers and seven drummers. [67] As the North American economy began to hum, army barracks, whether in Canada or Europe, held little enticement for young Canadians.

The Regiment rolled up its sleeves. Determined recruiting teams fanned out across the Maritimes. Bleury Street sent everything it had – from artifacts and battle trophies, to uniforms and paintings. The Advisory Board sent monies whenever required and made it clear the regimental family was one, and all shared in its battle honours and unique styles. Lieutenant Colonel John Bourne immediately set about working with Lieutenant Colonel Bill Seamark to confirm and standardize the minutiae of dress and customs that made the Black Watch distinct. They corresponded vigorously and Seamark visited Bourne in Montreal. There they carefully hammered out what would become regimental fundamentals in dress and custom for the next two decades.[68] The agenda included everything from uniforms to key traditions, from bugle calls to pipe tunes. Bourne set up a précis on mess customs. They even considered battalion pennants. Bourne presented Seamark with a battalion flag: a St Andrew's Cross with 1 RHC in red letters placed on one side: "It is customary to fly this flag outside your battalion headquarters when in the field or at camp, providing security regulations permit. This has always been the custom in Black Watch battalions."[69] Meantime, a trainload of tartan was ordered for the two Regular units. The government approved a contract for thirty-five hundred kilts. The diktats of regimental dress were drummed into the battalion ranks: "Putties rolled in threes, garter flashes cutting the centre seam of the lovat hose, kilt just clearing the floor when you kneel on both knees, don't ever wear battle dress unless you wear brown gloves with snap fasteners and you'd better have a plumed hackle." The care of the Hackle, a sacred artifact, was paramount within Black Watch catechetics: "You wet it, tie a string through the eye, swing it over your head to open it up and put it plume down in a beer glass to curl the edges."[70]

Although there were keen discussions regarding form and style; in the end, everyone agreed on the Red Hackle. When Colonel Paul Hutchison was invited by the lieutenant governor of Nova Scotia, the Hon Alistair Fraser MC, a former member of the Bleury Street mess, to attend the opening of the Nova Scotia legislature in 1954, he was keenly interested in the guard of honour mounted by The Black Watch RHC. Hutchison, ever the historian and regimental perfectionist, had a long chat with Lieutenant Colonel Seamark and subsequently wrote to Bourne: "The Guard was one hundred strong, very smart and well turned out all things considered, wearing the kilt. My only criticism would be that the Hackles are far too large and floppy."[71] It would be interesting to speculate what Hutchison would have said had he seen the Hackles worn by the Regiment in the new millennium. Harry Parker, who had recently handed over 1 RHC, confided: "I think Seamark was pleased that someone from Montreal was there to see the show."[72] It was a marked success. The Black Watch was letter-perfect with which the knowledgeable audience concurred. The lieutenant governor later wrote to Hutchison: "My Guard is the talk of the Town – they were smart and the cynosure of many eyes on Hollis Street and en route."[73]

Bourne and Seamark also cooperated on incidents of discipline.[74] Bleury Street tried to act as a Regimental Headquarters. What was *de rigueur* was smartness on parade, particularly dress that passed the RSM's and commanding officer's stern inspections. In 1954, Her Majesty Queen Elizabeth, The Queen Mother visited Ottawa. 1 RHC was ordered to provide the royal guard of honour as well as parade the pipes and drums.[75] There was great competition to be selected by RSM Finnie and his right-hand man, Drill Sergeant-Major McConnell. Meantime, the battalion was inspected by Major General EC Plow, GOC Eastern Command. As he inspected, the general paused to ask one smart Highlander if he was wearing his best battle dress. The private replied: "No Sir, I am saving it for the CO's parade."

It was a grand adventure. They took the train from Aldershot to Montreal, shepherded by Mr Finnie who stopped off to liaise at Bleury Street. They were then bused to Petawawa. The desire of the soldiers to appear properly Highland, dressed as Black Watch, was immediately evident. The annual inspection of the 2nd Battalion RHC on 7 May 1956 by Major General EC Plow, GOC Eastern Command was a milestone in the history of the battalion: "… for the first time, every man turned out in blue bonnet, hair sporran, diced hose and white spats. These articles are not issued by Ordnance, and are bought by the men through the kit shop."[76]

Garrison life was a skilled attempt to make the monotonous interesting. The battalions trained hard and played hard – each hoping for foreign deployment. There were minor diversions. In May 1956, the rebuilt pipe bands were considered good enough to be sent to a Tattoo in Hamilton, Bermuda which left the inhabitants 'goggle-eyed'. During Hurricane Edna, 1 RHC assisted apple farmers in the Annapolis Valley whose crops were nearly ruined. The farmers considered it "a deserving peacetime battle honour" and the "Jocks" picked sixty thousand barrels of apples.[77]

The First Battalion had been in Aldershot since its return from Germany in November 1953 and were becoming anxious. Finally, it was announced 1 RHC would be sent to Korea in 1955 to replace 2nd Bn Queen's Own Rifles. It was during this time that Colonel Hutchison suggested presenting a ram's head snuff mull to the battalion, to be taken with them to Asia. The snuff mull was originally presented to 1st Bn RHC by Hugh Paton, a prominent textile manufacturer and member of the mess, who had supplied kilts to the 5th Royal Scots. Lieutenant Colonel WH Seamark received it at Camp Sussex in mid-February 1955. To the battalion's great regret, after determined training and preparation, their posting to the Far East was "switched off" at the last minute: "Cancellation of our move to Korea did not come until the battalion was away completely on embarkation leave."[78] The snuff mull became a Black Watch artifact, eventually ending up as part of the Regimental fixtures of 2 RCR. The connection between Montreal and its Atlantic battalions was perhaps strongest during the period 1953–1963. Decades later, Brigadier General Don MacLellan reflecting on these early days remarked:

> The extent to which the Regiment had taken us, the new regular component to its bosom, how very much we were made to feel members of the regimental family ... We had been provided, from the beginning, with a wealth of moral and material support which made a great difference ... in marked contrast to the reception given other units lately embodied in the Regular Army from the Reserve. The Guards and QOR got a cold shoulder from the Militia – but the Montreal Black Watch enthusiastically embraced the new battalions, gave them access to everything, including the Battle Honours. They simply said, "How can we help?"[79]

The Regiment Rising: Dress and Customs in Three Battalions

So weave well the black threads,
The blue threads, the green threads,
Woof well the strong threads,
That binds their hearts to thine.

Alice MacDonell of Keppoch, 1894

The creation of two Regular Black Watch battalions was met with great approbation in the textile industry. The traditional supplier for the Black Watch had been the mills of Hugh Paton, but now purchase was orchestrated by NDHQ. Sources varied, but 'correct' regimental tweed still came from Scotland. The officer's tweed or 'Cantlie Tartan' was held by Stewart, Christie & Co as well as The Black Watch Depot in Perth. Officers continued to order suits made of the pattern that was a rustic brown with fine lines of blue, red, and green thread making an elegant hunting tweed and first-rate fall and winter suit. It was an exclusive, guarded weave that echoed the tartan of the soldiers of the Royal Highland Regiment in its early days and before power looms became general – a pattern as distinguished as the name it bears. The new Regular Force Highland regiment attracted bureaucratic decisions regarding dress regulations. The three COs (Parker, Seamark and Bourne) discussed orders of dress with vigour. It was decided that officers, and the RSM, would wear the *Skean Dhu* whenever the kilt was worn. Parker opined: "it gives the officers a certain distinction, and I feel – particularly in the Active Force – that the more of this we have, the better." Bourne did not approve of the battle dress blouse worn with trews: "never been done by the Black Watch – and I don't think we should change." The number of orders of dress were modified by simple political expediency. Seamark urged the Regiment to interpret and to conform to the seven orders of Army dress exactly:

> If we do this, no one at AHQ [Army Headquarters] can criticize us but simply agree that the existing dress regulations are not adequate for a Highland Regiment. If we put in 9 or 10 orders of dress, I feel quite positive ... that the official reaction will be unfavourable. I think they will say "7 orders of dress are good enough for the Canadian Army generally but the Black Watch have to have 10, therefore we will have to get them back in line." ... this will give us sufficient flexibility to add out own domestic supplements to the regulations.[80]

This was accepted. Sixteen years later, suspicious veterans would argue that one of the reasons the Black Watch was not popular with a government bent on introducing a new 'distinctly national' army was that the Royal Highlanders were simply too 'Imperial', and their dress requirements too antique (Imperial/Colonial understood) for a space-age military.

Mess behaviour and traditional forms of regimental dress were carefully coordinated; Bourne dispatched itemized mess customs as they had evolved in Bleury Street. Canadian Black Watch demeanour and deportment were mild transformations that began in the early nineteenth century, after affiliation with the Imperials, followed by modifications and amendments that had "winkled in" through the 1920s and 30s. The Regiment was given permission in March 1954 to wear the blue balmoral and the green coatee. It was decided to keep the hair sporran as part of the uniform rather than adopt the proposed white buff leather pattern. Some customs were not embraced, for example, pipe banners. The only personal banners that the Regiment possessed belonged to the 3rd Battalion, and these were of various designs. The Regular battalions decided that "if they wish to indulge in such luxuries, [e.g. pipe banners] will have to be acquired in the traditional manner."[81] There were differences of opinion. The high cost and conflicting heraldic opinions were also raised as concerns. The main conflict being the use of a crest and motto alone, as opposed to the coat of arms covering the surface of the banner. Field officers, it was quickly proved, showed little interest in the subject. The idea was new and in some cases foreign. Finally, it was decided by the Regular commanding officers in December 1957, that any field officer wishing to provide a banner could have either his personal crest and motto or coat of arms or complete achievement displayed, according to his preference – provided all were in accordance with the law of arms. By the time the battalions had settled in Gagetown, only one pipe banner had made its appearance. It was displayed when the Depot was granted the privilege of marching through the town of Sussex on 14 May 1958.

The First Battalion's complement began as a confederation of Canadian provinces; it was now half-filled with Maritimers and Newfoundlanders:

> … mainly Nova Scotians, but with a goodly smattering from the other eastern provinces, including a good representation of Newfoundlanders … The latter were especially interesting; they were physically very hardy, ever cheerful and undemanding; if the rations arrived, they fell to with a will – if not, they waited uncomplainingly.[82]

The officers were an interesting mix of veterans and keen young lieutenants. When a fire broke out in the Camp Aldershot officers' mess, a new subaltern bravely but recklessly ignoring his own safety, rushed in and retrieved the mess records. He then triumphantly presented the slightly scorched prize to the field officer of the day. The major carefully opened them, checked his mess bill, and casually threw them back into the fire.[83] One young officer recalled how inspections were guided by the company sergeant major, who particularly enjoyed using the young officer's own kit for his lesson on how to inspect defaulters parade: "Look in the pleats of the kilt, sir. Them folds is always got lint in 'em." With a twinkle in his eye he looked up "You'll catch th' buggers on that every time."[84]

As the Highland battalions became settled in Nova Scotia, The Black Watch became dominant. Not an easy task in a province that possessed three famous indigenous Highland regiments. When the finance minister visited 27th Brigade, Maritime newspapers published a cartoon showing him surrounded by a sea of Red Hackles. On 12 June 1955, the Black Watch was ordered to the Camp Gagetown training area to take part in the first peacetime concentration of 1st Cdn Div. Here, Lieutenant Colonel Ross DSO handed the 2nd Battalion over to Lieutenant Colonel W de N Watson DSO MC, completing a command of almost three and a half years.

Lieutenant Colonel William de Norban Watson DSO MC CD, 2 RHC

Lieutenant Colonel William deNorban (Bucko) Watson was an arresting senior officer, with an Errol Flynn moustache. He was compact, like a coiled spring, with riveting, critical eyes. His officers were both in awe and terror: "I played on his Company's hockey team – which Watson had forbidden. I broke my ankle, but never missed a parade."[85] William Watson joined Princess Patricia's Canadian Light Infantry early in the Second World War. Watson wore the kind of medals that made battle-hardened veterans take a second look. He was wounded in Italy during the capture of Villa Rogatti. "A" Company, commanded by Major Watson was allotted the defence of the northeast corner of the town. In the morning, intense mortar and artillery fire was directed upon the position and at 0730 hours the enemy infantry made a powerful and determined counter-attack in which one platoon of the company was overrun. Although in full view of the enemy and under a continuous and heavy cross-fire from a range as close as 100 yards, Major Watson moved from platoon to platoon coolly reorganizing the defence, co-ordinating the tasks of his platoon and encouraging and cheering his men in their stand.[86]

The recommendation for a Military Cross was passed on for immediate action by General Sir Harold Alexander, GOC 15 Army Group.[87] He next went on to win a DSO at the Hitler Line on 23 May 1944 where Watson still commanded A Company PPCLI, then the leading company on the battalion axis of advance – a route through wooded country, broken by fields of standing crops, against heavily fortified concrete and steel pill boxes, snipers and gun positions. The Germans were in over-watch positions and opened fire, cutting down swaths of men in two forward companies. The battalion paused, seemed to stagger, but:

> With magnificent leadership, Major Watson led his company through murderous German defensive fire of mortar, artillery and machine guns. In the blinding dust and smoke, although continually exposed to machine-gun fire, he coordinated the advance of his company through to the final objective. In the crossing of a wire obstacle twenty feet deep, studded with tree mines, Major Watson utterly disregarding his own personal safety under heavy fire, cheered and encouraged his troops through gaps made in the wire. Later when his officers and many of his senior Non-Commissioned Officers had been killed or wounded, under machine-gun fire from as little as fifty yards away, he reorganized the [forward] platoon, dealt with these machine-gun posts and continued to advance. [88]

Watson had been wounded in the attack but refused evacuation and continued to direct the battle. He was twice wounded during the war; finally ordered to England to recover, but soon returned as the commanding officer, North Shore (New Brunswick) Regiment, which he led from 4 November 1944 to 12 April 1945.

Watson was buttressed by the regimental sergeant-major, WOI Frederick Edward Blakeney, a Maritimer from North Sydney, Nova Scotia and a decorated soldier. He enlisted in the West Nova Scotia Regiment in 1939. As a corporal, he had been commended for distinguished conduct in 1940 and awarded the British Empire Medal in 1943. A year later, he won the prestigious Military Medal at San Lorenzo

Italy on 15 September 1944, as the platoon sergeant of 7 Platoon, A Company, the West Novies:

> During the attack, Company Headquarters was temporarily in a house at the foot of the feature. This building received several direct hits from heavy shells and the Company Sergeant-Major and six other members of Company Headquarters were wounded. Sergeant Blakeney immediately took over as Company Sergeant-Major at a time when the battle was particularly fierce. He quickly organized Company Headquarters and led them into the attack through very heavy shell fire and machine-gun fire from dug-in infantry and Tiger tanks ... the company was attacked by tanks and was very heavily shelled and machine-gunned. Sergeant Blakeney personally organized the company and supervised the digging in, setting a magnificent example to the men by his courage, coolness and leadership under fire.[89]

Blakeney then supervised the collection and evacuation of the company's casualties under great difficulties; there were no stretchers and the bearers all cut down. The house in which the wounded were being collected was hit six times by heavy shells and was under machine-gun fire. However, under Sergeant Blakeney's leadership, all the casualties were successfully evacuated. [90]

This dynamic duo added new riches to the coffers of regimental history. Blakeney was a 'traditional' RSM, but Colonel Watson was in every sense a 'character' – particularly well remembered by the 2nd Battalion's drummers (a body of men well-known for its characters). Their drum major was Michael Phelan, ex-Seaforth Highlander, ex-oilfield rough-neck, and a former professional prize-fighter who:

> ...ran the pipes and drums like a nineteenth-century Prussian Guard and this was no mean feat, since pipers and drummers are traditionally most difficult to handle. When faced with an uncooperative piper or drummer, the drum major would stand to his full height, draw his shoulders back, tuck in his chin and look at the miscreant as if he were made of dirty rifle swabs.[91]

Phalen's single goal was to create the best band in the world; his burning ambition was to introduce new black rod-tension drums into the band. But Colonel Watson was adamant – the battalion would parade with brass-shelled, rope-tension drums as long as he was around and that was that. "As far as I am concerned," *Bucko* used to say, "If you can't shine the shells and whiten the ropes, a drum isn't a drum." The drum major's plea that they sounded like Iroquois *tom-toms* did not faze the colonel one bit and Phalen was too much of a soldier to lose a competition to make his point. He finally got his rod-tension drums on the day Colonel Watson left the battalion. "The band continued to win competitions (no more than before), but at least they didn't have to shine the shells."[92]

Rocky vs. Bucko

General, we'll talk about this later.

Lieutenant Colonel William De Norban Watson, Gagetown, 1957

Watson, though a bit of a stick-in-the-mud, was old school when it came to his battalion, which he guarded with a fierce seigniorial authority. He left an indelible impression on his officers, one a future colonel:

It was the summer of 1957. Major-General Rockingham was commanding the 1st Canadian Infantry Division, concentrated at CFB Gagetown for summer training. I had just been commissioned a few weeks earlier and posted to 2 RHC. By good luck, I had a superb company commander and a great platoon sergeant. As the platoon commander of 3 Platoon, A Company, I was on top of the world. One of the major exercises that summer was Exercise SPITFIRE. An all-arms, live-firing exercise it was alleged to be the most comprehensive exercise of its sort ever carried out in Canada. Each company in the Division went through it in turn. Press coverage was extensive with much of it devoted to how General Rockingham was personally supervising the conduct of the exercise.[93]

The third day found the Black Watch at the ranges. The divisional staff arrived with the cacophony of peacocks. They discovered Lieutenant George Logan. On completion of the safety check, platoon commanders rendezvoused on a small knoll where General Rockingham decided to critique the company's performance. The general was impatient and turned on Logan as soon as he arrived, snarling: "Far too slow young man!" "Yes, sir!" Rockingham was determined to find fault: "Where is your radio set?" "Right here sir!" responded Logan, pointing to his radio man, standing beside him. Rocky tore into him with undisguised hostility: "Why aren't you carrying it yourself?" Logan went blank: "Suddenly I didn't know why I wasn't carrying it. I hadn't really thought about it. It was just the way it was when I joined the platoon." Rockingham closed in for the kill: "In my division, the officers carry their radios!" Suddenly, a voice from behind: "Sir, in my battalion, platoon commanders do *not* carry their radio sets." It was *Bucko* Watson coming to Logan's defence. Rockingham's eyes narrowed as he returned to Logan, about to unleash a stern tactics lecture – but was intercepted by Watson: "General, we'll talk about this later."

General Rockingham paused. He considered the Black Watch CO. The two warhorses were veterans of a dozen European battles, both wore DSOs. He then grunted and marched off, leading his zealous gaggle. Logan was spared: "I felt my heart beating with pride for my regiment and absolute love and devotion for my CO. I would have followed Colonel Watson anywhere. And, in 2 RHC, signallers continued to carry the radio sets."[94]

Watson was followed by five COs (CHE Askwith, WC Leonard, DA McAlpine, HJ Harkes, and WB MacLeod) who led the 2nd Bn RHC through the Regiment's golden age: a period that began in 1958 and took the Black Watch through two magnificent Royal parades, the 100th Anniversary and the Canadian Centennial – years with a surfeit of championships and recognition. The history was the same for the 1st Battalion. Following the reorganization under WH Seamark, a series of steady (yet innovative) commanding officers appeared: Lieutenant Colonels JME Clarkson, DS MacLennan, WA Teed, GH Sellar, WJ Newlands and GS Morrison. The Regiment's last battalion commanders, Scotty Morrison and Bentley MacLeod, were to endure the extra trial of training and operational deployment under the gnawing knowledge that they were to be disbanded. Yet they too achieved outstanding results.

Lieutenant Colonel JME Clarkson MC CD, 1 RHC 1956

Lieutenant Colonel John Michael Elliott Clarkson took over 1 RHC in January 1956. He was a University of Toronto graduate and had campaigned in Italy with the 48th Highlanders. He was later appointed as ADC to then Field Marshal BLM Montgomery. Clarkson's war career was distinguished: Mentioned in Despatches and awarded the Military Cross for an action in Ortona:

> On 23 December 1943, the 48th Highlanders of Canada had penetrated the enemy's defensive position ... West of Ortona to a depth of about two thousand yards ... [subsequently] the unit came under heavy shell and mortar fire and it was apparent that the enemy were forming up, about one battalion in strength, to counter-attack.

> At this time, word was received that a troop of tanks was available for support if a route could be reconnoitred and a guide sent to them. Lieutenant Clarkson with complete disregard for his personal safety and with great skill, personally reconnoitred a route for the tanks over one thousand yards of country occupied by the enemy, and in spite of heavy shell mortar and machine-gun fire, guided the tanks to the battalion area ... This action contributed directly to the ultimate withdrawal of the enemy from the area.[95]

Clarkson and his battalion were kept busy training and accommodating a growing list of requests for participation on ceremonial occasions. On 14 October 1956, The Black Watch mounted the Halifax Citadel Guard, which was highlighted by a pay parade on the Citadel square. The men were paid in cash by Lieutenant EM Knorr, the 1 RHC Paymaster. This was the first pay parade to be held in the Citadel since 1859 and destined to be an event completely eclipsed by cybernetic accounting. During a pay parade, the soldier or officer marches to a simple table where sit an officer and an NCO with nominal rolls and mountains of cash and behind them, an armed corporal. Once vetted and money received, the payee salutes and marches off. The paymaster is saluted no matter what his rank, for this is *The Queen's Money* and compliments are required.

Piping for the Queen and President

To the Regiment's delight, when Queen Elizabeth II visited the United States in the summer of 1957, the pipes and drums of 1st and 2nd RHC and the military band were invited to Washington to perform at a garden party held on the grounds of the British Embassy, where the Queen hosted the American President, Dwight "Ike" Eisenhower. The Black Watch piped-in the Queen and President with clear enthusiasm – and the former Supreme Allied Commander made a point of commending their play. The band fondly recalled that: "The Queen came over to us while we were on a wee break and thanked us for being there." It proved to be a busy expedition: "We played a parade down Constitution Ave, played at the Pentagon and a full-dress retreat at Fort Myers, Virginia, where we stayed – it was at Myers where [we] tasted our first pizza!"[96] Particularly popular was the pipe band's rendition of the US Marine Corps hymn *'From the Halls of Montezuma'*, which invariably brought cheers and ovations. A contingent was also requested to fly to New York and play at a state banquet held at the Waldorf–Astoria Hotel for the Queen. Pipe Major Duncan Rankine and three pipers went up, and much enjoyed 'The Big Apple'.

Lieutenant Colonels CHE Askwith CD

Following Bucko Watson was no easy task but the next 2 RHC CO was a suave Montrealer, who was at home with generals and privates. He was particularly at ease with Montreal Black Watch social circles, Kenneth Blackader, the Cantlies, McDougalls and Molsons being family friends. He joined the Regiment in January 1940 and was well thought of by Stuart Cantlie: "His quiet methods will produce good discipline and much respect from the ORs."[97]

Lieutenant Colonel Charles Hopewell English Askwith had studied at McGill expecting to be an accountant. He served with 1 RHC from December 1941 to February 1942. He was then posted as adjutant, 5 Bde Trg Wing 2 CDIRU until January 1943, and then sent on a series of staff positions (including Staff College) ending the war as GSO3, Headquarters, 3 Cdn Inf Div. Askwith was awarded the *Croix de Guerre* by the French in April 1945 (which he received alongside Campbell Stuart and CSM NW Price).

> Lieutenant Charles Askwith landed on the beaches of Normandy on D Day as Liaison Officer at Headquarters, Third Canadian Infantry Division ... For four days and nights during the battles of Gruchy, Buron and Authie this officer was constantly carrying reports backwards and forwards and during the period had no opportunity to sleep or rest ... At this time [9 July 1944] it was vital that special instructions be carried to the brigade commander. Without further rest Lieutenant Askwith immediately volunteered to take this message through ... Lieutenant Askwith ran the gauntlet over exposed ground and succeeded in reaching the commander [9 Cdn Inf Bde] ...[98]

Askwith had a fastidious, yet philanthropic style, and ensured the standards set by Ross and Watson were maintained. "He was a real gentleman, very quiet, quite thoughtful; he did not fit the mould of a parade ground soldier as his physique was more like an office clerk ... he was an excellent Military Assistant to the Chief of the General Staff ... was always fair and considerate."[99] Askwith was succeeded by WC "Bill" Leonard MBE, destined to be a major general and to exercise influence on the "modernized" army of the 1960s. In 1984, Lieutenant Colonel Askwith was appointed Usher of the Black Rod in the Canadian Parliament.[100]

Gagetown Garrison Duties

> In years gone past
> I was the class
> Of every major exercise
>
> Captain BE Harper, Ode to Lieutenant Colonel Clarkson, 1959

As the Black Watch battalions continued to train at Aldershot, 2 RHC advance parties were sent to coordinate its relocation to the newly built Camp Gagetown in New Brunswick. 2 RHC was scheduled to relocate, while 1 RHC deployed to Germany. WO I Ron Finnie was appointed divisional senior RSM of 1st Cdn Inf Division and performed his duties with his customary zeal and style: "When the divisional RSMs get together, it is no different. We bark orders at each other as well as at the privates."[101]

Their shooting was not bad either. The 2nd Bn again dominated the inter-service competition at the Bedford ranges in Halifax, in the early fall. WOI I Blakeney won the individual high-aggregate trophy. Both the CO and RSM had their eye on one specific trophy: The Hamilton-Gault, awarded annually to the Regular unit with the highest points in annual classification for the rifle. To an infantry battalion, it was the *sine qua non* of their profession. "The Jocks", as the Black Watch officers and NCOs were beginning to call their soldiers, were carefully trained and much rehearsed for competition: "Newer members of the battalion diligently studying pamphlets, memorizing the names of parts … etc." When the 1st Bn rifle team won the Eastern Command Rifle Meet – the credit was given to the skill and diligence of their coach, CSM "Nobby" Clarke.

Bastion of Military Boxing – Sergeant Les Mason, Canadian Champion

The Black Watch, as a regiment, became a bastion of Army boxing. The 2 RHC boxing team successively captured the 1955 and 1956 Eastern Command championship, and competed at the Army finals in Kingston, Ontario, which it won. The team, coached by S/Sergeant John Debison, went on to box for the Canadian Amateur Championships in Camrose, Alberta in April 1956, and again in 1957, where Sergeant Les Mason won, for the second year, the Canadian amateur welterweight title; he won the light welterweight class in the 1958 Olympic trials. Private Mike Christmas was runner-up for the bantam title. Although other sports and trials abounded, in the '50s and '60s, everyone was far more concerned with boxing. The 2 RHC team under Debison won the brigade and Eastern Command finals in Halifax and qualified for the Army championships in Kingston. As the decade ended, the Black Watch simply dominated competitions in the greater Maritime garrison.[102] Their biggest opposition came from the Navy teams: HMCS *Shearwater, Stadacona* and *Cornwallis*.

Each battalion stressed mastery of infantry skills. The First Battalion's 1 Platoon under 2/Lieutenant John Gazeley won the Sevastopol Trophy for speed marching. The battalion then swept the drill competition, winning the top four places, with 2 Platoon taking the Alma Trophy. CSM Nobby Clarke of HQ Company won his fourth "first" out of six COs' inspection of the barracks. The RSM was delighted: "We'd sure be lost without you Nobby – so how about signing that re-engagement form?" Meantime, the battalion QM stores suffered the "Scourge of the Earth" as the ordnance inspection team made a visit. They passed.

The veteran Clarkson had steadied the new battalion, adjusting to a flood of recruits, now mostly from the Maritimes. Major General Andrew Christie, then a junior officer in the Watch, recalled: "He enforced the rules … our confidence grew."

Lieutenant Colonel Clarkson would command for just over two years to be succeeded in 1959 by the colourful Don MacLennan. John Clarkson was popular: "He made us work but made us think."[103] His leaving was punctuated with receptions awash with *Moosemilk* (a potent and powerful brew that can only be mixed successfully by the sergeants' mess) and even a ditty along the lines of Gilbert and Sullivan:

> In years gone past I was the class of every major exercise
> By dint of guile in Monty's style Opponents I would mesmerize ...
> My scope is three-dimensional,
> My tactics unconventional,
> I am the very model of a (future) major-general[104]

Chapter 8

The Third Battalion RHC in a New Role and "Militia" Again

We are the Royal Highlanders, we come from Montreal,

And some of us from Westmount and some from Côte-St-Paul

And when we get to Russia, we'll show them who's the best

We're the boys who stop the bullets with the Molsons on our chest

The WWI Trench Song, converted in the Cold War by 3 RHC

A New Role for the Reserves and an Old Name Resurrected

"Do We Still Need the Militia?"[105]

By 1953, it became clear that some of the contributing Reserve units could not meet their training tasks nor could they produce sufficient recruits to keep their designated Regular battalion companies up to strength. General Simonds decided it was time for reorganization. The Reserves, he concluded, were too diffuse, burdened by organizational, administrative and training deficiencies, and were "competing unduly against one another for the limited manpower available."[106] Finally, it was evident that reservists found it increasingly difficult to achieve the same training standards as their Regular Force counterparts – a perpetual, if not endemic problem that was destined to remain into the next millennium. There were seldom sufficient numbers of experienced personnel to enable the Reserves to train themselves properly,

---

particularly with the advanced weapons and mechanized tactics that were part of modern doctrine. Simonds concluded that, given the limited time available that the average Reserve Force officer and man can devote to his military training: "it might be better for the militia to have its training standards lowered."[107]

Simonds convened the Kennedy Board in May 1953. Named after its chairman, Major General Howard K Kennedy CBE MC, it comprised general officers tasked with reorganizing the Reserves. The Board concluded that the Reserves had to be overhauled radically and put forward twenty-four recommendations, including a change of name. The Reserve force should henceforth be known as the "Canadian Army (Militia)" which was its traditional title and a complete reversal of the order passed in 1940.

Unfortunately, the old/new title *Militia* was thought to have out-lived its effective societal usefulness and had become increasingly unpopular. The designation would linger to the end of the century when *Reserves* became the preferred term, although *Militia* remained in use.[108] The six divisions of the Canadian Army Reserve Force were disbanded, and some thirty-five formation headquarters were replaced by *Militia Group Headquarters*. The "new" Militia was ordered to provide the nucleus of a partially trained and equipped force in the case of an emergency, and to be ready to augment or assist the Regular Force, as required. Given the push to space-age technology and the spectre of atomic warfare, senior RCAF officers asked: "Do We Still Need the Militia?"[109] In fact, this was only the beginning. The Black Watch would soon be denied its very *raison d'être*: infantry training.

Lieutenant Colonel John Bourne ED CD, 1953–1955

When John Bourne returned to the post-war Black Watch, many were surprised, as most were certain he would forever be a member of *the Devil's Brigade*. Bourne had reverted from a First Special Service Force (FSSF) battalion commander to major and kept that rank for another eight years. Bourne, the son of Dr Wesley Bourne, did not complete his studies at McGill in order to leave for Great Britain with 1 RHC. He was promoted to captain, but when he was posted back to Canada as an instructor, volunteered for the FSSF. His accomplishments as an original battalion commander in the FSSF (The *Devil's Brigade*) gave him a reputation that went before him.

He was no push-over in the mess. Legends abound. Reportedly, he threw an annoying, overly familiar officer over the mess balcony and onto the parade square during a mess dinner; and once decked his son who came up unexpectedly behind him. After a rousing mess dinner-in-the-field at Camp Farnham, Major MacDougall suggested that perhaps the duty piper (or better yet, the pipe major) might enter the CO's tent playing *Johnny Cope* "to help him better wake up" (Bourne was trying to dress himself after crashing-in at 0430 hrs) – but no one would dare!

Bourne joined his father-in-law's company, Atlas-Gest, and by the time he became lieutenant colonel in 1952, he was president of Atlas Construction. Having served as second-in-command to Jim Knox, as commanding officer, he selected the battle-scarred John Kemp as his own 2IC. The latter, undaunted by the loss of a leg on Verrières Ridge, valiantly continued in the Reserves and was clearly destined for command. John Gibb-Carsley was made OC of B Company and Lieutenants Alexander and Glen were promoted to captains. As RSM, WO1 Dynes was succeeded by WO1 RA Ablett, who had been with the Regiment since 1937.

When he was appointed commanding officer, the regiment held its breath. Bourne was feared, some say hated, as a major. His stern discipline and no-nonsense methods sorted out many a too-casual officer.[110] However, he became a respected CO and later, a beloved Colonel of the Regiment. His gruff exterior belied a keen, romantic mind. He loved tradition and he was determined to serve his Regiment, and the Queen Mother, possibly his favourite persona, with all the energy he had. The challenges of a post-war Reserve battalion became as nothing, when it was revealed the Black Watch would become a three-battalion regiment.

With undisguised wonder, Bourne watched the Regiment grow. At the church parade, held 30 May 1954, a newly formed BW Cadet Corps marched with the Bishop's College School (BCS) Cadet Corps. There was a palatable sense of energy within the armoury as the sports teams brandished a jaunty style in their contests with the Montreal garrison. The Regimental baseball team, called itself "Bourne's Cripples" and sported fractions (½, ¼, ¾, etc.) instead of numbers on their uniforms. This Highland posse included corporate CEOs, lawyers and merchants; even a future parliamentary secretary to the minister of national defence. Egan Chambers MC MP, played second base ("it was like running into a brick wall sliding in").[111] Their trips to Toronto to play their rivals, the 48th Highlanders, were legend. For the first time in nineteen years, the team won the Montreal Military baseball trophy; but their luck ran out against the Ontario champions, The Irish Regiment of Canada, in the final for the Eastern Canadian championships. Highland competition was even more serious in the Maritimes and overseas.

Root Root Root For the Home Team – The Regular Battalions

All Black Watch battalions were sports-mad. The 1st Battalion's soccer team, recruited and coached by L/Corporal W Murray, had been formed in Aldershot and dominated the East, going on to win the Canadian Army championship 7–0 against the Queen's Own Rifles. Later, in Hanover, Germany, they were entered in the BAOR *Knockout Cup* competition – the only Canadian team to take part. They surprised the British by reaching the cup final. The Black Watch lost 2–1 against a side that included six professional players plus two temporarily posted from HQ Lubeck for the occasion. They acquitted themselves most creditably, the BAOR newspaper reported:

> Yesterday in Hindenburg stadium, a mixed crowd of English, Canadian and German spectators witnessed the fastest and cleanest game of football played in Hanover for many a day. The teams, The Canadian Highlanders and English REME [Engineers] … demonstrated very clever show of team work.[112]

Training continued – albeit with a modicum of doctrinal uncertainty. The influence of foreign wars was keenly felt. The 3rd Battalion participated in Exercise *Little Korea* at summer camp and was the best organized and most realistic exercise in which they participated since the end of the Second World War. Shooting was much practised. Private Pearson qualified to represent Canada at the Bisley shooting competitions in England.

In the new year, the popular "The Ed Sullivan Show" invited the Bleury Street pipes and drums to perform in New York on 25 January 1953. It was a special Burns' Night Scottish programme; Sullivan enlisted Robert Sherwood's assistance to obtain his Regiment's pipes and drums on a coast-to-coast television hookup. Sherwood introduced the band. Speaking for a minute, "he epitomized the traditions of the Black Watch and his pride in having served with it."[113] Highland optimism continued as the usual summer attrition did not occur. The Bleury Street battalion increased in numbers. The Black Watch (RHR) of Canada Cadet Corps, formed in the armoury under Captain RA Dynes, had grown out of The Black Watch Boys' pipes and drums and formed its own junior pipe band that was sponsored jointly by the Regiment and the St Andrew's Society of Montreal. Dynes had been RSM from 1946 to 1952 and became the moving spirit of the Corps. In the first year, forty-eight cadets attended a special summer camp and successfully passed their courses. Another seventy applied the next summer. As recruiting for all three battalions swelled, soldiers even volunteered for extra drill on the parade square. The Regiment was authorized to complete its martial philharmonic with the addition of a Military Band in the spring of 1954.

Royal Performance and Determined Training

The Governor General of Canada, the Right Honourable Vincent Massey was the guest of honour at the fall reunion dinner in 1954. Over 160 officers attended. The piping was superb and praised by His Excellency. Shortly before, the Black Watch was asked to provide eight pipers for a grand dinner hosted by the English-speaking Union of

The United States in New York City, honouring Queen Elizabeth the Queen Mother, the Regiment's Colonel-in-Chief. Mr Massey also attended. The contingent was led by Pipe Major Hannah. When the group arrived at Uplands Airport in new uniforms, they drew "many admiring glances and words of praise – and perhaps aroused just a bit of envy in the Canadian Guards who were raising a pipe band of their own."[114] The pipers were a hit and were presented to Her Majesty. She declared to Lieutenant Colonel Bourne that they were "a credit to the Regiment." Directly afterwards, the Colonel-in-Chief visited Ottawa and the Black Watch was asked to send three pipers to Government House to play at the State Dinner. Brigadier Blackader, as Acting Colonel of the Canadian Regiment, was invited to attend the royal reception with his Regiment's commanding officers. He brought Lieutenant Colonel WM Seamark, CO 1 RHC, and Lieutenant Colonel John Bourne, CO 3 RHC (Lieutenant Colonel RM Ross, CO 2 RHC, had not returned from Korea). Queen Elizabeth requested that the Black Watch officers be brought together after the dinner so she might address them privately. "It was a memorable evening."[115]

The Blue Balmoral with the Red Hackle

In March 1954, all three battalions were given permission to wear the blue balmoral with the Red Hackle and the green Highland coatee. The parent regiment, the Imperial Black Watch, had recently adopted this uniform. In fact, the Canadian Black Watch became the larger of the two when, in October 1956, The Black Watch of Scotland was reduced to one battalion in the British Regular Army; it lost as well its independent Regimental Depot.

The tactical training was focused entirely on current Cold War experience and feared possibilities. The Militia battalion was told to practise both field craft and civil defence drills. While 1 RHC conducted nuclear attack exercises, training with "monitoring teams"; 2 RHC conducted combined schemes with the Centurion tanks of the Royal Canadian Dragoons. The 1954 Militia summer camps were made to emphasize practical training. Brooke Claxton, the minister of National Defence, who personally wrote to every Reserve unit, requested complete attendance. He backed up his letter by soliciting the co-operation of premiers, mayors and employers.[116] Colonel Bourne sent out a full complement of Red Hackles. Denied a tour in Korea, the 1st Battalion deployed to Camp Gagetown that summer. The camp was being constructed as the "the future Aldershot of Canada" – referring, of course, to the legendary British Army base in the Salisbury plains. The ultra-modern base was intended to house a full division poised to buttress NATO commitments.

The brigades established themselves in the field, living in tents but mostly out in the area. This large concentration culminated in a grand series of *atomic war games*, like Exercise *Rising Star*. The final assault took place in the pouring rain "but 1 RHC, nothing daunted, swept on to ultimate victory."[117] The summer ended with a memorable parade by the entire 1st Canadian Infantry Division, under the command of Major General John Rockingham DSO and Bar. Everyone was formed up in cohorts twelve deep on the Blissville airfield. Lieutenant General GG Simonds inspected and gave a rather stirring speech, which surprised veterans who had heard him before. The march-past was a remarkable sight, and the Watch left confident that they had prevailed. After all, there was nothing in the Division that could compare to the pipes and drums.

A "tremendous number" of officers and NCOs were sent on courses. In the middle of October, five officers went to the Royal Canadian School of Infantry in Camp Borden, Ontario, for Lieutenant–to–Captain examinations. "A real brain washing then ensued."[118] Officer training continued, their backgrounds reflecting no particular regional origin. Some were commissioned from the ranks of the battalion; a few were still veterans; but most came from universities (either military colleges or civilian *alma maters*). Typical summer groups for "Phase 3" training were RMC cadets or undergraduates from university Canadian Officers' Training Corps (COTC) contingents. A very small number might be from Montreal: McGill, Sir George Williams or Loyola College. They remained for three months and were often ("if they didn't look too dangerous") given a rifle platoon to command – but always under the watchful eye of an experienced sergeant. The COTC officers had the option of staying in the army; the RMC graduates were contracted for five years. The Black Watch seemed to attract a good number of top candidates.

Two Regimental Greats: Colonel Cantlie and Major General Ross

> Neither Montreal nor Canada will see his like again.
>
> Scotland's *Red Hackle,* bemoaning the death of Colonel George Cantlie[119]

In April 1956, Brigadier Blackader was pleased to order a special regimental parade; two hundred former officers, NCOs and junior ranks marshalled to demonstrate respect and affection for Colonel George Cantlie, aged ninety. Appropriately, it was held on a Tuesday evening working night. The Regular battalion in Aldershot sent representatives from all messes. The previous month, Colonel Cantlie had completed seventy years of continuous service with the Regiment, a Commonwealth record.[120] Major General JPE Bernatchez pinned the Canadian Forces Decoration (CD) decoration on Cantlie, elegant in Sam Brown Belt, cut-away tunic, and brown leather gloves.[121] The CD, crammed with three Clasps, had to be fixed near the shoulder seam of his jacket (Cantlie's queue of medals left little room for more). Brigadier Blackader described their honorary colonel as no less than "the Father of the Regiment" – a title significant in any military unit, but prodigious in the Montreal Black Watch, Canada's oldest Highland regiment.

At the beginning of the Great War, Cantlie had been selected as the London representative of Sam Hughes, Minister of Militia and Defence from 1911 to 1916; and yet he gave up this position and the certain rank of brigadier in order to lead his own battalion (the soon to be famous 42nd CEF) into battle. He survived two bloody campaigns, was awarded the DSO and though ordered home to recover, insisted on returning to Europe. Cantlie then commanded a second unit, the 20th Reserve Battalion, RHC. Appointed honorary lieutenant colonel after the Great War in 1920, he succeeded Sir Montagu Allan as honorary colonel in 1951.

George Cantlie had become a living landmark of Montreal, instantly recognized on his daily promenades down Sherbrooke Street, with cane and boutonniere – "a gallant old figure, bearing himself erect and with the dignity of service, every inch an officer and a gentleman."[122] Very much part of Montreal's *square mile*, the Colonel was one of the oldest members of The Church of St Andrew and St Paul and belonged to every prominent club in the city. His mansion, on the corner of Peel and Sherbrooke was directly opposite the Mount Royal Club, which he visited every day. It was at his club that Cantlie saw his first television broadcast (the Jersey Joe Walcott vs. Rocky Marciano fight on 15 May 1953): "I just sat down and the fight had ended," he lamented. That was also the last time Colonel Cantlie watched television.

To the sorrow of his beloved regiment and the regret of all who knew him, Colonel Cantlie died in the summer of 1956. The *Montreal Gazette* eulogized:

> Sherbrooke Street will never seem quite the same, now that Colonel George Stephen Cantlie is gone. His home was one of the last of the old residences that lingered on in the midst of change … Colonel Cantlie has been a link between past and present, a living tradition, a reminder of things to be respected and treasured. The dignity of service is his and the long years have been as kind to him as he is kindly."[123]

Cantlie's presence is made permanent by a strong portrait by the artist Alphonse Jongers that hangs above the Imperial snuff mull, next to the Colours in the Officers' Mess. The colonel is positioned to cast a steady guardian look toward the fireplace – the spot where the Colonels of the Regiment sit during mess dinners.

The warrior's passing was followed all too quickly by that of Cantlie's friend, ninety-four-year-old Major General James Ross. Dubbed 'The Grand Old Man of the Militia', he had signed on in 1879 and became a Lieutenant Colonel in the 5th Royal

Scots, The Black Watch antecedent. He was a famous marksman and commanded the Bisley Team. During the Great War, he was appointed Paymaster General of the CEF – *the most trusted man in the Canadian Army*. The General sniffed at the 1862 anniversary and took particular pains to point out the Regimental lineage extended to 1837 and beyond. After all, his family, friends and relatives had commanded Militia companies in 1812. The deaths of these two grand soldiers marked the end of the Regiment's living connection to the 19th Century.

> If there's another world, he lives in bliss
> If there is none, he made the best of this.
>
> Robert Burns

Lieutenant Colonel IR McDougall CD, 1955–1958

As long as Montreal remained an economic juggernaut, the Regiment had its pick of the best officer material in the City. Time passed surprisingly quickly. John Bourne began as CO RHC, then became CO 3rd Bn RHC, but before he had time to benefit from his work with the expanded regiment, he was at the end of his tour. Meantime, Major John Kemp was transferred by Hartland Molson to run the brewery's Toronto branch. To his great regret, Kemp was compelled to give up his turn at command. Lieutenant Colonel IR McDougall took over in May 1955 and selected WO1 T Turley CD as his regimental sergeant major, succeeding WO1 RA Ablett. The new RSM was "a war veteran and a rough and tumble guy."[124] The battalion's pipe major was a part of a Black Watch legacy, P/Major William J Hannah, assumed command of the pipes and drums in 1951. His father was pipe major from 1939 to 1946 – the first time in the Regiment that a father and son had been pipe majors.[125]

Lieutenant Colonel Ian Royden McDougall was the son of Group Captain GS McDougall OBE. He was educated in Switzerland, England and, at Westmount High. He was a Black Watch *auld* boy, chum of Knox, Petch and a European war veteran. He served in 1 RHC and was then seconded to the armoured corps where he became a squadron commander in the 8th Canadian Reconnaissance Regiment. McDougall was next posted to HQ 1 Cdn Army and in 1943, was appointed brigade major for 1 CIB. His service in Italy included conducting gutsy reconnaissances for his divisional boss, the brusque Major General Chris Vokes DSO (followed by Major General Harry Foster DSO in late fall), which got him into trouble. He was captured in December 1944 and spent the last five months of the war as a PW in Germany. Unshaken by his experience, he quickly rejoined the Reserve battalion as he began a civilian career in

Montreal. By 1948, he was director of marketing for Radio Engineer Products, and a Black Watch company commander; within seven years, he was the commanding officer.

Foreign Visits: Philadelphia RHC and USMC, 1956

There was concern about the declining strength of the Regiment. After the initial rush following the creation of the Regular battalions, the 3rd Battalion's numbers began to fall off and were soon declared very unsatisfactory. Although the paper strength was impressive, parade strength (actual attendance on parades, exercises, etc.) was disappointing.[126] By December 1955, the battalion reported that there were twenty-one officers and 248 Other Ranks; this was not the robust body seen before the war. The veterans found good work in a booming economy. Most were busy with new families, and the young men were committed to demanding jobs or finishing school. The advent of television made staying at home popular; attendance at the messes declined.

McDougall decided that in order to jump-start recruiting, he needed a bit of excitement and *pizzazz*. The regiment would trumpet (or skirl) its cause by bringing back the gusto of prewar days when exciting excursions made the armoury a stimulating place and gave the Watch international renown. He decided to take the battalion on an adventurous trek across the border.[127] On 8 June 1956, Lieutenant Colonel McDougall led his command on a two-day, goodwill visit to the United States. The 3rd Battalion, almost three hundred strong including the pipes and drums led by Pipe Major Hannah, journeyed to Philadelphia, whose name most appropriately, means 'City of Brotherly Love'. McDougall brought greetings from the Mayor of Montreal, His Worship Sarto Fournier. The Regiment was warmly received at Independence Hall for an exchange of gifts. Mayor Richardson Dilworth presented Colonel McDougall with the Philadelphia flag, which still hangs in the armoury, while Major Jim Macfarlane offered a Claymore to the mayor, who, in true Scottish fashion, gave a penny in return in order not to cut their friendship. The Regiment was then given that special distinction, the *Freedom of the City*: "whereas free men of the city, while with fixed bayonets, uncased their colours and marched through the streets of Philadelphia." McDougall commented: "To the best of our knowledge this is an honour which has been given to no other Canadian regiment by a city in the United States of America. And perhaps to no other foreign unit."[128]

At the formal dinner, the haggis ("great chieftain o' the puddin' race") was piped in; the snuff was passed (the battalion brought down ram's head snuff mulls from

Bleury Street) and the assembly drank the health of the Queen and the President. During the Regimental toasts, "Jim Macfarlane asked that this be done with full Highland honours [left foot on the chair and the right foot on the table]."[129] It became a late night; most officers did not retire until 3:00 am. At sunrise, the duty piper played *Johnny Cope* near the officers' windows to get them started. The Black Watch were guests of the United States Marine Corps at the Philadelphia Navy Yard. Host duties were also shared by the *First Troop of Philadelphia Cavalry*. The First Troop had been raised by Benjamin Franklin and served as General George Washington's bodyguard during the American War of Independence. The visit included a parade at Washington's Monument and a visit to Benjamin Franklin's grave at Christ Church – on the 250th anniversary of the American statesman's birth. At the monument, Lieutenant Colonel McDougall placed a wreath and Pipe Major William Hannah played *Lochaber No More* to commemorate both Franklin and the first American president. As well, the visit also marked a happy renewal of association with a historic Philadelphia reserve unit – the 111th Infantry Regiment of the Pennsylvania National Guard. The connection, which was with the Imperial Black Watch, began in the eighteenth century in the forests of Pennsylvania.

The trek proved a great success and Ian McDougall noted that recruiting improved in September. That fall, the 1956 reunion dinner welcomed as its guest of honour the Chief of Clan Fraser and perhaps Britain's most famous commando, Brigadier Lord Lovat DSO MC. Appropriately, the first march played by Pipe Major Hannah was 'Lord Lovat's Lament'.

Memorial Service St Andrew and St Paul, 6 October 1957

By These things Men Live.

Isaiah 38:16, theme of Padre Berlis's sermon, 6 October 1957

It was one of those glorious *Indian Summer* days, when warm sunshine is complemented by cool breezes from the St Lawrence and the trees along Sherbrooke Street are turning gold, bronze and red. Large crowds attended the regimental church parade on 6 October 1957. The Regiment unveiled a handsome bronze tablet to honour their fallen comrades of both World Wars. Captain the Rev RJ Berlis, who had been minister of The Church of St Andrew and St Paul since 1946, was still the chaplain of the Regiment. Sherbrooke Street was a sea of hackles. The parade comprised contingents from the Regular Force 1st and 2nd Battalions, as well as the 3rd Battalion and the affiliated Cadet Corps. Most treasured was the great number of Black Watch veterans from the Great War battalions, including Major General Eric

McCuaig DSO and Lieutenant Colonel IMR Sinclair DSO MC, who both commanded the 13th Bn CEF. They were followed by Brigadier Kenneth Blackader DSO MC and Colonel William MacTier MC, who won their Military Crosses with the 13th Bn RHC; and Colonel PP Hutchison who served in the 42nd and 73rd Bn RHC, and more recently as the Regimental Colonel during the war. These gallant soldiers led a veritable pride of lionized officers past the saluting base: Lieutenant Colonels Bourne, Knox, Ibbotson, Mitchell, Wallis and Mills.[130] The church parade brought out over 150 marching veteran members of the Association; who in turn were cheered on by another three hundred war veterans lining the street.

That day also witnessed a change of honorary lieutenant colonel in the 3rd Battalion as Bill MacTier succeeded Ken Blackader. Colonel MacTier was twice wounded in the Great War; the first time at Ypres, perhaps the Watch's greatest battle. He served the Regiment again from 1921 to 1934; and then commanded the 12th Infantry Brigade from 1940 to 1946. Later, the messes were filled with soldiers young and old as happy receptions were held. Invalid soldiers were driven in and carried up or down stairways to their respective messes. The Montreal Branch of the Regimental Association was particularly active. The Welfare Committee looked after the veterans, having interviewed over 127 members. There were eighty RHC soldiers and officers at the St Anne's and Queen Mary Veterans' Hospitals. They were visited twice a month. The Hospital Visiting Committee, led by WO Frank Smythe, Major G Jarvis and the curator of The Black Watch Museum, Sergeant Jackson-Hall, made an average of fifty trips a year, bringing cigarettes and other gifts.

Lieutenant Colonel WA Wood CD, Claymores and Football: Philadelphia 1958

Lieutenant Colonel William Archibald (Billy) Wood succeeded Ian McDougall on 8 January 1958. The Montreal battalion's new CO was a veteran. A Lower Canada College (LCC) Old Boy, he joined before the war and went overseas with Blackader. Selected for Staff College, Wood served on the staffs of XIII and V British Corps. He was made a staff officer in 1st Canadian Corps HQ in Italy, and served until 1944. Following his promotion to lieutenant colonel, Wood was posted to Canada in command of the *S16 Combined Operations Training Centre*. After the war, he reverted to a lesser rank in order to continue to serve his Reserve regiment. He was a manufacturer, the president of Whitehouse Holdings. Wood was charming "a very gentle, quiet, thoughtful man; his family collected clocks."[131] His relationships with Bucko Watson and Clarkson were subdued, lacking the spark that Bourne and

Seamark could ignite. The Regular battalions were now firmly established and less dependent on Montreal. Wood devoted himself to revitalizing the Third Battalion.

That spring, the Regiment's pipes and drums travelled to Fort Ticonderoga, New York – the site of the storied, albeit ill fated, Black Watch assault during the Seven Years' War. Remarkably, the star-shaped Vauban bastion, as well as the terrain around it, changed little since 1758. The event commemorated the 200th anniversary of the battle. It was a stately occasion and included Hervé Alphand and Sir Harold Caccia, the French and British ambassadors to the United States, and Georges Savarin de Marestan, the current Marquis de Montcalm,[132] descendant of the general who fought the battle in 1758, when the fort was still named Carillon. He presented his ancestor's sword to the Ticonderoga Museum. Colonel Paul Hutchison represented both the Canadian and Imperial Black Watch. The RHC contingent (the combined pipe bands from 1st and 3rd RHC) were joined by the *musique de R22eR*. Wood was inspired.

He decided to follow up McDougall's earlier success in Philadelphia and formally re-establish the historic ties with the 111th US Infantry Regiment, Pennsylvania Army National Guard (known as "The Associators"). The unit is considered the oldest infantry regiment in the United States, founded in 1747 by Benjamin Franklin. The Pennsylvania connection dates back to The Seven Years' War (or as it is known in American history, The French and Indian War) when, in 1763, the Imperial Black Watch attacked an Indian force at Bushy Run and lifted the siege of Fort Pitt (originally Fort Duquesne, now the city of Pittsburgh). The battle is regularly commemorated each year at the 111th's annual mess dinner, where there is a place reserved for the representative of the Black Watch. The chair remains empty if no member of the Watch is present.

Accordingly, Wood selected the 195th anniversary of the relief of Fort Pitt for the official visit. Fortunately, the arrangements were in the hands of a long-time admirer of the Black Watch, Colonel C Kennedy Allen, adjutant of Valley Forge Military Academy, and an ardent military historian. He had previously donated a splendid oil painting of the 42nd attacking Bushy Run. McDougall despatched Major Darcy McGovern and a robust selection of soldiers and bandsmen.[133] The event had the gusto and flamboyance worthy of PT Barnum. There was a band, Highland dance recitals, a demonstration professional football game, and even a mounted troop of the RCMP.

Major Darcy McGovern in Philadelphia: Dirks n' Gavels

On 13 September 1958, the 3rd Battalion Black Watch, including detachments from the pipes and drums from 1 and 2 RHC, returned to Philadelphia. This time there were no buses. The battalion flew and were met at the airport by a guard of honour from the 111th. The September visit marked the second time in 195 years that "The Black Watch Chair" would be occupied. [134] Major Darcy McGovern led the contingent. They began with a parade through downtown Philadelphia, followed by a performance by regimental dancers at Raeburn Plaza, kicking off the gala weekend. The formal banquet included a double-tiered head table, and was held at Philadelphia's exclusive *Union League*. The guest speaker was the adjutant general of the Pennsylvania National Guard, AJ Drexel Biddle, Jr. He was followed by the assistant to the Canadian military attaché to Washington, Colonel John B Allan, who presented a fine Highland claymore from the Queen Mother on behalf of the Imperial Black Watch to George H Roderick, the assistant secretary of the United States Army. Roderick in turn, handed it over to Colonel White, who was delighted, although it turned out that the 3rd Battalion's later offering, a dirk, would acquire even greater renown.

On Sunday, an exhibition game of CFL Football was played between the Ottawa *Rough Riders* and the Hamilton *Tiger-Cats*; it was nationally televised from Philadelphia's Municipal Stadium.[135] Despite a convivial reception, the Canadian version of the game (which originated at McGill University) did not inspire the Americans to convert to Canuck rules. At halftime, the 111th and Black Watch paraded and exchanged mementoes. The 111th colonel presented a wooden gavel, carved from a window of the original White House, burned by a British fleet in 1814. It is sometimes mistakenly introduced as a trophy from that war by over enthusiastic subalterns.[136] The Montreal battalion, keen to present a suitable memento to their hosts, turned to Bill MacTier, its honorary lieutenant colonel, literally at the last minute. He gallantly agreed to offer his own magnificent Highland dirk, which was beautifully carved and decorated with silver mounts, the pommels set with cairngorm stones. McGovern presented this to Colonel White. It was subsequently known in the American regiment as 'the MacTier Dirk'. Everyone agreed it was a successful visit. The Regiment returned the hospitality of the 111th Regiment by inviting a delegation to the annual 'Burns Nicht Supper' on 24 January 1959. Curiously, this camaraderie would be lost until the new millennium, when Colonels MacKay and Plourde reinitiated exchange visits and combined field-training weekends.

Joining and Serving the Regiment in Montreal – Pre Millennium

If you wanted to join the army, you were free to go down to the Craig Street Armouries and do so; but if you wanted to be a member of the Black Watch you had to be first considered and accepted by the junior officers.

Major Doug Robertson, 3 RHC

Of course, you still needed a sponsor in those days.

Lieutenant Colonel Hal Klepak, 3 RHC, on joining the Regiment

It was a tradition in Montreal's Black Watch that the respective messes should be supported and managed by the Regiment. Well after the war, the soldiers gave up 10 percent of their pay ("When we finally got paid – we had a paymaster famous for not paying anybody"); the senior NCOs donated 50 percent to the sergeants' mess and the officers gave up 100 percent. This continued up to the mid-1960s. However, they usually did not pay for their uniforms. Despite the feared expense of joining, few officers purchased entire regimental suites. The quartermasters' stores were full of Highland livery from the finest tailors in London and Montreal, donated by retired officers dating to the early 1930s, and before. Some simply inherited from their fathers or brothers.[137]

The top tailor in Montreal, if not Canada, was *Gibb's*. He made suits for prime ministers. Major Jack Gibb-Carsley was a member of the Regiment and was often heard to say: "Every gentleman should be in debt to his tailor." Subalterns recall arriving at his store on Mountain Street, being presented with bolts of cloth, measured, and advised that anything that may seem difficult will be hidden. The fittings were a blur of activity. Jackets were slipped on, "chalk marks applied, and ripped off one shoulder, then another, the threads offering no resistance ..." These were handed to a junior tailor and then, if Gibbs liked your style, he would invite you across the street to *Cafe Martin* for a drink. This was flattering but dangerous. Many a young executive risked his career: "I've just started at *MacBlanque and Sons* – I cannot be late after lunch!" "Piff!" sniffed Gibbs and ordered another whisky. Most suspected it was a test. The strong-willed excused themselves, went to work, and inevitably became executives and colonels.[138]

While most senior Regimental officers may appear to be brokers, insurance executives and lawyers, downtown Montreal was presided over by Black Watch merchants, whose stores lined St Catherine Street. Henry Morgan, who remained active in the 73rd Bn Association, owned a department store that had become one of the great Montreal business landmarks and now, as *La Baie*, remains prominent. Morgan's baroque facade overlooks Philips Square, facing Montreal's, indeed Canada's, most famous jeweller. Birks was massive and immediately daunting; the front doors were iron bulwarks with great bolts, heavy locks, fixed with a bronze family crest. The elegant Henry Gifford Birks, a loyal member of The Black Watch Regimental Association, continued to oversee the store. Members of the Birks family had served the Regiment in both wars, two of them fighting in France with the 42nd and 73rd Battalions. It was an association that would continue into the new millennium.

At the west-end of St Catherine Street stood Ogilvy's, the flank guard to the City's grand stores. It was run by Brigadier Aird Nesbitt. He bought Ogilvy's before the war in 1927, at a cost of $37,500. He was nineteen at the time and intent on simply "tarting it up" and selling it off, but he fell in love with the place and ran it for fifty-four years. During the war, though a Black Watch officer, he was seconded from 1 RHC to the Cape Breton Highlanders, with whom, as a company commander, he saw considerable campaigning in Italy. After the war, Nesbitt returned to Montreal, rejoined the Regiment and went on to command the entire military district. He was much devoted to his store. It is the only one of Montreal's four major west-end retailers still operating under its original name and is also known as the 'Grande Dame of St Catherine Street'. His aim was a unique Ogilvy look, and he sent forth his buyers to comb Faubourg St-Honoré, Knightsbridge and the Via Condotti for exciting ideas and handpicked merchandise. He turned Ogilvy's into a five-story *boutique*; he also added a floor to house an oak panelled concert hall, buying an Aeolian pipe organ that cost more than he originally paid for the store. Customers dined at The Tartan Room that served minced buffalo meat and Cornish pasties. Nesbitt maintained Scottish traditions. A kilted piper (invariably a corporal from the Black Watch) appeared to pipe out the last customers every Saturday afternoon. This ritual continues to this day although the piper now plays at noon, winding his way throughout the store. "The Brigadier" was beloved by his staff. The four hundred sales clerks had no punch clocks and could always have a word with their boss who liked to prowl the floors asking, "Who's abusing you today?"

The Regiment always had at least one doctor. The RHC medical officer in the 1960s was Major Jack Patrick MD, a McGill graduate affiliated with the Royal Victoria Hospital. He joined as a Black Watch officer and wore that uniform. He was a gynecologist and sometimes left mess dinners to deliver babies. The junior officers would all call as he left: "Make sure you wash your hands!" Sometimes he managed to get back to the mess in time to rejoin the gathering; and everyone would yell again "Make sure you wash your hands!"

He also delivered officers' children. On one occasion, he entered the *Waiting Room* (in those days fathers were expected to wait outside) and approached two Black

Watch junior captains, who promptly stood up. "Good morning Sir." "What are you guys doing?" The elder of the two held a cold thermos. "We're having a Martini." Patrick, with a twinkle in his eye: "That looks like a good idea. I think I'll have one too." He turned to the father: "Congratulations, you have a healthy little girl. And give me a little cup, I'll take it in to your wife who has been working hard all night."[139]

The Subalterns' Inquisition

If you can look onto the seeds of time
And say which grain will grow and which will not.

Shakespeare, *Macbeth*

It was apparent, to anyone who cared to look, that since the turn of the century, The Black Watch was not affecting to be Montreal society – it was. That remained true after 1945, when Montreal was still the engine that drove Canada, and where anything important or worthy of note could be found in the City. The officers were still from the upper strata and took parental care of their battalion. For example, Major Dan Downey put two of the soldiers in his company through dental college at his own expense.

Despite the fact that armouries no longer enjoyed their prewar clout of attracting businessmen and professionals in large numbers, potential officers were vetted in the self-same manner as in the days of the 5th Royal Scots – a tradition adhered to since the era of Crawford, Campbell and Caverhill. The due process of acceptance required that POs (potential officers) signify their desire to join by filling out a membership application, reinforced by the signatures of two members of the Regiment (a proposer and a seconder). They were next called by the Senior Subaltern and asked to appear on a parade night. POs were expected to mix with the junior officers. This was followed by an interview, which was considered almost as taxing as appearing before the Colonel. After two or three Tuesday nights, the candidates were discussed by the subalterns; their strengths and weaknesses were carefully considered and a consensus sought. The chemistry had to be there: *compatibility, personality,* and importantly, *would we want him in the family*? "Theirs was not the last word but pretty close to the last word." Symbolic of the democracy of the gentleman's club, everyone voted. Leonard Ferdon, notorious as the most strapped boy in Westmount's Roslyn School, was sent out from LCC to Sedbergh School, a tough school for tough Westmount boys. He arrived at the Regiment with Steve Angus, as recent graduates from McGill. In his interview, he was closely examined by one of the lieutenants, Johann Draper (a Canadian ski jumping champion) who heard of him:

Aren't you the blankety-blank with that terrible Great Dane, "Juggernaut"? Weren't you also making bombs out of shotgun shells and throwing them at streetcars on The Boulevard?

Yes.

But you have two gorgeous sisters?

Yes.

Ferdon passed this test with flying colours. Next, accepted officers were presented to the CO who could overrule, but tended to respect his subaltern's recommendation. The "medical" was conducted by the unit MO. After brigade headquarters stamped approval, the potential officer began initial training, wearing the rank badge of a second lieutenant, not "officer cadet" as was the custom in other regiments. The Black Watch did not recognize "officer cadets" and somehow, this was never challenged on courses, where everyone else wore a white tab beneath their single pip.

The "pure reserve" process differed from the Canadian Officers' Training Corps (COTC), which was a step closer to RMC training, but without a commitment to four years' service after graduation. COTC officers were trained in their universities and had their own messes. Conversely, under *Plan B Training*, Militia officers were instructed at their armouries, during the winter, on Tuesday nights, taking courses in map-using, military law, basic drill and regimental history. The "subbies" (subalterns) then attended a two-week qualification course given during the summer at Valcartier or Gagetown. It took about three years to become a full lieutenant, two years with a degree. At the end of the third summer, the gentlemen received the Queen's Commission as second lieutenants. In essence, they took the same courses as the Regular Force but more compressed and extended over a longer period. The instruction (and perhaps the instructors) was less intense. Ferdon, for example, joined in 1956 and was commissioned September 1959. It took about seven years to become a captain. The subaltern selection system was not foolproof nor was it exclusive to the Black Watch. Some officers slipped through – but in general, the Regiment was complimented on their officers' style. One cavalry officer noted: "Black Watch officers may sometimes be tactically challenged, but they are the most polite and pleasant in the garrison."

By the end of the millennium, the strict vetting of potential officers was somewhat relaxed, but the training, particularly after 2003, became more exacting. It was done exclusively by Regulars – veterans of Afghanistan. However, the subalterns (in an interesting display of democracy within a draconian society) still had some influence.

The First Colonel of the Regiment:
Brigadier KG Blackader CBE DSO MC ED CD

Rather imposing – strict, good looking, tall, and carried an air of absolute authority.

Major WE Stavert, of Brigadier General KG Blackader

Directly after the formation of the two Regular battalions, the Regiment requested authority to name Brigadier KG Blackader as Colonel-of-the-Regiment for The Black Watch, an appointment that, up to that time, had never been made in Canada. At last, after six years, in September 1958, the Adjutant-General informed Bleury Street that the appointment of *Colonel-of-the-Regiment of The Black Watch of Canada* had been approved.

Conferences and meetings of the Regimental Advisory Board now included representatives from all three battalions and the Regimental Depot. Lieutenant Colonel Val Traversy was appointed Vice Chair and became the "senior staff officer" to Blackader (in effect, the regimental secretary). The brigadier was "rather imposing, strict, and carried an air of absolute authority."[140] Jim Knox immediately set about preparing a draft to delineate the key aspects of the Colonel-of-the-Regiment's position, which went well beyond liaison and visits. The Brigadier saw his mission as twofold: "to foster *esprit de corps* within the Regiment [and] co-ordinate details of dress and to act in an advisory capacity to unit commanders on specific regimental matters so as to ensure uniformity." In 1960, Brigadier Blackader issued a detailed memorandum that broadened the functions of the *5th Royal Highlanders of Canada Armoury Association*. The regimental order, following DND directives, defined the responsibilities of his position, which he summed up succinctly: "The Colonel of the Regiment is concerned with every decision which will or could affect the Regiment as a whole."[141]

Brigadier A Hamilton Gault DSO ED CD 1882–1958

The year ended sadly with the death of a great warrior and a respected Black Watch officer, the revered father of The Princess Patricia's Canadian Light Infantry. Brigadier A Hamilton Gault DSO died in Montreal on 28 November 1958, aged 76. He came of an old and distinguished Scottish Canadian family; a score of its members (Kenneth Gault Blackader was a cousin) passed through The Black Watch of Canada as commissioned officers. Gault was a successful businessman, and from 1910–1912, Consul-General for Sweden at Montreal. He singly raised a veteran's battalion destined to become a legend in battle and a future member of the triumvirate that dominates Canada's Regular army. Despite his experience in South Africa, Gault was content to serve as the PPCLI second-in-command. Colonel Paul Hutchison recalled:

> At the Front, Gault was an outstanding soldier – always gay, completely fearless and amazingly gallant in action. He was the first Canadian during the Somme to be awarded the DSO and was Mentioned in Despatches four times and was wounded severely on three separate occasions. His last wounds resulted in the loss of a leg...With an artificial leg it became too difficult for him to continue to lead a unit in the trenches. Late in 1917 he finally consented to take command of a staging camp for his brigade reinforcements... many of us have vivid memories of passing through that staging camp – his gallant figure riding out to meet a new draft (Gault was a beautiful horseman and had been an expert polo player).[142]

Brigadier Gault was a passionate imperialist. From 1925–1934 he was the Member of Parliament for Taunton in the British House of Commons. Gault served Canada again in the Second World War helping both the PPCLI and Black Watch in their recruiting. He was promoted and commanded a training brigade in England. After each war, Hamilton Gault returned to Montreal and lived at his estate at Mont St-Hilaire, southeast of Montreal. He was a frequent visitor to the Black Watch mess, and well-remembered by his nieces simply as 'Uncle Hamie'. Gault left his mark on several generations: he was the model of a gallant soldier.

Dinners and Clubs – 1958

That fall, Major General the Hon George Pearkes VC DSO MC, Canada's Minister of Defence was the Regiment's guest of honour at the Reunion Dinner. It was the first major regimental dinner since the war. Well over two hundred officers attended, including representatives from 1st and 2nd RHC, The Black Watch Depot, and thirty-two serving officers from 3 RHC. Former officers numbered over 150. Brigadier Blackader presided. Major General JM Rockingham, officer commanding Quebec Command, completed the already dazzling head table. Regimental dinners are very much a pillar of Black Watch traditions, at all levels. Reunion Dinners had been held since the nineteenth century. That dinner was enthusiastically attended by former officers of the Regiment. Apart from a very few who appeared by special invitation, there are no guests and before the late 1970s, no women were present. The Reunion Dinner was usually preceded by the Regimental Advisory Board luncheon, where the guests of honour were given the opportunity to meet a number of the senior members in a less formal setting (if there was any such thing as an informal meeting of The Black Watch Board).

Lunches were held at the St James Club, the Mount Royal Club, or the Racquets Club, just up the street. The specific location was less a tradition than "the willingness of the Club to open on Saturday and who was paying the Tab."[143] Colonel Bourne used both the St James and the Mount Royal Club. The latter had been built by RB Angus and his friends. In later years Colonel Stephen Angus, as honorary colonel, moved the Board Luncheon to the sylvan Forest and Stream Club, set on a picturesque point in Lake St Louis, about forty minutes from downtown Montreal. The mansion was purchased from Frank Stephen, son of Lord Mount Stephen by friends of the Regiment, and the club's chosen name was a frugal Scottish compromise. The founders bought Stephen's entire silver service and simply adjusted the club's name to match the engraved flatware. One tradition is to serve the Queen Mum's favourite, lamb. Colonel Tom Price favoured deserts that reminded him of visits to Clarence House where the Queen Mother had served thick Devonshire cream: "My grandson brings it to me every Monday."[144] The dining room offers a splendid view of the lake, and by the time coffee was served, most regimental problems were temporarily forgotten midst conversation and war-stories. The members pride themselves that there are no speeches –any attempt being met with a barrage of mostly good-humoured abuse.

Storm Clouds on Horizon: Order-in-Council in 1959, National Survival

> National Survival, The new Militia, and re-entry operations – Och, it was a dog's breakfast ...
>
> A synopsis by a Black Watch officer[145]

Part of the reassessment of the Army and the Militia was influenced by the fact that the nation's missions had to be tailored to the very real threat of nuclear attack. The Soviets were taken seriously and in historical hindsight, perhaps too seriously, given the USSR's actual inability to launch an intercontinental attack in the 1950s and early 60s. Vast lines of interconnected radar stations were constructed across Canada; and bulky air raid sirens were constructed atop buildings throughout Montreal. Cold war tensions in Europe and Asia, together with increased NATO requirements, resulted in the Canadian Government assigning the Militia and Regular units to a "civil defence and national survival role [which] became the primary training activity with emphasis placed on traffic and population movement control, first aid, communications, decontamination, rescue of survivors, transportation of supplies ..."[146]

1 RHC began National Survival training in 1958; 3 RHC followed suit in 1959. "The jocks were exercised in the removal and handling of casualties in demolished buildings and rubble and giving first aid."[147] The concept envisaged mobile columns

(sometimes referred to as "Re-Entry Operations") pushing into cities after a nuclear attack, to perform rescue operations. Techniques included lowering a blanket-wrapped victim, secured to a stretcher, down a narrow ladder amidst debris and loose planking. It proved far more challenging than the soldiers had expected. The Black Watch Depot inserted *National Survival Training* into the Recruit Training Syllabus in 1960. During weeks twelve and thirteen of instruction, new soldiers were given fifty periods of rescue elements: reconnaissance, knots, lashings, casualty handling, crowd and refugee control and even firefighting. The St John's Ambulance taught First Aid, and successful recruits were given an SJA Certificate. By the end of the summer, two squads (fifty-seven recruits) had qualified. Priority was given to 2 RHC which was building towards a tour of duty in Europe.

The Militia was ordered to perform specialized tasks following a nuclear attack – everything from evacuating casualties, to jacking rubble, to first aid. Units were required to perfect communications (operating switchboards, establishing field telephones, running cables), to specialize in the detection of radiation, and to deal with chemical gasses. This, regardless of the fact that the Militia was not equipped with nuclear-biological-chemical warfare suits. Soldiers spent a lot of time learning to tie knots and manoeuvre on ladders, lowering casualties from multi-storey buildings. The troops' derogatory name for it was "snakes and ladders." Most Militia regiments were stripped of their martial duties and ordered to focus exclusively on *National Survival*. Traditional military training, except the most basic phase, came to a halt. This had a serious effect on the morale and structure of the Militia. "They voted with their feet, almost destroying the militia in the process."[148] One frustrated corporal wrote a passionate letter to the *Montreal Gazette*:

> Then suddenly, out of a clear blue sky, the Department of National Defence announced the Militia would henceforth have a civil defence role … the decision caused a havoc the results of which are still being felt by every Militia Unit. There are mutters of "Bucket Brigade" and "The Hook and Ladder Army" and visions of soldiers running about with a sand pail in one hand and a stretcher in the other … We were the only English-speaking unit to consistently parade 150 all ranks. Our Company strength dropped from 43 men to 10 … I sadly witnessed another Company, 38 strong, under this National Survival Training and emerge with eight men … the Unit is now down to around 50 all ranks and morale is at an all-time low … the scheme to train 100,000 civilians in civil defence via a six-week course with the Militia. Who can afford the time from work? Or is the Militia a haven for the unemployed?"[149]

Second World War veterans and new recruits both agreed they wanted nothing to do with *civil defence*.[150] Although the scheme met with disapproval by the army, it was welcomed by the public, for it provided a form of employment and income, as well as preparing communities for civil defence operations.

In addition to the normal training of militia, a newly elected Conservative Government under John Diefenbaker (21 June 1957) established a summer training programme: *Special Militia Training Programme* (SMTP). It was to be held in local armouries across Canada, involved in obtaining new volunteers from among the civilian population. It enlisted them in the Militia *under special conditions*, and offered a six-to-eight week basic recruit and civil defence training programme, which included drill, small arms instruction, rescue operations, first aid, and traffic control. It recruited teenagers, working men from industry, aboriginal peoples, and the unemployed. The scheme made veterans and senior NCOs grumpy. Black Watch officers noted that while some of those who joined were trainable, most were not enthusiastic and resented military discipline; they were more motivated by the pay cheque for eight weeks than anything else. The Reserves trained with guarded enthusiasm. Although unpopular, the programmes did demonstrate that the government was taking responsible steps to ensure survival by preparing the military to deal with a nuclear disaster.

Lieutenant Colonel D'Arcy McGovern 1959–62 – the Last War-Time CO

At the annual church parade weekend in May 1959, Lieutenant Colonel Wood handed over to Lieutenant Colonel D'Arcy McGovern. The new 3 RHC second-in-command was Major Bill Redpath; the regimental sergeant major was another veteran, WO1 JR Jackson, "quietly tough and a real pro."[151] The Methuselah of padres, about to be promoted major, was the Rev Rod Berlis.[152] D'Arcy McGovern was a long-serving Black Watch officer. During the war, he served with 1 RHC; then seconded to units in North Africa, and later posted to the Hastings and Prince Edward Regiment in Italy from 1943 to 1944. He returned to the Black Watch as a captain to participate in the winter campaign and push into Germany. He marked the end of the line. McGovern was "the last of the war-time veteran COs [in Bleury Street]." He worked as a market analyst and was a practical, sensible man. McGovern looked around the mess and admitted: "The Second World War [veterans] are getting too old to play an active part in a militia unit … we look forward to younger officers taking our places."

As a new decade approached, the ramparts of the Watch showed signs of wear. Veteran warrior Major Stan Duffield had moved to Vancouver where he managed the Canadian Imperial Bank of Commerce. He was not alone. The trek away from the city weakened the Regiment. Everyone was determined "this sinister trend" would be slowed, even if it could not be stopped. Interesting training was partly the answer. The 1960 and 1961 summer camps were conducted close to Montreal (Farnham was preferred) and concentrated on tactical training and war games, rather than drill and parades.

How Recruit Company Nearly Started an Indian War

In the fall of 1960, Stephen Angus was a senior lieutenant commanding the Recruit Company. One of his recruits, Private Jacobs, a member of the Caughnawaga Band of the Iroquois Nation, asked if the company would like to hold an exercise on the Reservation. Angus was interested, but only if the Band Council would permit it. Later, he received a call from an Indian Affairs Officer in Ottawa, asking what the *fuddle duddle* the Black Watch was up to. Apparently, Jacobs sought permission from the Council, but was denied. He then announced: "if they didn't give permission the Black Watch would come anyway whether they liked it or not!" Angus explained that Jacobs had no authority to make such a statement, and that he would deal with the situation. He immediately wrote to the Band Council, emphasizing the great respect the Regiment had for the Indians of Caughnawaga. He reminded them "We had been allies for years, and I thanked them for even considering the suggested idea." That defused the potential incident. Angus and his wife, Pamela, were invited to the Reservation where he was asked to take the salute at their Remembrance Day Parade. The Mohawks had a large number of war veterans on the reserve. "We had a wonderful time, they were wonderful hosts and we parted good friends!"[153]

Almost as an afterthought, the regimental baseball team won the Garrison Cup and went on to be Eastern Canadian Military fastball champions. [154] They are credited not only with victory, but the acquisition of inside screens to cover the rows of Gothic windows around the armoury. The regular smashing of panes by well-struck balls was the bane of the district HQ comptroller; but, no brigadier would ban a popular game that brought the regiments together. Many a wartime FOO, armoured recce or infantry officer who met in battle during the war were already friends, thanks to the pre-war league. The Cold War competitions were just as keen. One officer recalled, "I don't know how many times I hit a ball off the Battle Honour plaques on the east wall." These blasts were met with cheers as well as jeers. The baseball league waned in the 1970s and finally disappeared, replaced by floor hockey.

Chapter 9

The Black Watch in Gagetown and Germany

From 1 RHC's arrival in October 1959 until 2 RHC's departure in June 1965, Fort St Louis was the Regiment's European home.

Major Brian Cuthbertson, *The Black Watch Story*[155]

The Regular Battalions New Brunswick, New Home – Camp Gagetown 1958

It is suggested a strange attitude appeared to exist between the regular battalions of the Watch – but it is absolutely true and it stems from the tremendous rivalry between the two. Rivalry in everything from sports to drill, dress and everything in-between.

Lieutenant Colonel IA Kennedy CD

At Aldershot, the temporary summer camps in the pinewoods beyond Kentville were being vacated. The *auld* camp that had prepared officers and men for service in the Boer War, both World Wars, as well as NATO and United Nations commitments, was being vacated by the Black Watch. Both RHC battalions had been together in Nova Scotia since January 1955 and had established a close bond with the community for whom the move to Gagetown would have enormous financial implications. As one officer noted: "We are the economy."[156] Once, to demonstrate to the local merchants the importance of the Black Watch to the community, the RSM had the entire battalion paid in two-dollar bills.

In May 1958, the 2 RHC moved en bloc to New Brunswick. The just-built *Camp Gagetown* "with its brand new PMQ's (Private Married Quarters) was a wonderful improvement to the small apartments we had been used to." [157] It had been under construction for four years. Gagetown covered 427 square miles of mostly virgin forest, and (as the infantry was to discover) plenty of marshland. It was south of Fredericton, on the banks of the St John River. Scattered settlements, scarcely villages, were left empty as 'training aides' giving the place the semblance of a collective of ghost farms.[158] Conversely, the cemeteries looked 'lived-in'; they were fenced off, out-of-bounds and the grass was cut. Family visitors often left flowers, and the graves were maintained. A surrealistic atmosphere. Because the houses had been only recently abandoned, many veterans were reminded of France and Belgium in 1944. The Regiment liked to recount the tale of the pioneer sergeant who was steered off booze and a life of sin by a highly-effective Roman Catholic padre.

> Eternally grateful, the sergeant vowed he would repay the church for saving him from himself. His chance came a few weeks later when he was directed to paint the churches in the Camp Gagetown Training Area as a building preservation measure. He painted every Roman Catholic church a gleaming and sparkling white, and every Protestant church a drab army khaki.[159]

Gagetown seemed specifically intended for the Black Watch. Many of the original settlers had migrated from Scotland, thus giving it a distinctive Highland aura. As if to confirm the scenario, soldiers of the 42nd Regiment, Imperial Black Watch, had settled the area in 1787.

Camp Gagetown was formally opened by the Honourable George Pearkes VC, Minister of National Defence. The brigade was inspected and marched past – the parade stretched for five miles! It was no ordinary camp, but capable of housing at least a full division. The 3rd Brigade comprised all the components of a modern field force, including: infantry, a tank regiment, an artillery regiment, plus supporting engineers and ordnance units. There was plenty of space. Each arm had its own mess. The Highlanders were gathered at St Andrew's Barracks; the sergeants and officers' messes (St Andrew's, of course) set in groves of pine trees, away from the parade squares and tank hangars. Almost every day, winds carried the rattle of musketry from the ranges, the crack of *Centurion* tank-guns and the menacing '*Boom!*' of the guns of the Royal Canadian Horse Artillery banging away in the area. An inaugural mess dinner was held in the 2nd Battalion officers' mess. The new quarters were enthusiastically supported by Montreal. The Bleury Street mess sent over artifacts, art and helped get things off the ground.[160] The grand opening initiated a series of strenuous field exercises that tested everything imaginable and prepared the battalion for nuclear warfare, swamp warfare and tactical things in between. When the last ceasefire was ordered at the end of July, the soldiers went on leave en masse.

Concurrently, The Black Watch Depot bid adieu to Sussex, where they had been stationed for three years and had established a good relationship with the town. Besides the big move, mess talk focused on sports, as both units again dominated the command boxing finals – 2 RHC edged out 1 RHC by 2 points. The other major sport was on the ice. They swapped places in hockey – 1 RHC beat 2 RHC in the brigade final. However, the Watch never forgot that they were first and foremost, infantry. At the Eastern Command rifle competition held in June 1958, 1 RHC won the team competition with 3300 out of a possible 4550 points. Sergeant Gerald P Steacy from 2 RHC won the highest individual aggregate trophy and with L/Corporal O'Neil, qualified for the Canadian Army championships. They finished third.

The first winter in Gagetown was heavy with snow. The troops were occupied with winter exercises and shooting across frozen ranges. In the summer of 1959, the Black Watch team won the Letson Gold Trophy, emblematic of the Canadian Army team shooting championship. It featured the ten-man squad from 2nd Battalion RHC vs the 1st Battalion RHC in an all-regimental final. In sports, the 1 RHC softball team won the championship defeating RCAF Greenwood and took 1st, 3rd and 4th place trophies at the brigade track and field meet. At the 3 CIBG sports meet, a Black Watch team won the first aid trophy, cross country run and marching competitions. The pipes and drums dominated the regional Highland games. Within the 1st Battalion, the individual platoons competed for the Waterloo Trophy which was awarded to the platoon achieving the highest score on the range using all platoon weapons. Both battalions prepared for the Hamilton-Gault Trophy, awarded to the Regular Army battalion that attained the best results in completing the specified annual rifle qualification live-firing range course; a perfect result would require 100 percent of the soldiers on the posted strength of the battalion to qualify as 'marksman', the highest of three categories. The adjutant reported: "Our MO, Captain PJ Ferguson [1 RHC] made us sit up and take notice when he fired a perfect classification."[161] In reflection, it sometimes seemed that the greatest opponent to a Black Watch team was a team from another Black Watch battalion!

The summer manoeuvres were briefly interrupted in August, when the 2nd Battalion dispatched a one-hundred-man Royal guard of honour under Major CG Forrest DCM,[162] in support of Princess Margaret's opening of the Princess Margaret Bridge in Fredericton crossing the St John River. She next visited Gagetown to inspect the brigade; however, that evening Princess Margaret confessed to Lieutenant Colonel Watson that the thought of another parade was "rather boring." Nevertheless, following the division concentration, all units had cleaned and stored their vehicles. The royal parade was intended with personal weapons only, directly followed by a general leave; in deference to Her Royal Highness, the brigade commander advised all units that a demonstration exercise would be performed. "The required vehicles, tanks and guns had to be removed from storage, suitably camouflaged and all personnel had to dig out their field uniforms ... a demonstration exercise was hastily drawn up and there was only time for one rehearsal. It was chaotic ..."[163] However, the regal performance went off without a hitch. Of course, the troops then had to again scour the vehicles, tanks and guns returning them once again into storage before commencing their leave. A few, certainly not the Black Watch, considered the advantages of republicanism. Later, the Princess had tea at the headquarters' mess; the officers hoped that she found the morning's mechanized assault invigorating.

By November, newer members of the battalions were diligently studying pamphlets, memorizing names of parts and preparing for the *Leading Infantryman* Trade tests. Successful qualification meant an increase in pay, and soldiers could now set their sights on the specialty courses. The actual 'training cycle' and individual trade progression was complex:

> The cycle began in the autumn with annual refresher training followed by individual and winter training. In the spring, sub-unit (section, platoon and company) training began, followed by battalion and 'collective' (all-arms) training. This annual cycle culminated with a brigade/division concentration in Canada or a corps/army-group exercise in CE. Regular Army soldiers were paid for their rank and for their Trade Group level. To obtain Group 1 trade pay, the Infantryman had to complete one year of service and pass the Leading Infantryman test ... Trade pay could be as valuable as rank: a RCEME Craftsman (private) with Group 3 or 4 trade pay could earn as much as an Infantry Sr NCO with only a Group 1 or 2.[164]

The military routine was often set aside to aid the civilian government. Forty-five soldiers were sent to assist Springhill, Nova Scotia, which had suffered its second mine disaster in two years.[165] Some of the soldiers had relatives in the colliery.

Good-bye Bucko; Lieutenant Colonel Askwith

In January 1959, Lieutenant Colonel W de N Watson handed over 2 RHC to Lieutenant Colonel CHE Askwith. The Regiment would miss him, certainly his élan. "Bucko" tales would be a staple in all messes for decades. But training and competitions were unrelenting, and the Regiment continued its winning ways.[166] In May, the 2 RHC

Rifle Team won the Eastern Command annual rifle shoot by an unheard of margin of 699 points above the next team. Corporal HE O'Neil finally bested his mentors RSM Blakeney and Sergeant Gerald Steacy by winning the high individual aggregate trophy. In the training area, platoon and company exercises were held in any vacant quadrant or in any area considered challenging for infantry. The Jocks built 'hoochies' and lived rough when tents were not available.[167] By now, their tribal loyalty was so fixed that it transcended military strata. After the summer concentration, 3 RCHA sent a charge report to 1 RHC against one of their jeep drivers. The soldier had been ordered by his officer to keep the jeep on the road while he ducked into battalion headquarters: "Just after he disappeared into the woods, an artillery battery, with its towed 105mm guns, came along the road. The officer leading the battery ordered the driver to move the jeep off the road. He refused." On the Orders Parade the highlander was asked why he did not obey the officer's command. He replied, "Well, he wasn't one of our officers – he wasn't even a Second Battalion officer."[168]

The Golden Era: The Canadians in Europe

"Why are most of you from the same regiment?"

> British Army Official to Sergeant Gerald Steacy at the
> Bisley Rifle Competition, England, 1960

At last, selected to serve in the NATO brigade, 1 RHC sailed from Quebec City in the fall of 1959 aboard the *Empress of England*. Ken Blackader, as Colonel of the Regiment, saw them off. "The Germany period proved to have been the 'Golden Era' for the regular battalion."[169] The battalion arrived at Fort St Louis near Werl, West Germany and took over from 3rd Bn R22eR, the *Van Doos*. Their inauguration featured cold, damp, long hours, plus two weeks of rain, which prompted the usual digs about building arks. The sports teams concentrated on boxing and hockey. The battalion quickly entered the *Prix LeClerc* – a small arms competition. Unlike Aldershot or Bisley, they were tested by other NATO teams and did not win a thing. Lieutenant D Ludlow penned a wee dirge:

> But Black Watch marksmanship must improve
> For we missed the standard targets so we hear
> And made a total sweep of one dog, four sheep
> Three seagulls, seven rabbits and a deer.

Conversely, the Canadian Bisley team raised eyebrows. The Black Watch had won the Canadian Army Championship and the 2 RHC presence on the Bisley team was daunting: two officers, a WO1 and five soldiers. They won a challenge cup and placed second to the Royal Navy in rapid shooting. In England, Sergeant Steacy won the sitting shooting match; of the seven shooters, four were from 2 RHC. They beat all teams, including the SAS, to win the Hamilton-Leigh trophy. The top four Canadian shots were all Black Watch: Sergeant GP Steacy, Corporal HE O'Neil, L/Corporal JJ Breau and L/Corporal HS Pilkie. No one qualified for the final stage of the Queen's Trophy. "We felt wistful at our exclusion,"[170] reflected one member, but all left impressed with the organization, the quality of the Commonwealth competitors, and edified how a professional military rifle meeting should be run.

Fort St Louis was home to both 1 RHC and 2 RHC during the Regiment's NATO tours. It was built by the German Government for 4 Cdn Infantry Brigade Group, within an evergreen forest on high ground in the midst of the rich farms of the Ruhrland in West Germany. 1 RHC took over its barracks on 16 October 1959. They launched at once into mechanized operations training, and just as important, adjusted to the adventurous, carefree, mad-cap manner of the motorists, new traffic signs and autobahns. This was not quite *Blitzkrieg;* armoured assets were generally temporarily *grouped* from allied outfits. One officer noted, "To describe Dodge ¾-ton cargo-based manoeuvre training as "mechanized" is a real stretch. Genuine mechanized operations training for Canadian Army units in West Germany did not begin until M113A1 APCs were delivered in mid-1965, just as 2 RHC was returning to Canada."[171] Nothing, except perhaps driving around Montreal, could prepare Canadians for German drivers. Their commanding officer, a suave, international fellow, was determined that his battalion would make an impression on the continent, certainly on the BAOR. He started on the right foot since his RSM was WO1 RH Finnie.

Lieutenant Colonel DS MacLennan, CO 1 RHC, 1959

...physically very hardy, ever cheerful and undemanding.

Brigadier Don MacLennan of Newfoundlanders in the Black Watch

Lieutenant Colonel (Brigadier General) Donald Samuel MacLennan took command of 1 RHC early in 1959. He hailed from Winnipeg, the dead centre of Canada. During the Second World War, he had served in Italy as the 3rd Brigade intelligence officer where his boss was the colourful Brigadier JPE Bernatchez. As the war wound down, MacLennan volunteered for the Pacific. The plan was to deploy a Canadian division to support the Americans against the Japanese – retribution for Hong Kong. In mid-

1945, he was sent as an observer to General Douglas MacArthur's headquarters in Manila, and then attached to the 163rd Infantry Regiment of the 41st US Infantry Division. MacLennan participated in three operations against the Japanese. He led an American advisors' group tasked to support the *Moro* fighters.[172] The Philippine guerrillas harassed enemy rear areas and destroyed isolated strong points.

> We assaulted a strong Japanese position. The *Moros* used one hundred men Companies – and besides modern weapons, carried curious long wavy daggers – they were Clan units. I had a US Army FOO, along with air support, and naval gun fire. It was a messy but spirited action. The Japs surrendered after some bloody hand-to-hand work. To my surprise, I later got a gong for it.[173]

MacLennan was called to MacArthur's headquarters and presented with the Bronze Star, which was a unique decoration even among the exotic multitude of medals found on collective Black Watch chests. After the war ended, MacLennan remained in the Army, but did not join the Highland Battalion until the spring of 1953, as a senior major. He served in Korea and was aboard ship when the battalion was notified they were the 2 RHC. He recalled the battalion was popular with Canadian Headquarters: "General Allard loved the Black Watch; 'This is my regiment' he liked to say but that did not stop him from getting rid of us in the end."[174]

When the brigade commander decided to inspect 1 RHC, there was complete confidence. The predictable happened. As the brigadier arrived at Support Company, he recognized its popular OC, Major Dusty Rhodes DSO ("a major since God was a lance corporal"). Surprisingly, he asked to inspect Rhodes's pistol:

> In accordance with safety procedures, before presenting it for inspection, Rhodes pulled the slide back, whereupon it exploded into pins and springs all over the parade ground. Apparently, the mechanism had not been properly assembled ... [this initiated] a deal of ill-suppressed hilarity in the ranks of the Company. Dusty was furious and embarrassed, and after dismissal could be heard screaming for the head of his long-suffering batman, Private Mugford.[175]

Within the 1st Battalion, one rifle company was designated as 'Sports Company' in which were concentrated all the unit's jock-strappers. MacLennan decided to break it up and return the men to their own companies: "this appeared to make not the slightest difference to their performance in sports, might have even improved it, as we continued to win most of the events." Of the four rifle companies, one was a "predictably unpredictable company" and constantly in trouble. MacLennan tried an experiment; he decided that "trained soldiers should not be subjected to any more *chickenshit* than necessary." He relaxed the rules regarding kit stored in barracks. It could be kept (neatly, it was hoped) in lockers and cupboards. During the next brigade commander's inspection, MacLennan told him of his experiment. The brigadier was most interested and decided to visit that company's barrack rooms; the result was a disaster. The kit storage was chaotic. "Need I say more, Don?" the brigadier drawled – and that was the end of that misguided effort.

The mess began to socialize with the Navy. MacLennan was invited to dinner at HMCS *Shearwater*. He arrived looking *très* Highland, personal piper and all. After dinner, there were 'naval games' which included *Carrier Landings* (on a table in the dark, between rows of candles), *Buck-Buck*, and of course, *Indian Wrestling*, which involved throwing an opponent over by hooking his leg while both lay prone. The Black Watch CO participated in all these competitions to ever-increasing cheers. This initial evening was followed by a string of dinner invitations. Years later, MacLennan met *Shearwater*'s captain, now an admiral, who reminded him of that dinner and confessed that his female officers well recalled the event: MacLennan had been 'regimental' in his dress, raising the leg in each bout – revealing much.

MacLennan took the credit for introducing martial music classics to the battalion. Surprised that it was not being used, MacLennan asked the pipe major to have the pipers learn *The Black Bear*. RSM Finnie assembled the battalion and drilled everyone to "Hoy!" in the right places. It was first used at the brigade parade in Fredericton, on Canada Day 1959: "as the Black Watch neared the saluting base in a formation frontage of twelve files, and just before *Highland Laddie*; the pipes played *The Black Bear*! The "Hoys!" were thunderous; so much so that 2nd Battalion R22eR just ahead, was unable to hear their commands – their passing the saluting base was even more shambolic than was their wont."[176] Next, MacLennan and Finnie decided that the pipe band should learn *Squid Jiggin Ground,* but in secret, in order to surprise the soldiers and acknowledge the ever-growing number of Newfoundlanders in their midst. It was introduced as part of the incidental music during the next general inspection. The soldiers were much stirred: "One could almost hear the chests of the Newfies swelling with pride!" It was regularly played thereafter. They were happy battalions.

The officers of 1 RHC were devoted but sometimes exhibited old-school traits:

> I recall certain officers with evocative nicknames, there was *Ronald the Rodent*, sometimes, *Ronnie the Rat* … his hair abruptly turned whitish blond and he became known as *The White Rat* by the lieutenants and certain captains – he was then sent to Staff College and promoted to major – after that the subalterns referred to him as *The Ivory Rodent*.[177]

Life in an infantry battalion was exacting and sometimes harsh. Evaluation reports were often colourful, nay more, cruel. MacLennan recalled one particularly unkind summation: "I would not breed this officer." The most delicate part of bringing an officers' mess to full bloom was the education of the junior officers – unpredictable, innocent yet mischievous, courageous yet sometimes silly. MacLennan liked to say, "Subalterns in a battalion are like a litter of puppies."

The Royal Highlanders in Deutschland, 1959–1965

The Black Watch completed three rotations in Germany as a NATO contingent in the Canadian brigade:[178] the first from 1951–1953, as the 1st Canadian Highland Battalion; the next two as Black Watch from 1959–1965. The training in Germany with different European contingents was an adventure in itself. Four main areas were available: Haltern, Luneburg (better known as Soltau), Sennelager, and Putlos. One early bivouac by 1 RHC was in a wooded area near Putlos, far from any farm or village. It was discovered that a group of German Boy Scouts had decided to camp in the same location: "Boy Scouts have that rare faculty of rising in the break of dawn and emitting blood-curdling screams designed to represent the pouring forth of song. As the closest Black Watch tents were the officer lines, many a jock cast an incredulous glance at each officer believing this to be the source." The situation was promptly solved the following morning, just before dawn, when the pipe major led the pipes and drums gallantly through the officer lines, close enough to the Boy Scouts to terrify them with sounds the young lads had never heard. There was no sound from their *jugend* neighbours and they moved off by the afternoon. The First Battalion now owned the German forest.[179]

The battalion practised being panzer-grenadiers and quickly got the hang of mechanized operations. Sennelager boasted excellent ranges and plenty of challenging competitions. Exercises emphasised manoeuvre in support of a nuclear counterstrike against the Red Army, just across the border – something new and sobering. The Soviets were expected to storm across the north German plain. The Black Watch was often *grouped* with tank-heavy combat teams or armoured battlegroups. One assault, conducted before General Sir Richard Gale, Deputy Supreme Allied Commander Europe, was to demonstrate infantry-tank co-operation. It proved too great a temptation. Ordered into a flanking attack, with *Centurion* tanks crunching in to give close supporting fire, the company commander ordered his piper forward as they went into the assault: "the Jocks, were played in, destroying the enemy position, [supported by] field artillery, mortars, and tanks." With *Highland Laddie* wafting through the smoke, General Gale left with an ill-disguised grin.

The Canadians soon understood local references to *Dudelsackpfein* and became familiar with Werl's *Marktplatz*. They took to sports with a vengeance and before long dominated 4 CIBG in hockey and basketball. The battalion shocked the "all-star" RCAF team, which had not lost a NATO game, by trouncing them 9–1 and 12–6 in their first two games. The word went out: the Black Watch was in town and hard-nosed at that. Time quickly passed as winter drifted into a wet spring while the soldiers shrugged off the rains and practised their German. The leaves were wonderful and some of Europe's finest cities were only a drive away. Families became continentally minded. MacLennan managed to fly to London for an audience with the Colonel-in-Chief. The Queen Mother was, as always, totally interested in her Canadian Regiment.

In August 1960, Lieutenant Colonel MacLennan handed 1 RHC over to Lieutenant Colonel WA (Bill) Teed. He then went off to the National Defence College followed by a series of exotic postings in Laos, India, and Poland for the next two years. His assignments featured military liaison; he particularly enjoyed 'Honkers and Bangers' (Hong Kong and Bangkok). He and his equally exotic wife, a stunner, were popular in the embassy circuit. MacLennan next commanded the Staff College in Kingston. He retired in 1972, a brigadier general, part of a growing Black Watch senior stable.[180]

In Canada, the 2nd Battalion had Gagetown and winter all to itself. Their boxing team produced two Army champions. Pte WGR Stubbert won the Bantam Novice Crown and Pte JM McNeil the Welter Open Championship.

The Black Watch Military Band 1961

The Regimental Military Band was authorized in 1954 and spent its early years in Windsor Park, Halifax, under its Director of Music, Lieutenant DV Start. Within ten years, it grew from twenty members to an orchestra of fifty strong. It was a modified League of Nations including Canadians, English, Dutch, a Pole and an Australian, plus one Welshman and three Scots. A new director, Lieutenant HC Eagles CD, led the band to its permanent residence in Gagetown NB in October 1958. Within a few years, they developed an impressive series of combinations: three five-piece dance bands led by B/Sergeant Cecil Roberts, a New Brunswicker; B/S/Sergeant Jock Nisbet from Scotland; and B/Sergeant Henry Fielding, from England; together with a Chamber Music Group (B/Sergeant Martin Kouprie); a String Trio, led by B/Sergeant Brian Morley; and a vocal group called the 'Troubadours', led by B/Sergeant Carol van Feggelen. Resplendent in pre-war Highland band uniforms, the group was most impressive in kilts and feather bonnets. Often grouped with the pipes and drums, the

Military Band regularly took their varied *repertoire* throughout the Maritimes and in 1961, they toured the Canadian bases in Germany. They later were deployed to Germany, almost concurrent with 2 RHC – their artistic accomplishments included successful records produced with 2 RHC and the Black Watch of Scotland. The band was one of the Regiment's four Regular Force components – finally deployed to Montreal on return from Europe.[181]

Lieutenant Colonels Bill Leonard and Bill Teed – 1960–63

2 RHC bid farewell to Lieutenant Colonel CHE Askwith as Lieutenant Colonel William Clark Leonard took command in the summer of 1960. Leonard had served with the Irish Regiment of Canada in Italy and North West Europe, prior to and during the war. He was recommended for a Military Cross and later awarded the OBE:

> As Captain Leonard approached the crossing of the River Lamone the Germans started to shell the crossing intensely. Realizing the importance of his mission Captain Leonard pushed on until his scout car was knocked out by the shelling and he was thrown out into the ditch. Undeterred by this and the injuries he had sustained he immediately commandeered another vehicle, eventually arriving at his destination.[182]

His Black Watch command came in the middle of his military career. Eight years later, he would become a brigadier and commander of 1 Combat Group in Calgary. He would finish his career as a major general and as commander, Canadian Forces Europe. Under Lieutenant Colonel Leonard, 2 RHC won the Eastern Command rifle championship, and the Maritime and Eastern Command boxing championships.[183] The battalion was runner-up in the forced march, track and field, as well as the basketball and volleyball championships; but the main winter sport remained hockey, and competition was fierce. Yet it must be remembered that in 'the old Army' where boxing was king, hockey was considered the less violent sport. Battalion practices and inter-company games were as hard fought as brigade matches. The regiment favoured the team coached by S/Sergeant Jim Byrne (from 1 RHC), who also played. One spirited contest produced doggerel (a Black Watch tradition that goes back to the Great War) which shows both determination and Celtic resilience:

> *The rink was dim and foggy*
> *The boys were playing hard,*
> *When out of the dim, came that man Jim,*
> *And the puck struck the goalie in the lard*

His face was cut and bleeding

When they carried him off the ice;

The rest of the players, most of them sayers,

Said: "Now that wasn't very nice."

So Bill MacKay got hit in the eye,

That night he'll never forget,

For as you look at him now, with a nose like a prow,

He says, "Brother, I'm not done yet.[184]

In January 1961, 2 RHC established a Winter Camp at Summer Hill, deep in the manoeuvre area. The battalion practised a series of ten-man reconnaissance patrols that went out for three-day missions: no tents, one toboggan, sleeping bags, and limited rations. Some patrols moved only at night. Temperatures were consistently well below zero: 25 to 30 below was average, and in the heat of the afternoon, the temperature often climbed to zero. They were more than ready for Europe, looking forward to their rotation to Germany to replace 1 RHC.

In Germany, the First Battalion was packing up. Its CO, Lieutenant Colonel William Arthur Teed seemed the very model of a Highland clansman – large and rather austere. His wartime experience with the North Shore (New Brunswick) Regiment included an MID.[185] The colonel reminded Montrealers of Stanton Mathewson, who won the MC with the 42nd and once, out of bullets, punched out a German on Mount Sorrel. Teed was also burly, and never smiled for cameras, which was fine with his sergeants. The colonel was now chieftain to a rather large clan. His battalion numbered thirty-five officers, ten warrant officers, sixty-three senior NCOs and 855 men for a total of 963 all ranks. It was a large family indeed. A total of twenty-four hundred men, women and children were rotated from Canada to Europe, and back.

Teed's battalion had been well tested with the 4th Brigade completing four major exercises. During the Soltau Concentration, the Watch with great determination infiltrated through darkness and drizzling fog to surprise the foe.[186]. As new recruits appeared, old saws were replayed:

Mortar Sergeant: "Bring that base plate over here!"

New Private: "I don't see any plates Sgt, will my mess tins do?"

The battalion had become, in Teed's words, "acclimatized to NATO." There was one big difference quickly noted by platoon officers and sergeants: "training in Germany was unlike Camp Gagetown; one had to consult a map rather than simply estimate the objective was 1000 yards past the T junction at Hibernia on the right hand side near the barn with the caved-in wall and the Van Doo sign *Heartbreak Hotel*."[187]

Empire Hockey

Although both regimental hockey teams were formidable, the 1959 1 RHC hockey team was the powerhouse of the Canadian Forces, winning the 4 CIBG (Germany) championship four years in a row. While in Europe, the team played major exhibition games, one against the 1961 world champions, the "Trail Smoke Eaters" from British Columbia. The Black Watch international hockey fame peaked in April of that same year when 1 RHC was invited to send its hockey team to England to play the British National "B" world champions in a charity game to raise money for families of Canadian veterans in England. "Our team was flown to England compliments of the RCAF. The game was billed as *England vs. Canada*." The guests of honour were Field Marshal The Earl Alexander of Tunis, the former Governor General of Canada, and the High Commissioner of Canada, Mr George Drew. The match was held at the Wembley Empire pool, carefully frozen. British newspapers welcomed "a very powerful and sporting squad indeed." The game drew in excess of twenty thousand hockey fans.

The team returned to Canada and continued to play exhibition schedules as well as brigade competitions. They were considered one of the best teams in New Brunswick, confirmed in 1965, when they won the Southern NB Senior League Championship.[188] 1 RHC left Germany after a pleasant *Schützenfest* with the 192nd *Panzer Grenadier Battalion*, which included Belgian troops and German civilian marksmen. Old friendships were renewed and new ones made. The battalion teams finished off the tour with several trophies: 1 RHC had won the brigade hockey, softball and soccer championships in 1961. Despite good memories, everyone was focused on leave and returning to Canada after two years abroad. They were impatiently awaiting rotation back home. Some got testy. One CQMS charged into a company building and had the layout of the kit changed for inspection, despite protest, only to go outside fuming, then discover he was in the wrong company quarters.

In 1961, the venerable Great War *Tin Pot* was replaced by the US Army helmet, a deeper model which some soldiers preferred as a replacement for the metal wash basin they carried. This technology was coupled with a triumvirate of new section weapons from Belgium and England that replaced the .303 inch small arms in 1957/58: the FN C1 Rifle (7.62mm); the FN C2 (which replaced the *Bren Gun* as a section weapon; it had a larger magazine than the C1 and a heavier barrel with bipod); and, the *Stirling*

1 (9mm) Submachine Gun. All these were handled with the greatest glee. Meantime, RHC wags, tired of *National Survival*, and surly after winter treks proclaimed:

> Patrols, and not Survival
>
> We have become more the practical
>
> To accomplish our aim – that of being tactical![189]

Montreal: The Reunion Dinner

There was a brawny aggregate of seniors and generals at the fall reunion dinner held 28 October 1961. The battalions' colonels gathered before the great fireplace beneath the Colonel-in-Chief's portrait: 1st Bn Lieutenant Colonel WA Teed, 2nd Bn Lieutenant Colonel WC Leonard, and the 3rd Bn's Lieutenant Colonel DJ McGovern. The Depot Commander was Major DG (Tex) Cochrane, a talented country and western balladeer who gave up a promising career to continue his service in the Black Watch. Cochrane commanded The Black Watch Depot from 1960–1963. But prior to joining the Army during the Second World War, he had been a well-established country and western singer with an extensive fan base and a major record contract in the United States. It was thought that Tex might have been one of the greats along with Hank Snow and Wilf Carter. After joining the army, other than on a rare occasion following a mess dinner, he never picked up the guitar again.[190]

The guest of honour was General Sir Neil Ritchie, Black Watch officer, former Colonel-of-the-Regiment, and renowned desert warrior, who had been checked by the best, Marshal Erwin Rommel. There was much good news to report to the cheery gathering; at the reunion dinners, no wine is served but there are plenty of decanters of whisky along the tables. The 1 RHC shooting team won the NATO brigade competition. The stretcher-bearer team regained the coveted Connaught Shield (last won by a Canadian unit in 1958) in a tough contest that included forced marches, fieldcraft, and the treatment and evacuation of casualties across the roughest terrain. The hockey team again won the brigade title, played thirty-four games, losing only five. The 2 RHC boxing team won the tri-service championship; and the shooting team had represented eastern Canada at the Army Meet in Ottawa in August 1960, where Sergeant GP Steacy won the high aggregate prize. To rousing cheers, it was noted that the Toronto Branch was celebrating their thirty-fifth anniversary, though many a Great War veteran loudly insisted it was their forty-first, since Black Watch groups began to meet in the 1920s. To a great thumping on tables, Colonel HM Wallis was introduced as the new honorary colonel of the 3rd Battalion; he replaced the well-liked Bill MacTier in April 1961. Finally, there was a new Cadet Corps affiliation to report: Rothesay Collegiate School Cadet Corps (founded in 1891 and the oldest corps in the Atlantic area) had begun to drill as a Black Watch Corps.[191]

While the Regular battalions were preoccupied with European migrations and NATO *kriegspiel*, the Montreal training year concluded with a weekend exercise in Farnham; a Grey Cup party and the regimental children's Christmas party with Yule tree and be-hackled Santa, followed this. Outside the armoury, there was two feet of snow on Bleury Street.[192]

Preparing for the Royal Presentation of Colours

Montreal did not escape the slush and snow banks of winter until March. The streetcars were being replaced by buses; this decision later proved to be a poor one. However, the armoury would soon be next to a Metro station – the new subway planned to celebrate Canada's Centenary and the opening of the World's Fair. Training continued to centre on National Survival and a hot summer was marked by a return to Camp Farnham. McGovern, accompanied by a small but keen command element, led a large contingent, strengthened by recruiting in the new Montreal suburbs.[193] The 1961 concentration included ten Militia units and emphasized National Survival. The main exercise (Tyro 2) portrayed the theoretical explosion of a five-megaton device over Granby, east of Montreal. Its aim was to rescue those trapped inside buildings. Normandy veteran, Major General JM Rockingham, commandant of Quebec Command, ensured total participation by all units. The No. 10 Militia Group created Mobile Support columns and fanned out across the Eastern Townships, travelling to Bedford, Cowansville and Adamsville to assist casualties. Everyone was impressed by the realism. "Dummy casualties" were arranged at several locations to be met with as each column arrived at a village. "I am almost certain I saw a full colonel among the stretcher-bearers," recalled Major Bill Redpath. It was hectic work and good training. "Rocky" Rockingham, a DSO ribbon on his bush jacket, observed the efforts and later cautioned the assembled units: "Remember – nothing can substitute field training." National Survival was not well-liked, but it was recognized as extremely practical. Meantime, the battalion looked forward to the fall and social diversions, like the St Andrew's Ball.

The armoury was the busy hub of many activities. The Pistol Club of Montreal was formed during Ian MacDougall's term and included members of the Regiment, former officers and non-regimental members. It was an immediate success and met on Mondays, about twenty times a year. Members enjoyed the privileges of the mess and in appreciation donated a handsome selection of competition trophies that are still kept there. It was an eclectic collection that included a plaque with antique flintlock pistol, a Kiwi Bird on a base, a mounted whisky bottle with a ship inside, and even an erotic carving of 'Nubile Virgo Intacta' on a lettered base called simply 'The Sweetheart'. The Club soon attracted retired military types from across Montreal, all applying for formal admission as associate members of the Black Watch. By 1966, it boasted a hefty selection of troupers: infantry, paras and commandos. Most were businessmen, and many were not officers but former sergeants and privates. Several were graduates of Edinburgh and Oxbridge, and they all liked to party. The officers' mess was open on Tuesday and Thursday for lunch, and evenings for cards and other diversions. Social notices were published every week and included traditional regimental outings ("The A&A Golf Weekend"[194]) or totally leisure activities (from dances to dinners) – a renaissance of pre-war fun.

As a bright star on the horizon, there was the much-anticipated presentation of Colours to all three battalions by the Queen Mother scheduled for June 1962. This was guaranteed to put new life into the Montreal Watch, now buttressed by its splendid sister battalions from Gagetown. The event was to herald the Regiment's hundredth anniversary, for which Colonel Paul Hutchison would write a comprehensive history chronicling the Watch's evolution from the early 19th century to the present atomic age. The Regiment's Centennial Committee, chaired by Colonel WSM MacTier was hard at work planning the great occasion.[195] The year ended on a particularly sad note. The beloved archetypal warrior, a 13th Battalion RHC original and veteran of every major campaign from Ypres to the The Hundred Days, Lieutenant Colonel Hew Clark-Kennedy VC, died on 27 October 1961, in his 83rd year. His exploits were well matched by the great affection his friends and soldiers showed him, beginning with the Governor General of Canada, Georges Vanier.

Despite distances, all the battalions participated in the regimental Centennial. The spring of 1962 saw the gathering of a Who's Who of the Black Watch in Montreal: RSM WO1 RH Finnie; WO1 TF Charters and WO1 M Gurevitch from 3 RHC; and WO1 GW Wooten represented The Black Watch Depot. They were reinforced by a symphony of Pipe Majors: W Magennis; J Stewart, and the warhorse of skirling, WJ Hannah. Major Colin G Forrest DCM CD arrived from 1 RHC to assist Colonel MacTier and to co-ordinate the numerous event committees. Forrest was what the Regiment meant when it talked of an old soldier. He enlisted in the Royal Canadian Regiment in 1939 and was commissioned in 1945. He was awarded the DCM for one of those classic infantry actions that demonstrate the tenacity and valour of the private soldier:

On 18 December 1943, The RCR was attacking the important cross-roads on the Ortona–Orsogna lateral. The attack had succeeded in reaching several buildings, when extremely heavy enemy fire temporarily prevented "C" company from advancing further. When his Platoon Commander was killed and the Platoon Sergeant wounded, Private Forrest took command of the platoon and with exemplary courage and skill led twenty-one men remaining in it under heavy fire to a position in a gully strongly defended by the enemy. There the platoon dug in. Being unable to contact his company, Private Forrest decided to hold the ground he had gained until further orders were received. [He] maintained his position all night and successfully beat off all attacks. At first light on 19 December 1943, he led a patrol out of his position and succeeded in contacting battalion headquarters. He received orders to withdraw his platoon as an artillery barrage was to be put down in that area in preparation for an attack on the gully. Together with stretcher bearers and covering party, he returned to his platoon and although his men were almost completely exhausted, succeeded in withdrawing them with all their weapons and wounded ... His maintenance of the position in the gully denied to the enemy the use of ground that would have been of great assistance to him and greatly contributed to the success of the attack later put in by the battalion.[196]

Another veteran, WO2 GN Mills from the Gagetown Depot was despatched to Montreal to help whip the 3rd Battalion soldiers into shape on the parade square. As Moe Gurevitch, no slouch at parade drill himself, recalled: "His expert drilling is putting real life into training – one is filled with awe at the eloquence of the pacing stick – this mere piece of wood"

At the Bleury Street Armoury (sandblasted and repainted for the Royal Visit) training intensified; despite the previous *Survival* grousing, soldiers returned in greater numbers, and new recruits crowded the orderly room. A *Veterans' Company* was formed in early 1962 by several ex RSMs headed by WO1 R Diplock. Keen on parading before the Queen Mother, they not only sacrificed their time, but travelled long distances to parade. The body soon boasted sixty-one veterans (the maximum age permitted was fifty-five). Lieutenant Steve Angus was appointed company commander: "They accepted me because I was the grandson of Colonel Cantlie." Regrettably, the company (after training for three months) at the very last minute was refused permission to parade by small-minded bureaucrats.

'Summer Camp' lasted one week in early June and was held just across the St Lawrence River at Longueuil.[197] Though there were no buses across the Jacques Cartier Bridge, determined soldiers could have walked home to Verdun or Montreal in an hour. But of course no one was permitted to do this. The concentration comprised endless hours of drilling. Lieutenant Colonel McGovern demanded perfection and achieved it; all ranks forgave him for his hard driving when they listened to the applause that greeted them during the four days of military parades. Practice made perfect and brought unexpected dividends. In a dress rehearsal at Dorval Airport, the Regiment rehearsed the guard of honour, including greeting the Queen Mother as she alighted from the jetliner. Trans Canada Airlines (now Air Canada) made their staff available, and one of the stewardesses played the role of Her Majesty. She was a knock-out. McGovern was smitten. Right after the parade, he married her.

The Regimental Centennial

As 1961 began, 1 RHC prepared to return home so 2 RHC could replace it in Europe. Until that rotation, scheduled for October, both battalions carried on with their usual training routines – annual NATO exercises in West Germany for 1 RHC with 4CIBG, and the summer concentration in Gagetown for 2 RHC with 3CIBG. However, the unit rotation was thwarted by the East Germans on 13 August 1961 – the very day on which the 2 RHC advance party arrived in Germany – when they began to construct the Berlin Wall. This action heighten the strained relations between NATO and the Warsaw Pact and prompted Ottawa to postpone the rotation but 2 RHC was ordered to reinforce 1 RHC with some 125 personnel. This reinforcing draft sailed from Montreal aboard the QSS *Arcadia* which docked in Rotterdam on 1 October.

The reinforced 1 RHC remained in Fort St. Louis while 2 RHC languished in frigid Camp Gagetown until February 1962 when Ottawa ordered the rotation to commence. Following embarkation leaves, members of 2 RHC and their families began boarding commercial ships or RCAF special flights for West Germany. Most boarded the RMS *Saxonia* in Saint John NB or the *Ivernia* in Halifax, NS; both ships arrived in Bremerhaven in mid-March.

Second Battalion settled quickly into Fort St. Louis and the 4CIBG routine and, in October, Colonel Blackader visited the unit. This was followed in November by an inspection by General Hans Speidel, Commander-in-Chief of Allied Land Forces Central Europe, which made the few remaining veterans look twice; Speidel had been Field Marshal Rommel's Chief of Staff during the Second World War. Although he could have worn his *Ritterkreuz* around his neck, he preferred a tie.

Lieutenant Colonel Leonard's battalion had yet to make a major impression on the brigade in sports; however, the battalion managed a second place at the track and field meet. By the end of winter, they took first place honours in hockey. The new year found them working at three things: 1) normal training, 2) readying a colour party for the Queen Mother's presentation of Colours, and 3) preparing for a formal

Canadian (and Regimental) return to the beaches of France. The 20th anniversary of the Dieppe Raid was commemorated in July. Leonard despatched a 100-man guard of honour to the coastal town and its chalky cliffs etched into the memory of so many Canadians. Almost overshadowed by the summer's events in Montreal, it was a moving experience. The young soldiers were stunned at the diminutive size of Puys Beach where C Company had landed, while the actions of the Mortar Platoon on the main beaches remained foggy to all but regimental historians. In Montreal, at last, the great day dawned.

The Queen Mother, 8 June 1962

The Queen Mother arrived at Montreal's Dorval Airport on 8 June 1962: "a radiant figure in hyacinth mauve, wearing prominently her Black Watch diamond brooch."[199] The striking Captain Tom Price commanded the guard of honour; he seemed to capture what everyone imagined a Black Watch officer should look like, and immediately charmed Her Majesty. If she had a 'favourite' in the Montreal Black Watch, it may have been Price, who was always welcomed at Clarence House whenever he was in London. The greeting party included the Governor General and Mrs Vanier, Prime Minister Diefenbaker and the Mayor of Montreal, Mr Jean Drapeau. "C'est une journée magnifique" the Queen Mother responded to Mayor Drapeau's welcome. The Mayor later remarked, "Elle est tout a fait charmante."[200]

The Queen Mother's return, twenty-three years after her 1939 visit with the King, dominated city headlines with full-page greetings from corporations, front-page stories all exhaustively covered by television and live radio broadcasts. Thousands thronged the streets. The hottest tickets in town were to the presentation of Colours. Invitations to royal garden parties and the regimental dinner were particularly prized, but these were reserved for the Black Watch family. Lieutenant Thomas Dinesen VC arrived from Europe with another veteran of 42nd Battalion, RSM Page, under whom Dinesen served in the Great War. The courageous Dane was still quite fit and his 6'2" height allowed him to tower above fellow veterans. The Regiment had planned a packed schedule.

The first gala event was the Royal Ball, appropriately, at the Queen Elizabeth Hotel; it was an occasion never to be forgotten. Dining with their Colonel-in-Chief were forty-five DSOs and MCs from two World Wars and the Boer War. The glittering head table included General Sir Neil Ritchie, the Commanders of Eastern and Quebec Command, Major Generals FJ Fleury and MP Bogart and Lieutenant Tom Dinesen, VC. The Queen Mother wore white silk with brilliants, The Black Watch brooch, and a diamond tiara. Brigadier Blackader read a cable from The Black Watch of Scotland sending greetings to The Black Watch of Canada on the occasion of its centenary, which ended: "Good Luck go with you."[201] The dinner's highlight occurred when Her Majesty proposed the health of the Regiment. There was no rest, for the dancing lasted until morning; everyone was euphoric. During the weekend, Her Majesty visited the armoury twice, but the climax of the visit was the great parade at McGill's Percival Molson Stadium. All programmes were sold out, and a second printing was ordered. Copies were mailed to Black Watch members and veterans around Canada and across the globe.

The Parade – Molson Stadium

It was a magnificent sight and does infinite credit to the regiment, to the Canadian Army, and to Canada.

Governor General Georges Vanier, telegraph to Brigadier Blackader, 10 June 1962

Molson Stadium is perched on the south-east slope of Mount Royal. It overlooks the city and on this day, seemed suspended in the blue. On Saturday, 9 June, the stands were jammed with twenty-two thousand enthusiastic spectators. Stretched before them were two battalions and their colonels (2 RHC remained on duty in Germany, but its Colour Party was on parade), four 30-man guards, four Colour parties, the pipes and drums, the RHC Regimental Band, and cadres from each cadet corps. Two future colonels carried the Colours for the 3rd Battalion: Captains Stephen Angus (the new Colours) and Len Ferdon (the old Colours). All three battalion commanders were on parade: Lieutenant Colonels WA Teed, WC Leonard and DJ McGovern.

The parade, under the command of the Colonel-of-the-Regiment, Brigadier Blackader, gave the Royal Salute. Lieutenant Colonel Teed ordered his 1st Battalion to form a hollow square and three sets of drums were piled. The new Colours were then placed on top. The Consecration and Presentations by Her Majesty concluded with the Colonel-in-Chief addressing her Regiment: "May they [the new Colours] remind you of the valiant part the regiment has played in the history of your land. May they remind you, too, that the future of the Black Watch is in your hands." It was a perfect parade. Molson Stadium groaned with veterans, and many a hand pushed back a tear as the bands struck up *Highland Laddie* or *All the Blue Bonnets*.[202] The soldiers of both wars attended in remarkable numbers; veterans of Normandy and Holland looked young and fit, most in their mid-forties. The Queen Mother seemed to remember them all; she would often stop and chat, reminding a sergeant or corporal they had met on parade in England in 1942 or 1943. The veterans were charmed, indeed, smitten. The presentation ceremony was significant for the Highland regiment, for they received Colours from the hands of a Scotswoman, who grew up in one of the most historic of Scotland's castles, and whose family through generations have had their part in the battles and glories of the Black Watch. Those attending (and they included regimental families, cabinet ministers, lieutenant governors, generals and clergy) would long remember the Regiment marching off through the south-east archway, the pipes playing *The Black Bear* swinging white gloves, and spats gleaming in the sun, the three stands of new colours and the long line of bright Red Hackles in the men's bonnets.[203]

Venerable old militiamen, who had served with the 5th Royal Scots, immediately recalled Cantlie's legendary 1912 parade on Fletcher's Field for the Governor General, the Duke of Connaught. "This," they suggested, "was even better!" It was (as it turned out) the apex of the Black Watch's success in Montreal and in the Canadian Army for that century. By every measure of military and social success, the Regiment was entitled to be (as indeed it was) on top of the world. No one could imagine that in seven short years, victim of political machinations, the Regiment would be savaged.

The next morning, The Black Watch marched up Sherbrooke for its very special church parade. Five hundred and seventy-five of the Regiment filled the left side of The Church of St Andrew and St Paul, and an equal number of congregants filled the other. The balance of the parade waited on Redpath Street, with growing crowds surrounding the regimental church. Major the Reverend RJ Berlis smiled from his pulpit: "This Whitsun (Whitsunday, celebrating the birthday of the church) will always hold a special, shining glory." He then asked the Regiment "to feel the power of glorious tradition and the blessing of those comrades who have passed into the light of Heaven to join the Army of the Immortals." Her Majesty addressed the congregation. She recalled the famous battles in which the Regiment had distinguished itself: "Place names which stir the memory of us all, names which mark heroic deeds, valour and endurance and which have brought lustre to the history of our Regiment." The Communion Table was ablaze with red roses in memory of Lieutenant Colonel SST Cantlie, who was killed leading 1 RHC against Verrières Ridge. Her Majesty examined the great window, commemorating the 42nd Battalion in First World War: "When she was told about the Star of David and Lieutenant Myer Cohen, her eyes were seen to mist over."[204] The Regiment marshalled outside its Church; it then marched home through cheering crowds. The saluting dais was across from McGill's Roddick Gates.[205] This was yet another excellent day, in a flawless royal weekend that left everyone proud but exhausted.

For the Regular battalions, summer training could not help but be a bit of an anticlimax. But there was no pause. Training courses and exercises continued. The Gagetown Watch participated at the annual Massed Bands Concert in Halifax; the pipe band and regimental Highland dancers performed at the Seattle World's Fair. As expected, battalion sports were pursued with the usual vigour and enthusiasm. The First Battalion then trooped the New Colour in October, with the same pomp and circumstance as the Molson Stadium parade. In Germany, 2 RHC also trooped its own Colour a year later; in 1963, demonstrating that the battalion showed it had lost none of its dash on parade. At Fort St. Louis they celebrated the occasion by hosting Lieutenant Thomas Dinesen, who received the Victoria Cross while serving with the 42nd Battalion, CEF.

In Montreal, Lieutenant Colonel McGovern was chuffed. There was no way he could better his centennial summer. He left triumphant. McGovern's tour would have traditionally ended on the weekend of the spring church parade, but he sensibly stayed on to direct the royal ceremonies. He certainly had a colourful command, from Philadelphia to Molson Stadium. It was a fitting end for the regiment's last wartime CO. On 19 September 1962, Lieutenant Colonel WB Redpath took command of 3 RHC.

The Reunion Dinner, 17 November 1962

This is no ordinary Regiment. No one could come here and not sense there is something exceptional about it.

Governor General Georges P Vanier, 1962

The Regular battalions had ever-full schedules, while the Third Battalion would have to struggle to maintain the euphoria that marked the summer. The new commanding officer found himself face to face with a fresh reality: Montreal society, as it had been known for the past one hundred years, was undergoing a quiet revolution.

Lieutenant Colonel William Bradford Redpath was certainly impressive: 6'2", blond and fit, polished in uniform or suit. A product of Selwyn House and Lower Canada College, his father joined the Regiment in the Great War. Redpath himself enrolled in 1946, served in the ranks for two years, making Lance Corporal before applying to be considered for officer.[206] Redpath was a senior executive for Distillers Corporation and importer of spirits, which meant that in the 1960s, the messes were well stocked at prices that met Highland approval: "As long as Bill was around, there was always *Vat 69* behind the bar (we called it *Weasel's Pee*) – it became our consort to Molson's beer."

Redpath and his regimental sergeant major were inseparable. WO1 Moe Gurevitch was the first Jewish RSM in the Black Watch. He was a colourful man. As CSM of Support Company, he somehow managed to appear at exercises on a motorcycle. During far-away summer concentrations, he would provide treats from *The Main*, something true Montrealers could not live without: "He turned his A2 echelon three-quarter ton truck into a roving delicatessen; he always made sure there was something for the boys when we went up on exercise."[207]

The new CO's first official duty was to host the reunion dinner held on 17 November 1962. His Excellency Georges P Vanier, DSO MC CD LLD, Governor General of Canada was the guest of honour, joined by Major General the Viscount of Arbuthnott DSO MC, colonel of the parent regiment in Scotland, who had arrived to preside at the St Andrew's Ball. Lord Arbuthnott had already visited 1 RHC in Gagetown, to which he would return as reviewing officer at the graduation parade from the RHC Depot of 135 and 136 Squads. At the reunion dinner, the Viscount presented a splendid silver statuette entitled *The Waterloo Highlander*. It was the Imperial Black Watch's centenary gift to the Canadian Regiment.

The Governor General's association with the Regiment dated back to *The Hundred Days*, when his "dear comrade", Lieutenant Colonel Hew Clark-Kennedy gathered the remnants of the 24th and 22e (Van Doos) Battalions to continue a brigade attack. Vanier recalled: "Most of our officers, including staff, and other ranks were casualties so we decided to join forces … the night before he won his VC we spent together." It was in this battle that the Governor General had lost his leg, and Clark-Kennedy was awarded the Victoria Cross. They remained close friends throughout the years. General Vanier addressed The Black Watch with sympathetic words: "This is no ordinary Regiment. No one could come here and not sense there is something exceptional about it." He offered compliments on the Queen Mother's parade and praised The Black Watch traditions, noting that, in 1862 Lord Monck, then the Governor General and Commander-in-Chief, authorized the redesignation *The Royal Light Infantry of Montreal*. With a slight nod to the Viscount of Arbuthnott, he went on, with a twinkle in his eye:

> Since Governors General can do no wrong, you can imagine the consternation when forty-seven years later, in 1909, it was discovered the prefix *Royal* had never been approved. It took King Edward VII to straighten that one out … [and] the affair of the Red Hackle, that proud symbol of valiancy … worn by this Regiment since 1895 – a full ten years before it became allied with its Scottish kin. I wonder if I should reveal this in the presence of Lord Arbuthnott? It seems that here, too, royal approval had not been obtained. King George V straightened this one out.

There was a merry thumping on tables by an appreciative and discerning mess; these officers of the 1960s mirrored almost exactly the original Montreal regiment, for the most part descendants of Scottish immigrants. The Governor General was at home in this assembly. His benign smile, calm eyes and precision of speech, to say nothing of his silver hair and most debonair of moustaches, impressed all who saw him that night. Considered by many to be the best of our Governors General, this soldier with the noble limp, whose deep religious faith undergirded his distinguished career, spoke eloquently of the Black Watch and its heritage:

> Yes, independence – not to use a stronger word – is the deep, indelible mark of Scots. In proud boast of this heritage, The Black Watch badge is of St Andrew and his Cross. In its Greek origin, Andrew means *manhood*. Your badge is then, a reminder of manhood's ultimate sacrifice for the sake of his convictions, his independence ... the first Scottish settlers came to Nova Scotia in 1621; the MacDonalds settled in Quebec shortly after the old regime, the Ramseys and Frasers followed them, the McNabbs and Gaults opened up Ontario and the Selkirk settlers in the Red River Valley ... What is the magic of the Scot? May I venture to say it lies, among other virtues, in his strong religious sense, amounting sometimes to mysticism; his love of education, his high sense of loyalty, his pride, his self-reliance and his independence.

> The world needs today, or many parts of it at any rate, a dash of the Highlanders' romanticism and idealism. It needs something of the deep spiritual leaven that has surged through Scotsmen for long centuries ... that independence of spirit which held that every man was largely the captain of his own soul, the master of his own destiny.[208]

The next morning the 3rd Battalion marched to lay up its old Colours at the Regimental Church.

Hogmanay, 1963 and Foreign Visits

> The Centennial Year celebrations not surprisingly, therefore, left a deep mark on the Regiment. Officers, Senior NCOs and men re-dedicated themselves to Canada's Black Watch. Such dedication was to be sorely tested several years later ... However, as 1962 came to an end, optimism remained the order of the day.[209]

The Third Battalion was delighted by a splendid Centennial gift: wood-carvings, depicting the new Colours Guard. It was presented to the officers' mess by WO2 Ivor Watkins, who had been working on it since the Queen Mother's Colours Parade in June. Watkins whittled and painted each figure, with special emphasis on the battle honours, in exacting detail. The presentation was made to Lieutenant Colonel

Redpath during the sergeants' mess visit to the officers on the day after New Year's; later, the officers were entertained by RSM Moe Gurevitch and the members of the sergeants' mess. The customs of Hogmanay (New Year's Eve) were often coupled with the Regiment's New Year's Day Levee, due to the pressures of the holiday season.

Lieutenant Colonel Redpath planned vigorous winter training and prepared for an international visit to the United States, to participate in a Memorial Day Parade in Quincy, Massachusetts. The occasion commemorated the 236th Battalion – The McLean Highlanders of America (better known as "The McLean Kilties"). This visit was arranged by the Canadian Consul General and the Hon James Burke, member of the US House of Representatives. The invitation was in response to the 3rd Battalion's earlier invitation to two American sergeants, George J Matta and MF Johnston, to visit Montreal as the Regiment's guests, for the Presentation of Colours by the Queen Mother. The Americans originally enlisted in the 236th (The New Brunswick Kilties) Battalion CEF, which was also known as "The MacLean Kilties of America" in honour of the large number of enlistees from the New England states. Many transferred to the 42nd Battalion as reinforcements. Permission was given by the United States for the Royal Highlanders to come from Canada and recruit men from the Greater Boston area and other major cities in 1917, an event well recorded in Colonel Hutchison's regimental history.[210]

Redpath despatched Lieutenant Robert Gelston with a well-rehearsed guard of honour of sixty with additional pipers and camp followers. The visit included a military ball, a number of cocktail parties and the parade, where the Black Watch was given Congressional permission to march with fixed bayonets. They were most hospitably received. Their quarters "were a revelation to all of us, two per room, and what rooms! Radio and television!" War veterans shook their heads – this was splendiferous living. The visit was a great success and prompted congratulatory letters from the Consul General as well as a hefty reference in the Congressional Record.[211]

The Regimental Annual At-Home in April was more relaxed after the previous year's bustle preparing for the Queen Mother. A senior member of the Advisory Board remembers that at the spring dinner, Redpath skillfully sustained an amiable conversation while trapping a cockroach heading across the head table toward the guest of honour. Clearly, a gatecrasher from another unit! The CO faced other more serious survival challenges. The roof drain over the sergeants' mess clogged and a veritable lake built up, which finally erupted in little geysers from the WCs and flooding the mess and the rooms beneath. On another occasion, Lieutenant Colonel Bill Redpath was called well after midnight and advised there was a water problem. He arrived with his adjutant, Captain Steve Angus, to meet a plumber sent by the duty officer at District HQ:

He was good and we located an elbow in the Pipe Band room, which he used to clear the drain to the sewer on Bleury Street. Unfortunately, in doing so he had to open a trap cover in the Band Room and the water, with all the pressure from the pond on the roof came out with the force of a fire hose. The floor of the Band Room has never recovered and still is warped![212]

Later, the sergeants' mess threw a Beatnik party. The younger sergeants were in awe of the RSM and senior warrants doing the *Hokey-Pokey* and the *Twist* with equal dexterity.

The period after the Queen Mum's visit should have been stress-free but, in addition to housekeeping matters, political storm clouds were to be observed on the horizon. The election of Lester B Pearson's Liberal government in April 1963 initiated a precarious association that was to dominate military-political relations for the next two decades. The Pearson–Trudeau years, set alongside a volatile anti-war movement south of the border, proved difficult years for the Army. The unpopular Vietnam War resulted in something of an anti-military backlash in Canada, despite the fact that we did not take part in the war. Further, changing mores and fashions completely dominated, such as long hair and the *youth counter-culture* that affected recruiting, particularly in large cities like Montreal. Most importantly, in Quebec, the *revolution tranquille* furthered a certain hostility to the military. It was regarded as an alien federal organization contrary to the culture of Quebec: "Anglophone, and far too British-colonial in style and temper." It was, as the future prime minister, Pierre Elliot Trudeau noted: an interesting ideological debate, with two diametrically opposed philosophies – liberalism and the military mind. Coexistence within the governmental structure was to prove challenging, not to say uncomfortable, for the Army, as the government systematically redefined its military as an instrument of modern foreign policy.[213]

Regimental Items: Old RSMs, New Colonels, 1963

In his last six months as Colonel of the Regiment, Brigadier Blackader managed a full schedule. This included visits to: Her Majesty in Clarence House in London, 2 RHC in Germany on 23 August for a Trooping the Colour, and finally, New Brunswick. The NATO battalion was commanded by a Second World War veteran that Brigadier Blackader no doubt recalled, Lieutenant Colonel Duncan McAlpine. Everyone was in high spirits: the Second Battalion had won the NATO General Crerar Forced March competition; and A Company, under Major George McQueen, had just been presented with the 4th Brigade's "Skill at Arms Competition" trophy.

The Trooping of the new Colour was performed with great skill and was the first such occasion on foreign soil since the Great War. Previously, on 14 January 1919, appropriately in Germany, near Castle Ehreshoven, the 1st Bn (RHC) as the 13th Battalion CEF received its Colours from Major HRH Prince Arthur of Connaught. Later, on 29 January 1919, Major General Sir Frederick Loomis (who had commanded the 13th Bn at Ypres) presented Colours to the 2nd Bn (RHC) as the 42nd Bn CEF at Nechin, France.[214]

Blackader returned to Gagetown for a second Trooping, by the First Battalion – his last official act as Colonel of the Regiment. 1 RHC filled yet another shelf of sports trophies. The hockey team, coached by WO2 JY Byrne, brought victory in the Eastern Command hockey championships in March. Boxing, managed by Major WB Macleod, continued to dominate. The battalion's boxers won a most prestigious victory as they won the Army boxing championships on 5 April in Valcartier.

The parade earned Blackader's praise. The Trooping's execution was testament to the hard work of RSM Vic Lawson and his guard sergeants major who spent long hours bringing the guards to perfection. WO 2 Victor Chartier led a 3 RHC contingent to Gagetown for the parade in early October. He was accompanied by the serving RSM, Moe Gurevitch and a large court from the sergeants' mess. *The Tartan Times* chronicled the visit: "In the first afternoon, everyone attended a tea-party (no tea in sight) followed by the Trooping, followed by another tea-party (the tea still not in sight)."[215] The sergeants made do with whisky and *Moosehead*. At the mess dinner, Lieutenant Colonel Sellar presented a silver statuette of a Black Watch soldier in full dress to commemorate Brigadier Blackader's retirement and long service to the Regiment.

The battalion then gathered at a Trooping Ball, and the revelry extended well into the morning. The next day, bleary-eyed RSM Gurevitch, who was staying with RSM Finnie, leaned close-in trying to ensure a clean shave, and pushed against the cabinet drawer, shutting it. It was a memorable experience; Finnie well recalled the loud exclamations and subsequent oratory. The drawer had rudely closed on the RSM leaving him bruised, but unbowed.

Back in Montreal, on 2 November, after an autumn of field exercises and a range qualification weekend, the regimental reunion dinner honoured the new Colonel of the Regiment, JW Knox MBE ED. All battalion COs attended, including Lieutenant Colonels Sellar, McAlpine, Redpath, and Major LA Watling MC, commanding officer Black Watch Depot. Also present was Colonel HM Wallis DSO OBE MC, the Honorary Lieutenant Colonel of the 3rd Battalion. During cocktails, the latest issue of *The Tartan Times*, the Bleury Street version of *The Private Eye,* edited by WO2 Bobby

Miles, CSM of the 3 RHC "Depot", was circulated. It was full of news, gossip and anecdotes that were "refreshingly tongue-in-cheek."[216]

Jim Knox was still known as 'Gander Neck' and not only by veterans of the Second World War. In Highland attire, he seemed perfect as a colonel of the Black Watch – tall, a full moustache, dark piercing eyes and an austere, brooding face. In fact, he was rather shy and had a tremendous sense of humour, but only his closest friends knew that side. Despite his formality, Knox was considered more personable than his predecessor was, and the junior officers were a bit more relaxed in his presence. During the dinner, Lieutenant Colonel Sellar, on behalf of Regular officers of the Regiment, presented an oil portrait of HM Queen Elizabeth, The Queen Mother to the Regimental Headquarters officers' mess. Painted by Aubrey Davidson-Houston, it was commissioned for the Centennial and subsequently hung over the great fireplace in the Bleury Street mess.[217]

It was announced that the Black Watch would return to Mons on 9 November 1963, to commemorate the 42nd Bn CEF taking of the town on the last day of the Great War.[218] The mess was advised, to enthusiastic approval, that Colonel Hutchison's centennial regimental history, *Canada's Black Watch,* which was published in February 1963, was about to have a second printing. Hutchison, as former Colonel Commandant of the Regiment, thanked Kenneth Blackader and wished Jim Knox good luck on his tour. This occasion marked the end of a remarkable regimental career for Brigadier Blackader. A Great War veteran, decorated during The Hundred Days, as well as a veteran of the Second World War, Blackader commanded an elite "D-Day Brigade" and fought it deep into Normandy, against the best divisions in the Third Reich. He was awarded the DSO, again in battle, and before the Normandy Campaign ended, he commanded the 3rd Canadian Infantry Division. He was a no-nonsense officer with an imposing lineage and even more impressive regimental service of forty-seven years. Brigadier Blackader had taken over "the originals" recruited in 1939; he returned at war's end to serve as head of the Advisory Board, and later as the Colonel-of-the-Regiment.[219]

The Regimental Advisory Board also acquired a new vice chairman. Swamped with work at his company, Lieutenant Colonel Val Traversy declined the appointment as vice to Brigadier Blackader, who continued as chairman. Instead, he recommended, in the strongest terms, Lieutenant Colonel JG Bourne, whom he felt had been somehow overlooked.[220] If anyone could accommodate the powerful influence of the brigadier, it was surely John Bourne. Before the end of the month, Colonel Knox formally assumed his duties in Gagetown, where he was reviewing officer at the 1 RHC parade, and guest of honour at a mixed mess dinner. Bourne became vice chairman of the board.

Chapter 10

A New Army, a New Militia

It is not the strongest of the species that survive, nor the most intelligent, but the one most responsive to change.

Attributed to Charles Darwin

The Suttie Commission 1964

"... to carry out its revised roles more efficiently and realistically [to avoid disbandment]."

The Liberals came to power in April 1963. The following month, Prime Minister Pearson set up a special committee on defence, and requested a report on the Reserves from an ad-hoc committee: "The Commission on the Reorganization of the Canadian Army Militia" (1964). It was more commonly known as 'The Suttie Commission', as it was chaired by Brigadier ER Suttie and included many respected war veterans.[221] It was charged with recommending to the Minister of National Defence the best way of organizing the Militia to fulfill its four roles as the Reserve Army in Canada i.e. supporting the Regular Army; providing a training cadre; internal security operations; and, carrying out the National Survival programme. The commission concluded that a force of thirty thousand soldiers would be required and recommended various changes, which would allow the Militia "to carry out its revised roles more efficiently and realistically."[222] One of its suggestions was that the 25 Militia Group Headquarters be replaced by a smaller organization and, aided by "Militia Advisors" in the rank of colonel. What caught everyone's attention was the recommendation for large-scale disbandment of units and the amalgamation of those that remained. Wishing to avoid using the term 'disbandment' a *Supplementary Order of Battle* was devised. In the subsequent 1964 White Paper, the minister of national defence rattled the forces, particularly the Navy and Army, when he outlined the government's "unification" plans. The Canadian military was to become a single service, commanded by a single Chief of Defence Staff (CDS) and a single Defence Staff.[223] Folks held their breath, expecting more change. At this point, The Black Watch (RHR) of Canada could hardly imagine what the future might hold.

The distressing news in the new year was the sudden loss of the Third Battalion's well-liked commanding officer in December.[224] Major Tom Price was asked to succeed Lieutenant Colonel William Redpath. The change of command took place after the church parade on 12 May 1965. This was also the last church parade for Colonel HM Wallis before his retirement as Honorary Lieutenant Colonel 3 RHC; he was succeeded by Lieutenant Colonel JW Sharp CD.

Lieutenant Colonel John Wemyss Sharp CD

'Jake' Sharp was vintage Black Watch. A product of Selwyn House, Ashbury College School and Bishop's College School; he built a career in business and by the time of his appointment as Honorary Lieutenant Colonel, was the president of Phillips Security and chairman of United Pharmaceuticals. He was also president of the National Council Boy Scouts of Canada. Sharp reminded many people of Clark Gable. He married an attractive gal from the Eastern Townships and joined the Black Watch during the war serving as a 'reinforcement officer' seconded to the British Army. He was rated a keen, aggressive officer when he fought as a platoon commander with the 8th Argyll and Sutherland Highlanders in North Africa. In continuous action for two months, Sharp was wounded during the Battle of Longstop Hill in Tunisia, which was regarded as a major action. Mentioned in Despatches, he was praised for "exceptional powers of leadership...of great value to ASH."[225] Sharp commanded the Reinforcement Training School Canada 1944–45. He was a level-headed advisor as well as a bon vivant, well-liked by the Regiment and a hard-working honorary.

Lieutenant Colonel TE Price, 3 RHC 1965–67

Tom Evan Price was the *beau idéal*, the Black Watch version of Cary Grant; he looked dashing in anything he wore. Perennially tanned, his disarming smile lit up any room he entered. He invariably sent the debutantes into shy giggles at the St

Andrew's Ball; they blushed, deciding he resembled the rakish Black Watch officer their mothers had warned them of; but Price was innocently charming. He was able to put people at their ease immediately and was a great favourite of the Queen Mother. Whenever Tom Price visited London, he would be expected for lunch or afternoon tea at Clarence House.

Price was an Old Boy of Bishop's College School and a graduate of Bishop's University, Lennoxville. As the cadet major of Bishop's Corps, he was awarded the Strathcona Medal in 1948. He came from a military and business family in Quebec City. His father, Brigadier JH Price OBE MC, was much respected after the war for his valiant attempts to obtain special pensions for Hong Kong veterans, including soldiers from his own unit, the Royal Rifles of Canada, who endured suffering, as he did, in Japanese Prisoner of War camps. Tom Price joined the Watch in 1950. A stockbroker, he was later president of the distinguished firm of MacDougall, MacDougall and MacTier. Somewhat self-effacing, he was always selling himself short. He once said, "I don't remember if I ever passed Bishop's, and I am not a tactician – I'm the oldest captain in the Canadian Army."[226] In Valcartier, when he arrived with his second-in-command, the equally tall John Macfarlane, the other colonels dubbed the pair '*les grands Écossais*'.

By late 1964, the move to get people qualified, or out, had created a mass exodus. Many senior NCOs had to revert to the rank of corporal because they did not have the required qualifications. Most simply left, rather than take qualification courses with men half their age. Every Militia unit went through the same process. During this period, whatever disdain the Regular Force had for the Militia, increased in general. Throughout the centuries, the Militia was the poor cousin, getting hand-me-downs from the Regular Army. Their splendid record in the Second World War was forgotten. Some of the problem lay with the Reserve battalions, but much had to do with direction, qualification courses, and equipment made available from higher headquarters, which were run more like fiefs than military organizations. In truth, the Militia was not particularly efficient. It was almost *déclassé* to discuss doctrine or tactics in the mess. The decline began with the end of the war and continued intermittently. Standards varied; exercises were frequently bland and repetitive. When realistic schemes were attempted, all too often they exceeded the abilities of the units involved. To add to the concern, the 3rd Bn Black Watch was now considered no different from any other Militia unit. The Montreal battalion was no longer *non plus ultra* – a significant change, given its past century.

Lieutenant Colonel Price appointed a new RSM. WO1 Ivor Eugene ("Junior") Watkins succeeded WO1 M Gurevitch – a typical modern Black Watch exchange, with bits of the 'MacCohen' tradition. Gurevitch, Jewish and not originally RHC, turned over to Watkins, an Anglican from the Royal Canadian Navy. Watkins had several months commando training during the war and served with the Juno Beach harbour parties from 7 July to 21 August 1944 before returning to England.[227] He worked for the CPR in signals and communications and was a talented artist, with boundless initiative. He was also a perfect example of the training situation in the Militia vis a vis trade qualifications. Despite the fact that he had an impressive list of army courses and summer camps dating back to 1946, Watkins did not qualify *Militia Infantry Gp 1* until November 1967 yet he had been appointed to acting corporal, acting sergeant, and sergeant in 1947, 1948 and 1950 respectively. He passed a Sr NCO course in 1954 and was appointed RSM June 1965. It is noteworthy that RSM Watkins's 'Infantry Trade' courses were taken two years *after* becoming RSM. They were necessary in order to be eligible to parade before the Queen Mother in 1967. To his credit, he took the course with men half his age: "I'll get qualified, even if I have to train with young privates."[228]

The Montreal battalion looked forward to the 1963 Tri-Service Ball, and the sergeants' mess beamed at the results of the Burns Trophy shoot, for they edged out the officers: "It was in the bag until a certain old sweat got his point across." The new year would prove a difficult one for the battalion, although the challenges arose from what seemed to be a complementary development. Under the *Reorganization of Reserves,* the 3 RHC was redesignated as a 'major unit' with an establishment of three hundred all ranks. However, fewer officers were permitted. The battalion was therefore faced with an additional recruiting and training objective, coupled with a substantial reduction in the numbers of officers and senior NCOs. Regrettably, command was obliged to retire a number who had served the battalion well. While unit training had not quite abandoned National Survival, it now emphasized special-to-corps skills. The 3rd Battalion's task was to produce a trained rifle company of 150 all ranks and a heavy weapons platoon of fifty with assigned anti-tank weapons. These skills required new courses and qualifications.

The year was given a bit of excitement when Lieutenant Colonel Sellar invited twenty-two soldiers (all ranks) to be attached to 1 RHC for a major exercise in Newfoundland. The pipes and drums spent a week in Birmingham at the Alabama Highland Games, and then performed at the closing ceremonies of the New York's World's Fair. The Regiment now boasted six active cadet corps, going from west to east: The Black Watch Cadet Corps (135 all ranks); The Lachine High School Cadet Corps; Bishop's College School Cadet Corps (200 all ranks); the Oromocto High School Cadet Corps; Kings College School (152 cadets; Windsor, Nova Scotia); and the Rothesay Collegiate School Cadet Corps (No 130), Rothesay, NB. It was becoming increasingly apparent that the decade would provoke considerable military, political and social change. The future of the Militia was not clear. In fact, it was evident that the government had yet to make up its mind. Meantime, the Montreal Watch wavered between pre-war habits and post-war depression – a willingness to become modern and a determination to retain its prized traditions at any cost.

Terrorism in Montreal: FLQ attacks on the City – 1963

The significant factor in the topsy-turvy environment peculiar to Quebec (more specifically Montreal) was the issue of *separatism* – a nationalistic independence movement that was decidedly anti-federal, anti-military, and anti-Anglophone, particularly as it pertained to the great metropolis of Montreal, in effect, a bilingual city, where business was mainly done *en anglais*. The radical organization, Front Liberation Quebecois (FLQ), emerged as a violent, terrorist organization, stealing headlines via increasing violence in public demonstrations and eventually, overt acts of sabotage. These dark years began in 1963 with scattered bombings, then an escalation in March, when the military was attacked: three Westmount armouries had incendiary bombs exploded at their doors or basement windows. This was met with unusual calm and a refusal to believe that acts of deliberate terrorism could be happening here in Montreal. On 10 May, a bomb exploded outside The Black Watch Armoury on Bleury Street. Immediately, security patrols were ordered around the building. A week later, ten bombs were placed in Westmount: five exploded, and Sergeant Major Walter (Rocky) Leja was severely injured when the bomb he was disarming blew up. This brave army engineer had already dismantled two separatist bombs hidden in a mailbox. By the end of the year, a total of twenty-nine terrorist bombs had been placed.[229] On 26 September, FLQ conducted an armed bank robbery in Montreal, emulating the tactics of the FLN in Algeria and France, i.e. finance through robbery, terror through bombing. The next year was worse.

A dramatic escalation occurred early in 1964, jolting DND and the government. On 30 January, the FLQ staged a raid on the Les Fusiliers Mont-Royal Armoury. It was a stunning coup; an astonishing number of weapons and ammunition were hauled away, including fifty-nine modern FN assault rifles, four Bren Gun automatic rifles, thirty-four submachine guns, four mortars, anti-tank rocket launchers, grenades, and revolvers, and fifteen thousand rounds of ammunition.[230] This was followed a month later by a similar raid on the *62e Régiment d'artillerie de campagne*, a Militia unit in Shawinigan QC, where the haul was thirty-three FN assault rifles, pistols and ammunition. More bombs were exploded through the year and finally, murder was committed when the FLQ staged a raid on International Firearms, a Montreal business, which killed two employees.[231]

The two raids on Militia armouries provoked nasty cracks against the Reserves from senior officers in Ottawa. These were quickly reported by the press, imputing the Militia's reputation of social playboys who cannot look after their lethal toys. These in turn prompted a string of rebuttals from across Canada; a particularly effective one came from a former Black Watch hero and current Colonel Commandant of the Royal Canadian Armoured Corps.[232] Nevertheless, a sense of anxiety was evident in the garrison. Some regiments were considered suspicious, and the loyalty of their younger members questioned. Exercises were carefully monitored and for a while, ammunition. Pyrotechnics were tightly controlled, if not prohibited, even for ranges. It was much like the allegory of the duck. On the surface, the Montreal military appeared calm, gliding across Beaver Lake, while below, its feet were thrashing through the water. The City Militia went through its own particular *cafard* for the next ten years, with little sympathy or real understanding from the rest of the country. Montreal was in a particularly delicate position requiring measured in-house solutions: method rather than brute force.

That year, the Queen and Prince Philip visited Quebec City, arriving in Canada on the 100th anniversary of the Charlottetown Conference, which had led to Confederation. Forty Black Watch soldiers were present, tasked with crowd control – there were fears of violent protests by separatist elements. The soldiers remember it well: "October 1964 – we were on duty on the Plains of Abraham, overlooking the Royal Yacht *Britannia*, anchored in Wolfe's cove … our backs to the limousine facing the crowd, not the Royal Couple – it was unusual."[233]

The Queen Mother's Photograph: Pte Conway vs. RHQ

Early in the new year, Private James Conway wrote to Clarence House, on behalf of The Black Watch Men's Canteen, asking for a photograph of Elizabeth, the Queen Mother. This was approved. Captain Alastair Aird, the Queen Mother's private secretary responded: "I am commanded by Queen Elizabeth The Queen Mother to write and thank you for your letter … Queen Elizabeth has graciously pleased to agree to your request."[234] Private Conway was chuffed. The parcel arrived at the regimental headquarters but was promptly diverted to adorn an office. Conway was livid and sought justice from his colonel. Righteousness triumphed. Jim Conway became a celebrity in the men's mess and recalled his coup with great fondness as he continued serving as corporal, sergeant, and finally, as an officer.

The Exodus of Senior NCOs

Most of the militia problems were financial – budgets were limited.

Although NCO courses were available, far too many soldiers and NCOs required "Arms Qualifications" (certified Trained Infantryman, Machine Gunner, Mortarman, etc.). The chief aim was to qualify all privates as *Leading Infantryman Group 1* (there were four groups that formed the essential skills of the craft). Few soldiers had them. This was the case throughout the Militia. There were several causes; the chief ones were less emphasis on Infantry proficiency vs. survival techniques and budgetary restraints. All Black Watch soldiers paraded at the armoury on Tuesday and Thursday nights. In addition, there were Saturdays, weekend exercises, summer camps, and, attending qualification courses. These were usually held in the city. Often, soldiers returning from a course were given "acting" ranks without qualifications. As long as there was no stringent emphasis for qualification, sergeants were promoted within the regiment based on their efficiency and experience. Each unit took a turn in offering specialized courses, often scrambling to find qualified instructors. However, when District qualification courses were made available, attendance was not always possible for working men; some older soldiers, veterans for example, disdained to participate. Thus, the Militia continued to promote *as required*.

The removal of non-qualified NCOs (and officers) was ordered by Quebec Command shortly after the Queen Mother's visit. Some processed qualifications were based on previous military experience; some were transfers from the Cadet Services. The Junior NCO Course lasted 2.5 months: two nights a week, two weekends a month. Gradually, as the younger soldiers went on courses, they ended up with corporals and lance corporals more qualified than the sergeants. The warrants and sergeants were ordered to qualify or leave. In October 1964: two Senior NCOs reverted to Corporal, one a future RSM, the other a mess steward, because they had not taken the senior NCO course. It was very difficult to ask still-serving Second World War veterans to surrender their senior NCO stripes, even if they were unqualified and appeared on orders as 'corporal'. WO2 Jimmy Evans ran the orderly room from 1955 to 1965. Of him it was said, "Hell, he ran the building! When he retired they brought in a half dozen CWAC sergeants and privates to replace him."[235] Evans took loving care of the men on the regimental roll. Nonetheless, the battalion was forced to clean house. As late as the summer of 1966, out of the twenty-eight officers and 190 *effectives*, only four soldiers were qualified as *Group 1 Infantryman* (Sgt John Cher, Cpls Mike Cher, Dave Spence, and Gary Young); designated by their qualification badge (an ivory bayonet on the sleeve). Meantime, the officers were now without battle experience – Lieutenant Colonel McGovern was the last wartime CO.

From October 1964 to September 1965, 3 RHC lost twelve senior NCOs; another group left in 1966. A future commanding officer, Victor Chartier, joined as private soldier and reached the rank of WO2 with only one actual military trade qualification: Storeman. Moe Gurevitch called him into his office: "The new colonel wants you as RSM." Fate intervened; the next day, he was promoted by his civilian employer and posted to Quebec City.[236] Chartier was placed on the supplementary list, but returned in 1974, when he was quickly made RSM.

The decade witnessed a net decrease of seventeen senior NCOs in a twenty-seven month period. These were generally voluntary retirements; the reasons cited were demands of work, age and a depressing ennui regarding the state of the Militia. The sergeants' mess had been reduced by two thirds. By early 1968, the promotion of qualified junior NCOs quickly filled the vacancies and the sergeants' mess was back up to strength. Most of the senior NCOs now had at least two infantry trade qualifications.

University COTC Contingents

The best-qualified officers available to the Reserves were products of the University COTC (Canadian Officers' Training Corps) contingents. There were four in Montreal: McGill, Loyola, Sir George Williams and Université de Montréal. They boasted traditions that went back to the Great War and had produced a number of distinguished generals, one of whom, Frank Fleury, was in charge of Army personnel during this period. COTC training was exclusive to university students and required winter courses along with three full summers, where they trained with the student officers from the Royal Military College. The difference between the COTC and the ROTP was the contractual obligation to serve five years. The Regular officer cadets were given full tuition, clothing and living allowances whereas the COTC were paid only for the training taken. However, a summer of phase training usually allowed the officer to acquire his first half-year tuition; the remainder was acquired by way of bursaries or part-time jobs. The final product was a well-trained, reasonably experienced subaltern. Graduate officers were encouraged to select a Reserve regiment to which to apply for service as a commissioned officer. Lieutenant Colonel Macfarlane shrewdly made a point of attending the Loyola COTC mess dinners, accompanied by his personal piper. He was easily the most popular guest and delighted the Jesuits. His willingness to participate in mess games, particularly *Indian Wrestling* and *Buck-Buck*, made him a favourite with the officer-cadets: "Given the persuasive talents of the CO added to the prestige of the Regiment, it surprised no one to see the lion's share of the Loyola College COTC come to the Regiment."[237] They arrived to find a battalion hard at work to qualify NCOs, recruit soldiers and raise standards to meet the challenges of modern doctrine.

While the Regular battalions were at their prime, the Militia seemed sluggish. Of the twenty-eight officers listed during the Queen Mother's Trooping in 1962, fourteen remained in the fall of 1969. Major Stephen Angus, it appeared, was the singleton major and about to be promoted colonel. This "command gap" was solved when Ferdon and Sewell were promoted to field officer status.[238] The Militia, whose primary purpose for the past decade had been "National Survival Training", was readjusting itself to more traditional roles. This brief interlude, however, was immediately challenged by FLQ terrorist activities which totally disrupted the city as well as the Reserves.

The battalion incorporated two working companies supported by two bands (the military band at forty all ranks; and the pipes and drums at thirty). Privates and corporals were sent on formal, out-of-unit training to qualify as a *Leading Infantryman*. Several corporals were selected for the assault pioneer course and became skilled in working booby traps, mines, and explosives in general. Finally, as a complete break with the "pay book past", in 1967, NDHQ introduced a change: document inscription converted from the venerable "Regimental Number" to the citizen's nine-digit *Social Insurance Number* or *SIN*. Once again, old soldiers shook their heads.

The Auld Battalions

The 73rd Battalion CEF veterans marked their fiftieth anniversary on 26 March 1966, led by their own historian, Colonel Paul Hutchison. As per tradition, it was held in the Queen's Hotel just across the street from the old Bonaventure Station – the point at which they entrained for Halifax.[239] At the 73rd gathering, two prizes were regularly awarded after 1939: *Youngest Grandfather Present* and, *Second Oldest Member Present*.[240] The battalion, despite its lack of years and status next to the colossi (the 13th and 42nd Battalions CEF), was the most determined concerning anniversary reunions. It held fast until the last member had died. Their fiftieth included some of the more colourful members of the Black Watch: Colonels Morgan and Hutchison, and particularly Major General FF Worthington MC and Bar, MM and Bar. The general was famous as 'the father of the Canadian Armoured Corps,' and fondly remembered by the 73rd as a very brave corporal. Worthington, despite his firm identification with armour, never forgot that the Black Watch was his regiment (and he had plenty to choose from, including a couple of American outfits). Lieutenant Colonel Ivan

Ibbotson recalled that during the Second World War, when he was posted to 2nd Canadian Infantry Division as a brigade major, he regularly encountered two former 73rd officers: Colonel Jack Christie and 'Fearless Frank' Worthington. Though the dashing tank general commanded the dynamic 4th Canadian Armoured Division, whenever he met Ibbotson, "[Frank] always mentioned the fact that we served in the same battalion in the last war. The old tradition of love for the regiment is still very strong and I am meeting our men all over the place and they all are friends."[241] Major DC Campbell was still Secretary at the 56th *Anniversary of Departure Dinner*, but sadly, The Honorary President, HW Morgan MC and most of the honorary vice-presidents were now deceased. The average age was eighty. The 1965 regimental reunion dinner hosted Brigadier HC Baker-Baker, colonel of the parent regiment in Great Britain. All reference to the FLQ was avoided. Instead the general lamented the steady *Americanisation* of NATO and the adoption of the new (essentially US version) of the military phonetic alphabet. British and Canadians were now involved in the "discarding of sacred names"- now *Able*, *Baker* and *Dog* companies became *Alpha*, *Bravo* and *Delta*.[242]

Mobile Command

In 1965, as a precursor to the unification of Canada's armed services, all land forces were placed under a new entity called *Mobile Command*. In 1968, the 'Canadian Army' would cease to exist as a legal entity; as the navy, army, and air force were to be merged to form a single service called the *Canadian Forces*.

In Montreal, the year witnessed continued terrorist activities. The incidents turned international when, on 16 February, FLQ terrorist saboteurs were arrested in New York. Dynamite was found in their car. Their aim was to blow up the Statue of Liberty and other US monuments. Terrorist bombs continued to be detonated in Montreal at a rate of one a month. On 15 July, the FLQ raided the military base at La Macaza, Quebec and took a Provincial police officer as hostage. In November, the group exploded a small bomb at *le Palais du Commerce de Montréal*, during a Liberal Party convention.[243] The bombings, despite active RCMP and Military Police investigation, continued through 1966 and 1967.[244] Citizens were killed, monuments savaged and public businesses damaged. Perhaps because these acts did not disrupt day-to-day activities (in comparison to the security measures imposed throughout North America after the 9/11 terrorist attacks in New York and Washington) the reactions seemed too calm, almost blasé.

The Black Watch observed the first anniversary of *Mobile Command*, i.e. the Canadian Army, by shrewdly inviting its commander, Lieutenant General WAB Anderson to the 1966 reunion dinner as guest of honour. The venture proved a poor investment.[245] In the beginning, its very large headquarters (the St Hubert Air Base was twenty minutes from Montreal) increased the size of the already considerable Anglophone community on the south shore. It was also a source of part-time employment for the Militia. At any time, at least two dozen Black Watch officers, NCOs and other ranks were on six-month to yearly call-out contracts. However, this federal presence was an annoyance to French Canadian nationalists and eventually, DND shut the base down in the mid 1990s, moving the considerable staff, supporting garrison, and dependents to Ottawa. Regrettably, this eliminated a sizeable anti-separatist voting bloc, depleted English schools in the area, and removed an important source of extra employment that kept Reserve regiments alive. It seemed to many Montrealers to be an effective bit of anti-federal impairment, curiously effected by the federal government itself.

In February 1966, the 3rd Battalion conducted exercises in Gagetown, hosted by a demonstration team from 1st and 2nd Battalions. At that year's church parade, the Montrealers honoured Major the Rev Dr RJ Berlis, who observed his twentieth year as minister of The Church of St Andrew and St Paul. He was the last Black Watch wartime officer still serving in the 3rd Battalion. Meantime, The Black Watch Association held well-attended socials where the fun equalled the noise. The officers' mess could never quite match the gaiety of the sergeants' mess. 'Old Timers' were enjoying their best decade with dinners, dances and bowling. There was a Ladies' Military Whist Club every Friday as well as the steadfast Ladies' Montreal Tennis and Badminton Club, going strong since before the Great War. Bingo was popular, the numbers called by Sergeant Jack 'The Voice' Roe ("Shaddup, I kant hear-yuh!"). Special guest was WO1 Robert Blackwell, who had just taken over as RSM of the 1st Battalion from WO1 Herbert Firby – popularly (though out of earshot) known to many the lads as 'Herbie Firbie'. In the Second World War, the nickname/term 'Herbie' came to mean the typical ranker, or private soldier. It was adopted after Captain Bing Coughlin's popular cartoon series 'Herbie' that was published in *The Maple Leaf* in Italy and later in all editions through the war.

Regimental Traditions – The St Andrew's Ball

The guest of honour at the 1964 reunion dinner was Lieutenant General RW Moncel DSO OBE CD, famed as the 'boy brigadier' who rose to command during the Normandy campaign. The Regular battalions' Lieutenant Colonels Sellar and McAlpine joined Colonels Knox, Sharp, Wallis and Major LA Watling, who commanded the Depot, to form the head table. As ever, the dinner was followed within a fortnight by the St Andrew's Ball, traditionally held on the Friday nearest 30 November and held at the Windsor, with its two parallel ballrooms divided by *Peacock Alley*, where panache was king and romances began. However, this year the peacocks were forsaken for the new and fashionable Queen Elizabeth Hotel. In preparation, debutantes and their escorts met at The Black Watch Armoury to practise the "Centenary Reel", composed to mark the occasion; then a strathspey, with its unique steps, followed by the ever popular *Eightsome* and *The Dashing White Sergeant*. Forty debutantes and their escorts had been practising since October; many lived out of town, and others were away at school. Practices started after *rushing season* at McGill ended. The parade square usually had about thirty couples, and everyone was taught the *Waltz Country Dance* and *The Gay Gordons*.[246] During 1960s, the sessions were taught by Mrs Betty Speirs, who hailed from Scotland: "It's the boys who sometimes pose a problem." Since all Black Watch officers consider the Ball a formal "parade" and are expected to participate in key dances, it was normal to find at least two subalterns attending the practices. Helped by the duty piper and a record player, "the sessions featured rollicking reels and gay whoops. The dancers were soon good enough to step out in public."[247]

Black Watch at Harvard:
The Hasty Pudding Club Commemorate Robert Sherwood

That fall, Harvard's *Hasty Pudding Club* paid tribute to Robert E Sherwood, the six-foot-seven author, Pulitzer Prize winner and Black Watch veteran. He served in 42nd Bn CEF under John Herbert Molson. Sherwood was a long-time friend and advisor to President Roosevelt, as well as his speech writer. In 1949, he won a fourth Pulitzer in recognition of his screenplay for *The Best Years of our Lives*, an Academy Award-winning film. Before the 1966 St Andrew's Ball, Colonels Paul Hutchison and Tom Price took the train to Harvard to attend a dinner of the Hasty Pudding Club (founded in 1795) arranged to honour Sherwood, who had been an active member of the Club since 1918. Hutchison knew Sherwood in France, where it was believed that a kilt for the soaring Sherwood required 6 ¼ yards of cloth. At the dinner, it was learned that the *Pudding* was about the only thing that kept him in college, nearly got him fired, and lured him back in 1919-1920 to finish and stage the *Barnum Was*

Right show. Earlier in the war, Sherwood was so sure that he would be fired that he tried to enlist in the US Army. They would have none of him: "too tall," they said. So rather than court the ignominy of having Harvard can him, he raced to Montreal where "the Canadian Black Watch wrapped him up, sent him overseas, got him twice wounded, and has cherished him ever since."[248]

After the Centennial:
Lieutenant Colonel JIB Macfarlane Takes Over 3 RHC 17 October 1967

The Militia was being quietly reorganized from Mobile Command Headquarters. A new plan introduced General Military Training (GMT), which superseded the Recruit Training Programme and the Training Militia Programme. Militia COs now had little say about their battalion, a trend that would gather speed. These changes spurred Tom Price to ask to be relieved of command. He cited business responsibilities but made it clear to the Colonel-of-the-Regiment that he was annoyed that the battalion was no longer responsible for its own training. There were two sides to the argument; many Militia units appreciated GMT, glad to have another headquarters assume responsibility. Price, for one, did not welcome the new role.[249]

In October, after a fabulous royal summer, Tom Price handed over to Lieutenant Colonel John Ibbotson Buchanan Macfarlane.[250] The new CO had a sterling regimental lineage. He was the son and grandson of past commanding officers: Lieutenant Colonel WE Macfarlane MC and Bar, had been commissioned in the field after Ypres and completed the war having survived four wounds. He commanded the 3rd (Res) Battalion RHC. John Macfarlane's grandfather, Lieutenant Colonel IL Ibbotson, commanded the 5th Bn The Royal Scots of Canada during 1897–1901.[251] Macfarlane was the sales manager for a major paper company but seemed to have spent most of his life in a Highland battalion: a Boy Soldier in 1944, commissioned RHC in 1951, and then served with the 48th Highlanders (1952–65) before returning to become Price's 2IC. Major HG Mitchell CD became the new second-in-command.

At the fall reunion dinner, the CDS, General Jean Victor Allard, who always seemed very much at home with the Watch, was guest of honour. He presided as Lieutenant Colonel Tom Price was "mugged out" and presented with a silver cocktail shaker. The officers hoped Price might know what to do with it. Lieutenant Colonel Macfarlane, commanded his first church parade on 12 May 1968; Captain the Rev SA Hayes, successor to the retired Dr. Berlis, officiated as the new Regimental Chaplain. Hayes admitted it was "not an easy job to succeed Berlis who knew so many from the war – especially for one who was essentially an academic with no military background."[252] It was also the changeover of RSMs: WO 1 Ivor Watkins handed over the Regimental Sergeant-Major's cane to WO 1 Gerry McElheron.

Pipe Major William John (Willie) Hannah, 1967

Lieutenant Colonel Macfarlane inherited a battalion fresh with excitement from the Queen Mother's Parade as well as the exhilarating events of the Centennial Year.[253] Dozens had been seconded as call-outs to various projects – the Tattoo and Expo '67 in a series of never-ending guards of honour for visiting heads of state, while dozens of soldiers were sent on training courses in army schools across Canada. The pipes and drums squeezed in an international visit to New Orleans; and Pipe Major Harry Brown and Piper Gerry Paley spent four exciting days at the Canada Pavilion at *Hemisfair '68*, held in San Antonio, Texas. As was their tradition, the battalion commemorated their epic battle at the Annual Ypres Day Parade in Verdun, which was Pipe Major Hannah's swansong. The venerable musician retired, succeeded by Pipe Major George Greig CD. A portrait was presented on his retirement, and it hangs today outside the RSM's office beside the Battalion Orderly Room. P/Major 'Willie' Hannah, had been a piper in 1st Bn RHC during the Second World War and later pipe major of 3rd Battalion from 1951 to 1967. His father, P/Major Robert Hannah served in the trenches as the 42nd Battalion's pipe major and was P/Major of the Montreal Black Watch pipes and drums from 1939 to 1947. The Hannahs constituted a grand Black Watch family lineage that marked nearly a century of regimental piping.

That fall, the Earl and Countess of Dalhousie were invited as guests of honour for the 133rd St Andrew's Ball. As the Scottish Lord Dalhousie was a descendant of a former Governor General, it proved a fitting end to Canada's Centennial year.

The Black Watch Cadet Corps, 1967

Macfarlane inherited five robust cadet corps, three of which were among the oldest in Canada. The eastern corps were based in private schools like Bishop's or within The Black Watch garrison in Gagetown. The Montreal corps paraded out of the Bleury Street Armoury. Their well-being mirrored that of the 3rd Battalion, whose fortunes fluctuated according to the politics and economics of Montreal. The Centennial was invigorating. The Black Watch Cadet Corps enjoyed a banner year. The boys were worked hard both at Summer Camp (held in Farnham) and practising for the "Queen Mum's Parade in Gagetown" (as the lads referred to it). Cadet Major Kavanagh was selected for the National Cadet Camp at Banff, Alberta and Cadet CSM Ken Dingwell won a place on the Cadet Bisley team – the most prestigious shooting competition in the world. Captain JS MacAulay of 1 RHC was delighted to lead the team over that summer.

The Cadet pipes and drums numbered thirty-two members. They had played for Royal Scottish country dancers at Expo, and had also provided Highland contingents for the Old Fort on Île Ste Hélène, where they wore the uniform of the 78th Fraser Highlanders (circa 1759). The boys played daily at the Fort, the British Pavilion and at the popular Expo Pub, *The Bulldog*, earning the admiration of thousands of tourists. During their Expo duties, they played before HM Queen Elizabeth II, US President Lyndon Johnson and many other Heads of State – a rewarding summer for a group of lads not yet eighteen. The band competed at the annual Maxville Highland Games in Ontario and acquitted themselves well in competition against adult bands. Twelve boys were selected to accompany 3 RHC pipes and drums for a week in the deep south, showing the Red Hackle in New Orleans. The Cadet Corps, founded in 1953, supplied many recruits to the Canadian Armed Forces, both Regular and Militia. Several former cadets were serving as officers and warrant officers.

Militia Fights for Survival 1968–69

The decade produced a modern mechanized Army with tactical nuclear strike capability, but costs were mounting and cuts were required. By 1965, the Regular Force was far smaller than the Reserves, reinforcing the argument that the Militia must be reduced substantially in order to save monies and clear the deadwood. Consequently, Mr Hellyer's 1964 White Paper on Defence made a fact of the Suttie Commission's recommendation: that Le Régiment de Maisonneuve and the Victoria Rifles of Canada be axed from the Militia Montreal garrison. "A leak informed the Maisonneuves early enough to politick their way back to survival, while the Vics regarded it all with disbelief because the unit was 103-years-old."[254] In the end the Victoria Rifles were forced to stand down; their unique Cathcart Street armoury and its remarkable carved panels taken over, ironically, by Le Régiment de Maisonneuve. The VRC were stunned; the Black Watch strangely complacent. It should have taken heed. Canadian regiments were more important as political rather than military symbols. War records could suddenly be forgotten. In a modern Canada, *Maisonneuve* was now more acceptable than *Victoria*. The Black Watch shrugged, confident that nothing like that could happen to them and carried on.

Nationally, the government's priorities slowly shifted, away from traditional arms to air defence, space and missile defence. The Air Force was very much in vogue.

During the years between 1964 and 1968, Canada's military strength was reduced dramatically.[255] The bearskins and kilts of the Grenadier Guards and the Black Watch invited attention. The Montreal garrison became a political football. Montreal had three French-language infantry units and three English-language ones (although Westmount's Royal Montreal Regiment had itself redesignated as a bilingual unit).[256] The Royal Highlanders felt secure through their affiliation with the Regular Force via 1st and 2nd RHC and in their conviction that they were not simply "a social regiment" but a valued historical institution.

Chapter 11

The Regular Black Watch – Global Deployments

The Regimental System has created a family loyalty which has served the national interest. The Black Watch has always looked into the future while treasuring faithfully the best traditions of the past.

Colonel JW Knox, Philosophy of The Black Watch, 22 August 1967 [257]

Lieutenant Colonel GH Sellar, 1 RHC 1963–1966

Young lieutenant who survived the killing grounds of the Scheldt Estuary later commanded a Black Watch battalion and became a brigadier-general.

B Bourdon, *The Globe and Mail* October 2004

A very Black Watch CO – he was much like Bart MacLennan.[258]

On 16 April 1963, Lieutenant Colonel Teed handed over command of 1 RHC to Lieutenant Colonel Gordon Harper Sellar. The new CO was a Calgarian and had recently completed service as a member of the Canadian Military Training Team in Ghana. At the ceremony, Teed towered over Sellar, whose quiet efficiency and elegance belied the fact he was a hardened veteran and superb athlete: a skilled horseman and polo player, competing from the age of eleven. He made the varsity teams in hockey and football and was an excellent marksman. As a twenty-one-year-old lieutenant not long out of RMC, Sellar fought in all but a few of the twenty-two actions in which the Calgary Highlanders won battle honours. He commanded the Scout Platoon and on a daily basis penetrated enemy lines. Sellar fought in the Scheldt Estuary and Walcheren Island. His memory of that terrible causeway was vivid. He had watched grimly as a Montreal unit (the 1st Battalion, Black Watch) attacked valiantly, only to be stopped short of the objective with heavy casualties. He could not imagine that one day he would be the commanding officer of that very battalion.[259]

When the war ended, Sellar decided to stay in the Regular army, serving with the Princess Patricia's Canadian Light Infantry, before transferring to the 2nd Canadian Highland Battalion in 1952. After graduating from the army's staff college, he served in Korea with his new unit, now the 2 RHC. Lieutenant Colonel Sellar was thirty-nine when he took command. He would lead the battalion through New Brunswick marshes and Norwegian fjords. To the older members of the Regiment, Sellar reminded them of Bartlett MacLennan DSO, who had commanded the 42nd Battalion RHC in the Great War: debonair and passionately devoted to horses and the hunt.

Mechanized Infantry – 1 RHC

Gord Sellar took over the battalion garrisoned 'at home' in St Andrew's Barracks, Camp Gagetown. Within a year, 1 RHC was selected for the ACE (Allied Command Europe) Mobile Force.[260] This tasking involved a readiness to act as a mobile reserve in trouble spots on the flanks of the NATO alliance – this meant within the Arctic Circle. Sellar's first assignment, Exercise *Winter Express*, scheduled for rugged Norway, was interesting enough. They started training straight away, first for fitness, and then to perfect winter skills when the first snows fell. The ACE role involved, of course, mobility and by this time mobility meant movement by air. 'Air portability' was the by-word of the time and by spring, the whole battalion was so deeply enmeshed in air-training that one A Company wag wrote, "The integration of the services has gone too far."[261]

During this period, HQ Eastern Command organized and directed two major exercises with the RCN and RCAF, which included 1 RHC. The first, "Boat Cloak," took place in October 1963, and included eight destroyers, some smaller ships and a Flight from HMCS *Bonaventure*, the RCN aircraft carrier. The fleet set sail from Halifax to a bay off the Island of Madam, which was connected by a causeway to the East Coast of Cape Breton. The destroyers dropped anchor and soon Black Watch patrols went ashore and manoeuvred across the island to destroy "enemy targets." Aircraft out of Sydney played the role of an enemy aircraft.

En passant, Lieutenant Colonel Sellar had 1 RHC Troop the Colour on the Regimental Day 9 June 1965, which was well received in New Brunswick. A crowd of over three thousand attended. Major General GA Turcot, and Colonel Jim Knox, Colonel of the Regiment, took the salute. The day was sunny but chilly. The pipes and drums, under Pipe Major W Magennis and Drum Major WM MacKay, were joined by the Royal Canadian Dragoons Band, under their director of music, Lieutenant GVM Bogisch. Six 50-man guards completed the parade. The honour of carrying the Regimental Colour fell to Second Lieutenant R Gray, the junior subaltern. The aide-de-camp to General Turcot was Second Lieutenant Isaac Allen Kennedy, whose name would later pass into the mythology of The Watch.[262]

The battalion was also selected to be converted to an 'APC role'. This meant mechanized tactics and the ability to drive, maintain and fix their new M113 armoured personnel carriers. The American tracked vehicles were lightly armoured 'battle taxis' compared to millennium kit. However, in 1966, they were the cat's meow, and offered good cross-country capability. Now the infantry had to think about manoeuvring at speeds that blitzed past the standard foot-borne platoon. By the summer of 1966, there were enough APCs to equip one company.[263]

The Army Boxing Title; Shooting and Hockey Laurels

Regimental post-exercise diversions included two boxing competitions against the Navy. The boxers, all privates, edged the sailors, six bouts to five, at HMCS *Stadacona* in Halifax. In the return match at Gagetown, 2nd Bn RHC boxers won ten of the eleven bouts before a record crowd. It is worth noting that Privates Nelson Solomon, Joe Butts, Joe Foley, Bob Downey and Stan Dill notably won their bouts at both *Stadacona* and Gagetown. Private MH Coffie from Sydney NS became welterweight champion of Eastern Command. The finals took place in Quebec City. The Regiment next acquired another award of note: 1 RHC won the Army boxing title. It went down to the last round, decided by Corporal Art Snow, known throughout in the Regiment as a "bonnie fechter". His legendary bouts inspired fond memories by auld officers:

> ... if you were in the ring and had the misfortune of being on the receiving end of a punch by Arthur, it was usually lights out ... In '63/'64 the Canadian Military boxing tournament was held in Gagetown ... by the middle of the week the Watch was edging towards the grand aggregate trophy ... It came down to the last fight ... a heavy weight match between the Watch represented by our champion Art Snow and another brute, a corporal of military police from Quebec Command.

> When the two stepped into the ring it seemed as though the damned thing was near to collapsing ... but oh my – the wind from a non-connected blow was almost enough to bowl over an average-sized man. The force of their swings left each spinning in the ring ...

fortunately none thus far made contact beyond shoulder blows and almost below the belt ... they wound up in savage clinches which the ref was wearing himself out just trying to break them apart ... the crowd was in a frenzy ... screaming and shouting both encouragement and abuse to their respective champion. Part way thru the second round the ref called a halt and disqualified both on the grounds that they might do serious unintentional deadly harm to each other. It has always been my contention that the ref was really trying to save his own life.

As this was being announced it suddenly became obvious that the Watch had won the grand trophy which could not have happened even if there had been a draw. There were not just a few disgruntled, disappointed and financially distraught generals who returned to the hotel that night. Even generals on occasion have justifiable reasons for crying themselves to sleep![264]

In shooting, they were well represented on the Canadian Army Bisley team in July 1965: Captain WJ (Bill) Molnar 1 RHC tied for first in the Kinnaird Trophy shoot; Corporal Charles E Hockett placed second; Private Henry (Hawk) McKay placed eighth. The rifle team (drawn from junior ranks) came second and third at the Bisley competitions; the second team won the Eastern Command rifle championships at the Gagetown Ranges. [265] The 1 RHC hockey team reached the South New Brunswick League championships, but lost in the playoffs. The soccer team was runner-up in the Pearkes trophy. However, the softball team remained unbeaten, winning the Eastern Command and Atlantic Tri-Service championships.

Finnie Retires; 1 RHC Winter Training 1965–66

Mush, Gee, Haw and Whoa have replaced Quick march, Left, Right and Halt.

During the summer of 1965, RSM Ronald Finnie ended his love affair with the Army, retiring from The Black Watch in December, after thirty-five years of service. Joining the British Army in 1930, Finnie transferred to the Canadian Army in 1942, and held six RSM positions, including RSM 1 RHC, 1 CHB, Canadian Provost Corps, and Royal Canadian School of Infantry.

Winter Warfare training continued; this time the very regimental-sounding Exercise *Black Bear*. Colonel Bentley MacLeod, then serving as the Operations Officer during field exercises, recalled: "We all worked very hard for Gordon, who was a fair, calm and balanced leader. He was not given to histrionics but led by example. He got the best effort from all ranks."[266] Sellar decided to train in Newfoundland. He organized Ex *Ace High*, the largest military air move in Canadian history. The second joint exercise was designed to test the establishment of a hasty perimeter defence outside a strategic airfield. Lift was provided by RCAF Transport Command in Trenton. 1 RHC (including all vehicles, less large trucks) was moved from Fredericton airfield to Ernest Harmon Air Force Base in Stephenville, Newfoundland. A popular training opportunity for the Third Battalion occurred when twenty-two all ranks were attached to the exercise. The show was ably assisted by Lieutenant JF Arbuthnott of 1st Battalion, The Black Watch, who was with Sellar's battalion on exchange from the Imperials:

> He had used his personal net to obtain air support for the training from the United States Air Force 59 Fighter Interceptor Squadron at Goose Bay. This squadron had the Gaelic phrase "Freicudan Du" (Black Watch) as its motto and therefore served to Mr. Arbuthnott a legitimate source of not altogether authorized assistance.[267]

After the vehicles were lined up on the parade square in their 'chalks' ready to convoy to Fredericton Airport, there was a heavy snowfall and all they could see were the aerials sticking out of the snow. Exercises in Canadian snow meant soldiers muffled up to the ears in parkas and shuffling along on snowshoes. Army winter gear was reasonably efficient, but soon military *mukluks* (snow boots) were issued along with new kit – all white and with winter covers. A column of infantry, pulling toboggans even across open fields, would be almost invisible – especially if they stopped and went to ground. Trudging through Gagetown forest, they were totally obscure to the most keen scout or aircraft.

ACE Mobile Force – NATO in Norway 1966

As a prelude to Canada's NATO commitment for AMFL North, 1 RHC was directed to form "Ready Force."[268] At last, on 22 February, 1 RHC left for Exercise *Winter Express* in Norway. It was a major NATO effort; The Black Watch Battlegroup included 1 Troop 2nd Field Squadron, Royal Canadian Engineers; a signals element from 3 Signals Squadron; a logistics element from 3 Service Battalion; and "K" Battery of the 4th Royal Canadian Horse Artillery. In support of the battle group were three *Voyageur* and two *Kiowa* helicopters. Training in the rough bush of the Maritimes and Newfoundland made the Black Watch fit, even fitter than most of the NATO contingent, who were surprisingly road-bound, seldom venturing far from their main supply route. However, trekking across the Norwegian terrain on foot was challenging. Norwegian and Italian troops raced across the countryside on skis, but the Black Watch stuck to snowshoes. Sellar explained that skis were "useless in deep snow and soldiers need a lot of training before they became proficient ... Soldiers can be trained to use snowshoes in ten minutes – it takes weeks to teach a man to ski, especially when he has to carry a pack. We were slower on level ground." Sellar admitted, "but we had an advantage on mountain slopes. We could climb faster and higher."[269] Canadian troops performed admirably and while some NATO units were reluctant to stray from the highway, they trekked cross-country nearly all the time.

The exercise proved both stimulating and frustrating. There were frequent calls: "Where the hell are the umpires!?" Manoeuvres are surreal at the best of times: soldiers scrambling to assault a sleepy village while curious occupants calmly looked on – often joined by soldiers who preferred the part of a disinterested spectator. "What a way to run a war," muttered a burly Black Watch sergeant, as officers with white armbands finally arrived at a bridge he was attacking. "With live ammunition, it would have been over long ago." Language difficulties, which plagued the Alliance in its early days, were highlighted when the NATO Command Headquarters fell to a surprise attack. It was left unguarded when its defenders were suddenly pulled to prepare for a visit from Norway's King Olav V.[270] But that was what prompted the exercise in the first place – to discover weaknesses. In the end, it was well received by the soldiers: "The battalion was over its War Establishment of 837 – this is one of the best exercises the Canadian Forces have held since 1945." Later that year, at a NATO Defence Ministers' meeting in Paris, the Minister of National Defence, Mr. Hellyer, was publicly congratulated for 1 RHC's performance in the NATO training.[271]

Winter operations hold special challenges for Highland regiments, whether in Gagetown, Europe or Montreal, as only a piper can know. Only the piper has to remove his mittens to play! Old timers doubly appreciate the red-cheeked piper playing for them during a blustery arctic road march, knowing how his fingers must suffer. Predictably, the pipes echoed and re-echoed through the craggy fjords; and the sound of a *Pibroch* or lament seemed twice as melancholy under the Arctic sky. The Black Watch would long remember Norway. Lieutenant Colonel Sellar prepared to hand over to Lieutenant Colonel WJ Newlands, CD on 21 July 1966.[272]

Agent Orange

In 1966, the US military, with the permission of the Canadian government, tested herbicides, including *Agent Orange*, in selected areas within CFB Gagetown. The tests lasted three days in 1966 and four days in 1967. Soldiers working on the base at that time were advised that the chemicals would have no harmful effects on them. Portions of the training area were subject to testing of the defoliants *Agent Orange* and *Agent Purple,* which led to an inquiry as to its long-term effects upon the soldiers and civilian base personnel who were exposed to it. The affected areas had soil tests that measured dioxin levels at 143 times the Canadian Council of Ministers of the Environment ratings: "This caused many casualties amongst Black Watch soldiers – including Brigadier General Gordon Sellar whose exposure to the agent ultimately proved fatal."[273]

A Wicked Assault on Pipers, 1966

It would well have been amusing, had it not been a calculated slight. On 27 December 1966, *The Globe and Mail* and *The Montreal Gazette* trumpeted the news: "Some minion in the Department of National Defence announced (astoundingly on the eve of St Andrew's Day), that in the Army's opinion, a bagpiper wasn't a musician." It was one of those practical administrative solutions that demonstrated a complete ignorance, or perhaps rejection, of the customs and ethos that lent the Infantry a certain mystique. The reaction across Canada was near violent: "[We are] a race that can trace its ancestry through the pipes." A public debate ensued; dedicated pipe majors reminded Canadians:

> It takes about three days to fashion a set of pipes, about ten years to make a good piper ...
> In all of Canada there are perhaps a dozen good piping teachers, still fewer in the States ...
> The Pibroch, the classical music of the bagpipe takes years of learning and study, thousands upon thousands who have played the bagpipe have never reached the standard of being able to play the Pibroch (the big music).[274]

The government fell back in disarray and hopefully, shame. Finally, Minister of Defence Paul Hellyer proclaimed (appropriately on the anniversary of Robert Burns's birth, 25 January) that the Army now considered pipers as *performer-entertainers.* Wags quickly revised Burns's poem *The Jolly Beggars*:

> Their skills and craft have put me daft
> They've ta'en me in, and a' that;
> So pipers now musicians are
> Wi a' the'r blaw and a' that. [275]

4 CIBG in NATO: a Modern, Nuclear Army

The 1960s witnessed a period of military re-equipment not seen since 1941. The Canadian Army was supplied with what was then considered the best kit available. Its tanks (British *Centurions,* mounting 20-pounders then upgraded to 105mm guns) regularly won NATO gunnery competitions. Indeed, in a bit of hubris, the brigade donated the *Canadian Tank Trophy* for NATO competition (a large *Centurion* model cast in solid silver) which it invariably won. This lasted until the late 1970s, when new-generation armour appeared, completely outclassing the now-ancient Canadian tanks. But in the sixties, from M113 Armoured Personnel Carriers, to its own nuclear punch,[276] the brigade set the NATO standard. The Black Watch bristled with arms from mortars; new assault rifles (the Belgian FN); and its anti-armour platoon, soon to convert from 106mm Recoilless Rifles to SS-11 ATGMs (anti-tank guided missiles). The battalion had its own pioneer platoon, recce platoon and every cutting-edge accessory ultra-modern infantry could imagine. So up-to-date were they that to Ottawa critics, kilts and bagpipes seemed archaic, and somehow colonial. Closeted NDHQ grumblers were poised to sweep down on Highland regiments like avenging angels. There were hints aplenty. Nevertheless, the battalions preferred to remain oblivious, safe in the knowledge of their many awards and the fact they were the top regiment in the Canadian Army.

Lieutenant Colonel (Lieutenant General) DA McAlpine, Germany 1963–65: *Osae Waza*

> Winter's unusually long grasp on Westphalia has at last been unlocked; the snow at Fort St Louis and environs has quickly vanished.[277]

> The Army is a mighty and surprising machine.
> Captain DA McAlpine to Colonel PH Hutchison, from Belgium, 7 March 1945[278]

In Germany, 4 CIBG was probably the best trained and equipped Canadian formation which had ever existed in peacetime. Both 1st and 2nd RHC were, each in turn, one of the three Canadian infantry battalions, one armoured regiment, and one artillery regiment, which made up the teeth of Canada's heaviest brigade. Within the formation, the same sort of ambiance found in Gagetown prevailed, but always with a soupçon of *Deutsche.* The whisky was the same but the beer different: "You could eat the top foam, thick as whipping cream, and there was a whack of choices, beer we never heard of, one you had to order early because it took at least ten minutes to pour." And there was *Jaegy* (*Jägermeister,* pronounced *Yay/ger/myster*) which tasted like medicine but you got used to it, especially with beer. The Black Watch day-to-day vocabulary now included 'wie geht's?', 'das *macht* nichts', and 'macht schnell!' 'Prosit!' and the inevitable 'Ein groß Bier, bitte!' Everyone tried to use bits of the local language: 'Hier man spricht Deutsch' read one sign in the mess privy. Most did well. A mischievous note in the *Red Hackle*'s officers' mess report said: "Brian [Cuthbertson] finds English hard enough – German was quite impossible."[279]

Fort St Louis *Gemütlichkeit* was quickly absorbed by each Black Watch battalion. 2 RHC was nicely settled-in by the time a new colonel arrived in February to take command from the talented Bill Leonard. It was another Montrealer, Duncan McAlpine, who later wrote: "A sight I shall always remember, 2 RHC and support troops, some nine hundred strong, immaculate in parade order, stood silently on the snow laden parade square, waiting to say farewell to Bill Leonard."

In 1941, Second Lieutenant Duncan McAlpine, an 'attached' McGill COTC officer, walked into the Black Watch mess, donned the Red Hackle, and then promptly got himself into hot water. In his first assignment as duty officer in Camp Farnham, he was confronted by a contingent of savvy Black Watch sergeants and corporals. They had been assigned to train recruits in Aldershot, Nova Scotia and were much looking forward to leave in Montreal. They were sent back to Quebec but given weekend duty in Farnham. They beseeched the young officer with moving tales of being hard-done-by by the sergeants-major of other less friendly units. Besides, there was *nothing* to do in Farnham, just an hour away from Montreal. The raw junior subaltern was soon convinced. In his own mind, he was bestowing simple justice. He gave them leave. Three hours later, his commanding officer from McGill suddenly appeared with a visiting general and a gang of staff officers in tow. They expected to inspect Camp Farnham. McAlpine served two chiefs. As a university officer candidate, he answered to the McGill COTC CO, Lieutenant Colonel JM Morris; as a member of the Black Watch, he reported to the Regimental commander. It was a byzantine solution that could only be found in university and Reserve garrisons. The McGill commandant exploded and within a day, the RHC orderly room was under a deadly barrage of letters seeking cruel vengeance.[280] However, 'Snuffy' McAlpine (a nickname from the wartime 1 RHC officers' mess, later used only by close friends) was to find the good fortune that would follow him throughout his long and successful career. This time, his guardian angel was Paul Hutchison. The Regimental Commandant managed to patch things up; besides saving McAlpine's skin, he arranged for a quick posting to 2 RHC. McAlpine was next sent to Europe, ending up in Italy. He was somewhat in the shadow of his younger brother, Donald Ian, who joined 1 RHC, was attached to RRC and saw action in Normandy and France.[281] Duncan was seconded to the Carleton and York Regiment. After the war, he joined the 1st Canadian Highland Battalion, which became 1 RHC and returned to Germany: "Hanover, where the battalion was to be located, still bore the scars of war – streets were filled with rubble and people were living in cellars and bombed-out buildings."[282] Duncan McAlpine's star rose with the 2 RHC and continued to climb in the firmament. From 1975–1976 Lieutenant General McAlpine was Commander, Canadian Forces Europe ("probably the most cherished senior appointment available during the Cold War"). He would retire as a lieutenant general and end his career as the Honorary Colonel of the Regiment, escorting Prince Charles and the Duchess of Cornwall at the Presentation of Colours in 2009.[283]

The Wakefield Sword

In his three years as commanding officer 2 RHC (February 1963 to July 1966), McAlpine enjoyed a series of successes. He was well supported, with hard-driving leaders from his 2ic, Major Harry Harkes MC, to the rifle company OCs and the battalion's diligent staff officers. They would later recall, over a leisurely whisky, the parts they played in these "glory" years. There was plenty to boast about. 2 RHC held the 4th Cdn Infantry Brigade efficiency trophy, having won the 1963 Skill-At-Arms competition at Sennelager in June. In 1964, the battalion was particularly proud when Lieutenant MU Kelly's platoon won the Maple Leaf Marches, a NATO-wide competition at Hoogeveen, Holland, a Second World War Black Watch battle site. It was the first time in the history of the Marches (fourteen years) that a perfect score was given. This military test stressed basic infantry skills and was conducted over 25 km under adverse conditions, testing ability, bearing, leadership and discipline.

> 2 RHC entered a team in the General Crerar Marches in 1963 and 1964 and won on both occasions. Pipe Corporal Peter Hogg piped the team the 25 km … Mike Kelly led the team in 1965 with a perfect score. In 1964 the team was accompanied by the entire Bn pipes and drums who lead the team the last 3 kms back through the streets of Hoogeveen and later performed in the town square.[284]

On 6 November 1964, the Judo Team, led by Sergeant TJ Goodison and Corporal R Lavigne, team captain, won the Wakefield Sword, presented to the British Army Judo Championship Team.[285] Lavigne, a black belt, trained at the Kodokan Judo School in Japan. The Highlanders emphasized *Osae Waza* (superior *technique* rather than brute *strength);* this was the first time the team championship was won by a Canadian team. To add to these laurels, 2 RHC won the Canadian Army's brigade hockey championship. All of this was impressive bounty to offer Colonel Jim Knox when he visited in May 1964 as Colonel of the Regiment.

The Highland ethos of the Regiment was not neglected. Nourished from across Canada by the descendants of Scots and those who wished they were, the skills of Canadians doing 'highland things' amazed the Brits, winning accolades to the annoyance of some native Scots. In February 1965, Pipe Major WJL Gilmore, 2 RHC, took top honours competing against senior pipers and pipe majors of Scottish regiments in the British Army of the Rhine. The three-day event featured a series of competitions and 2 RHC pipers did well: Privates D MacIntyre, Corporals RA MacLeod, and W Harvey winning top prizes; Private RA Clarke placing second in Novice Piping; and Private T Rickets third in the Drumming Competition. Gilmore excelled in all events open to pipe majors – a feat that resulted in a special award from the Royal Scottish Piping Society. He also did well at the Massachusetts state piping championships. The pipes and drums of three battalions gathered in Montreal to record an album for Decca records, their third such recording.

Regimental Art: *Sanctuary Wood* then, Aphrodite

The part played by the Black Watch in the Great War was most famously depicted by Edgar Bundy's work *Landing of the First Canadian Division at Saint-Nazaire*, which portrayed the 13th Battalion RHC. That colossal painting hangs in the Canadian senate. However, the Regiment itself possessed no work worthy of its First World War campaigns until an unanticipated discovery by a Canadian banker on holiday in London. The *Recapture of Sanctuary Wood by The Black Watch, June 1916* had been created by William Barnes Wollen RI, a well-known British war artist and past member of the *Artists Rifles Regiment*. He had travelled to Mount Sorrel and made sketches of the ground shortly after the battle. He painted it in London, presented it to the Imperial War Museum, and it subsequently disappeared. The Canadian Watch was unaware of its existence until it was discovered forty-eight years later by Mr Harry Freestone, manager of the Bank of Nova Scotia: "It was gathering dust in a London junk shop." In April 1965, Mr Freestone offered it to the Regiment. He was flown to Germany, where he presented the painting to the 2nd Battalion: "After nearly fifty years of wandering, it now finds its rightful home." Today it has a place of honour in the BW officers' mess in Bleury Street.[286]

After the Christmas break, McAlpine's battalion went back into the field, exercising with British and German divisions, followed by the 1st Belgian Corps, in the snow-covered Eiffel Mountains during Exercise *Morning Star*. It went well, and McAlpine gave credit to his BHQ staff:

Captain R McConnell had the awesome job of keeping all the transport on the go. The other was Major P Hall-Humpherson (ops officer), who surely had the command post erected and struck dozens of times each exercise, yet always kept a steady stream of information flowing to brigade and, through the fog created by his inevitable cigar, co-ordinated fire and movement in a most competent manner.[287]

And then it all stopped. In the fall of 1965, they were back in Canada. But before the winter began, they were ordered to begin training for the Mediterranean: UN duty in Cyprus. They left in April 1966, circa Easter weekend.

After Germany, this was quite different. First of all, the place was beautiful: the pristine beaches, classical ruins, olive trees, the air scented by flowers and oranges, all reminiscent of the Island of Aphrodite. But there was a civil war going on. Cypriots (their homeland divided into Greek and Turkish enclaves) were hopelessly separated by religion, language, and a bitter struggle that ranged from politics to village blood feuds for the island's control. Provocations on both sides ranged from sniping, to digging trenches in unauthorized zones, to perversely aiming weapons at Black Watch soldiers on sentry duty: "This called for calmness, patience and diplomacy – mostly out-manoeuvring the other side (whether Greek or Turk) by guile and ploy. Sometimes it was simply standing one's ground." Major Bill Hamilton, C Company 2 RHC later wrote in his memoires:

> I dismounted (with my trusty olive wood cane) and strode up the hill toward the forward Turkish troops ... Pte Sangster, who seeing me coming up the slope, turned and said, "Sir, you see the Turk looking down the sights of his rifle at me. Well, if I go, he is going with me."[288]

The soldiers learned quickly. They were soon competent and, despite the hard work, having a swell time in the golden sunshine. In mid-summer, McAlpine handed over to his former second-in-command, Lieutenant Colonel HJ Harkes MC CD, another living legend of the Black Watch. However, McAlpine was hardly finished. He would go on to other exotic challenges, yet always, it would seem, orbiting the Black Watch, until in the end, he finally returned *officially*, in 1996, as lieutenant general and Honorary Lieutenant Colonel. When he said good-bye to 2 RHC, the out-going CO was given that most coveted of Highland regimental gifts, his own march: *Bonnie McAlpine,* which was composed by Pipe Major Bill Gilmour, rated as "easily the number one piper in Canada."[289]

Lieutenant Colonel HJ Harkes MC CD, 2 RHC 1966–1968

Lieutenant Colonel Harry Harkes was a soldier's soldier, who knew 2 RHC as did few others.

My career was made for me; I am a Scot.

Lieutenant Colonel H Harkes, 1 May 2012

Lieutenant Colonel Harold James Harkes took command of 2 RHC on 15 July 1966.[290] Harry Harkes was a war-savvy veteran, experienced in the ways of the Army and the Black Watch. He was born in a log cabin near Listowel, Ontario. He went overseas as a member of The Lorne Scots (Peel, Dufferin and Halton Regiment) in 1941; he was a sergeant at sixteen and soon selected for officer training. "At 5'10" I was taller than most young corporals." He graduated from RMC Sandhurst in August 1944 and was appointed platoon commander in The Royal Regiment of Canada. Harkes's first memory of the Black Watch is during the South Beveland (Scheldt) Campaign. "I actually observed the attack of 13 October 1944 ["Black Friday"], albeit from a fair distance." He next fought beside the Watch during the Hochwald Campaign. Harkes was decorated in action, first being Mentioned in Despatches, then awarded the Military Cross:

> …on 19 February 1945 when The Royal Regiment of Canada was given the task of cutting the Goch–Calcar road. "B" Company was advancing deployed over a wide front when the forward elements came under extremely heavy shelling and intense machine-gun fire, making the advance very hazardous, and slowing the progress of the attack. Unless the machine-gun post ahead was silenced, the flanks of the attack would be exposed to deadly cross fire.
>
> Although painfully wounded in the back he courageously pushed forward to a position 150 yards from the enemy. From here he was able to inflict some casualties, but the deadly hail of machine-gun fire forced his platoon to ground. Ignoring the pain of his wound and having absolutely no regard for his personal safety, he ran from section to section, shouting encouragement and reorganizing the platoon. As soon as the reorganization was completed, Lieutenant Harkes dashed forward leading his platoon across the open bullet-swept ground onto the enemy position, and succeeded in driving the enemy out, killing many and taking forty prisoners … Only after the positions were consolidated and his platoon reorganized, did Lieutenant Harkes allow himself to be evacuated to the Regimental Aid Post.[291]

After the war, Harkes completed Airborne School in Shilo, and was posted to the Cape Breton Highlanders as a training officer. Later, in 2 CHB, he was appointed

2IC of the Seaforth Company and eventually, OC A Company, which was The Black Watch Company. He served in Korea and was appointed military assistant to the brigade commander.[292] By the time he took command, there was little about the army, or soldiers Harkes did not know. He got on well with the Montreal crowd.[293] Fittingly, the new colonel's Regimental Padre was Father Romeo Plourde, dubbed "a soldiers' padre" for he preferred to be in the field with the men. Harkes's first RSM was WO1 CW Beacon CD (like Colonel John Bourne, a veteran of the First Special Service Force in the Second World War); followed by WO1 DB Reekie CD destined to be the last regimental sergeant major of 2 RHC. He was a highly esteemed person "of whom no one could think of a single bad thing to say."[294]

CWO Don Reekie: Archetypal Regimental Sergeant Major 1966–1970

"Sir, the only difference between charging a private soldier and a senior NCO is that the NCO gets a stunned look on his face when you tell him."

Reekie's advice to a young officer who was intimidated by his platoon sergeant.

It was said of CWO Don Reekie that he was a soldier without equal, not only in the Black Watch but in the entire Canadian Army. "He was the finest man I have ever known," wrote Colonel Ian Fraser. Reekie was born in Collingwood, Ontario, joined the Grey & Simcoe Foresters at the age of fifteen, and later transferred to First Canadian Highland Battalion in 1951. He was one of the youngest sergeants in the Canadian Army and served in Korea. "Don Reekie maintained that if the sergeants' mess was strong, the battalion was strong." He did not think much of Unification: "We expected Navy discipline, Army drill and Air Force food, but instead we got Navy drill, Army food and Air Force discipline."[295]

Cyprus proved a sultry yet often surprising tour, thoroughly enjoyed by the Second Battalion, who became partial to Greek culture, ouzo and *bouzouki*. Despite their readiness to enforce justice or stop political bullying, the battalion was at times prevented from taking decisive action, and often frustrated by UNFICYP mediators who seemed to regard them no differently than the bad guys. However, they bore it with Highland humour. Battalion wags reworked a popular hit song, to parody their United Nation-regulated world. It was called *The Ballad of the Blue Berets*[296], for when deployed on Peace-Keeping missions, all nations wore a blue beret with UN flashes – there were no Red Hackles seen in Cyprus:

Black Watch soldiers from the East

Not afraid of man or beast

Black Watch soldiers, here to stay,

The men who wear the Blue Beret.

No fear have we of the attack,

For UNFICYP will pull us back

This often happens twice a day

When you wear the Blue Beret.[297]

Harkes led them back in October 1966, ironically welcomed by Minister of Defence Paul Hellyer, who within three years would put paid to the battalion. Scarcely settled in, 2 RHC was scheming to find a way back to the Mediterranean. The title tune from *Zorba the Greek* was played incessantly on the billiards room jukebox, and just two months after homecoming, the battalion held a Cyprus reunion in the St Andrew's mess.

Lieutenant Colonel WJ Newlands, CD 1 RHC 1966

Back Home, another new CO took over the First Battalion. This colonel was from Kingston, Ontario, with a Bachelor of Arts from Queen's University, and a recent graduate of the US Armed Forces College. He joined in 1947, served with The Royal Canadian Regiment circa 1948–49, and was posted to 2nd Bn RHC in August 1953. Newlands was experienced: he saw service in Korea, had UN duty in Palestine, and was an exchange officer with HQ 4th British Division in Germany. On taking command of 1 RHC, his RSM was WO1 H Firby, succeeded by WO1 R Blackwell CD in November 1966 and by WO1 G Pyatt in July 1967. The handover took place in Sellar's office as the bulk of the battalion was on leave after a heavy exercise period. The formal part of the handover took place on the parade ground after the leave period when Newlands received the battalion from the Second in Command, Major JD Kinnear, in the presence of the Brigade Commander.[298]

Bill Newlands was looking forward to the Cyprus tour, but first there were assigned tasks for the Canadian Centennial: the Armed Forces Tattoo, Expo 67, and of course the visit of their Colonel-in-Chief on 12 July 1967. The battalion had already won the Maritime Tri-Service Trophy as part of a combined regimental hockey team with 2 RHC in early 1967. The entire Army seemed to be occupied with Canada's 100th anniversary. Montreal would play host to the planet in a spectacularly successful World's Fair, and the armed forces would inspire the country with a dazzling tattoo that pretty much absorbed every soldier or sailor, not posted to Germany or the Mediterranean. Lieutenant Colonel Newlands's battalion left for Cyprus, as scheduled, in mid-October.

The Black Watch and the Canadian Centennial, 1967

"The greatest road show in Canada's history."

It was one of the world's largest and most complex military tattoos, with a cast of seventeen hundred men and women from the Canadian Forces. They performed at Expo '67 (The World's Fair in Montreal) and toured Canada, offering performances in twelve cities. They travelled in two identical trains, each with approximately 250 performers, staging shows from coast to coast. Sergeant Norm Green and his platoon of thirty-five men and Pipe Sergeant John Stewart with a selected group from the pipes and drums were with the *Blue Train* travelling from Glace Bay, Nova Scotia, to Victoria, British Columbia. Sergeant Henry Dietz and Pipe Major Peter Hogg had a similar group on the *Red Train* that worked its way from Barrie, Ontario, to Vancouver, British Columbia. They racked up a total of eleven thousand railway miles – six weeks on trains. The jocks quipped: "Even a submarine comes up for air."[299]

The two groups joined in Victoria: Sergeant Bill McInnis and the Third Platoon from A Company, with the remainder of the band, joined the tour on the west coast. It was a Herculean effort. One Tattoo scene depicted garrison life in a Highland battalion circa 1782. It was recreated by 138 men and women in period costumes dancing five different Highland dances to the music of 108 pipers and drummers. The Tattoo portrayed Canadian forces in all wars. In one hectic scene, Pte Ken Langille tears himself from his NAAFI girlfriend and dashes off to his Spitfire, simulating the Battle of Britain. "A death defying act" was put on by Private Hooper and Corporals Scott, Smiley and Scullion. At the last minute, it was deemed to be far too dangerous and shelved by Major Ian Fraser, the Black Watch officer who was the director and producer of the Tattoo.

The Canadian Centennial Tattoo: Major (Colonel) IS Fraser ONS OMM CD

Ian Simon Fraser served in the Canadian Army from 1952 to 1983, retiring with the rank of colonel. He served around the world and was a graduate of the Indian Defence Services Staff College. He commanded 2 RCR; then successively, the Canadian School of Infantry and finally, the Canadian Airborne Regiment. But Fraser is best known as a creator of military spectaculars – widely acclaimed large-scale martial performances in Canada and the United States. Because of his success with a smaller tattoo in the late 1950s, Fraser was recruited to produce the Canadian Tattoo for the Seattle World's Fair in 1962. He was subsequently appointed to organize the

Canadian Armed Forces Centennial Tattoo, which was to coincide with "Expo 67", the prestigious World's Fair. The Forces tattoo reviewed the history of its three services and became the success of the year. More than two million people saw it, from coast to coast. It was a combination of Broadway extravaganza and military parade and helped make the 100th anniversary of Confederation such a splendid year-long party for all Canadians: 450 bandsmen stirred audiences with a lively medley of marches mingled with folk songs and show tunes. Two 23-car trains delivered troupes from Glace Bay NS on the east coast to Victoria BC on the west coast. The centrepiece was two weeks of open-air performances at Expo 67, in Montreal. The Black Watch, particularly the 2nd Battalion, provided a huge chunk of the performers: from drill sergeants through to gymnasts. There was even a daring motorcycle team from the Signals Regiment. Fraser made a half dozen trips to Europe to consult museum experts to ensure the many historical vignettes recreated for the show were accurate as to dress and equipment. He noted: "It is not a military parade and it's not straight theatre, but somewhere between the two." The media unanimously agreed: "... a splendid and most popular way to bring history to life."[300]

Braw Hard Workin' Hairy-legged Hielan' Men

> Braw Glenwhorple Hielan' men,
> Great, strong whusky-suppin Hielan' men
> Hard workin' hairy-legged Hielan' men
> Slainte Mhor Glenwhorple[301]

In St Andrew's Barracks, on a Friday night, the quintessence of a Highland regiment could be found in every infantry mess. Gagetown was essentially a Black Watch camp where strong, hard-nosed men behaved in a manner that immediately conjured up the auld Highland ways. Barely had the sun set when the piping could be heard from every corner of the camp. Westerners were introduced to the Atlantic brew *Moosehead Ale* (not quite *Molson's*) but good enough to inspire Sergeant Bob Miles to pen a dirge – *The Moosehead Lament*, which began: "*Och ye Amber and Frothy Brew, ye caressed ma lips last nicht / But t'day we're a through, we kicked out the licht!*" Far deadlier was the Westerners' introduction to Newfoundland *Screech*, which veterans agreed was a potion with far-reaching qualities. Garrison life straddled two centuries. Young men out of college suddenly found themselves within an Edwardian world while training for atomic age conflicts – it changed the habits of most:

> We had breakfast in the officers' mess. We were expected to attend coffee in the officers' mess at 1000. Lunch was at 1200 in the mess and Wednesday's lunch was a curry luncheon,

which we were expected to attend and which usually dragged on well into the afternoon. At the end of the day and particularly on Friday, all officers were expected to attend the mess and have a refreshment.[302]

Off-duty dress was not that onerous but nevertheless strict: "In the mess we were always required to wear a jacket and tie in the evenings during the week, but casual clothes were allowed during the day on the weekends. Travel on duty required a jacket and tie too."[303] Also evident in Gagetown, was an air of no-nonsense professionalism. It was big and, for Canadian infantry, grand. Everyone seemed to be training. Competition was fierce, particularly within the Black Watch from platoon, to company, to battalion; there was a determined desire to be the best in sports, in arms, or on the parade square.

There was a certain nonchalance about disturbing the repeated rumours that the military was to be drastically restructured in the Army. The focus remained on the NATO commitment and UN tours. When 2 RHC returned from Germany, Gagetown was groaning with Highlanders: "Two Black Watch battalions? – A critical mass!" cracked one former physicist turned staff officer. In January, Colonel JW Knox visited the fourth of the regimental commands, The Black Watch Depot, inspecting the trained recruits, the Regiment's life-blood. He was hosted by Major LA Watling, CO Depot. All three battalions were fully occupied while the Montreal unit continued to recruit and send soldiers on qualification courses. Further, there were now plenty of opportunities for Militia call-outs with their sister battalions. Secondments and visits to Gagetown by 3 RHC cadres invariably produced enthusiastic *born-again* Highlanders. Junior officers returned wowed by real regimental life.

On 11 February 1966, 115 soldiers from 3 RHC flew to Gagetown for a weekend refresher course and introduction to M113 APCs. The exercise included a fire-power demonstration by 1 and 2 RHC, supported by Royal Canadian Dragoons tanks.[304] The 3 RHC soldiers had the opportunity to get hands on practice with the battalion heavy weapons that cannot be fired at local training areas near Montreal. It was also one of the rare occasions when three Black Watch battalions were together in the field. The following year was Canada's centennial. Her Majesty, the Queen Mother, would be present when the Regiment trooped the Colour.

That June, an exultant clan reunion took place in Gagetown. The Black Watch at last stood together on parade: Lieutenant Colonel Newland's First Battalion; the Second RHC, under Harry Harkes; and Tom Price, who brought over his Third Battalion from Montreal. This would be the only time in the history of the Canadian Black Watch that the three would parade together in full strength, with bands and pipes skirling, before their Colonel-in-Chief.[305] Planeloads and trainloads of Black Watch society left Montreal, Toronto and Ottawa for Fredericton airport. It promised to be a great parade. It was.

RSM Don Reekie, had just succeeded WO1 'Tiny' Beacon as RSM 2 RHC; Beacon reportedly had worn out two pace-sticks, four pairs of leather boot soles, one gross of lead pencils, countless reams of foolscap and 363 aspirin tablets working out the details of the parade. Beacon was designated as Parade RSM. When 3 RHC arrived, it received extra drill under Beacon. Sergeant Bill Carlisle, who was part of the cadet contingent attached to 3 RHC, recalled "We were read the riot act about behaviour... and it was hot, the bottoms of our boots started to melt."[306]

The event was televised live coast to coast by the CBC. High television towers and press boxes were constructed around the square, bordered on its grassy verge by row upon row of chairs for spectators. There was some anxiety and last minute alarms: a bulldozer cut the television cable, and Colonel Knox was ordered to rest by the medical officer for severe laryngitis. Lieutenant Colonel Harkes, the senior battalion commander, was relieved when Knox arrived for the parade, somewhat hoarse but able to use his voice. Meantime, CBC sound experts rearranged the microphones around the parade – just in case. The soldiers at first regarded each other carefully, almost suspiciously, each guard preening and strutting as they milled around before forming up. The square could easily accommodate three football fields placed end to end. Then they were ordered into formation. And it all looked fine. The Regiment as one, the soldiers in summer-weight tan service dress with blue bonnets, hair sporrans, white spats and the Black Watch tartan.

Three Battalions together: The Royal Parade, 12 July 1967

> ...feelings of pride in the Regiment and devotion to her person, which are the hallmarks of the Black Watch soldier in every part of the world.[307]

The Queen Mother was greeted at Saint John airport by Governor General Michener. When the royal party reached Gagetown, they found the Black Watch arrayed in fifteen guards from the three battalions and the affiliated Corps of Cadets.[308] The line seemed endless. On the sounding of the "Advance" the pipes and drums, and the RCD Military Band struck up the familiar "Scotland the Brave" and the mass of the Regiment marched on in perfect cadence: "A sight that stirred men's souls; sweethearts and mothers had a lump in their throats as their lads appeared and couldn't have looked prouder." They halted, and stood immovable in their ranks awaiting the Queen Mother's inspection. The parade was everything hoped for – and more. This time there was light armour, as RHC personnel carriers lined the east side of the gargantuan Gagetown square, their steel tracks clattering a very non-infantry staccato when they roared into place.[309]

Her Majesty had a full day, which included unveiling a memorial Regimental Cairn, a Garden Party, and a Reception aboard the Royal Yacht docked in Saint John: "She mingled freely with the soldiers and their wives, stopping frequently to chat informally with them." Suddenly, it was over and the pipes and drums were playing, as the royal plane took off. "She won the heart of many a soldier, and increased in the older ones those feelings of pride in the Regiment and devotion to her person, which are the hallmarks of the Black Watch soldier in every part of the world."[310]

A Daunting Future: Unification and Integration

This is the most significant reorganization of the Canadian forces since the Second World War.

Lieutenant General WAB Anderson, Commander Mobile Command[311]

In December 1966, on the eve of the Centennial year, the commander of the army (Mobile Command) Lieutenant General WAB Anderson announced the approval of the new integrated force structure. It was to emphasize mobility, greater firepower, and a smaller administrative tail. Besides new equipment, there would be a new service uniform common to all arms, a new system of ranks, and a general restructure that promised to make things better and more modern. Regimental dress uniforms, the interested public was informed, would remain unchanged. However, this phrase was added: 'to be worn on appropriate occasions.' The Regimental System was being reviewed. The new uniforms would be 'Canadian', which veterans quickly understood to mean 'not British'. Initial angst regarding dress was heightened by the realization that regiments regarded as being too imperial were being considered for the chopping block. "Not-to-worry," the old guard was assured.

The annual regimental sherry luncheon, held just before Christmas and normally a festive affair, turned ominous when the visiting Colonel of the Canadian Guards mentioned that the Minister of Defence was, it appeared, evasive with regard to maintaining the present six Regular regiments. Sinister rumours spread that Mr Hellyer's ministry was seriously considering reducing the Regular Force on the pretext of increasing the 'older' Regular Force regiments to four battalions.[312] Although a disbandment of the Black Watch seemed unthinkable, a concerned Jim Knox convened confidential meetings at the St James Club. The single item on the agenda was 'the Black Watch should continue as part of the Regular Canadian Armed

Forces'. Senator Hartland Molson was asked to speak on their behalf to key MPs who were "friendly to the Regiment."[313] Several strategy luncheons were held, attended by senior Black Watch officers, serving and retired.[314] Regimental friends were requested to explore the possibilities of securing some commitment from the minister that he would assure the continuance of the Regiment. Although the cabinet insiders were polite and feigned interest ("My colleague thanked me for 'putting the matter to him in this way' and told me he would have a private chat with the Minister"[315]), in fact, there was no direct channel to the base of power. Senator Joseph Connolly met with Senator Molson, and then spoke to Mr Hellyer but "had not received a great deal of satisfaction."[316] The golden age of regimental influence, the Cantlie–Sam Hughes era, was well past. The *sui generis* Black Watch, despite its accomplishments and the prowess of its Regular battalions, suddenly found it had few friends in government.

In preparing its defensive battle, the Regiment prepared briefs, memorandums and statistical reports to be used in correspondence and in meetings to state the Black Watch's case in as a complete form as possible. The summaries stressed, in particular, the Regiment's integral part in the communities in which its units served. Scottish tradition with its special link to eastern Canada was emphasized. The accomplishments of 1st and 2nd Battalions were a matter of record. The Black Watch Regular battalions enjoyed a higher strength relative to authorized strength than any other English-speaking battalions of the Armed Forces. Its Regimental Depot was commended for the standard of its training and, by 1967, was training soldiers for other arms, including the Armoured Corps.[317] A form letter was prepared, addressed to Mr Hellyer, reminding him of his past assurances regarding the retention of key Regular regiments and noting, "These rumours persist despite your statement in the House ..."[318]

The government's plans included the creation of an 'airborne regiment' that would be formed at the expense of existing battalions. In an age of missiles and helicopters, the scheme to train parachutists, given the bitter lessons of the past war (e.g. Crete and Arnhem), seemed particularly misguided. Colonel Knox continued to lobby the FMC commander. On 22 August 1967, Knox was invited to discuss the proposed regimental structure of the Regular infantry battalions. The two-day conference was held in the Mobile Command HQ at St Hubert and included the six Colonels-of-the-Regiment in Canada. Anderson was chairman. The conference discussed everything save the critical question – guarantee for the future. The colonels left unsatisfied and pessimistic.

Centennial Losses: Blackader, Motzfeldt, Worthington

In Canada's centennial year, of the twenty-three Victoria Cross winners who still survived, three were Black Watch or originated in either the 13th or 42nd CEF battalion: Thomas Dinesen, Herman Good and the Hon Milton Gregg, the latter an RCR icon. Of these, Dinesen and Good managed to visit the Regiment and meet the young soldiers. The dark side of the year was the passing of Black Watch stalwarts and friends. Governor General Vanier died in March, followed by a great Black Watch soldier and first Colonel-of-the-Regiment, Brigadier Kenneth Blackader, on 28 April. He was seventy years old and served a half century with the Black Watch. His funeral was attended by every prominent senior officer in eastern Canada.

This sad occasion was followed by the tragic death of Lieutenant Colonel Eric Motzfeldt. The 'Great Dane', who had so often cheated German bullet and shell, died in a car crash en route to attend a regimental funeral in Montreal – "although he was told not to come."[319] Motzfeldt, only fifty-nine, was struck by a confused driver outside Gananoque on 31 July 1967. He had been the chairman of board of the insurance company he had founded and a beloved Black Watch veteran. After the war, Motzfeldt recounted how, while recovering from wounds in London, his arm still in a cast, he wangled a lift to Copenhagen, where he suddenly appeared at his mother's home. They had not been in touch for several years. News spread through the city, and soon Motzfeldt was escorted by one of the Danish princes for an audience with the King of Denmark. He was the first Canadian, perhaps Allied officer, to enter Copenhagen.[320]

The year ended with the announcement that Canada's foremost armoured soldier, the founder of the Corps and a loyal veteran of the Black Watch, General Frank Worthington, had died on 9 December. 'Fearless Frank' was a legend in two wars and although revered by Canadian tankers, never forgot his comrades of the 73rd CEF Battalion.

1 RHC: Lieutenant Colonel Newlands CD
to Lieutenant Colonel GS Morrison CD, 1968

An officer greatly respected by his peers and his subordinates for his professionalism, his sense of humour, and because he led by example.

1 RHC, having stood duty in Cyprus from October to mid-April 1968, shrugged off the Middle East and settled back into Gagetown, moving into a tented camp in early May. All companies practised tank-infantry cooperation drills until June. That summer on 8 June 1968, an unusual infantry parade took place to celebrate the Regimental Day; both First and Second Battalions conducted a 'roll-past' mounted in M113 armoured

personnel carriers. Colonel Knox took the salute. During the 1 RHC battalion sports day, A Company swept competition aside to win the regimental trophy. The major Exercises *Panzer Partners* and *New Broom* emphasized APC drills; becoming 'panzer-grenadiers' seemed to come naturally. Team-work with the RCD resulted in many troopers and jocks calling themselves 'Black Dragoons'. During the last exercise, Lieutenant Colonel Bill Newlands announced his posting. He gave a farewell address to the assembled battalion in the field. He was succeeded by a Maritimer.

Lieutenant Colonel Gilbert Scott (Scotty) Morrison was born in Halifax; he graduated from Dalhousie University where he had been a member of the COTC. He joined the Princess Louise Fusiliers (MG) Regiment and was commissioned in 1949, then served with 1 RCR in Korea. Morrison transferred to The Black Watch (RHR) of Canada in 1958 and was posted to 1 RHC in Aldershot. He saw service in Germany, attended the Indian Army Staff College, and served as Canadian Forces Liaison Officer at Fort Bragg, North Carolina. To celebrate Canada's Centennial, on Canada Day 1967, Scotty made a parachute jump over Fort Bragg dressed in his Black Watch kilt – proclaimed as a first in North America.[321]

2 RHC: Lieutenant Colonel HJ Harkes MC, CD
to Lieutenant Colonel WB MacLeod CD, 1968

On the Regimental Day parade, just before both battalions rolled past in their APCs, the well-liked Harry Harkes handed over command of 2 RHC to the young and dashing Lieutenant Colonel Bentley MacLeod. Harkes would be difficult to replace: "He was worshipped by the rank and file ... and known as *Harry the Hawk* to the officers and senior NCOs but to this day no one calls him by anything other than *Sir!*"[322] Less than a week later, the battalion participated in the Armed Forces Day parade; – ninety M113 armoured personnel carriers clattered past the reviewing stand and five thousand keen guests. Colonel Knox took the salute. In the summer, there was some cross-unit training with the South Wales Borderers, as well as several *adventure* attachments – some of which, the adjutants admitted, were 'swans'. In 1968, 2 RHC pipes and drums participated in the annual North American Highland Games championships at Maxville Ontario, in which they placed third overall. Then to add *Goombay* flavour to the regiment, they travelled to the Caribbean and took part in the Jamaican Military Tattoo in Kingston.

Both battalions also participated in a pair of exercises: *Naked Sword* and, with the Royal Canadian Navy, Ex *Nautical Ranger*. Black Watch officers were informed that despite recently fashionable Ottawa terminology, they were aboard a 'ship' not a 'water environment vehicle'. In spite of adverse weather, the training was a success, although many Jocks were greener than their combat uniforms. However, some of their ills left when they were issued the Navy's traditional rum ration. After the initial cycle, additional all-arms tactical training continued and the pace of armoured / mechanized indoctrination quickened. To counter the tendency to view such activities as routine, in December another amphibious training scheme with the Royal Canadian Navy was conducted. In the end, it was more *Dieppe* than *D Day*:

> Exercise "Web Foot" was a joint exercise during which Bn HQ, one rifle company and elements of Support Company of 1 RHC were embarked on a destroyer of the RCN for an assault landing in St. Margaret's Bay to capture a defended radio transmitter that was sending intelligence to a "foreign power". The Rifle Company, commanded by Major George Tibbetts landed in whalers; not exactly the latest thing in assault landing craft ... The weather did little to help the operation. The snow that had fallen the night before turned to rain, soaking the Arctic clothing and equipment ... [Finally] the Navy found that it was too rough to launch the whalers [for the pickup].[323]

Concurrently, B Company conducted fire power demonstrations for the Canadian Land Forces Command and Staff College, visiting courses, and 429 Tactical Transport Squadron, RCAF. In the brigade, they produced a best in show compilation that included Major Bill Pettipas as *Best Company Commander* and Sergeant Bill McInnis as *Best Dressed*.[324] Concerning this, the Army was conducting new uniform trials. The all-service outfit was in a basic dark green or forest green as it came to be known in the Infantry. There was some initial shock since it looked much like the United States Air Force style with matching forage cap for all ranks. Veterans gasped, while Highlanders began to grow anxious, as there was no version with a kilt included in the trial.

Black Watch Depot – The Last Graduating Class 1968

The year marked the end of the Regimental Depot. It was announced that the Black Watch was to begin a new role of exclusively training Senior NCOs. Old hands were suspicious. It seemed illogical to terminate a successful school that fed the Regiment its life-blood, unless something more sinister was afoot. Their dark predictions proved to be right. The Depot ceased to exist in December 1968. New soldiers would now be trained in regional centres; the English-speaking recruits were sent to CFB Cornwallis, NS. However, we must not forget that it had been an impressive run for the soldiers' *alma mater* begun in Aldershot, then briefly in Sussex, and finally established (and sadly terminated) in Gagetown. Fifteen years of existence and a total of 5,335 recruits trained. Most commendable. At first, the Depot provided only Black Watch cadres. Its standards were so high and the product so excellent, that it was tasked as well to train recruits from other corps of the Army. When the Depot's last Squad, No. 185 graduated in July 1968, it included only one Black Watch recruit.[325]

Colonel John G Bourne, New Colonel-of-the-Regiment

Lieutenant Colonel John G Bourne ED succeeded Jim Knox as Colonel of the Regiment on 1 November 1968. His long years in the Black Watch included a vigorous war tour when he was assigned to the First Special Service Force ('The Devil's Brigade') and campaigned from the Pacific to the Mediterranean. He became a battalion commander in Italy.[326] He now ran Atlas Construction, and was considered a hard but fair boss. Bourne was reserved and sometimes severe. His intense stare under dark unforgiving eyebrows made him completely daunting, even to senior officers. Subalterns were terrified to approach him and appeared ill at ease when he appeared in the mess. An unforgiving look was believed enough to destroy a career.

Major Douglas Robertson recalled: "John Bourne was not popular as a major; he was a tough second-in-command but he became a very likeable CO."[327] George Cantlie, as Honorary Colonel, would regularly visit RHQ. His standard greeting was usually: "Well Colonel, how are you doing? Do you need any money?" As Honorary, Bourne behaved in the same way. He ran the Advisory Board like a battalion and generally had his way in all things. He was stern. "You didn't say 'no' to John Bourne." He may have been unpopular as a disciplinarian company commander and second-in-command, but in the end, Bourne was a much-beloved Black Watch icon who wore the Regiment as a heart on his sleeve.

The Minister of Defence Attends the
Annual Reunion Dinner, 2 November 1968

Although they were not aware of it at the time, the Regular battalions' finale was to be directed by two officers from Atlantic Canada: Lieutenant Colonel Scotty Morrison CD from Nova Scotia and Lieutenant Colonel Bentley MacLeod OMM CD from Prince Edward Island. Their respective RSMs (not in attendance) were WO1 G Pyatt CD and WO1 DB Reekie CD. They gathered formally at the 1968 reunion dinner on 2 November, curious as to what the Minister of Defence might reveal. Both Morrison and MacLeod were scheduled to fly to London and visit Clarence House, where they were to be received by the Queen Mother. They hoped to bring good news.

The occasion was Jim Knox's farewell as Colonel of the Regiment. His guest of honour was the Honourable Leo Cadieux PC MP. It marked the first (and last) occasion upon which he had visited the armoury. His assisting officer was Brigadier HET (Pot) Doucet OBE, a Black Watch officer who had served on the staff during the war and became GSO 1 First Canadian Army. Colonel Paul Hutchison had argued that Brigadier Bill Leonard or Milton Gregg should have been the senior guest at the reunion dinner, not Mr Cadieux. Years after, John Bourne acknowledged he was right.

The head table groaned with dignitaries: General Sir Neil Ritchie GBE KCB DSO MC, Brigadier CB Topp DSO MC, Colonel HM Wallis DSO and Major General Paul Bernatchez DSO, who was both Commandant of Western Militia District and Colonel of the Regiment for the Royal 22e 'Van Doos'. Also present were Brigadiers JH Price OBE MC, JG Weir OBE ED, and the Honorary Lieutenant Colonel, JW Sharp CD. Officers from the three battalions filled the mess in an almost casual mix of colonels, majors and captains, 126 in all. At the far ends of the three extended tables sat the junior officers, including the latest group of subalterns in whom the Militia Regiment placed such great hope: COTC officers recruited from Loyola and graduates of McGill.[328] But that night they were swamped in a lagoon of Reserve and Regular officers which included Lieutenant Colonels Harkes and Newlands, supported by a flashy cohort of future colonels and generals – Logan, Kennedy, and Alden, to name but a few. The Gagetown crowd was particularly striking; self-confident and accomplished, their junior officers radiated panache. Yet all paled before the glitter of the Regiment's wartime officers, carefully positioned at each leg of the head table, to add even more lustre to an already impressive martial gathering: Aird Nesbitt, GR Sommerville, John Molson, Val Traversy, John Stikeman, GD Birks, and Erskine Buchanan, all residents of Montreal's *square mile*.[329]

Colonel Knox introduced the Minister of Defence, who began by noting that the achievements of the Black Watch were second to none. He called them the "vanguard of this illustrious company [the Canadian Army]." He referred to the accomplishments of the Regiment in the two World Wars, Korea, and their recent duty in NATO and UN peacekeeping deployments. Suddenly, he began to talk about *submarines*. His selected topic proved to be "the threat of Polaris-type long-range ballistic missiles [available to] the most powerful underwater force the world has ever known – the Soviet submarine fleet." He ended by citing Field Marshal Montgomery, reminding all that *we must not lose control of the seas* – this said with emphasis.[330] Mr Cadieux was no doubt aware that his department was planning to scuttle the very Regiment that was offering him hospitality. Could he not sense the feeling of almost desperate optimism in the room that night? It was therefore, with some audacity (later some called it duplicity) that the Minister faced his Highland audience in their own armoury, surrounded as they were, by their battle honours and artifacts. It was regrettable that his selected topic was so lacking in understanding. The audience appeared dismayed; many quietly grumbled, but stiff upper lips prevailed.[331] There was a measured reply, and finally, silver cups appeared as the head table toasted the pipers.

Lieutenant Colonels Wallis, Newlands, Harkes and the Depot CO, Major BE Harper, were presented with engraved cups. Mr Cadieux was presented with a copy of the Regimental History inscribed "With grateful appreciation from the Officers, The Black Watch." Finally, there was an engraved Perth Quaich cup for Colonel Jim Knox, his final gift as Colonel of the Regiment, a tradition since 1935.[332] It was made all the more memorable by the note that accompanied it from the Colonel-in-Chief, The Queen Mother. It expressed her "sincere appreciation for all [he] had accomplished during his tenure." Her Majesty noted: "Since November 1963, when Colonel Knox assumed his appointment, the future of the Black Watch has been under consideration; that the Regiment is to be maintained completely is due in no small way to the leadership and guidance of your Colonel." Mr Cadieux, who knew differently, averted his eyes and said nothing.

The Regiment then acknowledged the next in succession, John Bourne, who was to be Colonel of the Regiment, an appointment he was to hold for barely ten months. The subsequent year would prove calamitous for the Regiment.

25th Anniversary of Verrières Ridge 1969

On a more historic note, the Regiment acknowledged the 25th anniversary of the Normandy Campaign and its great battles south of Caen. The Mayor of St-André-sur-Orne, M Mauduit, a former member of the Resistance, had written to the Regiment advising them that the people of St-André wanted to name a street in honour of the Regiment. Two veterans led the visit, on 8 June 1969: Colonel Bucko Watson DSO MC, and Major Campbell Stuart *Croix de Guerre*. They were well received by the mayor and citizens. The RHC party presented a handsome statue of a Black Watch rifleman: "Aux citoyens St André-sur-Orne, en souvenir du 25 Juillet 1944."[333] Stuart lost his leg at their crossroads while adjutant of 1 RHC, coordinating a rearguard. Watson looked smart in summer tans and Sam-Brown; Stuart wore a dark suit, tan bonnet and Red Hackle. They took photographs on the newly christened *Rue de Royal Black Watch*.

1969 – Lance Sergeant Herman Good VC

Hogmanay and winter passed almost without notice. The Regiment was calm, but behind the scenes, Colonel Bourne had the Advisory Board and regimental friends hard at work attempting to deflect the feared blow. Sadly, April marked the passing of a Canadian hero, L/Sergeant Herman Good VC, who died at Bathurst, NB on the 17th. He served with the 13th Bn CEF in its great battles. During the fighting in Hangard Wood, part of *The Hundred Days*, he and Private JB Croak were both awarded the Victoria Cross for Valour – a memorable day for the Regiment. Good survived and lived a humble life in New Brunswick, often appearing unannounced in the armoury until he was recognized and then with a great flurry of respect, made welcome in the sergeants' mess. Sympathies from across Canada, including the Premier of New Brunswick, appeared. That left Brigadier Milton Gregg VC, who served with both Black Watch and RCR in the Great War, as the last surviving eastern Canadian recipient of the Victoria Cross.

A Pan-Canadian Regiment – Black Watch Demographics

> In February we awaited (in vain, as it turned out) word on the design of new cutaway tunics to be worn with the kilt in the coming move to a new green uniform for the Armed Forces. And then in March, we formally requested NDHQ that new Queen's Colours be prepared for presentation in 1970.
>
> Lieutenant Colonel Scotty Morrison, 1 RHC

A new uniform and a new rank structure was ordered; yet, dark rumours persisted. 1 RHC stayed busy with mechanized performances and demonstrations for visitors from staff colleges and other services, simulating what it was expected to do in Germany with a full battle group of tanks, APCs and artillery. The cold months were to be spent at the battalion winter warfare camp. The battalion's immediate preoccupation was all-Mediterranean. 2 RHC had served in Cyprus from March 1966 to October 1966, and 1 RHC were slated for Cyprus Duty from October 1967 to March 1968. Accordingly, 3 CIBG was tasked to conduct a Cyprus orientation exercise to help prepare 1 RHC for their deployment – Exercise *Pibroch Patrol* (18–24 June 1967). Lieutenant Colonel Harry Harkes, CO of 2 RHC, who had commanded 2 RHC in Cyprus, was named Exercise director:

> His Operations Officer, Captain Bob Campbell, utilizing the 2 RHC Cyprus Ops Log from their Cyprus deployment, developed the exercise scenario using the daily occurrence record. Captain Don Ludlow, the 3 CIBG G3 Int, used his magic to geographically orient the Gagetown training area to the Cyprus layout and had the maps overprinted. The Training

area was transformed, and all vehicle traffic drove on the left side of the road. The bulk of 2 RHC personnel were utilized as Greek or Turkish Cypriots and Exercise Control staff.[334]

Following the Cyprus tour of 1 RHC in 1968, Lieutenant Colonel Newlands remarked that the major problem with the Ex Pibroch Patrol was that by one month into the Cyprus deployment, the troops were so familiar with the scenario they began to lose interest. During the summer, Lieutenant Colonel Bentley MacLeod had switched 2 RHC over to 'Cyprus Establishment': two rifle companies in preparedness for their scheduled tour the following year. The CO instituted doubling days. This meant all ranks were to move in double-quick time whenever they were going from place to place in the unit lines, part of the fitness programme. The buoyant adjutant confessed in his final report he was looking forward to basking in an olive grove somewhere in Kyrenia district.

The tradition common both to the 1st and 2nd Battalions was that they were essentially a Maritime Regiment. This was a gradual evolution. In 1953, the battalions regarded themselves as pan-Canadian; but by the end of the 1960s, an Atlantic personality took hold. Initially, the Regular Black Watch was very much like the wartime Black Watch – a unit that attracted men from nearly every province. The real difference in the Gagetown battalions was a lack of soldiers from Quebec, in particular, from Montreal. Lieutenant Colonel Kaulbach noted: "Both the PPCLI and the RCR had battalions serving in 4CMBG in the late 1960's but were unable to provide sufficient reinforcements to maintain their required strengths. As a consequence, The Black Watch, the Queens Own Rifles and the Canadian Guards were all tasked to provide reinforcements."[335] By the end of the decade, as a three battalion Regiment, the Black Watch rested in two worlds. The association with the Bleury Street battalion evolved:

> There was a mildly strained relationship with the Montreal Black Watch – different philosophies; their wishes should be our wishes; distance was a good reason ... Though initially Black Watch Regiments were Pan-Canadian, there was now influence from Indians of Manitoba and of course, a strong Maritime influence.[336]

The officers included a substantial representation of RMC graduates, drawn from different parts of Canada. In October 1962, Brigadier Kenneth Blackader's inspection of the Depot in Gagetown, which was then training over two hundred recruits (a veritable battalion), recorded that the graduates presented a typical *historical* Black Watch recruit cadre. Of the fifty-six soldiers, the largest contingent (twenty-four privates) was from Ontario; twenty-six were from Atlantic Canada.[337] However, three years later, the majority were from the Maritimes (75 percent of 1 RHC and 68 percent of 2 RHC).[338] This was a normal military occurrence; the average Canadian soldier is happy to serve anywhere in the world, but if he is serving in Canada, he would prefer to be within striking distance of what he calls home. One commanding officer recalled:

> The disintegration of a very fine battalion occurred when 2 RHC returned to Aldershot NS from Korea. All those, and there were many, whose homes lay west of the Maritimes, took their release at the earliest opportunity or were transferred to western units. This mass migration could only be attributed to the location of the unit in Canada.[339]

The *westerners* became Maritimers by affiliation and demographic absorption. Much the same thing occurred in 12e RBC Regiment, where "Anglophone officers from other provinces found themselves becoming Québécois." [340] By 1968, while the majority of the soldiers were from the Atlantic Provinces (80% of the corporals and privates), the Regular Black Watch command cadres were from outside the Maritimes (65% of the officers and senior NCOs). While Scotty Morrison (and two company commanders, Ells and Manuel) were Nova Scotians, the deputy commanding officer (DCO; new for *second-in-command*) of 1 RHC was Major JA Pugh, born in Saskatchewan, raised in British Columbia.[341]

"Drastic changes" – 19 September 1969

> Regiments of one or even two battalions posed serious career, manning and morale problems related to the necessity of cross-postings … [it has been] decided to retain infantry regiments with the longest history of Regular force service : Royal Canadian Regiment, the Princess Patricia's Canadian Light infantry and the Royal 22e Régiment.
>
> Minister of Defence, Leo Cadieux, 19 September 1969

> "… though it was known that substantial reductions would be made in all of the Armed Forces for budgetary reasons. However, the Black Watch was not eliminated for such reasons, but for reasons of administration …"
>
> Colonel John Bourne

The official notice was expected, but it still shook the Regiment. Colonel Bourne called a meeting of the Regimental Advisory Board on 18 September at the St James Club at 8 pm to announce the cabinet decision. An official letter from Mr Cadieux to Bourne 15 September 1969 referred to review of defence policy and "the need to reorganize the Canadian Armed Forces. It is with regret that I must inform you that one of the decisions taken was to reduce the Regular element of The Black Watch RHR of Canada to nil strength."[342]

The Regiment Headquarters had been notified on Thursday 11 September 1969 that the two Regular battalions would be eliminated from the Regular component of the Army. There was stunned disbelief. Colonel Bourne issued a final *Order of the Day* that formally announced the 19 September decision and set the final Regimental parade for the spring of 1970, when the 2nd Battalion returned from Cyprus. The Colours would be cased then taken to Montreal to be deposited in The Church of St Andrew and St Paul. He next prepared a press release on behalf of the Regiment.[343]

It was argued that the newly-elected Prime Minister, Pierre Elliot Trudeau, seemed determined to extend Lester B Pearson's intent to visibly distance Canada from all British appurtenances. The new Canadian flag was such a change – eventually a popular one. The elimination of British Army influence on uniforms seemed another. The new look Canadian Army was almost completely North American in style. However, the kilt was difficult to 'Canadianize'.[344] It was a cruel political blow and seemed to many the imposition of a very restrictive brand of nationalism. Len Norris, the editorial cartoonist for the *Vancouver Sun* showed officers staggered by the news, collapsing on bar stools and couches in the officers' mess, holding a newspaper announcing *Canada Drops Queen's Own and Black Watch* – a senior colonel mumbling into his scotch: "Cut to ribbons ... wiped out ... totally annihilated ... by our own side."[345]

Colonel Bourne despatched carefully worded petitions on behalf of the Regiment, citing impressive arguments of history, military accomplishments, and culture – particularly its representation of Atlantic Canada's Scottish history. The Prime Minister replied politely, echoing the arguments of Mr Cadieux and his military advisors: "The experience of recent years convinced infantry corps officers that regiments of one or even two battalions posed serious career manning and morale problems related to the necessity of frequent cross postings." The principal author of the study, General Ramsey Withers, was originally a Signals officer. Mr Trudeau emphasized: "It was decided, nevertheless, that the need for efficient personnel administration of the infantry corps was of overriding priority."[346] In the end, after several formal pleas, Colonel Bourne agreed to soldier on and wrote to the prime minister: "We are pleased, however, that the 3rd Militia Battalion will continue to serve in Montreal. The Black Watch (Royal Highland Regiment) of Canada will always be ready to serve when called to the defence of Canada."[347]

Apocalypse Now: Announcement of Disbandment

"It was the worst duty I had to perform.

Lieutenant Colonel Scotty Morrison, 19 September 1969[348]

"There are few who can forget, indeed understand, the unwarranted decision that led to the demise of 1 and 2 RHC. It was the worst duty I had to perform," wrote Lieutenant Colonel Scott Morrison. The First Battalion was in the field, far out in the training area of Base Gagetown; it was a crisp sunny morning:

> The First Battalion gathered on a hilltop in the training area in Gagetown overlooking the
> St John River Valley and the glades of Queens County which have become as much a part
> of us as our homes across Canada ... the almost 500 available members of 1st Battalion
> gathered around me, seated on the ground with backs to the sun which shone on the St
> John River glistening behind them in the distance ... I was shaking with emotion inside. I
> think the soldiers sensed this and there was a hush among them as I read out the details.
> A few soft curses followed, there was a slow shaking of heads, and in the morning sunlight
> more than a few tears glistened on their cheeks.[349]

Morrison always recalled the cable: "It began: *Lochaber No More*. My highland grief goes to you all ... [it arrived] the day after the fateful public announcement of our disbandment."[350] Colonel Bourne had phoned both COs on Monday, 15 September, advising them that the two Black Watch battalions would be retired from the Regular Order of Battle within less than a year. Regardless, 1 RHC continued its field training and rehearsals for coming tactical demonstrations for the Canadian Army Staff College.[351]

Colonel MacLeod gave the news to his battalion at the same time, in the Gagetown Drill Hall. "I got a knot in my stomach just thinking of how the news would affect the men of my battalion." Ironically, on the previous 11 July 1969, 2 RHC had been notified it had won the Hamilton Gault Competition, marking supremacy among all Regular Force battalions in rifle classification, with 1 RHC in second place. Mrs A Hamilton Gault, the brigadier's widow, presented the award on 26 September, less than two weeks before 2 RHC's departure for UN peacekeeping duties again in Cyprus in early October.

The Maritimes felt it as a body blow. Canada, in general, was stunned. The major newspapers said it accurately, though without passion: *Sad Setback for a Proud Regiment*. It was a partial savaging of a regiment. Both battalions would vanish or scattered into battalions of "senior" infantry regiments. In the remaining months, training continued vigorously. 2 RCR was authorized to retain the pipes and drums, acknowledging the transposed Highland heritage.[352] The DCO of 2 RCR would be Major Ian Fraser; WO1 Don Reekie, the current Regimental Sergeant Major of 2 RHC was designated the RSM of 2 RCR. At the same instant, to complete the evisceration of a garrison deemed politically incorrect, in November 1969, the Commander of the Army directed the disbandment of Gagetown's 3rd Brigade and the creation of a *National Training Centre*. Ironically, a newly promoted Black Watch officer, Brigadier General Duncan McAlpine, was appointed commander of the new enterprise.

The furor prompted the CBC to produce a televised account of the Black Watch leading up to and including the final trooping scheduled for 6 June 1970. This included a historical narrative, photos, and interviews of veterans from two World Wars and Korea. Entitled 'The Ladies from Hell', it included interviews of veterans, current officers in Canada, and those on duty in Cyprus.

A Most Melancholy Reunion Dinner, 8 November 1969

... The old 3rd Militia Battalion will continue. This was the original source of the regular battalions and it will enshrine the traditions which they have so gloriously enhanced.

Telegram from Imperial Black Watch to Montreal, 8 November 1969

Within a month, they gathered at the regimental home for the annual reunion dinner. For the majority present, this was their last soirée as a Royal Highlander. The armoury was filled with officers, a record attendance of 178 officers; the numbers were so great that the dinner was moved from the officers' mess to the parade square below. It promised to be a sombre occasion, and with added whisky and piping, a potential Highland powder keg. Colonel John Bourne recalled the Scottish saying: *Twelve highlanders and a bagpipe make a rebellion,* and kept a tight leash on Black Watch passions. Midst dozens of gleaming silver trophies, beneath the great wooden plaques emblazoned with battle honours from past wars, the be-medalled and kilted host, resplendent in scarlet and gold, assembled for dinner.

Guests of honour were the former and present commanding officers of the Regular battalions. The head table also included: Colonel RL Rutherford OBE, the original commanding officer of the 1st Canadian Highland Battalion, which in 1953 was redesignated 1st Bn Black Watch; Lieutenant Colonel WB MacLeod CD who had flown in from Cyprus where his battalion was stationed;[353] and the former Colonel of the Imperial Watch and great friend of the Montreal Regiment, General Sir Neil Ritchie. Colonel Bourne endeavoured to keep his speech matter of fact, but was often forced to pause for enthusiastic or angered reaction from his audience. He then read a message from the Regiment's Colonel-in-Chief, Queen Elizabeth The Queen Mother. Her Majesty knew what was in their hearts: "It was with feelings of great sadness ... we lament the disappearance of these fine battalions ..."[354] From general to second lieutenant, all realized the dinner was a poignant *good-bye to all that*. When the pipes and drums appeared, blood boiled and highland whoops cheered each familiar tune. "In spite of our sadness at the removal of our two Regular battalions, never let it be said we are down-hearted." The Imperials mused:

> The one crumb of comfort in this present disaster is that the old 3rd Militia Battalion will continue. This was the original source of the regular battalions and it will enshrine the traditions which they have so gloriously enhanced. We must see to it that in this new phase of our joint history we will continue to stand shoulder to shoulder.[355]

The lament played by Pipe Major HH Brown of 3 RHC was *Lochaber No More*.

Political Surprise: The St Andrew's Ball 1969

The St Andrew's Ball was scheduled for Friday, 28 November 1969. Reel practices started in the armoury in mid-October. The guest of honour was Knox's friend and former fellow-battalion-commander, the monocled Brigadier Sir Bernard Fergusson DSO, who had been the last ADC to Field Marshal Earl Wavell and was the former Governor General of New Zealand. He was now Colonel of the Imperial Black Watch. To the Regiment's surprise, also attending, swanky in Highland evening dress, wearing the Elliot Tartan, was Prime Minister Pierre Elliot Trudeau. He was, *comme d'habitude*, charming. Several senior officers engaged him in conversation, sparring with the Jesuit-trained debater, and carefully watched by John Bourne: "Given what he knew about cabinet plans for us, I suppose it took some brass to show up at an RHR function."[356] Despite the temptation to attempt cold reason, the Black Watch remained polite, and just about cordial.

The Final Year in Gagetown

> The last trooping on June 6 was a day of sadness and triumph ... overcast, a fine drizzle of rain marked contrast to previous sunny days.[357]

The year began with a victory, but on the ice. *The Gagetown Warriors*, essentially a Black Watch team, swept both the New Brunswick and Maritime hockey championships. Thanks to locale and weather, the military activities conducted by the Regiment had very little to do with winter warfare. While the Second Battalion was basking in the warmth of the sun, 1 RHC wore parkas but walked on ground that was free of snow. The battalion dug far too many trenches as part of the annual staff college and visitor demonstrations run by 3 CIBG. Gagetown training was fixed on the next Hamilton-Gault Trophy competition, while the remainder of the battalion assumed most of the workload; supporting the Combat Team Commander's courses, which trained commanders in the tactics of mechanized warfare as per NATO doctrine.

The First Battalion publicly represented the Regiment. It turned out a smart 100-man guard of honour for the opening of the provincial legislature in Fredericton, New Brunswick. Major John Wigmore commanded the group that was resplendent in their feather bonnets, white spats, sporrans and kilts. The temperature was well below zero. The red cheeks and noses became interesting as tiny icicles formed at the tips of moustaches; pipers' fingers trembled on the cusp of frostbite; and the odd icy breeze startled the inner thighs as it darted up 'regimentally dressed' kilts. Of course, Scotland knows something of winter parades, but it is sternly noted by men from Montreal or Gagetown, nothing can match the bitterness of a Canadian February morning. Their drill was exemplary and drew applause from enthusiastic crowds. M/ Corporal Lenathen was moved to write:

> But we will carry on / Wherever we may be
> It could be with the RCR / The Pats or the Van Doo
> But there never be a finer sight / Than The Black Watch on review

Cyprus. 2 RHC, UN Duty, spring 1970

By the blue Mediterranean, 2 RHC enjoyed an agreeable winter. It was, despite their initial downheartedness, enjoyable duty. Brigadier General Bob Alden, who wore captain's pips at the time, recalled it as, "The best tour I ever had, with only 2 inches of snow in the Kyrenian Mountains." [358] The officers' mess was located in the Coeur de Lion Hotel, Kyrenia, which it shared with the sergeants' mess. Although squabbles by warring factions caused the cancellation of the St Andrew's Day Mess Dinner, the sergeants managed to properly celebrate 'Rabbie' Burns Day on 27 January. Old friends were remembered, including those who never left Cyprus. Two Regular Force Black Watch soldiers lost their lives while serving with the UN in Cyprus: Pte JPE Bernard, 2 RHC, 9 July 1966 and Pte JA Lerue, 2 RHC, 9 February 1970. Cpl VJ Perkin, 1 RHC, died on 18 October 1965 while serving with The International Commission for Supervision and Control (ICSC) in Vietnam.

The commanding officer's conference held at Camp Maple Leaf, Cyprus on 5 March 1970, was perhaps the last Regimental business meeting the operational Black Watch was to hold; Lieutenant Colonel MacLeod was host. Lieutenant Colonel Morrison reviewed plans for the final Trooping the Colour in Gagetown on the anniversary of D Day, and the Laying-Up of Colours Ceremony scheduled for Montreal on 14 June. Finally, a committee was established for disposing of Regimental property in CFB Gagetown. Donors of trophies would be given the opportunity to take them back; silverware bearing the Regimental Crest would be transferred to Montreal, while all expendable glass and dinnerware would be left in the mess for use by 2 RCR.[359]

Lieutenant Colonel MacLeod commanded the last foreign Black Watch deployment and third Regimental tour in Cyprus. Despite the situation, the urbane colonel did not lose his Highland sense of humour. The Black Watch was scheduled to hand over to The Royal Canadian Regiment before the end of May. That spring, MacLeod gave the incoming CO of 1 RCR a tour of his lines. He was careful to introduce him to the Regimental mascot – a donkey named *Yeltneb*. "This rare white donkey," explained MacLeod, "was presented in trust by the local Turkish Cypriot Mukhtar of Yeltneb (a dusty village nestled in the foothills of the Kyrenian Mountains) as a gift of gratitude for the many years of protection given Mukhtar's people by Canadian soldiers." He stressed that the Turkish community carefully watched the animal. "Should any harm come to it, they would be deeply offended." The RCR colonel understood completely, and made a point of offering compliments to *Yeltneb* and referring to him with praise when he met local Turks. He should not have been so trusting. The beast's name was *Ramazan*, and he had been purchased for £16 ("at least £14 more than he was worth").[360] *Yeltneb* was in fact *Bentley* (MacLeod's Christian name) spelt backwards. The Second Battalion reckoned it would have been worth the cash to see the reaction of 1 RCR when they finally discovered the truth about the donkey they were so tenderly caring for.

Before their return from Cyprus, 2 RHC was visited by Colonel Duncan McAlpine, as Director of Personnel. He would next see them as a promoted brigadier general and the new commander of Base Gagetown, as the former 'Camp' was now known. MacLeod took the battalion back to Gagetown, and they lost no time in making themselves noticed. The battalion hockey team won the base hockey finals, while the first aid team won the Maritime Region championship. This first aid team comprised WO George Pollock and Corporal Bert Burrows (both were RCAMC personnel posted to the Battalion Medical Section), as well as Corporal Rod Sweeney and Corporal George Ledwon (both Black Watch). They went on to the finals of the Mary Otter Trophy, emblematic of first aid supremacy in the Canadian Armed Forces. The

Regiment also did yeoman service for its community: Canada's crack shot, WO Gerald Steacy, was elected to the Oromocto Town Council in June 1969.[361]

Meantime, the 1st Battalion continued mechanized demos for professional visitors. They did well in the brigade evalutation held in Valcartier and were considered to be the best organized and best trained of all units participating. Meanwhile, the 3rd Battalion formed a 'Strike Company' under Major Duncan Nicholson and trained two 'Rescue Task Teams' teams. All this was in preparation for internal security operations and aid to the civil power (Sécurité Interne Programme D'Entrainement-Counter-terrorist).[362]

Regal Regimental visits were made. Colonel Bourne took the opportunity to make a last visit *en masse* to the Colonel-in-Chief. He led a contingent of commanding officers to England, where they were received at Windsor Castle on 17 June. His company included Lieutenant Colonels Morrison, MacLeod and Macfarlane, respectively of the 1st, 2nd and 3rd Battalions. This happy occasion was followed by an invitation from Her Majesty The Queen to luncheon, and to Royal Ascot in the afternoon.

CFB Gagetown: The Final Parade, 6 June 1970

Some wore mourning bands.

Montreal Gazette, 8 June 1970

The greater Black Watch family assembled at Gagetown for the farewell weekend, which included Trooping the Colour, receptions, and a Regimental Ball. The previous month witnessed two Freedom of the City parades. The first was at Saint John, and the second in Oromocto. CWO Don Reekie, the quintessential regimental sergeant major, put the men through exacting practices for each occasion, but was particularly fastidious in his preparations for the final Trooping. Postings had begun in January; many soldiers took retirement or release. The combined Black Watch had been diminished to fifty-one officers in the two battalions. Captain Don Fisher was the Regimental Adjutant.[363] The men put up with cold rain for some rehearsals and uncomfortable parade square heat when the days were sunny.

The final Trooping was as expected – melancholy and held appropriately under gloomy skies and brooding clouds. The parade commander, Lieutenant Colonel Scotty Morrison, accepted the parade from Lieutenant Colonel Bentley MacLeod, the parade second-in-command. The four guards were led by Majors JS MacAulay, RJ MacPherson, GN Laird and JR Wigmore. Lieutenants AC Bonnycastle and FM Fisher carried the Colours for the 1st Battalion while Lieutenants HWG Mowat and WS Habington carried the 2nd Battalion Colours.[364] The assembled battalions finally marched off the Gagetown parade square under a morning drizzle to the traditional *The Black Bear* and salvos of brawny Highland yells. Although *Nemo Me Impune Lacessit* is a grand motto for a regiment, the motto of the original 5th Royal Scots, *Ne Obliviscaris – Never Forget,* seems even more appropriate.

A few days after the final parade, Colonel Paul Hutchison opened a note from Major General CAP Murison CB CBE MC, who had served in the British Army in both Europe and the Middle East and was now retired in Vancouver: "We watched on TV the final parade of your Regiment at Gagetown – I have never seen a finer display – Your people were so magnificent and the occasion so terribly sad that I found myself with tears running down my face. Thank the Lord I wasn't at the Parade, the Heavens seemed to be providing enough moisture for the occasion!"[365] Murison was not alone. That fall, on 19 November, Colonel Bourne received a letter from the Colonel-in-Chief's private secretary, Captain Alastair Aird, in response to an album of coloured photographs of the Laying-Up of Colours and Final Parade: "Queen Elizabeth bids me to say that she looked at these pictures with tears in her eyes." [366]

Montreal: Laying-Up The Colours, 14 June 1970

Scarcely had the last *Hoy!* echoed through Gagetown when the Regiment arrived in Montreal to lay up the Colours at the Regimental Church. It was a heart-rending parade. More than six hundred troops marched along Sherbrooke Street: two companies from 1 RHC and 2 RHC, joined by 3 RHC, and Black Watch veterans, all led by a reinforced pipes and drums. The ceremony drew great media attention and, surprisingly sparked debate; letters inveighed against "the church's connection with the military tradition."[367] The minister of The Church of St Andrew and St Paul, Major the Rev RJ Berlis CD DD, past chaplain of the Regiment and a Black Watch war veteran, responded: "Military it may have been, but militaristic never! In all ranks, men were decent, honourable, valiant – yes, peace-loving. And yet they went in jeopardy of their lives to check aggression…"[368] The padre's rebuttal did not end discussion. Opinions, pro and con, continued to be published for another week.

It was an ancient ceremony. Montrealers watched as the Black Watch adjutant knocked on the door for permission to enter. The church was filled and some old sweats had to be turned away. Many had travelled from Ontario and the Maritimes. Veterans from both wars sat in the pews. Hundreds more stood waiting outside. Sherbrooke Street was jammed. "Have you got an extra program?" an American tourist asked. When told *no*, he commented "They should have sold them. They would have sold thousands."[369]

The service was solemn. Soldiers, veterans and cadets choked back tears. The Colours entered the sanctuary. They would be mounted in the vault of the nave of the Regimental Church, amidst a coterie of emblazoned regimental battle flags.[370] Later, Dr Berlis wrote to HM Queen Elizabeth, The Queen Mother: "Captain the Rev. Stephen A Hayes, conducted the Service with impressive grace and dignity."[371] It was, despite the occasion, a splendid parade. The Regimental column stretched from the church to past McGill's Roddick gates. In dazzling sunshine, the *tunes of glory* caromed off Montreal's buildings: "You should have seen them. You should have heard them. I thought my heart would burst with pride."[372] The salute was taken in front of Cantlie House. The battalions then retired to the Bleury Street messes for a long and proper wake. The Black Watch *anabasis* to the armoury was done with such resolute assurance, it might have been taken for a victory parade.

Epilogue

Colonel Bourne reverted from 'Colonel of the Regiment' to 'Honorary Colonel'. By the 150th anniversary of the Regiment, close to a thousand all ranks who served in those battalions have died. By 2016, close to fifteen hundred survivors recall their days of service in Germany, Korea and Cyprus with extreme pride and love in their hearts with the memories of their deceased comrades ever strong.

Back in Gagetown, the modern Army moved on. The two reduced Gagetown battalions (1 and 2 RHC) were merged into one and Scotty Morrison was appointed CO of the combined unit – subsequently designated 2nd Battalion, The Royal Canadian Regiment (2 RCR).[373] The battalion was briefly known as the "Cinderella Battalion." Wags grimly pointed out that at the stroke of midnight, the magic trappings of the Black Watch morphed into the RCR – thus Cinderella. The name stuck for about two years.[374] Bentley MacLeod was posted to the Staff College in Kingston as a member of the directing staff. Brigadier General Robert Alden OMM CD was the adjutant of 2 RHC during the close-out of the Regiment and did final personal moves and the finalization of Non Public Property.

We did not just become 2nd Battalion The Royal Canadian Regiment (2 RCR). Each member of the two Black Watch battalions in Gagetown was given his choice of regiment. Most selected The RCR because they were from the Maritimes and wanted to stay in Gagetown. Some who chose The RCR were posted to 1st or 3rd Battalion. Many chose to go to the PPCLI and some to the R22eR. The officers had fewer choices because of career implications however; those officers who were not serving in one of our two battalions on 30 June/1 July 1970 were given the option of selecting another regiment right away or changing when they were to be posted back to a battalion. I remained Black Watch until I was posted to the Recruit School in Cornwallis in 1974.[375]

It was still possible to find a Red Hackle in NDHQ as late as 1989 but the Regiment's Regular soldiers had been scattered and cloaked. The battalions they left had distinguished themselves in the trials of peacetime soldiering and in the frustrations of international peacekeeping. They provided guards of honour for the opening of legislatures, for governors general and for cabinet ministers. They paraded through cities, towns and villages. Black Watch soldiers performed in two World Fairs and, over the years, the pipes and drums of both Regular Black Watch battalions surpassed even Drum Major Phelan's fondest hopes – not only in competitions but in virtually every major military tattoo held in Canada, the West Indies, Europe and the United Kingdom. They played for presidents, kings and queens.[376] Though trained for war, they cheerfully picked apples following autumn hurricanes; they tramped the bush searching for downed pilots, lost hunters and children; they swabbed oil from Cape Breton's beaches; and they fought forest fires in all four Atlantic Provinces. They did yeoman service in Germany and in Korea. The Regular Black Watch battalions won, repeatedly, every sporting and martial competition available. They were disbanded for no military reason and through no fault of their own. No one could have done more or in better style.

Chapter 12

The Post-Apocalypse Black Watch
A Regiment of One Battalion

"It's a lie, it's a lie! Oh you know you're telling a lie,
You son-of-a-gun, you're telling a lie.
Oh you know you, you're telling a lie."

Regimental ditty, 73rd Bn RHC, CEF 1917

Ironically, as the Regular Black Watch prepared to dissolve, it was announced on 1 October 1970 that the 2nd Battalion had won the Hamilton Gault Trophy, awarded to the Regular infantry battalion with the best collective shooting record in the Forces. Further, the 1st Battalion RHC came next in the annual contest.

3 RHC Officers' Mess Notes, 1970.

Old Soldiers – The Black Watch Veterans' Reunions

Throughout the decades, the CEF battalions had occasional reunions. However, the 73rd Battalion CEF was hands down the most determined association of the three. The venerable veterans regularly convened, as per tradition, in the Queen's Hotel. In 1969, Colonel Paul Hutchison explained the Regiment's situation and presented the cabinet's reasons for disbanding the Regular Black Watch battalions. The members spontaneously broke into the 73rd song created in the trenches of France; their voices a bit rusty: "It's a lie, it's a lie! Oh you know you're telling a lie."

Colonel Hutchison decided that the time had come to gather together all The Black Watch officers who survived the Great War. He received the support of Brigadier CP Topp (author of the 42nd Bn CEF History) who helped him organize a three-CEF-battalion reunion. It required the backing of the Toronto Branch which had grown and now rivalled the Montreal Branch. In a few years, as more Montrealers migrated westward, it would become the larger association. The Atlantic Branch RHC Association would remain in the vanguard into the millennium.

The reunion dinner of the surviving officers of the 13th, 42nd and 73rd Battalions was held at the Bleury Street mess on Wednesday, 9 April 1970, attracting a vintage selection of veterans, many gazetted into the 5th Royal Scots before it became the Black Watch. There were twenty-five distinguished gentlemen, silver-haired, with impeccable polish and bearing hosted by Colonel Bourne. They all wore what was now *de rigueur* Black Watch mufti: the blue, green and red Regimental tie. There were twelve from the 13th; ten from the 42nd; and three from the 73rd. The assembled guests included six DSOs and nine MCs. Two toasts were made: *The Queen* and *Fallen Comrades*.

This gathering of comrades was a notable success and immediately inspired a second three-battalion reunion dinner held on 8 April 1971. This was to be the last. The warriors may have seemed immortal, but the gatherings were tiring, and as anyone past the four-score mark will attest, the staircase leading to the officers' mess is particularly taxing: "Where are the Sherpa guides?" quipped a stooped-over Highland colonel. Lest they thought he had grown too old, he followed up: "It's the weight of my medals, you see, and I only wore the nice ones." They all signed the menus and used their nicknames, which required some interpretation by later historians.[377] During cocktails, the members were shown the original *Red Hackle* magazine, published by the 73rd Bn RHC as they left for France on 4 March 1916. The secretary of the 73rd Bn CEF, Douglas Campbell, credited with "holding the organization together and always at their call", recalled a yarn from the battalion's training days before Vimy Ridge: The 73rd padre asked some soldiers if they got on with their sergeant. "Oh, we pray about him every night." "Have your prayers been answered yet?" "No, but we'll keep on trying."[378]

On 3 April 1971, seventeen soldiers gathered at the Montreal Cenotaph to lay a wreath, accompanied by a Regimental piper and bugler. They commemorated the fifty-fifth anniversary of the 73rd Battalion's departure from Montreal for the western front, honouring a pact made in the icy trenches of France in 1917. Again, there was plenty of snow on the ground. The piper played the lament and a bugler sounded the Last Post and Reveille. The next year, there were thirteen. The veterans were slowly fading. Douglas Campbell was candid: "For the past five years or so we've averaged about twenty to twenty-five people at the banquet, but it was never as low as this year … We can't expect all of them to attend I guess; one of them told me he was living on a meagre pension in Winnipeg so 'how the hell can I make it there?'"[379] Undaunted, Campbell prepared the mailing list for next year's reunion.

Soldiering On into the 1970s

> I remember not being a good platoon leader: I did not grip the situation, I was in mediocre physical condition for such a young man, and I was not alert. Though nothing was said to me, I was deeply embarrassed by my mediocre performance. Though I had a solid base of training in the COTC, I did not know how to command a platoon. Because the regiment's officers could not help me for lack of experience, I decided to train myself.[380]

If 1953–1970 constitutes a Periclean Age of Highland infantry in the peacetime army, then it is not surprising that the years immediately after the disbandment debacle were difficult and dark. 3 RHC ran a roller-coaster of the manpower stock market: Boom, Bust and Boom again. The Regiment was beleaguered not only by a seemingly disinterested government, but by a society turned topsy-turvy in morals, mode and manners. The Seventies would prove a most trying decade.

Through the 1950s and 1960s, the 3rd Battalion laboured to accommodate two groups: veterans (NCOs who had joined during or immediately after the war) and the much younger soldiers they had recruited since. The vast majority of battle-hardened veterans did not join the Militia battalion. The remaining veterans had received sergeant stripes after qualifications via local Jr/Sr NCOs courses but no trades courses. The Militia was an uneasy mix of the *qualified* and *unqualified*. The former, usually younger recently recruited Highlanders, were often at odds with older soldiers who showed little interest in doctrinal training or intensive courses away from the armoury. Part 2 Orders show a remarkable number of NCOs wearing sergeants stripes who were actually only qualified to the rank of private or corporal. They were either veterans or had joined (and served in Montreal) circa 1945–46.[381] The maxim regularly heard in the sergeants' mess was: "You just can't have war vets junior to rookies." Service with The Black Watch Cadet Corps was a definite bonus. Soldiers joining with a 'Cadet Leader Instructor' certificate were published in orders as "qualified Jr NCOs."[382] In 1963, the Black Watch had included four rifle companies (A, B, C, and D), Support Company, and two regimental bands – the pipes and drums with about thirty-six and the military band, which boasted forty members: "The square was packed solid with companies; the band was forced onto the ramp." The battalion often 'lent' section commanders to other garrison battalions for exercises; but by 1968, qualified section commanders were few. In practice, the battalion managed two working organizations, one of which, in imitation of the Regular battalions, was unofficially dubbed 'the Depot'. It was, in fact, B Company. By 1970, Regimental strength had fallen off to less than a hundred on parade, with rifle platoons averaging less than twenty soldiers. It was very difficult to field a three-platoon rifle company for an exercise. The quality of the training cadres varied greatly. One Regular Force officer, who had served in 3 RHC, recalled:

> My first militia exercise in the Black Watch and the only training event that I remember from that first year was *the Death March*: a winter exercise in early 1969 organized and directed by the Montreal Instructional ("I") staff. This was a motley collection of tired regular force officers and NCOs drinking their way to retirement with little energy and much negative attitude insofar as the militia was concerned. But they were certainly a group of experienced warriors with many vets of WW II and Korea in their ranks. Once I put aside my insecurities and hard-headedness, some of these were to become my mentors. I realize now that their antagonistic views of the militia were a reaction to the lackadaisical amateurishness of militia officers and NCOs.[383]

A support company that comprised an anti-tank, machine-gun and mortar platoon augmented the rifle companies. The modern weapons were kept in a Militia Pool at Longue Pointe, the army base in the east end of Montreal. For training and exercises, the Regiment used its two 30-calibre machine guns. These were hopelessly out-of-date weapons that were originally designed for use during the First World War. In addition, there were two 75mm Recoilless Rifles kept in the armoury. While capable of knocking out armoured cars and trucks, they could only scratch a modern tank. There were no mortars in the armoury and the ones available in Longue Pointe were never taken out on exercises. Nevertheless, selected soldiers were sent on courses to *qualify* on the mortar as well as the then prescribed Canadian Army anti-tank weapon, the 106mm Recoilless Rifle (RR).[384] However, ranges were difficult to book and opportunities to qualify proved exceptional and precious occasions. During its 1966 visit to Gagetown, 3 RHC was hosted, trained and given an inspiring 'Fire Power' demonstration by the Regular Black Watch battalions. At this impressive exhibition, the anti-tank platoon grabbed the opportunity to be part of the show as well as *qualify* on the Gagetown ranges. It proved to be the one and only time:

Every time you fired, you were burning off a hundred and fifty 1966 dollars a pop. The 150 qualification rounds we received came out of the Militia budget. We fired eighty and turned the rest over to the 2nd Bn so they could practise. They were eternally grateful. They only got a chance to shoot about five rounds a year.[385]

Perhaps the biggest difference between the old and the new Black Watch was the presence of a working daily staff, much of it contracted by the officers. Paul Hutchison ran a Regimental Headquarters with a large organization; twenty-five years later, Lieutenant Colonel Stephen Angus had to hire an adjutant over the summer. Until the early 1950s, the Regiment was open and working every day. The messes were full (too full, groaned the training officer), there was a vigorous social calendar, and every night seemed to have another activity. However, by 1970, the armoury was closed for most of the week. This annoyed some old soldiers. At one time, their presence was an inspiration to the young sergeants, but now more often than not, an annoyance. They grew tired of war stories and their advice. That, given the changing financial and political situation, made running a Regiment an arduous test.

Black Watch tradition and the weight of lineage created some friction over promotion or position. Because of it, a few promising officers left. Major JD Nicholson wrote to Lieutenant Colonel JIB Macfarlane: "promotion [is] determined by inter-family relationships and past family association with the Regiment. The Regiment requires leadership from non-traditional sources."[386] By the end of the 1970s, the Black Watch was a completely exotic mix of senior officers and future colonels – a healthy blend of Reservists, Regulars, businessmen, academics with backgrounds in infantry, signals and armour whose pedigrees included Scottish, English, French Canadian, Russian, and even Czech ancestry. The aim was to get rid of the career private. Though some were technically unqualified, all too often they became the workhorses of the Reserves. The 'qualify or out' scheme was well-intentioned, but the Militia was a complexity of problems. Montreal changed as the province of Quebec sought to become a unilingual nationalist state. It was made clear that 'Royal' institutions were annoying. Though the Francophone majority was largely unaware of the Regiment's sacrifices and its international representation of their city, it accepted the Black Watch for two reasons: the historic affection and intermarriage of French Canadians and the Scots, and the fact that the Regiment was a Montreal tradition. The Black Watch was as *Montréalaise* as hockey.

Lieutenant Colonel SF Angus – October 1970

> We are unique in the high level of affection existing ... For whatever reasons, we were never afflicted with the jealousy and resentment that characterize the relations between Regular and Reserve Battalions of some other regiments.
>
> The Third Battalion Report, *The Red Hackle*, December 1970[387]

> You can't do better than that.
>
> Colonel George Cantlie, upon learning his grandson had just joined the Black Watch

Although the Regular Black Watch had morphed into the Second Battalion RCR, there were at least two hundred Red Hackles to be found in the Canadian Armed Forces at various headquarters or working assignments around the country. Indeed, it was not unusual to find an RHC collar badge as late as the 1980s, in the oddest places, though they tended to drift into NDHQ. The eyes of Montreal and the wider Black Watch community were focused on Bleury Street. Very quickly a situation would arise that would present a far greater challenge than had been faced by any of its predecessors. Unexpectedly, the economic climate and infrastructure changed dramatically. A great migration was underway. On 6 October 1970, John Macfarlane handed command over to Stephen Angus; he was to be the "last CO of 3 RHC, and the first CO of RHC."[388]

Lieutenant Colonel Stephen Frederick Angus was Black Watch royalty. His maternal grandfather was George Cantlie, christened by Brigadier Blackader as *The Father of the Regiment*. His uncle, Stephen Cantlie and his first cousin, Stuart Cantlie, both commanded 1 RHC during the Second World War. Prominent Montreal families are included in the Angus family tree (Allan, Meredith, Molson, Lord Mount-Stephen). Stephen's paternal grandfather was Forbes Angus, the oldest son of Richard Bladworth Angus, whose consortium created the CPR.[389] That great centre of Canadian industrial might, The Angus Yards, long a landmark in the East End of Montreal, was named for RB Angus and built everything from locomotives to tanks.[390] Stephen Angus was a product of Bishop's College School (an early photo shows the ten-year-old scholar on school grounds wearing a dark suit with waistcoat). Angus graduated from McGill as a mechanical engineer and became sales manager for the Dominion Bridge Company (Industrial Products Division). He travelled widely, charming clients and sealing contracts. Angus was partly raised by his maternal grandfather. His second home was the Cantlie mansion on the corner of Sherbrooke and Peel.[391] He joined the Regiment as an officer-cadet in September 1956, the same night as future CO Leonard Ferdon. Angus married Pamela Margaret Bolton whose great-uncle, Harold Lea Fetherstonhaugh, an architect, had designed The Church of St Andrew and St Paul; her father, Richard Bolton was also an architect[392] who did the stonework for the Regimental Church. Another great-uncle, Robert Collier Fetherstonhaugh, was a noted military historian who published the official accounts of several Canadian Regiments, including the treasured *History of The 13th Battalion RHC 1914–1919*. Colonel Angus fondly recalled the day he announced: "Grandfather, I've joined the Black Watch." Colonel Cantlie beamed: "Stephen, you can't do better than that!"[393]

Alone, Yet Not alone – RHC 1970–1975

The Regiment, under Angus, inducted a new RSM, CWO Rodgers, who replaced CWO McElheron. The structure comprised a battalion headquarters, the pipes and drums, and two companies. Major Len Ferdon was the Deputy Commanding Officer and Major Bill Sewell was the Training Officer, assisted by Captain Herb F Hauschild. Lieutenant Alex Malashenko was the Adjutant; he had transferred in from the Intelligence Corps and quickly proved indispensable. The company commanders were Captain RF Starzynski (A Coy) and Major W Cook (B Coy). The Quartermaster was Captain TM Miller.[394] During this period the Regiment surely missed retired regimental quartermaster sergeant (RQMS) WOII Evans. He was rated 'a man of exceptional ability' in reference to his treasures buried in the basement of the armoury (the site of the regimental stores). Out of the depths appeared the impedimenta and minutiae required for each battalion exercise. No one dared ask where it all came from. In many ways, the 3rd Battalion operated on a combination of blind faith and good-natured optimism. Lieutenant Colonel Stephen Angus, with a nod to Dante, acknowledged that the late WOII Evans formed "a leading part of the RHC underworld."[395]

The Watch found stiff competition within the garrison from The Royal Montreal Regiment. Commanded by the flamboyant Lieutenant Colonel Rhett Lawson, its elite 'Strike Company' attracted notice and recruits. Although *National Survival Training* was pretty much done by 1968, rebuilding was slow. By the end of the 1960s, 3rd Battalion was in a low state when it was unexpectedly reinforced by four Regular Force trained COTC officers and a quartet of experienced reservists, including an academic who played the pipes. This fusion of new talent revitalized recruiting and training,[396] although at first was received with caution by some senior NCOs, who recognized the level of training brought to the unit by the new officers. There were a few tough moments, but there was no doubt that the COTC cadre stabilized the Battalion.

They were made platoon leaders and 2ICs in the rifle and support companies – the latter being under Major Duncan Nicholson. 'Dunc' was a Scot who had immigrated to Canada in the 1950s. He was a good man who left the Regiment in 1969 apparently because of a difference of opinion. He was a charismatic leader who would have made an excellent CO. From 1968 to 1972, training picked up. There was a new sense of seriousness, a sharper focus. "Exercises were tight … There was no horsing around … leaders were demonstrably committed … there were things to do … no more drinking on Saturday nights in Farnham." [397] 1970–1971 was a first-rate training year. The Regiment ran the Leading Infantryman course (LI). Its success was due to the leadership of the NCOs: Bill Carlisle, Ward Sweet and Gerry Lipscombe, who were section commanders and course students at the same time. "They grasped the opportunity to lead and gave it their all."[398] In addition, members of the battalion were given the opportunity for UN Call-Outs in Cyprus and Egypt.

Captain Alexei Malashenko

Captain Alexei George (Alex) Malashenko, a new but most enthusiastic transfer to the Watch, was formerly in the Intelligence Corps.[399] Malashenko was imposing at six-foot-three, three hundred pounds, and the sight of the gargantuan Adjutant, poised with a tiny glass of Drambuie, pinky finger akimbo, was burned into the minds of many a junior officer, particularly if Alex decided to impale his victim on the tip of his rapier-like wit. He was really a Highlander at heart and came to love the Regiment with a passion. Alex was also a keen military historian and, as he sometimes informed his peers, brilliant. This was not just an idle boast. Malashenko was quick, efficient and soon appointed Regimental Adjutant by Lieutenant Colonel Angus: "I was very fond of him. He was very bright and well informed, albeit a bit impatient and not always diplomatic. But he helped me a lot." As the District HQ did not provide the garrison battalions with a summer budget or staff, preparation for fall training was almost impossible. Lieutenant Colonel Angus personally paid Alex to work in the armoury's HQ during the summer months to ensure a successful launch in September. Malashenko's Russian heritage made him that interesting mix of chess player and Cossack. He clearly preferred the Black Watch to university. He was an efficient, if unforgiving, adjutant, but in the end, a much beloved major.

FLQ Terrorists: "The October Crisis" 1970

Montreal city politics have always been interesting. The political tensions created by FLQ terrorism made the situation delicate. The sudden police strike in 1969 resulted in frightening displays of vandalism and looting. The 3rd Battalion Strike Company began internal security training in the 1968–69 training year under Major Nicholson. It continued after his departure and intensified just prior to the *October Crisis*.

One platoon within Strike Company was designated to specialize in this type of training. A detailed syllabus on 'Internal Security' training was initially prepared based on CF doctrinal pamphlets as well as those of other NATO countries. The post *October Crisis* training benefited from the 'lessons learned' from Northern Ireland operations by the British Army. The fall of 1970 rocked Montreal and indeed, the rest of Canada.

The *October Crisis* was initiated by the kidnappings of a Quebec cabinet minister, the deputy premier and Minister of Labour Pierre Laporte (who was murdered soon after), and the British trade commissioner James Cross, by cells of the *Front de libération du Québec* (FLQ). Thus began a two-month period of dramatic events that dominated the decade and continues a topic of ardent debate today. Rattled by what was happening and fearful that municipal police forces could not cope with the situation, Premier Robert Bourassa and Jean Drapeau (mayor of Montreal) requested federal assistance. The Quebec government invited the Army into the province to help local police. Six thousand troops were stationed in Montreal by 15 October, guarding key areas and government buildings.[400] Accommodation needed to be found for the soldiers. Many were quartered in the city armouries. The Black Watch was informed that B Company, 2nd Bn the Royal 22e Regiment, would be based in Bleury Street and would require the use of all lecture rooms, offices, storage areas, as well as the messes.

In hindsight, deploying almost the entire army and suspending the civil liberties of Quebecers in reaction to a dozen terrorists seems like over-kill, but it was serious enough at the time. The city, indeed the province, was very much on edge. Mass arrests and detentions by provincial and federal forces annoyed a large proportion of Quebecers and this was reflected at the next election (1976) when a nationalist party was elected to form the provincial government. Its platform centred on separation from Canada. This would forever change Quebec, wreck its economy and reduce Montreal to a second-rate city. The effect on the English-speaking population and subsequently, the Black Watch's recruiting base, would be most serious.

The *October Crisis* occurred three weeks after Lieutenant Colonel Angus took command. As soon as it was clear what the Army requirements were, Angus and his deputy commanding officer, Major Len Ferdon, drove to the armoury. They were met by NCOs and soldiers, ready to mount a guard. The Montreal Pistol Club left its weapons in the rifle range vault, secured by a combination lock. The Regular Force major wanted to inspect, but no one present had the combination. The RQMS had yet to arrive. Angus and Ferdon considered the hefty lock. "Do you know the combination?" asked Ferdon. "Let's see," replied Angus, putting his engineering mind to work, "we're a highland infantry regiment; it's got to be simple. Try: 00–00–00." It worked. Most city regiments were indignant that their armouries were now garrisons for R22eR companies. Angus, in a gracious manner, took the opposite approach. He met the Van Doos' company commander, Major Charles Garneau and asked, "Is there anything the Regiment can help you with? Please feel at home." It was Highland hospitality at its best.[401]

It blossomed into a decent working association. "Our relationship with the R22eR and Major Garneau was so good we were able to continue training and even relieve them of some of their duties."[402] In the beginning, Van Doos performed sentry duty outside the armoury doors to free the police; troops carried live rounds but were not allowed to load until ordered. The Watch was the only Militia unit allowed to be in their armoury. "Charlie Garneau had the brains and personality to permit BW to continue training."[403] The Regiment posted a permanent officer and two NCOs on duty twenty-four hours a day for the duration of the emergency, which lasted almost three months (October–December 1970).[404]

Finally, after being pressed by Angus, the senior headquarters assigned several operational tasks to the battalion, which proved a real boost to morale. The Black Watch willingly shouldered any duty, no matter how minor. Platoons commanded by Lieutenants Boire and Klepak were sent to Camp Bouchard, the vast Canadian munitions dump. This was to give the Regular troops from the 5e Escadron du génie de Campagne and 2 RCR (former Black Watch) a break.[405] The guards were established over the weekend – something a Militia unit could easily manage. The crisis was over by the New Year. The incident made the Black Watch feel they had done something. It was a good example of a Militia organization supporting the Regular army. Strangely enough, the greatest hesitation came from the Department of National Defence, which had initiated these roles six years earlier.

B Company, 2 R22eR was filled with experienced older soldiers; many NCOs were Korean veterans. The Van Doos conducted courses for Black Watch soldiers, and the two units worked and relaxed together. While the Montreal garrison units cancelled their mess functions during the period, the Black Watch annual reunion dinner was held as scheduled. "Major Garneau was determined that this dinner, which brought together Regular and Reserve officers from across the country, would take place despite the emergency." Angus recalled, "We were able to hold our Annual Dinner in the armoury, and the Van Doos attended, dressed in *Combat* – the only uniform they had available.[406]

> All agreed it was one of the best dinners in years. A special pleasure came from the arrival of many of the officers of the 2nd Bn Royal Canadian Regiment, all of whom were Black Watch. They may have re-badged, but it certainly was not apparent that evening.[407]

The Black Watch's rapprochement with their guests was a restatement of the *auld alliance*, and Quebec's traditional affiliation of French-Canadians and Scots. "It was ironic that the actions of those who would drive us apart actually brought us closer together...We received substantial praise from Lieutenant General Turcot, Brigadiers Chouinard, Ross and the commanding officer of 2 R22eR." Lieutenant Colonel Guy Lessard wrote (in English) to thank Lieutenant Colonel Angus. He expressed praise for the "beautiful and gallant traditions" of the Regiment. Lessard assured Angus that the Black Watch hospitality was "a thing not easily forgotten." Angus replied: "Cette expérience a contribué, je crois, a développer une amitié qui durera longtemps entre nos deux groupes."[408]

Regimental Duty 1970

Angus's first formal parade took place at Christmas with the annual Regimental visit to its veterans at the Ste Anne's Veterans Hospital. It was a small gathering: the CO, four officers, the pipe major and members of The Black Watch Association and Women's Auxiliary. They gathered at the front of the hospital while Pipe Major Harry Brown tuned his drones. He informed the colonel that the route march could start any time now and explained to one of the doctors: "The pipes are something like women – it takes a while to warm them up."

Bagpipes have a telling effect on soldiers, particularly the veterans. The Association had visited its ailing soldiers regularly since 1948. One active member was Sergeant Jimmy Emo, a veteran of both wars. During Steve Angus's tenure, the remaining Great War veterans began to slip away: ninety-two-year-old Fred T Cannon, Arthur Gervais, WT Williams (who served under Colonel GS Cantlie, Angus's grandfather) and Joe Hamilton, another 42nd Bn soldier, who had been in Ste Anne's since 1921. One soldier's hollow eyes brightened when he heard the pipes and he managed to somehow bring himself to attention. A man about the same age stood behind him and sobbed uncontrollably.[409] The Regiment continued its Christmas and summer visits through the century and into the next, when there were few Second World War or Korean War soldiers remaining. However, by 2006, Afghanistan veterans began to appear in the hospital.

Training continued with the same emphasis on shooting and fieldcraft. The greatest obstacle to what they were attempting to do was often District Headquarters. The battalion did its best to recruit. "I managed with tenacity," recalled Angus. The guest of honour for the 1971 reunion dinner (the first by the Regiment as a one-battalion unit) was Minister of National Defence Donald MacDonald. His hosts, Steve Angus and John Bourne, were genial. It was a vaguely uneasy experience after the disbandment, but everyone was polite and smiled a lot.

Summer Student Training Programme, 1969–72

The government proposed to assist students seeking summer jobs by introducing a *Summer Student Employment Programme* (SSEP) across Canada. It was sponsored by the Department of Manpower and Immigration but administered by DND, comprising six weeks' work during July and August with no obligation to enlist in the Reserves at the end of the training session. Of course, given good training, many did, and were able to join the Regiment. In fact, SSEP trained students to become militiamen with basic infantry qualification. The initial training was in 1969 at Camp Dubé, in the CFB Valcartier training area. By 1970, it was done locally by Montreal units. The locations moved from armoury to armoury: in 1970, at the 2nd Field Artillery RCA (the Lacombe Street Armoury);[410] in 1971, at Le Régiment de Maisonneuve; and 1972, at the Black Watch.

In preparation, the Regiment selected a cadre of instructors. This nucleus was headed by Lieutenant Michael Boire, a COTC Loyola product, and ably assisted by Corporal William Carlisle as 2IC, and Corporals Allan Whitehall, Gerry Lipscombe and Jim Timmons as section commanders. Bill Carlisle recalls that CWO Chuck Levesque (SSF Veteran and RSM of the Centennial Tattoo) said that he had never seen soldiers work so well together.[411]

Sergeant Bill Carlisle

Corporal (later Sergeant) William James Carlisle was the classic Montreal Black Watch NCO; born in Côte St Paul, he grew up in Verdun. Both grandfathers served in the First World War, and one had been in the Boer War. He joined The Black Watch Cadet Corps as a young lad ("the older cadets kept us out of trouble and they weren't paid for it either"). Carlisle studied electronics; he became a sales manager for DuPont but weary of travel to Europe and Asia, he left to start his own general house repair business. He was taken on strength 1968: "We bought our own combat boots – the modern issues which were not in RQM but available in army surplus; we were only paid if there was enough money – that wouldn't happen today." MWO Gordon Scott, a Second World War veteran, was his mentor "He was the CSM of A Company; he told us how it really works, called him *Dad* – sometimes to his face – I think even senior NCOs referred to him as *Dad Scott*."[412]

The course was conducted at Le Régiment de Maisonneuve (the old Victoria Rifles armoury) and there were two platoons: The Black Watch (mainly English) platoon and the R de Mais platoon, which was French. "Though most training was done in the armoury, we did do a week of fieldcraft and battlecraft on the St Bruno Range." The course had two phases. Students who graduated as qualified Leading

Infantrymen qualified for a second summer of employment (SSEP2) at Valcartier in the advanced Junior Leaders Course. Given that the '70s was the era of hippies, psychedelic rock music, and a virulent anti-Vietnam war movement south of the border, getting students to cut their hair and subject themselves to discipline was an interesting challenge. Surprisingly enough, there were 350 applications to the Regiment but the course could only accommodate thirty recruits. In the end, the Boire/Carlisle team did quite well, and all their graduates joined the Black Watch.[413]

The 1972 SSEP, conducted at The Black Watch Armoury, witnessed the first training of women in the battalion. The command element comprised Captain Alex Malashenko as the company commander with two platoons of thirty led by Lieutenant Mike Boire (all men) and Lieutenant EDR Camolese (the female section was in his platoon). Fifteen percent of the candidates were female – considered ground breaking at the time.[414] The Black Watch Cadet Corps commanded by Major HA Darney, who succeeded Major JT Gibson, was also permitted to expand; on 19 May 1972, by Act of Parliament, the Army Cadet League voted to admit girls and young women to its ranks. Twelve girls went on parade with Black Watch Army Cadets in uniforms, but not in kilts.[415]

A Regimental Name and Historic Crosses, 1971

Two wooden crosses, first erected in memory of the dead from the 13th Battalion CEF, were presented by Lieutenant Colonel Stephen Angus on behalf of the Regiment to the Canadian War Museum in Ottawa. Rear Admiral Charles Dillon accepted them in late April 1971. The crosses were held in The Black Watch Regimental Museum. Originally, they were temporary memorials placed over the graves, after the engagement at Hill 70 on 15 August, and after the battle of Vimy Ridge in April 1917.

That year, in reaction to the removal of 1 and 2 RHC from the Army list, 3 RHC was redesignated, simply, *The Black Watch (RHR) of Canada*, and became, de facto, *The Regiment*. There remained, however, an impressive number of Highland Regiments (sixteen) in the Canadian Reserves. As Brigadier General Don MacLennan liked to observe, "We had more Scottish battalions than the Scots ever heard of."[416]

Lieutenant Colonel LN Ferdon CD, 1972

"There's no place like the infantry!"

Well into his second year, Lieutenant Colonel Angus was transferred to Toronto by his company. His last official duty was to be the annual church parade. However, it was cancelled due to the unsettled labour situation in the province. Regardless, a proper ceremony was held in the armoury where, on 27 April, Lieutenant Colonel Len Ferdon was formally appointed CO. This turned out to be the last occasion that the Regimental Military Band played with the Pipes and Drums. Angus recalled: "When I first joined they paraded with the unit every Tuesday night in uniform, along with the pipes and drums [but] ... They were removed from our establishment around the time of Tom Price, but we kept them on as "The Association Military Band". They were on parade when I handed over to Ferdon, but faded soon after."[417] The parade was followed by receptions for the families of the Regiment. The colonel regretfully bid good-bye to his cherished Regiment after eighteen months of command; but this was not the last the Black Watch would see of Stephen Angus.

Lieutenant Colonel Leonard Norcross Ferdon was a graduate of Sir George Williams University and an executive in Lawson Lithograph. He had joined with Angus in 1956 and served in all Regimental positions from platoon commander to DCO. Ferdon was also a rather decent piper. He could not have taken command at a more difficult time. The commanding officers who were to lead The Black Watch through the bulk of the 1970s (Ferdon and Sewell) would inherit the full tempest of political and social change from the October Crisis to the PQ election, from anti-war demonstration to the noise of adolescent rebellion. It was a period of extremely difficult recruitment and retention. The dazzle of the 1962 and 1967 parades and the Expo phenomenon were now only warm memories, gone as surely as were the two Regular battalions. WO Gordon Ritchie remembered "We called it 'The Dark Time'; we were not paid, wore poor kit, had poor equipment and hostile instructors."[418]

To make matters worse, several senior warrant officers retired, and three officers left. Dover went to England to join the Imperial Watch (but became a Gurkha); Boire selected tanks and joined a 12e Régiment blindé du Canada (*12 RBC)* in Valcartier. This was the old *Three Rivers Tank Regiment* and had been the first unit Bill Sewell had joined. Klepak went on to teach at *Le Collège militaire royal de Saint-Jean* (CMR), the bilingual Canadian Forces Military College[419] yet continued to parade with the Regiment as time would permit. On 23 May 1972, RSM Rodgers stepped down after a highly successful two-year tour in the appointment. CWO Ron Poirier took over the job.[420] The same month, as per a tradition that dates from the '30s, Lieutenant Colonel Ferdon travelled to BCS for the annual inspection of the Bishop's College School Cadet Corps. The corps paraded a large cadet contingent, commendable in an age when most private schools were abandoning any historic contacts or traditions with the Canadian military. The inspecting officer was Lieutenant General Jacques Dextraze, who was about to be appointed as the Chief of the Defence Staff. His Ottawa military assistant at the time was a Regular Black Watch officer, Lieutenant Colonel Andrew G Christie, who was considered a rising star.

Within a month, Christie was appointed as Commanding Officer of 3 (Mechanized) Commando in the NATO brigade, and soon after, promoted to the rank of Brigadier General. In 1977, he formed and assumed command of the new Special Service Force (SSF) as well as Canadian Forces Base Petawawa. He was more complex than he appeared, and was a keen historian. His rapid rise outside the Black Watch made him virtually unknown within the Regiment. His career highlight occurred on 20 June 1983, when he was made commander of the Allied Command Europe Mobile Force (AMF) – an eight nation, 13,500 man airborne/airportable quick-reaction force meant for deployment in times of crisis as a NATO deterrent. The general returned to Canada in 1989 and became Commandant of the National Defence College (NDC) at Fort Frontenac, Kingston, Ontario. [421]

The Black Watch generals' mews included other thoroughbreds: Major General Brian Vernon CD, and Brigadier General James S Cox OMM PhD who was commissioned into the Black Watch in 1967 and then served in The Royal Canadian Regiment from 1970 until his retirement from the Canadian Forces in 2001.[422].

The Last Black Watch General, 1965–2015

General Vernon joined the Regular army in 1965, serving with both battalions of the Black Watch; he later served with the Canadian Airborne Regiment and the Princess Patricia's Canadian Light Infantry in Europe. He commanded the Second Airborne Commando and 3rd Bn PPCLI. Later, he served as COS of the 1st Canadian Division, as Chief of Staff of Mobile Command and then Commander Land Forces Central Area retiring in 1996, thus ending thirty-two years of service with the Canadian Forces, though at the end, his career was marked by controversy. He left the military with adamant views.[423] But, he was remembered with a respect and fondness that was to resurrect him and temporarily resuscitate a Black Watch lineage in the new millennium.

In the summer of 2015, The Princess Patricia's Canadian Light Infantry announced the appointment of Major General W Brian Vernon as *Colonel of the Regiment, PPCLI.* He was the second former Black Watch officer to be named colonel of the Regiment, the first being Brigadier Andrew Hamilton Gault, another respected 5th Royal Scots/Black Watch officer, named to the position shortly before his death in 1958. Vernon's appointment was most popular amongst retired Royal Highlanders and prompted a wave of nostalgia from Pacific to Atlantic.

Montreal Marches On …

In the summer of 1973, Ferdon and Sewell, as CO and DCO, attended the Militia Command and Staff College in Kingston, Ontario, to qualify lieutenant colonels. Stephen Angus's sudden transfer occurred before Ferdon had time to take the course, and thus he commanded as an unsubstantiated colonel. That year, the candidates were billeted at RMC. Meantime, Major Graham Mitchell resigned and was transferred to District HQ. He subsequently became the interim commanding officer of The Royal Canadian Hussars.

That fall, Lieutenant Colonel Ferdon strived to invigorate his battalion by way of innovative exercises and recruits from the summer SSEP courses.[424] RHC soldiers augmented the 3rd Bn, R22eR in a winter exercise in Baffin Island, high in the Arctic. In January, three soldiers (Privates Cornut, Gloin and Powers) were attached to Ex *Pleine Neige* and subsequently took part in Ex *Patrouille Nocturne*, also in the far north. Black Watch exercises resumed in February followed by range practices. The central aim was to master winter survival skills of eating and sleeping rough in arctic conditions.

Meantime, Colonel Bourne flew to St-André-sur-Orne in Normandy to visit the Regimental battleground. The Black Watch visitors were warmly welcomed by the mayor and took photos standing in the newly renamed *rue des Canadiens*.[425] He returned for the Association Reunion, 14 October 1972, which attracted members from the Maritimes and as far west as Vancouver. General Sir Neil Ritchie was the guest of honour. The reunion committee was headed by Corporal Bruce Ducat, a veteran of Verrières Ridge; his co-chairman was the recently retired Lieutenant Colonel Stephen Angus.[426]

This event was followed by the annual reunion dinner on 18 November 1972. Canada's Governor General, the Right Honourable Roland Michener PC CC CMM CD was the guest of honour. Mr Michener joined the Regimental Advisory Board at luncheon in the St James Club, where he met senior members who had served during both world conflicts. The Great War battalions were represented by Colonel WSM MacTier MC from the 13th Bn CEF, Lieutenant Colonel GL Ogilvie (42nd Bn CEF), and Major Henry Morgan MC who represented the 73rd Battalion. The Second World War COs present were Brigadier Weir and Colonels Wallis, Mitchell, and Traversy, to name but a few. During the reunion dinner, Honorary Lieutenant Colonel Jake Sharp presented Steve Angus with a Quaich Cup.[427] As per tradition, the Governor General was accompanied by the Colonel of the Regiment and guests to visit the pipes and drums, whose mess is the band room, beneath the parade square. A merry time ensued, with much piping and every request was played.

Training in 1973: Exercise *Black Hussar*

The winter exercise with the Camerons of Ottawa on the Connaught Ranges was interesting. A Black Watch sergeant accidentally blew off a Cameron's finger (which was retrieved) with his shotgun, an unauthorized weapon. This became a drama that was discussed in the House of Commons and mentioned in *Hansard*. Lieutenant Colonel Len Ferdon navigated around and through the inevitable turbulance that eminated from the chain of command.

The next Regimental exercise involved supporting A Squadron, Royal Canadian Hussars. The scheme was to conduct a delay screen between Magog and Farnham as the recce squadron fell back on Montreal. The exercise included the anti-tank platoon of the RMR under Lieutenant Toby Glickman, mounted on jeeps and trailers, brandishing 106mm recoilless rifles, as well as a gun troop and command posts from 2nd Field Regiment RCA. The Black Watch Platoon (commanded by Lieutenant Ross Ehrhardt with Sergeant David Paull as 2IC) was split into assault sections each supporting a reconnaissance troop of RCH. The guns leapfrogged from the local school yard to church parking lots and practised maintaining fire support and communications. The Jocks enjoyed it: "It was interesting to say the least ... plenty of practice in delaying tactics gave us a healthy respect for the swift moving light armour ... our tank hunting teams learned that it was not easy to 'kill and fade'." Sergeant Paull, Corporal Hummell and eight privates went off to join A Squadron as assault troopers and enjoyed the experience, but held firm: "There's no place like the infantry!"[428]

Presentation of The Queen's Colour, June 1974

> When the bonnie pipes are skirlin' and the lads are on Parade;
> In the braw Glenwhorple tartan, wi' the claymore and the plaid
> When the sergeant-major's sober, and the colonel's no afraid.[429]

Hogmanay introduced what promised to be an exciting and busy year. It was said in Bleury Street that a Queen Mum's visit made for an additional company on parade. The preparations for The Queen Mother's 1962 visit strengthened the battalion at a time of decline. So too, Trooping the Colour in Gagetown in June 1967 boosted the Third Battalion; Colonel Macfarlane produced a worthy cohort to march with the two Regular Black Watch battalions. Despite the attention paid the military by Expo 67, the Montreal World's Fair had produced seductive job opportunities, which in the end drew away many of the new recruits and serving soldiers. The Third Battalion fell on hard times. During the late '50s and early '60s, the nominal rolls of the Black

Watch listed between 300 to 350 all-ranks, with a turnout of 175–200 on training nights. However, by the time of the *National Survival* training period, the effective strength had dropped to less than 150, which was halved after the October Crisis.[430] It required a royal visit to reinvigorate the battalion and attract new members.

The Army Council decreed that the Canadian Maple Leaf flag would replace the Great Union Jack flag as the Monarch's Colour. The new Canadian flag, based upon the maple leaf design, had flown since 1965 but for several years thereafter the Union Jack was retained as the basic design for the Queen's Colour of the Canadian Regiments. With time, what was considered an anomaly by some was changed. The Regular battalions received new Queen's Colours based on the maple leaf flag of Canada by the beginning of the 1970s. The visit of HM The Queen Mother on 27 June as part of her tour included the presentation to the Black Watch of the new Queen's Colour. The parade was scheduled for Monday 1 July 1974. Because of concerns over security, it was decided to hold the parade on the vast runway at CFB St Hubert, east of Montreal. Lieutenant Colonel Ferdon was determined that the parade would be flawless. He was the first to admit that Regimental drill had deteriorated over the years. He decided that his RSM, CWO R Poirier, needed help in the task and requested CWO AD Rodgers to return as RSM for the Parade along with the assistance from the HQ of RSM Ferris, R22R to oversee the training and facilitate dealings with HQ.

Her Majesty arrived at Dorval Airport in hot sunny weather, greeted by a guard of honour from the 2nd Bn, R22e Regiment. The royal caravan made its way across the St Lawrence to St Hubert. Her Majesty arrived to find the Black Watch steady in four formed guards on the wide runway of the airbase. Lieutenant Colonel Ferdon ordered the Royal Salute. Her Majesty then inspected her Regiment, together with the Cadet Corps and The Black Watch Association, in a specially-converted 'Royal Jeep' driven by Master Warrant Officer WCA 'Wilf' Holdam. Ferdon's battalion looked splendid, indeed, as did he. The CO had grown a striking moustache for the occasion. He stood beaming beside the Colonel-in-Chief as she inspected the battalion.[431]

The Black Watch paraded 190 all ranks; an impressive accomplishment for the Militia of the time.[432] The guard commanders on parade were No.1 Guard: Major WR Sewell, No.2 Guard: Major JAB Evans, No.3 Guard: Major RF Starzynski and No. 4 Guard: Captain HP Klepak. Lieutenant AJ Patrick carried the Regimental Colour on parade. A large massed band was formed by the pipes and drums (under the command of Pipe Major BD Bolton and Drum Major CA Leigh) and the newly uniformed military band (under the baton of Bandmaster R Munroe).[433] The stirring ceremony of the Consecration of the new Colour took place with the hollow square of the Regiment formed around the pyramid of drums. The Colonel-in-Chief presented the new Colour to Lieutenant Murray Cotton. The old Colours bearing the Union Jack were marched off: "Lieutenant M Mitchell had the singular honour of carrying this Colour past the troops. Few veterans' eyes were not brimming with tears as hundreds of years of tradition left the field."[434]

The presentation of the new Colour was followed by a walkabout where the Queen Mum mingled with Black Watch veterans and troops who were on parade. This was followed by a reception for Black Watch Officers, family and selected guests in the St Hubert officers' mess. Security was extremely tight. That afternoon, a 100-man guard of honour commanded by Major Jim Evans, saw her off from the airport when Her Majesty flew on to Ottawa. In the fall, the 1962 Queen's Colour was laid up in the Regimental Church, and the reunion dinner witnessed a change of command as Len Ferdon handed the Regiment to his DCO, Major Bill Sewell.

Lieutenant Colonel W Sewell CD, 1974–77

> I was an armoured officer, but I found it easy to adjust to the Black Watch; there were lots of BCS Old Boys…
>
> Lieutenant Colonel W Sewell CD, 14 February 2013

Lieutenant Colonel William (Bill) Sewell took over the Black Watch in October of 1974; Colonel Rhett Lawson, Commander District No 1, presided:

> At the Change of Command Parade we decided to alter the manner in which it was executed. Lieutenant Colonel Ferdon, the outgoing commanding officer, would present to me, the incoming commanding officer, the Queen's Colour, and then the Regimental Colour, signifying the acceptance of trust and protection of the Regiment and all that it stood for. Today we still perform the Change of Command in that manner.[435]

Chief of Defence Staff General Jacques Alfred Dextraze CC CMM CBE DSO and Bar was the guest of honour at the November reunion dinner. Since 1974 had witnessed the presentation of the Queen's Colour, Sewell agreed that Lieutenant Colonel Ferdon would host the dinner in acknowledgement of that achievement: "It is probably the first time that two commanding officers (sort of) sat at the head table." On this occasion Colonel JW Knox MBE ED presented a Perth Quaich to Colonel Paul P Hutchison, ED, the Regimental Historian, to honour him for all his varied service as an active and later as a retired officer.

Bill Sewell was from Trois-Rivières and had been a member of the Three Rivers Tank Regiment (now 12e RBC). He was a product of BCS, and consequently already known to the senior officers of the Black Watch when he arrived in Montreal. Sewell was also a graduate of Clemson University in South Carolina, known for its textile research as well as its prowess in football. He was an executive of Wabasso, a major Canadian textile manufacturer. The transfer from armour to infantry commander did not prove difficult. The Regiment was fortunate to have strong senior officers at this time in the persons of Major Bob Starzynski and Major Ross Ehrhardt; the attached RSS Officer was Captain Tony Butcher, who was also *of the family*.[436] He was formerly 2 RHC. He is remembered for his standard drink at lunch: *brandy and ginger*. Tony later retired home to South Africa. Sewell's officers also included Major Alasdair Ruthven, whose Regular Force experience with the British Army in Korea made him invaluable, and Major Jim Evans, who hailed from a long line of Montreal Black Watch officers.

The Watch, deciding it should do more challenging training, requested an area of Camp Farnham for a defensive exercise. The objective was to take a full company into the field to establish a defensive position that was to be developed and held. This specific area would continue to be developed in succeeding exercises and be used by other elements of the Regiment as an attack objective:

> That fall on a Friday evening, the Regiment embarked on buses to proceed to Farnham. At one point on the Eastern Townships AutoRoute the buses pulled over and the Regiment disembarked and proceeded to march as if in battle conditions down the access roads eventually leading to our area at Camp Farnham some 1 hour away. At one point we marched through a small town, circa 0100 hours and thankfully no one looked out the window to see soldiers armed moving through the town in combat formation.[437]

Sewell was concerned about his regimental sergeant major, CWO Al Rodgers, who had returned specifically to do the Presentation of Colours parade: "Our obligation to him was to find a replacement for him as quickly as possible. His recommendation was MWO Victor Chartier. Vic and I met to see if any chemistry existed, and if our principles of running the Regiment coincided; they did, and Vic became the RSM in the fall of 1974."[438] The Pipe Major was MWO Bruce Bolton, an experienced senior NCO. The new chaplain had just returned to Canada and knew nothing of the military or the Black Watch.

Padres Stephen Hayes and WR Russell

Captain the Rev William R Russell arrived in Montreal fresh from a nine-year ministry in New York City and New Jersey: "I was regarded as 'an American upstart' by some."[439] He was young, inexperienced in Black Watch ways but, it was agreed, looked like an officer. He had big shoes to fill. Russell succeeded the Black Watch war veteran, Reverend Dr 'Rod' Berlis, who had retired after twenty-five years of duty. The current regimental padre was Berlis's assistant, the Rev Stephen A Hayes, who had been called to be minister of St Andrew's in Cobourg, Ontario.[440] On a bitter winter's day early in 1974, an anxious William Russell was summoned to the St James Club to lunch with the Regiment's honorary colonel, John G Bourne, and his predecessor, Colonel James W Knox – a dynamic duo if there ever was one! He was found acceptable. There was much District HQ bureaucracy but "Colonel Bourne would have none of it. If I was to participate in the Colour Presentation – and by God, I was! – I was soon properly kitted out." Russell was taken to the quartermaster's stores in the bowels of the armoury – it became his most vivid Black Watch memory:

> As a young soldier struggled to find me just the right kilt, jackets, sporrans, trews, and the like, I confessed sotto voce: "I'm new to all this. What do I wear under the kilt?" He blushed vividly, then looked me straight in the eye and replied: "Yer balls ... sir!"[441]

Before the June presentation of Colours, Russell had confessed to the previous Colonel of the Regiment's wife, 'Tootie' Knox, that he thought wearing the black pulpit gown over his kilt made him look "sort of like a flasher with diced hose." The sympathetic Mrs Knox ordered Regimental blazer crests and had rue Ste-Catherine robe makers, *Milne et Frères,* create a black 'preaching scarf'. On the day of the Queen Mother's parade, it caught the eye of the attending senior Chaplains from Ottawa: "Quite irregular!" harrumphed the Chaplain General (Protestant). To which the Chaplain General (Catholic) replied "But quite attractive, don't you think?"[442] Russell was particularly delighted at having a personal piper, often Andy Kerr, who would play him into the officers' mess, the sergeants' mess or the men's canteen. He mentioned his pleasure to the Queen Mother during a Regimental garden party. "She gave me a funny look." The regimental sergeant major had overheard the conversation and later quietly explained to the padre why he was piped into the mess: "It's just so we know you are coming!"[443]

The padre was a passionate defender of his parishioners' rights. His public duel with the minister of culture, the Hon Camille Laurin, was both spirited and rather daring.[444] Russell subsequently left to head up the Canadian Bible Society in 1983. He was succeeded by the Rev JSS Armour who was destined to welcome royalty and later, on the occasion of its bicentenary, chronicle the history of his church, with special references to its connections with the military down through the years.

Carpentry and Exotic Travel

Lieutenant Colonel Sewell initiated a physical change to the Officers' Mess. It was decided that the big window facing out to the armoury floor was wasted space and could be converted into an impressive cabinet where the new Colours could be displayed in all their grandeur. Majors Starzynski and Ehrhardt as well as the Colonel pitched in: "The three of us built the Colour cabinet. We were going to formally unveil it at the Spring Mess Dinner. That evening I walked into my office to find someone was dressing in my bathroom. This was my introduction to Colonel Peter Cameron, the new District Commander."[445] The colonel was from The 48th Highlanders in Toronto and would prove a good friend to the Black Watch.

Colonel Bourne was invited to witness the Trooping the Colour of 1 Black Watch in Colchester, Scotland, in the presence of HM Queen Elizabeth, The Queen Mother. "Seven of us went; it was a wonderful occasion and impressive from the viewpoint that the commanding officer and the adjutant did the parade on horseback."[446] Sewell ensured the affiliated Cadet Corps were visited regularly. Two weeks after Colchester, he inspected King's-Edgehill Cadet Corps in Windsor, Nova Scotia. The Corps director was none other than the renowned Major RH Finnie (the ex-RSM of the 1 RHC). The Cadet Corps trooped the Colour and were impressive:

> The evening before, during dinner at the headmaster's house, Finnie turned to me and asked permission for the Corps to wear the Blue Balmoral and the Red Hackle. "He sort of insinuated that I might not return to Montreal in one piece if I didn't. I agreed, and they still proudly wear the Red Hackle today."[447]

Getting with the Times: Peace Keeping

Militia attachments became truly international in early 1974; this marked the first time that the Regiment sent two members on United Nations duty. Sergeant Mel Windsor was the first from the Black Watch to go over. He deployed in Cairo, and then was moved to open the old British base on the canal in Ismailia. His service paved the way for approval for the rest of the reservists. Sergeant Dave Paull went over in the winter of 1974 and served with then Corporal (WO) Gordon Ritchie from March to May 1975. The RHC soldiers in that group included Sergeant Carl Fischer, WO Roland ("Skunky") Labreche, Corporal Ernest Simpson, and Master Corporal Don Black who was the first soldier from the Montreal battalion to be deployed to the Golan Heights.

The first Canadian female detachment (fifty women) included Corporal Sherry Duplessis-Hummell, who arrived in July 1975. Sergeant (later Captain, the Rev Canon) RB (Bruce) Glencross was also in Egypt, as a duty driver, but this was before his ordination. By the fall of 1977, close to thirty Black Watch members were abroad, serving in either Egypt or the Golan Heights. Outside of Cyprus, no Black Watch Reserve officers served in the Middle East. The most travelled was WO Richard Cartmel who set a record for multiple foreign tours. He served four tours in both Egypt and the Golan Heights.[448] In the next ten years Black Watch soldiers – male and female – would be sent on United Nations attachments around the world: Cyprus, Egypt and the Golan; Regular Black Watch soldiers and officers (those that were left after 1970) served in Lebanon, Cyprus, Biafra, the Congo, and Vietnam (as observers).

Tradition vs. the Modern Army: the First BW Female Officer

At the end of October, Colonel John Bourne accepted an extension as Honorary Colonel which ensured for the Black Watch both experience and steadiness. That fall, the Regiment competed for the General Waters Trophy, emblematic of the best shooting unit in Canada. The trials were at the Mount Bruno Ranges with a large contingent of participants. When the Canadian results were tallied, RHC had won the Trophy (which was physically the Worthington Trophy ordinarily reserved for armoured units).

They intended to celebrate formally at the Reunion Dinner. The key guests invited were the Area Commander Brigadier General John Dunn and the District Commander Colonel Peter Cameron.[449] Brigadier General Dunn advised that his ADC, a female officer, would be attending. A chill went through the tradition-bound Watch. Colonel Bourne refused outright: "We've never had a woman at the Reunion Dinner!" Sewell was ordered to advise General Dunn. He requested a concession, explaining the Regiment's custom. Would the general mind using a different ADC? Dunn was livid. The next day Colonel Peter Cameron, Sewell's District Commander invited him to lunch at the St James Club. Sewell was informed General Dunn would *not* be attending the Black Watch Reunion Dinner, and further: "You will have a female officer in the Regiment within six months or seek employment elsewhere!" Sewell got busy. He approached Captain Jackie Percival, a lawyer by profession, who agreed to join the Regiment. In order to dress her in Regimental fashion, the senior colonels (and their wives) designed an elegant tartan skirt to complement the mess jacket. Captain Percival became the first Black Watch female officer.

The 1976 training year was indeed uneventful, although winter training was enlivened by a visit of fourteen (all ranks) to the 2nd Battalion 25th US Marines in Fort Drum. In an effort to encourage competition among his units the District Commander, Colonel PAG Cameron ordered a small bore rifle competition to be held. On a district parade (600 all ranks) in April 1976 Sgt Mel Windsor's team of well-drilled sharpshooters brought home both the Cameron Shield (winning team) and the Silver Bullet Trophy (best shot).

Sewell inspected the Bishop's College School Cadet Corps in May, which as an Old Boy was extremely satisfying. Happiness was short-lived. Following the October crisis, it was no great surprise (though a shock to the rest of Canada) when the Parti Québécois, bent on separation from Canada, assumed power. The new government promised to introduce legislation designed to eliminate English as the working language of business in Quebec.[450] Over the next decades, frustrated by stringent language laws, nearly two hundred thousand Anglophones would leave the Montreal area, a devastating blow to business, education and the traditionally English Regiments in the city.

In the midst of this political turmoil, Montreal was host to the Olympic Games. The 1976 event required extensive security. Most of the Regular Army personnel, deployed in and around Montreal, were involved; this meant plenty of call-out positions for Black Watch soldiers. WO Gord Ritchie particularly enjoyed being a driver. His tasks included: "doing taxi service for VIPs between Montreal and Bromont [site of equestrian events]; I once towed a dead horse (put down by the veterinarian after a bad jump). Another highlight was when we saw Princess Anne, who competed; Prince Philip and the Queen were also visitors."[451]

Once the Olympics were finished, the Watch returned to face modern Militia challenges. The military world was in the doldrums; the United States had just left an unsuccessful venture in Vietnam and was now turning its attention from jungle warfare to NATO. The British Army was severely tested in Northern Ireland, and the Soviet Union seemed to be building a formidable armoured force poised to swamp Western Europe. Concurrently, the Canadian Army was being quietly steered away from modern conventional war towards peacekeeping commitments. It was not capable of an operational or even independent manoeuvre. Its Airborne Regiment and Canadian Air/Sea Transportable (CAST) brigade were entirely dependent on the US/UK. The CAST brigade was trained to be inserted into NATO's northern flank (Norway), an adventurous mission that again could not be undertaken without extensive US support. Its NATO brigade was the only serious mechanized formation in its arsenal yet its tanks (British *Centurion* Mk 11), APCs and supporting air force were not capable of standing up to a Warsaw Pact force without lots of help. "The once state-of-the-art tank was beginning to show its age, though as late as 1975,

Canadian gunners could still outscore other tank types by considerable margins in exercises. The unsynchronized gearbox was also tricky for drivers to master, and faulty shifting could leave the fifty-five ton tanks rolling free in neutral on downward slopes, a condition nicknamed 'Mexican Overdrive.'"[452]

Back on Bleury Street, in January of 1975, Colonel Knox's comrade from battalion commanding days, Brigadier Bernard Edward Fergusson, Baron Ballantrae, Colonel of The Black Watch Regiment in Scotland, visited the armoury. He was not only an experienced soldier, but a military historian and the last British-born Governor General of New Zealand. He quickly belied his stern and be-monocled aspect by racing up to startled subalterns and asking, "I want to know what's really happening and I've learned what that means – speak to the subalterns." His father, a First World War general officer, had refused to allow him to go to Sandhurst wearing spectacles, which he needed as one of his eyes was weak, and insisted that he join that august academy wearing a monocle. "That monocle probably ranks as the most famous of its kind and when he was serving with the Chindits in Burma, it was necessary to have an air drop of monocles to make good his supply."[453] He served in many foreign places and was ADC to another great Black Watch Officer, Field Marshal Lord Wavell. Fergusson wrote an excellent biography of him as well as a number of highly readable books. Needless to say, the junior officers were charmed and delighted with this great soldier and author.[454]

Planning for the Future 1975–77

"… it was virtually impossible in the day's atmosphere to find officers."[455]

The political tensions in Quebec had marginally eased, but the prospects were not encouraging. The federal government was anxious to avoid a referendum on Quebec separation and thus reluctant to give support to institutions that were thought to antagonize the new regime. The Black Watch seemed to be one of them.[456] The best sources of future Militia officers were the downtown universities. However, graduates now tended to leave the province in search of greener fields. Further, as Militia training became less dynamic, trained officers and NCOs also left. In increasing numbers, executives were being transferred or migrating to better jobs. Of the university and COTC-trained officers that held such promise for the Regiment, four left to join the Regular army or went abroad to pursue graduate studies. The COTC had been disbanded in 1968, and officers who had enrolled in the new ROUTP programme were few. The alternate scheme (two-week summer camps to create Militia second lieutenants) did not allow sufficient time to master doctrinal fundamentals. On a brighter note, the 1976 Montreal Olympics sparked the first Montreal Indoor Highland Games (which later became the Montreal Highland Games). The inaugural event was held in the Regimental Armoury. Pipe Major Bolton and Captain Sandy Campbell requested permission to use the building facilities; Lieutenant Colonel Sewell gave it gladly.[457]

At one point, Colonel Sewell had five majors in the Regiment, but by Hogmanay 1977, he was down to none. Pressing business or family concerns had eliminated four, and the newly-promoted Major Hal Klepak was in England in the midst of graduate studies. Colonel Bourne held a dinner for all serving officers and Advisory Board members to review the situation. They concluded that in Montreal, "It was virtually impossible in [the day's] atmosphere for the Advisory Board to find officers."[458] They were unexpectedly saved by the district commander, Colonel Cameron, who informed Sewell that he was sending him an officer who would be a good fit. Captain Douglas Robertson, late of the Regular Force, had moved to Montreal from Fredericton, and was interested in continuing his military career in the Reserves. Sewell thought he would do nicely, and Robertson joined the Regiment. In May of 1977, he assumed command.

Before Lieutenant Colonel Sewell left the Regiment, he was asked by Colonel Cameron to continue his career at District 1 Headquarters. Sewell had already served a year at District as a Staff Officer in 1971, and felt that was quite sufficient. But it was Cameron's final request that he serve at District HQ until his change of command to Colonel Gilbert St. Louis. Sewell agreed; and then retired – but not from the military. He devoted himself to the Advisory Board and the supervision of the Black Watch's many enterprises as Regimental Secretary and resident *Solomon*.

Lieutenant Colonel GD Robertson CD PhD

... a "stranger", but became Black Watch pretty fast.[459]

Graham Douglas Robertson was born in Montreal. His grandfather emigrated from Dundee and served in the 5th Royal Scots just as the new armoury was built. His mother's great-grandfather, James A Ogilvy, founded Ogilvy's store and in 1927 sold it to Aird Nesbitt, then a rather young Black Watch officer. Doug Robertson's father was a major in the 17th Duke of York's Royal Canadian Hussars prior to the Second World War. He then joined The Royal Canadian Dragoons. After the war, he returned to Montreal and was second-in-command of the Hussars, soon to be simply 'RCH'. Robertson was a product of Westmount High School and received a full ROTP scholarship to attend the University of New Brunswick to study mechanical engineering. He joined The Royal Canadian Dragoons in May 1969 after graduation and briefly served in Germany, then rebadged to 8th Canadian Hussars. While in Gagetown, he completed a Master's in Mechanical Engineering. A Black Watch general, Duncan McAlpine, as base commander, approved a civilian appointment to attend Oklahoma State University to study for a PhD in mechanical engineering in December 1970. In May 1971, Dr Robertson was invited by the University of New Brunswick to return to the school as a professor. There he completed his PhD. In 1974, Robertson was assigned to the headquarters' staff of the Combat Training Centre. He served as the University Liaison Officer for the Maritime Provinces, and was appointed ADC to Lieutenant Governor Hédard Robichaud. He left the Regular Forces in 1975, transferring to the Militia (1st Battalion, Royal New Brunswick Regiment) and rejoined the faculty of UNB.

In the summer of 1976, Robertson joined Dominion Bridge in Montreal as a project manager for large manufacturing and construction programmes. He met with Colonel Peter Cameron and offered his services. With a fully trained background in the armoured corps, Robertson was prepared to follow his father into the Montreal cavalry; however, "With [both] the Hussars and Black Watch in my blood, Colonel Cameron steered me towards the Black Watch as they were in need of a senior officer to back up Lieutenant Colonel Bill Sewell."[460] He took command in 1977 and served in that capacity until 1980 when Dominion Bridge moved him to Niagara Falls to run Provincial Crane. He joined the District Headquarters Staff before retiring and immigrating to the United States in 1983. His career then turned to business. Robertson became president and part owner of Tesco Equipment Corp in 2000, turning it into the largest airline catering truck manufacturer in the United States. He ran for public office in 2012 and was elected to Florida's State Government.[461]

The General Waters Trophy 1978–79

The Regiment worked at building up its numbers. Recruiting was difficult but the summer influx of students kept things going. Their infantry skills were quite solid. In competition, The Black Watch continually achieved top national ranking:

> We won the General Waters Trophy two years in a row for being the best rifle team across all infantry regiments in the reserve forces. You would know the challenges of leading a volunteer part-time peace time unit. If your soldiers don't trust you and respect you, they don't show up for training. Regular units just don't understand the fragile connection between officers and NCOs and soldiers. Reserve units don't tolerate bad leaders for very long.[462]

Victor Chartier was the RSM. Robertson wanted to promote him to captain. "At first he was hesitant because [but] he accepted my offer and we see how well that turned out." Robertson noted how dedicated Pipe Major Bruce Bolton was to the Regiment. He approached the District Commander with the proposal that Bruce change his service designation to *Infantry*, and take on the role of RSM. Bolton would have to take all the necessary courses to qualify for the job but should he not complete the courses, he would have to relinquish the post. Colonel Cameron agreed, and Bolton became RSM in 1978.

It is customary for commanding officers of the Regiment to visit the Colonel-in-Chief during their tenure of command. At the end of May 1978, Lieutenant Colonel Robertson, accompanied by his wife and the adjutant, Lieutenant RF Clarke, visited England. The CO and Mrs Robertson were received by Her Majesty Queen Elizabeth The Queen Mother at Clarence House on 2 June. A few days later he viewed the annual Trooping the Colour at the Horse Guards parade from the VIP enclosure. A trip was then made north to Scotland, where the party was hosted at Balhousie Castle, Perth, by the regimental secretary and other dignitaries of the parent regiment. The links were further strengthened when, in November, Brigadier JC Monteith, Colonel of the Regiment, was guest of honour at the St Andrew's Ball. During this period, Major Alex Malashenko acted as commanding officer. Summer training allowed a break for a number of special activities, the most important of these being the Queen Mother's 80th birthday celebrations in London.

The Canadian Black Watch contingent included the honorary colonel, the CO, Lieutenant Jim Conway, Lieutenant Ian Cameron, RSM Bolton, Sergeant Major Labreche, WO Young, Sergeant Gio Carozza, Corporal Roger and Piper Kerr. The group was received royally by the personnel of the London Scottish, under the command of Major Patrick Layden. Hospitality was the order of the day and the generosity of this historic British unit left all ranks overwhelmed. For several days, the RHC detachment drilled at Chelsea and other barracks. Along with the other contingents, regimental quiffs took a pounding under the mercilessly efficient Guards' Senior NCOs, trying desperately to bring order to this disparate grouping. The show went off beautifully.

That summer, Lieutenant Colonel Robertson was transferred to Ontario. Succession was a major problem. There was but one qualified Black Watch major, and he was in Europe. Hal Klepak needed to get his research done for his PhD and Robertson needed a qualified DCO to take command. There followed an interesting meeting in London.[463] Directly after, Doug Robertson left for Niagara Falls.

During his command, Robertson recruited the second female officer in the Black Watch. Betty Ann Jones was keen and energetic and took over the QM. "The first evening I worked down there, I commented to one of my supply corporals how much I loved the pipes. He uttered a weary sigh, and said "Ma'am, it's obvious you haven't been here very long."[464] The Black Watch became both a *marriage de raison* and a *marriage d'amour*. Captain Jones married Major Alex Malashenko. Robertson much enjoyed holding a crown above their heads during their Russian Orthodox wedding. Betty Malashenko was effective and dealt well with the resistance she encountered from the old guard, who did not approve of this break with tradition.

Lieutenant Colonel Robertson left The Black Watch healthy and poised to expand. The real problem was the number of officers, a problem that had also plagued Bill Sewell. It was a new decade and a new CO returned from across the ocean.

Chapter 13

To the End of the Cold War

Lieutenant Colonel Harold Klepak CD PhD, 1980–83

You may wonder why I as a Czech hold these highland traditions so dear – it's because they work – they hold people together.

Lieutenant Colonel Hal Klepak

Of the post-war Black Watch commanding officers, only one can be termed international. Harold Klepak prided himself on Czech-Austro-Hungarian ancestry and an exotic multi-cultural youth. His Bohemian grandparents emigrated in 1909 but spoke German at home. The greater influence was his mother: "I was in the kilt when I was twelve and playing the chanter by the time I was in my late teens."[465] Klepak's father served with the Canadian and British navies, but ended up as a captain in the United States Navy, the naval attaché in Havana. Klepak was born in Virginia and raised in the British West Indies, Canada and Cuba. He currently uses the island as his base. He is a devoted academic, beginning as a lecturer at *Collège militaire royal de Saint-Jean* (CMR), then became a senior professor at Royal Military College, Kingston (RMC) as well as the Advisor on South American issues to the Minister of National Defence and the Army Commander. Klepak holds a BA from McGill and an MA and PhD from the University of London; his command of French and Spanish is flawless and he persists with his studies in Arabic. Klepak has written the definitive (to date) book on the Cuban Armed Forces "with the grudging acceptance of Fidel and Raúl Castro."[466] He is a consummate opera/theatre buff attending performances at least twice a week, no matter where he is in the world (which could be anywhere). He is, along with Major John Hasek (the parachutist, journalist, psychologist, and author), the second Czech Black Watch officer to gain international repute.[467]

Klepak's military career was inter-city, trans-provincial and trans-continental. "Canada gave me citizenship. I joined the RHC as soon as I left McGill in 1968... Of course you still needed a sponsor in those days, who was Major John Patrick, the RHC medical officer." Klepak commuted between the Watch and CMR St-Jean, Ottawa, and finally Europe. He was the ultimate military *tourista*, managing to secure secondments to regiments in England and France.[468] His appearance as CO was serendipitous. In the summer of 1980, Colonels Bourne and Robertson took him to lunch at The Royal Thames Yacht Club, during which Bourne impressed upon him the requirement to return to Montreal. The pressure was considerable ("You don't say no to John Bourne") however, shortly thereafter, the principal of CMR arrived in London and offered Klepak the post of setting up the Strategic Studies Programme at the college, which made leaving Europe and becoming CO of the Black Watch possible.[469]

Klepak was the perfect host and, throughout his command, the Black Watch became the social centre for Montreal garrison officers. His energy (and liver) defied most rugby teams. Klepak's officers were soon used to one dining-in per month and expected participation in the mess on Tuesdays and Thursdays. His contributions to the Black Watch officers' mess were the introduction of the *Cuba Libre* and a monstrous mess bill that came close to paying for the refurbishing of the bar.[470] This often meant long evenings and heavy heads; many a subaltern missed the last *metro* to Atwater, or the last bus to Ville St Laurent. "Despite the drift to Toronto and Calgary which reached epic proportions, the Regiment managed to hold [and build] its own in officer strength."[471]

Black Watch activities were managed by an eager hardworking staff. Both Major Alex Malashenko as DCO, and Major Vic Chartier, the former RSM, staffed field exercises. The incumbent RSM, Bruce Bolton retired on 14 September 1980, returning as pipe major, but leaving that important post vacant. Fortunately, Chief Warrant Officer GA (Gerry) McElheron, a previous RSM, was persuaded to leave his staff job at District HQ to return to the Regiment. "We couldn't have asked for better – intelligent, down to earth, got the job done and had a good time doing it."[472] Captain Drew Halpenny, attached from 2 RCR was the RSS Officer. Klepak opined: "Because Drew was the best RSS in the history of Christendom, Harvey got forgotten a bit." Captain Harvey Bailey was a no-nonsense officer from 3 RCR, posted – to his surprise – into Montreal. "He became a really good fellow and pro-Highland and RHC." Halpenny, 2 RCR, followed Bailey: "[Drew was] an excellent judge of people, delightful companion, tough but understanding; the best adviser and counsellor imaginable...he could be 100% RCR and 100% Black Watch at the same time. He loved everything about us and we loved everything about him." Hal Klepak's aim was to concentrate on officer development: "The junior ranks were not in short supply – officers, on the other hand, were rare."[473] He also believed that women were important to the Regiment's efficiency. Corporal Sherry Hummell recalls fondly: "Lieutenant Colonel Klepak put into process the idea that we all take some time to serve in each area of the Bn: BOR, Pay, QM, A Company etc, so that we could all replace each other when needed."[474] Klepak understood the power of personality and the effect it has on cohesion in a battalion. He avoided confrontation with brigade, was fluently bilingual and devastatingly charming in both languages. Klepak did not play the 'misunderstood Anglophone' regiment card but instead made headquarters quite comfortable in his presence.[475]

The Regiment strengthened its ties with the other Montreal regiments. Klepak suggested monthly CO luncheons at the United Services Club. This enabled the commanders as a group to analyse the often-draconian directives that emerged from the District Headquarters. This reservist 'band of brothers' included the commanding officers of The Royal Canadian Hussars, The Royal Montreal Regiment, Le Régiment de Maisonneuve and The 2nd Field Artillery.[476] A solid front was required because regrettably, the new Army had not changed much and odious attitudes to the Militia were not uncommon. For example, the officers' mess at Camp Farnham was open to the Regular Support Staff (including NCOs) and their civilian guests, but *out of bounds* to Militia officers who were the *raison d'être* for the base in the first place. Being treated like second-class citizens was a recurring complaint in the Reserve army circa 1970 to 1990. Many an officer found himself cold-shouldered in Base QM stores, or even the headquarters, by Regular NCOs relatively new to the forces. There was need to adhere to the basic principles and privileges common to all military personnel since the last century.

Honorary Lieutenant Colonel Jake Sharp retired in November. Colonel Sharp was the guest of honour at the annual officers' reunion dinner where he was followed, though never quite replaced, by the debonair Tom Price. Happy diversions, like the St Andrew's Ball were welcomed and attended *en masse*. With more regiments joining in, it became anew, a *de rigueur* social event for the garrison. The Ball returned to the Windsor Hotel, and *Peacock Alley* again sparkled with *haute couture* and dazzling smiles.

Highland Panzer-Grenadiers – the *Grizzly* AVGP

> Great hopes were placed on it in terms of providing more challenging training…Such hopes were not fulfilled and much frustration was caused.
>
> Canada's Black Watch 1962–1987 – an interim history

In another valiant effort by DND to revitalize the Reserves and encourage retention, the Black Watch was suddenly designated as *mechanized infantry*. They were tasked with mastering the new Militia training vehicle, the *Grizzly* AVGP (Armoured Vehicle General Purpose). It was a recurring problem: "People joined the Militia, came to like it, got bored with repetitive training and quit – units had the greatest difficulty in retaining even minimal standards…great hopes were placed on the Grizzly in terms of providing more challenging training." [477] *Grizzly* was a bracing title for what was essentially a six-wheeled van designed for urban operations. It boasted aluminum armour, a single machine-gun, and cramped quarters. It was a perilous cross-country drive. Worse, though it was essentially a bulky truck, the Black Watch was not going to actually receive any!

Grizzlies were to be kept in CFB Valcartier (a five-hour bus ride) for use on *militia weekends*. Montreal, a metropolis with hundreds of service stations and thousands of kilometres of good roads, hosting a complete Service Battalion and the home to Canada's central Ordnance Depot, which repaired everything from tanks to wreckers, was considered an undesirable base. The vehicles were kept in a Militia pool at Valcartier, and their availability varied. They could not be used until the unit qualified AVGP drivers and crew commanders. However, *conversion training* was limited to a couple of weekends a year. Preparatory courses (such as vehicle familiarization, driver training, tactical employment, 'de-bussing and em-bussing') could not be given until vehicles were available and crews trained. Frustration mounted as the promised delivery date continued to be delayed. Nonetheless, some training did take place. [478] Spaces on longer courses were limited, and scheduled at times difficult for militiamen to attend if they worked or were at school full-time. It would seem that the CF were creating programmes which excluded *bona fide* reservists and catered to leisured students and the unemployed. In the end, despite their mechanized status, the Black Watch mostly marched and remained, in effect, 'leg infantry'.

The 1980–81 training year brought exhilarating tasks. The Regiment participated in a challenging bridge demolition guard exercise at CFB Petawawa on 27–29 March 1981. Exercise *Pet Hackle* included A Company, elements of B Company, with augmentation by the Combat Arms Club of CMR, where Lieutenant Colonel Klepak worked. The officer-cadets of the college formed a separate platoon under Officer-Cadet Jay Mercer. Further, an expanded Summer Youth Employment Programme (SYEP) was instituted, together with the announcement that their Colonel-in-Chief would be visiting Toronto in July. The Regiment was partially responsible for the conduct of both these activities. It would help in the running of the SYEP, and it would provide a 100-man Royal guard of honour for the departure of Her Majesty from Lester B Pearson Airport in Toronto.

The day before the parade, the RHC contingent formed up at the Fort York Armouries alongside the Toronto Scottish, another of Her Majesty's regiments. In bright sunshine and sultry temperatures, the Regiment marched off to Old Fort York where a walk-about by the Colonel-in-Chief was held. With the historic fortress site as backdrop, the traditional pictures of Her Majesty with the officers and senior NCOs of her Regiment were then taken. That evening, the officers dined with Her Majesty at the state dinner given by the Province of Ontario in her honour. Then, the next day 6 July, the guard of honour commanded by Major A Ruthven, with CSM Labrèche as Guard Sergeant-Major, said good-bye to their colonel-in-chief at Toronto International Airport. The privilege of carrying the Colour went to Lieutenant Robert Clark; the Regimental Colour was carried by Second Lieutenant EG Eberth. "The men on parade earned praise from military and civilian dignitaries."[479]

Highland Winter 1982

In 1982, NDHQ Ottawa decided that the Army's *Shoot to Kill* marksmanship programme sounded a bit hostile for the times. It was reconstituted as the *Shoot to Live* programme. There were three levels of proficiency, and most Black Watch soldiers qualified in the top segment. To maintain interest during the long winter months, Klepak, in concert with his chum, Lieutenant Colonel Dan MacKay, CO of the Cameron Highlanders of Ottawa, instituted *Highland Winter*, a combination of winter-survival and Highland martial arts. The exercise practised infantry skills and soon attracted other Highland regiments from the adjoining provinces. RHC put up the cup,[480] the first hosting, and the mess dinner that went with it. *Highland Winter* involved tactics, survival training and a range competition. The units lived rough in arctic tents during what was usually a bitter, snow-filled weekend. The handsome trophy, a silver bowl made by Birks, was the gift of an enthusiastic Mrs Val Traversy and bore her husband's name. "The other regiments in the competition were delighted with the gesture as were all ranks of the Black Watch. It was particularly gratifying to be able to engrave the first victor's plaque for the base of the trophy 'RHC – 1982.'"[481] The second *Highland Winter* was held at the Connaught Ranges near Ottawa.

In the spring, a cross-border training exercise was conducted with the 104th US Armored Cavalry Squadron of the Pennsylvania National Guard.[482] To add even more colour, Professor Klepak again invited CMR's *Combat Arms Club* on exercises. In February, a three-unit competition occurred at the Connaught Ranges with three regiments each deploying a platoon. The RHC platoon was at full strength, under Lieutenant RF Clark, with Warrant Officer V Blazevic as second-in-command. The events were as varied as possible and tested individual, tent group and platoon skills. These included snowshoe races, pull-pole timed tent group activities, shooting, and toboggan races. The Black Watch team again won first place over-all.

The 1982–83 training year featured a series of AVGP-based exercises at Valcartier as well as further range work. But by the end of autumn, preparations began for another Highland Winter Exercise. This time the competition was hosted by the Black Watch in Camp Farnham and four units attended: The Cameron Highlanders of Ottawa; The Stormont, Dundas and Glengarry Highlanders; The Black Watch; and from as far away as Winnipeg, The Queen's Own Cameron Highlanders of Canada. This Regiment, it will be remembered, had long and deep ties to the Black Watch via the Cantlie family, particularly Lieutenant Colonel Stuart Cantlie, killed leading 1 RHC up Verrières Ridge. Lieutenant Brent Cowan led the Black Watch team to victory. News of the competition's usefulness spread quickly.[483] Reported during the Patrol Competition, the annoyed voice of a Highland officer heard at pre-dawn: "I'll kill the SOB who put point C in the middle of the swamp." Meantime, the Army's attention was completely focused on *RV 81,* the first great manoeuvres since the Second World War. Held that summer at CFB Gagetown, this military Olympics was, for former Black Watch members now serving in different regiments, above all, a *homecoming.*

Colonel WSM MacTier MC

It was a time of hectic change. The year ended sadly with the death of a gallant soldier and regimental stalwart, Colonel Bill MacTier. He had fought in the Regiment's first great battle – Ypres 1915, and continued to serve with the utmost loyalty in any function or on any committee the Regiment required. Bill MacTier had been Regimental Commandant from 1932 to 1934 and was a Black Watch officer whose demeanour and elegance made him a role model to every officer.

Ex *Quick Sword* – TEWT Advance and Quick Attack, 16 April 1983

A particularly ambitious exercise was *Quick Sword*. Crafted by Major Alex Malashenko and Captain Drew Halpenny, it was a brigade-sized, one-day Tactical Exercise Without Troops (TEWT). Klepak accepted the challenge to create a mega TEWT for eight units, each required to provide five to seven officers as candidates, RSS officers and drivers, in addition to a hefty support contingent.

The general scheme comprised a series of tactical problems emphasizing the advance and quick attack phases of war. It required considerable reconnaissance and planning. The Malashenko team plotted a series of *stands* in the Howick, Covey Hill, Chateauguay and Saint-Chrysostome areas of the Eastern Townships (60 km southwest of Montreal). It was an intricate, ambitious exercise. The exercise packages included maps, narratives and tactical problems for the eight syndicates. The logistical support plan was enough to discourage most planners. Save for The Royal Canadian Hussars, there wasn't another unit in the District, that could have produced this staff college exercise. It was a notable success. Lieutenant Colonel Klepak and his team, indeed, the Regiment, earned deserved kudos for a sophisticated effort that tested doctrine and officer skills – something their District would not attempt for another two decades. The Black Watch appeared to be at the top of its military game.

Lamentably, Lieutenant Colonel Klepak's third year ended abruptly. Command insisted he qualify at the Militia Command and Staff College in Kingston, and would not accept foreign or Commonwealth courses as equivalents. Following a contretemps with senior headquarters, Klepak resigned, and John Stothers took over within the week on 15 May 1983. When Hal Klepak assumed command, the Regiment had seven officers and mess life was listless. By the time he left, there were over twenty effective officers (including a good crop of second lieutenants) and rather innovative training.

Lieutenant Colonel John Charles Stothers CD

> The hallway lights were out, furniture blocked passages, doors were kicked in. It was great fun.
>
> Lieutenant Colonel Stothers, of the urban warfare exercise held in the armoury

John Stothers was from Hamilton, Ontario and an RMC graduate. He had previous militia experience with the 48th Highlanders but found himself in the Van Doos, his first Regular Force regiment in 1974. He served with the Canadian Airborne Regiment in 1975 and a NATO tour in Germany with the R22eR. He also served in Montreal as an RSS Officer with Le Régiment de Maisonneuve. He left the Army to continue his studies and was accepted into McGill's MBA program. He also applied to join the Black Watch. After graduating with his MBA, he accepted a callout at Secteur de l'est (Milice) on Atwater Avenue to run the 1981 Summer Training Program. During this period, a number of Black Watch officers had callout positions at Army Headquarters, now called *Force Mobile Command* (FMC), and created on 1 February 1968. FMC became one of six functional commands of the new integrated Canadian Forces. It was set up in St. Hubert, the old RCAF Station southeast of Montreal.[484] Colonel Bourne did not hesitate to offer command of the Black Watch to Strothers when Lieutenant Colonel Klepak resigned in 1983.

It turned out to be an exceptionally busy spring. Besides taskings to provide guards of honour, there was SYEP training to be organized, followed by the summer concentration. Stothers started the training year by appointing a new RSM. Chief Warrant Officer Dave Paull took over from RSM McElheron, who had provided yeoman service. Paull had a good sense of humour, was suitably authoritarian, but young at heart. The Regiment busied itself with *Grizzly* conversion, range qualifications and field exercises, which included a successful *Highland Winter III* – again at the Connaught Ranges, with The Stormont, Dundas and Glengarry Highlanders as well as The Cameron Highlanders of Ottawa.

Stothers was well buttressed by Alex Malashenko, Vic Chartier and his new RSM, CWO David Paull CD. His pipe major was the experienced Bruce Bolton and the new padre was Captain the Rev Jim Armour, who had received his training in the RCN. Stothers was new to the mess but learned quickly. One casual evening a steely-eyed Colonel John Bourne pointed to Stothers's *Van Doos* tie: "What the hell is that? I'm sure you're going to change it now!"[485] Perhaps John Stothers's favourite Black Watch person was the MO.

Captain DG Fraser MD

In the spring of 1984, the Black Watch was fortunate to again have a medical officer (MO) on strength. Derek George Fraser was a cardiologist, and proved to be a superb Regimental MO, perhaps because of his family connection. He was a graduate of Lower Canada College and McGill University. In 1970, he was chosen to be part of a precedent-setting project undertaken by McGill University and the University of Glasgow to develop the newly established faculty of medicine at the University of Nairobi, Kenya.[486] His father, Major George Fraser, commanded D Company 1 RHC and was killed during the Normandy campaign. A set of bagpipes played by the Imperial Black Watch at Waterloo are displayed in the officers' mess in his honour.

Captain Fraser, besides his regular presence at the armoury, attended every annual concentration and participated in Regular Force divisional exercises in Wainwright, Alberta. On his first Valcartier concentration, he became a casualty himself while tactically crossing a road during a combat patrol. Despite severe pain, he completed the patrol. Self-diagnosing a sprained ankle, he discovered that it was broken only upon returning to Montreal. He was a happy addition to the Regiment and much missed when he died from ALS in 2002, at the relatively young age of 61.

Recruiting and Retention

Service in Germany was one of the great plums of regular soldiering.

Brigadier General DS MacLennan

The Regiment's main concern was the same as it had been since the nineteenth century: recruiting and retention. "The retention of junior ranks was difficult due to low wages and sometimes uninteresting training. The recruitment process was too bureaucratic – long and tedious, even with a regimental medical officer present to do immediate examinations."[487] The only effective solution was to conduct exciting exercises. Stothers commanded a District defence exercise in Valcartier in 1985 where the use of live explosives to simulate artillery fire, and extensive use of engineer equipment to dig trenches, added to the realism. There were special occasions: early July 1985, the Regiment prepared for a visit of the Queen Mother to Ottawa. On 12 July, a 100-man guard of honour was provided. It was commanded by Major VG Chartier with CSM Gary Young as guard sergeant-major. This guard was notable because "Two women [Corporals Brenda McLellan and Lucette Robert] were on parade as part of the guard, surely a first for the Black Watch."[488]

One soldier ensured that a photo of the Black Watch appeared on the front page of *The Montreal Gazette* – unfortunately not the one Stothers hoped for. The jock had tarried late the night before the parade, and after an hour in the hot sun, fainted. When he came to, a medical officer was raising his legs to allow blood to move to his brain. The soldier raised his hand to his head, which had hit the pavement hard, and voilà, a photograph of a kilted Highlander apparently saluting while flat on his back. It was a natural and repeated in several national newspapers.

There was some creative training, which brought down the wrath of headquarters, and created paperwork for the Colonel. It proved, however, very popular with the troops. It began with troops rappelling down the front of the building. The *urban assault exercise* was really an attack on the armoury. It surprised, almost stampeded, the citizens and bus drivers along Bleury:

We only did it once. That was enough. The blanks, thunder flashes, and explosions were sufficient to alarm the locals; and the enthusiasm of the soldiers nearly wrecked the building … Two and a half platoons – about eighty all ranks. B Company was the enemy. The hallway lights were out, furniture blocked passages, doors were kicked in. It was great fun.[489]

This was followed by a less violent exercise that again produced soaked but happy troops: white-water rafting!

Overseas Visits

The next great Army manoeuvres were held out west in Wainwright, Alberta. *RV 83* deployed every regiment in Canada and substantial numbers of reservists were required in support. This meant a busy summer, but ensured all Black Watch members were militarily employed. In 1984, the Association organized a battlefield tour on the occasion of the 40th Anniversary of the epic battles for Verrières Ridge. Lieutenant Colonel Klepak agreed to act as guide. The group flew to Edinburgh and, after touring the city, proceeded to Regimental Headquarters at Balhousie Castle, Perth, where a cordial welcome was organized by the Regimental Secretary, Colonel Arbuthnott. They then took a coach to London and the Imperial War Museum and Lieutenant Colonel Strothers visited Clarence House. After crossing the Channel, the tour visited Vimy Ridge, where three battalions of the Black Watch fought together in the famous Canadian victory of 1917. The delights of Paris were sampled before touring the D-Day beaches and the Battle of Normandy Museum. This was followed by the visit to the battlefields around Verrières Ridge. The veterans were still fit enough to walk the bloodied ground. WOII Charlie Bolton, father to RSM Bruce Bolton, was wounded in the assault, and recalled his experiences on that tragic day. The townspeople of St-André hosted a reception in the Hôtel de Ville on Rue du Black Watch. The group then moved to the magnificently maintained Canadian War Cemetery at Bretteville-sur-Laize, almost in the shadow of Verrières Ridge. A particularly moving aspect of the tour was that several widows of soldiers killed in Normandy were seeing their husbands' graves for the first time. Next, the tour visited Dieppe, where C Company and the Mortar Platoon had taken part in the abortive attack in 1942.

Stothers continued building the Regiment and was pleased with the officer slate of twenty-five effectives on the rolls. The Regiment was greatly encouraged to learn that the Queen Mother would visit Montreal in the summer of 1987 to preside at a Trooping the Colour. This would be a most welcome return to a city where the Regiment had carried on steadfastly through two rather tough decades. Alas, John

Stothers would not be in the ranks; his tour ended after the annual church parade on 25 May 1986. He handed command to a true Highland workhorse, Vic Chartier. It was a historic occasion as the new CO was the first man in the Black Watch to have held the positions of regimental sergeant major and commanding officer.

Lieutenant Colonel VG Chartier OMM CD

My ball park was always the parade square.
Lieutenant Colonel Victor Chartier OMM CD, 8 February 2013

Victor Girard Chartier was born in Montreal, where he joined his school's Cadet Corps in 1949. He enrolled in the Black Watch in 1951. At once, he was confronted by such regimental worthies as Lieutenant Colonel Knox and WO1 Ralph Dynes MBE. He was in awe of Dynes, a large, much decorated soldier and decided immediately: "That's what I want to be, an RSM!"[490] Chartier recalls winning the Bren Gun competition and drilling on a very full parade square but "When the regular highland battalions were formed all the keeners volunteered; the Regiment was cut in half. I recall C Coy ordered to fall in one night; I was the only one on parade." His next CO was Lieutenant Colonel J Bourne, along with the new RSM, WO1 R Ablett, who wanted him to take the senior NCO course: Chartier was a sergeant at 19: "Only Al Rodgers was younger."

Vic Chartier's career encompassed Black Watch COs from Jim Knox to Bruno Plourde. He was present at memorable displays and militia concentrations. In particular, he had the good fortune to command the last grand Black Watch parade in Percival Molson Stadium before HM Queen Elizabeth, The Queen Mother. He liked to say, "The regiment and I fit together."

Chartier's company assigned him to Quebec City in 1964, and when he returned in 1975, he was almost a stranger. Lieutenant Colonel Bill Sewell had just taken command and promptly appointed Chartier as regimental sergeant major. The CO was direct: "The sergeants' mess is a disaster." Chartier decided the best way was to sit in the mess during a training night and feel the atmosphere. He concluded there was a palpable disconnect between the mess and the Regiment. New *ad-hoc* customs had been introduced, e.g. coming to attention at the door before entering the mess. "Highland regiments don't do this: ours certainly didn't." Other regimental traditions were either misunderstood or ignored from a lack of knowledge. Unfortunately, he did not enjoy immediate credibility with the senior NCOs: "I had been gone for eleven years and was seen as a 'parachute job' ... I knew I must retain a firm grip but a little psychology might help. One of my first orders was to stop the *attention at door*." It was a bit of shock treatment. The RSM then chaired a rather long mess meeting: "we established our aims, the duties of sergeants were confirmed and, in two months, things began to straighten out." The battalion appeared tighter. During Chartier's first church parade, Lieutenant Colonel John Bourne turned in his pew to Lieutenant Colonel Jake Sharp and grunted *sotto voce* (or as *sotto voce* as Colonel Bourne could manage): "Finally we have an RSM."

Chartier was regimental sergeant major under Bill Sewell and for another year and a half under Doug Robertson. He became an officer in 1978. Despite efforts, by the end of the decade, there were only seven effective officers left in the Black Watch. When Robertson first presented the opportunity, Chartier, the traditionalist, hesitated. "RSMs in Black Watch don't *cross the floor* – it rarely works." He declined. Then, the district commander, Colonel Peter Cameron invited him to lunch at the Beaver Club. The next parade night Chartier crossed the floor and became a captain.[491] As a staff officer, he worked for Lieutenant Colonels Klepak and Stothers. He learned to manoeuvre past Alex Malashenko, who, while ready to challenge him over staff duties, was equally prepared to help. There were skirmishes, but Chartier maintains: "What I saw in him was a brilliant mind, I respected him. Alex and I became very close friends when I was a captain."[492]

There were four majors eligible for the command billet. To his delight, Chartier was named the *Dauphin*. Stothers already asked Chartier to prepare for *The Queen Mum's Parade* in celebration of the 125th anniversary of the Regiment's first Colours. He organized the committee. "There were seventeen sub-projects in the plan. Little did I know I was to be in command." Lieutenant Colonel Chartier's RSM was CSM Paull ("enthusiastic, with a heart in the right place"), succeeded by Chief Warrant Officer MRG (Mike) Kelly MMM, an outstanding NCO ("fiery and exuberant, a true Irish man, a born soldier"[493]). The new DCO, Major Dan O'Connor, was a young Regular Force officer who had come to study law at McGill. Captain the Rev JSS Armour, having reached the compulsory age of retirement, was allowed to continue for the 125th Anniversary. He was followed in 1988 by Captain the Rev Bruce Glencross. However, Dr Armour, as minister of The Church of St Andrew and St Paul, continued as an honorary chaplain. *Comme toujours*, Colonel John Bourne remained his guiding authority. Despite its economic and political travails, Montreal could still boast a sizable stable of Black Watch blue bloods. Chartier almost choked when presented with a proposed budget of $90,000. Colonel Bourne simply said: "Leave that to me." Chartier was given an initial draft of $50,000 in a few weeks – "an advantage that present day COs no longer enjoy."

On 22 October 1986, Colonel AT Howard OBE VD died. At 95, he was a well-remembered and well-liked commanding officer (1936–38). He had come to stand for the Regiment's early heroic accomplishments. Howard rose through the ranks; he was a sergeant at Ypres with the 13th Battalion and was commissioned in the field just after the Somme in 1917. The traditional Levee on New Year's Day 1987 found key senior colonels absent. Honorary Lieutenant Colonel Tom Price was snowed in at Kennebunk, Maine, where he had spent the holiday with Lieutenant Colonel Jake Sharp. It was a long leave; everything, including all the cars, was buried. [494]

As the special year dawned, the Regiment was shocked by the sudden death of Major Malashenko on the evening of 13 January 1987. Chartier was intercepted at an O Group by his adjutant, Captain Gordon Lusk, and told the sad news. He ordered an immediate battalion parade where he announced to the assembled battalion that the DCO had died. Lieutenant Colonel Hal Klepak wrote:

> Always ready to spar intellectually with friends and foe, [Alex Malashenko's] sense of perspective and his thorough knowledge of military history and tactics had earned him a reputation as an expert in Montreal military circles. His "fireside" chats with young officers instilled a special pride and understanding of their responsibilities which they would carry for life.[495]

The military funeral was held at the Russian Orthodox Church on Laurier, just west of Park Avenue. It seemed the entire Montreal garrison attended; representatives from every regional regiment, as well as out-of-province Highland regiments. It was an awful way to begin such a promising year; an event keenly anticipated by the much-lamented Alex.

Later that month, the Regiment celebrated its 125th Anniversary on 27 January 1987 with a Drumhead Ceremony conducted in the armoury by the padre, Captain JSS Armour.

Black Watch Women, 1971–1987

> There were two clerks in the Orderly Room, but I was the only woman on the floor or in the field. I wore the uniform of the CWAC, not the kilt. For women that honour came during the 1980s.
>
> Private Karen Sutcliffe, 1972

The Canadian Army employed women in administrative, logistic and nursing roles since the Great War. The Reserves were allotted clerks as orderly room staff. They were part of the Canadian Woman's Army Corps (CWAC) and referred to, in a good-natured way, as 'Kwaks'. The combat arms qualifications and trades were closed to women until the late 1980s. In 1987, the Combat Related Employment of Women (CREW) trials started in the army and navy and the next year the air force removed all restrictions on the employment of women. The first Canadian Regular female soldier was qualified in the PPCLI in 1989; however, the Black Watch shares the distinction of having one of the first female infantry soldiers – if not in Canada, then certainly in Quebec.[496] Private Karen Sutcliffe was recruited in 1972 and placed on the Leading Infantryman Course. As a former Sea-Cadet, she attempted to join the Reserves: "When I walked into 2067 Bleury, the camaraderie was palpable. This felt like a family, even better, my wish to be 'a soldier' was considered possible. I wasn't dismissed by the recruiting staff. I had no illusions – I was walking into a man's world but I was given hope by the Black Watch." Sutcliffe's course was run by two experienced Black Watch NCOs, Sergeants Bill Carlisle and Roland Labreche. After qualifying, Sutcliffe served for two years in the BOR, B Coy, and then transferred into the Regular Force.[497]

Change came slowly – too slowly for the female soldiers in the Regiment. By the late 1980s, with the Queen Mother's visit and parade in full preparation, a determined group decided to nudge the Regiment toward a speedy and equitable solution, as indicated by NDHQ. Most vexing was the realization that recent recruits would be on parade; however, Black Watch females, some of whom had seen service with the UN and carried arms, were not included in the ranks with their regiment. Previous efforts were made; Captain J Percival had proposed bonnets and hackles, to mixed reviews from the Regiment's women.[498] The issue was not to do with uniforms but rather inclusion in all regimental undertakings.

Black Watch – Gender-Free, 1987–1991

As a result of your complaint to the Canadian Human Rights Commission, an extensive review of dress standards, policies, and regulations in relation to the kilted and other ceremonial orders of dress has been conducted at National Defence Headquarters. Consequently, explicit direction has been issued that makes the standards and regulations in this area clear and gender-free.

Major General Paul G Addy, Chief of Personnel Services, 29 November 1991

There was a formal objection. One of the leaders of the crusade was Corporal (later Captain) Brenda McLellan, who filed a complaint with the Human Rights Commission regarding their exclusion from the parade. Captain Betty Ann Malashenko and a number of female soldiers in the Regiment joined her.[499] In hindsight, it appears a necessary, self-evident adjustment, which would cause little disruption. However, that is to judge the situation in the light of gender equality today. In 1987, this was delicate ground; the militant attitude of the complaints unnerved the senior sergeants and officers who were anchored (the women might say mired) in century-old tradition. There was a mulish fear that the foundations of the Black Watch were in peril.

The complaint caused tremors in Ottawa. The area commander interviewed the CO; there was no directive[500] but minor changes resulted. Black Watch women were at the parade, but not quite 'on parade' – two carried the casings for the Colours.[501] The final result of the complaint was not realized for some time, but the conclusion remains important: The Human Rights Commission decided that the RHC female soldiers had, in fact, been discriminated against. Each complainant was awarded monetary remuneration, and received a letter of apology from the Forces' Chief of Personnel, which emphasized a gender-free Canadian Armed Forces. However, Major General Paul Addy did point out: "while the [Black Watch] policy was incorrect, it was clearly based on honoured tradition and was not intentionally discriminatory."[502]

This happened four years after the parade and two years after taking command. In 1991, Lieutenant Colonel O'Connor was still working to create a suitable Highland dress for female soldiers (he had proposed a tartan skirt, but the women rejected it).[503] He was unexpectedly given the findings of the Commission and ordered by DND to get on with it – gender-free uniforms. The Black Watch women would henceforth parade in kilt, sporran, blue bonnet and Red Hackle. This decision affected every Highland regiment throughout Canada.

Veterans on Parade: Refused

We will welcome Her Majesty Queen Elizabeth The Queen Mother – our Colonel-in-Chief – with honour and pride.[504]

"... but the hammer came down the day before the parade."
WO Gord Ritchie, of the BW Veterans training for the 1987 Trooping

Preparations for the parade were extensive but, in the end, it all depended on the soldiers of the regiment: the drill, the marching, and, of course, the numbers. It wasn't easy. The city's bus and *metro* workers were on strike. Difficult as it was to get to the armoury, it was nothing compared to getting to *CFB Longue-Pointe* (the old Long Point Garrison) far in the east end of Montreal, where the Black Watch rehearsed on the large parade ground. At one point, practice drills were cancelled. These were Militia problems – things their Regular compatriots often shrugged off. Chartier was resolute: "The officers, NCOs and soldiers of this regiment have no doubts about our ability to get the job done. Many of us are putting in sixteen and eighteen-hour days to make this happen correctly."[505]

Attempting to duplicate the spectacular trooping of 1962 was, some argued, unrealistic for a Reserve unit. They did not have the men, the money or the clout. Nevertheless, Colonel Bourne was determined. There were still sufficient Scottish warhorses left in Montreal to make this happen. The response from the Association, the Board, and the community-at-large was heartening. NDHQ (dotted with former Black Watch officers) cooperated and the City Council remained supportive. The CO was told to carry on with the parade – seen as the last hurrah for the Scottish community that once ran the city, indeed, the country. Chartier and his RSM were determined to reach a total of 150. The Regiment would be augmented by cadet officers, as well as good-sized cadets. Recruiting had been successful, and a platoon's worth of non-effectives returned to parade regularly. Further, there were the former soldiers: war veterans or members of the pre-unification army who were fixed on one last chance to march before the Queen Mum. Dozens volunteered, from great distances in Canada and the USA, several from overseas. One was still serving as RSM of an armoured regiment, yet he appeared at Longue Pointe as another soldier, ready to carry a rifle in the ranks. To Victor Chartier's great regret, NDHQ banned these imports at the last minute.[506] Consequently, the Trooping would be a bittersweet occasion for many.

Molson Stadium is cut into the mountainside, surrounded by trees and, in the background, the Scottish baronial towers of the Royal Victoria Hospital. Generations of Royal Highlanders have marched, manoeuvred, or jogged past the location, tramping up the mountain or onto Fletcher's Field, just further along Park Avenue. Behind the stadium sits *Ravenscrag*, the former home of Sir Montagu Allan, once Colonel of the Regiment. The armoury lies well below, on crowded Bleury Street, which, as it moves north, becomes Park Avenue. In early days, sleek tramways ran along that boulevard. Pine Avenue was lined by great family houses. The stadium stands on the site of the old Molson house. By 1987, the familiar route from the armoury to their mountain park remained in use by the Regiment. Even into the new millennium, platoons continued with fitness runs to the top of the mountain, and back, toughening up the jocks for brigade competitions or tours in Afghanistan.

HM Queen Elizabeth, Colonel-in-Chief – The Last Great Parade

Never have I been so proud of the Regiment.

Colonel John Bourne

Her Majesty first visited The Black Watch armoury where a Gold Award presentation ceremony for the *Duke of Edinburgh's Award* took place. Over fifty young Quebecers, boys and girls, had the honour of receiving their awards from Her Majesty, including three very proud members of The Black Watch Cadet Corps: Officer Cadet Pinard, who was then serving in the regiment, Cadet Captain Mark Mackisoc, and Cadet Corporal Alex Marcianesi. [507] There were official receptions, but for the Regiment, the visit began the next morning when the royal cavalcade drove to the stadium. The Queen Mother rode in a perfectly-preserved classic *Lincoln Continental* convertible limousine with the top down which was the same type and year she had used in 1962. As Her Majesty alighted from her limousine, the commanding officer gave the order: *Royal Salute – Present Arms.*

The Trooping of 6 June 1987 was the pinnacle of Victor Chartier's career, and also celebrated the Regiment's 125th anniversary. The Black Watch marched on in four Guards, Colour Party and formations from three affiliated cadet corps. The parade adjutant was Captain Gordon Lusk; the RSM was CWO David Paull. Major Dan O'Connor commanded the Escort for the Colour; Captain Paul Hindo was the Colour Guard Commander. The Pipes and Drums was under P/Major Andrew Kerr ("An excellent Pipe Major, one of the best, competent, intelligent, could be counted on to perform a task"[508]); the supporting brass band was the Royal Canadian Artillery band, a Regular Force unit from Kingston. But in fact, it was an all-Black Watch show: the Pipes and Drums were a compilation of RHC reserve, association and cadet bands and the Artillery band still had a large contingent of the Regular Black Watch Military Band from 1970. "Most of the BW regular force military band went to the Artillery band and there still was a legacy seventeen years later – i.e. they knew combined band music well."[509] It was positioned within the stadium at the entrance arch and instructed by Lieutenant Colonel Chartier to join in only at the last moment because the Pipes and Drums would begin playing well outside "to stir the blood of the crowd."[510]

Her Majesty was attended by the Lieutenant Governor of Quebec, the Hon Gilles Lamontagne and Colonel John Bourne. Her duty piper was Cadet Pipe Major Neil Cotie. A Black Watch piper woke Her Majesty each morning during her visit.[511] The Commander of Mobile Command, Lieutenant General James A Fox CMM CD, led the Honorary Colonels and host of Black Watch officers. The Regiment was drawn up in line with members of the Cadet Corps, commanded by Captain WH Gardner, behind the Regiment; behind them were about 250 members of the Association, commanded by Captain Ivor Watkins with their own pipes and drums. Their Pipe Major was William J Hannah, always known as Willie, who had been pipe major of the 3rd Battalion on the 1962 parade. The Queen Mother inspected the Regiment from an open jeep, specially altered as a review vehicle. She surprised everyone by gracefully hopping aboard like a teenager. Her driver, and the only Black Watch woman to appear midst the formed parade, was Corporal Debbie Leger. It was an experience she would treasure forever. The Queen Mother waved to the stands, and the crowd roared back its delight. The master of ceremonies was retired Lieutenant Colonel Hal

Klepak, who described each aspect of the parade in flawless French and English; he returned in the spring as guest of honour at the Red Hackle Club's mess dinner. The Regiment marched past in slow and quick time, then removed head-dress and gave three cheers to the Colonel-in-Chief, with the spectators joining in.

The stadium was packed. The war veterans were in their fifties and sixties, glittering with medals, still looking remarkably jaunty and debonair. Montreal's Anglophones, though dwindling in numbers, proved they could still fill a stadium with ease. The atmosphere was buoyant, and everyone felt young at heart. It had been twenty-five years since the Queen Mum's last Regimental visit, and the city hungered for a Black Watch show that would bring back the days of glory. The pressure on Lieutenant Colonel Chartier was simply enormous. Previous parades had the formidable bulwark of the Regular Force battalions to fall back upon. This time, the Regiment was quite alone. The eyes of Canada, and of a city that would accept nothing less than a triumph, were fixed upon him. And he did not fail them. Colonel John Bourne later wrote: "Never have I been so proud of the Regiment."[512]

Finally, and all too soon it seemed, the royal party left; a grand parade was over and the Regiment marched off to *Black Bear*. There was discernible emotion as the stadium stood and applauded until the last note of the pipes faded away.

The Regimental Dinner

This was the second occasion for a regimental dinner at the Queen Elizabeth Hotel; the first, in 1962, included the three battalions[513] and forty-five DSOs and MCs from past wars. Fewer were left, yet Her Majesty seemed unchanged. The Queen Mother, in brilliants, a soft blue gown, The Black Watch brooch, and diamond tiara, was radiant. At the regimental dinner, Her Majesty was presented with a suitably-inscribed silver salver, commemorating the 125th anniversary of the Regiment and the 40th anniversary of Her Majesty's appointment as Colonel-in-Chief of the Canadian Black Watch.[514] After dinner, Her Majesty stayed on, talking to the mess members and their ladies. She seemed reluctant to leave. The regimental dinner was highlighted by the Queen Mother's toast to Her Regiment but also included a surprise – the pipe band left playing a new tune, *Colonel Bourne*, which the Queen Mother pronounced "charming." On her return from the dinner, as she was escorted by members of the Royal Canadian Mounted Police down the long mezzanine, Her Majesty came upon a graduation dance held by a French high school in one of the grand salons. The music was quite loud, and the dance floor was crowded. Much to the astonishment (and the utter dismay) of her security escort, she walked into the room to watch the dancing. Suddenly, one young girl exclaimed: "Mon dieu, c'est la Reine Mère!" The orchestra stopped and the young people applauded. Her Majesty smiled and said to the orchestra: "S'il vous plait, continuer."[515] The tiring day came to an end, but it marked only the halfway point.

Church Service, Sunday 7 June 1987

The church parade was on a sunny day; the police allowed a bike marathon (*Le Tour de l'île*) to share Sherbrooke Street that Sunday, and spectators were treated to the odd sight of Highlanders marching along flanked by hundreds of cyclists whizzing by. A couple of *patriotes* booed the church as they cycled past. The crowd ignored them, and the area in front teemed with those hoping to catch a glimpse of the Queen Mother as she left the church. The church was full to overflowing. The regimental padre, Captain the Rev JSS Armour, conducted a moving and celebratory service. He thanked Her Majesty for keeping the promise she made twenty-five years ago when she unveiled the first clerestory window – that she would return when they were all installed. "And lo, she is here and our hearts are bursting with pleasure and pride."[516] The Honorary Colonel John Bourne then invited the Colonel-in-Chief to unveil the refurbished memorial tablets in the chancel. The two bronze plaques listed the names of the 836 officers and men of the 42nd Battalion, including their commander Lieutenant Colonel Bartlett McLennan DSO, who died in the Great War. It was in their memory The Black Watch Window was installed in 1920. The occasion also marked the fiftieth anniversary of the Queen Mother's coronation, and she was praised by Reverend Jim Armour for her "devotion to duty in peace and war … [and that] magical sense of making us believe that you are smiling directly at us … May good health, great happiness and every blessing attend your Majesty now and throughout the years to come."

Cheered as she came down the steps of the church, a Black Watch veteran cried out, "haste ye back, ma'am." The eighty-six-year-old Queen Mother turned and smiled at him: "Oh, I'll try," she said.[517]

That afternoon, amidst security and sunshine, a joyous crowd gathered at le Chalet du Parc du Mont-Royal for a garden party for all ranks of the Black Watch. The area includes a large terrace, the Belvedere lookout, which offers an unmatched panorama of Montreal, the St Lawrence River, the townships, and in the far distance, the Adirondack Mountains of New York State. Her Majesty again showed boundless energy, and seemed to have time to meet everyone and have a kind word for each. She departed to the tunes of *Auld Lang Syne* and *Will ye no come back again*.

The Royal Party left Dorval Airport on Monday 8 June in the pouring rain, befitting the melancholy moment. There was a quarter guard of fifteen soldiers, but no guard of honour for the departure, at Her Majesty's request. The royal visit was a triumph for the Queen Mother, and for the Regiment, an unqualified success. The next royal parade, in twenty-three years, would be made under siege, in an area that barely equalled a quarter of the McGill stadium grounds. Prince Charles, the new Colonel-in-Chief, grandson of the Queen Mother, would present Regimental Colours in The Black Watch Armoury on 10 November 2009.

Awards: The Proven Cup

Recruiting in the fall of 1987 concentrated on local areas around the armoury along St Joseph Street between the Plateau and Mile End. The Pipes and Drums were invited to participate at the Stone Mountain Highland Games in Atlanta, Georgia: "the weekend took its usual toll on the aggregate liver of the band."[518]

The next spring, the Regiment was rather keen on the presentation of the Proven Cup, which had been instituted in 1977 in memory of an inspirational trainer, Captain AB Proven, who had won the MM in the Great War. The Cup was in recognition of the best soldier in the Regiment for that training year. The first winner was WO Al Whitehall, who later, as a sergeant major in Afghanistan, survived a savage F-16 jet fighter attack. He was sent to Scotland to visit the Allied Regiment. The winner for 1985 was Corporal Raymond Joseph. The Regiment sent him to visit First Black Watch at Suffield Training Camp, the British training facility in Alberta. WO Gordon Scott Ritchie won in 1986, and he was flown to Scotland to visit 1 BW.

1987 – John Bourne Retires as Honorary Colonel

The Queen always called Colonel Bourne 'John'.

Lieutenant Colonel Victor Chartier

Colonel Bourne served until November 1987, when he decided to retire after fifty years of service. The officers' annual Reunion Dinner in November paid tribute to him. In attendance was the Hon David Arbuthnott, colonel of the parent regiment, who was guest of honour at the St Andrew's Ball. The theme that year was the Regiment's 125th anniversary. Colonel Bourne introduced his successors – surely a triumph for Bishop's College School. Tom Price was appointed Honorary Colonel, and Stephen Angus was welcomed back into uniform as the Honorary Lieutenant Colonel. Angus, an elder and former trustee of The Church of St Andrew and St Paul, would visit Montreal several times a month. Directly after the Reunion Dinner, they both attended the meeting of Honoraries in Ottawa. According to Angus, "We wore what was most comfortable as a uniform – we knew the fellows in the Honoraries did not know any different – no one could tell us we were wrong." They were a popular duo, but the evening belonged to John Bourne.

Throughout dinner, the guests exchanged anecdotes with friends and guests. Lieutenant Commander Gord Vachon was a naval officer, but such a regular visitor to the Regiment that he was dubbed *Senior Naval Officer Watch* (SNOW), which went well with his alabaster hair. He reminisced:

> It was at a sherry luncheon, when I was sitting diagonally across from Colonel Bourne – a truly devastating moment occurred in the life of this junior officer. As I was chatting to the officer next to me, I reached for my tomato juice and … knocked over the glass. The liquid took off across the thick white table cloth in the direction of Colonel Bourne, who merely glanced disapprovingly in my direction, at which moment the tomato juice came to a grinding halt. When I could breathe again, I realized that some officers really do have divine powers.[519]

Before Christmas, on 3 December, Colonel Bourne, Colonel Price, and Lieutenant Colonel Angus had the honour of being received individually by the Queen Mother at Clarence House in recognition of the changes in the honorary appointments. Bourne was devoted to the Queen Mum, and she was very fond of him. Victor Chartier noted: "The Queen [Mother] always called Bourne 'John'. When she left from Ottawa in 1985, Colonel Bourne was not in the departure line, but HM paused and called to him."[520] Despite 50 years of experiences in war and peace, his fondest memory was the 125th anniversary parade and the Trooping the Colour in her presence in 1987.

As John Bourne performed his duties, at all times in his shadow was the faithful Major William Ewart Stavert. He was the equerry to three regimental colonels: "I served KG Blackader as ADC, Knox and also Bourne, to whom I was almost a valet." Stavert was a product of Lower Canada College, Bishop's and had a law degree from McGill. His father was a director of the Bank of Montreal but thought Stavert was better suited to the courts. He worked at the esteemed Montreal firm of *Heward, Holden, Hutchison, Cliff, McMaster and Meighen*. Stavert remembers that while Colonel Paul Hutchison did not put on airs, "he was rather formal … If you weren't wearing a waistcoat he would ask – 'Aren't you chilled'?" Bill Stavert specialized in private law and trusts: "I got a Supreme Court judgement to change laws … I never did the same thing twice." Stavert joined the Regiment in 1956 and retired after the 1962 Colours parade. He continued to be the chief of staff to Colonel Bourne, ensuring he got to where he was going, and back.[521] Stavert's favourite excursion was to Cyprus in 1970, one of the last acts of Bourne as Colonel of the Regiment. It was tiring; the colonel made a special effort to visit all the Black Watch observation posts, no matter how remote. A pillar of the Advisory Board, Stavert remained a valued *eminence grise* of the Black Watch for the rest of his life. Having served nearly a dozen honoraries, he concluded, "Bourne was the best of the lot."[522]

After the royal parade, brigade exercises seemed anticlimactic, but Chartier was a trainer at heart. Even as the Regiment prepared for the grand trooping, they conducted a brisk exercise weekend two weeks before the big visit. In the continuing fall and winter cycle, all the usual training was conducted, and Lieutenant Colonel Chartier was tasked to command the 1988 District summer concentration. The planning started about January, and he decided to take the battlegroup out of camp and exercise in farming country about thirty-five miles west of Valcartier. "This gave my support staff plenty to do until June to clear farm lands for our exercise. We had helicopter support [but rather limited] due to weather, with the exception of a 30-minute recce I had. This was my final command other than completing my term in May 1989."[523] Chartier led the 'Anglophone Battle Group' and inherited a combined staff as well as all the regimental padres, about twelve. The rains would not let up, even as the troops crossed the start-line. After three days, a frustrated Chartier took a page out of General George Patton's book. He summoned the padres and announced they must intercede to have the rain stop. For each extra day of rain, he would arrest ("*sacrifice*") a padre. A couple missed the twinkle in his eye and exchanged concern. The Highlander seemed to mean it! The next day, the sun shone.

Victor Chartier's term as commanding officer officially came to a close after the spring church parade in May 1989.[524] The French Canadian Montrealer, now a Highlander, handed over to a former Regular Force officer from Ontario. Everyone feared the worst – another stranger. But, as is not uncommon in the history of this Regiment, the new man became more Black Watch than folks born in Griffintown, and he could play the pipes!

Lieutenant Colonel DF O'Connor CD 1989–1993

> We were simply very proud. That pride and distinctive style, the Highland uniform, was interpreted as arrogance by District HQ.
>
> Colonel Dan O'Connor, 18 February 2013[525]

Daniel Francis O'Connor was born on New Year's Eve, 1952, in Lindsay, Ontario. He was an army brat, growing up in Borden, Petawawa, Gagetown, Aldershot, and Germany where he delivered the *Stars and Stripes*. Duncan McAlpine, as CO of 2 RHC, was a customer. O'Connor's father served in the 48th Highlanders and was one of the original members of the 2nd Canadian Highland Battalion, which became the 2 RHC. O'Connor had always been keen on the Army. He joined the West Nova Scotia Regiment Cadets at age fourteen and soon was a corporal instructor, then sergeant. In 1970, he was accepted into The Royal Military College, Kingston, where he studied electrical engineering. He managed to participate in sports and the college gymnastic squad as well as the RMC Pipe Band, where he was named Pipe Major in his senior year. "Greg Mitchell and I introduced *Black Bear* as the march-off for cadet parades, a tradition maintained to this day."

His career demonstrated a lessening interest in communications (he was a qualified Signals officer) and a growing passion for mountaineering and parachuting. Two years with 2 Airborne Signal Squadron sealed the deal. He volunteered for all the adventure training available, became a pathfinder,[526] climbed Mont Blanc with the British, trained with Italian Alpini, and became a certified mountaineering instructor. He followed the path of least boredom and re-qualified as an infantry officer, thus becoming a member of the RCR. But, he was miserable. After graduating from the Long Armour-Infantry Course (a year in Bovington UK, 1982) he was, rather bizarrely, technically over-qualified for the infantry! He seemed doomed to staff work. O'Connor left the Regular Force in 1984 and joined the Black Watch that same year. Interested in studying business or law, he applied to McGill Law *and* the McGill MBA programme. He was accepted in both. "I decided to study both. That set the scene for the next few decades." He finally became a full-time lawyer and eventually started his own law firm. However, when O'Connor assumed command, he was still a McGill graduate student: "The Reserves became a part-time job; 'student' was my full-time job."

His attachment to the Black Watch was serendipitous. John Stothers was an RMC classmate. Despite family history, O'Connor forgot the Black Watch was in Montreal. He and John met as an officer was showing O'Connor the armoury. Stothers immediately invited then Captain O'Connor to a dining-in where he was met with polite reserve and muffled groans: "Not another Regular Force officer from RMC?" After dinner, well aware that O'Connor had led the RMC band, Colonel Stothers called for the pipe major's pipes and thrust them into his hands: "Here – play these." O'Connor stood up and began – it was *Highland Laddie*. He could not have made a better entry into the Regiment.

His first job was 2IC, A Coy under Major Grant Rust, "a blood and guts officer, he knew his stuff, he was confident and had Regular Force experience."[527] Their work was cut out for them. By 1989, the Regiment was an average Reserve unit. O'Connor recalled, "I had no preconceived animosity, had no expectations; I was tolerant beyond belief ... it was in not bad shape for a militia unit; a scattering of good NCOs and officers, and promising corporals on their way up." The Regiment needed more officers. Even though O'Connor was soon promoted as the fourth major, most junior officers had not completed their last phase of training. In January 1987, O'Connor was appointed DCO, in place of the late Major Alex Malashenko. He assumed the task of coordinating all the administrative aspects of the anniversary activities, particularly the planning for the Queen Mother's visit in June. That administrative order grew to a thick stack of papers, affectionately known as 'The Brick'.

His RSM was CWO John Rodger, described as "a big time Glaswegian, very Scottish, a good soldier; he kept peace in the sergeants' mess, and served O'Connor well."[528] O'Connor's first major exercise was *EnGarde 90*, the biggest Reserve exercise ever held in CFB Gagetown, involving over four thousand soldiers. Everyone went into the field. This was followed by another large concentration in 1992; by now, everyone, men and women, were wearing the same uniform, including kilt and hackle. Despite the fact he was in his fifth year, "I was still regarded by some as a parachute." O'Connor became good friends with Dr George Fraser. The captain was the hard working MO and beloved in the Regiment. They both lived in Montreal's West Island and often drove home together. Fraser complained about the mess, the junior officers, and the costs. Finally (perhaps to change the conversation) O'Connor decided to appoint him as the president of the mess committee (PMC). "But I can't – I'm the MO." "Well, I'm the CO and I'll fix that." George Fraser gave a wry smile: "OK, I'll do it."

At the next reunion dinner, Fraser decided to calibrate the Monteith Bowl, a silver vessel on the mantle above the fireplace and directly below the Colonel-in-Chief's portrait, always filled for the reunion dinner with exactly two dozen red roses.[529] Fraser announced to O'Connor: "We'll save money; I'll put in one dozen roses – no one will be the wiser." The CO wasn't completely sure about this … and he was right. The night of the reunion dinner, as the head table made its way upstairs and into the mess, Colonel Bourne entered, stopped, and turned to O'Connor: "Dan, why are there not two dozen red roses in the Monteith Bowl!?" This was corrected. Fraser next bought two dozen silk roses for the bowl. Handsome, and they would never have to be replaced. That worked.

The Purple Network

> The underlying assumption is that [padres] have no rank … In a tiny and secure sense, we work outside the chain of command
>
> Captain Canon Bruce Glencross, CD

Jim Armour handed over duties to Captain the Rev (later Canon) Bruce Robert Glencross CD, a soldier padre, who had done as much time in the Militia. Glencross held degrees from McGill, Wycliffe Hall, Oxford, and a clattering of gongs for UN service. He joined the Governor General's Foot Guards (in Ottawa) in 1972 and worked his way up to sergeant, seeing UNEF service in Israel and Egypt. He became Regimental Padre in January 1988, and wore four medals on parade. "Not since Berlis," noted John Bourne.

Besides his deistic allegiance, he served under seven RHC colonels (Chartier to MacKay: 1988–2008) and was devoted to the Regiment. He got on well with them all, but he seemed to work best with Dan O'Connor: "As wonderful and straight-laced as they come, strict military bearing ... he was dying from a pernicious cancer, but he believed in his own survival; we both know the reason he survived – a miracle!"[530] The Anglican padre was modern yet in many ways old school. He understood and used *The Purple Network* (padres) and the British padre tradition of assuming the rank of the person they speak to. "The underlying assumption is that they have no rank ... in a tiny and secure sense, we work outside the chain of command, how else could I report the morale of the troops to the CO?" His favourite duties were "working with the soldiers (who always cooperated), several selected me to marry them and take the marriage preparation course."[531] The Regiment's opinion of their padre was made evident when Captain Glencross was voted as the recipient of the coveted Proven Cup signifying *best soldier*: "It was my proudest moment in the Black Watch."[532]

The Oka Crisis and Cinematic History 1990

In the summer of 1990, the Montreal area again witnessed the deployment of the Canadian Forces to deal with what was termed 'The Oka Crisis'. At issue was a land dispute between the town of Oka and the Mohawk reserve of Kanesatake, northwest of Montreal, which began on 11 July 1990. Confrontations ensued and blockades were erected. In solidarity, Mohawk in Kahnawake, on the south shore across from Lachine, blockaded the approaches to the vital Mercier Bridge, which passed through their land. Quebec requested support from the Canadian Army, which was their right under the constitution. Provincial and national leaders participated in negotiations between the Mohawk and Quebec, and the barricades came down on 26 September 1990. The Reserves were not mobilized, although many RHC soldiers received call-outs. The occasion was judged to be skillfully handled by the military. The feared violence was avoided and peace between Mohawk and Quebecers restored. However, it was, at the time, viewed as a very serious confrontation. Above all, the professionalism of the army was commended. During the crisis, 2 RCR, commanded by Lieutenant Colonel Greg Mitchell, one of Lieutenant Colonel O'Connor's RMC chums, was stationed in Kahnawake. Just before their redeployment, O'Connor invited the officers to join their fellow Highland officers for dinner in the Bleury armoury, in combat dress, as their mess kit was unavailable. It turned out a truly memorable affair. Lieutenant Colonel Mitchell came back in November for the reunion dinner as guest of honour. His speech was a report (with maps) of the recent operations during the Oka Crisis. Mitchell was rated by many as "the best we've had in many a year."[533]

The on-going crisis did not prevent the Black Watch from training. During a company exercise in Farnham, they became film stars. The CBC was producing a major series about Canada in the Second World War. The third episode (*In Desperate Battle*) was a two-hour docudrama that covered the Normandy Campaign and featured the Black Watch attack on Verrières Ridge. The ill-fated 25 July assault was re-enacted by the battalion, albeit in modern kit. Major scenes covered key confrontations with the brigadier and the final charge. Lieutenant Colonel O'Connor starred as Major Philip Griffin, who assumed command of 1 RHC. The Black Watch segment met with considerable acclaim and as one producer quipped to O'Connor: "Made you and your boys immortal."[534]

The Freedom of the City of Montreal, World Scottish Festival, 1992

…The Freedom of the City, bestowing upon it the privilege of marching through our streets on ceremonial occasions with drums beating, Colours flying and bayonets fixed.[535]

Perhaps O'Connor's best day was the Freedom of the City parade in 1992. A group of leading citizens headed by Mrs David M Stewart orchestrated a formal petition requesting this honour for the Regiment. The year marked the 350th anniversary of the founding of Montreal. In their petition, they wrote: "The Black Watch's association began more than 230 years ago … this Scottish Regiment first comprised part of the Montreal garrison." The Black Watch reflected a diverse ethnic and linguistic character:

In consequence of the Auld Alliance between Scotland and France many of these troops had previously served in the French Army and were fluent in the French language thus resulting in a close rapport with the local inhabitants … Scottish immigration continued to be of great importance in the academic, religious and economic development of the City.[536]

The petition had a hidden agenda; its petitioned dates coincided with the schedule of the World Scottish Festival (a weeklong fête 15–23 August 1992) presented by the city's Thistle Council. Heralded as the largest French-speaking city in the world outside of Europe, Montreal's heraldic shield and flag feature the thistle, emblematic of Scotland. The *Auld Alliance* has a special meaning in Quebec where the Scots served *l'ancien régime* in Canada.[537]

The Regiment's request to participate in both the Freedom of the City Parade *and* the World Scottish Festival meant leaving the militia summer manoeuvres (MILCON, held in New Brunswick) a few days early. This annoyed the senior District and Area staffs and there was some tension with headquarters.[538] However, permission was granted; the event had the enthusiastic blessing of NDHQ, as well as the municipal government. It would seem the Scots still had friends in high places. Therefore, the Black Watch left MILCON early – much to the displeasure of senior staff officers.

The Freedom of the City Parade took place Sunday, 16 August 1992. The Black Watch formed on the south portico of City Hall. From this bluff could be seen the old Montreal landmarks, so familiar to a Regiment that traced its roots back to 1862 and earlier: le Champ-de-Mars, Craig and Bleury Streets, and of course, Mount Royal. Next to the Ceremony of the Keys at the Tower of London, this is the oldest ceremonial format still in existence:

> The march to the Hotel de Ville (City Hall) was simple and dignified and without fanfare… soldiers did not fix bayonets and officers kept claymores in their scabbards … The commanding officer knocked three times using his claymore; was permitted entry and greeted by Mayor Jean Doré, once the proclamation had been read, Lieutenant Colonel Dan O'Connor ordered the Regiment to fix bayonets, draw claymores and the Colours uncased.[539]

Thousands of Montrealers lined the streets. The Regiment marshalled two hundred soldiers that day. The DCO was Major Gary Dover, who organized the ceremony on behalf of the CO; the parade adjutant was Lieutenant Charles Barlow; and the Guard Commanders were Major Brent Cowan and Captain Bruce Bolton. The parade senior NCOs included Warrant Officers Young, Carozza, Kelly, Hamel, Barron; Sergeants Bourdon, Irvine and Munizaga. Lieutenant Greg Lowe commanded the Colour party. The city cheered them all the way back to the armoury. They returned chuffed and glad it was over. The march back was up the incline and O'Connor kept a close eye on the honorary colonels, who shrugged it off: "Climbing the stairs to the mess was the main effort, but we were greeted with a whisky-soda."[540]

The Scottish Festival came next, and if the Regiment was triple taxed with guards and ceremonies, the pipe band was run ragged. The events included Clan Gathering, the Tartan Ball, a full Tattoo at the Montreal Forum, Highland Games, and a Grand Ceilidh. The Watch was present at all, and the armoury hosted many receptions and soirees.[541] After the MILCON wargames, parade, and festival, the Regiment was quite exhausted. There was no time left for holidays. The next week, everyone went back to work or studies.

Relationships with District HQ and Succession

Damnant quod non intelligunt[542]

O'Connor's bosses were Colonel George Javornik (RMR), followed by Colonel Jean Gervais (Le Régiment de Hull). Their staffs did not appear to like the Black Watch very much; District saw the Black Watch as a stuck-up regiment. "But we were simply very proud. That pride and distinctive style, the Highland uniform, was interpreted as arrogance by district HQ."[543] The Regiment did, at times, bend the rules and create interesting situations, as O'Connor admitted:

> I arranged for two of my junior officers to get on an upcoming serial on the parachute course in Edmonton. I may have bypassed Dist HQ. We got the two guys flown out west – Peter Danyluk and André Demers. Peter passed and got his wings; André later joined Regular Force, went on to command the 3rd Bn of the Van Doos, and then was promoted full colonel. As subalterns they proved to be daring but not too canny. The same duo, with Mark MacIntyre, decided to clean up the Armoury. They climbed onto the roof, enticing pigeons with bread and then shooting them with pellet guns. The police came, filed a report. Later, the District Commander, Colonel Jean Gervais was not pleased. When he found out two of them were in Edmonton at the airborne parachute depot, he was totally cheesed.[544]

The Regiment boasted three and eventually six field officers: Majors Bruce Bolton, Brent Cowan, Gary Dover, Gordon Lusk, Brian Lloyd, and Grant Rust. There was the challenge of keeping up with the incessant CO's demands. As one might expect, there was competition, good-natured rivalry and a few irritations. The deputy commanding officer was one of the COTC originals from 1968. Major Gary Donald Dover was a product of Montreal North. He was from Ville St Laurent, across the mountain and on the north side of the (then) *Canadair* runways. Getting home from Bleury on a Tuesday night was a torment for suburban officers; waking up in the last subway car in Atwater Terminus was invariably a risk.

Dover graduated from Loyola College and the Infantry School in Borden as a COTC officer. He served the Black Watch for two years then joined the British Army, attending RMA Sandhurst (where he won the sword of honour for academics), the Royal Military College at Shrivenham, and the Army Staff College at Camberley. It was intended he join the Imperial Black Watch, as clearly, the Canadian Regular battalions were doomed. To Colonel Bourne's surprise (and annoyance), Gary joined the Gurkhas. He served with the 2nd Bn King Edward VII's Own Gurkha Rifles (The Sirmoor Rifles) in Hong Kong and various peregrine spots. Dover was posted to Northern Ireland during the more violent years; then transferred to the British Army Intelligence Corps and at last retired, returning to Montreal in 1989. He rejoined the Black Watch and worked eventually under four COs – though not consecutively.[545] During the initial period, he was employed as an intelligence officer at FMC Headquarters, but paraded as a Black Watch officer. Later, he started his own furniture business. It was his need to initially work at FMC that created difficulties, given the directive that forbade Militia COs to be on call-out in a lower or equivalent rank.

As DCO Dover helped sort out the regimental bureaucratic backlog. Supported by Bolton, he wrote a proposal, *The Way Ahead*, to reorganize the unit's subsections as well as critical enterprises. This included the formation of a regimental foundation, the creation of a regimental secretary, systemizing the operations of the pipes and drums, organizing a business-like regimental kit shop ("before it was basically a box in Sandy Campbell's office"),[546] and a practical way to finance Highland gear for the soldiers and young officers. In the end, it proved a very shrewd proposal. The RHQ worked well enough in a decade where the Army, NATO, and budgets changed dramatically. Bolton encapsulated:

> Dan was a good CO, not quite totalitarian but determined, driven, headstrong, worked hard and fought a real rear guard – the regiment was in challenging times, budgets, man power and various projects, the unit fund was in difficulties and O'Connor had his DCO sort it out.[547]

Dover got used to the new Militia and his commanding officer's style, but field exercises were what he enjoyed best. A favourite reminiscence is the summer concentration of August 1992, conducted in CFB Gagetown. Dover commanded A Company; his umpires were suspicious Van Doos:

> We were ordered to do a frontal attack against Jerusalem Ridge, silly, really. We decided, with the CO's blessing, to do it with the pipers leading. The umpires were dumbfounded, then livid: "You can't tactically do this!" As the field commander [I] threatened them with disciplinary action if they stood in the way ... The attack went very well. It was cinema, the Regina Trench, Vimy ... and yes I know I just spent twenty years in the Brit Army ... perhaps a bit romantic, too regimental, but a ceremonial part of our history. Everyone loved it.[548]

It may not have helped Lieutenant Colonel O'Connor's career. These were stringent days for everybody. The CF was downsizing, quickly closing down its German bases in Lahr and Baden, and eliminating garrisons in Chilliwack and St Hubert (the old FMC Headquarters): "hacking left, right and centre, painful, savage cuts to the Army." Dover recalled: "Dan O'Connor got some of the best turnouts in decades; we could consistently average sixty on our parades and exercises … [but] he was nearly sacked a couple of times … and told District Commander to *shove-off* [sic] when the Regt was starved of man-days and couldn't pay soldiers."[549]

Lieutenant Colonel O'Connor tended to do everything to excess. What other CO could boast four degrees and seven children, while juggling a half-dozen more projects than any ordinary lawyer would handle, many of them *pro-bono* efforts for the Regiment and its members. By 1993, O'Connor decided he had no one to succeed him as he prepared to hand over command. There were the usual personality clashes, difficulties regarding civilian employers, and family demands, but a major reason was the regulation against Militia COs as *call-outs*, especially in FMC Headquarters. Three of the majors worked at FMC. The rule was exactingly enforced by Colonel Jean Gervais. Lieutenant Colonel O'Connor concluded his majors were not eligible and approached his superiors for assistance. "I asked the Army (through chain of command) to provide an interim CO for the Regiment." O'Connor handed over to Ian McCulloch in May 1993. It seemed the end of a brief Highland career, but as we shall see, it was simply the end of Volume I in the regimental life of a parachuting, mountaineering, bagpiping barrister – Lieutenant Colonel of The Black Watch (RHR) of Canada.

Notes to Part V

The Black Watch of Canada
and The Cold War, 1946–1992

1. BWA. CBC Radio Broadcast Charles Miller, Lamont Tilden 31 November 1945.
2. P/Major WO2 CW Stevens MMM CD/RJJ, 14 March 2013.
3. Hutchison, 248.
4. Bill Carlisle/RJJ, November 2013. See: TBWA Archives, Toronto.
5. Ibid., 249.
6. Anne Stewart, regimental archivist. RH 001, Spring 2001.
7. Ibid., 251. This was the last Black Watch visit by FM Wavell; he was succeeded by Gen Sir Neil Ritchie as Col of the Imperial Black Watch.
8. Hutchison, 254.
9. Losses included the Molson Family gift to the Regiment, a painting depicting *The Battle of May-sur-Orne July, 1944* by Sherriff Scott. Another Scott painting of SSM Craig was also destroyed as well as an oil showing "a piper marching resolutely under fire."
10. RH, No 98, October 1950, 23. Hereafter, RH.
11. RH, January 1951.
12. BWA. HSB Vol VII; RH, January 1951.
13. The Cdn force sailed 30 July 1950 and included three Canadian destroyers (HMCS *Cayuga, Athabascan, and Sioux*). The force was supported by the RCAF's 426 Sqn and a number of fighter pilots attached to the US Fifth Air Force. The UN Force was augmented by other UN countries in rapid succession: Australia, Belgium, Canada, Colombia, Ethiopia, France, Greece, Luxembourg, the Netherlands, New Zealand, the Philippines, Thailand and Turkey. The Union of South Africa provided air units; Denmark, India, Norway, and Sweden provided medical units. Italy provided a hospital, even though it was not a UN member.
14. WO Gordon Ritchie CD, *The Forgotten Flower; The Unofficial and Unauthorized History of the 1st Canadian Highland Battalion*, (Montreal: 2012), 17.
15. On 4 May 1951, the regiment mobilized two temporary Active Force companies designated, "E" and "F" Companies. "E" Company was reduced to nil strength upon its personnel being incorporated into the 1st Canadian Highland Battalion for service in Germany with the North Atlantic Treaty Organization. It was disbanded on 29 July 1953. "F" Company was initially used as a reinforcement pool for "E" Company. On 15 May 1952, it was reduced to nil strength, upon its personnel being absorbed by the 2nd Canadian Highland Battalion for service in Korea with the United Nations. "F" Company was disbanded on 29 July 1953.
16. See: Brian Cuthbertson, "The Black Watch Story: Atlantic Canada's Regiment 1951–1970"; Unpublished manuscript, September 2007. Hereafter, Cuthbertson. See also: Maj Robbie Robertson memoir *An ageless Company, My Time in the Canadian Infantry*; Sean Maloney, *War Without Battles: Canada's NATO Brigade in Germany*

1951–1993, (Toronto: 1996); and, extracts, *The Camp Gagetown Gazette, The Beaver; The Cdn Army Journal* (1950–1960).

17. Col A Craig Cameron, "The Heart and Soul of 1 RHC, May 1951 to June 1970", RH, No 018, Winter 2012.
18. Cameron, Ibid. For another list of nicknames from 1st and 2nd RHC, see: *Canada's Black Watch* 126–127.
19. DHH. Rutherford, Richard Lewis, Major (Acting Lt Col) – Officer, Order of the British Empire – Infantry (Queen's Own Cameron Highlanders of Canada and Brigade Major, 6 Canadian Infantry Brigade) – awarded as per *Canada Gazette* dated 15 December 1945 and CARO/6276 dated 18 December 1945.
20. Ibid.
21. Ibid.
22. 48th Highrs Davidson tartan and motto *Dileas Gu Brath* (Faithful Forever); Seaforths with MacKenzie tartan – *Cuiich'n Righ* (Help the King); Cdn Scottish, Hunting Stewart tartan, *Deas Gu Cath* (Ready for the Fray); and NNSH with Murray of Atholl tartan, *Soil Na Fear Fearil* (No Retreating Footsteps).
23. BWA. Manuscript, Sgt Don Roy, "Don Roy's Narrative," Part I, 13. Also, *Internet*: donroy@westman.wave.ca.
24. Cuthbertson, 2. Basic Training was carried out at or as near as possible to the location of the parent regiment by officers and NCOs of the new company augmented by personnel from the PPCLI and RCR. Four officers from these regiments were taken on strength of 1CHB: Capt John Hardy and Major Bob Graves were RCR; Lt George Finley and Capt Charles Barter were from the PPCLI.
25. Pte RD Cain, cited in Cuthbertson, 2.
26. Cain; Ibid., 4.
27. Ibid.
28. *The Canadian Bagpipe Band.*
29. Cameron, Ibid., 2 Part I, " WO Ken Mitchell MMM"; Asked why he laid a hand on an Officer, *Moose* replied: "I didn't know if I should salute or burp him." The Black Watch had received some "awfully young looking officers."
30. 1 CHB officers on board: Lts Hugger, Hamilton, Capt J Hardy (Adj); Major Boswell; Capt JG Pearson; Lt G Tibbetts, Capt C Glue (QM); CSM WL Frost; Pipe Major K Lee; Chaplain Major DR Anderson.
31. Hanover BUP, 26 July 1951.
32. RH, No 101, July 1953, 30.
33. RH, April 1952, 21.
34. RH, July 1953, 30.
35. Ibid., 13.
36. Col A Craig Cameron, "The Training of an adjutant", RH, No. 014, Winter 2010, 21. Finnie once shut down the Kentville Cleaners and taught the staff, including the bookkeeper how to press a kilt; he then supervised their practice until he was satisfied the soldiers' pleats would be correct.
37. Cuthbertson, 15.
38. John Marteinson, *We Stand On Guard: An Illustrated History of the Canadian Army* (Montreal: 1992), 376.
39. DHH. Parker, Harry Hugh Alexander, Major (Acting Lt Col) – Officer, Order of the British Empire – Lake Superior Regiment [Motor] Deputy Assistant Adjutant and Quartermaster-Gen, 4 Canadian Armoured Brigade – awarded as per *Canada Gazette* dated 15 December 1945 and CARO/6276 dated 18 December 1945.
40. Ibid.
41. Hutchison, 268.
42. 2 CHB comprised A Company The Black Watch (Montreal); B Coy, 48th Highlanders (Toronto), C Company The Seaforth Highlanders (Vancouver); D Company, The Canadian Scottish (Victoria) and Support Company, The North Nova Scotia Highlanders. Lt Col RM Ross; Maj G McLean Logan, Adj Capt Kitch Tracy. RSM Fred Blakeney; RQMS Sgt Hal Young. Pipe Major Duncan Rankin. See: Atlantic Branch Newsletter 4/99; and, TB/MB, 8 January 2014.
43. BWA. Don Roy Narrative, Part I, 16.
44. Ross Infantry (Queen's Own Cameron Highlanders of Canada) – awarded as per *Canada Gazette* dated 10 October 1942; confirmed by CARO/3580 dated 2 September 1943. On 30 August 1943, Ross was recommended for the MBE by Maj-Gen ELM Burns, GOC 2 Canadian Division: "Major Ross has displayed ability, energy and soldierly qualities of a very high order … he has carried out his duties with outstanding zeal and efficiency." This was followed, on 29 August 1943 by a recommendation for the Canada Medal.

45. Ibid.

46. DHH. *Canada Gazette* and CARO/6074, both dated 22 September 1945.

47. Lt Col WB MacLeod, memoirs.

48. BWA. Lt Col WJ Newlands, Memoir Notes, Hereafter, Newlands.

49. Cpl Mulligan recalls that: "each company of 1CHB was represented by a small section of men on the coronation parade, and that he is the last living member of the RHC contingent." TB/MB, 8 January 2014.

50. BWA. Ibid., Newlands, 3; MacLennan/RJJ. Harkes/RJJ, 1 November 2013. Hereafter, MacLennan. Harkes was with the advance party: "Each rifle company in turn was sent to Jasper Camp for a short period of simulated mountain training while the unit was in Wainwright."

51. "No one cuts (attacks) me with impunity" – the motto of The Black Watch; much like, in braid Scots: "Wha daur meddle wi' me" – "Who dares meddle with me."

52. The Commonwealth Division had three brigades: 25 Canadian brigade, 29 BR and 28 Commonwealth Bde.

53. Photograph 2 CHB WD, October 1953.

54. DHH. CHB Redesignated The Black Watch (RHR) of Canada CAO 76-2 358/B D/26 October 1953. Min of Defence, Brook Claxton announced publicly on 12 October 1953 the creation of a new peacetime division that would include new Regular battalions: The Black Watch, the Queens Own Rifles of Canada and the Canadian Guards.

55. The Defence Committee was to meet 6 October; 2 CHB sailed 8 October. BW required 48 hrs. See: Lt Col W (Bill) J Newlands, "Notes on 2nd Highland Bn / 2nd Bn Black Watch RHR May 1952–October 1955", unpublished article written September 2002, Kingston. Sources included Lt Col David Dodge (Maj, OC C Coy); written notes by Brig Don MacLennan (Major, OC D Coy and Bde Major 25 CIBG); Lt Col Harry Harkes (Maj OC A Coy); Brig Gordon Sellar (OC C and D Coys in Aldershot and Support Coy; LO1 US Corps in Korea); Maj Bill Stewart (Lt 10 Pl); and by Newlands (Capt, 2IC C Coy and OC D Coy).

56. Note: 2 RHC redesignated 2nd Bn The Black Watch (RHR) of Canada; authorized abbreviated designation is "2 RHC." Badges, headdress provided under seal in the custody of Capt JS Melbourne: 6 October 1953. There are more dramatic variations of this incident, both colourful and clandestine. USN *Marine Lynx* sailed at 1530, 8 October 1953.

57. WD 2 CHB 15 October 1953.

58. RHC Boxing Team won the Eastern Command Championship in March 1955; Sgt LT Mason was judged the best boxer.

59. BWA. Don Roy Narrative, Vol II, 1.

60. 2 CHB War Diary opened 11 October 1953; Pt I & Pt 2 Orders published each month. The command slate in Korea (as of 18 December 1953) listed: Majors GA Logan, Bn 2 IC; JC Clarke OC HQ Coy; Capt HJ Harkes, OC A Coy; Maj GA Donaldson, OC B Coy; Maj DWR Dodge, OC C Coy; Maj DS MacLennan OC D Coy; Capt Rev RW Peirce was padre; Capt HM Power, Adj; Lt AW Gemmill (RCOC) was RQM. Also: RH, January 1954, 27.

61. BWA. WD 2 RHC, Korea, 24 December 1953. 1 CHB began a War Diary in 1 October 1953 while Chatham Barracks Germany. The 1 CHB newspaper was "The Kilt and Sporran."

62. IS Fraser, *Atlantic Branch Newsletter* Vol 2012 No 3, November 2012, 2–3.

63. Sgt Gerry Steacy, correspondence, 5 October 2013; "The remaining three were Pte Elvin Sabean (26 December 1954), he died when a vehicle rolled over; and Ptes Clifford Earhart and Robert Christie (15 February 1954) … they both died on Active Service." 2nd Bn Black Watch soldiers who lost their lives while serving in Korea: Pte Ralph Elvin Turnbull (1 January 1954), Pte Robert Alan Christie (15 February 1954), Pte Albert Clifford Earhart (15 February 1954), Pte Clifford Joseph Laframboise (14 June 1954) and Pte Elvin Stanley Sabean (26 December 1954). Three Regular Force Black Watch soldiers lost their lives while serving with the United Nations Forces: Cpl VJ Perkin, 1 Black Watch (RHR) of C, ICSC (18 October 1965), Pte JPE Bernard, 2 Black Watch (RHR) of C, UNFICYP (9 July 1966) and Pte LA Lerue, 2 Black Watch (RHR) of C, UNFICYP (9 February 1970).

64. "I was A Coy Comd. During a defensive exercise Gen Allard ordered A Coy from one high position through a valley to another high position by night to see if such a move was practicable. The next morning the Gen wanted to observe the result of the move, which was positive. That is when we did our little mountain climbing!" Lt Col H Harkes/RJJ, 12 July 2012.

65. WD 2 RHC 24 October 1954.
66. AH Matheson, "Requiem for a regiment", *The Atlantic Advocate*, June 1970, 24–25.
67. BWA Seamark/Bourne February–March 1954 through to 1955.
68. Ibid., Bourne/Seamark Correspondence 22 January 1954 etc.
69. Bourne/Seamark 22 April 1954.
70. Ibid.
71. BWA. PPH/Bourne 22 February 1954. Re RHC Dress, Lt Col Tud Kaulbach notes: "During the Aldershot years, officers of 1st Bn wore 5/8-inch pips and dark Fox puttees whereas 2nd Bn officers wore 1-inch pips and light Fox puttees. Dress was standardized in 1965 Dress Instructions so that all Regular Army units wore 1-inch pips with light puttees and kilt but dark puttees with battle dress trousers." TB/MB, 8 January 2014.
72. HHA Parker to Bourne 30 January 1954 and, PPH/Bourne 1 March 1954.
73. PPH/Bourne 5 March 1954.
74. Ibid., The Payne incident, September 1954; 2/Lt ED Payne. Bourne was a driving force from Montreal regarding the conduct of a young officer arrested on a train. "Punishment meted out seems like a pretty tough one, but I guess it will set the necessary example." Seamark/Bourne 27 October 1954.
75. 13 November 1954; see RH No 113, July 1955, 31.
76. Report, 2 RHC for RH, July 1956, 31.
77. Seamark/Bourne September 1954.
78. BWA. Seamark/Bourne, 28 September 1954 and 15 February 1955. The presentation appears to have been at Camp Sussex where 1 RHC was briefly deployed from January to summer 1955; back to Aldershot by fall. See, BWA File "Letters between commanding officers 1st, 2nd, 3rd Bns BW 1954–1956."
79. Interview. Brig Gen DS MacLennan, 8 February 2010, St Sauveur QC.
80. BWA. Seamark to Bourne 19 February 1954; Also, Parker/Seamark/Bourne 30 January 1954 etc. By the millennium, the Black Watch sported seventeen orders of dress. In 2012 (150th Anniversary) there were fourteen orders of dress for officers (a half dozen simply added or removed one or two articles of dress), a lesser number for soldiers and NCOs, and a slightly higher number for the pipe band. The differences were not excessive in mode; several being simply: "with or without" (tie/glengarry/bonnet/sword/full vs. leather sporran. etc).
81. RH 125, July 1958 and BWA. Bourne /Parker 18 February1954.
82. BWA. Brig Gen DS MacLennan, "Some Personal Reminiscences", unpublished memoir, March 2002.
83. AH Matheson, "Requiem for a regiment", *The Atlantic Advocate*, June 1970, 24–25.
84. Ibid., 26.
85. Lt Col HJ Harkes/RJJ, 2 May 2012.
86. DHH. Watson, William De Norban, MC, Princess Patricia's Canadian Light Inf; *Canada Gazette* 18 March 1944 and CARO/4296, 1 April 1944; "in recognition of gallant and distinguished services in Italy."
87. Watson joined PPCLI on 12 March 1942 as a lieutenant; promoted captain, major; served as adjutant (December 1942 to 29 July 1943); wounded in Italy on 6 December 1943 (remained on duty); wounded again on 10 December 1943 and on 23 May 1944; struck off strength from the Princess Patricia's Canadian Light Infantry on 29 March 1945; commanding officer, North Shore (New Brunswick) Regiment from 4 November 1945 to 12 April 1946; commanding officer, 2nd Battalion, The Black Watch (Royal Highland Regiment) of Canada 1955 to 1958. Decorations include: DSO, MC, 1939–1945 Star, Italy Star, France and Germany Star, Centennial Medal, Canadian Volunteer Service Medal and Clasp, 1939–1945 War Medal, United Nations Cyprus Medal, and CD with Clasp. His Military Cross was an immediate award; initiated by Lt Col CB Ware, CO, PPCLI.
88. DHH. Watson, William de Norban, MC – Distinguished Service Order ; as per *Canada Gazette* dated 30 September 1944 and CARO/4986 dated 14 October 1944. Initiated by Lt Col CG Ware, PPCLI; supported by MajGen Chris Vokes, GOC 1 Cdn Div; endorsed by Lt Gen ELM Burns, 1 Cdn Corps; Lt Gen OWH Leese, GOC Eighth Army; approved, Gen Alexander.
89. Cpl FE Blakeney, BEM, WNS Regt, *Canada Gazette* 9 January 1943 and CARO/2983 4 January 1943. MM: awarded as per *Canada Gazette* and CARO/5283, both dated 20 January 1945.
90. Ibid.
91. Mathewson, Ibid.
92. Ibid.
93. Col G Logan/RJJ, Dorval, 10 November 2012; Correspondence, 25 November 2012.

94. Ibid.

95. DHist, *Canada Gazette* dated 6 May 1944 and CARO/4452 dated 10 May 1944; Mention in Despatches – awarded as per *Canada Gazette* dated 9 March 1946 and CARO/6431 dated 8 March 1946.

96. BWA. Don Roy II 10.

97. BWA. CHE Askwith Pers File. Evaluation 1 RHC, Maj SST Cantlie, 21 January 1942.

98. DHH. Askwith, CHE, Lieutenant. *Croix de Guerre avec Etoile d'Argent* (France), (HQ, 3 Cdn Inf Div). 8 January 1945; awarded as per CARO/5625 dated 28 April 1945.

99. Lt Col HJ Harkes/RJJ 7 October 2013.

100. Lt Col C Askwith, 84–85. The Black Rod informs Members of the House of Commons they are summoned to the Senate to hear the Speech from the Throne that opens every session of Parliament (or witness the Royal Assent that enacts bills). The title comes from the ebony stick carried, used to knock on the doors of the Commons.

101. *Gazette* 13 July 1957.

102. 1 RHC grognards are quick to point out that the fixation for boxing was a 2 RHC thing: "1 RHC was dominant in all other sports and attracted more interest in the military and civilian communities than did boxing." RFM/MB, 5 January 2014.

103. MGen Christie, 22 February 2013; RH April 1959, 37.

104. Capt BE Harper, RH 1959, Ibid.

105. Major-Gen WHS Macklin, "Do We Still Need the Militia?", *Saturday Night*, 9 June 1956.

106. DHH. Letter from Lt Gen GG Simonds, CGS, to the Gen Officers Commanding summarizing the findings of a conference to restructure the army Reserve force, "Organization, Administration and Training of the Canadian Army Reserve Force", HQC 2001-3/1 (CGS), 12 December 1952, D-Hist: 112.1 (D160).

107. Ibid.

108. Stephen J Harris, *Canadian Brass: The Makings of a Professional Amy, 1860–1939* (Toronto: 1988), 146–147. Hereafter, Harris. See: DHH. "Report of the Board of Officers on the Organization of the Canadian Army (Reserve Force), 14 January 1954, Part III, 140. See also, CP Stacey. The report stated that there was no requirement for a framework of brigades and divisions in peacetime. Recommendations included reducing the infantry and artillery components and increasing the number of armoured units (with armoured units also taking over the anti-tank role). The Board's recommendations were largely accepted in March 1954.

109. MGen Macklin, Ibid.

110. Interview Thomas Bourne; Maj W Stavert/RJJ, 2012.See also, Bourne, BW Part IV, Second World War Chapter 2. John Bourne was married to Joan Dawes in 1943 in St Helena Cathedral, Helena, Montana where his unit, 1st Special Service Force, a joint Canadian and American unit, was stationed.

111. SF Angus/RJJ, Hudson QC, Erin Ont, 2011, 2012. «Bourne's Cripples» included Egan Chambers, Darcy McGovern Alistair Pratt, Jim Macfarlane.

112. Cited by No. 34486 LCpl W Murray, 1 RHC. RH, October 1954, 33.

113. Hutchison, Ibid., 226.

114. RH, No. 11, January 1955, 33.

115. Ibid.

116. Brooke Claxton to Bourne 1 April 1954.

117. RH, January 1956, 35.

118. RH, January 1956.

119. RH, October 1956.

120. Internationally heralded, the colonel appeared in the globally syndicated column, *Ripley's Believe It or Not* : "Active soldier 70 years!"His brief resignation during the period of turmoil under Lt Col Strathy was passed over in Dist records. The CD represents forty-two years of service; additional service had been recognized with a Colonial Auxiliary Forces Officers' Decoration (VD) awarded in 1907.

121. TJK/MB, 8 January 2014. Kaulbach notes: "Only the officers of 2nd Bn were required to have brown leather gloves with 'dome' fasteners (snap fasteners were at a later time). Dress regulations only called for 'brown leather gloves'."

122. *The Montreal Gazette*, 31 August 1956. Cantlie died 30 August 1956. The Col put on no airs. Once, his grandson Steve Angus, bumped into him leaving the Mount Royal Hotel, a fashionable downtown auberge: "Hullo Stephen, I just stopped off to have a pee."

123. Ibid., 31 August 1956; 21 March 1957. Col Cantlie was first appointed Honorary Lt Col directly after the Great War in 1919, he succeeded Sir Montagu Allan as Honorary Col of the Regiment in 1951. GS Cantlie was the son of James Alexander Cantlie. His mother was Eleanor Simpson Stephen, sister of Lord Mount Stephen. Survived by one son, Lt Col SD Cantlie and four daughters, Mrs R Hampson, Mrs GS Lyman, Mrs IE Angus and Mrs HG Lafleur.

124. Chartier, 8 February 2013.

125. BW P/Majors during post-war period: P/Maj E Peden, 1945 (1 RHC); P/Maj R Hannah, 1939–1946, P/Maj FG Hinton, 1947–1951, P/Maj WJ Hannah CD, 1951–1967. When WO2 Gaudard retired as RQMS, WO2 FG Hinton took over.

126. NAC Annual Hist Report. Strength 3 RHC: thirty-eight Offrs, 10 WOs, thirty-eight Sr NCOs and two hundred ORs. As at 31 December 1956. Two parades: church parade 3 June 56; Philadelphia 8–11 June 1956: forty-four officers, 240 ORs. Three Camps in two locations. Farnham, and Valcartier in 1957; avg attendance seventy-three all ranks.

127. RHC used eight buses. Sgt (Lt Col) Victor Chartier's bus (which carried the Regimental Colours) broke down at Chazy NY: "We arrived late, as the USMC were changing the guard at Washington's Monument and Maj Gibb-Carsley wouldn't let us off the bus. But in the end, they had to wait for us – because we had the Colours."

128. The Philadelphia Inquirer, Montreal Gazette: 10, 11 June 1956. RH 118, October 1956, 22.

129. BWA. HSB Vol VIII, 1956–1960; also, CB Topp, The Legionary, June 1956, 34.

130. The Colour bearers were 2nd Lt SF Angus, Queen's Colour; and 2/Lt RN Southward, Regimental Colour. Pipe Major William Hannah; the saluting base was Strathcona Hall, in front of the Roddick Gates, McGill.

131. Maj W Stavert, Intvw/RJJ, 29 October 2012.

132. Red Hackle 1958 October, 9–11.

133. NAC Annual Hist Report. Special Parades: twelve Officers and 149 ORs. Considerable, given the 3 RHC strength in 1958 was thirty-one officers, twelve WOs, thirty Sr NCOs and 170 ORs. The other special parade was Bn Shoot at Mt Bruno in October, Camp was held in Gagetown 14–22 June 58 (eleven officers, fifty-five other ranks).

134. Account by Mr C Kennedy Allan, June 1956. See: BW Annual reports 1956, 1958. Red Hackle April 1957, 58.

135. Renamed John F Kennedy Stadium; subsequently demolished in 1992.

136. The gavel was carved in 1950 from an East Room window of the White House by the new architect, Lorenzo Winslow. Chapman, 84.

137. Col SF Angus, 3 RHC, later, RHC. Erin, 1 September 2012.

138. Ibid.

139. Col SF Angus et al; Erin, Ont, 1 September 2012.

140. Stavert, Ibid.

141. Blackader supervised both Regimental Funds and the Advisory Board; co-ordinating via an annual Regimental Conference and assisted by active committees: armoury, officers' messes, Black Watch Associations, Regimental Museums and Archives.

142. BWA, PPH, notes Gault Bio, RH April 1959.

143. Before the creation of The Black Watch Foundation, the Hon Col picked up the cost of the Luncheon, sometimes helped out by friends.

144. SF Angus, Ibid.

145. Sandy C/RJJ intvw, USC Montreal, September 1990.

146. GCA Tyler, The Lion Rampant, p. 83; BWA 008 3653-1 'National Survival Training'; RH 1959; also, Photos Lt SF Angus on Trg 1958 Hudson Heights.

147. Red Hackle January 1959; Harris et al.

148. John Boileau, "New defence units a bad idea –Territorial battalions in Canada are simply redundant", Halifax Daily News, 21 February 2007.

149. Cpl Alan MacAllister, Montreal Gazette, 26 September 1961.

150. See: George M Urquhart, The Changing Role of the Canadian Militia, 1945–1975 (Victoria: 1978), 76; and, Joseph T Jockel, Canada in NORAD, 1957–2007: A History. (Montreal: 2007) D.Hist: 112.043 (D2) The Commission on the Reorganization of the Canadian Army (Militia) Part 1, June 1964: "Canada, Department of National Defence, Special Commission on the Re-structurinq of the Reserves" (Ottawa: CCGP 1995), 6.

151. Chartier, 8 February 2013.
152. RH, January 1962, 40; in later years, Padre Emeritus James Armour was anxious to point out that, *the venerable* Berlis "was only forty-eight years old in 1959."
153. SFA/RJJ November 2012. "…they presented me with a book, *The Caughnawaga Indians and the St. Lawrence Seaway*, which had been constructed partly on some of the Band Lands, which they were upset about."
154. RHC Fastball Team, 1962 Champions: I Macauley, TW Litchfield, DJ McGovern, JF Macfarlane, AR Pryde, TE Price, WA Edge, RM Southward, WF Benson, EE Chambers, CD Cushing, LW Patrick, JAB Evans, JF Turcot, J Bonthron.
155. Ibid., *The Black Watch Story*, Chapter 5, 56.
156. MacLennan, 8 February 2010. Also: *Atlantic Branch Newsletter* 4/99. IA Kennedy/RJJ 6 December 2013: "… it had more to do with letting the town council and the people of Kentville know that is was the money from over two thousand BW soldiers that was keeping that 'village' afloat." 2 RHC left for NB; 1 RHC did not move to Gagetown until it returned from West Germany in 1962.
157. BWA. Don Roy II, 10.
158. The first large-scale exercise at CFB Gagetown was held in the summer of 1954 when the 3rd Cdn Inf Brigade conducted six weeks of training. In the summer of 1955, the 1st Cdn Inf Div carried out a complete formation exercise.
159. Mathewson, cited in RH 168, August 1970, 24.
160. "After the war, the Montreal Militia became petit bourgeoisie; the 1960s saw the last moneyed COs in Black Watch history. Nonetheless, the Gagetown mess was initially funded by the Montreal mess: Blackader called a dinner and a pile of cheques was produced, in fact, the Gagetown Black Watch mess was favoured by Westmount money …": intvw Lt Col Vic Chartier, Honorary Lt Col BW, Mtl, 2011.
161. Red Hackle July 1959.
162. The Guard included: Lt DS Manuel, 2/Lt RS McConnell, WOII GN Mills, WOII CB Laidlaw, Sgt AL Chipman and Sgt GS Berry. See RH January 1959, 37.
163. CC/MB, 5 January 2014.
164. Lt Col T Kaulbach/MB, 8 January 2014. To obtain Group 2, soldiers had to successfully complete another period of service and a specialty course (Machine Gunner, Mortarman, Anti-Tank Gunner, Infantry Signaller).
165. 260 km from Gagetown. Two separate mining disasters occurred in 1956 (thirty-nine deaths) and 1958 (seventy-five deaths) in different mines within the Springhill coalfield, near Springhill, Cumberland County, NS.
166. Including: the 1959 boxing championship and Eastern Command rifle shoot, a 2 RHC win. 1 RHC won 3 CIBG track and field meet, 2 RHC was 2nd. BW also won the first aid trophy competition.
167. Red Hackle July 1959; RH October 1959.
168. BWA. Col C Cameron, "The Training of an Adjutant, 1 RHC 1958–1959", unpublished monograph, 2010, 11. The charge was dropped and dismissed on the technicality that there was a conflict of commands.
169. Cuthbertson, 82.
170. CDQ 1960 *The Canadian Army Rifle Team in Bisley*, 49.
171. TB/MB, 8 January 2014
172. *Moro* fighters were Muslim guerrillas fighting the Japanese on the island of Mindanao. The word *Moro* is derived from the Spanish word for "Moors" and alludes to its Islamic inhabitants.
173. MacLennan, 2.
174. Ibid.
175. Ibid.
176. Ibid. Some BW officers argue this actually occurred during Div Parade at Blissville airstrip in 1958.
177. Ibid.
178. The Canadian brigade in West Germany was initially the 27th Brigade in 1952, replaced by 1st Cdn Inf Bde in 1953, by 2nd Cdn Inf Bde in 1955 and 4th Cdn Inf Bde in 1957. It became 4th Cdn Inf Bde Gp in 1958 and finally, 4 CMBG in 1 May 1968 – three years after the last RHC battalion left the theatre.
179. RH 134, October 1960, 36–37.
180. Ibid.
181. TK/RJJ, October 2014.
182. DHH. Leonard, William Clarke, Capt; Member, Order of the British Empire *Canada Gazette* dated 15 December 1945 and CARO/6276 dated 18 December 1945.

183. 1961 Sports. Boxing: 2 RHC beat Army (and Navy) opponents: ten of eleven bouts. 1 RHC Small Bore Team won Bde Championship and Hockey Championship Bde; 2 RHC 1961 Shooting Team won Hamilton-Leigh Competition plate.

184. RH, Winter, January 1961.

185. DHH. Teed, William Arthur, Capt – Mention in Despatches – Infantry (North Shore [New Brunswick] Regiment) – awarded as per *Canada Gazette* dated 9 March 1946 and CARO/6431 dated 8 March 1946.

186. RH January and April 1961, 28; RH January 1962. The 1 RHC team lost to the British team in the BAOR Championship at Sennelager; BWA Scrapbook.

187. Ibid.

188. The *Smoke Eaters* won their first Allan Cup in 1938 and won a trip to the 1939 world championship, which they won. They won another world championship in 1961 and another Allan Cup in 1962. Black Watch 1 RHC hockey team: Capt RF MacDonald, "First Bn Black Watch Hockey Team (1959–1965) – Highlights": 1959–1962 4 CIBG champions, Germany; 1963–1965 Camp Gagetown champions; 1964–1965 3 CIBG sports meet champions; Southern NB Sr League champions. RFM/RJJ December 2013; Oromocto Sports Hall of Fame – Inducted 6 November 2004.

189. *Red Hackle* April 1961; BWA Highland Scrapbook Vol IX 1958 – January 1963.

190. Simon Fowler (sic), *Canada's Black Watch* (Fredericton: 2008), 37.

191. Highland Scrap Book Vol X 1963–1965; some refs have Rothesay/BW affiliation official in December 1962.

192. RH 61, 16.

193. Maj WB Redpath, Maj Ian Eisenhardt, Lts LN Ferdon, JCD Tree, DM White. WO2 M Gurevitch and WO2 JJ Evans. Lt Col McGovern ordered a parade in Rosemount, and began to attract numbers of recruits from the area.

194. *Athletics and Alcohol.*

195. Advisory Board of the Regiment 1962: Brig KG Blackader; Lt Col GL Ogilvie, Gen Sir Neil Ritchie, Col JD Macpherson, Col IL Ibbotson, Col HM Wallis, Lt Col FM Mitchell, Col ALS Mills, Lt Col VE Traversy, Col WSM MacTier, Lt Col JW Knox, Col AT Howard, Lt Col JG Bourne, Col PP Hutchison, Lt Col JR McDougall, Maj HW Morgan, Lt Col WA Wood.

196. DHH. Forrest, Colin Grant, Corporal (A.6091) – Distinguished Conduct Medal. Royal Canadian Regiment; awarded as per *Canada Gazette* dated 18 March 1944 and CARO/4296 dated 1 April 1944. Forrest graduated from the Australian Army' Staff College in 1954 and transferred to the BW. Retired 1970 with the rank of Col. Died in Ottawa, 6 February 1998, aged seventy-seven.

197. RH 1962–63; photos Longueuil Camp June 1962.

198. RH October 1962, 142.

199. Hutchison, 302.

200. The subalterns with a one hundred man Royal Guard of Honour were Lts SF Angus, RC Gelston and JCD Tree.

201. Present at the dinner was CO 1st Black Watch of Scotland, Lt Col NGA Noble.

202. The Parade. COs: 1 RHC Lt Col WA Teed; 2 RHC Lt Col WC Leonard MBE, 3 RHC Lt Col D'Arcy J McGovern; RHC Depot, Maj GD Cochrane. Officiating Chaplains: Col The Rev JP Browne, MC, Dep Chaplain Gen; Maj The Rev JL Rand, Command Chaplain; Maj The Rev RJ Berlis, Regimental Chaplain. Guard Commanders: #1 Maj JG Mimms, #2 Maj MA McTague, MC #3 Maj DG Armstrong #4 Maj BE Harper. Colour Parties: 1 RHC: Lt GN Laird, Lt CJ Devaney; 2 RHC Lt RS McConnell, 2/Lt JS Forrest; 3 RHC Lt SF Angus, Lt RC Gelston; Old Colours 3 RHC, Lt LN Ferdon, Lt JAB Evans. RSMs: 1st Bn. WO1 RH Finnie; 2nd Bn WO1 TF Charters, 3rd Bn WO1 M Gurevitch; Regtl Depot WO1 GW Wooten. Bands: Dir of Music Regimental Band, Lt HC Eagles; Bandmaster 3rd Bn Sgt EJ Memess. Pipes and Drums: 2 RHC. Sgt M Phelan, 3 RHC. Sgt C Wilson. Pipe Majors: 1 RHC P/Maj W Magennis, 2 RHC P/Maj J Stewart, 3 RHC. P/Maj WJ Hannah. Officers Commanding Cadet Corps: The Black Watch Cadet Corps. Capt MA Hoey; Bishop's College School Cadet Corps, Cadet Major Robert McDonald; King's College School Cadet Corps, Cadet Major M Jardine; Oromocto High School Cadet Corps, Lt A Staples. The 3rd Bn Colour Party: Lt L Ferdon, Lt J Evans, Sgt G Betts, WO2 QR Miles, Sgt N Naughton. See BWA, BW Scrap Book Vol IX 135.

203. *The Gazette*, 9 June 1962; Hutchison 309–310.

204. Edgar Collard, *The Gazette*, 8 September 1973; see also this history, Volume 1, Part 2 Great War: Lieutenant Myer Tutzer Cohen MC, killed at Passchendaele in 1917. Previously, the daring subaltern became Scot by acclamation. 1st Cdn Div Comd, Sir Archibald Macdonell DSO: "I hereby confer on him the brevet rank of 'Mac' to

be used whenever he likes, but he must always be MacCohen in the kilt." 42nd WD, Topp Collection. Message, Macdonell to 42nd re Lt Cohen, 30 September 1917; D Morton; JSS Armour/RJJ: Rev Berlis: "He became just that, except the MC was now after his name, rather than before." See Part II WWI, 71.

205. Hutchison, 305–314.
206. BWA. Pers File WB Redpath.
207. Interviews Angus, Chartier; Ibid.
208. BWA, HSB Vol IX, "Governor Gens Remarks at Mess Dinner BW (RHR), 17 November 1962.
209. Klepak, *History BW* Chapt 1 12.
210. HSB Vol X, p21: The Congressional Record, 88th Congress. 1st Session, 1 April 1963; see also Hutchison, 102–112.
211. RH July 1963, 57; "The Black Watch at Quincy Mass" Ibid.
212. SF Angus/RJJ, correspondence, 9 September 2013. The "Pipe Band mess" is officially an annex of the WO and sergeants' mess, and considered the *Pipe Band's Canteen*. It has a chequered history: it was ordered shut down ("out of control") in the 1950s.
213. See: Samuel P Huntington, *The Soldier and the State: The Theory and Politics of Civil-Military Relations* (Cambridge: 1972), 83; also: Peter Haydon, "The Changing Nature of Canadian Civil-Military Relations in the Aftermath of the Cold War"; "The Soldier and the Canadian State: A Crisis in Civil-Military Relations?" *Proceedings of the Second Annual Conflict Studies Workshop, UNB*, eds. DA Charters and JB Wilson (Fredericton: Centre for Conflict Studies, 1996), 51.
214. See BW histories: RC Fetherstonhaugh, 312; CB Topp, 306–307; PP Hutchison, 139; and, HSB Vol XIII 1968–75.
215. BWA. HSB X, p 67: *The Tartan Times*, #30, October 1963. *The Times* was published until Miles retired in 1970.
216. RH, TT and BW Scrapbooks, October 1963.
217. BWA, HRH Scrap Book #10, 8.
218. BWA. See Regtl Hist and, "Chapter II The Second Battle of Mons", Col PPH subaltern's dairy HSB #10 87.
219. BWA. Pers. Lt Col VE Traversy, Correspondence 1948–1962; 1963.
220. Traversy: "… in spite of the fact that he has supported every type of Regimental affair from baseball-games to Royal Parades he has never been given more than a 'Joe's' post." BWA. Correspondence VET/Knox, 5 September 1963. Traversy saw the Vice post as a *buffer* between the Brig and Col Jim Knox.
221. The eight other officers who made up the Suttie Commission were Brigs FT Jenner, EG Eakins, IS Johnston, DG Cunningham, V de B Oland, Paul Triquet, JP Carrière and Lt Col BJ Legge.
222. Regimental taskings, see also Lt Col H Klepak RHC History 1962–87, manuscript BWA, 64, 100. Cols Angus and Macfarlane "agreed that the 1970–71 training year should include some slight IS [Internal Security] training for the most advance platoon of A Company … [new syllabus became] the basis for some limited specialized and very different training from the norm." Course devised by then Lts HP Klepak and GMAC Boire.
223. DHH; DND: The White Paper on Defence (1964), 19. Although the decision to reorganize the militia in 1964 was made by the Liberals to coincide with their plans for broader changes within the Department of National Defence, the idea appeared to have been inspired by several reports on defence matters that preceded it.
224. Lt Col Redpath tragically took his life at the Ritz Carleton Hotel over Christmas. He left a note and a Red Hackle, but the contents were never revealed by the two regimental officers (one was Lt Col MacFarlane) who were first to arrive.
225. BWA. Sharp File. Maj LH Brown BM 5 CIB; 31 July 1943; DHH, JW Sharp, MID *Canada Gazette* dated 13 November 1943.
226. Price/Angus intvws, scholastic file BCS. Col Price had unimpressive marks in BCS but his natural style made him a constant choice for Head Boy. The Head Master BCS felt Price represented the *ideal BCS graduate (grades aside)*. Price finished BCS and then received a BA Hist/Econ from Bishop's University; he joined his uncle, Tom MacDougall in 1959 "as a very junior clerk – his salary was $2400"; he rose to be President and then Chairman.
227. BWA. Ivor Watkins V44071, Certificate of Service, Royal Canadian Naval Volunteer Reserve 3 August 1942–12 September 1945. Watkins returned to Canada September 1944 after almost a year in Europe. He attended Sr NCO Provisional School in 1954, was appointed Quarter Master in 1955 as Acting Warrant Officer.
228. BWA. Watkins Record of Service. I Watkins D598100. Watkins retired and then worked with the BW Cadet Corps. He was commissioned as Lt and retired as a/major. Pres of BW Assn, and volunteer in BW Museum.

229. FLQ Bombs 1963: 23 February Incendiary bomb CKGM Radio; 8 March three incendiary bombs at three Mtl / Westmount Armouries; 1 April x3 bombs Mtl; April 6 bomb CBC Mtl; 3 May three bombs Mtl; 10 May bomb explodes at Black Watch RHR; 16 May bomb expl Montreal Refinery; 17 May 10x bombs in Westmount, five exploded; Sgt Maj Leja blown up; bomb at Cdn Forces Recruiting Centre; 20 May Victoria Day bomb; x75 sticks at Montreal armoury; 13 July explosion damages Queen Victoria monument in Quebec City; 22 August bomb damages CPR RR bridge at Kahnawake (south shore Montreal); 26 September armed robbery in Montreal by FLQ terrorists; 9 October, two bombs placed Montreal Post officers, disarmed. Also, "Firebomb found at BW armoury – FLQ terrorists", *Montreal Gazette* 16 July 1963.

230. FLQ 1964, 30 January raid FMR Armoury: x59 FN; x4 Brens; x34 SMG; x4 mortars; x2 rocket launchers; x3 grenades; x5 revolvers and 15300 rnds ammo. It was feared there were accomplices within the regiment.

231. FLQ attacks 1964: Raids 30 January and 20 February on DND Armouries; 29 August Intl Firearms (murder). Bombs: 21 April bomb (disarmed) Queen Victoria monument at McGill; 30 May bomb (disarmed) statue Boer War Quebec City. 2 November, bombs explode causing damage to CFCF radio/tv station tower an English media outlet.

232. Maj Gen FF Worthington rebuttal to Mtl Star 21 February 1964. "'…professional officers who have great influence in the Defence Department said the militia's reputation of being a club of social playboys …' [is a] savage crack that tarred all unfairly and so soon after the Second World War."

233. BW. WO M Cher, 18 October 2012.

234. BWA. HSB XII, 248. Correspondence Aird/Conway, 23 October 1964.

235. M Cher, 18 October 2012. WO M Cher joined in October 1963, serving with his brother, also a Sr NCO. John Cher transferred to the Service Bn in 1974; WO Mike Cher SOS to Supp Reserve, June 1971.

236. V Chartier/RJJ Interview, December 2012. "I was a kid at the time. I also felt it was fairer for Ivor Watkins to take over." There were transfers into 3 RHC: from the disbanded Victoria Rifles. "I became a staff sergeant and took a Sr NCO course on the orders of RSM Ablett or no promotion."

237. Klepak, 65.

238. Officers active in 3 RHC circa 1967 were: CO, Lt Col TE Price retired May 1967; Lt Col JIB Macfarlane 1967–70. Majors SF Angus, HG Mitchell, JD Nicholson; Captains JAB Evans, LN Ferdon, MA Fraser, SRG MacLeod, TM Miller, WR Sewell, Lorne H Walls; Lieutenants GW Carter, HM Darney, R Ehrhardt, HF Hauschild, RF Starzynski; RSM WO1 I Watkins. OC Support Company, Major JD Nicholson (formerly 11 Regt, RC Sigs) resigned, and Major Graham Mitchell (formerly 37 Field Regt) also resigned, was transferred to District HQ and was seconded to RCH as 2 IC. See: BWA. JD Nicholson to Lt Col JIB Macfarlane, 9 September 1969.

239. On 13 September 1964, forty-one veterans of 13th Bn CEF attended a reunion luncheon at the armoury; the annual reunion dinner was held 31 October 1964, the guest of honour was Lt Gen RW Moncel DSO OBE CD, Comptroller Gen of the Canadian Forces.

240. BWA. 73rd Bn CEF Files; handwritten 73rd CEF reunion dinner awards, stats and nominal roll: see HSB Vol 1 42.

241. BWA. IL Ibbotson File. Ibbotson/Davis 14 March 1943. On 11 November, five surviving members managed the Cenotaph, veterans of the Somme and Vimy. Thirteen showed up for the anniversary.

242. BWA. Highland Scrap Book Vol XI 1965–1968. The 'old' UK and US alphabets were essentially the same. The new NATO alphabet was adopted to make pronunciation simpler for non-English speaking members of the Alliance. BWA. HSB Vol x1 p42; PPH, RH; In 1968, on the 52nd Anniversary, thirty veterans appeared at Queen's Hotel.

243. Bombings, 1965: 30 April, bomb expl *Place Victoria*; 1 May bomb expl outside US Consul; 14 June bomb expl at RCMP HQ, Quebec City; 1 July bomb expl Westmount City Hall; 2 July bomb expl CKTS Radio, Sherbrooke; 15 July, raid on la Macaza base, hostage; 28 July bomb expl HQ CIBC Bank, Montreal; 2 August 2x bombs CP RR bridge/ tracks; 1 November bomb Palais du Commerce.

244. Acts: 1966. 5 May 1966, bomb exploded in a shoe factory; one killed; 22 May bomb expl *Dominion Textile,* Drummondville; 3 June bomb expl *Centre Paul Sauvé* Lib Party convention; 14 July bomb expl – one killed at *Dominion Textile*, Mtl. 1967. 1 January bomb expl mail box outside Mtl *American Trust*; 12 September 2x bombs at Macdonald High School, an English secondary school; 11 May bomb expl at the *7Up* plant; 24 May bomb US Consul, Mtl; 25 September bomb damage John A Macdonald statue in Dominion Square; 14 October bomb expl HQ *Union Nationale* party; 12 November 2x bombs *Eaton's* dept store; 31 December 4x bombs around Montreal.

245. FMC (*Force Mobile Command*) was commanded by a Lt Gen, responsible for all army ground forces in Canada. It was formed to maintain combat-ready land and tactical air forces capable of rapid deployment for NATO service in Europe to United Nations and other peace-keeping operations. Tactical Air Group would consist of CF-5 tactical ground-support, *Buffalo* transport aircraft, heavy and light helicopters.

246. "My first St Andrew's Ball was a great time. The adjutant, 'Herbie' Hauschild, a German who mirrored all the clichés, fixed me up with a young lady who needed a date. We did Scottish dancing practises together and danced well at the Ball." Correspondence; GMACB/RJJ, October 1999.

247. *Montreal Star* 16 November 1966.

248. *The Hasty Pudding Gazette*, Vol 1, No 1, Fall 1966.

249. BWA. Price File. Correspondence TW Price / JW Knox, 5 September 1967. RHC had been a "regional reserve" but now was ordered into FMC, insignia and all.

250. BWA Pers File TE Price TD 47386. Price requested early retirement on 14 September 1967 because of business commitments.

251. Lt Col J Macfarlane, Intvw Pointe-Claire, May 2009.

252. Capt Rev JSS Armour, correspondence/intvw June–December 2012.

253. 3 RHC HQ: 2 IC Maj HG Mitchell [later appointed CO of RCH] ; ADJ Capt WR Sewell; Trg Offr Maj SF Angus OC B Coy: Maj LN Ferdon; OC Strike Company: Maj JD Nicholson; OC A Coy: Maj JAB Evans ; RQM Capt TM Miller; Padre: Capt SA Hayes; OC Spt Coy: Lt HF Hauschild; 2 IC B Coy RF Starzynski; 2 IC Spt Coy 2/Lt GMAC Boire; 2 IC A Coy 2/Lt GD Dover; Pl Comd 2/Lt Ehrhardt; 2/Lts Lloyd; Pompeo; McMartin; BHQ 2/Lt HP Klepak.

254. Larry McInnis, "After regular force cuts, it's militia's turn", *Gazette* 3 October 1969.

255. <u>Canadian Army strength</u>. At the end of the Korean War (July 1953) there were 48,458 officers and men in the Canadian Army active force; the strength of the Canadian Army Reserve force was 7,629 officers and 39,243 men. In 1960, 47,000 Regulars, 40,000 Militia; by 1964, the strength was 49,800 Regulars, 46,000 Militia. By 1970, the *unified* CF totaled 98,000 – the Army strength was 46,000 Regulars. By the date of the Black Watch presentation of Colours (2009), the CF had a strength of apx 68,000, plus 27,000 Reservists (Militia), 5000 Rangers, and 19,000 supplementary Reserves. By the fall of 2014, the establishment of the Army Reserve was 26,000 (a "funded strength" of 19,471, or 70% of establishment). According to Solomon, Militia Strength was 33,704 in 1947. By 1964, 32,000 and reduced to 19,344 by 1970 (post-Unification). Strength in 1979 was 15,000; 1985, 15,500; 1995, 18,347; 2001, 14,600; 2008, 17,293; 2010, 21,000; 2014, circa 19,000. See: DHH; *Canada Year Book* 1945–1980; David N. Solomon. "Sociological Research in Military Organizations" in *Canadian Journal of Economics and Political Science*. Vol XX, No. 4, Nov 1954 and, BGen D Patterson /RJJ Nov 2014.

256. Montreal: Cdn Grenadier Guards, Black Watch, Royal Montreal Regiment; French Cdn Regts: Régiment de Maisonneuve; Fusiliers du Mont-Royal and 4th Battalion Royal 22e Régiment with the 6th Battalion Royal 22e Régiment just east of Montreal in Ste-Hyacinthe. The Royal Canadian Hussars were an "English" unit as were 2nd Field Artillery and 3rd Field Engineers but all were quickly becoming bilingual. The period also featured the first year of revised General Military Training (GMT) courses. Summer camp (30 June–6 July 1968) was held at CFB Valcartier.

257. BWA Knox Files. Memorandum 22 August 1967.

258. Col SF Angus, Erin, 1 March 2013.

259. Buzz Bourdon, "Col Gordon Harper Sellar, Army Officer and Horseman 1923–2004", *The Globe and Mail,* 17 December 2004, S9. Sellar scouted forward with Majors Ross Ellis and George Hees (later a Tory cabinet minister), going from trench to trench, talking to the exhausted men. Sellar described that walk as the "longest of my life." He took command 16 April 1963.

260. AMF (L) – ACE Mobile Force (Land component). There was also AMF(A) air force component. AMF was responsible for both flanks of NATO; the Cdn battle group was exempt fm the southern flank (Turkey).

261. RH 1966; Klepak Ibid.

262. Pde followed by an all ranks garden party, two "smokers" and three formal balls. Church parades were held, fol by march past – Col Knox took the salute. Key pers: Gd commanders and their Gd sergeants-major: Escort to the Colour, Major J Kinnear and WO2 HE Firby; No.2 Guard, Major CC Watt and WO2 JT Byrne; No.3 Guard, Capt KL Wollison; WO2 GR Pyatt; No.4 Guard, Capt JW Cummings; WO2 DW Gillrie; No.5 Guard, Capt HFH Pullen and WO2 RR Blackwell; No.6 Guard, Capt B Cuthbertson and WO2 JF MacIntyre. The RSM was WO1 VI Lawson.

263. RH 1965/66; officers' mess notes 1 October 1965–30 September 1966; "B" and "C" Companies were the first equipped.
264. Lt Col IA Kennedy/RJJ, 11 June 12. In rebuttal to Kennedy, Lt Col Kaulbach noted: "The fact that he could box 'worth a damn' is corroborated by his KO-ing three opponents (all with his left hook) in eliminations leading to the final competition described." TK/MB, 8 January 2014. Snow re-mustered to Cook in 1984 from which MOC he retired a lean, fit Warrant Officer." WO Snow was elected president of the Atlantic Branch in 2011.
265. TK/RJJ, October 2014: "Eastern command rifle championships were held at Bedford or Gagetown. The national championships were (and still are) conducted at Connaught Range."
266. Buzz Bourdon, "Gordon Sellar, Army Officer and Horseman 1923–2004," *The Globe and Mail*, 17 December 2004, 59.
267. Klepak, Ibid., 16. Prior to this, 1 RHC participated in a Comd AMFL conference at Bardafoss, Norway in 1964. The BW group consisted of the CO, 4 Majors, the MO and the Recce platoon complete with all its jeeps and trailers including Dyna-track rugged terrain vehicle provided by the US Marine Corps. RFM, CC/MB, 5 January 2014. Begun in 1961, the exchange program between the BW/RHR and RHC was an important program to enhance relations between the two regiments. RHC officers who served with 1BW included Lieutenants BC Cuthberson, RP Alden, MG O'Brien and RI Burns. BW officers who served in 1RHC were Gary Garford-Bless and JF Arbuthnott.
268. This Force was commanded by CO 1 RHC and included from 1 RHC the Bn HQ operational element, the Bn Recce Pl, two Rifle Coys, Recce Sqn of the Armoured Regt, 1 RHC's support Lt Arty Bty, the support Tp from the Fd Sqn, a composite Pl from the Svc Bn, and one aircraft from the RCHA AOP Flt.
269. Lt Col Sellar, *Montreal Gazette* 4 June 1966; also, BWA. Brig Gen GH Sellar, *Memoirs*.
270. Capt RF MacDonald recalls: "One of the highlights of the Norway deployment was the visit to the BW of the new King of Norway. At the time, the Bn was doing user trials on a new *Ski-doo*, made by *Bombardier*. I was detailed to take the King on a demonstration drive. He was very impressed with the concept but thought the machine was under-powered. I reminded him how big a man he was." RFM/MB, 31 December 2013.
271. Ibid., Klepak Hist, 17.
272. *Montreal Gazette* / Sellar, Ibid. Promoted to brigadier general in 1972, Sellar served three years in Ottawa as Director-Gen of Land Forces Reserves and Cadets and then retired to Kingston. Over the next thirty years, the brigadier spent much of his time indulging his life-long love of horses, participating in horse shows in Canada and the United States. Bourdon, Ibid.
273. Greg Thompson, Minister for Veterans Affairs worked with veterans to help with claims for the compensation package. On 12 September 2007, the Govt of Canada offered a one-time ex gratia payment of $20,000 as the compensation package for Agent Orange exposure at CFB Gagetown. On 12 July 2005, Merchant Law Group LLP on behalf of over eleven hundred Canadian veterans and civilians who were living in and around the CFB Gagetown filed a lawsuit to pursue class action litigation concerning Agent Orange and Agent Purple with the Federal Court of Canada. On 4 August 2009, the case was rejected by the court due to lack of evidence.
274. Ibid.
275. Ibid.
276. This included the *MGR-1 Honest John* rocket – the first nuclear-capable surface-to-surface missile in the US arsenal with a 30 km range and 20 Kt or 1500 lb warhead.
277. Ibid., 2 RHC 1963 strength in Germany was 786; of these, 363 were married, with 747 children.
278. BWA. Pers DA McAlpine. Correspondence: Capt DA McAlpine/PPH 7 March 1945.
279. RH April 1964.
280. BWA. DA McAlpine Pers File. Correspondence: JMM/PPH 10 July 1941 (to August); PPH War Diary 1941.
281. BWA. Ibid. Donald Ian joined 1 RHC in 1943; seconded to RRC. His patrols received attention: see: Ross Munro, *Montreal Star* 25 August 1944; Allen Kent, *Toronto Telegram*, 29 September 1944.
282. Simon Falconer (sic), "Canada's Black Watch" 2008.
283. Duncan McAlpine: born in Montreal, McGill COTC, commissioned BW at 17, 1942. An original offr in 2 RHC, transf 1 RHC, Italy Second World War; NATO HQ 1959; 1963 Lt Col and CO 2 RHC, Fort St Louis, W Germany (BAOR). Peace-keeping Cyprus 1965; Director Personnel Devel; BGen 1970, comd, CFB Gagetown. Asst Dep Minister (Mil) Personnel. 1973 comd Cdn military contingent to International Commission for Control and Supervision (ICCS) in Vietnam. MGen 1974, Chief of Pers Development; posted to Lahr.1975–1976 McAlpine was Commander, Canadian Forces Europe. Ottawa 1977, appointed Asst Dep Min (Pers) as LtGen. Appt

Hon Lt Col of The Black Watch (RHR) in 1996 and Hon Col May 2000. D 2010. Hosted HRH The Prince of Wales, presentation new Colours in November 2009.

284. TK/MB, 8 January 2014; See also John Marteinson, *We Stand On Guard* (Toronto: 1992), 395.

285. 1964, 1965 team included: Sgt TJ Goodison Cpls GWE Dobson, Cpl R Lavigne, LCpl GC Ross; Ptes D Keddie; JBS Showell, J Vanier, and FR Lowe.

286. CB Topp, "The Black Watch at Sanctuary Wood", *Weekend* Magazine No24, 1966 p36–37. Wollen was perhaps more famous for "The Battle of Quatre Bras" which was acquired by the Imperial Black Watch in the fall of 1950.

287. McAlpine, RH, Ibid. "Hall-Humpherson was the rock on which the excellent unit field operation rested." Harkes/RJJ, 1 November 2013.

288. BWA. Capt JWB Hamilton "Cyprus Incidents" 12 November 2001.

289. Don Roy, *Memoirs*, Vol II, 10.

290. Lt Col McAlpine returned to Montreal as a senior staff officer at "Mobile Command", the recently created *Army Headquarters* at St Hubert airbase, 8 km east of the city.

291. DHH. Lt HJ Harkes, Royal Regiment of Canada; awarded MC as per *Canada Gazette* dated 10 November 1945 and CARO/6193 dated 12 November 1945. Corrections to data in above citation after intvw with Lt Col Harkes 5 October 2013.

292. "My appointment in AHQ was as Military Assistant to The Quartermaster Gen and later as G2 Equip in The Directorate of Infantry just prior posting to 2 RHC." Harkes/RJJ, 1 November 2013.

293. "The [Montreal] Black Watch was kind to me; Cols Jim Knox, Price and Bourne were friends. As COs we went down to Montreal and got on well with the officers of the 3rd Battalion." H Harkes/RJJ 2 May 2012.

294. Col Ian Fraser, "In Memory of Don Reekie" *BW Assoc Atlantic Branch Newsletter*, Vol 2012 No 2, August 2012.

295. RSM 2 RHC 1966–1970; 2 RCR 1970–1971; and Canadian Airborne Regiment 1976–1978; Reserves, RSM Western Area 1978–1981. Nova Scotia tattoo 1981–2010 as Assistant Director; died 4 May 2012. "The incredible international reputation the Tattoo enjoys is due in no small measure to the impact Don Reekie had on the production." Ian Fraser, Ibid. and, RH "Don Reekie" Summer 2012, No. 019, 10. See also: Ian Fraser, BW Assoc Atlantic Branch Newsletter "In Memory of Don Reekie" Vol 2012 No 2, August 2012.

296. Parody of the popular "The Ballad of the Green Berets" written by Robin Moore and S/Sgt Barry Sadler. Patriotic hit song 1966, became a major hit, reaching No. 1 for five weeks.

297. "Battle of the Blue Beret". The battalion paymaster, Capt Larry Donohue, wrote the words.

298. Lt Col Newlands/RJJ, Mtl, September 2012 and 18 September 2013. MajGen McAlpine/Klepak 30 January 1987. WO1 Blackwell was succeeded by WO1 Pyatt on 12 July 1967. The formal handover between Sellar and Newlands took place later.

299. A Company 2 RHC, with some help from other companies, contributed 148 personnel as performers in four of the thirteen scenes in the CF Tattoo.

300. Philip Smith, *Montreal Star*; *Weekend* No 35, 1967. The DND Centennial Planning Staff was led by Brig C Arnold Peck. Col Fraser sandwiched yet another production: the first Nova Scotia Tattoo in 1979. Marking the first International Gathering of the Clans outside Scotland. Opened by HM The Queen Mother, it became an annual event. In 2006, it was awarded royal designation by Queen Elizabeth II on her 80th birthday. Ian Fraser was in charge until 2007, when he stepped aside as executive head, but remained as Artistic Director of the show. By century's end, Ian Fraser had authored books, plays and directed over a thousand martial shows.

301. BWA: HSB Vol X 91; as sung in the messes of all three battalions.

302. Brig Gen James S Cox OMM PhD, *The RCR Journal*, Regimental History "The Young Officer", memoirs circa 1965. "… at that time, an officer was expected to support the mess by running up a big mess bill – and paying it off regularly … Happy Hours invariably lasted until at least 2100, when most married officers had to go home, because their wives had come to get them and were standing in the mess foyer (women were not allowed in the bar)."

303. Ibid.; Officer Cadets were delighted by a pay raise in 1965: "… to $355 a month. By the time I was Lt it was almost $500 a month, $5 of which was siphoned off in a pay assignment to pay for regimental dress accoutrements … Officers carried ashplant walking sticks. Junior officers ALWAYS had to have their platoon commander's notebook on them."

304. The First Battalion had just completed Ex *White Caribou*, D Company, 2 RHC was the enemy force.

305. On Parade as well: Maj BE Harper CD, Cadet Corps Chief Instructors: Maj JT Gibson CD Montreal; Cadet Offr RH Finnie CD Kings College Edgehill; Capt ND Honeyman Rothesay Collegiate; Capt MO Noland, Oromocto; Maj SF Abbott CD, BCS.

306. Carlisle Ibid.

307. RH December 1967.

308. BW Guards 1967 Parade: one from Depot, six from 1st Bn, four from 2nd Bn; two from 3rd Bn, and one each from two Black Watch Cadet Corps: Montreal and Bishop's College School. On Parade: Cadet Chief Instructors: Maj JT Gibson CD, BW RHC Cadet Corps; Capt RH Finnie CD, King's College School; Capt ND Honeyman, Rothesay Collegiate; Capt MO Nowlan, Oromocto HS; Maj SF Abbott CD, Bishop's College School.

309. BWA. Highland Scrap Book Vol XI, 1965–1968. Headlines in Montreal and Fredericton papers: "Limited Seating at Black Watch Review", 11 July 1967. It was also the thirtieth anniversary of the appointment of HM Queen Elizabeth the Queen Mother as Colonel-in-Chief. King George the Sixth appointed her to succeed her father-in-law, King George the Fifth, as Colonel-in-Chief of The Black Watch; it was her twentieth as Colonel-in-Chief of the Canadian Black Watch.

310. RH December 1967; The Centennial Regimental Cairn was later relocated to the Town of Oromocto (just beside CFB Gagetown) it honours the members of 1st and 2nd Battalions of the Black Watch who contributed extensively to the community from 1954 to 1970.

311. Cdn Forces Bulletin. Vol 1 No 5, December 1966.

312. BWA Knox File. Sherry Luncheon notes, 22 December 1966. Col Rowley/Col Knox et al. Gen Anderson had forecast that thirteen Inf Bns would be reduced to twelve; the "Regimental System" was under review; battalions in NATO (Germany) would rotate on a man-for-man basis. "A massive re-badging would be required."

313. BWA Knox Correspondence H de M Molson /Knox 20, 23 January 1967.

314. The initial exploratory session included Senator Hartland Molson, Brigs KG Blackader, JH Price and JA Nesbitt, Cols JG Bourne, VE Traversy, JPG Kemp, JW Sharp, JW Eaton, and Neopole. The Regimental Advisory Board circa 1966–1967 comprised: Brig KG Blackader CBE, DSO, MC (Chair); Brig. WH Seamark (Vice Chair); Col VE Traversy (Secretary) and Members: Cols GL Ogilvie, JB Macpherson MC, HM Wallis DSO, OBE, MC, ALS Mills DSO, WSM MacTier MC, AT Howard OBE, PP Hutchison, IL Ibbotson, FM Mitchell, HW Morgan, Gen Sir Neil Ritchie GBE, KCB, DSO, MC, JW Knox MBE, JG Bourne, JME Clarkson MC (1 RHC), WC Leonard, MBE (2 RHC) and WA Wood (3 RHC).

315. BWA Knox Correspondence, Memo 19 January 1967 BWA; and, H de M Molson/Knox, 20 January 1967.

316. BWA Ibid.

317. The Army switched its combat arms basic training to a regional system circa 1960/61, which saw all combat arms recruits from the Atlantic Provinces undergo basic recruit training at The Black Watch Depot. Geographic location had probably more to do with this than the standard of training.

318. BWA Ibid. At the time of The Black Watch meetings, DND reported the strength of 1 RHC was 683 vs authorized strength of 792; 2 RHC was above str: 679 vs 623. The 1 Cdn Gds held 500 vs 655 auth; 2 Cdn Gds 546 vs 792. The 1st and 2nd QOR were 180 and 145 men down, respectively; 1 RCR and 2 RCR, serving in Cyprus and Germany were kept up to strength as was 1 PPCLI. 2 PPCLI, in Canada, was two hundred men down. Also: Knox Files. Model letter to Min of Nat Defence. Undated.

319. Stavert, Ibid. Motzfeldt driving to Hubert Welsford's funeral.

320. PPH, correspondence to RH, No. 160, December 1967.

321. RH, No 015, Summer, 2010.

322. Lt Col IA Kennedy/RJJ February 2013. Re Harkes: "He would have had more promotions but fell afoul of fools in higher places and unfortunately told them so."

323. A Keith Cameron, "The Royal Canadian Navy and the Unification Crisis", JA Boutilier, *RCN in Retrospect 1910–1968*, 340.

324. The "Best" List (mainly created by A Coy, 2 RHC also included: Best Looking – Pte Paul Melanson, Best Soldier – WO2 Ron MacKinnon, Best Athlete – Cpl Dunc McLean, Best Highland Dancer – Cpl Danny Desmond, Best Instructor – Sgt John Marr, Best Drinker – Pte Brian Bourn, Best Barrack Room Lawyer – Pte Len Lancaster, Best Hockey Player – Pte Carl Aymar, Best Marksman – Cpl Ken Reid, Best Apple Polisher – Pte Cecil Hooper.

325. Last Recruit Course BW Depot: February 1968: sixty-three Cpls qualified Sr NCO; forty-six BW candidates, sixteen from RCD, one from CFB Chatham. 10 July 1968, No 185 Squad: twenty-six RCA recruits, six RCASC,

one RCEME and one BW recruit. The depot stated training soldiers from other Combat Arms trades in 1960. The first (103 squad) to go through from January to June 1960 had a mixed squad of twenty-five Black Watch and twenty RC Signals. TB/MB, 8 January 2014.

326. See Black Watch Hist Pt IV, Second World War, Bourne, Chapt 2.

327. Robertson/RJJ Intview, Erin, Ont 19 September 2012.

328. The group included 2/Lts Michael Boire, Gary Dover, Brian Lloyd, Jack Pompeo; George Carter, Bruce McMartin, and Hal Klepak.

329. Reunion dinner, 2 November 1968. The Head Table, LtoR: Cols JME Clarkson MC, JIB Macfarlane, AT Howard OBE, Brig CB Topp CBE DSO MC, Lt Col GS Morrison, Brig WC Leonard MBE, Col HM Wallis DSO MBE MC, Col JBJ Archambault; Gen Sir Neil Ritchie GBE KCB DSO MC, The Hon Leo Cadieux, Col JW Knox MBE, Lt Col JG Bourne, MajGen JPE Bernatchez CBE DSO, Brig WH Seamark, Brig JH Nesbitt, Brig JH Price OBE MC, Col IL Ibbotson, Maj WJ Cummings, Brig JG Weir OBE, Lt Col JW Sharp. The "legs" were entitles *13th; 42nd;* and *73rd.* Col Paul Hutchison fractured his pelvis in September 1968 and could not attend.

330. BWA. Knox Files. "Speech by the Hon Leo Cadieux at the regimental reunion dinner Sat, 2 November 1968."

331. Brig Doucet later claimed the speech had been inadvertently *switched* at the last moment. One stern glance cut short a musical attempt: "When the speech was going on and we all started to listen to the threat of Soviet submarines off of our East Coast, the three of us began to sing 'We all live in a yellow submarine'. Col Bourne heard us and if looks could kill we would have been hanging from the sergeants' mess balcony. Actually, it was fun." Lt Col WR Sewell/RJJ 10 December 2013.

332. Originally made by John Cornfute in 1772. The *Quaich* is a two handed cup – the Cornfute design in silver or pewter.

333. In fact, the statue should have been presented to the citizens of St-Martin-sur-Orne, where most of 1 RHC's fighting took place.

334. Lt Col TJ Kaulbach/MB, 8 January 2014.

335. Ibid. Maj TJ Kaulbach commanded C Company of 2 RCR from February 1969 to July 1970: "My company was about 70 percent RCR, 15 percent Black Watch and 15 percent Guards and QOR of C. In July 1970 3 Mech CDO was formed of 60 percent 2 RCR and 40 percent 1PPCLI. The name and colours of 2 RCR and 1PPCLI were repatriated to Gagetown and Winnipeg respectively. 3Mech CDO went to Baden Soellingen and the same percentages of Regimental representation prevailed, that is, 15% were former Black Watch Snr NCO's and men."

336. Lt Col HJ Harkes/RJJ 2 May 2012.

337. HSB Vol IX, p261; twenty-four Ontario, one Quebec; three BC, one Alberta, one New Brunswick; seven Newfoundland, twenty Nova Scotia. Top recruits 1965. White Belt winners: KA May, Ile Perot Quebec; RJ O'Callaghan, Sydney NS; F Howard-Smith, Kars Ontario. 1966 top Recruits: HA McLeod Kars Ontario; GJ LePage Halifax NB; NL Hamilton, Georgetown Ont. 1962. Graduates No 121 Squad, the year's visitors included The Duke of Devonshire. Col Knox accompanied Blackader. Three Squads were graduated in 1962; Blackader presented silver spoons to the top marksmen. Several Depot soldier played for the battalion teams.

338. BWA. HSB. Vol IX; see also: Knox File. Lt Col WJ Newlands/Knox, 15 August 1967. Newlands: "Of forty officers, twenty-eight are not Maritimers, of forty-nine WOs, Staff Sgts, Sgts, thirty are non Maritimers and of 611 Cpls and Ptes, only 122 are non Maritimers." Lt Col HJ Harkes/Knox 3 August 1967: "Approximately 68 percent of 2 RHC consists of Atlantic Province personnel."

339. Lt Col WJ Newlands/Knox, 15 August 1967.

340. BWA. HSB Vol IX, Knox File; Newlands, August 1967; and, Maj GM Boire/RJJ 17 November 2012.

341. Ibid., Harkes/Newlands/Knox/Kaulbach.

342. BWA, DHH. Bourne Papers; Min Def Cadieux/Bourne 15 September 1969. BWA 69 HSB 44, Bourne 23 September 1969 HSB, 44. The remaining Regular battalion of the QOR became the 3rd Bn PPCLI; the remaining battalion of the Canadian Guards Regiment became the 3rd Bn RCR, and finally, the remaining two Black Watch Regular battalions would be distributed amongst the Army, the bulk becoming the 2nd Battalion RCR. In addition, armd and arty regts were cut: The Fort Garry Horse; 4th Regt Royal Canadian Horse Artillery. The remaining Cdn Infantry Regts would be reduced from six to three. The eleven infantry battalions reduced to nine. The regiments kept were the three "original" Permanent Force units: The Royal Canadian Regiment, Princess Patricia's Canadian Light Infantry and The Royal 22nd Regiment. Each of these would now have three battalions as selected serving battalions were reduced to nil strength. See *Gazette, Star, Globe* 23–26 September 1969.

343. BWA. Bourne 15 September 1969. "This notification came as a shock, even though it was known that substantial reductions would be made in all of the Armed Forces for budgetary reasons. However, The Black Watch was not eliminated for such reasons, but for reasons of administration ... It is interesting to note that the greatest reservoir of recruits for all branches of the Canadian Armed Forces lies in the Maritime Provinces ... No one can contest that the efficiency of the two Regular battalions of The Black Watch has been second to none among the existing infantry battalions in the Armed Forces since 1953. It is most fitting that Canada's Senior Highland Regiment be the representative Infantry Regiment of the Atlantic Region as there is such a great proportion of the population of the Maritimes that is of Scottish descent. However in the new organization, the Maritimes will be deprived of its representatives Infantry Regiment in the Canadian Armed Forces."

344. *Montreal Gazette* 6 October 1969 Editorial.

345. HSB XII, 126; *Vancouver Sun*; *Telegraph Journal* Saint John NB, 27 September 1969.

346. BWA HSB, 48: Bourne Correspondence: Trudeau/ 25 September 1969.

347. Ibid., HSB XII, 45–47.

348. Mathewson, *Atlantic Advocate*, Ibid.

349. BWA. Morrison. "Lochaber No More – A Dark Day for the Regiment," Memoir written by Col GS Morrison CD 1928–2010. "Lochaber No More" is the Regimental lament.

350. Morrison, Ibid., Lt Col Donald Cleghorn, a retired BW officer from Montreal. Telegram to 1 RHC in the field September 1969; Lochaber is a district in Western Scotland.

351. Ibid.

352. What remained of RHC was merged into 2 RCR. "One officer from The RCR had been posted to 2 RCR in the summer of 1970 thus 2 RCR was not made up 'entirely' of former 1st and 2nd RHC personnel." TJK/MB, 9 January 2014.

353. Representing the First Battalion were Col HHA Parker OBE CD, Brig-Gen WH Seamark CD, Col JME Clarkson MC CD, Brig-Gen DS MacLennan CD, Col WA Teed CD, Col GH Sellar CD, Lt Col WJ Newlands CD and Lt Col GS Morrison CD. The COs from the Second Battalion were Lt Col RM Ross OBE ED CD, Col W de N Watson DSO MC CD, Lt Col CHE Askwith CD, Brig-Gen WC Leonard MBE CD, Col DA McAlpine CD, Lt Col HJ Harkes MC CD. Cols McAlpine, Sellar and Harkes, serving outside Canada, were unable to attend. Lt Col Harkes completed a three-year posting as Cdn Liaison Officer in the Pentagon 1968–1971; Cdn Army Staff College and USMC in Quantico ("I've been educated beyond my capability – twenty-six courses"); a UN observer in Pakistan, and retired 27 March 1975.

354. HM Elizabeth R/Bourne 8 November 1969. HSB, 61.

355. BWA. HSB, 1970, 76. *Telegram*, 1 BW 8 November 1969.

356. SF Angus, 1 September 2012.

357. Ibid., Morrison, *Lochaber No More.*

358. Intvw Gen RP Alden/RJJ October 2011.

359. BWA. HSB Vol XII *Minutes Colonel's Conference, Camp Maple Leaf,* Cyprus 5 March 1970, 87.

360. Captains Terry Power and Ron Durst (the battalion's RCOC Quartermaster) concocted the cunning plot after a long lunch with their neighbouring British battalion.

361. RH 1970, BW Cadet Corps Pipe Band won the Province of Quebec championship in their grade.

362. BWA. Internal Security BW 010 Box 15; See: 3 RHC Trg Syllabus: ref is en français ("Sécurité Interne Programme D'Entrainement"). Strike Company, Maj D Nicholson. See: Pt I Orders dated 10 June 69.

363. See Appendix: "Officers of The Black Watch (RHR) Gagetown, Oromocto, NB – as at 1 April 1970."

364. 1 RHC. Majors: DA Fraser, CN McCabe, JA Pugh; Capts PS Bury, RL Fillman, J Fuller, WM Leonard, DA Mills, AG Miller; Lts DC Bondurant, AC Bonnycastle, GW Carter, JS Cox, FM Fisher, DG Jack, RD MacKay, MJ Smith, AR Turpin, JD Beavis; 2/Lt KK Johnson. Adj. Capt Fisher (Pde); 2 RHC. Majors: WH Eastwood, IS Fraser, GN Laird, JS MacAulay, JR MacPherson. Capts RP Alden, GW Garforth-Bles (1 BW), P Goldie, RM Gray, JD Harris, BV Johnson, RM MacAlpine, DS Martin, IE Patten, TPA Power. Lts: EM Anderson, MS Campbell, JFJ Jamieson, WA Leavey, DM Mair, AL Maitland, HWG Mowat, MR Newman, GP Nichols, RC Wen, KL White. NB. At that time there were 3x BW BGens: WC Leonard, DS MacLennan and WH Seamark; 5x Cols: JME Clarkson, DA McAlpine, GH Sellar, WA Teed and W dcN Watson; 7x Lt Col: AC Cameron, GD Corry, JS Edmondson, JH Hardy, HJ Harkes, GL Logan and WJ Newlands.

365. BWA. PPH Files, June 1970.

366. HSB, 225, 226. Murison/Hutchison, 5 November 1970; and, Clarkin/Bourne 19 November 1970. The parade was nationally televised by the CBC. Excerpts became available circa 2009 on the *Internet* via *YouTube* collections (various refs: Black Watch, Canada, Gagetown, 1970).

367. The occasion was criticised in a letter to the *Montreal Star* as "an appalling spectacle in contemporary society." C MacAuley, 25 June 70. There were several rebuttals and comments . *Star*, 25, 23, 30 June; 6, 14 July 1970.

368. *Montreal Star* 25 and 30 June 1970.

369. Larry McInnis, "Tears choked back as Black Watch disbands" *Montreal Gazette* 15 June 1970 and, Tim Burke, *Montreal Star* 15 June 1970.

370. Lt Mike Boire carried the 3 RHC Regimental Colour; he was a platoon commander in A Coy with Capt Jim Evans whose son was born that year, would become a Black Watch officer, and marry Boire's daughter forty years later!

371. Archives, The Church of St Andrew and St Paul; File 33 Correspondence, Document: RJ Berlis; SA Hayes 1963–1993; Maj RJ Berlis to HM Queen Elizabeth the Queen Mother, 17 June 1970.

372. Ref: BWA. RHC 1110-1. Lt Col GS Morrison, *The BW RHR Laying–up of Colours Ceremony*, Montreal 13–14 June 1970. Quarters Longue Pointe: from Gagetown: twenty-one Offrs, fifty-two Sr NCOs and 203 Cpls/Ptes. On Parade: 1 RHC 132; 2 RHC 132; 3 RHC 169; Cadets 142, Association one hundred: with Administration Section, Total 681.

373. Morrison took over 2 RCR made up entirely of former members of 1st and 2nd Bns Black Watch. A few weeks later, 15 October 1970, the battalion was suddenly ordered to Montreal for internal security ops in aid of the civil power ("The October Crisis"). They remained on duty until December. Later, Morrison served as DS at the Land Forces Command and Staff College. Promoted Col, he was posted to Heidelberg, West Germany to HQ Central Army Group. After retirement, Morrison was appointed to the Regimental Advisory Board.

374. Lt Col CN McCabe, et al. 25 May 2016, May and November 2015.

375. Correspondence BGen RA/RJJ 2010-12. In 1970 Capt Alden attended the Army Staff College as one of the last members of The Black Watch 1971 Maj Alden led a Coy in 3 Mech Cdo, Cdn Airborne Regt (CAR). 1977 Lt Col Alden aptd DCO of the CAR. The family found itself on the move ten months later in June 1979 as Bob took over command of 3 RCR then part of 4CMBG in Germany. 1986 Germany, HQ CFE in Lahr. 1988 BGen Alden in Heidelberg as Deputy Chief of Staff Operations, Central Army Group (NATO). 1992 aptd Commandant of the Army Staff College and the Deputy Comd 1 Can Div.

376. Mathewson, RH August 1970, 24.

377. Reunion dinner of the surviving officers, 13th, 42nd and 73rd Bns. Among the present were (with their preferred names/nick-names): Col ALS (Arthur) Mills DSO, Maj Henry Morgan MC, Maj Hugh Scott MC, Brig CB (Toppo) Topp DSO MC, Col Lorne C Montgomery OBE MC, Lt Henry Birks, Col TS (Sid) Morrisey DSO, Lt Col Ian Sinclair DSO OBE MC, Lt Col Hugh Johnson DSO, Col CT (Bert) Howard OBE, Maj David (Davey) Carstairs MC, Lt Col Erskine (Buck) Buchanan, Group Capt Gerald Birks MC, Col Hugh Wallis DSO OBE MC, Lt Col JM (Jim) Morris MC. The BW summer Garden Party, held at Col Keiller Mackay's estate saw a hundred Black Watch members. The May 1969 Red Hackle Dinner (41st) held at the King Edward Hotel. Guest of honour was Major William Denison, Mayor of Toronto, descended fm a grand Cdn cavalry family. Most prized guest was Col the Rev GGD Kilpatrick, DSO.

378. HSB, 197. Hutchison Papers; *The Black Watch Association (Montreal Branch) Newsletter*, December 1970, 7.

379. *The Montreal Star* "Black Watch: 1,069 went, 13 Remember" 3 April 1972.

380. Maj GMAC Boire, correspondence / RJJ November–December 2012.

381. BWA 3 RHC. Pt 2 Orders 1965–1966.

382. BWA. Pt 2 Orders issued by Quebec Command #467, 19 December 1963.

383. Boire, ibid.

384. The complement of Support Company included soldiers "qualified in theory." The first 106 RR anti-tank course was offered at 4 Personnel Depot in Longue Pointe in 1965. Eight Black Watch soldiers qualified and then in turn ran regimental courses to qualified more. Subsequent courses were conducted at Camp Valcartier in 1966–67.

385. WO M Cher, 17 October 2012.

386. BWA JD Nicholson to Lt Col JIB Macfarlane, 9 September 1969. Lt Col Ferdon: Nicholson was irate when Steve Angus returned from an absence and made CO; he resigned: "I needed a break."

387. RH No 169, December 1970, 29.
388. SF Angus remembers thinking: "I'm sitting in the CO's office with the sword of Damocles over my head."
389. Angus Family Archives (AFA). CPR group included: Angus, George Stephen (his boss at Bank of Montreal), MacIntyre and James Hill; later joined by Lord Strathcona and Cornelius van Horne) as general manager.
390. AFA. CPR Train Order No. 218: "Please arrange that work be suspended, and all trains stopped for a period of two minutes, commencing at 1:45 pm Eastern Standard Time today, as a mark of respect to the Late RB Angus." When he died, 19 September 1922, every CPR train was stopped for the man who connected Canada from sea to sea.
391. AFA. The mansion purchased from Montagu Allan, built for his daughter on two lots. The modern Cantlie House, an apartment hotel, was built on the property after house and stables were torn down.
392. Designed St James Club, Standard Life Building, Canadian Embassy Berlin, Gander Airport, etc. Another Fetherstonhaugh was Dean of Engineering U of Winnipeg.
393. SF Angus/RJJ Interviews Montreal/Toronto/Erin, 2009–2013. Hereafter, Angus.
394. BWA. Officer Appointments September 1970: A Coy 2 IC, Lt RF Ehrhardt, OC 1 Platoon Lt GM Boire, OC 2 Pl Lt HP Klepak; 2 IC B Coy, Capt A Pamment, OC 1 Pl Lt E Camolese. Accounts Officer, Capt JAB Evans, Asst QM, Lt BA Lloyd.
395. BWA. HP Klepak, *Canada's Black Watch 1962–1987 – The Regiment Continues*, unpublished manuscript, 1987, 59. Hereafter, Klepak.
396. COTC officers Lts Boire, Dover, Lloyd, Pompeo; and Lts/Capts Klepak, Starzynski, Ehrhardt, Evans, Malashenko.
397. Maj GM Boire, Memoir Notes, January 2013.
398. Ibid.
399. Malashenko joined No1 Int Trg Coy as a private in September 1966.
400. Premier Bourassa and Mayor Drapeau sent a letter to PM Trudeau declaring an "apprehended insurrection" was at hand, calling on the federal government to intervene. Mr Trudeau imposed the *War Measures Act,* emergency legislation dating from the First World War, which temporarily suspended civil liberties. The army remained in Quebec until 29 December. The Act was quickly replaced by a series of public order regulations, lasting until the summer of 1971.
401. Angus, Ibid., "We fed them for the first couple of days."
402. Ibid.
403. Ibid., and, RH April 1971, 29.
404. FLQ activities from 1963 to 1971: 200+ bombings, three raids on armouries, three kidnappings, eight deaths, and more than fifty injured.
405. 2 RCR strength (after absorbing 1/2 RHC) was: thirty-eight officers, one hundred WOs and Sr NCOs, 542 Jr NCOs and ninety-four privates. NAC Hist Report; as at 1 January 1970 – 30 June 1970. Lt Col GS Morrison, CO 2nd Bn The Royal Canadian Regiment.
406. S Angus/RJJ, 26 July 2012. "Later I was able to call to John Bourne for Maj Garneau, who had applied for a position with the Duke of Edinburgh Awards. He got the job thanks to Bourne's intervention." See also, Klepak, 37.
407. BWA. RH, December 1970, 29–31.
408. HSB, 240. Correspondence: Lessard/Angus 12 and 21 January 1971.
409. Interview Col S Angus/Jarymowycz September 2009; July 2010, 11; see also, Tim Burke "The skirling of the pipes", *The Montreal Star*, 21 December 1970. One octogenarian was Harold Lea Fetherstonhaugh, the architect of The Church of St Andrew and St Paul (Pamela Angus' great uncle); he loved being on the ward with the soldiers. "He asked the pipe major to play *Bonnie Dundee* and when Brown obliged, he wept" … Angus turned to Tim Burke, the columnist who joined him on this visit: "A visit like this gives you a strange feeling. You feel good and then you don't feel good."
410. In 1970, BW was allocated thirty spaces which offered employment to its own officers and NCOs. BW platoon was commanded by Lt Mike Boire, NCOs: Sgt Gordie Johnson and Corporals Paul Stevenson and Mike Brazeau. Maj Wayne Cook was appointed to the composite staff and made a company commander.
411. Sgt WJ Carlisle, Intvw/correspondence, 19 November 2012.
412. Ibid.
413. BW Historical Report, summer trg, 1970.

414. DHH. SSEP records, see also, BWA. SMTP BWA 008 3653-1; see: BWA Unit Annual Historical Report (UAHR) 1 January 1972 – 31 December 1972 RHC. 5 July 1973. Lt Col LN Ferdon.

415. The first commanding officer was Capt Ralph A Dynes, a former regimental sergeant major. The mess steward, Sgt Henry Dollard, was assisted by his son; this was now a three-generation affair, for Sgt Patrick Dollard had served in the mess since the war.

416. MacLennan, 2011. Scottish Regts in CF Reserves: 3rd Bn RHC Mtl; 1 and 2nd NSH; Cameron H of Ottawa; SDGH Cornwall; Lanark and Renfrew Scottish Regt, Pembroke; The Toronto Scottish; The 48th Highlanders; Lorne Scots Brampton Ont; Highland Fusiliers of Cda, Galt, Ont; Argyll and Sutherland Highlanders, Hamilton, Ont; The Lake Superior Scottish Regt, Thunder Bay, Ont; Queen's Own Cameron Highlanders of Cda, Winnipeg, Man; The Calgary Highlanders, Calgary, Alta; Seaforth Highlanders of Cda, Vancouver; Canadian Scottish Regt, Victoria BC.

417. Col SF Angus/RJJ, 25 Feb 2014.

418. WO Gord Ritchie/RJJ Intvw 5 November 2012. "On exercise we seldom had blank ammo and were instructed to yell 'Bullet! Bullet!' during the exercise attacks."

419. The tri-services colleges of the RCN, RCAF and Cdn Army were combined after the Second World War: Royal Military College of Canada RMC, formed in 1874; Royal Roads Military College RRMC Royal Roads, renamed from Royal Canadian Naval College 1947; in 1952 Collège militaire royal de Saint-Jean (CMR) was added. After 1995, the DND ordered all mil trg and education re-directed to RMC Kingston, Ontario. In July 2007 the military college at St-Jean, which was closed in 1995, reopened again.

420. RSMs: the rank WO1 ceased being used as of unification in 1968, replaced by Chief Warrant Officer (CWO).

421. On 14 June, 1982, Christie apptd DCOS (OPS) at CENTAG HQ, Heidelberg, Germany where he was also Acting COS for the next six months. In July 1986, he assumed the appointment of Assistant Director of the NATO International Military Staff (IMS) for Plans and Policy responsible for the development of NATO military strategy, nuclear plans and policy.

422. In 1993, BGen Cox was appointed Commander, 1 Cdn Mech Bde Group. In 1995, Director Gen Land Force Development in Ottawa. After retiring from the Canadian Forces, Brig-Gen Cox became the Executive Secretary of the Canadian Association for Security and Intelligence Studies.

423. Vernon, *MacLean's* 30 September 1996: "In 1972, as a result of a management study, it was decided to combine the department of national defence and Canadian Forces headquarters. We took apples and oranges and created tangerines as a result. We now have military people involved in areas where uniformed people should not be – government policy, protection of the minister and so on. We very much have bureaucrats involved in armed forces policy like the mounting of operations … My view is that the military operators should be running the organization – and not a collection of bureaucrats."

424. 1972 Student Employment Programme July 1972: ten females (CWACs) and thirty-four males, sixteen short of the allotted quota. See: *Montreal Star* 11 July 1972, story and photos.

425. RH April 1972; Major Alexandre Mauduit.

426. Committee Members: R Daniels, B Powney, B Wilson, J O'Brien, J Small, R Williams and A Bates. The Head Table was packed solid: Maj Gen Duncan McAlpine; Cols Bourne, Knox, Hutchison, Buchanan and Dubuc; Lt Cols Traversy, Ogilvie, Ferdon (the CO), McGovern, Ritchie, Sharp; Maj Kavanagh, Miller and Maj the Rev R Berlis. Much welcomed were the presidents of the three Association Branches: J Vaughan (Toronto BWA), RE Henley (Pacific Coast BWA) and R Ablett (Montreal BWA).

427. Angus, Ibid., also, see HSB XII p 297. The fall and winter social events included: The 101st St Andrew's Ball; and the 45th Annual Red Hackle Dinner 13 January 1973, The Royal York Hotel in Toronto. Col Hutchison was guest speaker.

428. BWA. RH August 1972, 29; WO R Hummell/RJJ, 18 September 2013; BW section ldrs: Cpl Lipscomb and Cpl Snell. OC A Capt Starzynski and CSM Gord (Dad) Scott; Sgt Cantwell was CQMS. The Sqn OC was Maj RJ Jarymowycz. This combined exercise was repeated then paused for security reasons after the 1974 election. The joint exercises were re-established when Jarymowycz and Klepak were COs of RCH and RHC in the early 1980s.

429. *Glenwhorple*, song. HSB, Vol X, 91.

430. Annual reports for 1971, 72 and 74 show an all-time low in regimental strength returns: 137, 97, 106 all ranks.

431. See *Red Hackle* Winter 2010 No. 014, 36.

432. With Honoraries. WO Gordon Ritchie/RJJ Intvw 5 November 2012. "The total unit strength reached a high of 187 for the 1974 St Hubert Trooping parade, and then progressively dropped to 157 at the end of the 70s."

433. The parade was shaped by RSM, CWOs Al Rodgers and G Ferris of the Royal 22e Regiment, who acted as Parade Coordinator. To complete the make-up of the "family" parade were The Black Watch Association led by former RSM RA Ablett and The Black Watch Cadet Corps under the command of Major JT Gibson, CD.

434. Klepak, History (draft 2), 95.

435. Lt Col Sewell/RJJ, correspondence, 8 December 2012, interview 18 January 2013.

436. Sewell's experienced officers were Majs R Starzynski, R Ehrhardt, Jim Evans, Capts A Malashenko, Alasdair Ruthven, Hal Klepak.

437. Sewell, Ibid.

438. Ibid.

439. RJJ/Russell, August 2012; See also: Capt Rev Dr William R Russell, "The 1974 Queen's Colour: A Memoir", RH No 015, Summer 2010, 26. Russell later earned a DMin at Princeton.

440. Rev Berlis, WIA in Normandy, later served with the Forestry Corps and Corps HQ in Europe before returning to RHC.

441. Russell, Ibid.

442. Russell, Ibid.

443. Russell, Ibid.

444. The Church of St Andrew and St Paul Archives; Sermons 262: Rev Wm Russell 1979–1980; Russell letter to The Hon Camille Laurin Min of State for Cultural Development Palm Sunday 3 April 1977, protesting the self-admitted "restrictive law" and disregard of relevant provisions of the BNA Act "on the pretext that bilingualism has not been fully recognized in Canada's other provinces … As a Christian, I protest the white paper's warlike overtones in such phrases as 'a reconquest by the French-speaking majority in Quebec.'"

445. Sewell, Ibid.

446. RHC Party: HCol Bourne, HLt Col Sharp, Lt Col Sewell (with wife), Major Starzynski, RSM Chartier (with wife).

447. Sewell, Ibid.

448. WO G Ritchie/RJJ 30 September 2013; "We had a BW god-father – Lt D Anderson working at District HQ, who filled in as many slots as possible with BW people. People continued to be sent over until they closed Egypt in 79. None of our people went to Golan heights after 79." UN Postings included: Sgt Rolland Labreche, MCpl Sherry Duplessis-Hummell, Cpl D Cyrus, Cpl/Pte Mike King, MCpls Lenny Kiriluk, Richard Kundra, Michael Lemieux, Tom Miles, Graham Smith, Pte Wallace, MCpl/Cpl Gary Traikov, Cpls/Ptes Michael Tremblay, Tom Irvine, Wallace Todorov, and Sam Weissfelner. MWO Peter Gannon served in Egypt with RMR. G Ritchie, 1 October 2013: "[Cartmel's] tours were with the 3rd Fd Engineers, he later saw the light in the mid 80's and served in the Watch until retired."

449. District No 1 Commanding Officers 1970–1997

1970–1971	Col JR Dori, RCIC (FMR)
1972–1974	Col GS Dubuc, RCIC (R de Mais)
1974–1976	Col RAC Lawson, RCIC (RMR)
1976–1979	Col Peter Cameron, RCIC, (48th Highlanders)
1979–1982	Col Gilbert St Louis, RCA (2 Fd)
1982–1984	Col Thomas Stafford, RCA (2 Fd)
1984–1988	Col George Javornik, RC Sigs, RCIC (RMR)
1988–1990	Col John Cochrane, RCAC (RCH)
1990–1992	Col Jean Gervais, RCAC (R de Hull)
1993–1996	Col Mike Pronkin RCA (2 Fd RCA)

450. 1976 Election. 15 November PQ majority 41.3 percent vs. Liberals 33.78 percent. In 1971, before the PQ's first election, the Anglophone population sat at 788,833. By 2011, the total had dropped to 599,230.

451. Intvw G Ritchie/RJJ, October 2012.

452. Don Dingwall, *The Centurion in Canadian Service* (Service: 2005).

453. Obituary for Lord Ballantrae that appeared in the London Times, 29 November 1980.

454. Klepak Hist (Draft) 100. Later, Victoria Schofield published a biography of Wavell in 2006, then in 2012, a history of The Black Watch (UK).

455. Klepak, Ibid.; Sewell, Ibid.

456. Introduced by the first Parti Québécois government of Premier René Lévesque, *Bill 101* was granted Royal Assent on 26 August 1977. The Charter's provisions expanded upon the 1974 *Official Language Act* (Bill 22), making French the official language of Quebec. Prior to 1974, language was subject only to the requirements on the use of English and French in Article 133 of the BNA Act, 1867. Bill 101 has been amended more than six times since 1977.

457. Sewell/RJJ 26 September 2013.

458. Ibid.

459. Angus, Ibid.

460. Correspondence/Intvw the Hon. GD Robertson/RJJ December 2012 –16 February 2013.

461. Ibid., Robertson joined the district headquarters staff of Col Frank Ching in Hamilton as the senior operations officer. *Tesco*: "I was a registered professional engineer and hold patents from various machinery designs developed over the years … I am serving as Supervisor of the Lake Ashton Community Development District." For a change, Robertson also volunteered to teach mathematics at an inner city ghetto school in Fort Lauderdale from 2005–2011.

462. Ibid.

463. Klepak Hist, 104–105.

464. Maj BA McBey/RJJ Correspondence, 27 January 2012 "He was very brave to bring a woman officer into the Regiment."

465. Correspondence Klepak/RJJ, 17 April 2013; Fond: 2011, 2012; May–September 2013.

466. Klepak/RJJ, 13 October 2013.

467. BW Officer, Hasek served in Ghana, Vietnam and Cyprus; the first commander of the Sky Hawks Parachute Team, retired in 1981, worked as journalist, published *The Disarming of Canada* (1987). Founded "Education for Democracy" EOD), a non-profit organization bringing 1500 volunteer English teachers to Czechoslovakia fm Canada, US, UK and Australia. EOD renamed "John Hasek Society" in 1994 after Hasek's death – causes were unclear, with some speculating that he had hit a mine in his car, or due to a collision with a Serbian military vehicle.

468. Ibid., Piper, St Laurent Pipe Band; Military: Black Watch RHR in 1968; Platoon OC A Coy 1968–70, 2IC B Coy 1970–72, Adjutant 1973–74, 1975–78 ; A Coy OC; CO 1980–1983. Attachments : Platoon OC X Para (London TA)1972–73, Officer Trg Offr 76e Régiment d'Infanterie, Vincennes 1974–75, Ops Offr lst Bn 51st Highland Vols (BW Bn of composite regiment)1978–80. Strategic Analyst NDHQ 1969–76, visiting Prof CMR 1976–78, Strategic Analyst NATO 1978–80, Professor and Founder, Programme in Strategic Studies CMR 1980–94. Retired: from Reserves 1984, from RMC 2007. Academic: Royal Military College when CMR closed 1994. Adviser to the Foreign and Defence Minister for Inter-American Defence Affairs 1992–2002; Adviser to CDS for Latin American Army Affairs 2001 to date.

469. Klepak/RJJ February, April, May 2013. See also Klepak, *BW History 1962-1987*, (Draft, unpublished).

470. Klepak, a true laird, insisted on treating every guest or group of officers.

471. Ibid., 100–101.

472. Lt Col Vic Chartier OMM: correspondence and Intvws/ RJJ 2009, 2012–2013.

473. Klepak correspondence, Ibid., Also see, Klepak Draft Hist, 102–104.

474. MCpl S Hummell, correspondence 26 April 2013.

475. Boire/RJJ 2 January 2014.

476. Lt Col Steve Goldberg, Lt Col RJ Jarymowycz, Lt Col (later Col) George Javornik, Lt Col (later Brig Gen) Marc Préfontaine, Major (later Lt Col/Col) Bob Brooks (712 Sigs Sqn). The Grenadier Guards were in a different Militia District.

477. Klepak, 93,101; (initial Draft, 107–8).

478. Ibid.

479. Ibid., 109.

480. Col Bourne was prevailed upon to inquire of Mrs. Val Traversy if the commissioning of a silver trophy for the "Highland Winter" competition, a prize that would bear Lt Col Traversy's name, would be appropriate. Her reaction was enthusiastic. Klepak: "People tend to think we invented it but Dan's [MacKay] input was key…he did a great job of getting it off the ground with Highland regiments in Ontario and then Nova Scotia."

481. Klepak, Ibid., 112.

482. Troop A Philadelphia City Cavalry "The 'Father and Son Ex', May 1980, with Officer Cadets Brent Cowan and Gord Lusk; Piper Cpl MacLellan … an armoured recce ex – mostly driving around Fort Indian Town Gap."

483. Intvws Cowan, Klepak May 2013; See, Klepak Hist (initial Draft), 108–110.

484. FMC was created prior to *Unification* of the three services; commanded by a Lt Gen, and had responsibility for all army ground forces in Canada. Replaced by Land Force Command, NDHQ Ottawa. ARMY HQs: Militia 1867 to 1940; Army 1940 to 1968; FMC 1968 to 1997, LFC 1997–2013, Canadian Army 2013–present.

485. Chartier, Ibid.

486. Upon his return to Montreal in 1973, Fraser practised clinical cardiology at both St Mary's Hospital and the Royal Victoria Hospital. For over thirty years, George taught at both the undergraduate and postgraduate levels at McGill University's Faculty of Medicine. A special fund and memorial dinner (held at RHC mess) was established.

487. Lt Col G Stothers/RJJ Correspondence.

488. Ibid.

489. Ibid.

490. Chartier, Intvws: 10 January 2013 and 8 February 2013. RSM was CFR'd: Capt Dynes, and made head of BW Cadet Corps.

491. Ibid., He was given three options: to become district chief warrant officer; to be appointed as a capt in the district staff or, option 3, to become an officer in the Black watch. "I'm not a headquarters guy"; "… the decision was amongst Robertson, Cameron, me and of course my wife."

492. Ibid.," Alex and I pulled strings from different ends … he presented a non-military *image*, but I respected his knowledge and I needed that approval …"

493. Maj G Dover Ibid.

494. Maj G Dover; and, BWA. Bolton Papers; G Ritchie intvw. Cost projects included: Regimental gala dinner at Queen E, rental of Stadium, walk about on Mount Royal, church parade reception, departure/arrival guards, extra costs beyond allotted man-days, private dinners, royal accommodation at a private home for HM and her staff. The Regiment raised monies via a *Regimental Cook Book* while the pipes and drums put out a new record. Both sold out. BW Committee: Chair Maj DF O'Connor, Maj B Lloyd, Capt EA Malashenko (to January 1987), Capt GT Lusk, Capt BD Bolton, Capt J Conway, Capt R Ferguson, Capt DG Fraser, 2Lt GC Lowe, CWO Paull, WO A Kerr; Lt Cols Sewell, Stothers.

495. Klepak Hist.

496. DHH/ NDHQ. Barbara Dundas lists Pte Heather R Erxleben (PPCLI) as "Canada's first female infantry soldier" with photo fm PPCLI, 26 March 1989. See: Dundas, *A History of Women in the Canadian Military*, Ottawa: 2000, 130. DHH opinion. Dr Ken Reynolds/Dr Steve Harris, 20 November 2012:" Obviously, there have been women in uniform for decades, including those that were in the CWACs, WRCNS and RCAF (WD) on the eve of Unification. Those formations disappeared in 1968 with the creation of the CF and the women were folded into the new personnel structure. I would not think that a CWAC serving with a Reserve unit in the 1960s or 70s would be considered "infantry" … If, as it appears, Pte Sutcliffe was not a CWAC, was she actually a qualified infanteer? I ask because, as I understand it, the combat arms qualifications/trades were closed to women until the late 1980s. In 1987 the Combat Related Employment of Women (CREW) trials started in the army and navy. In 1988 the air force removed all restrictions on the employment of women … Erxleben may have been the first qualified Regular force infanteer and may very well have been preceded by a qualified infanteer in a reserve force unit [emphasis added]."

497. BWA. Pte KA Sutcliffe. Scrapbook Memoirs, 2012. Her memories are partly melancholy: "As a woman, I could not wear Highland dress … I did not march in the church parade or the Remembrance Day parade … I waited at the armoury for the men to return."

498. MCpl S Hummell: "The first female officer, Capt Percival was trying to get the Balmoral and Hackles for the females as well but we did not like them actually, as they just did not look good on us because of our hair – we just wanted to have at least The Black Watch Cap Badge and the chance to be included in all things Black Watch as we knew we had the right to." Correspondence SH/RJJ 18 April 2013. Lt Col Chartier pointed out that the recruits were well-practised by the time of the parade. VC/RJJ 24 September 2013.

499. Partial: MCpl Duplessis-Petruch, MCpl S Hummell, MCpl D Leger, Cpl C Prader, Cpl Toffi. Uncnfmd: Cpls L Robert, N Royal. Capt BA Malashenko: McBey/RJJ Ibid.,: "These women were as proud and passionate about

the Regiment as the men and felt that they had been betrayed." Particular assistance by MCpl Sherry Hummell, April–July 2013.

500. Chartier: "Gen Belanger … not once did he say – indeed nor did anyone – *you must have females on parade*."
501. Cpl B McLellan carried casings; Cpls Prader and Royal were stretcher-bearers; Cpls Hummell and Toffi assisted with seating VIPs. Hummell: "I called us the 'cigars, cigarettes, *Tiparillo* girls'." Correspondence. Maj Betty Ann McBey, Cpl S Hummel 26 April 2013. One BW female soldier, a nurse, was responsible for VIPs.
502. DND. Letter to MCpl Duplessis-Petruch, and other members of BW, from MGen PG Addy, Chief Personnel Svcs, 29 November 1991. Each complainant received $750 from the Human Rights Commission; see Hummell, McBey et al.
503. O'Connor considered skirts in BW tartan. The first considered option was to copy the 48th Highlanders, where clerks always wore a plain brown tartan skirt.
504. Klepak, 126.
505. Ibid.; Chartier/RJJ; " I have full confidence in my staff and soldiers, and I know all plans are in place and we will welcome Her Majesty, Queen Elizabeth, The Queen Mother – our Colonel-in-Chief – with honour and pride."
506. The restrictions stated all troops would be 031 rated (infantry trained), leaving out veterans and others.
507. Friday 5 June was the first day the soldiers were able to rehearse in Molson Stadium, where they were to troop the Colour the next day. It was also a busy day for the Colonel-in-Chief. The first event was a luncheon given by the Government of Canada at the Ritz Carlton Hotel for three hundred guests consisting of government and civic officials and many distinguished Montrealers. At 4:30 that afternoon, there was a reception at the Four Seasons Hotel given by the Provincial Government, hosted by Premier Bourassa for 150 guests.
508. Maj G Dover, Interview RJJ July 2013.
509. Lt Col Bolton/RJJ, 25 February 2014.
510. BWA. Bolton Papers. 1987 Organization Files. RHC fifty man Gd of Honour welcomed HM in front of Montreal City Hall 1700, 4 June on 6 June Trooping: 190 grand total; on parade: fourteen officers, 128 NCOs and ORs plus forty-two in the BW pipes and drums. Command: Lt Col Victor Chartier; Pde Adj Capt Gordon Lusk; RSM CWO David Paull. Escort for the Colour: Maj DF O'Connor, Capt Paul Hindo, 2Lt Andrew MacKay, MWO Mike Kelly, MWO Peter Gannon, WO Traikov, WO Alden, Sgt Millard, Sgt Apple. No 2 Guard: Maj Brent Cowan, Lt Jacques Galipeau, Lt James Bradley, MWO Victor Blazevic, WO Maura, WO Ritchie, Sgt Barron. No 3: Guard. Capt Bruce Bolton, Lt David Jones, 2/Lt Greg Lowe, MWO Rolland Labreche, WO Hummell, WO Cartmel, Sgt Kelly, Sgt Bourdon. No 4 Guard: Capt James Conway, Lt Alain Bissonnette, 2/Lt Hugh Dimock, MWO Gary Young, WO Rodger, WO Windsor, Sgt Irvine. Regimental pipes and drums: P/Maj Andrew Kerr, D/Maj Charles Leigh; Association pipes and drums: P/Maj William Hannah, D/Maj CS Christie; RCA Band Capt JRG Leblanc; Black Watch Association: Capt Ivor Watkins; Combined BW Cadet Corps: Capt William Gardner.
511. HM stayed at a private home in Westmount (the family moved out for a month) with her private secretary: Sir Martin Gilliat GCVO MBE, and her personal staff which included ladies in waiting, two secretaries, three equerries, plus deputy steward, footman, dresser, second dresser, hairdresser, and security.
512. BWA JG Bourne File. 6 November 1987.
513. The 1st (Lt Col WA Teed CD) and 3rd Bn RHC (Lt Col McGovern CD); the 2nd Bn (Lt Col WC Leonard, MBE) was in Europe on NATO duty, but the Colour Party, Band and CO attended.
514. It was her fiftieth anniversary as Col-in-Chief of the imperial BW. On 1 December 1947, Her Majesty Queen Elizabeth was formally appointed as Colonel-in-Chief of the Canadian Black Watch; the Regiment commemorated the occasion with an inscribed jewel case.
515. Chartier/RJJ.
516. Armour/RJJ; the padre was beaming and daunting in full kilt and accoutrements. At his first church parade, he was hustled into a side passage by two subalterns who switched his spats, for the disapproving eyes of Col Bourne had been fixed on them all through the service.
517. Armour, Ibid.
518. BWA. Bolton Papers 1986–87.
519. LCmdr G Vachon/RJJ, correspondence, 16 June 13.
520. Chartier, Intvw, Ibid., HM paid a brief visit to the armoury to present the Duke of Edinburgh Awards to Black Watch Cadets.

521. Stavert Intvw RJJ, 29 October 2012. "We had an unwritten rule; I drove him to armoury and fetched his drinks during; after dinner, he was sometimes pie-eyed but in a nice way; I took him to his door, left key on the ledge."

522. Stavert, Ibid.

523. Chartier/RJJ 25 September 2013.

524. Lt Col Victor G Chartier OMM CD A de C died on 6 April 2016 after a lengthy battle with cancer. He was eighty-two years old. Capt Rev Jim Armour noted "his wife, Doreen, was as much 'regiment' as he was." JM/RJ 15 May 2016.

525. Col O'Connor/RJJ Intvw as at 18 February 2013.

526. O'Connor was a qualified parachutist; a total of about 113 jumps, half free fall.

527. Maj WB Cowan/RJJ, intvw, 1 May 2013.

528. Maj G Dover, Ibid.

529. Sir Montagu Allan of Ravenscrag, Hon Col of the Regiment, on the occasion of HM's appointment as Col-in-Chief in 1937 presented the silver bowl. It is correctly referred to as a "monteith"; a vessel that was originally fashioned to rinse and cool wine glasses. Monteiths function as elegant centrepieces.

530. Capt Canon RB Glencross/RJJ Intvw and correspondence, 30 November–2 December 2012. Lt Col McCulloch: "Part soldier, part secular saint, committed to his Master's degree." Lt Col Plourde: "The only exception to all my military connections since 1972, to understand and to be successful in militia and Regular force."

531. Glencross, Ibid.

532. Ibid. At the end of Glencross's career in 2008. Glencross became the second longest serving Black Watch padre after Major the Reverend Rod Berlis: twenty-one years vs. twenty.

533. O'Connor/RJJ, 12 October 2013.

534. See: *The Valour and the Horror*, Part 3, "In Desperate Battle"; CBC, NFB, Galafilm, Radio-Canada. Directed by Brian McKenna. The series won both kudos, and protest (from the RCAF) for the second episode dealing with *Bomber Command*. The Verrières Ridge scenes were filmed on the day Oka surrendered and since Farnham was used as a holding centre, the entire sequence was filmed in the cramped confines of the back Rifle Ranges. Surprisingly, the attack (sportingly assisted by a Platoon from the Royal Montreal Regiment) was a good piece of historical cinema, and went on to be used in high schools across Canada.

535. BWA RHC 1110-3 and, Anx A "Freedom of the City Parade", 23 July 1992.

536. Ibid., World Scottish Festival; see also BWA. Bolton Papers, *Scottish Festival Preparation*, 1992.

537. Ibid., Claude de Ramezay, Governor of Montreal whose chateau still graces the city centre, was Scottish.

538. The Dist Staff opined that the COs of CGG and BW tended to refuse any district directive, usually without consequences. "[They] got away with it." Maj GMAC Boire, SSO 1 and G3, D1 HQ 1990–1993.

539. Ibid., BWA. RHC 1110-3; Anx A "Freedom of the City Parade"; *Gazette* 17 August; Bolton Papers, 10–17 August 1992.

540. Angus/RJJ, Intvw Ibid., Armour/RJJ: "Col Tom Price gave a speech, part of it in French during the ceremony."

541. Festival events included a Scottish Film Festival, Theatre Festival, Music Festival, cultural exhibitions and seminars at McGill. BWA. Adjutant/RSS Papers 1990–2010; Report, LCOL DFA O'Connor/Comdr Number 1 Militia District HQ, "City of Montreal 350th Anniversary Celebrations, BW RHR Participation", 6 February 1992; 16 September 1992.

542. Cicero: "They discredit that which they do not comprehend."

543. O'Connor/RJJ. Ibid., "Was the BW unjustifiably haughty, arrogant, we didn't think so – [but] Jean Gervais could not be convinced."

544. Ibid.

545. As Int Offr Maj Dover served in BAOR, MOD London, Cyprus and Army HQ Salisbury; His BW COs: Macfarlane: 1967–68; O'Connor 1991–1993; McCulloch 1993–1995; Lusk: 1997–1998.

546. Dover, Ibid., "previous honoraries bankrolled the Regiment; by the 1990s, they did not have that kind of money."

547. BD Bolton/ RJJ, Ibid.

548. G Dover/RJJ 10 October 2013.

549. Intvws BD Bolton and G Dover April–July 2013.

Part V

Illustrations

Commanding Officers, 1 CHB / 1 RHC, 1951–1970

LCol RL Rutherford OBE CD
1951–1952

LCol HA Parker OBE CD
1952–1954

LCol WH Seamark CD
1954–1956

LCol JME Clarkson MC CD
1956–1959

LCol DS MacLennan CD
1959–1960

LCol WA Teed CD
1960–1963

LCol GH Sellar CD
1963–1966

LCol WJ Newlands CD
1966–1968

LCol GS Morrison CD
1968–1970

Commanding Officers, 2 CHB / 2 RHC, 1952–1970

LCol RM Ross OBE ED CD
1952–1955

LCol Wm de N Watson DSO MC CD
1955–1959

LCol CHE Askwith CD
1959–1960

LCol WC Leonard MBE CD
1961–1963

LCol DA McAlpine CMM CD
1963–1966

LCol HJ Harkes MC CD
1966–1968

LCol WB MacLeod OMM CD
1968–1970

Commanding Officers, The Montreal Battalion, 1945–2020

LCol IL Ibbotson ED
1945–1946

LCol FM Mitchell ED
1946–1947

LCol VE Traversy
1947–1949

LCol JW Knox MBE ED CD
1949–1952

LCol JG Bourne CVO ED CD
1952–1955

LCol IR McDougall CD
1955–1958

LCol WA Wood CD
1958–1959

LCol DJ McGovern CD
1959–1962

LCol WB Redpath CD
1962–1965

Commanding Officers, The Montreal Battalion, 1945–2020 (continued)

LCol T Price CD
1965–1967

LCol JIB MacFarlane CD
1967–1970

LCol SF Angus CD
1970–72

LCol LN Ferdon CD
1972–1974

LCol WR Sewell CD
1974–1977

LCol GD Robertson CD
1977–1980

LCol HP Klepak CD
1980–1983

LCol JC Stothers CD
1983–1986

LCol VG Chartier OMM CD
1986–1989

LCol DF O'Connor CD
1989–1993

LCol IM McCulloch CD
1993–1996

LCol GT Lusk CD
1996–2000

LCol BD Bolton MMM CD
2000–2003, 2003–2005

LCol J Potter MC
2003

LCol TEC MacKay CD
2005–2009; 2016–2017

LCol GB Plourde CD
2009–2013; 2017–2020

LCol CR Phare CD
2013–2016

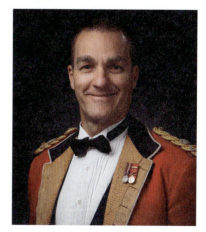

LCol F Roy CD
2020–

Regular Force RSMs, 1951–1970 (incomplete)

WO1 RH Finnie CD
1952–1953; 1954–1962
1 CHB / 1 RHC

WO1 FE Blakeney MM BEM CD
1952–1961
2 CHB / 3 RHC

WO1 TF Charters CD
1961–1964
2 CHB / 3 RHC

WO1 H Firby CD
1964–1966
1 CHB / 1 RHC

WO1 EF Cain CD
1964–1965
2 CHB / 3 RHC

CWO CW Beacon CD
1965–66
2 CHB / 3 RHC

CWO DB Reekie MMM CD
1967–1970
2 CHB / 3 RHC

RSMs, The Montreal Battalion, 1945–2020

WO1 E Bleasdale
1945–1946

WO1 R Diplock MBE
1946

WO1 AF Turnbull DCM
1947–1949

WO1 R Dynes MBE
1949–1952

WO1 R Ablett
1952–1955

WO1 T Turley CD
1955–1958

WO1 JR Jackson
1959–1960

WO1 M Gurevitch CD
1960–1965

RSMs, The Montreal Battalion, 1945–2020 (continued)

WO1 I Watkins CD
1965–1968

CWO GA McElheron MMM CD
1968–1970; 1980–1983

CWO AD Rodgers CD
1970–1972, 1974

CWO R Poirier CD
1972–1974

CWO VG Chartier OMM, CD
1974–1978

CWO BD Bolton MMM CD
1978–1980

CWO DI Paull CD
1983–1987

CWO MRG Kelly MMM CD
1987–1990

CWO J Rodger CD
1990–1994

CWO T Miles CD
1994–1998

CWO P Gannon CD
1998–2001

CWO C Hamel CD
2001–2006

CWO JC Barron CD
2006–2010

CWO R Unger MMM CD
2010–2013

CWO M Carmosino CD
2013–2017

CWO SD Campbell CD
2017–2020

CWO FD Mamen CD
2020–

The Church of St Andrew and St Paul

Above: The Black Watch Window.
Top right: The visits of Her Majesty Queen Elizabeth The Queen Mother to the Church in 1987 (colour) and 1962 (black and white).
Bottom right: Black Watch memorial plaques inside the Church.

Padres of The Montreal Battalion since 1945

Maj Rev RJ Berlis CD
1945–1965

Capt Rev SA Hayes
1965–1973

Capt Rev W R Russell
1973–1983

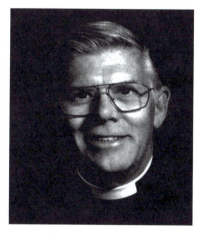

Capt Rev JSS Armour
1983–1987

Capt Rev B Glencross CD
1987–2008

Capt Rev RR Topping
2008–2009

Capt Rev David Godkin
2013–2015

Capt Rev Alain Brosseau
2016–2017

Capt Rev Gary Karamoukian
2018–2020

Colonels of the Regiment

Brigadier KG Blackader CBE
DSO MC ED CD
1958–1963

Colonel JW Knox MBE ED CD
1963 – 1968

Colonel JG Bourne CVO ED CD
1968–1970

A Company, Black Watch, July 1951. The 1st Canadian Highland Battalion (1 CHB) comprised four rifle companies and a support company. Designated Reserve battalions were tasked to recruit and train a single company each. The Black Watch immediately formed its company under Major Allan Paterson Boswell, the manager of the Black Horse Brewery in Montreal. His hurriedly assembled command was ready by 20 May and marched in the annual church parade: "Our training was carried out in the armouries and the Greater Montreal areas... the company strength was only 67, including just one officer – the Company Commander."

A Company of the 2nd Battalion RHC moving forward in Korea during 1953.

1 CHB in Germany C 1951, Lt Col RL Rutherford OBE CD and officers.

Above left: 2 RHC B Company officers and senior NCOs with the company's assigned KATCOMs in Korea. Major GA Donaldson (front row, fifth from left) and to his immediate right, Lt IS Firstbrook.

Above right: SSgt Donald Fisher (later Regimental Adjutant) is on the right.

Members "D" Coy boarding train for Gagetown 1955.

Regular Battalions in Transit

Deployment to Europe meant moving families by ocean. This RHC family arriving in Germany is Major Peter Hall–Humpherson, his wife Doris, and their daughters Marcie and Vicky.

Soldiers of the Regiment in "C" Coy, 2 RHC boarding train for Gagetown 1955.

Smartness on and off parade. Exacting standards carefully monitored and directed by senior NCOs

Above: Camp Aldershot – Private Wilf Holdam (right) and an unknown private of 1CHB stepping out.

Left: WO1 RR Blackwell (left) succeeds WO1 EH Firby as RSM 1 RHC, 1966

Camp Gagetown – 1955 1 RHC Accommodation Area.

Above left: *National Survival Training* was required from the Army in 1960. The Black Watch Depot inserted National Survival Training into the Recruit Training Syllabus – new soldiers were given fifty periods of rescue elements: reconnaissance, knots, lashings, casualty handling, crowd and refugee control and even firefighting. The St John's Ambulance taught First Aid, and successful recruits were given an SJA Certificate. Priority was given to 2 RHC which was building towards a tour of duty in Europe.

Above right: Field training in Gagetown; note the WW2 weapons: Bren light machine gun and Lee Enfield.

Right: Gagetown was much the "ghost camp"; recently lived-in villages and farms dotted the area; churches and cemeteries were off-limits and carefully tended.

2 RHC marching through Downtown Fredericton NB, 1959.

1 RHC marching past the Bürgermeister of Werl in Germany, 31 August 1960.

Gagetown was the biggest training base in the Commonwealth, with the largest parade squares. The troops in the picture are marching on the Blissville airfield.

The magnificent carving of St Andrew was commissioned and dedicated to the RC Chapel in Fort St. Louis by the Roman Catholics of 1 RHC, and repaired and re-dedicated by the Roman Catholics of 2 RHC. In Fort St. Louis it stood in front of the RC Chapel. 2 RHC brought it to Gagetown in 1965 where it rested, again, in front of the RC Chapel, and then relocated to Montreal.

BLACK WATCH TROPHIES—Fred Kelly, centre, director of physical education for Acadia University, paid tribute to the outstanding sports achievement of 1st Battalion, The Black Watch (RHR) of Canada during a dinner for unit athletes at Camp Aldershot. On hand were some 27 trophies won by the battalion in both Army and inter-service sports competition during the past year. The battalion chalked up a record in sports that led all other regular army units. With Mr. Kelly are Capt. Lloyd Hill, left, battalion sport officer, and Lt.-Col. J. M. E. Clarkson, commanding officer. (National Defence photo).

Honor Top Canadian Army Sports Unit

ALDERSHOT—The 1st Battalion, The Black Watch (RHR) of Canada, took a "long count" of their 27 major sports trophies won during the past year and found that the unit had topped all others in athletic competition throughout the Regular Army in Canada.

To celebrate the occasion, popular commanding officer Lt.-Col. J. M. E. Clarkson, MC, CD, brought together nearly 150 of his stellar athletes at Camp Aldershot for a turkey dinner "on the house."

WINNING COMBINATION

Guest speaker Fred Kelly, director of physical education at Acadia University, told the husky young highlanders he had never met "a more winning combination than is here tonight." Mr. Kelly, a former Army major, praised the recent upswing in military sports activity and commended leadership Col. Clarkson has given in athletics since taking command of the battalion one year ago.

Maj.-Gen. E. C. Plow, CBE, DSO, CD, in a letter to the battalion, lauded the "fair play and highly competitive spirit" of their athletes. Gen. Plow said that their outstanding record of achievement was a credit to not only the Regiment but to the whole of Eastern Army Command.

Capt. Lloyd Hill, battalion sports officer, said his teams captured all softball and soccer titles in both Army and inter-service competition. Last summer the 1st Battalion walked away with the Army divisional sports meet at Camp Gagetown on points in track and field events and taking the grueling speed march competition.

In addition, the unit led the command in both indoor and outdoor rifle shooting competitions. And the Rothesay, N.B., Highland Games the Pipe and Drum Major of the 1st Battalion carried away five out of six trophies awarded.

"This is just the beginning," Col. Clarkson told his men at the dinner. "Next, I want the Armed Services Senior Hockey League championship." The Black Watch team representing Eastern Army Command, play their first home game in the league against Stadacona at Kentville this Saturday.

Both units dominated the command boxing finals. The 2 RHC Boxing Team won the tri–service championship. Their boxing team produced two Army champions: Pte WGR Stubbert won the Bantam Novice Crown and Pte JM McNeil the Welter Open Championship. The 1 RHC Boxing Team, managed by Major WB Macleod, won the Army Boxing Championships in 1963.

Cpl Doug Wilson, Captain Black Watch Hockey Team, 1 RHC, winners of the 4th Cdn Inf Bde Group Trophy in Germany. The Highlanders swept the series four straight. They next hosted Team Canada on 15 April 1961 at Wembley Stadium played before former Governor General Earl Alexander of Tunis.

A SCENE FROM SOLTAU ...

Above: Jeep mounted, 106mm recoilless rifle. Before advent of reliable anti-tank guided missiles, it was the infantry's only available longer range weapon.

Left: Armoured manoeuvres in Germany in Centurion tanks.

Below: M113 APCs on manoeuvres. The aluminum armoured "battle taxis" were better protection than trucks or half tracks and had better cross country performance. Each carried an infantry section of ten soldiers. Their only weapon was a 30 cal MG, replaced in Europe by a robust, though ancient, 50 Cal HMG — a weapon still used in the new millennium by many armies.

Soldiers of the 1st Battalion, the Black Watch move into the attack accompanied by a tank from the 8th Canadian Hussars as the first serial of the Soltau exercises gets under way. (PR Photo)

Above and bottom: 1 RHC in Norway 1965 as part of ACE (Allied Command Europe) Mobile Force. Led by LCol GH Sellar, Exercise *Winter Express*, The Black Watch Battlegroup included 1 Troop 2 Field Squadron, Royal Canadian Engineers; a signals element from 3 Signals Squadron; a logistics element from 3 Service Battalion; and "K" Battery of the 4th Royal Canadian Horse Artillery.

Right: The Norway manoeuvres included new kit: the Canadian-made Ski-Doo was deployed and tested and shown off. Capt RF MacDonald, Transport Officer 1 RHC, demonstrates the vehicle to King Haakon of Norway.

Black Watch in Cyprus

2 RHC had served in Cyprus from March 1966 to October 1966, commanded by Lt Col (Lt Gen) DA McAlpine CMM, CD, and Lt Col (Colonel) HJ Harkes MC CD; 1 RHC under Lt Col WJ Newlands CD served from October 1967 to March 1968. The last UN tour was by 2 RHC, led by Lt Col (Colonel) WB MacLeod OMM CD - the last foreign Black Watch posting and third regimental tour in Cyprus.

Top left: Cyprus terrain was rugged. Above: A typical OP. Left: LCol MacLeod and Col John Bourne in 1970, with regimental mascot *Yeltneb* - before donating him to the 1 RCR in a bit of mischievous Highland humour.

Black Watch Signal Section

Lt Col WA Teed took 1 RHC to France to participate at the Remembrance Ceremonies held 6 November 1960. Above, the Black Watch Guard of Honour stands fixed and perfect before the great memorial.

Drummer Calvin C Wilson, a WWII RHC veteran from Verdun, Quebec, charms two French youngsters in front of the memorial atop Vimy Ridge.

Above: The Trooping of the new Regimental Colour by 1 RHC (October 1963, Gagetown, NB) was performed with great skill and was the first such occasion since 1943. The parade also marked the last official act as Colonel of the Regiment for Brigadier KG Blackader.

Numbered above: **1** – SSgt JW Hughes; **2** – WO2 EH Firby; **3** – Maj JD "Jock" Kinnear; **4** – Capt DP Ludlow; **5** – Maj DS Paisley; **6** – Lt John Hasek.

Left: Lieutenant (LCol) Richard M. Gray receiving the Colour from RSM VI "Bull" Lawson CD. The occasion was the 1 RHC trooping 9 June 1965 in the presence of Maj Gen GA Turcot, GOC Eastern Command, and Lt Gov J Leonard O'Brien was also present, his last official engagement as Lt Gov of NB. The Commanding Officer was Lt Col Gord Sellar CD, Capt Dick Patterson was the Adjt. Capt Laurie Joudrey was the commander of the Escort to the Colour; Gray carried the Colour.

The Hamilton Gault Trophy. Ironically, as the Regular Black Watch prepared to dissolve, it was announced on 1 October 1970 that the 2nd Battalion had won the Hamilton Gault Trophy, awarded to the Regular infantry battalion with the best collective shooting record in the Forces; the 1st Battalion Black Watch placed second in the annual contest.

Canadian Army Bisley Team, 1965 – ablaze with Red Hackles

During their 18 years of Regular Force service, RHC battalions won trophies in all disciplines from shooting (right) to the Connault Shield for First Aid (below left and right). Below right is the 1 RHC stretcher bearer team that won the Connaught Shield in 1960 as the best team in the British Army of the Rhine.
Front row: (l to r): Pte SW Clements, Pte AT Marr, Pte PPJ Fitzpatrick, Pte Lapointe. Back row: Sgt RD Smith, Pte LM Pitts, Pte LPE Hubbard, L/Cpl RB Falconer, Pte KA Allen, and Cpl J Bell.

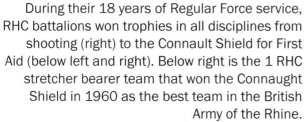

RHC Advisory Board, 1962

Front row (l to r): Major GD Cochrane (RHC Depot), LCOL WA Teed 1 RHC, COL PP Hutchison, General Sir Neil Ritchie, Brigadier KG Blackader, HM The Queen Mother, LCOL WSM MacTier, LCOL HM Wallis, COL GL Ogilvie, LCOL WC Leonard 2 RHC, LCOL DJ McGovern 3 RHC

Second row (l to r): LCOL WA Wood, COL JG Bourne, Lt Col FM Mitchell, COL AT Howard, COL ALS Mills, COL Andrew Fleming, COL IL Ibbotson, LCOL VE Traversy, COL JW Knox, LCOL IR McDougall

The Queen Mother at the Sergeants' Mess, Montreal 10 June 1962.

Front row (l to r): RSM RH Finnie, 1 RHC; HM The Queen Mother; RSM GW Wooten, RHC Depot.

Back row (l to r): RSM M Gurevitch, 3 RHC; RSM D Giles, 1 BW (Scotland); RSM TF Charters, 2 RHC.

Officers' Mess 3rd Battalion – 31 May 1959

First row (l-r): Capt AR Pryde; Maj RE Miller ED; Maj WB Redpath CD; Lt Col D'Arcy McGovern; Maj Ian Macaulay; Capt CS Bradeen, Jr; Capt WC Boswell.

Middle row: Lt WE Stavert; Lt AW MacLean; Lt Peter A. Webb; Capt G Johan Draper; Capt Ian Roberts; Lt JW Biddell; 2/Lt AR Aird; 2/Lt SF Angus.

Back row: 2/Lt Robert C Gelston; 2/Lt LN Ferdon; Lt John LC Macintyre; 2/Lt WH Wilson; 2/Lt RM Southward; 2/Lt Sidney Mentiply; 2/Lt LD Burpee; Lt SA Wilgar.

Note above fireplace, a humbler picture of HRH The Queen Mother and monteith bowl, with roses.

Molson Stadium, Presentation of Colours on 8 June 1962 by HRH the Queen Mother.

Lt Stephen Angus is framed over the drums above. Molson Stadium was filled to overflowing for the occasion.

The Canadian Centennial Tattoo was directed and produced by Major (Colonel) Ian Simon Fraser ONS OMM CD - gigantic and complex, with a cast of 1700 men and women from the Canadian Forces. They toured Canada, offering performances in twelve cities, travelling in two identical trains. The show incorporated well over a hundred Black Watch soldiers, in various period costumes. "It was a Herculean effort" – one Tattoo scene depicted garrison life in a Highland battalion circa 1782. It was recreated by 138 men and women in period costumes dancing five different Highland dances to the music of 108 pipers and drummers.

Gagetown 1967: The grand Black Watch Centennial trooping which united the three battalions in a splendid parade. The COs gathered for a royal portrait at the St Andrew's Barracks Officers' Mess. L to R behind the Queen Mother: Lt Col WJ Newlands CD, 1st Bn RHC, Lt Col HJ Harkes MC CD , 2nd Bn RHC, Colonel JW Knox MBE ED CD, Colonel of the Regiment, Lt Col T Price CD, 3rd Bn RHC, and Major BE Harper CD, The Black Watch Depot.

Amongst the many trips by the Pipes and Drums across Europe and North America were included a few more exotic excursions.

Left: Major (Lt Col) J MacFarlane CD, accompanied the band to Churchill Downs, Kentucky for the Derby in May 1966

Below & bottom right: In April 1956, the rebuilt pipe bands were considered good enough to be sent to a Tattoo in Hamilton, Bermuda which left the inhabitants 'goggle-eyed.'

Above left: More recently, a select grouping of the pipe band travelled to Beverly Hills, California, where they performed in a number of Hollywood events in April, 2011. The BW Hollywood Stars (l to r): P/Maj C Stevens, Sgt R Larman, Ppr S Jette, Dmr A McCulloch, Ppr A McGuckin, Dmr M Poxon, Ppr S Lawson, Cpl H Vanden Abeele, MCpl A Wilson, Ppr A Walsh, MCpL J McCarthy, CD, Ppr A Leger. Front kneeling: MCpl Ramsay, Sgt Dittmar, Cpl Reid.

The Regular Black Watch in transition. This 1970 photo captures the senior officers of 2 RCR (all former RHC) dressed for dinner, looking like chums of Ian Fleming or James Bond. As this was a 2 RCR Mess Dinner, the CO, Scotty Morrison, deemed it inappropriate for the officers of Canada's senior line regiment to appear in Highland dress for the occasion since the new CF (Midnight Blue) mess kit had not yet been approved. The sole option thus was dinner jacket. From left: Majors Stu MacAulay, John Forrest, Bud MacEachern, Lt Colonel Scotty Morrison, Majors Chuck McCabe, Ian Fraser, and Doug Fraser.

Part VI

The New Millennium, War, and New Challenges: 1993–2022

Chapter 14

Ending the Century

Lieutenant Colonel IM McCulloch CD, 1993–96: Bosnia and Archives

The decision to reduce militia pipe bands to just two paid members started to hit home in the House of Commons and the local press ... Members of three different parties stood up in the house to question the DND decision ...

Lieutenant Colonel IM McCulloch

Unlike previous Black Watch Regular Force commanding officers, the new CO arrived in the army via Carleton University (Journalism) and not RMC. He was commissioned into The Royal Canadian Regiment (RCR) upon graduation. Lieutenant Colonel Ian Macpherson McCulloch was a Maritimer from Halifax who was educated in Scotland and Switzerland. He served in a variety of regimental and staff appointments in Canada and the USA, and later acquired a Master's Degree in War Studies from the Royal Military College of Canada. McCulloch was promoted to lieutenant colonel in 1993, and in that year, assumed command of The Black Watch of Canada, a Reserve unit. This was not unusual.[1] McCulloch was recommended by Brigadier General Bruce Archibald, the senior RCR officer in FMC (Army) Headquarters: "When Archibald asked which regiment I preferred, I said without hesitation ... the Royal Highland Regiment!" He was subsequently interviewed by Colonels Bourne, Knox and Price at the Mount Royal Club: "Bourne grilled me on my education and career." McCulloch revealed he had worn a kilt since the age of three, had attended Fettes College in Edinburgh, and had played in three different pipe bands as a drummer.[2]

The lunch ended, and Colonel Bourne seemed satisfied: "... the next day I was called into General Gordie Reay's office to be congratulated on my appointment to command the Regiment."[3]

The Black Watch was in the fortunate position of having a full-time, staff-trained, regular commanding officer available every day.[4] In effect, the Regiment was now run by the Regular Force; and as luck would have it, there were RHC connections. "My RSS officer arrived the same time as I did – Captain Rob Boyd, 2nd Battalion Royal Canadian Regiment, a veteran of Gulf War One and Croatia, and more importantly, son of Lieutenant Colonel John Boyd, a former Black Watch Regular." Boyd was employed principally as adjutant ("he made me look good"). However, McCulloch did try to get authority from the RCR Home Station in London to grant him permission to wear kilted order but "[this] was turned down despite the RCR being entitled to wear the Maple Leaf tartan."[5] Captain Boyd stayed two years, retired, then pursued an MBA in Paris; he was replaced as RSS officer by Captain Pat Weir, PPCLI, who was decorated in Bosnia.

McCulloch was supported by a new regimental sergeant major, CWO Thomas Miles ("Damned good at what he did – technically proficient, good disciplinarian – but pretty tough on people – he was one of the first members of the 3rd Battalion to serve overseas on call-out.")[6] He had served in the reserves since 1973. McCulloch's senior officers included Majors Dover and Lusk, but the bulk of the RHC officers were new and inexperienced. Lieutenant Tom MacKay was a platoon leader: "We had no lieutenants, [because of] an exodus to the Regular Force, Chris Phare and I were the only qualified platoon commanders; 2/Lts from Phase 2 were not qualified [but] we had a bumper crop of six new officer cadets."[7] With Captain Bruce Bolton, the new CO had the combined knowledge of an RSM and pipe major to work with.

The drive to create a Regimental Foundation predated McCulloch and was a continuing subject of discussion between Colonels Tom Price, Jim Knox, Lieutenant Colonel Steve Angus, and Major Bill Stavert. As the century closed, it became increasingly apparent that the Regiment could not continue to operate as before, a *sui generis* icon supported by Montreal's business moguls. Angus underscored the situation:

> It had always been a concern to me that we were fast losing the people who could (without personal pain) provide finances to support the Regiment at a time when its needs were increasing logarithmically. The days of the individual patriarchal dominant leader were disappearing; changes were coming. It was not possible to demand the self-sacrifice (no pay, etc.) of the past, and it was important to build consensus and participation.[8]

Major (then Captain) Bruce Bolton assisted McCulloch in formalizing The Black Watch Business Council,[9] which resulted in the incorporation of The Black Watch Canada Foundation. At the same time, Lieutenant Colonel Vic Chartier became the first regimental secretary.[10] The Regimental Foundation was one of the more important projects McCulloch and Bolton established with the full support of the Regimental Advisory Board.[11]

His Militia Moment

The Black Watch was tasked to provide a recce platoon for the new "10/90 battalion" established by headquarters. In one of his first projects, Lieutenant Colonel McCulloch obtained Advanced Reconnaissance Course vacancies from the Infantry School in Gagetown. Captains Charles Barlow and Chris Phare were the first course graduates. The next year started off with a bang. McCulloch ordered an ambitious exercise in Huntingdon, part of the Eastern Townships, now renamed the Montérégie Region of Quebec. The staff secured District 1 HQ authority and clearances in terrain not used before. It was a progressive effort, based on Staff College SOPs and current doctrine employing a theoretical battalion structure. The Black Watch managed a rifle company with two full platoons but only one officer (Lieutenant TEC MacKay). The other platoon was commanded by WO John Barron. The recce platoon, somewhat below strength, was also commanded by a warrant officer. The CO prepared battle group orders straight out of the Kingston Staff College format. The armour, artillery, engineer, and air-support was 'notional'. He delivered a professional O Group in the field; his audience included the company commander, Major Gordon Lusk, with an attendant platoon commander dragged there by Lusk, who felt rather alone. Listening to full battle group orders, Tom MacKay recalled:

> I think we were more concerned about the buses and getting the men back to Montreal. Bitter reality. It may have been then that Ian looked at us; though it was a great exercise, we could see him deflated, giving battalion orders to a single company commander with one platoon officer ... it was his militia moment.[12]

However, field exercises and parade square bashing became a *bagatelle* when a new directive was announced which struck at the very essence of The Royal Highland Regiment.

The 1993 Pipe Band Calamity

We became a volunteer pipe band.

> Lieutenant Colonel Bruce Bolton, twice Pipe Major, The Black Watch

We met the enemy – they were from our side.

> Lieutenant Colonel SF Angus 1993[13]

The Regiment was considered typical of the Montreal garrison. Paper strength conflicted with the turn out for exercises, which averaged anywhere from sixty to one hundred all ranks. The Montreal reserves persevered without modern equipment, but at least the Black Watch had highland style and that *sine qua non* which distinguished them from other infantry regiments – the pipe band. The band had even amended old conventions: The Watch introduced its first female piper, Corporal Carolyn McLeod, in 1993. And then, disaster struck.

An economical senior staff officer in NDHQ decided that pipes and drums were decidedly passé in a *Star Wars* army. Certainly, it could be argued, the Reserves did not need them. And think of the money saved! Heretofore, the band had its own budget; authorized bandsmen and a separate financial code for expenses. A total of forty training days (per soldier) was allotted. The draconian changes garroted military music in Reserve bands across Canada; their budgets rolled into funds for training and administration, already severely reduced. The quota of pipers was slashed from an establishment of thirty to <u>two paid members per battalion</u>. Highlanders blanched: "What a disaster! We had to shove folks into infantry positions; we became a *de facto* volunteer pipe band." Ten years were to pass before the situation righted itself, and even then, unsteadily. Pipe Major Brian MacKenzie, who endured the great cut recalled: "I had to advise a lot of people they were out of a job."[14]

> The challenge was to build a voluntary band; we advertised, tried to attract student pipers and drummers; they could make a few bucks by playing for social occasions, weddings, ceremonies, corporate events that continues today. I ended up with ten pipers and drummers, the government allowed a pipe major, and two official band positions ("code #871, musician") drummers – <u>but not pipers.</u> Corporal Kieran Boyle (a tenor drummer) was a medic for example. It had to be all volunteers.[15]

The protests of the Regiment reached the House of Commons. The Minister of National Defence, the Hon DM Collenette, was approached by Warren Allmand MP and some progress was made. Although reduced to the status of a volunteer band, The Black Watch Pipes and Drums was "entitled to a cadre of seven paid musical instructors, a full suite of instruments and a variety of maintenance grants to assist it financially."[16] This left only two active reserve battalion bands in the city: The Black Watch and Les Fusiliers Mont-Royal. In order to be paid, pipers were camouflaged, employed as technicians and store clerks. In one instance, a skilled piper who had volunteered to cross-train and successfully qualified as an Infantry Weapons technician was employed in the QM. The pipe major showed remarkable patience as he negotiated for the piper's freedom to train with the band. He finally exploded when the lad was not permitted to wear the Royal Stewart kilt. His passionate letter to the CO eventually brought justice.[17]

The Black Watch rear guard was effective, indeed, too effective. McCulloch recalls:

> I ran afoul of Area Commander, Armand Roy, who called me in on the mat over the pipes and drums brouhaha (I have the wound stripes to prove it) when our covert and not so covert PR campaigns against the decision to reduce militia pipe bands to just two paid members started to hit home in the House of Commons and the local press (print and TV). Members of three different parties stood up in the house to question the DND decision: Warren Allmand (Lib); Bill Blaikie (NDP) and I believe it was John Fraser the speaker of the House ...[18]

In the end, as the only highland unit in Quebec, the Regiment was permitted seven paid positions. That was more than most bands in Canada. There were exceptions: The 48th Highlanders Pipe Band was allowed to remain at full strength (thirty-five to forty members) because it was considered to be *an important band* in Toronto.[19] Perseverance did, however, pay off. The Black Watch Pipes and Drums morphed into a reserve association union that "swelled with volunteers when former band members learned they would not have to do annual battle fitness training, weapons qualification or be subject to the code of service discipline – they could just focus on what they loved to do most: play the bagpipes or drum."[20] By combining the regimental Pipes and Drums with the pipe bands of the association and the cadets, the Regiment could muster anywhere from thirty-five to forty-five musicians on larger parades.[21] On grand occasions (royal visits, church parades), Montreal still reverberated to the skirl of the pipes and the beat of the drum.

Corporal Kieran Boyle and the Case of the Missing Pipes

In the fall of 1995, after Sunday band practice, regimental bagpipes were stolen from Corporals Vince Steeves and Stéphane Ethier. The latter's were the prized *Stewart bagpipes*, superb silver-mounted Henderson pipes – a link to the past. They had been donated by the family of Sergeant James Stewart, a Regimental piper who had died from tuberculosis. "This is part of the Black Watch family tradition ... We issued them to be played; after practice, the pipers went to a restaurant and left the pipes in the car; the back window was smashed and two bagpipes missing." Pipe Major Brian MacKenzie alerted the piping community through Montreal and then contacted the media. This resulted in news reports and a CBC skit, which was seen in Hamilton, Ontario. It was watched by a young lady who worked in *Arnie's Surplus* store. She was a former Montrealer and past member of The Black Watch Cadets. A couple of fellows tried to pawn bagpipes that day. She called The Watch. MacKenzie then called Corporal Kieran Boyle, a former drummer in the band, who lived in Hamilton. He was dynamic. He contacted the police, visited *Arnie's*, and interviewed shop owners in the area. Not impressed with the police investigation, Boyle became a Black Watch Sherlock Holmes. He searched out likely hang-outs, describing the perpetrators. Finally, he got a lead and staked-out the Hamilton YMCA. When the suspects showed up, he signalled the police. Six cars arrived. The recovered pipes were flown back to Montreal and met at the airport and armoury by TV News crews and reporters. "Everyone was now fascinated by the recovered pipes – Boyle was awarded a commendation."[22] P/Major MacKenzie felt the unnamed young lady should also be commended; he drove to Hamilton with a regimental plaque and gift, but she had left, moved west, never to be seen again.

Black Watch Archives

Eheu! Fugaces, Posthume, Posthume / Labunter anni[23]

Horace, Book 2 The Odes.

It was dirty, darkish and damp, I was covered with the dust of a century after a day's work, some boxes had not been opened since the first or second world war ...

Terry Copp, Canadian historian, of the early BW Archives

Regimental training was normal: ranges and district exercises. Keen on military history, McCulloch organized a "Staff Ride" to the battlefield at Gettysburg, PA. About a dozen Black Watch officers and NCOs attended. They were later joined by a cadre of their confreres in the 111th US Regiment ("re-establishing the links which had fallen by the wayside").[24] They toured the famous battlefield and discussed military history circa 1863, later enjoying lunch with "The Associators" at the Spring City Armoury near Valley Forge. These were the G.H.W. Bush years. Soldiers and officers were taught new terms; the Red Army was now referred to as "The Threat." There was a resurgence in doctrinal training. New philosophies of war were in vogue: the essence of Yankee manoeuvre warfare, *AirLand Battle*. Its developers and their graduates were known as *Jedi Knights*.[25] The Canadian Army was much impressed by the American cultural and technological renaissance – from new ground-attack aircraft and gunships, to the superb M1A1/2 *Abrams* main battle tank. The Kingston staff college curriculum was revamped, and militia officers were expected to know far more doctrine and tactical techniques than their fathers could have imagined. Tours in Bosnia were professionally beneficial, but also introduced modern social difficulties. Prudently, Lieutenant Colonel McCulloch introduced a seminar on post-traumatic stress disorder (PTSD) for the families of returning Bosnia-Sarajevo veterans.

Much like Colonels Klepak and Robertson, McCulloch was an academic. His historical passion was reflected in his interest in the Regimental Museum, to which he added the Korea and peacekeeping exhibits. Perhaps his great legacy was the reorganization of the Black Watch archives. As CO, he published a number of papers and completed his Master's in War Studies for RMC. Seconded to McGill under Professor Desmond Morton, he chronicled the 7th Canadian Infantry Brigade in The Great War, which included the 42nd Battalion CEF (Black Watch). As he conducted his research, McCulloch became aware the archives (a cavern-like vault in the basement, accessible by a circular iron staircase) were in abysmal shape. It had been threatened by floods, and recently suffered considerable water damage. Terry Copp, one of the great Canadian military historians, recalled his own early research: "It was dirty, darkish and damp; I was covered with the dust of a century after a day's work; some boxes had not been opened since the first or second world war."[26]

Lieutenant Colonel McCulloch established proper archives, using one of the armoury classrooms. After consultation with Professor Morton, he invited Ms Barbara Wilson of the National Archives to advise. He next secured the assistance of Ms Johanna O'Neil and Maura Pennington, both recent graduates of archival sciences at McGill, and both RCR wives. Pennington eventually became the first Black Watch archivist, followed by Ms O'Neill, and later, Ms Anne Stewart.[27] This marked the beginning of the present Black Watch Archives (BWA), which remain the envy of most Canadian regiments.

Security in the Regimental Museum required serious attention, particularly after twenty rare campaign medals were discovered missing. McCulloch replaced the volunteer curators, changed the locks and along with the introduction of university-trained archivists, hoped to establish order and control in both the Museum and Archives. It was a limited success, but led to improved management in the years to come. The stolen medals were not recovered.[28]

Black Watch in Bosnia, 1993

The end of the Cold War brought considerable change to the Canadian Forces, though sadly, the demise of the Warsaw Pact did not produce the anticipated relief and savings. Instead, western militaries were called upon to intervene in religious and cultural conflicts. When Yugoslavia wrecked itself via civil strife, the United Nations Protection Force (UNPROFOR) was deployed as a peacekeeper. However, such separatist wars required a new form of peacekeeping to maintain control, in the face of human rights atrocities. The so-called Third Balkan War was marked with brutal ethnic conflicts and genocide. *Peacemaking* replaced *peacekeeping* and called for a more traditional employment of troops. Canadians first arrived in the Balkans when war broke out in 1991. Eventually more than forty thousand members of the Forces served in the region. Twenty-three soldiers were killed while serving in Bosnia-Herzegovina. The first Black Watch personnel assigned for UN operations arrived in Bosnia (former Yugoslavia) on 29 October 1992. The Black Watch participation was limited to volunteers who served on limited tours. Of particular interest was an experimental all-reserve platoon. Gathered from volunteers throughout the Quebec regiments, its first (and only) officer commanding was a Black Watch officer, Captain Chris Phare. WO M Snoddon was one of the corporals. Phare, destined to command the Regiment, recalled:

> Up to that point, it was the biggest leadership challenge I had. The Van Doos didn't want us there; we were set up for failure. But we were determined, pressed on. It was a challenge to maintain discipline and morale ... I realized the need for excellent, not just competent NCOs on operations. Here training can allow us to experiment, in operations, it was different.[29]

The new padre was helpful. Captain the Rev Canon Bruce Glencross had served in the Middle East and was therefore acutely aware of the problems foreign service could create for reservists. In the great scheme of things, they were neither fish nor fowl to the Regular Force command, particularly when placed in the battle groups. Glencross was recommended by Lieutenant Colonel the Rev William Fairlie, Command Chaplain for the Army. These were again interesting times. DND Ottawa was going through *operational envy* and now insisted that chaplains in reserve units need to be as operationally ready as those in the regular units. Lieutenant Colonel Chartier asked Fairlie to help find a successor to Dr Armour. He agreed and quickly delivered: "Bruce Glencross was a young cleric in the Diocese of Montreal, who was willing to serve. The CO urged me to find a Presbyterian, but I told him that we were not allowed to discriminate and Bruce had a Scottish name. All worked out well."[30] Canon Glencross recalls:

Going from *Peace-Keeping* to *Peace-Making* in Bosnia with our hands tied! I interviewed soldiers from Bosnia – they didn't want to admit anything was wrong, really it was the beginning of PTSD (post-traumatic stress) being recognized in the Militia after service abroad, it required extra to work with the RSM in interviews of ex-Bosnia veterans.[31]

The reservists, once their tour was completed, were cast adrift. Having bonded with their comrades under stress, they were, quite literally, abandoned at the airport. Several suffered trauma. The family aspect of The Watch helped. McCulloch's PTSD seminar for the families of returning veterans was the right start. Lessons learned from Bosnia deployments would help the Black Watch in their next war, a decade away. As late as 2013, a considerable number of Black Watch Bosnian veterans still served in the Regiment. These included the commanding officer as well as warrant officers Keith Fuller and John Lawton and Sergeant Don Desy. The one who saw the most action was MWO Steve Campbell, who had served as a platoon warrant officer with the 2nd Battalion, Princess Patricia's Canadian Light Infantry during the Medak Pocket battle, March 1993.[32] Providing in-regiment professional care grew more difficult as the Army decided to group doctors in medical companies, and attached practitioners (though there was a number that wished to serve the Black Watch) were no longer permitted. The last Regimental MO was Captain Gordon Roper.

Bosnia was never really resolved. Worse still, the over-extended Canadian Army became involved in East Africa resulting in the Somalia Affair of 1993 – an incident involving a Somalian intruder. It appalled the Canadian public and brought to light internal problems in the Canadian Airborne Regiment. Military command was soundly rebuked, leading to a public inquiry that cited problems in CF leadership. The affair led to the disbanding of Canada's elite Canadian Airborne Regiment, damaged the morale of the Forces, and led to the reduction of military spending by nearly 25 percent. These were truly arduous times for the Reserves – often the first to suffer cuts in budget and equipment. Still, the Regiment managed to have the museum refurbished and the St Andrew's stained-glass window (originally from Werl, Germany) installed as part of the NATO-Peacekeeping exhibit.[33]

In the early 1990s, the Regiment paraded thirty officers and 150 other ranks. It was not unusual to field a rifle company at concentration (MILCON). By the fall of 1994, the complement was twenty officers, twenty-four NCOs, 129 ORs for a total of 173 all ranks. They had placed third in the *Mary Otter Competition* for No1 District, which was good news at the annual Reunion Dinner. The guest of honour was the deputy commander of the Army, the ever-charming (and musical) Major General Romeo Dallaire OC CMM GOQ CD.[34] The general had just returned from Africa as former Force Commander of UNAMIR, the ill-fated United Nations peacekeeping force for Rwanda, and was still suffering from the effects of that horrible experience. However, the reunion dinner emphasizes family hospitality, traditional food and drink, and the wondrous effect of the pipes, able to cast a spell over any occasion. The sombre mood of the general lifted and he accepted the pipe major's invitation to visit the depths of the Pipes and Drums canteen where the Gaelic ways still lived and merry tunes were played. His executive assistant confided: "It was the first time I have seen the general laugh since getting back from Rwanda."[35]

Mess life was a bit more relaxed since the colonel required less time in the mess. Previously, there was a dining-in or social event once a month. This did not include mixed soirees or such *de rigueur* occasions as the reunion dinner, debutantes' reception, Christmas party, and Levee.[36] Officers were expected to stay until excused by the CO. It had always been that way. The mid-nineties were easier, but only slightly. Captain Bruce Bolton was one of the company commanders; Major Dover was the DCO but was soon followed by Gordon Lusk. Four new captains left for HMCS *Donnaconna* or the Regular Force just as Lieutenant Colonel McCulloch took command. Finding new subalterns proved a challenge, and training would require experienced hands. McCulloch invited a former officer, Captain (Colonel) Patrick Kelly, to leave the RMR and return to the regiment. Kelly took over from Gordon Lusk to command A Company when Gordon moved to DCO.[37]

In April 1995, under the Hon David Collenette, Minister of National Defence, a special commission on the restructuring of the reserves was created. The reporting team was chaired by the former chief justice of Canada, the Right Hon Brian Dickson and included Lieutenant General Charles H Belzile and the noted Canadian military historian, Jack L Granatstein. The Dickson Commission's recommendations were published on 30 October 1995. The report proposed that the Army Reserves, steadfastly called *The Militia*, should provide platoon-sized cadres for incorporation into Regular Force units proceeding on peacekeeping duties. The historic Militia Districts, dating back to the early 19th century were to be eliminated and replaced by seven Militia brigade groups, each commanded by an officer in the rank of colonel. The existing Area Headquarters were retained but reorganized and became Total Force Area Headquarters, commanding all Army troops in their area of responsibility. Three aims were highlighted: *Cost Effectiveness, Historical Performance,* and *Footprint and Link to the Community*. The net result was that Headquarters grew bigger and the Reserves smaller. In practical terms, "conforming to *Total Army Establishment*"[38] was married to the closing of armouries, sharing facilities and a threatened *restructure,* which would soon affect the Black Watch dramatically. Despite good intentions, little changed on the floor except that there was more paperwork, business plans and detailed long-range-training-forecasts at a time when the average reserve battalion could manage less than 150 soldiers. Though field training averaged about two platoons on exercise, the same administration was required as for a full regular battalion.

In his third year as CO, McCulloch travelled regularly to Kingston for graduate studies, as well as researching and writing his Master's thesis. He was, in his own words, "less conspicuous ... I was a 'part time' CO."[39] Meantime, the Black Watch was being watched and criticized – something that would become alarmingly evident during Lieutenant Colonel Lusk's first ninety days.[40] Lieutenant Colonel McCulloch's tenure as CO was completed in the summer of 1995, when he visited, unaccompanied by the Regiment's honoraries, with HM the Queen Mother at Clarence House, to brief her on the state of the Regiment. In the early spring, with Montreal still dirty with old snow and slush, McCulloch handed over command of the Black Watch to Gordon Lusk on Sunday, 31 March 1996, in an orthodox parade held in the armoury. Lieutenant Colonel McCulloch left to become the deputy director of the newly-formed Directorate of History & Heritage (DHH) in Ottawa.[41]

Colonel Tom Price

In early May 1996, a week after church parade, the Regiment was stunned by the news that Colonel Thomas Evan Price had died of a heart attack. The dashing Tom Price was much beloved and considered in the prime of life. Queen Elizabeth the Queen Mother sent condolences to his wife.[42] The Montreal garrison turned out for the funeral at the Regimental Church perhaps the largest funeral ever held there. Price was well-regarded throughout the province, and the country – he was *toujours, le grand écossais*. His old friend and school mate, Stephen Angus, became Honorary Colonel of the Regiment, while a venerable Black Watch veteran, diplomat and general, Duncan McAlpine, who joined the Regiment in 1941, and only recently retired from the army as a lieutenant general, became the Honorary Lieutenant Colonel.

Lieutenant Colonel GT Lusk CD, 1996–2000: At the Edge

It was quite stressful. We were worried we would disappear. Gord carried that burden.[43]

Lieutenant Colonel Tom MacKay

Gordon Thomas Lusk was forty-three when he took command of the Black Watch. He was born in Sudbury but devoted to Atlantic Canada ("the Maritimes formed my character"), and like Doug Robertson, an engineer from the University of New Brunswick. Lusk began his military career with Toronto's 48th Highlanders and later moved to Montreal to join the Black Watch in 1980. His early days were spent as a staff officer at Army Headquarters in St Hubert, before he started his own general contracting business. A careful manager, he was determined to get the Black Watch out of the red with District (now Brigade) HQ and clear up the backlog. He would scrupulously follow all directives. Lusk was welcomed by the battalion: "We were relieved to have a regimental officer back in charge."[44] Initially, his DCO was Major Dover, soon to be followed by Major Bruce Bolton. The year began well. The new CO was placed in command of the Militia Concentration (MILCON). However, the reserves *per se* were in a state of flux. Change was sweeping through the system.

The Canadian Forces comprised sixty thousand regulars and nearly thirty thousand reservists, but few reserve units could produce cadres for operational tasking without a concentrated two to three-month preparation under experienced instructors. The year after the report of the Dickson Commission,[45] DND introduced amendments to the National Defence Act, which was almost fifty years old, and extensive revisions to the Queen's Regulations and Orders (QR&O) with special emphasis on the summary trial process. The impact of Canada's Charter of Rights demanded more extensive and better legal counselling. Further, the 'District' system (in place since before Confederation) was replaced by an ambitious 'brigade' concept. This meant one less promoted reservist, now the deputy commanders in each *Area*, with total control by Regular Force headquarters, which now orchestrated *brigades* run by full colonels (not brigadier generals) of the militia. Disappointingly, the new scheme produced neither greater efficiency nor easier access to equipment. A partisan journal, *The Militia Monitor*, complained of "*voodoo accounting* ... disentangling Reserve and Regular dollars."[46] The hoped-for-legislation required to protect reserve employment did not come about. *The Gazette* noted: "It is shameful that a sergeant in the Black Watch had to give up his job in 1993 because he wanted to serve as a United Nations soldier in the former Yugoslavia."[47] The Black Watch found itself part of 34 Brigade: *le 34e Groupe-brigade du Canada,* part of *Secteur de Québec de la Force terrestre* (SQFT), renamed *2nd Canadian Division* in 2012.[48] Predictably, all the much-vaunted change produced was an ever-increasing crush of administration with brigade headquarters churning out more paperwork than Second World War divisions. Perhaps, to his surprise, Minister of National Defence David Collenette found himself siding with the reserves, as NDHQ concocted new plans for efficiency, only to find it reduced Militia funding by diverting it to other projects. He, therefore, worked closely with the honorary colonels "to stop the decline of the reserves. Too often the regular senior staff seemed not to share my view, which was particularly odd given that during my time, reserve forces constituted 20–30 percent of active strength in Bosnia and Croatia."[49]

Black Watch Ordered Disbanded, August 1996

Go home and tell your soldiers you will be disbanded.

Major Gen Alain Forand

His knife see rustic Labour dight
An' cut you up wi' ready sleight

Robert Burns, To a Haggis

Despite the minister's support, in the summer of his first term, Tuesday, 27 August 1996, Lieutenant Colonel Lusk was summoned before the newly appointed SQFT area commander, Major Gen Alain Forand CMM SC CD. Lusk arrived accompanied by his Honorary Lieutenant Colonel, Lieutenant General Duncan McAlpine. They anticipated trouble but could never have guessed what awaited them. They were summoned inside. "It was a short meeting ... we didn't get to sit down." General Forand was brusque: "Go home and tell your soldiers you will be disbanded."[50] The Black Watch was all but cashiered. Its pipe band was eliminated. The battalion reduced to a rifle company and company headquarters, commanded by a major. Case closed.

Lieutenant General McAlpine made a few phone calls, one of which was to the Minister of National Defence. He was not alone. Three regiments in Montreal: The Canadian Grenadier Guards, The Royal Montreal Regiment, and the Black Watch, had been threatened with the guillotine. The Honorary Colonel of the Royal Montreal Regiment and former District Commander, Colonel George Javornik, was a charter member of *Reserves 2000* (a private group of lobbyists committed to the interests of the militia): "It was in this latter capacity that I, on a conference call from New York, raised the spectre to the Minister of National Defence [The Hon David Collenette] of shattering the post-Quebec-separation referendum fragile peace. How? By publicly exposing that the Quebec units slated for downsizing happened all to be Anglo units. What [am] I to tell those Honorary Colonels all set to go to the press?" The next day, according to Javornik: "The Minister [requested] the Commander of the Army [Lieutenant-General Maurice Baril] to cease and desist all and any such downsizing initiatives across the whole country."[51]

The alleged plan was to regroup the three Montreal Anglophone infantry regiments into a single English-speaking battalion, with three rifle companies to represent historic units; other solutions ranged from the practical to the bizarre.[52] The final scheme was worse, and spelled nothing less than torpid termination. The Grenadier Guards and The Royal Montreal Regiment were advised that they would become rifle companies in the 4th Battalion R22eR (the Van Doos battalion in Laval, across the Rivière-des-Prairies, north of Montreal). Reduction to 'minor unit' status was an iron-fisted attempt by bureaucracy to save money by reducing the size of the reserves across Canada.[53]

Rescinded

The Restructure of the Reserve was not an exercise in popularity.

General Maurice Baril, CDS[54]

It should not have been totally unexpected. Major General Baril, as area commander, had briefed all the honorary colonels at FMC headquarters earlier that spring. "For most of them this was a surprise; much more than they were expecting." No one believed this would actually occur. However, Baril was "determined to reduce that social club; we were starving for troops and money."[55] As soon as it was decided that the Reserves were to be restructured, the order of execution was signed by General Baril as Chief of Land Staff and forwarded to the area commanders ("Alain Forand did not act on his own"). However, the specific mechanics were staffed in Montreal at SQFT headquarters.

By Friday, 30 August, it was completely turned around. Lusk received a call and was told to forget about it and carry on. General Baril, as Army chief, acted after meeting with the minister of national defence: "I rescinded the order personally." In Montreal, the incident was remembered by Major General Alain Forand (later appointed Colonel of the Regiment, Royal 22e Régiment) as essentially *a Militia solution*:

> Units that were selected were those judged to be not performing or maintaining sufficient number of personnel … This was based on the recommendation of my staff. I wanted it to be done by my senior militia officers: Unfortunately, after the evaluation criteria were assessed, it was the three Anglophone infantry units, and perhaps a fourth, the 3rd Field Engineers [in Westmount] who were designated. I summoned them to my HQ – there was no discussion. [56]

Brigadier General Jean Gervais denies he or any Militia officers participated in the selection.[57] Upon reflection, Forand allows that "perhaps we moved too fast in Quebec compared to the other Areas." He referred to the meetings held that evening as his "Black Tuesday."[58] In retrospect, the selection of the three Anglophone regiments in Montreal invited speculation. Had these units been eliminated, the greater part of English Montreal's military history would have disappeared, together with the ties that bound regiments to the community. Curiously, senior Reserve generals were certain "it was not a witch hunt, although it did not make a whole lot of sense."[59] Worse, it seemed to extinguish all hope still held by the Black Watch for the resurrection of its lost Regular battalions. Despite efforts, the Minister of National Defence was stymied, not by those against the military, but by the Regular Force: "On a number of occasions I expressed a desire to reconstitute the Black Watch as a Regular regiment, particularly after the disbandment of the Airborne Regiment. This was opposed by the Army."[60]

The incident made a lasting impression on the new colonel. "We were being judged by a 'Viability Study'[61] – it drove my four years and was my chief priority," reflected Lusk. The battalion was rated by 1) Attendance, 2) Operational Capability, 3) Finances, 4) Individual and Collective Training, in addition to 'Unit History' and 'Footprint within the Community': "We took it very seriously; however, the Francophone units were not at all concerned about disbandment."[62] It seemed another example of the two solitudes. That, plus the seemingly unbridgeable Militia vs. Regular Force divide – a deep-rooted misunderstanding of the militia's particular ethos, limitations, and needs. Military historian Desmond Morton surmised: "[given] the political influence the militia could mobilize, it was to the government's benefit that the two sides were in open warfare. It usually is."[63] The named regiments, their heads resting close to, if not actually on the chopping block, were concerned.[64] It smacked of betrayal. Routine battalion training now held critical consequence. Lieutenant Colonel Tom MacKay, then a platoon commander, recalls: "It was quite stressful. We were worried we would disappear. Gord carried that burden."[65]

That fall's reunion dinner took a different theme: the guest of honour was Robert Côté OC ADC, who headed the Montreal police bomb squad during the turbulent 1960s and 70s. He recounted hair-raising stories of their activities and noted: "Many people believe that the October Crisis was an event by itself. In fact, the October Crisis was the culminating point of a seven-year long period of terrorism in Montreal." That winter, the Regiment trained with renewed vigor. Lusk concentrated on retention and administration: "We cleaned up finances, attendance, and back paper work". Lusk also refurbished his RHQ team. The RSS Officer and RSM required attention. He welcomed Captain Peter Radman CD, 2 RCR, as his new regular staff officer. Radman had a rich Regular Force and militia background, and would become synonymous with the Black Watch for the next fifteen years. Lusk noted Radman's immediate effect: "I cannot say anything but good things; I could not have done it without him."[66] The unit was further reinforced in February 1997, when Captain RF Clarke CD and Captain Andrew GM Kerr CD joined Regimental Headquarters, an adjunct to the Advisory Board. Its membership rose to twenty-seven members, most of whom served as COs in Regular or Militia battalions of the Regiment.[67]

With the Imperials in Ticonderoga, 1997

The regimental church parade, held on 4 May 1997, was highlighted by the superb performance of the *Almelo Christelijk Mannenkoor* (Almelo Christian Male Chorus) a male chorale from Holland standing in for the church choir. There were several references made during the service to the debt owed by the Dutch people to the Black Watch, among their liberators in the Second World War. Their visit was arranged by that distinguished veteran, Okill Stuart, the ninety-three year-old-brother of the 1 RHC adjutant, Campbell Stuart. The memorable service was conducted by the Black Watch chaplain, Captain Bruce Glencross, assisted by the Honorary Chaplain, Dr JSS Armour.

The Regiment was to experience a summer of history. Lieutenant Colonel Lusk, with fond memories of being fêted with Lieutenant Colonel Klepak by the prominent Pell-Ducharme family at Ticonderoga in 1981, decided to order a Black Watch excursion into the USA, in the style of McDougall and Wood. He led a hefty contingent that included a substantial pipe band to the old fort on Lake Champlain in New York State. The dedication of a commemoratory cairn to the assault of 1758 marked the occasion. It also marked the first time the Imperial Black Watch had returned to the site since the Seven Years' War. The First Battalion Black Watch had just completed duties as the last British garrison in Hong Kong. The crown colony soon after reverted to Chinese control. On their way back from the Far East, their CO, Lieutenant Colonel Alasdair Loudon, agreed to visit the Fort. They arrived in uniforms still wet from the torrential downpour during the Hong Kong Parade. They were joined by Brigadier Garry C Barnett OBE, Colonel of the Imperial Black Watch, who was delighted to see Lusk's Canadian Royal Highlanders. They made the unveiling of the memorial there truly special, particularly as the 1st Battalion was only represented by a very small party since the remainder was still returning from the Hong Kong handover. The event included a parade through the town of Ticonderoga as well as parties chock-full of cosmopolitan New Yorkers and Bostonians. Bruce Bolton recalls, "We were lost in the shuffle; it was assumed by everyone that the CO, myself and the band were British and with Lieutenant Colonel Loudon."[68]

Undaunted, Lusk's next conquest was closer to home. The Black Watch was granted the Freedom of the municipality of Ormstown. Nestled in the Chateauguay valley, south-west of Montreal, in what some folks call 'the western townships', Ormstown is one of the few remaining rural areas still populated by English-speaking farmers descended from Scottish and Loyalist immigrants. The parade took place on Sunday, 4 October 1997. Mayor Chrystian Soucy welcomed Lieutenant Colonel Lusk and the Regiment. It was a not a grand parade but presented with the same attention to detail and deportment as with every Black Watch ceremony. There were two twenty-five-man guards, as well as the pipes and drums. The Colour Party was commanded by Captain Charles Barlow; CWO T Miles was parade RSM.[69] The Regiment was well-received, and Lusk was pleased to report another 'Community Foot Print' (one of the newly designated Militia Roles) to his brigade headquarters.

Gracious in Tough Times: The Reunion Dinner, 1 November 1997

In October 1997, an arbitrary decision by the Chief of the Land Staff lopped $16,900,000 from the Militia budget, while promising that the paid ceiling would remain at sixty-five training days allocated annually for part time (Class A) soldiers. "As the Regular army establishment failed to do any serious mobilization planning, but began instead to assess the viability of Militia units, many of which were prevented by imposed manpower ceilings from recruiting viable numbers, relations between reserves and regulars once more deteriorated."[70] Nonetheless, the guest of honour for the Reunion Dinner was the new Chief of the Defence Staff, General JMG Baril CMM MSM CD.[71]

He spoke of the Regiment's illustrious history and dedicated service to Canada, noting his own focus on supporting Canadian servicemen and women with equipment and training. The speech had a familiar ring to it and echoed the optimistic sentiments that former Army Commanders had presented to the Black Watch since the 19th century. Given the events of the previous summer, the Regiment was still not certain who had ordered their disbandment. Nevertheless, in good highland fashion, they received General Baril with cordiality. General Duncan McAlpine thanked the CDS, recalling he had served with Baril in the 1970s and was certain he shared his own high hopes for the future of Canada's Reserves. McAlpine held a suspicious stiletto in his hand, but any concerns were evaporated as he blithely presented the guest of honour an engraved silver Black Watch letter-opener, and a copy of the regimental history.[72] The Reunion Dinner was followed by the annual Remembrance Day Parade. The garrison turned out at the Montreal Cenotaph, across the park from the Sun Life Building. A strong contingent of Black Watch veterans was prominent at the ceremonies and did credit to the Regiment. Of particular note was ninety-five-year-old Corporal Roy Henley, a First World War veteran, still active in the Association, who lived in Ottawa. He stood steadfast and saluted proudly during the ceremony and acquitted himself well during a televised CBC interview. These were fleeting but precious days for the Great War veterans still attending regimental parades; however, Second World War and Korea veterans filled their gaps, and their Red Hackles dominated the crowd.

Black Watch Veterans Recognized

Black Watch veterans were recognized throughout Canada for accomplishments beyond regimental confines. Lieutenant Colonel Bill Molnar, awarded the Queen's Medal, Commandant of the Canadian Bisley team in 1996 and a renowned marksman, was selected for induction into the Canadian Forces Sports Hall of Fame. At the same time, Lieutenant Colonel Chuck McCabe OMM CD, commandant of the Connaught Ranges since 1992, retired from the Forces after forty-four years of service in the Militia and Regular Force. He would not drift far from the Regiment. He was followed at Connaught by another Black Watch officer, Lieutenant Colonel Bryan Johnson. This fusillade of bulletins was followed by the news that Lieutenant Colonel Thurston (Tud) Kaulbach OMM CD had just retired as Executive Director of the Dominion of Canada Rifle Association, a position he had held since retiring from the Army in 1991.

To alert everyone that the army of the past was about to come to an electrifying close, the Regiment announced it had launched an impressive home page on the World Wide Web. The site was maintained by Captain Andrew GM Kerr CD, spectrally dubbed *the Webmaster*.

Khaki Pattern Tam Adopted

The modern Army tinkers with *vogue*, less by design and *chic* and more by cost and availability. At the urging of the soldiers and with the support of the Advisory Board, the CO selected the British Army pattern khaki tam o'shanter to replace the aging stock of khaki balmorals. The officers wore the fawn balmoral in lieu of the tam. The new headdress was to be worn with combat uniform only; the blue bonnet (balmoral) would continue to be worn by all ranks with service dress and all orders of regimental dress. The replacement was scheduled for the spring of 1998.

Valcartier 1998 – Unit Viability Assessment, Tactical Evaluation

In the 1997–98 training year, the Black Watch, like all other units in Canada, was evaluated across six different categories, including collective training. The officer selected to command the tested platoon was Captain Tom MacKay, who was well aware of the responsibility resting on his and his men's shoulders: The consequence of failing these evaluations was thought to be amalgamation with another regiment or reduction to nil strength and closure of the unit.[73]

Preparation began in earnest in early 1998 with section level drills progressing to platoon level tactics. Every aspect of the quick attack was broken down into elemental parts and rehearsed. This encouraged everyone.[74] The test was conducted in Valcartier in the spring of 1998. The enemy force (an infantry section) and the evaluators (a captain and warrant officer) were Regular Force, from the Vandoos. MacKay issued orders quickly. They sent scouts forward (a tactic little used by other units but one that put them in good stead with their evaluators) then the fire team deployed into carefully selected over-watch positions.

> We had advanced about 800m when the lead section came under contact ... [it] wasted no time in winning the firefight; GPMG team delivered a withering volume of fire onto the enemy position. The two sections not under contact moved rapidly and under cover to an assembly area ... My orders were delivered quickly and the section commanders were efficient in getting their troops ready to move out for our assault. Sergeant Siket moved forward independently to take command of the *Firebase* ... We arrived opposite the enemy trenches already in proper formation facing our objective at a 90° angle – the soldiers fixed bayonets, and on my command, charged forward onto the enemy.[75]

The evaluators offered MacKay kudos for the assault and praised Sergeant Siket's command of the firebase. "He said that our performance was as good as any Regular Force platoon he had seen." The platoon bested all the units from its own 34th Brigade, and tied with the top regiment from 35th Brigade.[76]

The battalion's high standards were further acknowledged in a letter Lusk received from Lieutenant Colonel JAG Champagne, commanding the Infantry School at Gagetown. The entrance tests for RESO training were conducted in the field for the first time and many candidates failed. However, Colonel Champagne was moved to write complimenting Lusk on the results achieved by the six Black Watch candidates: "This is an exceptional record ... I recognize the significant investment in time and resources to achieve this ... not only were you the largest unit represented, but the only unit to achieve a 100 percent pass.[77]

Operation Recuperation: The Ice Storm 1998

Blow, winds, and crack your cheeks! rage! blow!

King Lear Act III. Scene II

The New Year would prove memorable, not for reasons political or indeed military, but for matters meteorological. Quebec was devastated by a spectacular ice storm that struck on 6 January 1998. Dozens of hydro towers collapsed, crippling all of Montreal, most of the South Shore, and a wide swath of Eastern Ontario and Quebec. The army was mobilized; over twelve thousand soldiers worked closely with political, civil and public safety authorities to resolve the crisis. Lieutenant Colonel Lusk was notified on 9 January that all members of the Regiment were to assist the Regular Army units in disaster relief operations. By 1930 hrs on Saturday 10 January, the first full Black Watch platoon under Captain Tom MacKay had been deployed; this was followed quickly by a second platoon, plus a support section. By Monday 12 January, all of A Company was deployed to the South Shore in support of 3 R22eR (the Van Doos) assisting civil authorities in the evacuation of homes, the clearing of downed trees, and patrolling evacuated areas. At the height of operation, over eighty-five members of the Regiment were deployed. This was a considerable effort for a reserve unit where most soldiers were working, or attending university. The entire effort to deal with Op *Verglas* (Ice storm) lasted a month (7 January to 8 February) and utilized most of the Regiment's resources.[78]

Once things returned to normal, standard training was reinstated. This included a winter indoctrination exercise, *Frozen Hackle*, to take place in February, which was usually the coldest month. However, "Just to mock the soldiers, with their toboggans and arctic tents, Mother Nature brought rain and most of the snow melted. As a result, the newer soldiers had a rather distorted view of what winter warfare really means."[79] Things got much better in April. Captain MacKay and Sergeant Siket took the ready platoon to CFB Valcartier where it was evaluated in tactical problems. They conducted a textbook attack and came back with an appraisement of 92 percent, one of the highest marks in the brigade.

On the first of May, a most congenial event took place with the Black Watch honouring Colonel John Bourne on the occasion of his eightieth birthday. On one of the warmest, most humid nights in years, one hundred serving and former officers and their ladies paid tribute to his unfaltering service to the Regiment for over sixty-one years. HM The Queen Mother was most fond of Bourne, and Colonel Angus read her message of warm congratulations. Colonel Scotty Morrison, the last CO of 1 RHC, offered a humorous but nonetheless moving account of Colonel Bourne's dedication to the welfare of the former regular battalions prior to their disbandment. If the muggy weather did not remind John Bourne of campaigning in Italy, then a letter from Colonel Thomas Gilday, a comrade from their *Devil's Brigade* days, did. It contained hitherto untold tales of Colonel Bourne's early exploits in the Second World War.

Following the regimental church parade on 3 May 1998, to hearty applause from the assembled battalion it was announced that Corporal Len Maillet was the winner of the Proven Cup. This traditionally involved a visit to the Imperials in Scotland.[80] MWO Peter M Gannon CD was promoted to chief warrant officer (CWO) and assumed the position of regimental sergeant major. Gannon was a nineteen-year veteran of the Black Watch; "his first eight years were spent with the Royal Montreal Regiment before he saw the light in 1979." He succeeded CWO Thomas Miles CD whose own regimental career encompassed twenty-five years.

Fort Drum – 1998

That August, the 34 GBC summer concentration was conducted in the United States. Exercise *Tambour Roulant 98* was held at Fort Drum NY, a large US Army training base just southeast of Kingston, Ontario. It included *Les Fusiliers Mont-Royal* (FMR) as well as support from the reserve helicopter squadron, 438 ETAH from St Hubert.[81] Earlier in the month, Lieutenant Colonel Lusk travelled to CFB Gagetown to attend the graduation ceremony for Phase 2 Infantry and was well-pleased to witness four Black Watch officer cadets receiving their "pips".[82] Two of the new second lieutenants, Glenn Cowan and Sean Hill, were selected to command the BW platoons in Fort Drum. Emphasis was on patrolling; one *'Escort Patrol'* (designed for a valued specialist) protected the internationally known musicologist, Major Bruce Bolton. It is reported that he kept pace with the patrol, to the pleasant surprise of the troops. After ENDEX, the BW contingent headed home, welcomed by a dinner of steak and potatoes cooked by the RSM. The cold Canadian beer was also very welcome. Concurrently, the pipes and drums under P/Major Jordon Anderson, after a two-year hiatus, competed at the traditional summer games, placing a respectable third at both the Maxville and the Montreal Highland Games in the Tier 4 competitions.[83]

That fall, on 3 October 1998, Gordon Lusk conducted another Freedom of the City Parade. It took place this time in Huntingdon, down the highway from Ormstown, on the Chateauguay River, just fifteen kilometres from the American border. This picturesque farming and manufacturing town was a training base during the Second World War and home to many Black Watch recruits. At City Hall, Mayor André Brunette, welcomed the Regiment and presented a city flag, which still hangs in the armoury. The parade passed close to St Andrew's Church, drawing keen local support. Little did the enthusiastic crowd, nor indeed the Regiment, appreciate that included in the march-past were four future commanding officers, two of whom would go to war in Afghanistan.[84]

By the time of the reunion dinner, Lieutenant Colonel Lusk was able to report a quite exceptional year: their deployment during the Ice Storm was noted and praised, as was an overall rating of 83.5 percent in an exacting evaluation. There was also a commendation by the brigade commander. The guest of honour was the distinguished Canadian military historian, Dr Jack L Granatstein OC FRSC, member of the Dickson

Commission and that year's winner of the Vimy Award. He would serve as the head of the Canadian War Museum in Ottawa from 1998 to 2000 and was a driving force behind the building of a modern repository worthy of the nation's military heritage.

The Dubuc Trophy, February 1999

The best was yet to be. It was announced in the new year that the Black Watch had won the Dubuc Trophy. In an evaluation of military training, administration and efficiency, they triumphed over all regiments in 34 Brigade. It was a testament to the work of the past three years, which had begun so ominously with a threat of extinction.[85] In spite of this, nothing really changed – it was not formally presented until 2001, after Lusk had retired.[86]

The decidedly anti-colonial, not to say anti-British, trend towards modernization was ever present. In Ottawa, there were still calls for removal of non-Canadian culturally based units, in other words, the highland regiments whose kilts and accoutrements were considered alien and the cause of excessive expenditure. All of this was met with a vigorous reaction from across Canada. Newspapers trumpeted, "Reserve Regiments face uncertain future. Despite the reassurance of the new defence minister, Art Eggleton, that "the highlanders were not in danger," [87] doubts lingered.

The year's training was marked by other events. The sergeants' Burns' supper lived up to its uproarious reputation. There was the usual over-dramatic poetic recitation, and any attempt at a speech was met with rude calls to 'Sum Up!' The supper was bolstered by a good attendance of out-of-town guests, and a grand time was had by all. Just before the St Patrick's Parade, with its ever-popular appearance of the pipes and drums, the officers' mess held a dining-in on 11 March 1999 to mark the retirement of their honorary chaplain Jim Armour, as the minister of The Church of St Andrew and St Paul. Colonel Angus spoke warmly of his service to the Regiment.[88] The elders of the church were invited to attend, in an attempt to strengthen the link between the Black Watch and the congregation.

St Jean Baptiste Parade 24 June 1999

We were well-received and it was friendly.

Lieutenant Colonel Lusk

Montreal is very aware of the Black Watch, from the 'Ogilvy Piper' to the pipes and drums marching in the trio of city parades that bring out families in the hundreds of thousands – the Santa Claus parade; the St Patrick's Day parade; and the

Remembrance Day parade. In Verdun, The Watch has always appeared at the Legion's Ypres Parade. The 2nd Ypres was the first time in history a British Regiment (the Imperials) put the words "affiliated to ..." in its recruiting posters in recognition of the 13th Battalion's gallant defence. The Regiment's participation in summer's Highland Games, winter's St Andrew's Ball, and international appearances at Ticonderoga, New York, Philadelphia, and Hollywood in 2012, expand its renown. No other Montreal regiment is capable of reminding the city of its special identity and association with a storied past. It was, therefore, an occasion for surprise when the *Société Saint-Jean-Baptiste* – that bastion of Québécois nationalism and seeming foe to all things Anglophone – invited The Black Watch pipe band to participate in its annual and now rather political, Saint-Jean Baptiste Parade. Before RHQ could catch its breath, Pipe Major Jeordie Anderson accepted the invitation with true Scottish style ("A gig is a gig"). This was, in hindsight, a good regimental benchmark: so secure is the Black Watch in Quebec that it may appear in parades meant to further sovereignty. Moreover, to accept The Watch, in separatist terms, was not to become a *vendu* (sell out), but rather a shining example of the Scottish-French Canadian *auld alliance*. It was not particularly popular with the band. They were greeted by both cheers and whistles; however, there were more *hurrahs* than *boos*. The Black Watch was viewed as politically modern by some, though frowned upon by higher levels of command. The pipers said they would prefer not to do it again as it was not a particularly affable experience ("We were squeezed in narrow streets, hooted at times; finished, got on a *metro,* and went back to the armoury for a whisky."[89]) However, it was surely a bit of *in-your-face* highland bravado.

Lusk's Third Freedom: 11 September 1999 Verdun

By the end of the century, the Black Watch was honoured with eight Freedoms of the City. Just before the dawn of the new millennium, it would march in a ninth (Colonel Lusk's third). That seemed a surfeit of special parades, but such ceremonies served a higher purpose: "The troops got sick of doing parades, but it made us more difficult to kill – we hoped."[90] The Verdun Parade had a special meaning for the Regiment. While Vimy Ridge is its most famous action with three Black Watch battalions attacking together, Ypres was its first and arguably, its greatest battle. The annual Ypres Parade is a tribute to the great numbers of soldiers who left that city to join the 13th Battalion CEF, and subsequent units (including 1 RHC during the Second World War). Verdun was a working-class city, a mix of Scottish, Irish, English, and French; though by 1999, few of the original families were still there. Verdun had become a nostalgic visit for Montrealers, who had left the province or lived in outlying suburbs.

"Due to extensive road construction, we were forced at times to march down the back alleys of Verdun on what seemed to be garbage day. There were not a lot of spectators lining these sections of our route."[91] Although a modest crowd attended the parade, a proud cohort of veterans determinedly showed up. The Regiment looked smart; the drill was crisp, and when the pipes broke into *Highland Laddie,* many a steely eye became moist and gnarled hands closed tightly around walking sticks. It was a fitting parade with which to close out a momentous century.

That fall, the pipes and drums visited Rhode Island, transforming an *Oktoberfest* in a decidedly non-Germanic style. The month ended on another historical note as the Quebec Thistle Council passed a resolution urging the preservation and maintenance of the Bleury Street armoury as a home for the Black Watch and establishing it as a Scottish Community Centre.[92] The annual reunion dinner featured The Hon John Allen Fraser PC, a distinguished parliamentarian and former speaker of the House of Commons.

Gord Lusk had been determined in his goals. Far earlier in his career he had considered retirement but was asked by his friend, Lieutenant Colonel Victor Chartier: "What is it you want in the Army?" "To be CO of The Black Watch." "Well, I guess you had better stay." Besides winning the Dubuc Trophy, his efforts would become more apparent as time went by. "Lusk was opinionated, aggressive and sparred with Brigade, but was good with details, which was appreciated."[93] His tenure was commended: "Gord and Bruce may be credited with straightening out the unit finances which had been in a mess for a long, long, time."[94] The Regiment now boasted an experienced team and had overcome the bugbear of the 1980s – succession. Lusk had a qualified CO waiting in the wings and a strong list of future candidates.[95] Arguably, his best gift to the regiment was yet to come, in the form of *Canada's Red Hackle*, an international publication that chronicled the Black Watch progress through modern times. In May 2000, following a spirited church parade, Lieutenant Colonel Gordon Lusk handed over command to a Black Watch warhorse, former Pipe Major and RSM, Bruce Bolton. This marked the first time in Regimental history that a pipe major had risen to the rank of lieutenant colonel.[96]

Chapter 15

The Highland Millennium

Lieutenant Colonel BD Bolton MMM CD, 2000–2003: The Piper as *Laird*

You cannot be aloof as an officer, you must have a pulse.[97]

Lieutenant Colonel BD Bolton

The novelist Evelyn Waugh could never understand why the Army insisted on turning outstanding warrant officers into mediocre officers. In The Black Watch experience, this was not the case – Victor Chartier and Bruce Bolton are two fine examples. Bruce Douglas Bolton joined the Black Watch on 21 October 1960, his tenth birthday. He took the streetcar from Notre Dame de Grace to the armoury and signed on as a boy piper in the Learner's Programme run by the St Andrew's Society. He was no stranger to the building; his brother had already joined, and his father, a well-respected sergeant major, was a battle-scarred veteran of Normandy and Holland. Bolton served in The Black Watch Cadet Pipe Band until 1970. He was recognized for his organizational skills, and within four years was appointed Cadet Pipe Major: "We were very successful and about four times as large as the Regimental Pipe Band."[98]

Bolton signed up with the Regiment. By then he had graduated from McGill with a BSc and joined the MacDonald-Stewart organization. He was soon supervising the Stewart Museum (then the *Montreal Military and Maritime Museum*) and eventually was appointed Executive Director.[99] As part of his portfolio, Bolton supervised *The 78th Fraser Highlanders*, a historical re-enactment group that incorporated chapters across Canada and the United States. He also enjoyed a rapid rise within the Black Watch: "There was hardly anyone left with energy – I was a corporal within months, a sergeant within two years, a WO within three. I was CWO by 1977."[100] In 1978, when the Regiment needed a new RSM, Lieutenant Colonel Doug Robertson decided his pipe major might be the answer. Bolton recalls: "I was hesitant. But in the end, I think I was an OK RSM." He concentrated on tradition – the regimental way of doing things. After completing his tour as RSM, he reverted to pipe major, and set about training his more talented pipers as successors.[101] Many of his protégés, cadet and militia, would become pipe majors.

In 1983, the Regiment urged him to become an officer. On the way, Bolton accumulated considerable experience. He was placed in charge of Non-Public Funds and regimental finances. He was invested into the prestigious Order of Military Merit (MMM) as a member. This award is presented to soldiers, sailors, and air personnel who have demonstrated dedication and devotion to the call of duty. Bruce Bolton was the first non-commissioned officer in the Black Watch to receive the MMM. When Lieutenant Colonel John Stothers, the new CO, invited him *to go upstairs*, the pipe major accepted: "I had got on famously with the officers, and I had a ready replacement in the pipe band, Andy Kerr – I didn't need any coaxing to go into the officers' mess." However, Bruce Bolton's primary military skill was piping: "I had no infantry qualifications. I had to endure Aldershot as a captain taking tactics courses with eighteen-year-old pups and then two weeks in Gagetown on major qualifying – there were six of us on that course."[102] He moved through key regimental jobs, including quartermaster and DCO. Finally, in 1998, Bolton was selected for command. He cringed. This meant attending Staff College at Kingston, which was a national qualification attended by well over one hundred Canadians and many guest students from foreign armies, some of whom wore recently-won battle ribbons. Further, the staff course, with a long winter preparatory segment, had become doctrine-heavy, emphasizing operational manoeuvre in brigade level TEWTs. Bolton was a piper, not a tactician. The Major became concerned and threw himself into the jam of staff work, combat appreciations, and battle-planning with careful tutoring.[103] To the Regiment's relief, and his own, Bolton passed.

The new CO was well-supported by The Black Watch Advisory Board which was, as they grew old, gruff but kind. Colonel Bourne visited RHQ regularly and was matter-of fact: "Here's your cheque". Bolton recalled his first Board meeting in the mess, then a major. He was to present the regimental accounts. He sat quietly in a dim corner awaiting the great gods of the Regiment. At 11 am, he thought he heard Colonel Jim Knox, whom he had only known as a shy man, seldom speaking:

"He used to send me congratulatory notes when I was pipe major. I don't think he said two words to me in ten years." Suddenly, Bourne and Knox swept in like two dreadnoughts in full steam, and Knox said in an assertive voice: "I need a #@*% martini!" Evidently, the two vied with each other to see who would have the first cocktail before lunch. Bolton was speechless ...[104] Bolton next worked closely with Colonel Bourne during the fundraising for the 1987 celebrations: "That's when our relationship started to blossom."[105] By the millennium, Bourne had warmed to his CO. They worked well together and because of this, Bolton became well-accepted by The Black Watch Advisory board, their *imperial senate*: "Remembering my dad, I was Charlie's boy, someone they could trust."

The Black Watch felt it was under intense scrutiny; it always seemed they were looking for something. As CO, Bolton decided to placate the Brigade Headquarters: "I thought I would take a more conciliatory approach. I was shrewdly political. I played up regimental differences and made sure I cooperated with everything, no matter how silly." He was also fortunate to have inherited a well-trained staff in BHQ. His second-in-command was a battle experienced officer from the British Army, Scottish born John Potter MC; Major Tom MacKay was the operational company commander; CWO Peter Gannon was his RSM (eccentric but very regimental) soon succeeded by CWO Claude Hamel ("who was a gem ... knew what was going on, and he was there all the time"[106]). CWO Claude Hamel CD hailed from Sweetsburg; his uncle was a member of the Regiment in the Great War. Hamel held all major NCO command and administrative posts within the Regiment and a number of posts as senior instructor within the District Battle School. A senior service representative with Xerox Canada, he was appointed RSM 11 November 2001. Bolton also appointed a promising new Pipe Major to head the band, WO Cameron Stevens.[107] The RQM was controlled by the devoted Sergeant Ross McLellan, a Class B regimental call-out and Black Watch through and through. Captain Peter Radman was the Regular Force staff officer and Corporal M Gosman ran the orderly room. It was claimed that Gosman covertly ran the Regiment. In fact, the Black Watch administration team, headed by WO Yves Cantin and Sergeant McLellan took top honours in G1 and G6 assessments by the Brigade HQ. Recruiting was also revamped. Bolton created the "Vimy Platoon" for all new soldiers as preparation for Area's Basic Military Qualification (BMQ) courses. *Vimy Platoon* proved the perfect *regimental* solution. It was immensely popular and continues to the present.

Good COs had eased the battalion into modern, but not necessarily regimental, methods: "Gradually things were done differently; people didn't understand why things were done. Initially, I standardized – the Burns Shoot, for example."[108] As an elder and chairman of the Board of Trustees at The Church of St Andrew and St Paul, Bruce Bolton was eager to strengthen the relations between the Black Watch and its Regimental Church, which he deemed had become "somewhat stand-offish." His friendships with the former padre, JSS Armour, and future padre, RR Topping, proved helpful in this regard. It was normal for officers and soldiers to be married or baptized by the Regimental Padre, even if they were not Presbyterian. Bolton enjoyed the best of ecclesiastical worlds: "Bruce Glencross had military experience; he was the army padre, and Armour was the philosophical padre."[109]

Honorary Colonel Lieutenant General McAlpine, 2000

At the millennium Reunion Dinner, Lieutenant General Duncan McAlpine, already a legend, presided as the new Honorary Colonel. He pointed to the great portals leading into the Officers' Mess: "I walked in through those doors as a lieutenant in 1941." There was hearty applause and thumping on tables. In the previous spring, Colonel Stephen Angus had decided to step down as Honorary Colonel in favour of McAlpine, and devote his time to helping the Regiment as chairman of the Advisory Board.[110] The new Honorary Lieutenant Colonel was another regimental first – a former RSM, Victor Chartier. His easy manner and bilingualism would be most useful in the meetings of Quebec Honoraries. Lieutenant General McAlpine's first parade as Honorary Colonel took place in the new year as the Black Watch celebrated its birthday. During the Drum Head ceremony on 23 January 2001, McAlpine presented the *Canadian Peacekeeping Service Medal* (CPSM) to Black Watch recipients; a total of fourteen officers and NCOs were presented their medals, which commended service on operations from Bosnia, to Golan, Cyprus and Egypt.[111] The occasion was doubly festive. Previously, the talented Pipe Major, Andy Kerr, had written *Colonel John Bourne* as a march; on this occasion, Pipe Major W Gilmore (retired from the Regular Force) played a new tune, *Duncan McAlpine*. It was declared a *braw bricht tune*.

The Canadian Red Hackle Magazine, 2000

Historically, Bolton's legacy might be the launching of the *Canadian Red Hackle*, but kudos must go to Lieutenant Colonel Gordon Lusk. The magazine, started by the 73rd Battalion CEF as they left Montreal in 1915, was to become the official organ of the Imperial Black Watch, published in Scotland, and distributed throughout the Empire and Commonwealth from the Great War to the present.[112] The Canadian section was limited to about a page or two, if the colonel on Bleury Street ensured the due report was written and sent. When Gordon Lusk replaced Victor Chartier as Regimental Secretary, the idea of publishing a Canadian journal began to formulate. The first edition was aimed at the Canadian Black Watch Associations as well as the Regiment's serving members: "We wanted to have our own magazine to bind the family together, the east and west coast, the cadet corps ... previously it was newsletters sent out by Vic [Chartier], but we felt a need to create a better method ... From the fall of 2000 to Spring 2001, we put together our first issue."[113] the Black Watch regimental journal was entitled *Canada's Red Hackle* and published in the spring of 2001 as a chronicle of The Black Watch (RHR) of Canada, The Black Watch Association Branches, and the affiliated Cadet Corps. The layout graphics, design, and advertiser hunting was done by retired Warrant Officer Dave Willard, formerly 1 RHC. Gordon Lusk remains in charge as the *Red Hackle* editor-in-chief.[114]

Queen Elizabeth, The Queen Mother, 4 August 1900 – 30 March 2002

Lieutenant Colonel Bolton's first official act was the celebration of the 100th birthday of the Regiment's Colonel-in-Chief. There was to be a grand parade in London to which The Black Watch of Canada was asked to send a contingent. Although now CO, Bolton gave command to his predecessor, Lieutenant Colonel Gordon Lusk, who has this favourite memory of the Queen Mother:

> I was commanding a composite Guard composed of Black Watch and Toronto Scottish in Toronto. My sash got tangled with the claymore: every time I saluted the Queen Mother, the sash would go up – the one time I needed perfection ... At the grand old age of eighty-seven, she didn't miss it. Later, during the inspection she asked, sotto voce: "Did you get it free yet?"[115]

Just two years later, Bolton returned to London with regimental officers and soldiers for Her Majesty's funeral in Westminster Abbey on Tuesday, 9 April 2002. The Queen Mother died ten days earlier at the age of 101. The funeral proved one of the great events in Lieutenant Colonel Bolton's tenure as commanding officer. It is difficult to describe the special bond between the "Queen Mum" and the Black Watch. Highly respected for her devotion to duty as consort and Queen Mother, Elizabeth was much loved for the personal interest she took in the fortunes of her Regiment and its soldiers. The fact that she was brought up in Glamis Castle and that her brothers served in the Black Watch during the First World War was also in her favour. The Black Watch (RHR) of Canada was to have three Colonels-in-Chief during its 150 years of history: King George V (1912–1936); the Queen Mother (1937–2002); and now Charles, Prince of Wales.

The orders for the Queen Mother's state funeral (OP *Taybridge*) were kept in a vault for years, updated from time to time. It included the full schedule, and the regiments permitted to attend. Major Tom MacKay led the official RHC contingent, which was selected by Bolton.[116] It was a difficult time for the Imperial Watch. It was announced earlier that the Regiment would be reduced to battalion strength and lose regimental status. Newspapers blared: "Internal bloodletting triggered by the Treasury vs. Whitehall … other regiments regard the Black Watch, rightly or wrongly, as clannish, aloof and insular." It was further stated: "All that stands between it and possible extinction is the perceived wrath of its royal patron."[117] Now that was passé. The two allied battalions of the Black Watch met during the funeral parade rehearsals for their joint royal patroness. At the RSM's O Group, CWO P Gannon put his balmoral and Red Hackle next to the Hackle of the 1st Black Watch RSM. They eyed each other warily, smiled, and then sat down together.

It was a solemn yet spectacular procession. Lieutenant Colonel Bolton took Master Corporal Kevin Camire with him to the service; they both sat in the fifth row in the nave of the Abbey; he was the only commanding officer there with an NCO. Master Corporal Camire had just won the Proven Cup. In Montreal, a memorial service was held at the regimental church that night. The church parade that year was conducted in special memory of Her Majesty. The Church of St Andrew and St Paul was filled to overflowing; the padre declared it the largest turnout for church parade in recent history. The battalion included twenty Bosnian peacekeepers. The guest preacher was the Right Rev Andrew S Hutchison, Bishop of Montreal and Ordinary of the Canadian Armed Forces.

Training for the Taliban via the Dubuc Trophy

In the summer of 2002, The Black Watch Association Montreal Branch organized a veterans' return to Normandy, specifically Verrières Ridge.[118] On 25 July, the fifty-eighth anniversary of the battle, three Black Watch pipes major (Bolton, Kerr and MacKenzie) played the regimental lament atop Hill 67, overlooking May-sur-Orne, St-Martin and St-André. A plaque honouring the fallen of 1 RHC was formally unveiled.

That year, the Regiment paraded about 140–150 persons; they were really lucky to get one hundred out on exercise. The numbers were average for the brigade, and the Watch trained with the same tenacity as it administrated. The work paid off with incontestable results: rated against all the regiments of 34 Brigade (some fifteen units) the Black Watch was again awarded the Dubuc Trophy, the second time during Bolton's term of office. Bolton said: "We won the trophy because we were able to train and practice, but I also give the credit to Gord Lusk, then Peter Radman the RSS officer – they helped me organize a competent team." Winning the trophy certainly sweetened relations with headquarters. All this would change dramatically when Canada became involved in the war in Afghanistan.

The first Canadian infantry unit deployed into Afghanistan unobserved in the fall of 2001. It was a covert manoeuvre, and then in the new year, the public was gradually made aware of the formal involvement of Canadian troops in combat operations – the first since the Second World War and Korea. The appearance of Canadian infantry south in Kandahar was not a surprise to Bruce Bolton; the colonel received a note from one of his former officers, Lieutenant Glenn Cowan, who less than two years earlier, had graduated from Phase 2 and commanded a Black Watch platoon in Fort Drum. He was now a platoon commander in the PPCLI, but part of him was very much RHC:

> … the area we are landing in is the most heavily mined region of the theatre and Taliban forces have the ability to strike with artillery … I will be deploying to Afghanistan as an officer in the PPCLI but I will always be an ambassador of the Black Watch.[119]

Soon, the war affected the Black Watch and the nation. There was a swell of public support for the Army. Soldiers, sailors, and airmen were enthusiastically praised – even in Quebec. The soldier-as-hero reappeared in the Canadian media in sentiments not seen since the Second World War. Volunteers appeared in greater numbers. Dozens of Black Watch officers, senior NCOs and soldiers volunteered for foreign service and were soon deployed abroad. The armoury acquired a different atmosphere. Within a year *bona fide* war veterans, wearing the admired Afghan decoration, appeared on the parade square training recruits. There was a greater sense of purpose to Reserve training.

The Changing Pages of RHC history
Colonel John G Bourne CVO ED CD, 1918–2002

He could spot a phoney or a good guy from a mile away.

Colonel SF Angus, September 2013

Colonel John Bourne died on December 8, the same year as the Queen Mother. Besides the devoted service shown to his regiment, Bourne, a successful CEO, served for seventeen years on the National Council of the Duke of Edinburgh's Award Scheme and was responsible for organizing the programme in Quebec. His efforts enabled fifteen thousand young people of the province to participate. To raise such interest in a fundamentally British scheme during a time of anti-English-Canadian political upheaval in the province was a considerable feat. A prominent newspaper editorialized: "Colonel Johnny Bourne, who has died aged eighty-four, commanded a force of Canadian and American soldiers in southern Europe; later, in the face of separatism, he nurtured the loyalty of Quebecers to the Crown."[120] He was remembered as a hard soldier with a no-nonsense disposition. However, "John Bourne did not motivate or lead through fear – he was loved by the officers."[121] His written memoirs reveal an imaginative chronicler with a romantic's appreciation for the military, and the world *in toto*. It was a side he tried to keep hidden yet was discerned by his regiment. No one dared contradict or interrupt John Bourne: "At one of his last mess dinners, he was distracted and rose to thank a guest, and then delivered his speech (which was dull the first time) a second time: the officers just sat there and quietly listened."[122] The Regiment buried him atop Mount Royal; in a dense Scottish mist, the pipe major played his favourite lament, *Flowers of the Forest*.

In the fall of that unhappy year, Bolton appeared to thrive on over-work. His last months would include final suppers, training weekends, and a Freedom of the City Parade. The annual reunion dinner was decidedly impressive; the guest of honour was the former Canadian CDS and international diplomat, General AJGD de Chastelain OC CMM CD CH. The general was deeply involved in the Northern Ireland peace process, and the chairman of the Independent International Commission on Decommissioning in Northern Ireland.[123] A *potpourri* of general officers and senior guests attended. De Chastelain, a passionate Scot and skilled piper, paid close attention to the music that night, and offered compliments to the CO. He was the ideal person for Lieutenant Colonel Bolton's final Regimental Dinner. At the end of the month, the St Andrew's Ball of 2002 celebrated 167 years of Scottish heritage in Montreal. The Viscount and Viscountess Dupplin were the guests of honour. In the new year, the creation of the "Mega City" prompted another regimental march to City

Hall, where the Regiment was received by Mayor Gérald Tremblay, presented with scrolls and another banner to hang over the parade square. It was a smart parade and the pipes and kilts drew applause from Montrealers as the battalion marched up Bleury Street.[124]

Bolton retired in the spring of 2003, after forty-three years in the Regiment.[125] Following the regimental church parade on 4 May 2003, Lieutenant Colonel Bolton handed-over to his DCO, a British war veteran with desert sand still in his map-case.[126]

Lieutenant Colonel J Potter MC, 2003: *Desert Storm* à *Montréal*

Is sleamhainn leac doras an taigh mhòir.[127]

John Potter seemed just what the Black Watch needed: a warrior *au courant* with modern doctrine, experienced in both staff and combat operations, and a Scot. He was born just south of Glasgow, in Hamilton. He was commissioned into the Royal Highland Fusiliers in 1979 after graduating from university. Potter served in Northern Ireland, Germany and UN peacekeeping tours; and then went to war in *Operation Desert Storm* (1990) where he was Mentioned in Despatches, then awarded the Military Cross:

> Major Potter commanded B Company in 1 Royal Scots Battle Group ... Major Potter's Company was heavily involved ... He moved around constantly encouraging, leading, directing and chastising, without regard for enemy fire or mines ... During the Battle Group attack on yet another position, Major Potter led his Company through a turmoil of dust, direct and indirect fire, to execute a classic rolling up operation ... By this time Major Potter's Company had been in action for 48 hours ... He was cool under fire, calm in contact, resolute in danger and pursued the enemy with clinical ruthlessness.[128]

Potter was promoted lieutenant colonel in 1993 and took command of 5th Battalion, The Royal Irish Regiment, deployed in Northern Ireland. He retired from the British Army in 1997 and immigrated to Canada where he was hired as risk management coordinator with Bombardier Transportion. Potter reactivated his commission with the Canadian Forces, joined the Regiment under Lieutenant Colonel GT Lusk, reverted to the rank of major, and assumed the position of OC B Company with WO Hamel as his sergeant-major. Later, Lieutenant Colonel Bolton appointed him DCO.

Experienced in conventional as well as anti-terrorist ops; Potter created a buzz when he joined. "Humorous, sarcastic, quick-witted. Familiar with Highland traditions ... Bruce did DCO work: budget, Non Public Funds – Potter told great stories;

knew tactics; we were excited he would be CO."[129] Potter was keen on introducing modern training to the rifle companies. Alas, all this proved difficult within limited budgets, and it took some adjustment for Potter (not only to Canada's climate but its military culture). The new CO's heart seemed to be still in the Middle East, but he made a vigorous start, resolutely working to streamline and try new schemes. Tom MacKay was his DCO and recalls Potter soon had his *militia moment*. He jousted with the tribal support that allows a reserve regiment to survive and has been in place for centuries: the CO and the Advisory Board. Lieutenant Colonel Potter decided he was not comfortable with the byzantine reality of the Canadian militia and the Advisory Board. He tried to force change – it was not well-received. Finally, citing regimental conflicts and pressing personal matters, John Potter offered his resignation in the early fall. It was accepted.[130] The Black Watch turned at once to Bruce Bolton (who was just about to return his kit to the quartermaster stores) requesting he reassume his post as CO for a second tour. He warily agreed, accommodating his civilian and family schedules. Bolton's repeat appointment as CO was effective 21 October 2003, giving him just enough time to prepare for the Reunion Dinner and the St Andrew's Ball.

The Piper Redux: Lieutenant Colonel BD Bolton MMM CD, 2003–2005

For we're no' awa' tae bide awa', / For we're no' awa tae le'e ye,
For we're no' awa' tae bide awa', / We'll aye come back an' see ye.

The returning colonel had looked forward to a bit of rest, but he barely had time to hang up his bonnet. Things seemed the same, but Bolton soon discovered he had a bugbear in brigade headquarters – John Potter. "The brigade commander was a cynical man who didn't like the Black Watch but loved Potter, and wanted him as next brigade commander – [Potter] was appointed as deputy commander of 34 Brigade."[131] Bruce now had to deal with his former DCO and fellow RHC commander as a senior staff officer who held a decided attitude toward his former regiment. They were constantly at odds. Potter, with very recent inside-knowledge, began to badger the Black Watch for everything from finance to subaltern dinners. He applied the strict letter of the law, and Bolton had to put in extra hours to sort things out. He was annoyed, especially since some issues stemmed from folios assigned to his new overseer only twelve months earlier.[132] He bit his lip and carried on directly into the St Andrew's Ball. The 2003 edition was practically a Black Watch production: Captain Andrew Kerr was ball chairman, retired Pipe Major Brian MacKenzie was in charge of floor committee and Lieutenant Colonel Daniel O'Connor was the president of the society. It was a Montreal (as well as regimental) tradition: "We have always had Black Watch representatives on council – this ensured we are not forgotten." Church parades became even more interesting. Bolton (with his padre's help) invited prominent ministers from the chaplain general's office to preach. The Rev James Peter Jones was memorable, as was Brigadier Father Murray Farwell who became the Canadian Forces Chaplain General.[133]

New Reserve Units: PSYOPS

In 2003, the Reserves were restructuring, yet again, to meet 'Army of Tomorrow' requirements. All Areas were required to introduce Psychological Operations (PSYOPS) with a *Centre of Excellence* designed to convey selected information to modify the behaviour of groups and individuals. The aim was also to enhance civil-military co-operation (CIMIC) capability, i.e. the military means by which a commander links to civilian agencies active in a theatre of operations.[134] It was signed off by Lieutenant General RJ Hillier, the dynamic and Pattonesque figure who had revitalized the CF internally and made the army popular. This defined 750 new positions for reservists across Canada. The emphasis was now entirely on Afghanistan and the employment of re-trained reserve cadres. There was, as well, interest in expansion and revitalization. The bitter reality was that without the buttressing of reserve cadres, the Afghanistan mission could not possibly succeed. Attempts to organize another local 'Highland Winter' exercise were simply over-taken by events.[135] The reserves were increasingly burdened by the requirement for more and more regional courses, which tended to minimize the *raison d'être* of an effective unit – its regimental armoury. It took an ever increasing amount of time to create a Black Watch senior NCO; normal career progression planned for fifteen years and seven basic courses, including six specific infantry qualifications without which a soldier could never become a CWO and RSM. The Reserves continued to be a hefty, expensive (though not particularly large in actual numbers) association: seventeen armoured units, fifty-one infantry regiments (of which fourteen were Highland!), seventeen artillery regiments, four anti-aircraft units, and ten engineer regiments or squadrons.

Backhanded Thanks ...

What an insult!

Lieutenant Colonel BD Bolton

The aim was to keep the Black Watch ticking over and to groom Tom MacKay for command. It became unexpectedly hectic, for by 2004, the participation in Afghanistan had become a full-fledged operation and the call for Reserve volunteers increased beyond anticipation. Concurrently, the country's attitude towards the military soared. Enthusiasm and adventure brought a flood of recruits. Vimy Platoon was filled. Bolton did not yet realize it, but the Regiment was approaching another of its periodic golden eras.

After a year and a half of intense regimental work, at the 2005 church parade, Bruce Bolton turned the Regiment over to a younger colonel, but one who had served the Regiment for over a dozen years. The commander of 34 Brigade, Colonel Jacques Lachance CD, presided. The Honorary Colonels, Duncan McAlpine and Victor Chartier were there to see Bruce off. However, Bolton would continue to serve as a dynamic member of The Black Watch Advisory Board.[136] Inexplicably, just after he handed over command and formally retired, Bolton received a letter from *le commandant adjoint* of *Secteur du Québec*, Brigadier General Marc A Préfontaine. The letter discussed Bolton's ranking on the 'merit list' and his suitability for promotion. He was rated in the bottom third. This, after he had been fervently urged to return and resume command following Lieutenant Colonel Potter's sudden departure. The usually taciturn Bolton shot back: "What an insult!"[137] He urged similar letters not be sent to retiring officers: "I am not sure that when my great grandchildren request a copy of my military record in thirty years they will understand the context of this letter." Brigadier General Préfontaine, a decent chap, privately agreed. The Reserve brigade's approach to their 'merit list' was in imitation of their Regular Force confreres and tended to confuse fancied operational requirements with militia reality. When an urgent need arose, age and modern doctrine became a trifle as long as a fellow could run a battalion. Later, when a crisis had been averted, bureaucratic regulations were resurrected. Bolton's willingness to be parachuted-in to help out both the Black Watch and Secteur du Québec headquarters was forgotten. His only good news was that the battalion floor hockey team won the brigade championship for a second year. His Westminster Abbey seatmate, Sergeant Kevin Camire, accepted the trophy as team captain.

Bolton's ability to pursue several vocations without losing his balance testifies to his managerial skills. Looking across his many-faceted career, he allows, "It was a long haul." His talent, he insists is: "I tend to be surrounded by good people."[138] The affection in which he is held is anchored in the pipe band. When Bolton was promoted to executive director of the Macdonald Stewart Foundation, MCpl Jeffrey McCarthy wrote a jaunty pipe tune, *The Director Steps Up*, and to celebrate Bolton's assumption of command, he composed *Lieutenant Colonel Bruce D Bolton, MMM*.

The Black Watch Pipes and Drums – Oldest in North America

Now goe the foes to wracke

The Kerne apace doe sweate

And baggepype then instead of Trompe

Doe lull the back retreate

Perhaps the most visible part of The Black Watch (Royal Highland Regiment) of Canada, the Pipes and Drums embody the unit's tradition and history. It is the oldest organized pipe band in North America and has been ranked among the top Canadian Forces reserve bands. The RHC pipes and drums is more than a band; it is an institution, a near private fiefdom and an entity unto itself. Arguably, it is the pipes that make The Watch a familiar and beloved Montreal tradition, far more than kilt, hackle or tartan – such nuances are lost in a city that is associated with hockey, a clutch of world-class breweries and universities, and insists on viewing everything through a *français* lens. It is the pipes that bring cheers, draw tears and arouse ardour and highland war whoops as the Regiment marches by, in a steady, unhurried pace, while the pipe major deftly orchestrates pieces as diverse as *Cock of the North* to *The Maple Leaf Forever* to *Vive la Canadienne*. The pipes have their own canteen, *the band room*, as sacred as any of the messes and admittance is by invitation only. The basement lair is decorated with trophies and pictures depicting 150 years of active martial music in peace and war. The bar is bedecked with ribbons, plaques, mementoes and trophies. Overseeing all are the mounted horns of *Flora MacDonald*, the regimental goat that led the 13th CEF Battalion's pipe band as they marched from Passchendaele to Vimy Ridge and finally, through the *Hundred Days* and into Cambrai: "Her usual place at the head of the Regiment. She swung into step as soon as her beloved pipes struck up one of the tunes she knew so well." This is a battle memento for after all, bagpipes are not instruments, but weapons of war.

The Black Watch School of Piping and Drumming

I foresee, in the near future, when the Black Watch will march behind a hundred pipers and drummers.[139]

The Black Watch pipes and drums have weathered many a storm, from German artillery searching them out in the rear trenches, to machine gunners and snipers targeting out the piper leading his battalion into battle. This maliciousness was later matched when their own headquarters savaged pipe bands, reducing them to two musicians in the 1990s. It required a decade before P/Major Stevens could muster thirty-five, of which only eleven were in the Militia. By 2012, the Reserve portion of the band rose to twenty-two.[140] Pipe Major Brian MacKenzie recalls: "… over the years, we developed so many; they succeeded exponentially, but they all moved away seeking jobs – my lead tip Daniel Dagenais has helped me maintain and develop the band [pipe major is the conductor, *lead tip* is the lead drummer]. But the future lies in our students."[141]

The Black Watch pipes and drums are moreover, a thriving school. In an era when the Army has disbanded its piping schools and will only *test* pipers in CFB Borden, the Regiment provides an increasingly rare military service in Canada. The Association band and the school of piping, drumming and highland dancing happen on Monday and Wednesday nights and Saturday mornings. The regimental band practises Thursday nights. Every Saturday morning, the armoury is again filled with music. At one corner of the parade square, a half-dozen dancers practise the sword dance. In other corners, groups and singletons play on pipes. In classrooms and archive offices, new students are taught the rudiments of the chanter. It has become a formidable enterprise led by Pipe Major Cam Stevens, the chief instructor. The cadet programme runs on Saturdays and is guided by retired Pipe Major Brian MacKenzie, Joseph Boran, Bruce Bolton, as well as three drummers from the regimental pipe band.[142] Stevens is enthusiastic: "The school is thriving! Saturday morning is for the youngsters nine to thirteen-year-olds, and, of course the Cadet Corps' pipes and drums."[143]

The regimental pipe band is completely booked with parades and performances. In 2012, it performed in 156 separate engagements, including three concerts, six parades, and nine mess dinners.[144] The present band, gathering its two Association bands and the cadet pipers and drummers, can march nearly one hundred strong. The Black Watch school aims to develop over a hundred armoury-based pipers in the decade. The future lies in both cultures. By 2012, half of The Black Watch Association's new pipers were Québécois, some speaking halting English. Young men and women are instructed on the pipes on a Saturday morning. Their mentor speaks rudimentary *français* with an NDG accent, but the intonation is all on the chanter. The nascent pipers listen attentively, then attack *All the Blue Bonnets over the Border* as the metronome ticks away.[145]

Black Watch Stalwarts – *Slainte deagh*

The band's list of alumnae is varied and exotic and includes legendary pipers and devotees who supported them as passionate converts. The band's collective of great pipers includes legends from the First and Second World Wars as well as the Hannah father-son team that carried the Regiment through the Cold War. Sergeant Drum Major Calvin (Cal) Wilson played with the Second World War band 1 RHC, and was drum major of the 3rd Battalion, serving nearly twenty years and retiring in 1972. In September 2013, the band gathered over sixty members to mark Sergeant Ross Larman's fortieth anniversary of joining the Regiment. The esteemed bass drummer, with Colonel Cantlie's seventy years noted, was then the longest serving member of the Regiment, eligible for three bars to his CD in 2015. It must also be recorded that Major Alexander (Sandy) Campbell and WO Robert (Bob) Fulton both had a tremendous influence on the development of piping and drumming students over the years. Another prized talent is Captain Andrew GM Kerr CD, the regimental keeper of data. Kerr is better known as the former pipe major (1983–1993) and creator of over a dozen brisk pipe tunes, the best known being *Colonel John Bourne*.[146]

The musical fire of the regiment forever branded Corporal Lionel Chetwynd – internationally acclaimed screenwriter and film director. He served in 3 RHC March 1957–April 1959, and has long been a loyal supporter of his Regiment. Chetwynd credits the Black Watch with giving him the direction and impetus that led to degrees from McGill and Oxford and a subsequent film career that included Oscar and Emmy nominations.[147] His affection for the Black Watch was again demonstrated in 2012, when Chetwynd insisted NDHQ send The Black Watch Pipes and drums (*No other regiment would do!*) to participate in a Hollywood gala memorial to the fighting soldier. This involved a journey to California and appearances on a series of television interviews and a continental special. Another alumnus of the Pipes and Drums was the then Command Chaplain for the Army. Lieutenant Colonel Rev Bill Fairlie played with the Black Watch from 1987 to 1992, dressed as an other rank: "The pipers under Andrew Kerr were unsure what to call me. I told them my first name was fine, since I was not on official business … They decided on 'Colonel Bill'."[148]

Its pipe majors tend to remain as teachers and Association workers. The trio of Bolton, Kerr and MacKenzie is daunting in itself; P/Major Cam Stevens further added to the lineage. He was the last Canadian piper to play in Southern Afghanistan. The CDS specially requested Stevens to accompany him to Kandahar for the stand-down ceremony as the Canadian brigade concluded operations and redeployed to Canada. He has represented his Regiment, Army and Nation in Dieppe, Vimy and in a dozen official memorials. When he speaks of the pipes, he becomes scholarly as well as zealous. He can lecture at length on traditions, tune origins, and the classic Pibroch.[149]

Piping is a significant part of the social life in the Regiment – from parades to dinners, from parties to barbecues. The annual Black Watch summer BBQ was traditionally held at the Angus Farm in Erin, Ontario. Colonel Stephen set up a grand tent with tables, chairs and infantry-sized grills. The event was a clan gathering; all ranks, families, friends, even favoured guests from other regiments. Although there was much to do, and the colonel's house a treasure of highland and RB Angus railroad artifacts, the best part seemed to be the performances of the combined pipe band – a conglomerate of the Toronto and Montreal Associations. These elder statesmen were buttressed by the battalion's pipes and drums, and loosely led by Lieutenant Colonel Len Ferdon. Folks arrived from far away, glad to find friends and catch up on regimental buzz.

The highland fellowship included stalwarts like the Carlisles and Hummels as well as more unconventional Black Watch personalities. CSM Gary Wayne Patrick Young is what the uninitiated described as a *character*, but in fact he is typical of the bond the Regiment effects. He was CSM of B Coy, once called *the Depot*, after the example of the Regular Force battalions. Young is from Pointe St Charles. He joined the cadets in 1956 and the battalion in 1960; a sergeant in 1964 and a warrant in 1967 ("his ear piece is directional," muttered one of the younger sergeants). Gary Young became another icon and well-known to generations of new officers when, on retirement, he became the mess steward. He is much appreciated by The Black Watch Ladies Badminton Club, which meets to play on Fridays: a tradition from before the Great War. CSM Young organizes their weekly luncheons and refreshments. He is notorious as the regimental raconteur: "He has more jokes than Henny Youngman." Any highlander who needed a lift sought out Sergeant Major Young, for he always has an anecdote that brings smiles to all faces. Young and his chum, Mike Cher, are regular Friday features at the armoury. Both like to recount a fellow patriarch's meeting with the Queen Mum. Sergeant Gordie Betts had met Her Majesty on parade in England in 1942; twenty-five years later, at the 1967 Gagetown Parade, the Queen Mother midst inspection, stopped before Betts: "Nice to see you again". Another twenty years later, Betts formed up with the Veterans at the Troops at Molson Stadium. Her Majesty paused: "A pleasure to see you again." "How ... ?", asked his surprised chums. Betts never hesitated: "I'm very good looking!"

Forming the Future: The Cadet Corps 1953–2013

The Black Watch family of cadet corps enjoys a distinguished history. It began in the nineteenth century with the Highland Cadet Battalion (HCB), heralded as *"facile princeps*, the premier position in point of equipment and organization among kilted cadet corps of the empire."[150] The regiment was augmented in the 1930s by the affiliation of The Bishop's College School Cadet Corps. After the Second World War, there was an attempt to revive the cadet movement that had been dormant for nearly eight years. This was done by re-establishing the HCB, which had moved away from Black Watch sponsorship. Sadly, there were clashes between the two commanding officers. Although the regiment had a formidable corps in Bishop's, it was decided to raise a Montreal cadet corps directly from the armoury. The Black Watch (RHR) of Canada Cadet Corps No. 2497 was created in 1953. By 1970, the Regiment boasted five impressive corps (including the HCB in Lachute, which was welcomed back with enthusiasm). Three of these corps were the oldest active corps in Canada: Bishop's College School and King's Edgehill School Cadet Corps were self-operating; and Rothesay School which, in 1995, decided to disband its cadet corps. The Oromocto Corps was briefly taken over by 2 RCR after the regular battalions were disbanded. The Regiment took more time with the corps closer to Montreal (indeed, right in the armoury) which was considered more fragile. In 2000, it briefly added another: "The Bombardier Cadet Corps."[151]

The armoury corps was shepherded through the tougher decades by Majors Gibson and Darney, Captains Bob Clark and Vic Knowlton. Major Mick Darney emigrated from Kinghorn, Scotland and joined The Black Watch Cadet Corps as an instructor. He made sure his son was a cadet. Darney became the cadet training officer and then the corps' commanding officer; he was also the police chief of the Town of Hampstead. Major Darney was succeeded by Major Sandy Campbell, and then, by his son, Captain Mike Darney, who insisted he remained "a minor player in the Black Watch history, but a long standing one." Darney was also Scottish-born but went to school at Cardinal Newman High School, a tough all-boys' school run by the Christian Brothers in what is now fashionably called *Le Plateau*. Young Captain Darney was particularly keen on weekend schemes and manoeuvres:

> We ran some extreme weekend cadet exercises; the Regiment was generous: a 2–1/2 ton truck, winter kit, pyrotechnics of every type, BFAs and FNs [Blank Firing Attachments and 7.62 mm rifles]; unlimited blanks … we even had pistols. Plus a gung-ho staff of excellent instructors from the battalion like Warrant Officer Rolly Labreche.[152]

Training was much the same to the end of the century. The Bleury Street organization acquired new life circa 2002. With publicity from Afghanistan, the Reserves and Cadets attracted more interest. Captain Victor Knowlton OStJ CD A de C, ably supported by Captains Charles Tawa and Catherine Lord, enjoyed a full staff and fifty-five eager cadets. They were encouraged by enthusiastic parents, the cadet league and the Regiment.[153] Former Pipe Major Brian MacKenzie instructed the cadet pipe band, assisted on Saturday mornings by Lieutenant Colonel Bolton. The senior pipers were talented, and several marched with the regimental band. The cadet shooting team participated in the biathlon regional finals at CFB St Bruno. The millennium cadet corps changed commanding officers in 2013; Captain Karl Morel CD, an experienced soldier who served as senior NCO in several reserve units, assumed command on 16 February 2013. He commanded until the winter of 2014 and was succeeded by Captain Wayne Dover CD, whose DCO was Lieutenant Andrew W Baddeley – who assumed command of The Black Watch Cadet Corps in the fall of 2014.[154]

Lieutenant Colonel TEC MacKay CD, 2005–2009

He showed me the Ritchie Tiger.

Lieutenant Colonel Thomas Edward Charles MacKay was very much the traditional, pre-Cold War, Black Watch officer. His background was old school. Like John Bourne, he graduated from Selwyn House. His grandfathers were military. His sister attended Bishop's College School and marched, in uniform, in the regimental church parades. His brother Andrew was senior subaltern in the Black Watch and suggested he join. MacKay was familiar with the Regiment. He was now thirty-three but fondly remembered being shown about the officers' mess by his uncle, Colonel Tom Price, as a little boy: "He bought me a soft drink and showed me the Ritchie Tiger" – a magnificent tiger skin presented to the Regiment by General Sir Neil Ritchie. After university, MacKay became a broker, like most of the family, beginning as a futures trader, and then moving on to investment banking. He joined the Regiment in 1991 and was initiated into the Black Watch brotherhood during the traditional subalterns' dinner: "In those days the *show me your brand* (a ritual rite of passage) was not a custom … Still, it was a most memorable evening."[155] Over the next decade, he became a fine-looking, reflective senior subaltern, and an experienced platoon and company commander.

MacKay's second-in-command was a Bosnian war veteran, Major Chris Phare, to be followed shortly by Mike Walker. MacKay's adjutant was the staunch Peter Radman, assisted by Captain Derrick Farnham, who was soon to succeed him. The regimental sergeant major was CWO John Barron CD, originally from the Verdun, then Chambly. He had served and trained on bases throughout Canada and Germany, and had been the Colour Sergeant for the Black Watch at The Queen Mother's ninetieth birthday parade in London. A senior analyst for the BMO Investment Banking Group International, he diligently served the Regiment holding all senior NCO positions, and was selected as an instructor on the WO leadership course in 2005. They were supported by the robust pipe major, a former classmate from Selwyn House, MWO Cameron Stevens. Stevens was a shrewd fellow and familiar with private school praxis. MacKay recalled: "Cam Stevens got me caned one day in gym class."

The guiding spirit was Lieutenant General Duncan McAlpine. Now in his eighties, he was less active, but his calm presence and sage advice were a comfort. His wartime Black Watch nickname was 'Snuffy', but around the millennium Watch, he was 'the Dunc.' It was said privately, with a soldierly affection. As Honorary Lieutenant Colonel, Victor Chartier did the running around. He had been appointed chairman of the Quebec honoraries council and directly advised the area commander.[156] His counsel was both timely and valuable to MacKay, although he did not always take it. The young colonel, keen on being both modern yet traditional, rediscovered what all COs had to learn. Things looked different from the commander's chair, and the senior headquarters remained as inflexible as it was when Paul Hutchison ran Bleury Street. He philosophized, echoing the frustrations of most Reserve commanding officers:

> It is the modern *Catch-22* of Militia – the government neither using its reserves nor allowing them the equipment and funds to train. This slowly deteriorates us ... there is a complete misunderstanding of the part-time soldier, the dedicated civilian who works and wants to serve his country. I think DND has visions of folks hanging around the armoury waiting for call-outs. The difference between the Strategic Militia and an Operational Army Reserve that augments the Regular Force is it never mobilizes. We simply rotate in and out.

Adjutants at Work: Captains Radman and Farnham

Captain Peter Radman came to us from the RCR and was the RSS adjutant for a record period of 13 years. He served five years in the Reserves with the Royal Canadian Hussars (Montreal); Regular Force service with the Royal Canadian Dragoons, including two years with The Gloucestershire Regiment (Tidworth); six months with The 2nd Battalion, 34th Infantry Regiment (Fort Benning); and three months with the 2nd Battalion, The Royal 22ieme Regiment (Gagetown RV81). Finally, he was posted to Montreal and the Black Watch – his reserve experience, being a Montrealer, and bilingual made it an easy fit.[157]

Serving under five RHC commanding officers, he became a true member of The Regiment: fiercely loyal to his CO's at a time when RSS officers were expected to show loyalty to higher headquarters as opposed to the regiments where they were employed. He took a genuine interest in all aspects of Regimental life in addition to wearing multiple hats: adjutant, operations officer, and financial officer for budget preparation. Most notably was his involvement, along with Reverend Richard Topping, in post-deployment interviews of our personnel returning from missions.

About halfway through his tenure, he received a posting message to return to Regimental duties. Our Honorary Colonel, Lieutenant-General Duncan McAlpine, suggested to Captain Radman that the Regiment would be amicable to his continued employment, if he wished to remain with us. The wish was clear, phone calls were made and the posting was cancelled. Upon Captain Radman's retirement in 2010, Lieutenant Colonel Plourde gave him the distinct honour of addressing the battalion on Church Parade. His comments were no surprise: "Soldiers of The Black Watch, it has been an honour to be part of our family."

Captain Radman was replaced by Captain Derrick Farnham – a *modern* officer. Derrick returned from Oxford to write his PhD thesis in Montreal. To better survive, he joined the Reserves. Before he knew it, he was a Black Watch officer and soon volunteered to serve in Afghanistan. Returning a veteran, Captain Farnham applied for the Class B position to serve as Radman's replacement until a Regular Force RSS officer would be posted in. Farnham knew nothing, but was willing to learn; besides, in the Militia, errors could be covered up between succeeding Tuesday nights. The Army, very much on a war-time footing, was short of experienced captains. Farnham was the typical Black Watch 'stranger' and followed the aeonian path of officers who appeared in the Regiment over the past century. He became thoroughly Black Watch. In a learn-as-you-go approach, Farnham mastered traditions, protocol and all the indulgences and facets that made up the Royal Highlanders. He dealt with the two concerns that dominated that period: Black Watch cadres despatched to serve in Afghanistan, and the scheduled presentation of Colours by the new Colonel-in-Chief, Prince Charles.

Running the Regiment in Peace and War: *parades dangereuses*

> In the Militia, you can't simply transfer-away your problems like the Regular Force. When you deal with volunteers you must learn to accept; the truly bad are released...but you must work with the others.
>
> Lieutenant Colonel Tom MacKay

Training the regiment was now an uncommon undertaking. Many of the best left for Afghanistan or exotic call-out posts. The DCO, Major Mike Walker, ended up in a UN headquarters in Haiti. He was a family man, and it seemed a safer place than Kandahar – that is, until the great earthquake nearly took his life.

Meantime, MacKay devoted himself to officer training. Tuesday nights were interesting. After the battalion lectures and dismissal parade, the officers gathered in the mess around the CO who stood them a drink and engaged them in discussion – military, doctrinal or current events. Questions were asked, opinions expected, challenge and debate encouraged. Most rose to the challenge. It was a collegial gathering and rather impressive. Regrettably, MacKay's patrician style was not always appreciated by his superiors. In contrast to Bolton's oil-on-troubled-waters approach, MacKay was prepared to stand his ground if challenged – on *any* point. He got on famously with his first brigade commander, a Van Doo. The next appointee was a military policeman and former CO of the Service Battalion. MacKay considered him "a miserable, angry fellow." He did not warm to Tom or the Black Watch. Perhaps it was the collective style of the garrison, in particular, the CGG, RMR and Black Watch commanding officers. They sought consultation, discussion and explanation. Their traditions were: discuss, have-it-out, then salute smartly, and get on with it – in the spirit of *Auftragstaktik*. It was not the preferred approach in SQFT. The Black Watch was again regarded as difficult, and Tom *uncooperative*.

Although he resolutely followed orders, MacKay's dossier included two venial sins. The first was the 8 May 2006 church parade. The route from the armoury to The Church of St Andrew and St Paul was a regimental (indeed a Montreal) tradition: up Bleury, west on Sherbrooke, to the church. "That year the city (the Borough of Ville-Marie) refused our request and provided us with the alternate route, citing an ambiguous city ordinance that Sherbrooke Street had to be kept open as 'an evacuation route for hazardous waste materials.'"[158] The Black Watch was told to take its battalion, band, cadets and veterans, and tramp along side-streets, then shoulder its way up Bishop Street to appear on Sherbrooke, a third of a block from the church. "It made little sense and reeked of pettiness. We only took a part of Sherbrooke Street when we marched."[159] The Regiment's visit to its church acquired the makings of an incident when Saturday's *Gazette* published a front-page story (with maps and photos) "Black Watch Parade – Post 9/11 Rule Scotches Route."[160]

On a quiet, sunny Sunday morning, the battalion, pipe band, Colour party and a cohort of veterans, marshalled in the armoury. Outside, waiting, were the police cars and motorcycles of the escort. At 1020 hrs, noting there were few cars downtown, MacKay asked the officer commanding the escort if the parade could use Sherbrooke instead. He replied, "We have no problem with you going along Sherbrooke Street." RHC then marched to church along the traditional route. This quiet parade, in a city that generally yawned at its Reserve regiments, ignited the media and sparked a minor tempest. *The Gazette* triumphantly (mischievously?) reported: "Defiant Black Watch takes traditional parade route!"[161] Media attention … the brigade headquarters was not amused.[162] Judged by city-hall bureaucracy, MacKay had sinned. Regimentally, he was a hero. It did not stop there. A city-wide debate ensued. Subsequent letters to *The Gazette* applauded but not all. A sarcastic sniping came from a fellow militiaman, the ex-CO of the Grenadier Guards. "*Et tu, Brute*" thought MacKay and buried himself in administration and letters of explanation.

MacKay had about redeemed himself but just as the dust settled, it was 2008 – the 400th anniversary of the founding of Quebec City. It was to be a provincial, national and international commemoration. The area commander, the enthusiastic Brigadier General JGJC Barabé decided to celebrate the occasion with a grand procession of all the regiments. All the bands would play the tunes of glory, and all the regimental Colours would be paraded. The Black Watch was told: "Just send your Colour Party." It was here that MacKay committed his second heinous sin. He noted, "Colours without a full guard" was *verboten* in the drill manual. Both he and the CO of the RMR, Lieutenant Colonel Colin Robinson, citing CF drill pamphlets and DHH advice, declined. In the end, General Barabé, very disappointed and angry, shrugged and backed off, absolving those units who did not wish to participate. MacKay felt it was a principled stand. Although his stodgy decision did not land him in trouble, it did not help his cause ("My stock went down after that"). He received a poor evaluation as CO. He tried not to brood, instead turning to training and preparation. However, hierarchical hot water became secondary as world events in Afghanistan overtook the Regiment.

MacKay concentrated on training, then dispatching his soldiers to augment Regular Force battalions. At the same time, he grew increasingly aware that the presentation of new Colours loomed on the horizon. The Black Watch would host His Royal Highness Charles, Prince of Wales and Duke of Rothesay – it would prove his greatest regimental undertaking. In 2004, the Prince assumed the title of Colonel-in-Chief of the Canadian Black Watch following the death of Queen Elizabeth, The Queen Mother.[163] Accompanied by his wife, Camilla, the Duchess of Cornwall, this was his first visit to his Canadian Regiment. The event injected energy into the armoury. *Esprit de corps* mushroomed as the royal visit neared. There was even minor mischief. The subalterns decided to decorate. Everyone was vexed when a perfectly decent sign above the door of the officers' mess (in correct Latin) was replaced by *Sortie* for no intelligent reason. Zealous second lieutenants discovered a dusty artifact above a basement side-door, and when no one was looking, replaced the *Sortie* sign with *Exit*! MacKay pretended not to notice.

This was to be Tom MacKay's final regimental moment. He was to have handed over in May, but the designated commander, Lieutenant Colonel Bruno Plourde would not return from Afghanistan until mid-October. The adjutant, Derrick Farnham, was saddled with two tasks: receiving returning Afghan veterans (which included briefings to parents and partners), and sorting out the detailed protocol for Their Royal Highnesses and the schedule of the grand parade. It was decided to hold the parade inside the armoury, rather than risk rain in Molson Stadium. During the preparatory planning, the chairman of the Black Watch family, Colonel Stephen Angus, calmed anxious hearts: "This is a good opportunity for us to do what we are *capable* of doing, in a familial atmosphere. It will be at *home* and that's a good thing." This proved a wise decision. When it was announced by the media that there would be seating *by invitation only*, the orderly room and regimental secretary were flooded with calls. The Regiment established a strict security system to supervise admittance.

HRH Prince Charles Presents Colours to The Black Watch, 9–11 November 2009

"A wonderfully mad eight days for the Regiment."

The presentation of Regimental Colours by the Colonel-in-Chief, His Royal Highness Prince Charles, took place on 10 November 2009. The Black Watch had not hosted royalty for twenty-two years, and this time it would be a royal couple. The Watch eased into an operational rapport with Clarence House, highlighted by a long audience with Prince Charles in January. MacKay was accompanied by Honorary Lieutenant Colonel V Chartier and the Honorary Colonel designate, Lieutenant Colonel Dan O'Connor. It was the first time RHC officers visited their new Colonel-in-Chief. "We celebrated by going down to Jermyn Street in St James's and buying decent silk regimental ties."[164] Senior Foundation members fondly recalled that special relationship the Regiment enjoyed for over a half century with the much-beloved 'Queen Mum.' That this was a new era was made clear to all when both Queen Elizabeth's familiar portrait and the monteith bowl filled with red roses were moved to the west wall of the mess, and a handsome portrait of the Prince, dressed as Colonel of the Black Watch, was fixed above the great fireplace. Precision, in short order, was required. In the end, MacKay allotted a fortnight's time: two weekends, a quartet of Thursday and Tuesday evenings, plus a Monday dress rehearsal. It was a hectic pace for the battalion was at school or at work; many soldiers were on call-out, posted to courses in distant bases; still others just back from tours in Afghanistan. The incoming commanding officer, Lieutenant Colonel Bruno Plourde, arrived from Kandahar a few weeks before. Plourde sportingly waved aside immediate command and busied himself driving back and forth to Quebec City airport to meet each overseas flight and escort Black Watch soldiers, now veterans, back home. The day before the Royal Visit, another plane-load of veterans, including four Black Watch soldiers, landed. They were picked up and delivered to Bleury Street. Half of them managed to get their highland kit together and to appear on the parade.

In the armoury, everyone pitched in – from repainting the basketball backboards in regimental colours, to refurbishing the messes. Tom MacKay had just begun work at Army headquarters in Ottawa. He was a *commuting colonel* with an exhausting timetable. The CO was assisted by the regimental secretary, Lieutenant Colonel Bill Sewell, who managed all sundry tasks in prompt style. Perhaps the hardest working officer was the regimental adjutant. On daily duty, Farnham sorted out a hockey sock full of tasks. He was supported by that ever-present bulwark of Black Watch administration and minutiae, Warrant Officer Ross McLellan, and the BOR staff: WO Chad Shaw, Sergeant François Martin and MCpl M Gosman. Farnham was used to tough undertakings and this was an exceptional challenge:

> We did not receive orders for this visit until very, very late. This obliged us to work with tentative plans, but allowed us the freedom of working independently of the Brigade...The size of the parade square was a factor; very, very small for the format required. The CO and RSM were constantly toiling to make the parade work in such a confined space. We never practised as an entire group, but always at half-strength.[165]

The Afghanistan veteran found himself troubled by conscience: "I found myself thinking (even with my wild enthusiasm for the Royals) – 'This is not the most important thing I will do today.' We still had soldiers in Kandahar, and I was eager to check my email to learn that they were out of Afghan airspace and safe … this was more important than the parade. But perhaps only soldiers would understand this."[166] On the night of the parade, the royal couple, after a day of visits to Montreal cultural centres, made ready at the MacDonald Stewart Foundation building. The Prince was helped with his Black Watch paraphernalia by Lieutenant Colonel Bruce Bolton.

It would not be a royal parade in Quebec without some sort of political reaction. There was a minor but noisy demonstration outside the armoury. It delayed matters by a half hour. Aware Their Royal Highnesses would require more time, MacKay ordered the regiment to *ground arms and stand easy*. One retired officer commented: "Now *that* was impressive; I know they did not rehearse *that* part – it's a good test of a regiment, reacting to the unexpected and doing it with matter of fact precision." The entourage's intent was to avoid a confrontation at the front, on Bleury Street. When both the security services and the RCMP seemed stumped, Bolton guided the convoy via a hidden lane to the back entrance of the armoury. The Royal couple was concerned – not by the demonstration – but by being late and causing their Black Watch family to wait. This left an impression on the Honorary Lieutenant Colonel, Dan O'Connor, who had met the Prince and Duchess at the north-east entrance and led them through the basement warren to appear magically at the great doors.[167]

The armoury was packed; the balconies of both messes overflowed, and the parade square was filled to its furthest edges. Major Michael Boire was the bilingual

Master of Ceremonies and everyone, save the Honorary Colonel, Duncan McAlpine, was apprehensive. In the basement, the Red Hackle Club was crammed with cadets and soldiers. The RSM, CWO John Barron, stood silent on the edge of the square. The battalion and Colour Parties crowded into classrooms, checking each other's dress, bantering, trying to ignore their nervousness.[168] The anticipation of the crowd was palpable when Boire finally announced at precisely 1630 hours: "Ladies and Gentlemen, The Black Watch, Royal Highland Regiment of Canada." The massive inner doors opened and clad in Stewart and regimental sett, feather bonnets flying, thirty-three pipers and drummers led by Pipe Major Cameron Stevens and Drum Major Michael Lanno, marched onto the square playing the always stirring *Highland Laddie*.[169] It was exhilarating – the trump card that only a Highland regiment can play – the skirl of bagpipes and a beloved march that stirs the passions of soldiers and civilians alike, and lights up a cavernous armoury.

Four complete guards, buttressed by two Colour Parties for the old and new Colours formed within what was now a crammed drill square. It seemed to those watching from the sergeants' and officers' mess balconies, that they overlooked a field of red hackles. General McAlpine watched with wistful satisfaction. Four generations of Black Watch veterans witnessed this presentation of Colours, making the long trek from different parts of Canada: the West Coast, the Maritimes, and a strong contingent from Toronto led by their dynamic president, Sergeant Bill Carlisle. It was, at the risk of exaggeration, a *perfect parade*: the four guards formed a dark-green phalanx, flanked by the pipes and drums.[170] Supporting the Regiment were their cross-town comrades, The Royal Montreal Regiment, who provided sentries for the armoury. "It is times like this when you find out who your friends are," noted Carlisle. In addition, four Cadet Corps affiliated to the Black Watch were represented by ten members each. They flanked the ramp leading up to the parade square and were the first to greet the royal couple. Three of the delegations showed ardent determination: Bishop's College School from Lennoxville in the Eastern Townships (No 2 in Canadian lineage), The Highland Cadet Battalion from the foothills of Lachute (No 4), and King's Edgehill School from Atlantic Canada, Windsor Nova Scotia (No 254). Together they comprised Canada's oldest Army Cadet Corps.[171]

The Prince was in excellent form and immediately put the crowd at ease: "First of all, I just wanted to say how very sorry my wife and I are to have kept you all waiting so long – I hear there's a little local disturbance."[172] The heir to the throne praised the efforts of his Regiment over the decades; he made reference to those who had just returned from war and to anxious loved ones at home. The Prince claimed a special relationship: "My son served in Afghanistan."

The Colonel-in-Chief then inspected with close attention the four guards, pausing to speak with every third or fourth soldier. The ceremony subsequently moved forward to the consecration of the new Colours, on an altar of drums, conducted by three padres: the Rev John P Vaudry, Lieutenant Colonel G Chapdelaine, and the Chaplain General of the Canadian Armed Forces, Dr Brig Gen David Kettle. The drill was particularly crisp.[173] After the new Colours were smartly marched past, and the parade dismissed, the Prince and his cheerful wife, the Duchess of Cornwall, spent the next hour moving through members of the Black Watch family, gathered in the officers' mess. They then proceeded to the parade floor, where many more awaited them. The royal couple stayed later than planned, striving to meet everyone possible before departing to catch their plane to Ottawa for Wednesday's National Remembrance ceremonies.

The Regiment, dismissed by the RSM, and buoyed by their experience, set off to party! Lieutenant Colonel MacKay ordered an all-ranks dance to celebrate the parade and welcome returning Afghanistan veterans. To spare the unit extra work, it was held at the Hyatt Regency, a swank hotel and a short walk from the armoury. It proved to be a bonnie soiree. This was but the first stage of a dramatic and demanding week.[174] Wednesday, 11 November was the Montreal Garrison's Remembrance Day Parade, held for the first time in decades, on the McGill University campus. Thousands crowded into the McGill quadrangle to participate in honouring Canada's fallen. The Watch, weary after an enthusiastic dance, paraded proudly in strong numbers, the pipes and drums drawing the downtown crowd's attention. This was followed by yet a third parade. It was held that Saturday, 14 November when Lieutenant Colonel MacKay relinquished command to Lieutenant Colonel Plourde. There were fewer active members present than on the previous Tuesday, but as the Association president noted: "With course commitments and taskings, the active members of our Regiment do not get much time off these days – they are going 24/7."[175] Nevertheless, the armoury was filled with supporters and family, and the ceremony was again impeccable. Major Boire was back for an encore as MC. It signalled the end of the Black Watch's most ambitious week in decades – the capstone being undoubtedly the dazzling presentation of Colours. Tom MacKay had reason to feel proud. It had proved another historic occasion and most importantly, he handed over a regiment that was in splendid form.[176]

Chapter 16

Regimental Business

Associations of the Black Watch

The Black Watch has the strongest regimental association in the Canadian Army.

Lieutenant General Stuart Beare CMM MSM CD, 2011[177]

"We have been known to get temperamental at times; grumpy ... The Black Watch has personalities, we are a family and have the pros and cons of a family – but God help anyone who says a word against us."

Black Watch veteran

Holding the regimental family together was not easy. The enemies are time and distance. Time is particularly unforgiving as the veterans age. The vast distances of Canada, incomprehensible to Europeans, challenge any endeavour. In the end, from Halifax, Fredericton, Ottawa, Toronto and Vancouver, the Regiment is delicately held together by the battalion in place. It is in its city, in the sanctuary of the Regiment, that its Colours, battle honours, trophies and countless artifacts are guarded. It is impossible to possess the tactile reality of a fortress-like armoury, to hear the tramp of soldiers being piped off to war, and not sense the warrior's burning pride.

There always seems to be a bit of internecine conflict in the clans. It sometimes flared in the modern BW associations as the remnants of the Regular battalions drifted further away. Family solidarity was the guiding principle of Colonel Stephen Angus who, as chairman of the Advisory Board – the baronial regimental senate of wise men – ensured its roots carefully extended to all cities and provinces.[178] The position required charisma, patience, a certain hardness, but mainly, an absolute vision. The greater Regiment survives because of its history, traditions and unconditional devotion of its members. This proved most critical as the Regiment approached its momentous anniversary.

In November of 2011, the RHC Board invited all the presidents of the Associations to Montreal for discussions concerning the anniversary: Gord Ritchie (Montreal), Art Snow (Atlantic), Terry Seaver (Upper Canada Branch/Ottawa), Dave Leslie (Pacific Branch), and Bill Carlisle (Toronto), who was made chairman of the 150th Association committee.[179] The branches are unique, each with a distinct personality. The Toronto Black Watch Association (TBWA) is a stand-alone organization. The difference is historically important. Though the Directors of the TBWA have come to use the expression "Toronto Branch" to be inclusive, this is an independent incorporated association that is eighty-six years old, incorporated in 1934 but its first meeting was held in 1928. It flourished after the Second World War and at one time boasted two full time clubs in Toronto. Attendance waned as society changed. The 22 February 1982 fire that burned down the BW clubrooms in York Street was spectacular, but had minimum effect on the Chapter's fortunes as it turned out:

> We were being evicted anyway – our lease was not being renewed as the building was slated for renovation in the form of demolition. We had just finished an auction on the day of the fire, and most of our fixtures were sold off, but we lost valuable documents. In our heyday when we were making money in the clubroom, it was a vibrant business with a staff of six full-time employees plus TBWA Directors. Members included a cross-section of folks from railroad yard bosses to senior VP's and the odd president from the insurance and financial industry; they all drank together, often *and* in quantity.[180]

The Toronto Branch has remained dynamic as demonstrated by their very active welfare programme, pipe band, and well-attended annual gala, *The Red Hackle Dinner*.[181] The Atlantic and Montreal branches have similar programmes and events. The Montreal Branch was formed in 1929, initially to deal with the needs of old soldiers; its regular visits to Ste Anne's Veteran's Hospital and incorporation of veterans from other regiments in the 11 November parade, and subsequent armoury reception are notable. The Atlantic Branch became particularly energetic after the disbandment of the Regular battalions in 1970 and conducts yeoman work with the largest aggregate of Black Watch veterans in Canada. The Associations' role, in concert with The Black Watch Advisory Board and Foundation, is to support, guide and in some cases, control projects in support of regimental undertakings. In the years immediately before the 150th Anniversary, these included regimental reunions and a plethora of special projects: a regimental anniversary stamp (an RHC Board project), an anniversary artistic print, and historic publications.[182]

A National Historic Site, Regimental Museum, et al

During the regimental anniversary, two events attracted national notice: the declaration of the Black Watch armoury as a Canadian Heritage site and the reopening of the regimental museum. The first was attended by the Governor General (and former Principal of McGill) His Excellency, the Rt Hon David Johnston and the Hon Peter Kent, minister of the environment. Larry Ostola, Director General, National Historic Sites, read the heritage dedication and unveiled a great bronze plaque that was affixed to the stone wall beside the front gates. Ostola noted he had once served in the ranks of the Regiment.

The impetus for having the Bleury Street armoury designated as a National Historic Site began in 2003 when Black Watch Museum curator, Anne Stewart, Lieutenant Colonel Bruce Bolton and Lieutenant General Duncan McAlpine submitted the first application, in hopes that the designation would arrive for the armoury's 100th anniversary in 2006.[183] The process included much documentation and letters of support. Bolton recalls: "Our submission emphasized the community aspect of the building which resulted in an approval in 2008. With the 150th anniversary looming, it was decided to have the official plaque unveiling during the anniversary year." This occurred directly after the 150th Anniversary Trooping the Colour at Fletcher's Field on 12 September 2012.[184]

The second important event of the anniversary year was the re-opening of the first phase of the completely refurbished and redesigned Black Watch Museum. Mr. Peter Webster, Chairman of the R.W. Howard Webster Foundation, the major sponsor, cut the ribbon at the Museum's heavy oak door illuminated by the great Perth Street lamp fixed at the entrance, a generous gift from Major CR Trenholme of the Canadian Grenadier Guards in 1965. The lamp originally lit The Black Watch barracks in Perth, Scotland 150 years ago.[185] The museum proudly features two recent accessions. The first item was a splendid life-size portrait of the Regiment's (and Canada's) first Victoria Cross recipient, Corporal Frederick Fisher VC, by G. Home Russell. It was originally presented to Westmount Academy by his mother after the Great War, and generously donated by the school to the Regiment in its anniversary year. The second item is a painting by acclaimed war artist, Edgar Bundy: *Portrait of Major General Sir Frederick Oscar Warren Loomis,* signed and inscribed by Loomis, the most accomplished Black Watch general in either World War.[186]

Another project to receive pan-Canadian, as well as international, notice was the issue of a Black Watch commemorative stamp, a handsome work of art featuring four regimental soldiers circa 1899, circa1918, a piper, and a modern BW soldier in Afghanistan kit. The project was chaired by Colonel George Logan OMM CD[187] supported by the regimental secretary, Lieutenant Colonel Bill Sewell CD, a keen philatelist: "I remember getting a phone call from Jean Charest's secretary asking who we were and what business were we in. It was really funny – but we got the stamp."[188] Sewell worked with Canada Post to obtain "a special Frank mark on our First-Day Cover which we did, with it being Montreal versus Antigonish." The stamp was launched in a special presentation in the officers' mess on October of 2012. To add to numismatic interest, the Regiment ordered specially minted regimental dome coins. These became vogue in the American forces and quickly imitated by the CF; popular with soldiers, particularly those posted to foreign spots and used as *challenges* or as gifts. It was initiated by Montreal Branch President, Gordon Ritchie.[189] The coins were presented to the soldiers gratis.

In 2008, the Atlantic Association, with Black Watch Foundation assistance, published its own history of Canada's Black Watch, *An Illustrated History of the Regular Force Battalions, 1951–1970,* based on an initial draft by Major Brian Cuthbertson PhD. In Oromocto, the town beside CFB Gagetown, the Atlantic Branch succeeded in renaming a street *Black Watch Avenue* in 2012. The Regiment's Museum produced a book devoted to the rare artifacts found in the museum and messes: Earl Chapman's *Canada's Black Watch 1862–2012 – Legacies of Gallantry & Service.*[190] The Women's division produced an anniversary calendar, with yeoman assistance from The Black Watch Archival Staff. The Regimental Foundation's dedicated support was significant in ensuring all these projects were realized.[191]

An artistic project that proved successful was a striking regimental print portraying 150 years of Black Watch history by the celebrated war artist, Katherine Taylor. The idea was presented by Bill Carlisle but initially deemed too expensive and risky a venture by the Regimental Foundation. In the end, Bill did receive RHC Inc approval to proceed on a self-financing basis. An "Anniversary Print Syndicate" was formed comprising of Bill Carlisle (Chair), Michael Boire, Margaret McGiverin Carlisle, William Davis and David Willard. The plan was to cover the cost of the original painting by selling limited-edition prints from the original. Taylor was hired. The vibrant result became a collector's item; its centrepiece is the Canadian Black Watch Soldier, in full-dress uniform, supported by a montage of major milestones in RHC history. The original artwork was presented to Lieutenant Colonel Plourde during the 150th Anniversary Remembrance Dinner on November 10, 2012. A framed print was donated to the Junior Ranks Mess.[192] The effort was a commendable accomplishment by the small syndicate, with kudos to Bill Carlisle's leadership. Lamentably, a parallel art project suggested by the Honorary Colonel, a bronze statuette of a Black Watch soldier in the Great War created by André D Gauthier OMM, a noted Canadian sculptor, was considered prohibitively costly and rejected.

What promised to be an enjoyable experience, creating a 150th anniversary regimental whisky, proved to be a highland headache. The 1962 100th anniversary spawned a magnificent metal container, embossed with Black Watch scenes and a very drinkable scotch within. Montreal Association President Gordon Ritchie, thus inspired, sought to secure something close, if not as glamorous, then at least as palatable. This was enthusiastically supported by HCol Dan O'Connor. Ritchie started the ball rolling. The suppliers proved difficult. Disappointments followed; eventually, Lieutenant Colonel Bill Sewell and the HCol found themselves spending much time trying to finish the project within reasonable financial boundaries. Things did not look promising and O'Connor almost despaired. As luck would have it (a Black Watch staple), the guest of honour for the 2011 St Andrew's Ball was Lieutenant General Sir Alistair Irwin KCB CBE, former Adjutant-General to the Land Forces in the United Kingdom and thoroughly Black Watch. At a regimental luncheon, O'Connor bemoaned the state of affairs. It turned out that Sir Alistair's family were involved in Scotland's whisky industry. Problem solved.

Anniversary Highland Dinners

Let the war-pipes ring ...
Here's to the lad brought home to be King[193]

The Montreal Highland dinner was held in February. The first was in 2011; the guest of honour was Peter McAuslan, Montreal's master brewer and president of the St Andrew's Society. The anniversary year guest of honour was Dr Larry Ostola, Director General, National Historic Sites, Parks Canada. The mess was crowded with civilians, for this was the Regiment's introduction to the uninitiated. The *Toast to the Haggis* was recited in full with exaggerated accent, but as always, received encouraging cheers. The highlight was the pipe major playing *MacDonald of Kinlochmoidart's Salute*. The Piobaireachd (Pibroch) is the classical music of the great highland bagpipe. It takes over ten minutes to play and requires an ear for music and a highland background. A brave venture by P/Major Stevens, but politely received by a modern audience of professional and business executives who were probably hoping for "Scotland the Brave" or "Amazing Grace". Lieutenant Colonel Plourde was determined to bring back Highland tradition to a Montreal that was in danger of slipping its moorings. In the end, the solemnity of the piece brought a thoughtful silence, then thunderous applause. In Toronto, *The Red Hackle Dinner*, the 81st, was particularly well-supported. Although the Toronto dinners date back to the twenties, the Red Hackle Dinner is associated with the Toronto BW Association organized after the Second World War, and it first president, the decorated warrior, Captain Joe Nixon.[194]

The Honorary Colonel's Dining-In 2012: The American Ambassador

"I don't think an American has seen so many Red Coats since the British captured Washington."

In the spring, the pipe band gave a series of concerts in Montreal and produced (with the cadet and BW Association bands) a CD for martial music aficionados. The RHQ saw a change of adjutants; Captain Guay was posted back to Valcartier and was replaced by another RSS Captain, former MWO, Captain Gaetan Larochelle. Like most Van Doos, the new adjutant took a bit of time to get used to the ways of the Black Watch. That May, the Honorary Colonel's 150th Anniversary Dining-In became one of the great dinners in Black Watch post-war history. It was moved from the officers' mess to the armoury floor, for over 220 attended. The guest of honour was the United States ambassador to Canada, David Cary Jacobson.

During his well-received speech, Jacobson looked over the array of uniforms and quipped: "I don't think an American has seen so many Red Coats since the British captured Washington and burned down the White House." The occasion brought out a coterie of senators, consul generals, generals and illuminati of Montreal society. Friends of the Regiment arrived from across North America, as well as Europe.[195] Before dinner, Senator Colin Kenny presented eight Jubilee Medals in the officers' mess.[196] Almost unnoticed in the festive crowd was Lieutenant William McKenzie Wood, diplomat, former Chargé d'affairs to Israel, and one of the last surviving officers of 1 RHC in World War Two. He was a veteran of Verrières Ridge, the Scheldt and a prisoner of war late in the campaign. It proved to be his last regimental dinner; Lieutenant Wood died shortly before Remembrance Day, aged 90.

The next morning, the church parade repeated the previous November's *Sea of Hackles*. The combined band excelled itself, marching eighty-four pipers and drummers up Sherbrooke Street ("largest number in regimental history" claimed former Pipe Major Bolton[197]), leading a proud parade of soldiers, cadets and veterans. This time the war veterans were equally distributed; as many serving soldiers marched within the two regimental guards as with the Association. The service was conducted by the interim padre, the Rev Jeff Veenstra, and the sermon delivered by the Rev JSS

Armour, the honorary chaplain, who spoke most feelingly of the Regiment's proud heritage and the symbolism of The Black Watch Window. Dr Armour was padre when the 125th anniversary was celebrated in 1987.

Atlantic Personae

In 2012, The Black Watch Advisory Board meeting featured an affable addition – a robust deputation from the Maritimes as well as the west coast. Usually Major Ronald McConnell unofficially represented the Atlantic Association; this time, Lieutenant Colonel IA (Ike) Kennedy OMM CD attended. Renowned in the Canadian Army, and accomplished in four regiments, he made no secret that his heart belonged to the Black Watch. Isaac Allan Kennedy resembled von Manteuffel in stature and a grumpy George Patton in style. He is a complex man with the gift of what Kipling called the common touch. His men, whether jocks, paratroopers or reservists, were devoted. Ike was happiest under a Red Hackle or jumping out of an airplane into the cold winter night. His desperate romanticism, barely hidden under the cloak of a hardnosed field-soldier's demeanour, disguised the artist and the *boulevardier*. As a captain, Kennedy was famous for exotic cars, bespoken suits and a vast library. His *Marcos* (the only one in Canada) brought an international snap to the officers' parking lot. The best-dressed fellow at any party, Kennedy had his clothes flown in from his London tailor. By the time he retired, his memorabilia of Black Watch and parachutist artifacts could fill a small museum– in fact, it did. His house became a mecca for visiting officers. There, the Edwardian who loved tramping through the bush with a bombastic green bandana atop his head, was juxtaposed by the gourmet chef. He retired as lieutenant colonel; his last mission was to turn-around a militia regiment going through rough times and make it ready to receive new Colours from their Colonel-in-Chief, the charismatic Princess Diana. He performed virtual miracles.[198] The Princess of Wales' Own Regiment suddenly dominated drill, training and shooting in eastern Ontario. His rifle team competed against and bested Regular Force squads in title matches – which both shocked and delighted NDHQ. Kennedy captured the imagination of central Canada's militia. A bulwark of the Atlantic RHC Association, Ike won a prominent place on the Black Watch mantle reserved for its more colourful *grognards*.

Reunions at Home and France

The next month was June – summer at last. It featured the Black Watch clan gathering in Kingston, Ontario, which was selected as a site because it was almost half-way between the Maritimes and Toronto (even though it was not). "The aim was to have one barbecue that would cover the triangle of Montreal, Ottawa, and Toronto."[199]

The event featured a barbecue-reunion, and a tattoo inside Old Fort Henry, the magnificent fortress overlooking RMC, protecting Kingston's harbour. It is still in use as a tourist attraction and hosts the Fort Henry Guard (university students who re-enact all aspects of an 1860's British garrison). Their Tattoo is world famous and this time was augmented by the Black Watch pipes and drums as well as devoted volunteer re-enactors modelling a series of historic Black Watch uniforms. The reviewing officer and guest of honour was an old regimental friend, Lieutenant General Sir Alistair Irwin.

In the summer of the same year, Canada observed the seventieth anniversary of the Dieppe Raid; Lieutenant Colonel Plourde travelled to that historic Normandy port, with Pipe Major Cam Stevens MMM, who was one of two picked pipers in all official CF ceremonies. There they joined a DND pilgrimage that included four hundred veterans. Stevens' great-uncle commanded the Mortar Platoon in the Dieppe Raid (and felt by the Regiment to have deserved a DSO). Stevens visited the beach in the evening, and standing close to where the landing craft had docked, played a lament "and finished many a dram of scotch." By then, Stevens was the second longest serving Pipe Major in The Watch. The great pilgrimage then moved to Vimy and another solemn commemoration ceremony where Stevens readied himself to play a stirring *Pibroch*. He was forbidden to do so by a senior staff officer from Ottawa.[200]

Battalion Training and Competitions 2011 to 2013

> Ultimately, it was the *camaraderie* of our team that saw us through....We pushed each other constantly. Defeat, letting down your friends, was not an option for us.
>
> Corporal Sebastian Barry[201]

In October 2012, for a second straight year, the Black Watch team won the annual 34th Brigade March and Shoot competition. It was held at Farnham, in the Eastern Townships. Annually held, the event is the Grey Cup for the Montreal Garrison's infantry battalions. The competition is based on a fully equipped battle-ready infantry section.[202] This was followed by a year of vigorous training and exercises. Field exercises began on New Year's Day; officers, NCOs and soldiers gave up holidays to attend Ex *Noble Guerrier* in Camp Lejeune, North Carolina. The week-long exercise (1–8 January) featured a selected combination from 34 Brigade Battle Group (now part of the *2nd Canadian Division* – formerly, *Land Force Quebec Area*); over 650 troops took part. The exercise confirmed doctrine and technique. Command was tested, and as usual, *lessons-learned* regarding planning and liaison. The Black Watch provided the exercise command element, the responsibility assigned to Lieutenant Colonel Bruno Plourde. They were visited by the commander of the Canadian Army and praised for their dedication and professionalism. Many of the senior leaders were recent veterans and had considerable experience working with the US Army. The soldiers completed the range work and battle tests quickly, and most were back in Montreal by the weekend. It was a different experience from Valcartier and winter's blasts; but many spent as much time aboard aircraft and in airports as they did in the training area.

While *Retention* remained the Reserves bugbear, by 2011 it was not exclusively a militia problem. The Regular Force French-speaking regiments, despite the impressive growth of support for the military in the province, found themselves desperately short of home-grown officers. At one stage, the Van Doo's platoon officers were mainly Anglophones, posted directly after graduation from RMC. They hurriedly brushed up on their classroom *français*, mastering their soldats' local and Van Doo slang. Nearly a dozen R22eR officers were former Black Watch; officers leaving the Bleury Street battalion found themselves with many chums in the R22eR Mess at the Citadelle, that splendid fortress that overlooks *le fleuve Saint-Laurent*.

In March, the battalion participated in Ex *Guerrier Nordique*, braving minus 35C temperatures in an inhospitable environment. This was followed by a combined exercise with the RHC brothers-in-arms, the 1st Battalion 111th US Infantry Regiment. Two exercises (*Highland Yankee* and *Early Thaw*) were conducted and brought together veterans of Iraq and Afghanistan. However, this time it was in Valcartier snow.

Lieutenant (later Major) Loic Maxim Baumans returned from a tour in Afghanistan, having served with 1st Van Doos and the headquarters of 2nd Battalion R22eR as influence activity advisor. He arrived home trained, experienced, and eager to pass on his knowledge. He became part of the RHC Training Team.[203] The exercises were a refreshing change from the century-old routine of driving to Camp Farnham or Valcartier – they used the available areas around Montreal. There were previous local training exercises (the exception not the rule) but this changed with Afghanistan. Militia training began to forsake bucolic escapades for urban scenarios: house clearing and sector security, all part of the continually evolving FIBUA (Fighting In Built-Up Areas) doctrine, something Canadians have been masters of since Ortona, 1943.

A series of schemes, from 2009 through to 2012, were situated at the old terminal in Mirabel airport, an abandoned prison, and the port of Montreal. The reconnaissance and exercise traces were conducted by WO Brasseur and Lieutenant Baumans. The exercise in the port was particularly worthy of note, as it incorporated FIBUA ops.[204] The pitfalls of Reserve exercises are that failure can occur at brigade or unit level; the planning cycle is key:

> The administrative preparation involved the Fire Dept, Police, Port Security, structural engineers, preventive medicine, environment and resource conservation – lots of green lights required; everyone must say *yes*, one objection can kill the exercise; lastly the agreement of the land holders, who must also agree.[205]

Baumans noted that most of the brigade headquarters staff were not from Montreal, particularly the Regulars, "who assume (wrongly) that Montreal is anti-military, and any exercise will be met with hostility. The opposite is true." The modern Army is risk-averse. It is desperate to avoid civilian conflict. Commanders are daring and yearn to create, support, encourage exciting, stimulating exercises, training schemes, but generally a too-careful, pessimistic staff hobbles them. By late 2012, The Watch "started to feel effects of budget constraints, ammo was at a premium, gas expensive, limited pay; we had to fight for pretty much everything. We started to feel the effect of the post-Afghan crunch. This is true in every unit of brigades across Canada."[206] Further, by 2012, recruiting was made far more difficult to conduct: "The army has become generic: overt cultural styles, like the Black Watch uniforms, make *modernists* uncomfortable."[207] When the Black Watch recruiting team gave a presentation to an assembly of potential recruits gathered by the brigade headquarters: "We were allowed *one* slide to explain the Regiment." Cultural differences were to be minimized; highland traditions were discouraged. Recruits were encouraged to join a uniform army: "We became extensions of the recruiting centre – we can still do it, but we just can't advertise it."[208]

Chums with the 111th US Regiment

> Lieutenant Colonel Mike Wegscheider and I agreed to plan a reciprocal joint training between our units ... I think that it was the first instance where both units agreed and successfully brought the historical/protocol relationship to the operational arena since the 1950's reinstatement of our affiliation.
>
> Lieutenant Colonel Bruno Plourde CD

Plourde was dead keen on following up the relations re-established by Tom MacKay. He took a group of officers to attend the 111th mess night in Philadelphia and invited them back to Montreal for the reunion dinner. Combined training was an important part of international relationships and traditional camaraderie. The Black Watch was asked to participate in the 111th US Army National Guard training weekend

16–18 November 2012.[209] Plourde accepted in a flash – *Certainement!* Thus began a series of training opportunities that was of benefit to both strengthening old ties. As they manoeuvred and then relaxed together, they became friends. The exercises were happy reunions as much as serious tests of military skills. Plourde and his HQ team attended a planning conference in Plymouth, Pennsylvania (the HQ of the 1-111th US) for a two-phased joint exercise in the summer to follow-up joint winter exercises in Valcartier March 2012, the last training weekend of the reserve calendar. "The 250-year-old link is a good thing – let's keep it going." The reciprocal training was well-supported by both regiments' headquarters.

Brigadier General Gary O'Brien, Chief of Staff Army Reserves, gave Plourde his *nihil obstat* and Major General Wesley E Craig, the adjutant general of Pennsylvania and commander of the Pennsylvania National Guard, was just as eager about the historical liaison. Most helpful was Brigadier General Giguère, who agreed with Lieutenant Colonel Plourde that this was the opportunity for both to *think strategically* and as Bruno put it so well: "play with the American *Gucci* items … remember, we are perpetuating the oldest link between a Commonwealth and an American unit." The exercises were a great success. The Americans enjoyed winter training in Valcartier using Canadian kit and the Black Watch greatly valued the modern ranges and wealth of vehicles available to the National Guard. The mess dinners were most enjoyable as well. During 22 June–5 July 2013, the Black Watch joined the 111th US at Fort Indiantown Gap (near Harrisburg, Pennsylvania) to participate in Exercise *Highland Yankee*, part of a larger exercise, *Highland Associator*. The exercise stressed platoon tactics and recce patrols; the *live-fire* portion was dramatic (a better range than available at Valcartier). It was rated as extremely successful.[210] Part of the exercise planning cycle involved 'guesstimation' because of a rather basic fact that has always driven militia training: "In the Reserves you really cannot order attendance on exercise; for an accurate number of soldiers, you can only count who gets on the bus on Friday night. Same for Tuesday or church parade – see who forms up on the square. People work, study, have exams, family commitments or simply, they are burned out. Volunteer training takes its toll."[211]

The March and Shoot Hat-Trick

"We did not rest …"

Nothing demonstrated more clearly that this was another golden age for the Black Watch than their iron-fisted hold on brigade infantry standards. The Regiment won kudos for its performance at home and abroad. The presentation of Colours by Prince

Charles set the hackle ever higher in the battalion bonnet. It could have begged that age-old crack: "Very pretty, but can they fight?" They could – and did. The procession of combat veterans with commendations for battle was uncontestable. To further drive the point, the regiment acquired a shelf-full of trophies for infantry skills – a string of victories that delighted the battalion and earned the plaudits of their competitors.

The term "team effort" is routinely used to describe infantry competitions and in this case, is certainly true. However, that would be to overlook the fact that Sergeant Devin Batchelor led regimental teams to two successive victories. He was pivotal in planning, organizing and training each group.[212] The 2013 event featured the testing of a complete infantry section competing against representative teams from six garrison regiments: The Grenadier Guards, The Royal Montreal Regiment, Les Fusiliers de Montreal, Le Régiment de Maisonneuve, 6th R22eR and the Black Watch.[213]

Training was brief, beginning at the end of January and conducted twice a week at night, and every Saturday. Preparation emphasized physical drills as per competition standards. The training included range practice, communications, general military knowledge and lots of navigation practice. Weapons were carefully stored to avoid past problems where "rifles smacking against kit lost their zeroing." The march portion was orienteering point to point, interspaced by *stands* where the team was tested on military knowledge: "Everyone got 100 percent at each stand." One test consisted of stretcher-bearing for a distance of eight hundred metres (using filled jerry cans to give weight). This proved tricky on the icy roads. Setting up the ten-man arctic tent was a breeze: "We practised in the armoury and cut any corner to shave time – we pre-taped our toboggan harnesses and got a much faster start than other teams." The tent set-up required getting the stove going and brewing tea. The standard required was a sixty-metre move with a packed toboggan, setting the arctic tent with a kettle of boiling water inside of five minutes. Striking the tent ("Pull Pole!") and packing up took three minutes.

> There was one minor navigation failure, a six hundred metre error, quickly adjusted, but we did 1.2 kms extra. The stress that hit us when we realized we were wrong gave us a boost of adrenalin; we flew to the next point. Because we were the first team, we had to *break trail* through the dense woods. Hard to manoeuvre a toboggan … We opted for no snowshoes but there was enough snow to make it tough. We did not rest to avoid cramps.[214]

Snow blew across in a stiff wind as the team drove on: "We smoked everyone." The finished march of over ten kilometres took two hours and forty-five minutes. After shooting, it was clear no one was going to beat them.[215] The triumph proved Sergeant

Bachelor's last hurrah with The Watch. Like so many of his mates, he transferred to the Regular Force in April 2013 as a master corporal in 2 RCR.

The remaining battalion exercises were held in the spring, but Camp Farnham, and certainly Valcartier, had large reserves of snow in the tree lines; the early rains made field craft frustrating. Thick clinging gumbo stuck to everything – older officers recalled a bit of doggerel *at the drop of a balmoral* ...

> Mud, mud, glorious mud / Nothing quite like it for cooling the blood
> So follow me follow, down to the hollow /
> And there let me wallow in glorious mud.[216]

CWO Mike Kelly MMM CD
the First Army Reserve Chief Warrant Officer

Fall training was dampened by the bitter news that former Black Watch RSM, Chief Warrant Officer MRG Kelly MMM CD, died tragically from a fall on 25 August 2012. Mike Kelly enrolled in 1970 and was appointed Regimental Sergeant Major of the Black Watch in September 1987. Following his term as RSM, Kelly transferred to the Eastern Area Battle School at CFB Valcartier as the School CWO. In January 1992, he was transferred to Quebec District Number 1 Headquarters and appointed the District Chief Warrant Officer, a position that he held until the new 34 Canadian Brigade Group was created in April 1997. He was subsequently employed as the school standards warrant for the Brigade school. His reputation for balanced judgment and professional knowledge led to a transfer to Army HQ in January 1998. Kelly reported to Brigadier General Kenneth Quinn, the Reserve Advisor to the Chief of the Land Staff. He was made responsible for NCM training and career projects. Two years later, CWO Kelly was transferred to Land Forces Doctrine and Training System HQ in Kingston, where he advised on issues relating to Reserve NCM career progression, training and leadership training.

The Black Watch beamed with pride when CWO Kelly was appointed the first Army Reserve Chief Warrant Officer by the Chief of the Land Staff, Lieutenant Gen William Leach on 1 July 2000. He followed in the footsteps of another Royal Highlander, CWO John Marr, who was the first Canadian Forces Chief Warrant Officer (1987–1991). *CFCWO* constitutes the senior non-commissioned member appointment in the Canadian Forces, a post created in 1978. CWO Marr began his Infantry career in 2 RHC. Kelly reported to Brigadier General Herb Petras, Director General Land Reserve, regarding policies and related issues of concern for non-commissioned officers. He travelled across Canada to the four Land Force areas. He had already hung up his Hackle to wear the trappings of an Ottawa NDHQ chief warrant, but at the end of his tour as Army Reserve chief, he was again called to duty, and this time it came with a bearskin attached. CWO Kelly accepted an appointment as the Regimental Sergeant Major of the Canadian Grenadier Guards in November 2004, serving until his retirement from the Canadian Forces in 2006. In the end, Kelly reached the highest strata possible for a Black Watch, indeed any non-commissioned, officer in the Canadian Reserves.

Major Mike Walker

The 2010 Haiti earthquake was rated at a catastrophic magnitude of 7.0 on the Richter scale. It struck on 24 January 2010. There were fifty-two aftershocks and a death toll of nearly 160,000 people. Major Mike Walker was almost crushed in his headquarters and just managed to escape. Immediately, he plunged into rescue work, for which he was subsequently decorated with the *Commendation for Bravery*: "assisted strangers in a foreign land in a time of great need and under volatile and dangerous conditions. All Canadians can be proud of their exemplary action ... despite the shock and devastation experienced, [Walker] sprang into action following the earthquake, risking his own life to help rescue many victims from the rubble."[217]

Chapter 17

The Black Watch at War and Beyond, 2002–2022

On patrol … and suddenly, out of nowhere: kids. All they want are pens; they come up to you and tap their hand "Pen! Pen! Pen!"[218]

Sergeant Bjorn Dittmar

Part 1: The Home Front

Canada's role in the Afghanistan War began in late 2001. The first major contingents of regular troops arrived in theatre in January–February 2002. The Canadian battle group took on a larger (and far more dangerous) role in 2006 after troops were redeployed into Kandahar province. For the first time since the Second World War and Korea, Black Watch soldiers and officers were sent to battle. When Lieutenant Colonel Tom MacKay took command of RHC, the Canadian involvement in Afghanistan had grown to twenty-five hundred personnel; of these twelve hundred comprised the front line battle group, well-reinforced with reservists, many of them Black Watch. They left Bleury Street for training in Gagetown or Valcartier, and after a robust three-month refresher, were seconded to Regular Force battalions or special PSYOPS units working directly with the local populations. They deployed into the centre of the maelstrom in Kandahar, which was the most dangerous, most Taliban-infested region south of the Kush. It was not far from the Pakistan border and 150 kilometres from Quetta – the venerated War College where many a Black Watch Officer had studied.[219] During this period, MacKay worked to re-establish ties with their allied

American unit, the 111th US Infantry. On 5 November 2005, he attended their mess night, and left impressed: "They just had an entire rifle company returned from Iraq. It was an all-ranks dinner, and they honoured the four soldiers killed. I was taken with their traditions, unique things they hold dear. As they read the roll a subaltern would call out a quote from a past battle." [220] MacKay and McCulloch (in 1992) had heretofore been the first Black Watch officers since the 1958 grand visit to sit in the Black Watch chair. He vowed to revitalize this historic association.

As the battle group in Kandahar grew into an intricate juggernaut, the Army became strapped for soldiers. Reservists were either sent across vast oceans to backfill positions of soldiers already deployed, or they were offered Class B positions (temporary contracts) "in places where we would never have sent reservists before, which included the leadership school and the recruit school." [221] Members of the Regiment served everywhere, including the Area HQ, as well as the burgeoning PSYOPS and CIMIC organizations. The Afghan support groups alone required up to three thousand Canadians. During his command, MacKay had sixty Black Watch soldiers and officers on fulltime service, both exciting and frustrating: "It wasn't mobilization, but the atmosphere was darned close; best yet, there was tons of money sloshing around … The Regular Force seemed to think all you needed was a FIN Code, and you hired a *milicien* … this is how we mobilized the reserves without actually doing it." [222] The unit was constantly generating soldiers for pre-deployment training, supporting them while deployed, and then re-integrating them on their return. All of these demands for Militia personnel meant that while over 40 percent of the Black Watch worked with the CF, only a few of those of the Class B were able to train with the unit.

Augmentees to Headquarters such as ISAF, IJC or NTM-A were identified singularly and generally trained through the Peace Support Training Centre in Kingston for six weeks training. Soldiers who volunteered to train with the battle groups (BG) were selected individually and "endured a far too long a period of training during the pre-deployment and mounting phase with some rotations seeing routine contracts between fifteen and eighteen months." [223]

As to the actual employment, it was "a piecemeal affair with Reservists sprinkled about the BG." [224] There were some components that were comprised of more than 50 percent reservists where it was felt the task could be carried out by Reserve cadres. It came down to trust and confidence in the Militia: "The R22eR and RCR were better integrators with the PPCLI lagging behind … " [225] The leadership of the Army Reserve justifiably lauded the accomplishments of the Reservists but recognized the system begged improvement, as did the regiments. MacKay noted:

"Despite the previous decade's experience re-generating reservists for operations in the former Yugoslavia ... we were still sending only individual augmentees to serve with the Regular Force battle groups." Bosnian service had taught RHC that soldiers returning from operations had some difficulty reintegrating into unit life, because the people they shared their deployment with were no longer around them. The closest the Black Watch came to sending any kind of formed capability was when Sergeant Bjorn Dittmar led a five-man PSYOPS detachment, four of which were Black Watch soldiers. Subsequently, soldiers who served alongside their mates from the Regiment reintegrated easily.[226] The Black Watch reached out as a true clan and developed a routine that involved a series of meetings with the families before, during and after the deployment. The meetings addressed the families' concerns over the physical dangers of the mission in Afghanistan as well as their concerns over the potential for mental illness and how best to help their sons and daughters reintegrate upon their return home. These meetings also provided the families with an opportunity to meet each other and develop a secondary support network of people sharing the experience. MacKay insisted: "This may have been the greatest service we provided to the families as many of them developed close bonds with each other."

The soldiers underwent a series of interviews, before and after deployment, to ensure that they were well-prepared for active service and able to reintegrate on their return. While overseas, Black Watch soldiers were regularly sent *care packages* from the Women's Division and The Black Watch Association branches.[227] This proved extremely popular and became a model for other Canadian units. The parcels were noted by Regular Force soldiers who served alongside and often commented that the Black Watch was fortunate to receive such consistent support. It was simply a clannish concern – a solid tradition dating back to the Great War. Whether a toque or a *Canadiens* hockey T-Shirt, it was *home* and much welcomed. Parcels were sent every six weeks; toilet paper was gold still, even after the Second World War. The soldiers requested writing pads, candies with Canadian flags, pens to give to kids, lip balm, energy drinks, canned goods, books; each box weighed thirty pounds. At Yuletide, the Regiment launched *Operation Santa 2012* guided by Bill Carlisle and Gord Ritchie. The project included follow-up letters to each Black Watch soldier on active service.[228]

Although the knowledge gained from overseas postings was invaluable, the Regiment was not to benefit from this experience for very long. As of 2009, the retention of soldiers coming back from Afghanistan was less than 50 percent. Lieutenant Colonel MacKay was vexed, considered solutions, and would soon put his theories to the test. His years of command prepared MacKay for his next goal in life. He had taken a sabbatical from his business interests to work in the Army Headquarters in Ottawa as a Staff Officer. His aim was to serve in Afghanistan and re-establish his military credentials away from SQFT. Serendipitously, the former CO of the Cameron Highlanders, Colonel Patrick Kelly MSM CD (also a former Black Watch soldier and officer), was the Director of Army Reserves and about to deploy to Afghanistan.[229] MacKay was offered the position of *Army Reserves 2*, Acting Director, for the year. He did well, receiving the Army Commander's Commendation in December 2011. Within two years, MacKay finally went to war, despatched to Kabul as the Director of Afghan National Security Force Operations. He was away almost eight months, returning a wiser and more thoughtful man.[230]

Part 2: Outside the Wire – Fire Fights and Air Strikes

> When asked, the Reservist has always delivered alongside of their Regular Force counterpart. Those who could persevered and those who could not, disappeared ... In the end there was one; one team, one organization, proud to be going into the fight and deep inside everyone was the uncertainty how each of us would perform.[231]
>
> Major General David Fraser, commander in Afghanistan, 2006

> Boys, take pride in wearing the Hackle! You are among a select and elite few.
>
> Lieutenant Glenn Cowan, to Black Watch soldiers[232]

The Reserve battalion in Montreal finally went into battle, and members of the Regiment returned with new decorations, commendations, and in 2014 a new battle honour.

Modern, asymmetrical warfare proved radically different from any previous Black Watch experience. The enemy was everywhere, yet nowhere. The contacts were regular, and casualties were continuous. The infantry battalions experienced daily fire-fights, mortar attacks and the ever-present mines (IEDs, Improvised Explosive Device) as well as the deadly suicide bomber attacks – enough to drain the strongest soldier. While the Forces had been in constant peacekeeping/peacemaking operations throughout the 1980s in Cyprus, and Bosnia in the 1990s, Afghanistan was something new. "Combat was something that had been talked about ... something that the CF had yet to experience ... an environment that was only theoretically understood."[233] Afghanistan was to stretch the CF experience to its furthest boundaries – its operations testing both the institution and the individual soldier. This was a routine of relentless war, an ever-present enemy and no safe 'rear areas' in which to relax. Outside of their fortified bases or armoured laagers in the unforgiving terrain, the soldier was a constant target, on roads, dirt tracks or precipitous mountain crags. While enjoying total command of the air, the ground war was an unending purgatory, where death lingered around every corner or seemingly friendly village square. The more scholarly recalled Kipling's *Arithmetic on the Frontiers*, written about Afghanistan fighting in the late 19th century, yet still very relevant:

> A scrimmage in a Border Station
> A canter down a dark defile;
> Ten thousand pounds of education
> Drops to a ten-rupee jezail
> The Crammer's boast, the squadron's pride
> Shot like a rabbit in a ride.[234]

Black Watch soldiers were fed into battle as individuals, pairs or section teams at best. There were no all-Reserve company-sized units deployed to Afghanistan, nor for that matter, any all-Regular companies, save for the 3 PPCLI deployment in 2002. "Afghanistan featured platoon/troop-sized units, made up of many Reserve unit contributors that did convoy escort or force protection duties. They were typically inside Regular company/squadrons that had that task also."[235]

They were strangers in a strange land. Their burden was to prove themselves to the regimental clan to which they were assigned. Though they were often as well-trained as any Regular Force corporal, they had to adjust to the routine, the terrain, and their immediate comrades. Major General David Fraser CMM MSC MSM CD MA, commander, Regional Command: South Afghanistan in 2006, saw it differently: "There were no regiments in-theatre. There were no arms in theatre." Preconceived notions of what combat was going to be like were replete as were the prejudices and regimental banter about each other:

> This situation was not mean-spirited but a result of tremendous pride and lack of understanding of the other. Training beat that out of each of us because the standards necessary to achieve the operational effective levels demanded that we work together as a team.[236]

Most made friends quickly, and in battle forged solid bonds. Yet at the end of their stint, they were cut adrift, sent home, and in many regiments, on their own when they left the plane. Fortunately, this did not happen in the Black Watch.

At the front (a misnomer since everywhere was potentially *the front*) soldiers quickly learned tricks of survival not taught at the Combat Arms School back home. It was a psychedelic world of battle. The skies filled with bizarre aircraft – from gunships, to ground attack aircraft, the radical *Osprey* and the ever-present robotic killer, the Drone. It was very much a cyber-war; the flesh and blood highlander was augmented by *molti roboti*.[237] There were military units from other countries. This was a war that emphasized the psychologist, the lawyer and the linguist as much as the tactically skilled. While soldiers bore some resemblance to the *Tommies* or *Herbies* of past wars, they were *Starship Troopers*. The Canadian-designed digitized camouflage (desert *CADPAT*), battle armour, knee and elbow protectors, helmets with cameras, infra-red receivers, and the ever-present macho sunglasses that added to the mystique. On top of that, firepower: small sections rivalled Normandy-era companies. They were soon bolstered by the best tank in NATO – not surprisingly a German product – the ultra-sophisticated *Leopard* 2A6M CAN, augmented by the all-Canadian LAV III and *Coyote* eight-wheeled armoured combat vehicles. With body armour, earphones, cell phones and GPS, they looked exactly like what they were – millennium infantry. No veteran from past wars knew what to make of them, except when they moved to contact, and assumed the familiar skulking choreography that has denoted infantry for centuries. There were still scouts, snipers and, invariably, battle casualties.

Corporal JP Warren KIA, July 2006

> When I took command in May 2005, I was asked, "Whom are we going to war with?" … Fifteen months later I found myself burying a Black Watch soldier killed in Kandahar by a Taliban suicide bomber.
>
> Lieutenant Colonel Tom MacKay

On 22 July 2006, a vehicle driven by a Taliban suicide bomber detonated midst a Canadian convoy near Kandahar. The blast killed Corporal Jason Warren and the driver of the vehicle, Corporal Francisco Gomez of the PPCLI.[238] Jason was only a couple of weeks away from the end of his rotation and had already survived numerous firefights and close calls. He was a Quebec City native, and had enrolled in the Black Watch in February 1999:

> The enemy attacked repeatedly and staying together, we were strong. But at times the enemy was successful as he was in July when we lost Jason along with Corporal Frank Gomez – both died fighting and serving for a cause they believed in. While both soldiers came from different regiments they were one in spirit and effort … a shared passion to do what they believed in. They did this willingly.[239]

As word spread, soldiers gathered at the armoury. The junior ranks' mess was opened. MacKay, visibly shaken, addressed those who had gathered. Corporal Warren was on his second operational mission. He had previously served on Operation *Palladium*, in

2002. He was the only soldier from 34 Brigade lost in Afghanistan and the first Quebec-based soldier to die.[240] Media attention was enormous. Satellite trucks appeared at the armoury, demanding interviews. Major Christopher Phare was designated assisting officer to the Warren family. They requested a regimental funeral. The Watch prepared immediately. The ops officer, Mike Walker, and Captain Peter Radman sorted out the many details.[241] Corporal Warren's and Corporal Gomez's remains were brought home together on the same flight. The Chief of Defence Staff (CDS), the Minister of National Defence and the Governor General all attended the repatriation. Corporal Warren's bearer party was entirely from the Regiment – all friends of Warren.[242]

The funeral took place on 2 August 2006 at the regimental church. The service was conducted by both Canon Glencross and the new padre, Captain the Rev Richard Topping. It was an impressive, exacting funeral. The congregation included representatives from all units in 34 CBG, the Commander of SQFT, the Chief of Staff for Army Reserves, and the Lieutenant-Governor of Québec. At the request of the family, Lieutenant Colonel MacKay gave a eulogy with Corporal Tom Meisner and Gerry Warren. "Corporal Meisner's tribute to his friend was so stirring that the entire church broke into loud applause as he finished." Warren was interred at the National Cemetery in Ottawa, attended by the CDS, General Rick Hillier.

Staff Officers, Afghanistan

…within the pool of his trade and the ocean outside of it …

Captain Rod DeCastro

The war required competent staffs. Captain Derrick Farnham was made interim RSS officer: he was thirty-eight years old, bilingual, had lived in India, and was about to write his doctoral dissertation. He was both the uber-competent staff man, as well as the ever-observant regimental adjutant.[243] Farnham's graduate studies were centred on German philosophy – Hegelian idealism, mixed with a soupçon of Nietzsche, just right for a highland regiment. In Afghanistan, he was appointed Kandahar provincial reconstruction team liaison officer at the military airfield: "I briefed the colonel of the *Effects cell* in the morning, the general of the Canadian Kandahar contingent in the evening, and the regional command south CIMIC cell irregularly." He travelled, visited and liaised. He once flew to Maywand with a briefcase filled with one billion Afghani dollars. Yet, he was quite serene: "Maywand was utopian. It was poppy harvesting time … the Taliban made certain we were perfectly happy in a tranquil environment."[244] He had grown a beard and shaved his head. With a deep tan, he was part Mullah, part Greek olive-oil merchant. At Maywand, he was pleased to discover that the 'influence officer' working with the British Parachute Regiment was none other than a recent member of the Black Watch, Captain Rod DeCastro, who had joined the Regular Force, and was now a Van Doo. He decided his time with The Watch and subsequent service with the R22eR complemented each other nicely:

[In Afghanistan], I worked as an aide to a general who had little love for the Reserves ... I would say that 75 percent of what he appreciated about me as an officer I learned at the Black Watch. The BW instilled in me the notion that an officer should be able to swim easily within the pool of his trade and the ocean outside of it – comfortable conversing on politics, the arts, current affairs, etc. The Black Watch was my officer's 'liberal arts education.'[245]

Colonels at the Front

The two most senior Black Watch officers to serve in Afghanistan were Colonels Plourde (deployed October 2008 – September 2009) and MacKay (November 2012 – June 2013). Plourde had bags of operational experience from Africa to Europe, but Afghanistan was completely new. Initially, he was assigned as liaison officer with the Afghanistan national security forces (ANSF) op command and control centre – the first Canadian in the position. He fit in well. The bearded French Canadian looked rather like a menacing Pashtun on most days. His war was often simply based on luck – not being where the suicide bombers were: "I commanded a team of 3 NATO members from UK, Netherlands and Canada ... [previously] a suicide attack at the provincial parliament in downtown Kandahar [created] a 15m-wide crater and blast that took away the tiles from the building for up to 75m – quite impressive." During his deployment, Plourde interacted directly with Americans, coalition officers and members of Afghan security forces. "That changed my life both as a soldier and as a person. Working in partnership with the Afghan national police (ANP) was a stimulating but slow and sometimes frustrating endeavour. Attacks on police stations and IED strikes were part of our routine."[246] WO Snoddon recalled:

Lieutenant Colonel Plourde was an unknown figure to many soldiers of the Regiment ... It definitely came as a surprise when during my tour in 2009 I received a *Facebook* message from this Lieutenant Colonel inviting all Black Watch soldiers to ring him up at Kandahar Air Field – he would pay the coffee. I remember speaking to soldiers that came back into the FOB who had taken him up on the offer. [They met up] with a lieutenant colonel sporting a full beard who spoke with glee about the thrill of acting as the turret gunner in a vehicle driven by a US sergeant-major and how much it 'sucked' to have to come back to the echelon with all those rules. The guys loved it and could all relate to him, it never felt like you were sitting down with a politician … that word spread quickly through our ranks and even to soldiers we worked with from other regiments. More importantly … we felt confident knowing we'd be coming back to work for someone who had actually walked a mile in our MK III's, an 'operational' CO as we referred to it.[247]

Plourde suffered through the bureaucratic part of his job. He recalls each participating nation wanted 'to do good' and be recognized for it. "We even got a bunch of self-proclaimed missionaries in a 'bus of love' that tried to go across the country!"[248]

Three years as a senior staff officer at Army HQ gave Tom MacKay éclat. He was bureaucratically smooth but still an idealist. He yearned for the front. And he was in luck. MacKay was selected to deploy with *Operation Attention* and promoted to full colonel; but, like his war, the rank was temporary: *Acting While So Employed* (AWSE). MacKay spent thirty-two weeks in-theatre as director of Afghan National Security Force Operations within the ISAF Joint Command HQ. He commanded four Train/Advise/Assist teams working across four ANSF headquarters in Kabul.[249] His own headquarters was beside the Kabul International Airport, in a fortified Afghan Air Force base (KAIA–North). He discovered: "The Afghans are incredibly brave and tough soldiers with a strong sense for tactics born out of decades of fighting. [They] were overcoming the hybrid Afghan military culture of Soviet training and Mujahedeen experience." His closest call occurred in his last week. He awoke at 0430 to the sound of explosions and gunfire. "Quickly strapping on full fighting order and C7 rifle (my pistol was with me at all times). I ran into Sergeant Rutherford of the Para Regiment (UK). He immediately became my fire-team partner and we set off for the gate." The enemy had tried to breach the wall to the Afghan Air Force base, which would have given them a relatively easy approach to the International Airport. They were defeated. MacKay well recalls "the initial rush of excitement of being under ground attack."[250]

Comrades in Arms: RHC and 3 SCOTS – *Ceud mìle fàilte*

Coinnichidh na daoine far nach coinnich na cnuic[251]

The senior leadership of the Army rarely fails to state that they could not have done the task without the Reserves and that the Regular and Reserve components gained enormous confidence in each other through the experience of conflict.

Colonel David Patterson, A/Director Army Reserve, NDHQ, 3 November 2013[252]

Sergeant Devin Batchelor was raised just blocks away from the armoury and grew up the archetypical bilingual Montrealer. Laconic, lanky, and confident, with a quick mind and a pitiless sense of humour, he is a natural leader. Batchelor was deployed to Kandahar twice. Like many Black Watch soldiers, he was a PSYOPS team member. RHC cadres worked in areas assigned to a tactical infantry commander, supporting missions against opposing forces. Their tasks included encouraging popular discontent with the opposition's leadership, and combining persuasion with a credible threat to degrade the Taliban's ability to conduct or sustain military operations. A master corporal at the time, Batchelor's initial PSYOPS team members were all Montrealers and mainly Black Watch; Sergeant Bjorn Dittmar was in charge. The team included Corporal Leonard Maillet, Corporal Tom Meisner and a soldier from The Watch's downtown neighbour, Le Régiment de Maisonneuve, Corporal Etienne Comtois. Concurrently, other Black Watch soldiers deployed in surrounding sectors: MCpl Matthew Ramsay was with B Company 2 R22eR with Corporal Ryan D'Alesio; Sergeant Brian Hill and Corporal Matthew Anderton were with A Coy. Corporal Alexander Reid was with the PRT Provincial Reconstruction Team at Camp Nathan Smith as defence and security team.[253] Devin Batchelor's favourite experience occurred when his team worked out of Forward Operating Base (FOB) Ma'Sum Ghar, and was detached to Regional Battle Group South. To their delight, they found themselves with the Allied Regiment – the 3 SCOTS, Black Watch. They were surprised to see them – in fact, they were unsure just who they were!

The Imperial Black Watch was now the 3rd Battalion, Royal Regiment of Scotland (3 SCOTS). In 1967, the regiment lost its *Territorial* battalions, which were amalgamated into the 51st Highland Volunteers. It was the last British military unit to leave Hong Kong in 1997. Furthermore, during the 2003 Iraq War, the Black Watch fought in Operation *Telic*, the initial attack on Basra. It continued to occupy the Basra area until 16 December 2004 when it was announced that the Black Watch was to join with five other Scottish regiments (The Royal Scots, The King's Own Scottish Borderers, The Royal Highland Fusiliers, The Highlanders, and The Argyll and Sutherland Highlanders) to form the *Royal Regiment of Scotland*, a single regiment consisting of five regular and two territorial battalions.[254] As with the other Scottish regiments, The Black Watch retained its former name, with its battalion number as a subtitle. Further, the battalion was permitted to retain its most famous distinction, the Red Hackle on the Tam O'Shanter.[255] In 2009, the battalion deployed into Afghanistan as the reserve battalion of 19th Light Brigade, based at Kandahar. It was during this tour that elements of the Canadian Watch had the opportunity to conduct operations with their sister unit. Once introductions were made, it was *Schottenfreude* – a Scottish joy; a fraternal reunion midst the sober test of enemy fire:

I alone was attached to B COY [while] Sergeant Dittmar and Corporal Maillet were attached to A COY as a PSYOPS capability. It was a "disrupt" operation that would last four days in the heart of Zhari District in an area called Nalgham. It ended up being a very "violent" four days. Soon after we inserted by Chinook Helicopter we were met by Taliban gun fire for the rest of our stay (in intervals of course).[256]

It was the group's first real contact with the enemy: "At first the firefights were exciting. The enemy was firing from far away so I could never really see them. However, that changed – there is definitely a change in attitude when friendly soldiers are injured or killed."[257] Batchelor recalled his main sensation was "Anger – the feeling when you realize they are shooting at you." Sergeant Dittmar and Corporal Maillet, with A Coy 3 SCOTS, were taken under fire as they arrived. The lead section, including members of the Afghan National Army, were hit. It was in this action that Dittmar received his *Mentioned in Despatches*.

The team spoke with warriors' satisfaction about their experience with the Allied Regiment: "The 3 SCOTS were an amazing unit to work with. Very professional at all levels … These guys were motivated, smart fighters that took great care of each other."[258] Soon after that operation, Batchelor deployed again with the 3 SCOTS for another 'disrupt operation' into Zangabad – a place he returned to on his second tour in Afghanistan (March – June 2009). This time he was appointed commander of the PSYOPS Section.[259] They were then attached to A Coy, 1 R22eR ("a great company to work with"). When the hot months arrived, there were more contacts, more IEDs and more firefights; some were pretty rough towards the end. His tour ended that summer. Sergeant Batchelor and his mates returned in time to be on parade for the presentation of the Regiment's new Colours by HRH Prince Charles. He then promptly redeployed back into the maelstrom of Kandahar as leader of another PSYOPS team in 2011. This time, he was the only Black Watch representative, but the rest were from Montreal and Quebec.[260]

Warrant Mathew Mark Snoddon spent sixteen of his thirty-four years in the Regiment and on exotic call-outs. Had the Regiment been still a part of the Regular Force, he surely would have found himself among their ranks following in the footsteps of his great uncle. With three bars to his Campaign Star and a cluster of other medals, plus a Commander's Commendation, he was almost out of place at Farnham exercises or correcting drill on the armoury floor. Snoddon's Afghanistan tours took place from 2007 to 2011, each with less than six months at home before returning to pre-deployment training. During these periods, he balanced the need to reconnect with family and the obligation to parade with the regiment. All his deployments were into Kandahar, and as he gained experience, he advanced from 2IC to Tactical PSYOPS Team Leader.[261] During his tours, he did almost two years 'outside the wire' as some have come to say. He remembers his first operation, three weeks on an isolated hilltop with a battalion reconnaissance platoon being rocketed and mortared, sometimes several times a day:

> We'd all lost a close friend when Jason Warren died. I'd be lying to say it didn't drive many of us to volunteer to go overseas. It also opened my eyes to the preparation that each of us needs to do before going to war; an obligation to your family and loved ones to 'set things straight'. I decided I'd write letters to all them explaining my reasons and that I'd keep a journal so my family would know what I did overseas if I was killed (Over three tours I never missed a day). Writing the letters was the hardest thing I'd had to do until that point in my life. So I kept putting it off. The first night I set off from Kandahar Air Field and arrived at Forward Operating Base Ma'Sum Ghar late at night. The next morning we found out a soldier had been killed when he hit an IED driving down the same road right after us. We were deploying on the Battle Group's first major operation the day after and I found myself staying up late writing those letters to family when I should have been sleeping.[262]

The effect of war was never apparent back home. On parade, Warrant Officer Snoddon looked dapper in a kilt or in camouflage combat uniform giving lectures on a Tuesday night – cool, almost casual. But pressed to describe combat, he recalled the brutality of war: "Seeing horrible wounds on fighting men and little children. The crunch of bone as we manipulated them trying to stop the bleeding – like when you snap chicken wings." Despite all this, he remained a highland romantic, speaking with satisfaction about "getting detached to the Royal Gurkha Regiment for ops – a historical regiment I had heard so much about. Hearing firefights start [and] your team in the thick of it." Like most soldiers, Snoddon confesses nothing could be hidden from mother: "She could tell in my voice every time I was worried – mom always knows when you're lying!"[263]

Ladies From Hell – the nom de guerre made real

> The vast majority of patrolling I did was on foot.
>
> Sergeant Kimberly Anderson CD

The millennium Watch deployed its soldiers, both men and women, to the battlefield: something unthinkable in the Second World War. War was suddenly a very real vocation. Being a soldier was now far more complex than Loomis, Cantlie or Dinesen could have imagined. The routines of seemingly safe psychological warfare elements were suddenly on the front lines. There were no "safe" missions. PSYOPS patrols would develop into skirmishes; firefights often became battles. Sergeant Kim Anderson and WO Stephanie Cyr regularly ended up in the thick of things.

Marie Danielle Stephanie Cyr was a well-educated soldier (BA, Political Science; Certificate Social Psychology, McGill; a Masters in International Relations, Queens University). During her thirty-four years, Cyr saw the effects of war in Bosnia (two tours), the Congo, and Afghanistan (two tours). A reservist *condottieri*, she has spent more time away from the Regiment than serving in Bleury Street. Her exotic postings were both exciting and dangerous. She was awarded two commendations; the second was from the Chief of Defence Staff, for operational duty; however, she declines to speak about it:

> I don't believe that anyone can really be prepared for war as intense as fire fights can be; [however] I feel that the training and the experience gained from the Regiment trained me well to react to combat. There are many moments where skills obtained over the years [become] second nature.[264]

Sergeant Kimberly Ellen Jane Anderson worked out of Kandahar during 2011 as a tactical CIMIC (civil–military cooperation) operator, at times attached to missions she is not cleared to discuss, even today as with all overseas missions. Her work-place would sometimes be only reached by air:

> My Location was at COP Robinson in Talukan Panjwai'I; conditions were remote, austere and violent. My movement to and from KAF was done via Chinook [helicopter]. I spent much of my time there working on and coordinating school projects which had been petitioned for by the local elders. One of the more prominent elders was killed by the Taliban a few hours after submitting the petition to me. That had a huge impact on me. The school was named in his honour and those believed responsible for his death were later killed.[265]

IEDs were a constant threat and Anderson's operating base was fired upon routinely. She recalls: "The vast majority of patrolling I did was on foot." Anderson is a Montrealer. She likes to be called Kim; she is tall, fit, with a ready smile, and an eye for detail. Armed with a college degree in Police Technology and a Bachelor of Arts, Anderson joined The Watch in May 2000; by 2008, she served in the Arctic, the Middle East and in Guli, in Northern Uganda. She exudes a quiet, friendly confidence. On parade or on exercise, Anderson is respected; her *Afghanistan Medal* simply puts the icing on the cake – she is an infantry professional. "I attended Shuras in Mushan and Talukan. Two Canadian friends at my operating base were critically injured along with about a dozen Americans when a suicide bomber blew himself up in the bazaar a few hundred metres from our operating base." Black Watch females had certain advantages as soldiers, which they applied effectively:

> As a woman, I was able to talk to other local women and they were able to speak to me about their concerns. I created a small project for women in the community as well. The only difference for me with being a women soldier is that I was easily recognizable. The local population especially the children knew my name.[266]

There was never a shortage of volunteers for the positions offered and the Reserve Force met every demand placed upon it by the Regular Army. "My personal experience, though in a formation HQ, was that there was absolutely no difference between a Reservist and a Regular once we started training together, and our Allies were always 'surprised' when an individual's affiliation was identified as they could not differentiate."[267] The only way to tell the difference was the odd occasion when balmorals with Red Hackles were worn; but no matter where they served, in the end, the soldiers who left Montreal considered themselves Black Watch. As one RHC veteran wrote: *The tartan bite never heals.*

New Battle Honour "Afghanistan" – 9 May 2014

In March 2014, Canada's twelve years of operations in Afghanistan drew to a close; it was the longest armed conflict in Canadian history. To this end, on 9 May 2014, Prime Minister Stephen Harper announced that eligible units of the Royal Canadian Navy, the Canadian Army, Royal Canadian Air Force and the Canadian Special Operations Forces that participated in the South-West Asia theatre of conflict have been bestowed with the "Arabian Sea" or the "Afghanistan" Theatre Honour.[268] The Black Watch (Royal Highland Regiment) of Canada was awarded the Theatre Honour "Afghanistan".

Specific honours such as "Kandahar" or "Zhari-Panjwai'i" will be awarded to Regular Force units. There is intent to recognize the contribution of so-called "Force Generators" that would include reserve units. The criteria may involve numbers contributed and a line being drawn (fifty or more, twenty-five or more, etc.). As noted previously, no reserve regiment sent a complete company or platoon to war, but then, no Regular Force regiment deployed a complete company either.[269] Anywhere from 25 percent to 40 percent of the troops in frontline units and support outfits were from Militia regiments. The largest purely reserve organizations deployed were the CIMIC companies attached to either the Task Force Headquarters or latterly, the Provincial Reconstruction Team. There were, as well, Reserve PSYOPS platoons attached to the battle group. Finally, there were many individual augmentees at all levels of the formation and in the headquarters, up to ISAF-level. Despite a century of international experience, the process remained abecedarian: "The single greatest complaint received from soldiers and leaders was that it appeared that every time we deployed a reservist it was almost as if it was the first time we had ever deployed a reservist, with gaining units, the Regular Force, having to figure out how it worked."[270]

These recent and rather young veterans were a complex group to lead and remould into reservist life in an armoury. Fortunately, the commanding officer was experienced with foreign postings, and had just returned from a tour in Afghanistan.

Lieutenant Colonel Bruno Plourde CD
The Regular Reservist, 2009–2013

Is ann den aon chlò an cathdath (The tartan is all of the one stuff)

I am passionate about this. If you want the militia to be as qualified as the regular force, why have a regular force? We are citizen soldiers not soldier citizens![271]

Bruno Plourde turned out to be a shining example of the auld alliance, as thoroughly highland as he was *Canadien*. Fluently bilingual yet with enough of a *Québécois* drawl to make it clear he was decidedly not an *Anglo*. It would be difficult to find a commanding officer more committed to his regiment's dual culture – in his case, three. He was born and raised down river at Lévis, across from the ramparts of Quebec and a few kilometres from the raging waters of the Chaudière River. His first military experience was with Le Régiment de la Chaudière in 1980. He served as an NCM until accepted into the officer programme in 1983. Seemingly continuously on call-out and in a variety of headquarters, he was subsequently posted to the 4e Battalion du Royal 22e Regiment (Laval). Plourde finally became a member of the Black Watch in 1994. A training injury to his knee prevented him being accepted as a full time regular, but as a reservist, he was permitted to volunteer for attached service, and foreign postings. During the next two decades, he served in several operational deployments including Bosnia (Herzegovina). He was promoted lieutenant colonel in 2002 then served as a senior staff officer in the Congo ("always flying the St Andrews flag"). He was finally posted home as a Reserve advisor Secteur du Quebec HQ.

Plourde was a ship without a port, with little prospect of command. That changed when Brigadier Christian Barabé recognized his potential. Barabé needed a G5; Bruno straddled the cultures, and he wore the Red Hackle, which made the choice easy. He was posted back to the Black Watch as the next *Dauphin*. To Plourde's gratification, the general permitted him to complete his full tour in Afghanistan: "When you return from the front, you'll be a rock star."[272] Plourde deployed in Afghanistan at Headquarters ISAF Regional Command (South); he recalls with satisfaction serving at the same time as some twenty Black Watch soldiers deployed in his area. He met them as often as he could. Operationally, he was part of the CIMIC operations, and to ease the interaction with the locals, sported a thick black beard: despite the Canadian CADPAT camouflage uniform, Plourde looked more Taliban than Black Watch!

By the time he returned to Montreal to take command, Plourde had a chest full of medals[273] and more operational service than any other Black Watch CO since the last war, aside from John Potter, who had served in Northern Ireland and been decorated for Desert Storm. He was appointed as G5 Reserve at the Secteur du Québec headquarters, with responsibility for "everything related to reserves, from long term planning to structure, to op readiness …"[274] As far as the Regiment was concerned, Plourde could not have been better placed.

Directly he returned, instead of leave, he began ferrying contingents of RHC returning Afghan veterans from Quebec's airport to Montreal (three hundred km), often daily. The last group arrived just in time to participate in the Presentation of Colours. Three days later, he was officially appointed as commanding officer, RHC. The Regiment had a solid representation of war veterans, well-distributed in each of the three messes. Unlike the past four decades, these veterans were young, and several had already signed up for a second or third tour with the Kandahar Battle Group. The CO, adjutant, the RSM and several officers, as well as over a dozen NCOs and privates had seen battle.

Plourde was now part of another Black Watch "golden age" which seems to appear every twenty or so years. There were reasons. Most credit the war in Afghanistan, which changed training and provided opportunities to soldier professionally in ways not witnessed since 1939. However, substantial acknowledgement is due to the precursor commanding officers. Things fell into place. Plourde: "I credit fate. Right mix of circumstances. I never did anything special. Tom MacKay built it up, recruited, trained, sent the platoon to Afghanistan … while I served it abroad." Plourde was a graduate of the Canadian Army Command and Staff College, the Canadian Forces College in Toronto, and the United States Marine Corps University. Further, as a senior staff officer, Bruno could do a better job looking after his Regiment; he was *plugged in* to the Secteur. Captain the Rev Bruce Glencross wrote: "I know of no other regular force officer who understood the militia/regular difference better than Plourde."[275]

As a francophone, Plourde took the edge off long-term perceptions of The Watch that even after a century, still lingered in the city and the province. He made a point of explaining his adopted third (Highland) culture: "We were not *les blokes!*" Lieutenant General Duncan McAlpine, the Honorary Colonel, was Plourde's favourite regimental officer. He had been anxious about being considered an "an outsider" but was quickly set at ease in his first interview: "I was warmly welcomed by the general; I will always remember his smile, his cheerful look. Since that first day the Regiment has made me feel at home."[276] He was determined "to break down myths about The Watch".

The Highland Dinner, a Plourde brainchild, was a good example. He decided to raise money for the men's mess and *reintroduce* The Royal Highland Regiment to the city and the civilian community of the province. Visitors arrived from as far away as the Rimouski in the east and Chateauguay, and Toronto in the west. Guests from every garrison unit, as well as a hefty representation of business and professional Montrealers were invited to "a highland evening" and promised "a complete experience – from haggis to pipers and dancers". Officers and NCOs, scattered amongst the guests, rose during each course to offer brief vignettes about artefacts around the room or regimental traits. The dinners were successful – and benefitted the Regiment. The aim was to make Quebecers realize the rich traditions of the Black Watch as a Montreal icon.[277]

The Regular Force Support Staff in the Millennium Watch

Training became more demanding but far more interesting as returned veteran soldiers trained both recruits and the first company. One of Tom MacKay's last projects was to order a mock plywood village constructed in the middle of the parade square. It was finished by WO Hinse, the ops warrant. The most recent house-clearing drills were taught which inspired soldiers. Alas, jocks who volunteered for Afghanistan were lost to the regiment for well over a year:

> [CF training was] a highly inefficient system as it strips valuable leadership and capability from the armoury floor for far too long a period of time. The concomitant effect is drawing employees away from work for the same period of time which is well outside the legislated protection that now exists in each province and territory.[278]

The Regiment bustled with activity. Plourde acquired a new adjutant to replace Farnham. Captain Roger Guay CD, the new RSS officer: a former Van Doo sergeant major and a "good fit" in the Regiment. Guay immediately busied himself staffing the brigade's ambitious exercises. His right-hand man was WO Pierre Serge Brasseur CD, a nineteen-year-veteran. Compact, competent and dangerous, Brasseur was a parachutist, ranger, mountaineer and tactician. He served everywhere, and completed two tours in Afghanistan. He confessed his only fear was "the sergeants' mess war stories". A skilled boxer, he often rescued imprudent highlanders from skirmishes in Montreal bars. WO Brasseur perennially looked like he just crawled back from a long-range patrol. His half-beard was the result of a skin condition: spending a frozen night trapped in the middle of a blizzard, clinging to pinions on the sheer face of a mountain. Brasseur was a problem solver and confidant; Black Watch soldiers in difficulties found him a ready friend. Combat veterans had someone to talk to. He had little trouble sorting out training exercises; he had worked with Americans before, under far more trying conditions.

This helped as ever-larger exercises were held in the United States and featured working with American units on modern bases with very up-to-date ranges. The Regiment attended every exercise from Valcartier to Farnham, from Fort Drum to Fort Pickett. The colonel was smitten with the complex cultural character of his unit: The Black Watch Saltire accompanied them on long route marches and parades in the bush: "The ceremony of bestowing Red Hackles to recruits was performed with the pipes playing, signifying that they were taken into regimental family."[279]

Honorary Colonel Lieutenant General Duncan McAlpine 1922–2010

> He was decisive when required – he was clever, sly, yet diplomatic.[280]

The new year brought sad news. The Honorary Colonel had died in Florida on 23 January 2010. Lieutenant General Duncan McAlpine was an inspiration to the Regiment – kind, yet with a sharp side, a man who cared very deeply for the Black Watch: "Our last great connection to the Regular Force." He was described by one superior as "evidencing an aggressive bumptiousness ... Over time, though, the traditions of the Officers' Mess and some firm guidance smoothed his rough edges."[281] McAlpine continually emphasized the Regiment's traditional support for cultural values in Québec. "I had been told from day-one he was a delegator; that was his reputation in the Regular Force RHC ... He was decisive when required – he was clever, sly, yet diplomatic ... a talent to use those around him."[282] Daniel O'Connor, who had been constantly at regimental business as a member of the Advisory Board, was designated as Honorary Colonel of the Black Watch. O'Connor was already national president of *Last Post Fund*,[283] on the executive in the St Andrew's Society (of which he was elected president in 1996–1998), and a full time barrister. The new Honorary Lieutenant Colonel was not a Montrealer. Lieutenant Colonel Charles (Chuck) McCabe OMM, CD a native of New Glasgow, NS, had been a member of several Militia units then joined the Black Watch in 1957, and served in both Regular battalions.[284] Upon retirement as a Lieutenant Colonel, he transferred back to the Reserve Force and settled in Ottawa. He was appointed Commandant of the Connaught Ranges.

Farewell to a Wartime Padre: Captain, the Rev RR Topping, PhD

One of the best padres we had – intelligent, funny, totally devoted and extremely frustrated with the Army.

Lieutenant Colonel Tom MacKay

In the midst of Afghan war, a new padre appeared at the armoury. He was an academic and knew nothing about the army. But he was tenacious even if, as it eventually came to pass, he had to face-off against the Area HQ padre-in-chief. The minister of The Church of St Andrew and St Paul, a Brampton native, unilingual, and a life-long civilian, raised serious reservations in SQFT Headquarters. MacKay retorted: "He is already trained to do his job – I don't care if he marches." Topping was quickly aware that in his regiment "there was more deferential, great respect accorded the position of padre – [I had] inherited a legacy". He went *porcus* – uniform, exercises and parades. "When I demonstrated a turn to Major Phare and asked, 'how was that?' He shrugged and said, "You are only going to be a chaplain."[285]

Undaunted, Topping visited the Black Watch archives and reviewed the files of war-time padres. He was influenced by a letter written during the Second World War by the 1 RHC chaplain, Captain E Cecil Royle, to a family in Red Deer, Alberta. "It was a sad letter, regarding the death of their son in combat. Royle consoles the family by drawing attention to the soldier's Christian witness."[286] He was even more determined to minister to returned veterans. He was initially frustrated, faced with unilingual francophone resources. Topping had to ask friends in other provinces for English versions in order to offer potential PTSD soldiers effective guidance. "I saw all the soldiers from theatre, initially about fifteen, met them immediately, and then followed up in three months and six months."[287]

The padre was best remembered for his sermons. He was a charismatic speaker with a captivating style, a delightful wit, and an appreciation for the soldier in the ranks. Topping recalled the complexity and simplicity of his highland soldiers – unorthodox, yet real. In Trenton Airport, at a repatriation ceremony for soldiers lost in Afghanistan, the Regiment formed part of the honour guard. Topping stood beside the Governor General of Canada, Michaëlle Jean.

In December 2010, Dr Richard Topping was posted to British Columbia – about as far away as you could possibly go in Canada. He left to become Professor of Studies in the Reformed tradition at St Andrew's Hall, a theological college on the University of British Columbia campus. He was not formally succeeded as padre until January 2013 when Captain the Rev David Godkin, a Lutheran minister, became the new Black Watch chaplain.

Millennium RSMs

> He thinks he is an officer ... he rethinks everything we do.
>
> Lieutenant Colonel Bruce Bolton

Bolton's comment (which could apply to a few Black Watch RSMs, including himself) was not meant to be unkind. There is a great divide, both physical and psychological, between the sergeants' and officers' messes. The millennium batch of RSMs were as accomplished and educated as many officers were in the 1960s. Plourde's RSM, CWO John Barron, had seen the battalion through the Colours presentation and was now prepared to retire. He was "a good militia leader – understood well that regardless of what we wanted to achieve, grandiose stuff, aim was to get out to training area, get some sleep and be fresh for real training; reality of civilian life, more important than military life was to leave early Sunday to be fresh for work on Monday."[288] Barron's practicality and no-nonsense work ethic made him very popular. He was presented with the Proven Cup, the acme of the Regiment's respect.[289]

Barron was succeeded by CWO RM Unger: "Smart, experienced, calm, cool and collected."[290] Robert Michael Unger was from St Lambert, across the river. Fluently bilingual with degrees in Communication and Marketing, he transferred to the Regiment in 2002 having spent his early militia years with the CGG and in Vancouver with the Seaforth Highlanders. He was a veteran, deploying to Afghanistan in July 2006 as the operations warrant officer of a PSYOP cell. Like Plourde, he grew a great beard to relax the locals, except Unger ended up looking more like a friendly bear. During the Colours Parade, Prince Charles asked: "When did you go to Afghanistan? Would you go back?" "Yes!" replied Unger, "But my wife won't let me." The Prince laughed and gave a knowing wink.

Unger was appointed RSM effective May 2010 – one of the first to enter the job as MWO, without a chief warrant officer's course. He was quick to point out that "there were others who did a job while wearing lower rank although qualified in a trade but without the Leadership course. It is not very easy for a Reserve NCO –

working, family – to take three weeks off." He explained the challenges faced by a Reservist RSM, little appreciated by the Regulars:

> Soldiers (perhaps it is laziness) prefer to wear combat [uniforms]; when we have a kilted parade, often some soldiers don't show – perhaps up to 20 percent and that affects collective training … They will of course parade on the "important days" … for example at church parade we had forty soldiers kilted on parade but we had another thirty soldiers away on course – therefore the battalion seventy soldiers "at work" plus, nine officers, fifteen senior NCMs and fifty in pipes and drums of which twenty are serving soldiers, the rest volunteers.[291]

Unger was well-supported by Pipe Major Stevens ("Pipey" as he was affectionately known by senior ranks): "Stevens has taken the band to its present strong state in the last ten years of him being P/Major." Unger's first challenge was preparing for the 150th Anniversary of the Regiment in 2012. He could not have asked for a better time to be the RSM. However, there was hard work ahead. Lieutenant Colonel Plourde briefed him simply: "This will be like any other year, but on steroids."[292]

Remembrance and Honour

The poppy
Its scarlet mass deployed across fields
Individually fragile, floating on air, yet resilient;
Determinedly surviving storms and icy blasts
It is at once the soldier of the front.

The annual Remembrance Day Parade was moved to the McGill Campus and The Black Watch Armoury was again selected as the marshalling point. The garrison regiments were grouped into one guard; the Black Watch fielded two by itself. They were joined by a Naval contingent and a large guard of cadet officers from *Collège militaire royal Saint-Jean*. It was a spectacular event. The garrison was drawn up in a hollow square. For the first time the 2nd Field Artillery Regiment did not give its salute from the Mount Royal lookout but instead deployed in front of the McGill Arts Building. Each time the guns fired, all the security and car alarms on campus went off. The Black Watch, led by Lieutenant Colonel Bruno Plourde, was the largest of the garrison units, and vied with the CMR cadets for panache. They looked particularly natty in green coatees, blue bonnets with blazing hackles; their ranks boasting over a dozen decorated Afghan war veterans.

The Regiment's birthday was marked by the traditional *Trooping*; however, Plourde decided not to hold drill practices but simply conduct the parade and blessing of the Colours on a normal training night. It was a gutsy move. Tuesday, 31 January turned out to be a rotten night since the snow, swept around by fierce winds, made travel daunting. There was a small but committed crowd in the armoury. Most wondered who would brave the weather. They were pleasantly surprised. The RSM produced two fifty-soldier guards, a Colour Party and P/Major Stevens paraded a callithumpian pipe band that included thirty-six pipers and drummers. It was a splendid parade, and everyone applauded the soldiers for their sporting effort, braving a Montreal winter storm to bash the square. During the parade, it was announced that Regimental Sergeant Major Robert Unger and Pipe Major (MWO) Cameron Stevens had been awarded the Order of Military Merit by the Governor General of Canada.

Properly Dressed On Parade: The Regimental Uniform

A uniform was something a soldier wore when he wasn't fighting.

James Laver[293]

During the Aldershot years, officers of 1st Bn wore 5/8-inch pips and <u>dark</u> Fox puttees whereas 2nd Bn officers wore one-inch pips and <u>light</u> Fox puttees.

Lieutenant Colonel Tud Kaulbach[294]

Military dress, and its associated complexities and vanities has been misunderstood and sometimes derided by civilian critics. The subject is mosaic and as sophisticated as perhaps vainglorious. The uniform and the soldier parallel civilian fashion – all uniforms reflect what is worn "in the street", from business suits to workman's dungarees. For all their urbanity, money, and education, the 5th Royal Scots were surprisingly ignorant about specifics within the parent regiment until the mid-thirties. This changed by the Second World War. The military uniform *per se* had evolved dramatically. By the mid-20th century, "a uniform was something a soldier wore when he wasn't fighting."[295] In battle, there was no longer a noticeable difference. In a combat zone, the Red Hackle distinguished the Black Watch from dozens of different NATO and foreign outfits. However, it is the nuances in dress that characterizes one unit from another. These are the essences of unit ethos. This aspect of the regimental system adds immeasurably to élan and pride. It is the cornerstone of the drill-sergeant's parade square philosophy: "That will not do (pointing to an offending article of clothing) you slovenly soldier! It may be all right for the *XYZ Fusiliers* but it will never do for The Black Watch!" Discernible difference makes easier the demand for higher standards. To disgrace one's uniform is a phrase everyone understands, and in their unique dress (the Red Hackle and kilt), the Black Watch is preeminent. Indeed the Black Watch is one of the few reserve units that can parade a battalion in full highland dress with advance warning, and send out a fifty-soldier guard at a moment's notice.[296]

It is not enough to be in the Black Watch; the soldiers and officers must look every inch the part. Well into the millennium, the Black Watch mess was still near-Edwardian; young men in university suddenly found themselves extras in *Tunes of Glory*, and looked expectantly over their shoulders for Major Jock Sinclair or Colonel Basil Barrow. Beyond the stone walls, the city revelled in the 21st Century; in the Black Watch officers' mess, the Second World War had barely ended. Captain Rod DeCastro's recollections from Afghanistan explained it well:

> The Black Watch instilled in me a particular expectation of what it means to be an officer that has served me in good stead. Seemingly, obvious things – standing up when speaking to a superior, when the CO enters a room; entertaining guests, conduct at a formal dinner … greatly facilitated my transition to the Regular Force.[297]

It had ever been thus in both militia and regular battalions. Brigadier James Cox had been a subaltern in Gagetown, in the centennial year: "In the mess we were always required to wear a jacket and tie in the evenings during the week, but casual clothes were allowed during the day on the weekends."[298] Regimental dress was more Daedalian. Though clear within the unit, rococo distinctions were usually scorned by uninformed civilian critics and penny-pinching Ottawa bureaucrats, often referred to as *civil serpents*. Cost and availability were the main bugbears in highland dress.[299] The Dress Committee investigated all suppliers, from the traditional Montreal sources like Scully's, Gaunt's and Johnson's to England, Scotland and finally, Pakistan (the best bet and often the only affordable option for most). Officer's mess kit (serge or barathea waistcoat, tartan vests, and scarlet Doeskin shell with quilted lapels) could cost as much as $3,620 (2013 C$) depending on quality of cloth and the number of fittings. Cheaper versions tend to look just that. Most of the items were available for issue from the regimental quartermaster stores – thanks in a large part to the disbanded Regular Force battalions who returned their inventory to Bleury Street. By the time of the 1987 Queen Mother's Trooping of the Colour, the QM still held 579 blue and 690 khaki Balmorals, 148 Hair Sporrans, 1280 Kilts and 245 Red Hackles.[300] There were eight Claymores. Most subalterns acquired mess kit from brother officers: majors who could now purchase bespoke uniforms or simply donations to the regimental stores from retired officers or their families. Many a junior officer attended his first Reunion Dinner dressed in a retailored Doeskin made before the Second World War.[301]

The Regimental Dress Committee, a far more serious matter in the Black Watch than most reserve regiments, comprises the commanding officer as chair, the DCO, Adjutant, RSM, Pipe Major, and the Regimental Quartermaster, with a representative from the RHC executive. Agendas were carefully controlled and meetings considered all matters, from purchases to the wearing of combat clothing in winter, inside the armoury ("sleeves up or down?"). The Regiment's uniform was a complex collection of martial accoutrements and intricate pieces of Scottish highland dress.[302] In addition, there was an item of civilian dress, de rigueur for officers, the *Cantlie Tartan* suit – made solely for proven Black Watch officers, cut from the *regimental hunting tartan*; the bolts of cloth available to tailors only via imperial regimental headquarters in Scotland.[303] The garment, a wonderful fall or winter outfit, was augmented by regimental or personal tie, a choice of buttons (including leather or bone) and the finest polished brogues. Since the outfit identified the wearer as a member of an exclusive martial caste – it was both unidentifiable and unavailable to mere mortals, which added to its aura. Regrettably, by the 150th anniversary, few senior Montreal Black Watch officers wore one.

That ultimate Scottish weapon, the Claymore broadsword, was unaffordable if purchased from Wilkinson Sword in England. Black Watch Claymores (as most swords in the CF) were purchased from Germany – EUF Hörster, the Solingen area armourers, whose forges made excellent and cheaper swords. By 2000, Wilkinson Sword had switched to selling razor blades and sold their sword business machinery, tools and equipment to Weyersberg, Kirschaum & Cie of Solingen, the oldest producing sword factory in the world. New Claymores (officer and NCO types were different) varied in cost; by 2014, anywhere from $1000 to $4000. Claymores made in Pakistan were considerably cheaper. One dared not think what past generations of Black Watch warriors from the past wars might have said.

Trooping The Colour, Fletcher's Field 2012

"When you wear this Red hackle, it makes you stand a foot taller or so."[304]

By 2012, this grand maxim had just about become true. Red Hackles purchased from England reflected their new Highland Regiment with its smorgasbord of representative battalions, including The Black Watch, as 3 SCOTS. The Red Hackle, heretofore an embellishment on the bonnet, displaying understated *panache*, had become a burning bush, well over three inches, rampant and ablaze. A close formation of The Watch was beyond *a sea of hackles* but rather a torrent of lava. Seniors noted the difference and muttered into their cups. The parade, held on 29 September on Fletchers Field

(*Parc Jeanne-Mance*) returned the Regiment to a historic site, where Colonel GS Cantlie had received the Colours from the Duke of Connaught on the regiment's fiftieth anniversary in 1912. The parade took place in the open area directly north of the Grenadier Guards Armoury on a grey, rainy day. Above Plourde's battalion loomed Mount Royal, the great iron cross barely visible in the mist. It proved a daring venture for a reserve unit with humble numbers.[305]

The trooping demanded complex, multifaceted organization. It was mainly staffed by the Black Watch RSS team: Captain Roger Guay, WO Brasseur, and a small team of Black Watch NCOs. The presence of the Governor General required liaison with the representatives of the City of Montreal Police, RCMP and Military Police. Brasseur emphasized they received spectacular support on a real labour-intensive parade. Preparation included building and setting up seventy street barriers, a dais for the Governor General (in three parts), large tentage, red carpeting, two large bleachers for the crowd, and transportation. In addition, reinforcements from *la musique des Fusiliers Mont-Royal*. Onsite support included elements from the 51 Field Ambulance, the RMR and the Van Doos. The Regiment, with Afghan postings and soldiers away on courses or call-out employments, managed 114 all ranks.[306] Three practices were conducted at CFB Longue Pointe (although in hindsight, they would have been better using the sports field rather than the base's parade square). Marching on grass is strikingly different and plays havoc with smart drill and normally trouble-free manoeuvres. It was a spirited parade, and reminded some of the opening segments of *Barry Lyndon* when a raised militia regiment marched past. The *Feu de Joie* went off quite well but the winds carried away the staccato reports, which make the event so spectacular. Lieutenant Colonel Plourde's headset malfunctioned, and the final march-past was not the battalion's best. Everyone smiled through clenched teeth. However, the Governor General and the crowd, mostly family and civilians, did not seem to notice.

The soldiers left grousing; it had been an awful parade, they said, the antithesis of the Colours Presentation with the Prince. But they were quite wrong. Newspaper photos and news clips on television closed in on individuals and soldiers, or followed the governor general and Plourde. To everyone's delight, as a Canada-wide bit of news, it turned out well. Critiques were left to old corporals and drill sergeants.[307] The parade, despite the gloomy drizzle, attracted a substantial number of the faithful. The Regiment arranged for buses to transport the audience from the armoury to the parade and back. A distinguished guest was Lieutenant Colonel WJ Newlands CD, one of two Regular Force battalion commanding officers remaining. Newlands led 1 RHC in Canada and Cyprus. Still agile, he smiled, climbed aboard his bus and said nothing mean about the parade. Plourde and RSM Unger advised everyone to get on with it. They turned to a more controlled event.

The Remembrance Dinner, 10 November, a Saturday evening, replaced the annual Reunion Dinner for the anniversary year only. It was *une autre grand spectacle*: over 250 all ranks, on the armoury's parade floor.[308] It was followed by a larger-than-ever Remembrance Day Parade; everyone downtown seemed to gather at McGill. The garrison's units deployed in greater numbers, again joined by a snappy cohort of CMR cadets. The Grenadier Guards produced their own complete guard, as did the Navy; the remaining city's regiments paraded a combined contingent, while the Black Watch, in two impressive Guards, (Colour Party and a hefty pipes and drums), carried the centre of the parade. It had indeed been *a year on steroids,* and everyone agreed they needed a break. Christmas could not have come at a better time.

Châteauguay – Two Hundred Year Battle Honour

On the eve of the 150th anniversary, RHQ received an acknowledgment from Ottawa that the Regiment had been awarded a new emblazonable battle honour (as well as a general *War of 1812* honour). The battle honour (now its first) acknowledged the defence of Montreal (The Battle of Chateauguay) and brought to mind that, despite its pan-Canadian and certainly Maritime connections, The Black Watch (RHR) has always reflected a substantive cultural and historical connection to its province, but more specifically, the city of Montreal.

As Canada acknowledged the War of 1812, the Regiment was offered and accepted "the perpetuation via the 5th Battalion, Select Embodied Militia."[309] The Regiment traced its origins to Scottish immigrants whose first recognized unit was the *Highland Rifle Company,* subsequently, a part of the *Montreal Light Infantry*: "the first distinctly Scottish military organization ever raised in Montreal."[310] A proud tradition the Black Watch is determined to continue. The official citation emphasized the *5th Select Embodied Militia* rather than the *Highland Rifles*. Either way, The Watch was *officially* two hundred years old.[311]

Honouring Their Own: The Regimental Boards

Respice, Adspice, Prospice[312]

Bruno Plourde left his mark on the Black Watch and on its armoury. He was responsible for a face-lift, the like of which had not been seen since the Second World War. Following the church parade in May 2012, the Regiment and family gathered at the armoury to witness the unveiling of the Regimental Boards. The addition of the oak tablets that decorate the three walls enhanced both the old bronze memorials and city banners beside the great gothic windows. Plourde left the armoury a far handsomer place than he found it.[313] Reservists often complain that the Regular Force are overbearing and ignore them. Conversely, retired members of the two Regular Black Watch Battalions (disbanded 1970) complained that when they visited the Bleury Street armoury, "It was all about the 3rd Battalion." Plourde was determined that as the regimental headquarters, the armoury's walls should reflect a comprehensive history and exalt members of all battalions (including The Regimental Depot): commanding officers, regimental sergeant majors, and the pipe majors. Twelve handsome oak boards, inscribed in gilt lettering, now embrace the parade square. The armoury had not looked this good ever, exclaimed a senior colonel who knew the difference. Lieutenant Colonel Bruno Plourde possessed the temperament and expertise to guide the Regiment at a time when it could have plummeted just as rapidly as it soared – he had an effervescent style, buttressed by boundless energy. The result was a series of vintage years with notable accomplishments that won the Regiment regional, national and international acclaim. He was colonel and le seigneur; his regiment was both clan and famille; Plourde liked to say: "La Milice, c'est comme un village … The Reserves are like a village."[314]

Lieutenant Colonel Christopher Phare CD, 2013–2016

Nemo regere potest nisi qui et regi.[315]

Lieutenant Colonel Christopher Roger Phare assumed command in May 2013, following the regimental church parade.[316] The CO was a Montrealer with over two decades of service in The Watch. The new RSM was CWO Mario Carmosino CD, a twenty-seven-year veteran of the Regiment.

Phare seems younger than he is, but his credentials go back six colonels. A Bosnian war veteran and participant in more exercises than he can recall, Phare carried the Colours for the Canadian delegation at the August 2000 Birthday Parade for the Queen Mother in London: "The Toronto Scottish tried to dominate, but we were senior." On the front page of every newspaper, there was Chris Phare next to the Queen Mum. As a subaltern, he had officered through an era that mixed work with dottiness.[317] Captain Phare attended the Jamaican Defence College, served a second tour in Bosnia and volunteered for advanced infantry courses in Gagetown. His tour in Bosnia, commanding a rifle platoon completely comprised of Reservists, gave him unique credentials well before the juggernaut that was Afghanistan. His adventures kept him out of the advancement loop. Officers who joined with him, were promoted before him. Phare became a senior executive with 3M Canada in Ottawa; his commitment to the Regiment included driving in from the capital several times a week. He noted that MacKay and Plourde would be tough acts to follow, particularly as Canada's participation in the Afghan War ended. The last troops returned at Christmas 2013. The commander of 34 Brigade, Colonel Luis De Sousa, announced: "This is the first time since the Korean War that the Canadian Army will not have a significant contingent deployed overseas." Many of the veterans became bored and simply left; the adjutant found work teaching and faded away; the DCO resigned; younger NCOs joined the Regular Force, or went west looking for work.

For the 150th Anniversary Trooping, held at Fletcher's Field, September 2012, in the presence of the governor general, Major Phare ensured he looked immaculate. As he marched on, he became aware of RSM Unger's reproachful stare. He forgot to wear his medals! A year later, 11 November 2013, a beaming Lieutenant Colonel Phare led his intrepid battalion onto the McGill campus to participate in the Remembrance Day service. Again, the Black Watch more than matched the guard of CMR officer cadets as well as the combined Montreal garrison formations.[318] It is interesting to cite the media coverage: "The Army, Navy *and* the Black Watch gathered at the cenotaph today …"[319] In Montreal, the Regiment is considered *une force unique*. From Vancouver to St John's, the Black Watch is the one regiment everyone knows.

On the first of May, 2016, after the annual spring church parade, the Regiment held a change of command ceremony in the armoury. Chris Phare retired and handed over the reins to a familiar officer: Lt Colonel Thomas MacKay CD. The "new" CO returned to lead the Black Watch and, by chance, inherited an important occurance in Montréal's *histoire*: the 375th Anniversary of the City. The next year would be busy with parades, a Highland Tattoo (orchestrated by Major (ret) Brent Cowan) and new honoraries. MacKay, serving as Deputy Director of Army Reserves in NDHQ Ottawa, would commute to Montreal to guide the Regiment's progress and evolution.

The Regiment looks ahead to another century, confident that it will prosper because the Black Watch is a practical, proud regiment; its successes have never been easy; its triumphs were built on sacrifice, determination and Olympian self-esteem. From the earliest battles defending their homes in 1812, to the extraordinary efforts on the battle fields in Europe, the march of time has singled out Montreal's Regiment, Canada's very special Regiment.

Highland Coda

Downtown Montreal on a cold January evening – if one walks past the armoury, one can make out *Highland Laddie* from within the grey stone, much as it was a century past. It is, in its antediluvian Gordian way, a military church, whose sacred history tells the story of a fighting regiment, whose very existence has been as threatened as much by its own side, as by foreign campaigns. The synergy of a highland battalion is a galvanizing force for a citizen seeking stability, discipline and the inspiration of tradition in an impersonal, chaotic world. In its 200th year as a Montreal militia, and 150th as a formed Regiment, The Watch remains not only a fearsome weapon of war, but an intricate icon, at once the story of its City as well as a distinct community within its country. It is hackles and kilts along Sherbrooke Street. It is Burns' Suppers and Snuff Mulls. It is a bilingual battalion composed of men and women with equal service and battle commendations. It is an internationally respected pipe band. The Black Watch are the *New York Yankees* of the Canadian Army, love them or not, – everyone knows who they are. Their triumphs and defeats are the stuff of legend, and even those not of the military, identify with them and seek some association. As the decades slipped by, each battalion (be it the 13th, 42nd, 73rd, First or the Second RHC) has mused upon their brief days in the sun, proclaiming with conviction that *they* were the finest infantry in the Army. Millennium veterans now recall their service in Afghanistan with the same soldierly nostalgia. The Black Watch argue that once you have spent time in the Regiment, you will be forever transformed. Colonel Paul Hutchison wrote, "I too once served in the Black Watch. This is my tribal Regiment." Soldiers, young or old, consider the parade square, the thousands of hours of drill and instruction, and look up in wonder at the prodigious wooden memorials, covered in battle honours with difficult-to-pronounce names, battles that could wash Bleury Street with Black Watch blood.

If one is inadvertently alone in the darkened armoury on a winter's night, there is the chance of hearing sounds of hearty ruckus, of soldiers making-merry. Should one disturb these spirits, there will be a rising rumbling. Then, from the basement stairs, over the balconies of the sergeants' and officers' messes, will pour the awesome ghosts of four thousand Highland warriors, chasing the intruder out of their hallowed bastion, into the snowfall of a cold Montreal night, and up Bleury Street towards the mountain, until the last echo is faint … but never, never gone.

Nemo Me Impune Lacessit

In memoriam

Roman Johann Jarymowycz
19 January 1945 to 19 January 2017

Epilogue, 2013–2022*

Regimental histories, by their very nature, must remain unfinished. So long as the regiment still stands in service its story will continue, unabridged, carried on by the men and women who proudly wear the uniform of the Canadian Armed Forces. In our case, that means the swinging kilts and the red hackles of Canada's Black Watch.

As far as regimental histories go, Dr. Roman Johann Jarymowycz left The Black Watch with a fitting opus. In length and reverence, it is perhaps unequalled in Canadian military writing. Despite having himself proudly served as a cavalry officer *par excellence,* Lieutenant Colonel Jarymowycz's respect for the Black Watch, perhaps falling just short of outright love for the Regiment, is palpable throughout this very large book.

This epilogue is a *mise a jour*, loosely tracing the events of the years since Lieutenant Colonel Jarymowycz's work left off. It is not a history, nor should it be read as one. Rather, it is one vantage point overlooking the ongoing events at the Regiment, seen largely through the eyes of the Unit's Commanding Officers. It is a brief coda, capping off Roman's herculean history of Canada's senior highland regiment: The Black Watch.

---

* This Epilogue was written by Alexander McGuckin. He started in the Regiment as a cadet piper, moved to the Pipes & Drums, and is now an Officer. Roman Jarymocyz considered Alec to be one of his star students in his High School classes, and especially as a member of the school's debating team.

Lieutenant Colonel Christopher Phare, CD

Lieutenant Colonel Christopher Phare took command of the Black Watch after Church Parade in May 2013.[321] A Regimental stalwart who first donned the red hackle as a cadet at the tender age of 12, Chris' passion for the Regiment is perhaps best epitomized by the simple but powerful closing phrase of the speech he gave upon assuming command: "I LOVE THIS REGIMENT!"

Chris Phare's tenure began a time of transition for the Regiment, the Army Reserve and, indeed the Canadian Armed Forces as a whole. As previously covered by Roman Jarymowycz, Canada's role in the war in Afghanistan was winding down, ultimately ending in 2014. "My only real concern when taking over," reflected Chris, "was succession planning and budgets, because things were changing after the Afghanistan war."[322] Budgets were being cut across the military, but the scalpel trimmed the most from the Army. Fortunately, through the last six months of Lieutenant Colonel Bruno Plourde's command, Chris was Deputy Commanding Officer (DCO), which allowed him the opportunity to develop a training plan and usher through a "slow burn transition instead of a 'bang' date."[323]

In planning for his command, Chris Phare and his team broke down the Unit's responsibilities into five distinct operations, each with a specific mission: OP HIGHLAND SOLDIER, tasked primarily with individual training and maintaining individual battle task standards (IBTS); OP HIGHLAND WARRIOR, which focused on collective training at the unit, brigade, or international level; and OP HIGHLAND READINESS, which incorporated recruiting, personnel management, mandated training, professional development, and Unit training activities. These were rounded out by OP HIGHLAND CITIZEN, the Unit's plan to connect with the population at large, including Pipes and Drums activities and public events such as the Remembrance Day parade; and OP HIGHLAND CITADEL, which focused on maintenance of equipment and the physical assets of the Regiment, including the armoury building itself.[324] These plans were detailed, ambitious, and as Chris Phare emphasized, they demanded strong communication to succeed, "If you go back to the op plans for 2013–2016, the centre of gravity in every one of those for me was communication. Communication was the key."[325] Indeed, when asked, he identified improving communication "not just with our soldiers, but with the entire Regimental family," as one of the principal goals during his time as Commanding Officer.[326]

Another early aim was to improve collective training opportunities for the Unit. In this, the shadow of Afghanistan presented another challenge. Budget cuts aside, there was a push down the chain of command to return to the basics of soldiering; after a long war that impacted how the CAF trained and fought, the army wanted to once again stress the fundamentals. "We were ordered to train only up to the section level. A lot of our planning was to fulfil that requirement to have sections trained up to a certain level, but simultaneously to add training that would be interesting to the soldiers."[327] An early success in creating exciting training opportunities was the development of an urban operations training system comprised of modular walls that fit onto the armoury's parade square. The structure, which could be configured in many different forms to generate unique scenarios, was completed through the tireless work of Captain Jay Hinkson, WO Pierre Brasseur, and a host of other NCMs.[328] The ambitious goal of using walls to host a live-fire "simunition" exercise (firing specially designed paint rounds through the C7 service weapon) in the armoury was met with skepticism and resistance at the Brigade level: "Everyone at Brigade told us we couldn't do it, but we did," remembers Lieutenant Colonel Phare.[329] In the end, the exercise was a resounding success, and the higher-ups took note:

> … because of our success, the Brigade decided they were going to seize our walls – they decided they belonged to them because we used their budget money, so anyone could request it. We had no problem with anyone requesting the walls, but they were staying here![330]

Phare was quick to point out that, although the live-fire exercise was a highlight of his time as CO, it was achieved through the hard work of the NCMs who shepherded the project: "The CSMs and Brasseur, they really made this happen. I just signed off on it."[331]

There were training opportunities outside of the armoury, too. In the summer of 2013, a platoon of Black Watch soldiers trained with the 1-111th Infantry of Pennsylvania, joining their scout platoon for a live-fire and urban operations training exercise, dubbed EX HIGHLAND YANKEE II.[332] A reconnaissance detachment from the Black Watch participated in a helocast exercise in Valcartier that same September. A Company's 1 Platoon participated in EX SOLDAT AGUERRI, and in the winter of 2014 a contingent of soldiers flew to the arctic for training. The latter is chronicled in an article in *Canada's Red Hackle*, written by Lieutenant David Serapins, who laconically quipped of the climate that, "we may have had a mission, but the cold was our enemy."[333] Joint Task Force 2, one of Canada's elite special operations units, staged an exercise out of the armoury, which involved Black Watch soldiers. The Pipes and Drums were active as well with a notable performance in the winter of 2015 at the Canadian Parliament's annual House of Commons Robbie Burns Dinner. It was also during this period, at the request of Corporal Brook Vivian, President of the Red Hackle Club (Junior Ranks Mess), that two lasting changes were made in the

Unit. The first was the inclusion of the Junior Ranks annual mess dinner – the Fred Fisher Dinner – as an official event in the Unit calendar. The second was a plan to renovate the Junior Ranks Mess, a request that was supported by Lieutenant Colonel Phare and would be ultimately completed in 2019.[334]

Another significant event in 2014 was the presentation of the Afghanistan battle honour which was mounted on the east wall of the armoury. This project was spearheaded by CWO Mario Carmosino. "The reason this was important to us as a command team was because of the Afghanistan vets in the Unit. We wanted them to have their battle honour up while they were still serving."[335] It was designed to match, in substance and style, the gold and brown boards that have for decades hung above the Sergeants' mess, as an acknowledgement of this generation's sacrifice. The honour was unveiled after Church Parade in the spring of 2014, with the family of Corporal Jason Patrick Warren, who was killed in Afghanistan in 2006, present for the ceremony.

In the spring of 2016, the Regiment lost one of its titans when Lieutenant Colonel Victor Chartier, OMM, CD, died in April. Victor Chartier joined the Black Watch in 1951 as a non-commissioned member, rose to the position of Regimental Sergeant Major, commissioned as an officer and eventually served as CO and then Honorary Lieutenant Colonel of the Regiment. He was the first RSM to become Commanding Officer. As Honorary Lieutenant Colonel Bruce D. Bolton related in his eulogy, "Vic was unpretentious, faithful, loyal, committed to his community, and a mentor."[336] It was a loss the Regiment would feel for years to come.

Looking back at his command, Lieutenant Colonel Phare is quick to identify areas where he perhaps fell short of complete success. The armoury's infrastructure problems were not resolved, owing largely to bureaucratic hurdles. He notes also that the relationship with the 1-111th in Pennsylvania had not flourished quite as much as he would have liked. The challenges presented by the end of the war in Afghanistan, too, presented a greater obstacle than anticipated:

> The usual emphasis on collective and individual training made it difficult to maintain the interest of many soldiers… This contributed to the Afghan vets joining the Regular Force or just getting out – it just wasn't of interest to them anymore… I didn't realize the full impact when I took command, but over the next couple of years I had to keep adapting to try to generate interest in the collective training and do things that interested those soldiers who were still there and had combat experience.[337]

Lieutenant Colonel Chris Phare handed over command of the Black Watch to Lieutenant Colonel Tom MacKay in the spring of 2017. Despite plans to retire after relinquishing command, Phare was convinced to remain in uniform, and he began to teach on the Army Operations Course (AOC) at the Canadian Army Command and Staff College in Kingston. Looking back on his 25 years with the Regiment, he posits nostalgically that "every good thing in my life can be connected to my time at the Watch … I owe the Regiment more than I have given."[338]

Lieutenant Colonel Thomas MacKay, CD

In the spring of 2016, Lieutenant Colonel TEC MacKay became only the second officer in the history of Canada's Black Watch to serve two terms as Commanding Officer.[339] In preparing for his return, Tom playfully recalled, "I wanted to ensure that I didn't totally blow up my good reputation from my first term. I felt like I did a pretty good job my first time around and potentially there was nowhere to go but down!"[340] Speaking more seriously, though, he was aware of his unique position: "coming back, I had all these great experiences that I wasn't able to draw on my first time as Commanding Officer. I really wanted to use those to help progress the Unit, to build upon everything that had been done before me."[341]

After finishing his last term as CO in 2009, Tom MacKay remained involved in the Regimental family, but he also continued to work full time at National Defence Headquarters and had deployed to Afghanistan as a colonel in 2011–13. By 2016 his resumé and his experiences were impressive. And he hoped to leverage that experience to the Unit's benefit: "I wanted to help the Unit do well with some of the evaluation metrics that the Canadian Army Headquarters looked at to evaluate Reserve units." These included maintaining a low rate of unit members on non-effective strength (NES) and a "very high number of trained, effective soldiers."[342]

In tandem with Tom MacKay's appointment as CO in 2016, the Canadian Army initiated the *Strengthening the Army Reserve* (STAR) program which saw the unit's establishment increased by one rifle platoon, from three platoons to four in a rifle company. This was a small but meaningful increase. It was also an opportunity, since it offered the Unit a chance to demonstrate that it could, in fact, fill new positions. In time, this could lead to more growth. As Lieutenant Colonel Mackay expressed in the March 2017 issue of *Canada's Red Hackle*, "the entire team at Canada's senior highland regiment is enthusiastically embracing the challenge of swelling our numbers."[343]

While the moment seemed brimming with opportunity, Tom MacKay was quick to acknowledge that his second term faced early obstacles. "When you cross the line of departure in your command," he recalled, "you are ultimately faced with the challenges of the day."[344] One major test, in November 2016, was a series of impending renovations at the Bleury Street armoury. These included structural work on the building's roof, which would render the building out of bounds for months. The optimistic view of the building upgrade was straight forward and true: the regimental home was getting a much needed upgrade, an investment that was a good sign for the long-term health of the Regiment. The armoury is "a familiar place," Lieutenant Colonel MacKay noted, "and that familiarity is one of those intangibles that is worth so very much to an Army Reserve unit in its mandate to connect with the community."[345]

What proved more difficult was relocating the Unit during the renovations. "It was," Lieutenant Colonel MacKay remembered, "incredibly disruptive to training."[346] No longer able to parade at 2067 Bleury Street, which had fast become a dust-covered worksite, the Regiment was welcomed by the Canadian Grenadier Guards at their armoury on rue de l'Esplanade in the Plateau Mont Royal. The Pipes and Drums had their training relocated to the Côte-des-Neiges armoury, home of the Royal Canadian Hussars and the 2 Canadian Field Artillery Regiment. And while the Black Watch had for decades paraded on Tuesday evenings, training was moved to Thursdays in order to accommodate the Regiment's new *environs*. For citizen soldiers with civilian jobs and families, this change, while seemingly minor, had the potential to be extremely disruptive to their schedules, and could impact attendance.

As the renovations stretched on, traditions had to be modified. The annual City of Montreal Remembrance Day parade, which had historically stepped off from the Black Watch armoury, was relocated. The soldiers of the Regiment instead departed from the Régiment de Maisonneuve's Cathcart Armoury before marching to the cenotaph at Place du Canada. The Officers' Reunion Dinner was held at the nearby Rackets Club instead of the officers' mess. And without access to the parade square, the Junior Ranks Christmas dinner took place at the CGG armoury. "We struggled to find the same kind of rhythm to our activities," Tom MacKay recalled, "and the effect on morale was noticeable."[347]

Nevertheless, training and Regimental life continued through the renovations and the troops eventually returned to the armoury. The Black Watch was assigned responsibility for housing 34 Brigade's Influence Activities (IA) capability, a task which fell to C Company. The Watch was also made responsible for training the Brigade team for the Canadian Patrol Concentration (CPC), a gruelling undertaking held deep within the unforgiving expanse of CFB Wainwright, Alberta. "It's a very difficult patrolling exercise for anyone, Regular Force or Reserve," Lieutenant Colonel MacKay noted. Much to the Brigade Commander's pleasure, the Black Watch team not only finished the concentration – an accomplishment onto itself – but placed well.

The Regimental family was active under Lieutenant Colonel MacKay's command. The flagship event of 2017 was a military Tattoo, held at Montreal's Bell Centre on 8

April 2017, commemorating the 100th Anniversary of the Battle of Vimy Ridge. The display of military pomp and flair, which was organized with the support of the Black Watch Foundation by Major (retired) Brent Cowan, Victor Knowton, and countless other volunteers, was a unique show for the thousands who attended, including the Mayor of Montreal, Denis Coderre.[348]

OP LENTUS, 2017

While the spring of 2017 was exciting for the Black Watch, it was also very, very wet. After a snowy winter gave way to a warm and rainy April, water levels around the island of Montreal quickly began to rise, causing the most dramatic flooding the city had seen in a hundred years.[349] As the situation became dire, the possibility of a military component to the government's response became more and more likely. By the weekend of Church Parade 2017, Tom MacKay recalled having to slip out of Regimental meetings in order to respond to calls and emails as the Unit prepared to deploy volunteers to arrest the flooding damage.[350]

By the Sunday morning of Church Parade, the Unit's soldiers, who were ready to deploy, arrived with their kit and worked through the verification process at the Battalion Orderly Room. The armoury was alive with activity; troops were preparing to fight the floods and members of the Regimental family gathered expectantly, waiting to form up for Church Parade. "It was an exciting time," Tom recalled, "as much as you don't want to deal with natural disasters, you don't want there to be a flood; you don't want there to be a war either but when it's happening, and you are getting ready for it, it's a very exciting time. There is just this incredible increase in the adrenaline and energy of everyone as you get spooled up."[351]

Whether or not Church Parade would go forward became an immediate question. After consulting with senior officers and RSM, Lieutenant Colonel MacKay opted to go forward with a scaled-back parade marked by one visible exception: the Unit would march in their battle dress uniforms, not in full dress or ceremonial kit. "The decision to march in Church Parade was a difficult one," he recalls. On the one hand, the Black Watch's leadership was keenly aware that a parade in these circumstances, with homes and communities succumbing to flood waters, could seem indelicate. At the same time, if done correctly, it could serve as an "opportunity to call attention to the fact that we are going out the door ... to draw attention to the fact that the Unit was deploying on OP LENTUS."[352] It was the first time since the end of the Second World War that the Black Watch marched in its annual Church Parade in battle dress. Lieutenant Colonel MacKay was quick to note that, "we weren't expressly forbidden by the chain of command from [parading], but I also wasn't asking permission."[353]

It was a risk, to be sure, but as the photos of that day attest, it achieved its goal.[354] Rather than looking insensitive, the parade underscored the sense of urgency gripping the city. The decision to march through the driving rain was defiant of the natural disaster itself, not its victims; it was an acknowledgement that there was work to be done, that the Regiment was ready to help, and that the Black Watch marches undeterred.

In the wake of this unusual Church Parade, the Regiment quietly passed a milestone in its modern history. Pipe Major (MWO) Cameron Stevens, MMM, CD relinquished his appointment after 17 years at the helm of the Pipes and Drums. He was replaced by MWO Daniel Smith, CD who had joined the Regiment in 1976 before transitioning to a career in the Regular Force. Pipe Major Stevens' tenure had been among the longest of any Canadian Black Watch Pipe Major. The Regiment also changed RSMs in a muted post-parade ceremony, saying goodbye to CWO Mario Carmosino and welcoming CWO Stephen D. Campbell into the role.

The Unit deployed a platoon of soldiers to OP LENTUS on 7 May. They were placed under the leadership of Capt Jay Hinkson and Sgt Matthew Ramsay. Over the next forty-eight hours the orderly room worked to churn out a steady flow of volunteers, resulting in a Black Watch contingent on the ground numbering well over thirty soldiers, not including the rear echelon staff supporting the deployed members.[355] The soldiers worked long days, especially at first, preparing sand bags and building retaining walls so water could be pumped out and dry zones could be established.[356] There were light-hearted moments too: among the filed promotions carried on OP LENTUS, one was to Private Daniel Mason, who was promoted to the rank of corporal while "standing chest deep in the La Prairie River."[357]

The deployment was a success and it marked a high point for the Reserve Force in Quebec, a province which, in the shadow of the October Crisis and the Oka Crisis, sometimes had a complicated political relationship with the use of soldiers for domestic operations. The support of troops during the Ice Storm in 1998 began to reframe this relationship. By 2017 Lieutenant Colonel MacKay felt there had been a paradigm shift, and that domestic operations like OP LENTUS had the potential to become more common, despite the structural challenges faced by a system dependent upon volunteer service during emergencies:

> The Army Reserve in Canada is not designed particularly well to respond to domestic emergencies ... but it does work. It works because the men and women of the Army Reserve want to do this. They joined because they want to serve; they want to go on operations whether domestic or overseas or both, and they volunteer.[358]

Although he planned to complete a two-year term as CO, Tom Mackay's command was cut short when the Army named him Director of Army Reserves and promoted him to colonel in August 2017.[359] He lobbied to stay on as Commanding Officer until the end of his term, but the Army dismissed the idea of a full colonel commanding a Reserve regiment. A month after his promotion in September 2017, Colonel MacKay, in Black Watch dress complete with the red gorgets of a full colonel, handed over command of the Unit to a familiar face – someone intimately acquainted with the demands of commanding Canada's senior highland regiment. Someone the Regiment was happy to welcome home.

Lieutenant Colonel Bruno Plourde, CD

Lieutenant Colonel Bruno Plourde was preparing for retirement. Having served more than three years in command of 2 CRPG (Canadian Ranger Patrol Group) after completing his time as Commanding Officer of Canada's Black Watch from 2009 to 2013, he was putting the finishing touches on a long and distinguished career. But the promotion and departure of Colonel MacKay, combined with a lack of field officers at the Black Watch available to assume command, created a need for someone who could step into the role of CO as quickly and seamlessly as possible. The moment called for someone who would have the confidence of both the troops and the Regimental family to keep the Black Watch on course. And so Bruno Plourde became Commanding Officer of the Unit, for a second time, in September 2017.

Lieutenant Colonel Plourde's goal upon assuming command was simple: growth. He wanted to "prove the Unit could be autonomous ... and to complete [its] operational mission."[360] Part of growing the Regiment and solidifying its operational effectiveness was ensuring that a maximum number of junior leaders – non-commissioned members and officers alike – were qualified and prepared to assume new roles. This would "position the Unit for better sustainability and autonomy," particularly when it came to filling future Commanding Officer and Regimental Sergeant Major appointments. By March 2020, RSM Stephen Campbell was able to report in his message to the Regimental family that "since the spring of 2018, we have promoted over twenty-five new leaders, MCpls and Sgts ... this sets up the Black Watch strong for the future decade."[361]

This undertaking came with challenges. Despite a push to recruit more soldiers, the training pipeline was sometimes unable to accommodate the influx of eager new members. The result was what Bruno referred to as "a significant backlog in training and huge loss of potential soldiers that quit the CAF before training because they were waiting too long."[362] Additionally, a considerable number of experienced NCMs and officers took full-time army contracts working at military schools, bases, or Brigade and Division Headquarters. While many continued to parade with the Black Watch on a voluntary basis, the high number of leaders tasked-out on long-term contracts was a perennial challenge for the Unit.[363]

Despite these challenges, training continued and the Unit participated in a host of annual exercises. The Black Watch was again tasked with training the two 2nd Canadian Division Reserve teams for the Canadian Patrol Concentration. As Bruno himself summarized in *Canada's Red Hackle* magazine, "under the outstanding leadership of Sgt Devon Best, both teams trained, deployed, and successfully completed the competition that saw elite teams from our NATO partners abandon it due to its extreme difficulty."[364]

Throughout this time, members of the Regiment continued to deploy on operations outside of Canada, including OP IMPACT in Iraq, OP REASSURANCE in Latvia, OP UNIFIER in Ukraine, and OP PRESENCE in Senegal/Mali. These deployed members are often the focus of the Black Watch's Regimental association. Along with the Family Division of the Regiment, the association branches host events, visit hospitals, and provide care packages to support the Black Watch members deployed on missions around the world. These care packages are produced with the support of the Black Watch of Canada Foundation, and they have been known to stir envy in the hearts of soldiers from other units when they are opened by our deployed soldiers.

On the domestic front, the spring of 2019 once again saw water levels rise in Quebec and parts of Eastern Canada. As it had in 2017, serious flooding began to overtake parts of Montreal, necessitating a substantial response from local and provincial authorities. The Black Watch was called into service under the auspices of OP LENTUS, and members deployed alongside approximately 2,500 CAF members who filled sandbags, performed wellness checks, cleared routes, and helped to evacuate residents.[365] The mission officially lasted from 19 April to 5 June 2019, for much of which a consistent flow of Black Watch soldiers volunteered to rotate through and help their community – putting service before self – something they had been asked to do before and would be soon asked to do again.

Outside the perennial rhythms of training, Bruno Plourde's command was marked by several notable moments. The Black Watch strengthened its relationship with the 1-111th Infantry Regiment of Pennsylvania, with representatives from each Unit continuing to attend each other's annual mess dinners. As a sign of kinship and to mark the strong inter-regimental bond, Bruno was proud to present the 1-111th with a pipe banner – a uniquely highland gift. While there had been some hope of organizing collective training between the two Units, because of logistic and bureaucratic obstacles, it ultimately did not come to fruition.[366]

The Regiment sent a contingent to Buckingham Palace, having been invited to our Colonel-in-Chief's 70th birthday and patronage celebration on 22 May 2018. Bruno described the garden party event as a "once in a lifetime experience," delighted that some members of the Black Watch group had the opportunity to "exchange a few words with The Prince of Wales and The Duchess of Cornwall."[367] Lieutenant Colonel Bolton affectionately recalled how *personal* the event seemed, despite its size and scope: "it was wonderful, you were there with 3,000 of Prince Charles' best friends, and you were made to feel important."[368] In March 2019, Lieutenant Colonel Plourde, along with Honorary Colonel Daniel O'Connor and Honorary Lieutenant Colonel Bruce Bolton, again travelled to London with Sergeant Devon Best to meet with Prince Charles. The meeting marked perhaps the first occasion where a non-commissioned member joined the senior leadership in providing the Colone in Chief with an update on the health of the Regiment. By all accounts, Sergeant Best and The Prince of Wales shared a lively conversation and got along well.[369]

Alongside the high moments, however, came a moment of great sadness for the Regimental family: the death of Colonel Stephen Frederick Angus, CD on 4 November 2018. Colonel Angus was Commanding Officer of the Regiment from 1970 to 1972 and Honorary Colonel from 1996 to 2000. Regimental historian Roman Jarymowycz described Steve Angus as nothing short of "Black Watch royalty." Lieutenant Colonel Plourde characterized Colonel Angus as one of the "pillars of our Regimental family." His death marked the end of an era for the Black Watch and, in many ways, signaled the end of a regimental golden age. It was an immeasurable loss.

The Pipes and Drums 2018–19: Mons, Normandy, and Edinburgh

The heartbeat of a highland unit is, in fact, a drumbeat. The Regimental Pipes and Drums have long considered themselves the guardians of tradition; the sinew that binds the past to the future. As warfare becomes more modern and weapons and uniforms change, the skirl of the highland bagpipe and the deafening crack of the drum serve as audible testaments of the Regiment's history. They remind us, with each parade, where we came from.

On an annual basis the Pipes and Drums represent the Black Watch at well over 100 events – Regimental functions, Remembrance Day services, and parades throughout the city. In November 1918 as a part of OP DISTINCTION, the Pipes and Drums sent members to augment the combined Pipes and Drums of the Canadian Armed Forces in Mons, Belgium to commemorate the end of the First World War. They joined members of the Nova Scotia Highlanders, the Cape Breton Highlanders, and the RCAF as they paraded at locations across France and Belgium, including a rainy morning preformance alongside Prime Minister Justin Trudeau at the Vimy Memorial.

The trip culminated in a ceremony in Mons town square on 11 November. There the regimental pipes and drums were joined by a re-enactiment Pipe Band comprised of many former regimental pipers and drummers from across Canada, each wearing the period uniform of the 42nd Battalion. This group had received a hero's welcome the day before at Wallers, France, a town which was also liberated by the 42nd Battalion in October 1918. Marching with the band – although not quite in step – was Flora Macdonald the Second, a goat draped in Royal Stewart Tartan. Flora II was a mascot befitting the 42nd and she had a proud lineage; the original Flora Macdonald had been adopted by the battalion during the war and was killed in fighting just outside of Wallers. Her antlers can still be found in the band room at the Black Watch armoury.

The Mons ceremony was significant. A picture taken on 11 November 1918 shows the Pipes and Drums marching from the very same town square. They were announcing an end to the protracted fighting which had absorbed Europe since the late summer of 1914. One hundred years later, after the nationally-televised commemoration ceremony was over, the Black Watch again marched through the streets of Mons, the echo of *Highland Laddie* and *Black Bear* reverberating through the medieval town's narrow streets.

Back home in Montreal in January of 2019 at the annual Regimental Birthday parade, MWO Daniel Smith, having reached the age of mandatory retirement, left his position as Pipe Major of the Black Watch. The Pipe Major's dirk was given, along with the appointment, to Adam Wilson, CD, who was simultaneously promoted to Warrant Officer on the same parade.

Less than a year later in June 2019, four members of the Pipes and Drums returned to France to participate in ceremonies commemorating the 75th anniversary of the invasion of Normandy. Upon their return the pipers and drummers were thrust into preparations for the Edinburgh Tattoo.

The Tattoo, which has run for 70 years, is recognized as the pinnacle of military music and pageantry. For the first time since the year 2000, the Black Watch of Canada was invited to participate in the event, having been asked to lead the Canadian Armed Forces contingent, which also included members of the Nova Scotia Highlanders and the Stormont, Dundas and Glengarry Highlanders. Preparation began in the winter of 2019 and continued through the summer as the contingent participated together in The Royal Nova Scotia International Tattoo in June and July.

At the beginning of August, the band travelled to Edinburgh where they undertook a frenetically paced, five-day workup under the direction of the British Army to prepare and rehearse the tattoo's meticulous timing, music, and choreography.

They then began a month-long run of nightly shows (two on Saturdays) which were seen by more than 100,000 live spectators and countless more as the show was re-aired internationally on the BBC. Lieutenant Colonel Plourde flew to Scotland on a whirlwind trip to watch the Black Watch perform in the Tattoo, as did Lieutenant General Jean Marc Lanthier, Commander of the Canadian Army; CWO Stu Hartnell, Canadian Army Sergeant Major; and Paul Hindo, Honorary Colonel of the Canadian Army, who had started his military career with the Black Watch.

From early on, the Pipes and Drums distinguished themselves. They were asked to form the outside flank of the massed Pipes and Drums, opposite the 3rd Battalion, Royal Regiment of Scotland, better known by their ancestral name, *The Black Watch*. It was the first time in almost twenty years that the two regiments had paraded alongside each other. As Pipe Major Adam Wilson saw it, "it has been far too long since our storied Pipe Bands have been able to share performance space, and with both Pipe Bands in Edinburgh for the Tattoo absolutely no opportunity for rekindling a relationship was wasted."[370] Indeed, on the last night of the Tattoo, after marching down the famed esplanade of Edinburgh Castle into the streets below, the Senior Drum Major of the British Army, a 3 Scot, reformed both bands together and put them at attention while the rest of the Tattoo participants began to say goodbyes and disperse. On his word of command – "Black Watch, by the centre, QUICK MARCH!" – the two regimental bands came together as one and stepped off playing *Wa'Saw the 42nd*, a suitably Black Watch tune. The surrounding crowd looked on with respect and bemusement at the sight of two legendary highland regiments, usually separated by an ocean, marching seamlessly together along Edinburgh's cobblestone streets.

OP LASER

From the early days of 2020, the presence of a new and deadly coronavirus which was rapidly spreading in Wuhan, China, began to garner international media attention. The virus – later dubbed COVID-19 – soon appeared in concerning numbers in countries around the world. By March 2020, with case numbers rising across Quebec and North America, unprecedented lockdown measures were imposed in a bid to slow community transmission of the coronavirus.

Meanwhile, through various directives from the CAF and in an effort to contain the virus, training at the Regiment – and most use of the building – came to a halt. The Watch had to be quick to adjust. Some training moved online. In an unprecedented change, The Regimental Church Parade was held virtually, as was the change of Honorary Colonels, from Daniel O'Connor to Bruce Bolton. Jonathan Birks was named Honorary Lieutenant Colonel, taking over the position from Bruce Bolton. The Change of Command parade, which was planned to follow the annual Church Parade, where Lieutenant Colonel Plourde was scheduled to hand over command of the Regiment to Lieutenant Colonel Francis Roy, was postponed until September, It would ultimately take place as a digital ceremony. In a very short period of time, the Regiment was forced to adapt its traditions to accommodate extraordinary circumstances.

In the backdrop of these activities, the Black Watch prepared to support OP LASER, the CAF response to the COVID-19 crisis. More than 80 members of the Regiment volunteered for full-time domestic operational (Class C) contracts, effectively signaling their willingness to support their community in whatever way they possibly could. Most of these contracts began on 5 April 2021 and required a five-month commitment. They joined the more than 7,000 members of the CAF Primary Reserve who volunteered for full-time service.

Reporting had begun to emerge from Quebec and Ontario that the situation in the provinces' long-term care facilities was taking a worrying turn. Infection rates were accelerating, and so was the mortality rates of residents. The facilities' staff members were becoming ill at an alarming rate, leaving a tragic void for the vulnerable sick patients with increasingly few staff members healthy enough to care for them. As the magnitude of the situation became blatantly clear, Quebec Premier François Legault requested support from the CAF to help stabilize the situation in the province's long-term care facilities.

The Black Watch soldiers were reformed into two platoons. They undertook specialized training from the CAF Medical Branch and the Red Cross. They were then sent to work in CHSLDs (Centres d'hébergement de soins de longue durée – residential and long-term care centres): one platoon at CHSLD Valeo in St. Lambert under the command of Lieutenant William Richardson and Sergeant Jimmy Ray Thompson; and the other at CHSLD St. Andrew in NDG, under the command of Captain Zach Duma and WO Adam Wilson. Each platoon was paired with a medical team. The infection rate amongst the residents at these centres was high when the Regiment arrived. *The Montreal Gazette* reported that on 30 April 2020, shortly before the troops arrived at CHSLD St Andrew, 81 percent of the residents in the facility were Covid-positive.[371]

The troops working in the CHSLDs had daily contact with Covid-positive residents. While their duties varied, most soldiers helped by bathing, feeding, and providing hygenic care. In quiet moments they sat with the centres' occupants and kept them company. These were rate new faces for patients who, for over a month, had been unable to leave their rooms or receive outside visitors. While these restrictions were necessary infection control measures, the isolation was a tremendous emotional burden for the residents, one that members of the regiment tried, in their very small way, to alliviate. At both CHSLD Valeo and CHLSD St Andrew the platoons stayed in place until the situation stabilized, residents began to get better, and staff began to return. When it was over and the platoons prepared to leave, the moment was, for many, bittersweet. Lieutenant Richardson captured a common feeling in *Canada's Red Hackle* when he wrote "we hope to return to CHSLD Valeo in happier times."[372]

In order to mitigate the risk of further spreading COVID-19 in society at large while working in the CHSLDs, both platoons were required to isolate in hotels with little direct contact with the outside world. The Regimental Association, the Family Division, and the Black Watch Foundation provided care packages to ensure that the troops were not in quarantine without some essential creature comforts, including much-appreciated snacks to supplement the daily meals provided by the military.

OP LASER, along with OP LENTUS and other domestic operations, rely heavily on Reservists to ensure their success. Lieutenant Colonel Plourde, reflecting on the role that members of the Primary Reserve play during these operations, noted that "the Black Watch and the Reserve Force in general are a perfect fit for the CAF/Canadian Army domestic operations response. I would even argue that reservists are better suited for domestic operations than our full-time colleagues because of [the reservists'] link to their communities."[373] However, he was also quick to note that domestic operations of this nature are not without their challenges, both for the individual members and for the institution:

> The biggest challenge is to have the institutional chain of command accept that a reservist doesn't have the availability of a Regular Force soldier. Our institution is getting better at the recognition that a reservist is supported by legislation or laws that will protect [their] civilian employment because of service while on domestic operations. [I]t is key that the chain [of command] recognizes that, once deployed or engaged in an operation, the Reserve Force doesn't have the institutional depth to continue to do 'business as usual' as the Regular Force/full time army does.[374]

Lieutenant Colonel Plourde identified the Regiment's contributions to OP LENTUS and OP LASER as being among the highlights of his second term as Commanding Officer, and expressed tremendous pride in seeing the members of the Regiment work together:

> Infantrymen/women, pipers, drummers, volunteers, support staff, all working very hard, in very difficult and complex circumstances to make things happen. In adversity (floods, covid) I was driven by the pride and dedication of the members of the Unit and the support from the Regimental family. My highlight was to be able to serve with them. My regret — not being able to thank them in person.[375]

Lieutenant Colonel Francis Roy, CD – A New Decade, A New Challenge

At a ceremony held on 12 September 2020, Lieutenant Colonel Bruno Plourde handed over command of the Regiment to Lieutenant Colonel Francis Roy, CD. RSM Stephen Campbell retired and CWO Francois Mamen, CD was appointed as the new RSM. The ceremony, which took place in the officers' mess, welcomed a skeleton crowd: a few dignitaries, spouses, and a piper. This was a necessary condition of the world in the fall of 2020: with a pandemic still raging, large gatherings and parades were strictly forbidden. The event was live-streamed on a social networking site, allowing the Regimental family to participate, albeit at a distance.

Lieutenant Colonel Roy took command of the Unit during a difficult time, but it was a unit fortified by the support of a strong Regimental Family. The four cadet corps affiliated with the Black Watch carried on despite the pandemic, finding new and adaptive ways to train. The Black Watch Scottish Arts Society, established in 2015, continued its mission of teaching Montreal's future pipers, drummers, and highland dancers. Black Watch Association branches in Montreal, Ottawa, Kingston, Toronto, Western Canada, and the Atlantic provinces likewise found new ways to remain active. Often, this meant learning to leverage the potential of digital meeting platforms to bring people together. The Colonel's Circle, an extension of the Black Watch Foundation populated by influential Montrealers, was established to support the regiment and solidify its long-standing prominence in the community. When their usual in-person gatherings in the officers' mess were no longer permitted, they began hosting a lecture series, held on a virtual platform, featuring experts in the fields of history, international relations, and the military. General Wayne Eyre, the Chief of the Defence Staff through most of 2021 and 2022, and who was then the commander of the army, was an early presenter at this digital podium.

Canada's Red Hackle magazine, which for 20 years has been the seasonal news source on all things regimental, was now supplemented by a new, punchy monthly email newsletter aptly titled *The Red Hackle Express*. As the pandemic world relied more heavily on digital platforms, the Black Watch Foundation and the Royal Highlanders of Canada maintained their website – but they still took care to ensure that the analog was not forgotten, dutifully overseeing the upkeep of the Black Watch Museum and Archives.

The soldiers of the regiment have witnessed unprecedented uncertainty since the spring of 2020. For each challenge that the regiment has faced, though, it has also found a solution. When the armoury was given a reduced maximum occupancy as public health protocol, the unit split its in-person training to two nights a week. When required, training was held virtually. While the nature of that training may have changed, it certainly did not stop. An early focus in fall 2020 was placed on maintaining Individual Training (IT), ensuring all members were able to progress with career courses, creating a healthy pipeline of trained soldiers and future leaders. In the spring of 2021, 34 Brigade announced collective training exercises, which had been halted during the early days of the pandemic, would again be part of the training calendar. In both the 2020–21 and 2021–22 training years the Black Watch was tasked to lead a platoon in the Arctic Response Company Group (ARGC), a national tasking focused on training to protect Canada's North. And in December 2021, the Canadian Armed Forces were again mobilized as an aid to civil the power, asked to help the Province of Quebec inoculate Quebecers as the new Omicron variant of Covid-19 was rapidly cutting through the provincial population. The Black Watch sent a platoon of soldiers and two platoon commanders to support these vaccination efforts as a part of OP VECTOR. And, in another unconventional milestone, the regiment celebrated a subdued 160th birthday ceremony on Microsoft Teams, a virtual meeting platform.

Perhaps more than any time in recent memory, the Unit's future is not of its own choosing. External events, both domestic and international, will play a large role in how we train and fight – and in how we interact with the world around us. As the Regiment continues into the uncharted territory the coming years are sure to offer, the history of the Black Watch makes one thing certain: through adversity, just as it has through success, the Black Watch marches on, and the regiment will continue to adapt – and thrive.

Nemo Me Impune Lacessit

Notes to Part VI

The New Millennium, War, and New Challenges: 1993–2022

1. RHC was one of ten Canadian Militia regiments that requested a Reg Force CO, DCO or RSM that year; that same spring Lt Col Robert Scantland, 2 R22eR, was appointed CO of a reserve unit, the Canadian Grenadier Guards.
2. Ian McCulloch, Interview/correspondence RJJ, 13 November 2012, 3 May 2013, 26 September 2013; hereafter, McCulloch. Father: Cdr PLS McCulloch, RCN, a Korea War veteran.
3. Ibid. "The one question that I still remember vividly was when Colonel Bourne leaned over and asked if I was Catholic. Nonplussed, I responded that … the McCullochs, were now Church of England but originally Presbyterian from just north of Inverness and that my mother's family, the Macphersons were Catholics from Glenlivet and were out with Charlie. That seemed to be the end of the interview …" McCulloch felt District HQ was miffed at RHC: "continually at war, the BW was black balled."
4. Ibid., For personal family reasons, the Montreal posting was preferable to a Regular Force base. Appt to RHC: "[BGen Archibald suggested] … MGen Tom Defaye commanding LFWA could approach the Army Commander to have me considered."
5. Ibid.
6. Maj G Dover, Ibid.
7. MacKay 30 October 2013. "I was forced to be Senior Sub. We trained them and they passed with a 98 percent, tied for first in Province, in retrospect, it was probably meaningless to the Brigade staff."
8. Col SF Angus/GMACB, 18 Feb 2014.
9. BWA. Bolton Papers. Box 2 1180-9 (Secretary) 20 September 1994 initial memo (Maj G Dover); November 1994 – June 1995 etc. First meetings winter. Capt B Bolton Secretary, 1994.
10. Appointed August 1996.
11. Ibid., and Bolton Papers/Intvw 28 September 2013. McCulloch: "Most of the initial paperwork with the feds re charitable status etc was done during my watch. Colonel George Milne of the Calgary Highlanders was invited … he met with me and Bruce Bolton. Bill Stavert might also have been present. I delegated Bruce to staff it to completion given his museum foundation expertise…Colonel Milne was behind the Winter Olympics fundraising in Calgary." Foundation project had been strongly advocated by Cols Price and Angus; "After years of discussion … McCulloch pushed for its establishment" BDB/RJJ 15 March 2014.
12. Lt Col TEC MacKay / RJJ, 12 October 2011. McCulloch opines: "… for me my militia moment was at the operational level – getting the various Regimental institutions sorted out and humming again." McC/RJJ 18 November 2013, re Exercise: "All my trg objectives were met … The recce platoon (augmented by six Maisonneuve colleagues from the 10/90 recce platoon) counter patrolled as a very active enemy force … In another large exercise down near Hemmingford, the unit did a separate company advance to contact ex … The *pièce de résis-*

tance for that exercise was when A Coy secured a farm … on what they thought was their last objective [then] someone shouted 'Armour!' and they were counter-attacked by an armoured half-track full of recce platoon and a Ferret [armd car] both belonging to a collector nearby who rented out armoured vehicles to American film companies!"

13. Angus / Potter, 30 July 2003, re restoring budget and authorized strength of Pipe Band.
14. BWA, Bolton Papers. Intvws Bolton/Stevenson. Notes, October–November 1993.
15. P/ Maj Brian MacKenzie / RJJ, 4 November 2013.
16. BWA, Ibid., Allmand/McCulloch 20 October 1994; Collenette/Allmand 19/September 1994.
17. BWA. Ibid., Sgt JD Anderson/Lt Col Lusk correspondence, 13 May 1998. Cols Angus and Price summoned to District HQ Atwater to discuss the BW Band. An explosion was barely averted. Price: "Boy were you uptight Steve".
18. Ibid., McCulloch.
19. Bolton, Ibid., 28 September 2013.
20. McCulloch, Ibid., Bands were guaranteed annual funding for transportation and equipment allowances for up to thirty members.
21. Adjustments by the Area HQ (after much protest from Regiments throughout) permitted a brigade band, bands for 6 R22eR and FMR, and ten extra posts for The Black Watch pipes and drums.
22. P/Maj BS MacKenzie/RJJ, 5 November 2013.
23. "Alas! Posthumously the fleeing years gallop by …"
24. Ibid., "We were joined by the future Comd of the army, Marc Caron … photo of RHC group by the BW cairn in Carlisle Barracks, PA [from which pt] the 42nd / 77th Foot marched to relieve Fort Pitt in 1763".
25. Correspondence, Gen Donn Starry, Lt Gen Holder, MGen Huba Wass de Czege. May–July 2008. *The School of Advanced Military Studies* (SAMS) was begun in Ft Leavenworth; its graduates were usually dubbed *Jedi Knights*.
26. Terry Copp/RJJ, Intvw Erin, Ont, 21 September 2013.
27. <u>Black Watch Museum and Archives Leadership</u>: David O'Keefe 1991–94; Maura Pennington, 1994; Johanna Douglas-O'Neil, 1994–95; Linda Brown, 1995; Haidar Moukdad, 1994–95; Russell Switzer; Anne Stewart, 1998–2003. Stewart retired as Curator/Archivist, Kit Shop manager and secretary to RHQ: "After more than five happy and interesting years working for the regiment"; David O'Keefe, 2003–2009, supported by Phil Godfrey and Cal Kufta; Cal Kufta, 2008–2013, supported by a number of valued employees and volunteers including Eliot Perrin, Eliza Richardson, Mike Cher, and Cynthia Jones; Upon Kufta's departure from Montreal, the Museum and Archives have been run by Cynthia Jones as Collections Manager and Mike Cher as Coordinator. Throughout nearly this entire period, stability and continuity were ensured by Lt Col Bruce Bolton, who provided guidance and oversight of the Museum and Archives.
28. Volunteers: Ivor Watkins was appointed curator, and, with Gordon Ritchie, placed in charge. Security remained a problem. Ritchie: "Control was lax. The commissionaires had the key but anyone could sign it out." McCulloch: "Our most valuable medals were not touched as they would have been recognized instantly on the specialized market but at least twenty more obscure but valuable medals had disappeared … I called in the SIU but they sent a female private fresh out of recruit school to do the investigation and the lost medals were never recovered." The incident would continue to be a sore point with the Regimental Advisory Board and was never satisfactorily concluded. SFA/RJJ, 18 February 2013.
29. Lt Col C Phare/RJJ, 30 April 2013.
30. Lt Col Rev W Fairlie/RJJ, 16–18 December 2013.
31. Capt Rev RB Glencross/RJJ 30 November 2012. McCulloch recalls, "Captain Rob Boyd the RCR RSSO, a Bosnian vet himself, established a weekly support group for all Bosnia-Croatia vets in the Montreal Area which met once a week for coffee at the Cafe Sarajevo downtown."
32. Also, Sgt Hugh Lawton, M/Cpls Don Collins, Len Maillet, Martin Prince, Jose Perez and MCpl Orser. Operation Medak Pocket (9–17 September 1993) was fought by the CF (2nd Battalion, PPCLI); four Canadian soldiers were wounded.
33. McCulloch: "I always strategically planned Maj events in March at the end of the fiscal year so that I could take advantage of all the money that DistHQ had held back – the BW was there to help out Dist avoid their annual dilemma of handing back thousands of dollars they had been too stingy to disburse during the rest of the year."

34. Reunion dinner guests of honour during McCulloch's term: 1993 – Colonel John Knox; 1994 – MGen Romeo Dallaire, DComd Army; 1995 – LGen Duncan McAlpine. McCulloch and RSM attended the 1995 Reunion of the 1st and 2nd Bns, BW, in Camp Aldershot with six pipers from Montreal.

35. McCulloch Ibid., and correspondence 30 September 2013.

36. For review of Cdn Militia (and Regular Force) Mess life, see: Anthony Kellett, *The History of Messes in the Canadian Army*, (Ottawa: April 2014). Examples of RHC Mess circa 1920s to modern era, *passim*.

37. McCulloch Ibid., "I allowed Capt (now Col) Patrick Kelly back in the regiment … Part of the deal with Pat was that he would backstop Capt Bruce Bolton and make sure that Bruce passed both his Maj and Lt Col qualifying courses." Col P Kelly, correspondence 6 June 13: "[Ian McCulloch] was highly supportive of my return as it lent stability back to A Coy and aided [the] intention re training of junior officers. Ian was outgoing …"

38. *Special Commission on the Restructuring of the Reserves Report*, DND Ottawa:1995, 76. BW: "no RESO trained militia officers have made it to command in BW despite having two to four officers on course every year since its inception … Upper level courses were not conducive to old timers who have established jobs, families; pay and benefits out of balance; retention is the critical factor; the enrollment system is simply out of control."

39. McCulloch/RJJ, 20 October 2013.

40. McCulloch was not aware of the brewing storm: "Colonel Gervais and later Colonel Mike Pronkin dealt fairly with me and pretty much left me alone."

41. McCulloch: In 2000, Assist to the Dir Gen Health Services, MGen L Mathieu; Posted 2004–07 on staff HQ Supreme Allied Command Transformation, Norfolk, Virginia. Appointed to Directing Staff at the Canadian Forces Staff College, Toronto in 2008. Books published: Osprey Publishing (UK): *British Light Infantryman of the Seven Years War, 1756–1763, North America*, and *Highlander in the French & Indian War*; Robin Brass: *Through So Many Dangers Memoirs and Adventures of Robert Kirk, Late of the Royal Highland Regiment*, and, *Sons of the Mountains: A History of the Highland Regiments in North America, 1756–1767*. McCulloch has also written articles for *The Beaver, CMH* and *RH*.

42. Col Price died on the 17th Hole of the Royal Montreal Golf Club 12 May 1996; he was Chairman of "3 Macs" the investment firm. He never forgot his ties to The Black Watch or the Queen Mother. "A picture of Colonel Tom in full regimental dress towering over the Queen remains in his old office as a memento at MacDougall, MacDougall and MacTier." Ferrabee/Harrison, Ibid., Correspondence B MacD/RJJ, 27 September/2 October 2013.

43. Lt Col Tom MacKay/RJJ, 30 November 2012.

44. Ibid.

45. Dickson Commission Report 1995: seven hundred briefs, three hundred witnesses; three commissioners: a former chief justice; a retired general and a historian. Examples discussed: "… in the past few years Exercises where less than seventy-five people show up for a weekend's training have not been uncommon etc." In fact, that was a good turn-out for most units.

46. *The Militia Monitor*, July/August 1995.

47. *The Gazette* 16 March 1996.

48. On 20 April 1997, BW became part of 34e GBC: 2 reserve brigades incorporating units of the 3 previous Quebec Militia Districts:
    34e GBC Order of Battle: The Royal Canadian Hussars, Le Régiment de Hull, 2 Field Regiment RCA, 3 Field Engineers Regiment, The Canadian Grenadier Guards, The Black Watch of Canada, 4e Bn, Royal 22e Régiment, 6e Bn, Royal 22e Régiment, Les Fusiliers Mont-Royal, Le Régiment de Maisonneuve, The Royal Montreal Regiment, 51e Bn des services du Canada.
    35e GBC: The Sherbrooke Hussars, 12e Régiment blindé du Canada (Milice), 6e Régiment d'artillerie de campagne, 62e Régiment d'artillerie de campagne, 10e Escadron du génie de campagne, 35e Régiment des transmissions, Les Voltigeurs de Québec, Les Fusiliers du Saint-Laurent, Le Régiment de la Chaudière, Le Régiment du Saguenay, Les Fusiliers de Sherbrooke, 5e Bn des services du Canada.

49. MND David Collenette/RJJ correspondence, 12 October 2013.

50. Lt Col G Lusk/RJJ, Intvw 30 May 2013; hereafter, Lusk. The Grenadier Guards were summoned that same day: "MGen Forand advised that we were to be reduced to a coy – no discussion." Lt Col R Garber CD, who as DCO, accompanied RMR CO, Lt Col H Hall. Correspondence H Hall/ R Gerber 14–15 October 13.

51. Colonel G Javornik/RJJ correspondence 1 June; 7 October 2013. Gen Baril officially assumed Comd Canadian

Army 17 September 1996. The mechanisms of the plan to eliminate Montreal Anglophone units is unclear. The incident requires further research and analysis.

52. Plans included: The CGG to move to Ottawa, amalgamate with GGFG and become the Canadian Guards; The Black Watch, senior highland regiment, to move to Nova Scotia, the Citadel in Halifax. The RMR was to remain in the City and inherit with the RHC Pipe Band (in City of Montreal Tartan). Col C Branchaud/RJJ, 18, 20 October 2013.

53. MGen FJ Norman CD / RJJ 14 October; Colonel H Hall/RJJ 15 October 2013. Other units in Canada were not yet warned; and in Quebec, Le Régiment du Saguenay was also advised it was to be reduced. The unit that initially profited in this deconstruction was the R22 Regiment (4th Battalion).

54. Gen M Baril/RJJ Intvw, 16 October 2012.

55. Ibid. The Reserves were not sympathetic to the Regular Army's proposals. Baril: "We always thought the militia was not working with us." The Militia Honoraries, at least those from English Regiments, were not completely certain what the meeting meant. Angus: "We had 'briefings' ... and few of them, led to anything, and, were not specific anyway. You didn't ask questions because you were talking to a room full of different agendas, and there was always the danger of arming a competitor, or a group of them, with knowledge he/they would use against you. The conferences were held entirely in French in that dreadful building in St Jean, Quebec ... finally after suffering through enough of them, I learned to quietly absorb them, and disregard them in the knowledge that saner heads would prevail." SFA/RJJ, 16 October 2013. Baril was made Chief of Land Staff (the Army) in September 1996. In September 1997, Gen Baril was appointed CDS by GovGen Roméo LeBlanc, on the advice of Prime Minister Jean Chrétien.

56. Ibid. According to Gen Forand, the SQFT Militia Officers who selected the units were SQFT Deputy Commander, BGen Jean Gervais, (R de Hull); Lt Col (BGen) Louis Denis Pelletier (Les Fusiliers de Sherbrooke), and perhaps Colonel Roger Chouinard (R de Mais). The Chief of Staff was Colonel (BGen) Daniel Pepin. This evaluation, in fairness to Lusk, was based on BW performance under the previous CO, circa 1993–1996.

57. BGen J Gervais/RJJ, 21 October 2013: "... no assessment was made by the Militia staff on the matter". Gen Forand emphasizes he was following instructions: "It was the order I was given ... We did it quickly – there were a total of six units selected "

58. *Reserves 2000* used a more dramatic term: "the night of the long knives", Colonel J Selkirk/RJJ 16 October 2013.

59. Gen FJ Normand, Ibid; Dr JL Granatstein, member of the SCRR trinity, in ref to criteria for *reserve reduction*: "SCRR did not specify where and how, and we had no idea of what was to be done. We had been finished eight months before August 1996. I think our sole criteria were size of units and viability. At least a real Coy, with a Pl for training. The reason for combining was to get at least two or preferably three Coys. We looked at demographics, and we worried about rural units. And we did not even suggest who would make decisions ... SCRR didn't go into details for individual units." Granatstein/RJJ, 17–19 October 2013. BGen Jean Gervais, SQFT Deputy, denies Militia Cols on SQFT HQ staff had anything to do with the decision: "no assessment was made by the Militia staff on the matter and I clearly remember having voiced our position on the matter to the Commander where we were worried that the involved units would eventually disappear on the long run, although they were supposed to remain in their individual armouries ... The study, if it was any, could have been done by the SQFT staff under Colonel Pepin [Chief of Staff Colonel (BGen) Daniel Pepin] ... I do not know if some criteria were established." Gervais/RJJ 21 October 2013.

60. Collenette/RJJ 13 October 2013.

61. The *Unit Viability Process* began in 1996 and was completed in 1999. It was to be the criteria upon which the future of units would be decided. Results were never officially published but were obtained through Access to Information (ATI) and prompted a media interest in March of 2000. The ATI information showed that forty-one of 120 or so units were not viable, including exactly half of the CSS units. "Only two Quebec units were on the non-viable list, 3 Fd Engr Regiment and of all things 51 Svc Battalion, which in terms of numbers, at least, was one of the largest units in the country." Colonel J Slekirk/RJJ 17 October 2013.

62. Mackay, Ibid., and, Lusk, Ibid.

63. DM/RJJ, 9 January 2014.

64. Ibid., Lusk: "Even though we were at the top of the list every year, it didn't mean anything". SQFT HQ saw things differently; MGen Forand later referred to it as a "wake-up call."

65. MacKay, Ibid.

66. Lusk, Ibid. Capt Radman replaced Capt Harris Silver Harris, RCR.

67. Maj General AG Christie CMM CD, Brig Gen Robert Alden OMM CD and Colonel Ian Fraser OMM CD, were invited to serve on Regimental Advisory Board; Colonel Angus directed RHQ to assume supervision of the Museum and the Archives, the Regimental Kit Shop was to be managed by RHQ on behalf of The Black Watch Foundation.

68. BWA. Bolton Papers Box 9. Barnett/McAlpine 8 August 2002. Bolton/RJJ September 2012; Victoria Schofield/ RJJ correspondence, 8 October 2013. The Regiment received a note of thanks from Capt Sir Alistair Aird GCVO, Private Secretary to HM Queen Elizabeth. Fort Ticonderoga memorial cairn dedication was recorded on film by the 982nd Signal Company US Army Reserve. CO 1 BW with entourage of eleven, including Lt Col Ronald (Ronnie) James fm the Ministry of Defence; "… Colonel Loudon gallantly took the credit for the band". GL/RJJ, 15 Mar 2014.

69. Ormstown Parade: DCO Maj B Bolton; Pde Adj Capt P Radman; No1 Gd Capt Barlow/MWO Carozza; No2 Gd Capt Cyr, MWO Hamel; Pipe Maj BS MacKenzie. Maj G Dover, OC B Coy left the battalion in December 1997, having served as a subaltern from 1968 and then interspacing a twenty-two year career in the British Army.

70. Colonel Jack English, *The Role of the Militia in Today's Canadian Forces* (September 2011; Canadian Defence & Foreign Affairs Institute and Canadian International Council), 14.

71. Gen Baril had been promoted from head of the Army (Land Force) to CDS 0n 17 September 1997.

72. Lusk/RJJ 9 October 2013: "Gen Baril was always a good friend of ours during those days."

73. Lt Col T Mackay/RJJ 19 October 2013.

74. Ibid. On previous exercises, it was asked: "Are we being evaluated or just camping with guns?" The RSSO, Capt Peter Radman (RCR), and the CSM, MWO Claude Hamel, supervised all field training and led extensive reviews after every segment. All participated, from private soldiers up through section commanders – the platoon felt well-prepared and confident going into the evaluation. MacKay reflected: "The approach to this task was the most detailed and methodical training I had ever participated in as a militia officer."

75. Ibid.

76. Ibid. Perhaps the highest compliment came from the enemy force, a section of Regular Force privates and corporals being forced to work a weekend in support of the Militia: "They expressed genuine admiration for the Black Watch soldiers, complimenting the aggressiveness and speed of the assault."

77. BWA. Lt Col JAG Champagne/Lusk, 8 May 1998.

78. Diary of BW involvement was placed on BW website URL. Lusk, Ibid. "BW provided Platoon into *Montérégie* (Chambly Carignan) that went door to door, saving folks isolated in their homes; with no electricity from carbon monoxide poisoning or freezing."

79. BWA Bolton Papers. BW RHQ Newsletter, June 1998.

80. BWA. Lusk correspondence; 6 May 1999 Lt Col RJK Bradford 1st Battalion BW re hosting Proven Cup winners.

81. Lusk; Bolton; Fort Drum Ex 13–16 August 1998.

82. The four graduates: 2Lt Sean Hill (joined Reg Force as a Pvt soldier); 2Lt Glenn Cowan (joined Reg Force as officer PPCLI); 2Lt Jason Barbagallo (now Military Police); 2Lt Chase Robinson (joined USMC as infantry officer, deployed to Iraq twice, retired to Toronto as an investment banker circa 2013).

83. On 18 September 1998 the MS *Black Watch*, a Norwegian cruise ship visited Montreal. Feted RHC and pipe band who performed on the main deck with the backdrop of downtown Montreal and Mont Royal.

84. Huntingdon Freedom of the City, 1998. Lt Col Lusk; DCO B Bolton; Pde Adj Capt T MacKay; No1 Gd Capt C Barlow/ WO Barron; No2 Gd Capt B Plourde/Sgt Quesnel.

85. This included military and civic exercises: air crash evac, Lakeshore General Hospital evac, door-to-door interaction with citizens to provide emergency action instructions and, Y2K drills. Lusk/RJJ 20 November 2013.

86. The occasion was the 34 Brigade Dinner at St-Jean 17 March 2001: *The Colonel Jean-Claude Dubuc Trophy* was presented by Col Préfontaine, Commander 34 Bde, an old friend of the Regiment; this was followed by a presentation on parade to the entire battalion at Bleury Street the following Tuesday. Bolton insisted Lt Col Lusk attend on both occasions and receive due recognition. Lusk commented later: "I was perturbed since I felt we deserved it while I was still commanding, but then again I did not have a lot of fans at higher HQ. We busted our butts throughout this whole viability process and I think we were at the top of the heap and they did not like that." GL/RJJ 15 March 2014.

87. *Calgary Herald* 24 September 1998; 1–2 October 1998, "Reserves: Infantry at risk"; *Montreal Gazette, Toronto Star, Globe & Mail, Calgary Herald*, et al: "Highlanders not in danger say top brass"; and, *Montreal Gazette* 16 March 1996, Buzz Bordon, "Reserve Regiments face uncertain future."

88. The padre, accompanied by his very charming Scottish wife, was not leaving. He would continue to serve the Regiment, as both mentor and historical advisor, well into the new millennium.

89. Intvws P/Majors Stevens, MacKenzie, Lt Col Bolton/RJJ, 2012–2013. Lt Col Lusk remembers it differently: " We were well-received and it was friendly … they used and still do use our armoury as an assembly place."

90. Lt Col T MacKay, 30 October 2011. A final total of ten Freedom of the City Parades 1956–2003.

91. Lusk/RJJ 24 November 2013.

92. RHC Pipe Band Rhode Island visit: 8–11 October 1999; Thistle Council Resolution, 29 October 1999.

93. Bolton, Ibid. "He tended to be direct – his forthrightness got him in a lot of trouble".

94. Maj B Cowan/RJJ July 2013; Bolton/RJJ: "Toward the end of previous term nothing was happening; the CO [McCulloch] was totally absorbed in his own education; Lusk conversely, took an interest in everything from soldiers to staff work." Lusk recalls his division of work: "Bruce did finances; I handled attendance, recruiting."

95. Black Watch 1999–2000: DCO Maj BD Bolton; OC A Capt CG Barlow; Capt TEC MacKay Adjt; Capt CR Phare, 2IC A Coy; Capt B Plourde Ops Offrs; Capt PJ Radman OC B Coy/RSS; Lt SB Nashrudi; 2/Lt T Atkinson A/Adj; 2/Lts JE Barbagallo, GR Cowan, S Hill, W Jones, Armstrong-Whitworth; O/Cdt JC Robinson; H/Capt BR Glencross; CWO PM Gannon RSM; MWO C Hamel CSM B Coy; WO JW Barron CSM A Coy; WO Cantin Ops WO; Sgt JD Anderson PipeMajor; Sgt M Carmosino; Sgt DD Desy; Sgt RM McClellan, RQ; Sgt KP O'Connor RQMS; Sgt JJ Quesnel; Sgt MF Romanauskas; Sgt AY Tasse; Sgt Thibault; Sgt MJL Voghel. Total: Lt Col; one Maj; six Capt (inclu RSS and Padre); seven Lts; one O/Cdt; four WOs; ten Sgt; nine MCpls – sixteen offrs; twenty-three senior NCOs.

96. Parade included change of Honorary Colonels: SF Angus stepped down in favour of Lt Gen Duncan McAlpine.

97. Lt Col BD Bolton/RJJ intvw 7 January 2013.

98. Ibid.

99. Bolton was the Frasers Regimental Adjutant for North America – with garrisons in Ottawa, Toronto, Kitchener, Winnipeg, Calgary, Vancouver, Washington State, Quebec City: about five to six hundred members.

100. Ibid.

101. Bolton went back to the pipe band 1980 [Cpl Art Dickson had reverted to piper], "they needed me back."

102. Interview Lt Col BD Bolton, 24 October 2012. Hereafter, Bolton.

103. Colonel Pat Kelly tutored Bolton in the combat arms. Kelly/RJJ.

104. Bolton.

105. Ibid., 15 Mar 2014

106. Ibid.

107. Bolton: "The ten pipers we got was a local decision, everyone else was cut to two. There was jealousy. Ian McCulloch persuaded Brigade to adjust musician positions and locally, we were given a separate deal. Ten pipers. McCulloch was liked at Bde HQ" Bolton's Pipe Maj, Sgt Jordie Anderson, resigned in 2000. "When I became CO I thought the band was becoming a commercial operation and I set up new rules." BWA Bolton Box 9, Memorandum 10 August 1999; Clarke/Bolton 20 June 2000.

108. *The Burns' Shoot* prize is the Robert Burns bronze statue. A splendid piece executed by Hugh Cairns in 1910; it was awarded to Pipe/Maj MacMillan Fraser at Panama Pacific Inter Exposition in San Francisco in 1915. Fraser presented it to the warrant offrs and sergeants' mess where it became the prize for the annual Regimental shooting contest conducted between the officers' and sergeants' messes. Chapman, 80.

109. Bolton., Ibid.; Dr Armour holds degrees from universities in Toronto, Edinburgh, New York and Newfoundland. He published a history of the congregation *Saints, Sinners and Scots: A History of The Church of St. Andrew and St. Paul, Montreal, 1803–2003* in which he emphasized the many connections between the church and the military, particularly the Royal Scots/Black Watch. Armour also completed the official history of The Royal Montreal Curling Club, and later became both mentor and the "CommaTsar" of this history of the Black Watch.

110. Angus/RJJ, 25 Feb 2014. "It was my choice. A gift to Duncan, because for him it was then or never. He was H/Lt Col, willing to stay in that job … I had two years to go in my appointment."

111. Canadian Peacekeeping Service Medal (CPSM). Service outside Canada for min of thirty days (not necessarily consecutive).

112. BWA. The original *Red Hackle*, 1st Issue, published by 73rd Battalion CEF 1915, is preserved in BW archives (see: Red Hackle, 73rd Battalion, and, HSB Vol XII, Page 14). The later with editorial board signatures, and menus from ship taking them to England.

113. Lusk/RJJ 22 October 2013.

114. Ibid. "I was the first Editor of *Canada's Red Hackle* and the Regimental Secretary; in the early 80s, permission was granted by The Black Watch of Scotland to use name … Support from Lt Cols V Chartier, B Bolton and Capt Andy Kerr." As at 2012, The Black Watch 150th Anniversary, twenty issues had been published, the readership numbered approximately three thousand from across Canada and around the world. Willard: "LGen McAlpine and Bruce asked me to take on *Canada's Red Hackle* magazine, I was tickled pink. I designed the publication, [did] all the typesetting". Willard edited the RH under Lt Col Lusk 2001–2011. DFW/RJJ, 24 October 2013:

115. Lusk, Ibid. Parade in Toronto, July 1989.

116. Bolton, Ibid. Bolton met with the designated CO of 1 BW, Lt Col Mike Riddell-Webster, he later visited Canada in August. MCpl Camire joined Regular Force, became officer. Four with MacKay for Op Taybridge. MWO Barron, MCPL Len Maillet; Cpl Scott.

117. Ian Bruce, *The Herald*, 16 May 2001, 13. "Imperial Black Watch reduced from Regimental strength". The year before, two RHC soldiers (MCpl Jonasz and Cpl Thompson) visited 1st Battalion BW in Germany, 3 October 2000.

118. Led by Lt Col Bolton, the party included Capt Andrew Kerr, Pipe Maj Brian MacKenzie, Cpl Bruce Ducat, Cpl Jim [, Sgt Gary Young, and Private William Booth.

119. BWA. Bolton Papers. Lt Glenn Cowan, 3 PPCLI email to Lt Col Bruce Bolton, 17 November 2001.

120. *The Telegraph*, "Colonel Johnny Bourne" 11 February 2003.

121. Colonel SF Angus, 30 March 2013.

122. Colonel SF Angus Intvw Hudson QC, Erin Ont, 2011.

123. de Chastelain was responsible for decommissioning of arms by paramilitary groups and later, as part of the Good Friday Agreement, he was the neutral adjudicator selected to oversee disarmament of Republican and Loyalists in Northern Ireland. He made an impact on the way that Britain viewed the IRA once he became involved.

124. The Freedom of City Parades: Philadelphia, 1956; Sussex, NB, 1958; Werl, Germany, 1960; Oromocto, NB, 1970; Saint John, NB, 1970; Montreal 1992; Ormstown, QC, 1997; Huntingdon, QC, 1998, Verdun, QC, 11 September 1999; and, Greater Montreal "The Mega City," 2003.

125. The Quebec Thistle Council instituted the General de Chastelain Piping Awards, presented to anyone in Quebec for being a top all-around piper and an example of the Scottish community; later became sponsored by the Black Watch. Gen AJGD de Chastelain was CDS and international diplomat; guest of honour at two St Andrew's Balls.

126. 4 May 2003 Change of Command Pde: RSM CWO C Hamel; Queens Colour Lt Haslett; Regimentl Colour Lt deCastro; Gd Commanders: No1 Capt CR Phare; No 2 Lt Barbagallo; Pde Adjt Capt Kerr; Pde DCO Maj T MacKay. The Bolton march, by Cpl McCarthy has an inscription: "Once the Pipe Maj, then Regimental Sergeant Maj, he is now our 'Millennium Colonel'!!" Bolton Papers, 23 October 2013.

127. *The chief's house has a slippery doorstep.*

128. "Later, after a surrender, Potter gave clear instructions for the tending of enemy wounded and the burial of the dead … ensured that the worst of the wounded were carried forward with the Battle Group." Supplement to *The London Gazette*, 29 June 1991; MC Maj John Potter (509149). Potter joined the British Army: as Lt in 1979, the Royal Highland Fusiliers; Lt Col 1993 appointed CO Royal Irish Regt.

129. MacKay, Ibid.

130. "The new CO was taking us on a different course, we were going to change along British Army lines, RHC traditions were to be forgotten … [the old guard] thought it was revolutionary and became unnerved." Lt Col Lusk recorded meeting re RHQ operations and structure of Red Hackle; he cited Potter: "… and frankly, my opinion is all that counts." Bolton Papers: Lusk to Angus, June 2003.

131. MacKay, Ibid.: "Potter had a Scottish accent; married to a French Canadian; Colonel Duhamel immediately appointed him."

132. Bolton, Ibid., Lt Col Potter as Deputy Commander of the District pursued a minor Mess incident and challenged RHC financial records and Mess accounts. Bolton bit his lip and chose not to offer a stinging rebuttal – *that* (he decided), would remain Regimental family business.

133. Lt Col Paul Acton, Office of the Chaplain General NDHQ / RJJ, 23 October 2013. Reverend James Peter Jones was the Presbyterian Representative of the Interfaith Committee on Canadian Military Chaplaincy (ICCMC).

He was a civilian, father of a former Black Watch officer; Lt Col Bill Fairley was an Anglican. Lt Col Sylvain Maurais. BWA. Capt Rev B Glencross, "If He preaches they will come!" Monograph. "… Brig Gen Murray Farwell responded positively to our invitation and we were blessed with the largest attendance in several years at the Church."

134. CIMIC capability, connected with Universities and Colleges, included for a new Field Engineer Regiment in Quebec City suburbs. Money was the key, LFQA received less than Atlantic and Central but more than the West.

135. Attempt in 25 January 2004 by Lt Col PN Kelly (CO, Cameron Hghrs, Ottawa) to Bolton to re-institute the Highland Winter Competition (Tent groups, toboggan pulls and route march in snow shoes, navigation etc.).

136. Former COs were normally invited to sit on the Board. By 2015, the retired commanding officers serving as members were: Colonels Angus, Ferdon, Sewell, Robertson, Klepak, Stothers, Chartier, O'Connor, Lusk, Bolton, MacKay and Plourde.

137. BWA. Bolton Papers, Box 9: CO Correspondence 2000–2005; BGen M Préfontaine/ Bolton, 22 November 2005; Bolton/ Préfontaine, 3 December 2005. Bolton's last Reunion Dinner as CO was held Annual Reunion Dinner, Saturday, 6 November 2004; the guest of honour was BGen JR Gaston Côté OMM CD, Commander, Land Force Quebec Area Headquarters. Bolton service: 1960–2005, for a total of forty-five years' service in uniform.

138. Lt Col Bolton has a wife and two daughters; he is an elder at The Church of St Andrew and St Paul; served as chairman of that church's Board of Trustees; a senior executive at the MacDonald-Stewart organization; and a moving force behind the 78th Fraser Highlanders. Commodore of the Canadian Forces Sailing Association; President (2011–13) and former Ball Chairman and President of the St Andrew's Society; Vice President of the Quebec Thistle Council, and, Chairman of the Board of Governors, Trafalgar School for Girls ('the English-Scottish school on Mount Royal slope … Many BW officers' wives and girlfriends came from Trafalgar: Pam Angus, Margaret Stavert, etc … '). Last but not least, every Saturday morning, he tutors aspiring pipers in the armoury.

139. Bolton, report to the RHC Advisory Board, F&S Club, 9 November 2013. See also: *Red Hackle* #18, 2012.

140. Pipes and Drums circa 2001; six Military members (on establishment) (Sgt CW Stevens P/Maj; Sgt RG Larman, D/Sgt Cpl AZ Marcianesi; Cpl JC McCarthy, Pipe Sgt; Cpl SD Wilson QM; Pte ML Lanno Drum Maj; 5x Military Volunteers: Cpl JV Morsani; Pte JW Firth; Pte W Kerby; twenty-four Civilian Volunteers including the Lead Drummer, GM Hay. Total: thirty-five (eleven Military; twenty-four Volunteers). BW pipers moved west and soon led bands in Simon Fraser University and several famous Police Pipe bands across Canada.
Pipes and Drums 2013: twenty Military members (on establishment): Pipe Maj MWO CW Stevens; Drum Maj MCpl ML Lanno; Pipe Sgt Sgt AJ Wilson; Drum Sgt Sgt RG Larman; Drum Sgt Mcpl H Vanden Abeele; Drum Instructor Mr M Poxon; Mcpl M Langevin; Mcpl JC McCarthy; Mcpl A Leger; Mcpl TL McLaren; Cpl A Marcianesi; Cpl S Morin; Pte S Jette; Pte D Bowes-Lyon; Pte J Whyte; Cpl T McKinnon; Cpl AC Appleby; Pte J Miller; Pte V Larocque; Pte P Limeburner. Two Military volunteers: WO T Dougherty; Cpl J Morsani. Twelve Civilian Associate Members: Mr E Brahma Mr S Lawson; Ms A McCulloch; Mr R Rice; Mr R Quinn; Mr A Walsh; Mr C MacFarlane; Mr D Dagenais; Mr R Labreche; Mr A McGuckin; R Kerr; Mr X Bolivar. Total: thirty-four (twenty-two Military; twelve Volunteers).

141. Sgt B Mckenzie/RJJ. BWA October 2013.

142. MacKenzie, Ibid. and, MWO C Stevens/RJJ 12 December 2013. "BW Instructors: Lt Col B Bolton, Julie Perron, MCpl Maxime Langevin, Daniel Dagenais, Brian Viens; MCpl Hugues Vanden Abeele (former cadet who came from this system), Cpl Tommy McKinnon, and Mike Poxon (also a former cadet who came through this system – and a champion side drummer who is constantly being sought out by the highest level pipe bands at the Grade I competition level) – joined occasionally by others from both the Regimental and Association pipe bands."

143. Ibid. Wednesday night is The Black Watch *School of Piping and Drumming* – students are taught theory and the practical side of the instruments by instructors from both the Regimental and Association pipe bands. Instruction generally runs from 1900hrs until 2100hrs.

144. MWO C Stevens/RJJ February 2013. The average calendar for regimental military parades is about ten per year: Remembrance Day Parade, reunion dinner, regimental birthday parade, church parade, Highland Games (at least two per year), St Patrick's Parade, Santa Claus Parade, and brigade parades (if any).

145. Lt Col B Bolton: "We are gradually becoming a Québécois regiment the longer we can survive.… large numbers

of French Canadians are descended from Scots … their DNA infused with Scot blood. The future of The Watch Pipe Band alone depends much on the increased support of French Canadian pipers and drummers.»

146. Kerr's military compositions: *Lt Col Robertson* (1979); *Timeless Halls* – 1980; *HMCS Huron* – 1981; *Sesquicentennial March* – 1985, *The Man from Lyons Brook* – 2007, and *Colonel Johnny Bourne* – 1987.

147. With RHC "Chetwynd turned his life around"; attended McGill Law School and Oxford. Later, Columbia Pictures. *The Apprenticeship of Duddy Kravitz* [Writers Guild of America Award]; continued to direct (*The Hanoi Hilton*).

148. RHC Hollywood contingent 2012: P/Maj CW Stevens, MCpl AJ Wilson, Sgt RG Larman, Cpl H Vanden Abeele, Alec McGuckin, MCpl JC McCarthy, M Poxon, S Lawson, Pte S Jette, A Walsh, Cpl A Leger. Afghan vets: Sgt B Dittmar, MCpl Matthew Ramsay and Cpl Alexander Reid. Featured was actor Gary Sinise "Champion for the Wounded Warrior project"; nominee Academy Award, Emmy and a Golden Globe Awards (*Forrest Gump*, *Apollo 13*, CSI NY). Lt Col Bill Fairlie/RJJ 16 December 2013: The colonel continues to play in Ottawa with RCMP band and is rector of St. Margaret's Anglican Church.

149. Tips: " Officers toast pipers first: *slanch a va, bonney pibroch* – The pipers reply *Slainte* … if time permits play *Caller Herrin* [sequal to *Black Bear*] – exit playing the first part of *Black Bear* so the *hoys* can be given." Re the BW Cadets: "I see great things in the Cadet Pipe Band … and new students attend in greater numbers." Bolton adds: "Tunes for dancers: Eightsome Reel 6/8s played spritely; Gay Gordons 4/4s …"

150. Adam, 276. See also, LAC RG24 v 1760 *Development of Defence Forces of Canada*. In 1909, fifteen thousand cadets were provided with the Ross Rifle.

151. BWA. Bolton Papers. Suzanne Bergeron/ Bruce Bolton, 09 October 2013. MWO Wilf Holdam, retired from the Black Watch to join the Air Cadet Instructors, organized the affiliation of 588 Air Cadet Squadron. In 2000, New Sqn OC, Capt Suzanne Bergeron agreed BW affiliation beneficial: "Our unit was situated in a French environment and the cadets needed an English-speaking structure." The Regiment supported Sqn for all activities, sports, [kit] for bush exercises; "Via BW Capt R Clarke … our cadets participated in a winter survival exercise with BW cadets and some BW cadets came on Sqn spring exercise … Cols Bolton and Chartier were invited as reviewing officers for special parades." Regrettably, despite active support from the Regiment, "resistance at the sponsoring committee level was high …" Bergeron's successor was not at all interested in maintaining BW affiliation.

152. Darney/RJJ, 8–12 December 2012.

153. QM Officer Capt Anthony Gucciardo, Adm Offr 2/Lt Arcuri, pipes and drums Instructor, WO Brian MacKenzie; Shooting Coach Ms Nancy Brown and Highland Dancing Instructor, Ms Heather Bremner.

154. The Black Watch (RHR) of Canada Cadet Corps 2497, 1953–2013; for Commanding Cadet Officers, see Appendix, Volume 3, page 474. VK/RJJ 3 June 2014.

155. MacKay interview 29–31 October 2012, Ottawa and Montreal. "*Show me your brand* began in the mid-nineties, introduced by Mike Blanchette or Luc Cyr". Meantime, Maj Brent Cowan claims it was he who discovered the implement and burned *RHC* into the floor. The short-lived medieval ceremony involved the Great War branding irons, the fire place, secrecy, and strong nerves. It was quietly retired about the time of the Black Watch sesquicentennial and the arrival of a graduate philosophy scholar turned adjutant. Hereafter, MacKay.

156. Ibid. "I was able to establish a good relationship with the commander. It was effective: a Scottish unit and we also spoke French – I invited BGen Barabé for a dinner of RHC honoraries, Tom MacKay was CO and host (he had been having difficulties [sic] with Barabé at the time) … nine pipers and drummers wearing *No1* dress played. The Brigadier asked: 'Expensive uniforms?' Chartier replied: 'Yes, we need help.' The result was a budget supplement for $35,000 for RHC."

157. He was transferred to the infantry, The RCR. After exciting tours as an exchange officer in England [1983–85, with The Gloustershire Regiment) and a half year in Kenya, he was given his turn as a Regular Support Staff (RSS) with a militia regiment – 2nd Battalion, The Royal New Brunswick Regiment (The North Shore Regiment, today). Regimental duty 1980–83 (2 RCR) then, 1988–91 (1 RCR) where he served as Adjutant. Then posted to Army HQ 91–97, and in 1997 seconded to Reserves as RSS officer.

158. MacKay/RJJ 6 December 2013.

159. Ibid.

160. Jeff Heinrich, *The Gazette*, Saturday, 7 May 2006, 1: "Black Watch Parade – Post 9/11 Rule Scotches Route."

161. *The Gazette*, circa 9–12 May 2006. The incident inspired a flood of letters, emails and blogs to *The Gazette*. An article by Jeff Heinrich, *The Gazette* 9 May 2006 cited Lt Col Bolton's rebuttal: "We were never defiant. We went

<u>with</u> the police. It was all discussed. They said: 'We have no problem with you going along Sherbrooke Street'. If they had said *no*, we would have gone the other route. We cannot and will not portray ourselves as going against the law." A subsequent letter from Lt Col Gordon McWhaw (CGG) questioned MacKay's actions and military discipline.

162. MacKay December 2013: "This was one instance where being an Anglo unit was beneficial because the controversy played out in the English media and 34 CBG never took notice until it was almost entirely played out. I remember receiving a phone call from the Brigade COS around mid-week after the parade … exclaimed "What did you do?!" I explained the situation and he asked me to follow up with a written report which I provided via email. I never heard a word about it from the Brigade Commander Colonel (later BGen) Lachance at the time."

163. BWA. Correspondence re HRH Prince of Wales from Capt David Basson, The Welsh Guards, Equerry to HRH The Prince of Wales to BDB 23 November 2004. HRH Charles, The Prince of Wales KG KT GCB OM AK QSO CD PC ADC. The Prince was created Prince of Wales and Earl of Chester in 1958. In 1968, The Prince of Wales installed as a Knight of the Garter; Knight of the Thistle in 1977. In June 2002 The Prince of Wales was appointed to the Order of Merit. Prince Charles appointed Colonel-in-Chief of The Black Watch, 2003. Correct imperial regimental toast: "Our Colonel-in-Chief" Vice seconds: "His Royal Highness The Prince Charles, Duke of Rothesay." Mess members reply: "The Duke of Rothesay". In 2003, a Black Watch Battlegroup deployed in Iraq (Op Telic) as part of 7th Armd Brigade based on 1st Battalion The Black Watch (RHR) supported by A Sqn The Royal Scots Dragoon Guards and Egypt Squadron, 2nd Royal Tank Regiment. They had trained in Canada in 2002 in preparation.

164. MacKay, Ibid.

165. Capt D Farnham/RJJ, 8 December 2009; 25 November 2013: "The new recruits, many of whom were completely untrained, were the exception, coming out consistently in great numbers (up to thirty) … While the planning was going on our soldiers were returning from Afghanistan [often one at a time]. The incoming CO went to meet them all."

166. Farnham/RJJ, 8 December 2009.

167. O'Connor: "The first thing the Prince said to me was to apologize for being late; as we moved through the labyrinth beneath the parade square, the Duchess twice mentioned concern that the families and troops had been kept waiting."

168. The entire parade was broadcast "live" to all messes and would become a historical DVD organized by Captains Robert Frank and Victor Knowlton, former CO of The Black Watch Cadet Corps. Noteworthy guests included the Lieutenant Governor of Quebec, the Honourable Pierre Duchesne, and the Commander of Land Forces Quebec Area, BGen JRMG Laroche OMM. The master of ceremonies was Maj (recently retired) Michael Boire CD, who kept the assembly relaxed during the demonstration's more trying moments, as the parade awaited the arrival of the Royals.

169. The great doors are adorned by a magnificent stained glass window depicting the BW Regimental Badge. A gift from Anita and Major Gary Dover.

170. Presentation of New Colours Parade as part of OP BLEURY, 10 November 2009:
CO, Lt Col TEC MacKay; DCO, Lt Col B Plourde; RSM, CWO J Barron;
OC 1 Guard, Maj CR Phare; SM 1 Gd , MWO R Unger;
OC 2 Gd, Capt A Tardiff; SM 2 Gd, MWO M Carmosino;
OC 3 Gd, Capt D Bowes-Lyon, SM 3 Gd, MWO S Campbell;
OC 4 Gd, Capt D Farnham, SM 4 Gd, WO F Mamen.

171. Bill Carlisle. He wrote later: "It is times like this when you find out who your friends are. We can certainly count the Royal Montreal Regiment amongst them. It was some of this Regiment's personnel who were providing sentries for us outside the Armoury thereby allowing the maximum number of active Black Watch to be on parade. They unfortunately took some of the brunt [of the demonstration's antics]…while performing their duty on our behalf!" <u>Cadet Corps</u>: BW Cadet Corps, Montreal; The Highland Cadet Battalion, Lachute, QC, BCS Lennoxville, QC, Kings Edgehill, Windsor, NS.

172. *The Gazette*, 11 November 2009; the Prince stressed he was sensitive to the demands on the active members of the Regiment in this time of war. This was driven home when he mentioned Corporal Jason Warren by name.

173. During walk-about, all ladies wanted pictures and affably snuggled close. "Be careful" kidded Charles, "lest this photo ruin your reputation." In another lighter moment, the Prince, attempting to take hold of the Queen's Colour, found Maj Chris Phare, would not release it. There was a split second meeting of eyes: "Salute first,

sir!" whispered Phare. Charles calmly responded with an elegant royal salute. After, Charles and the Duchess of Cornwall, retired to the Colonel's office to meet with the families of two soldiers recently lost in Afghanistan.

174. Saturday 7 November was spent "pounding the square" in practice; the reunion dinner was that night; Sunday and Monday featured additional drill on the square. A final rehearsal was held Tuesday morning, just before the Colours Parade.

175. WO G Ritchie, Sgt W Carlisle. 14 November 2013.

176. In November 2015, it was announced that upon the retirement of Lt Col C Phare, Lt Col Tom MacKay would assume command of RHC for a second tour beginning May 2016. He would continue to work at NDHQ in Ottawa and commute to Montreal.

177. Chief of Force Development in 2008; responsible for the CF Warfare Centre, in addition to strategic planning, Joint Capability Development, and CF Doctrine.

178. The Past/Present Members 1993–2013, including RHC Generals: WC Leonard; DS MacLennan; GH Sellar; WH Seamark; DA McAlpine; RP Alden; AG Christie, Brian Vernon; Recipients of The Order of Military Merit (OMM) or Order of Military Merit Member (MMM, for noncommissioned) Member: BGen RP (Bob) Alden, Col IS Fraser, Col GL Logan; Lt Cols: B Bolton, VG Chartier, TJ Kaulbach, IA Kennedy, CN McCabe, CWO RM Unger, CWO MR Kelly, and P/Maj C Stevens.

179. BW Association Membership. Canada-wide as at November 2013 was listed as: 3,237 (Capt A Kerr, BW Data Archivist, Membership, November 2013). Previous breakdown shows a steady decline; Black Watch Associations as at 2011: Atlantic Branch: twelve hundred (as at 2013, 1057), Montreal: four hundred (2013, 375: "This total includes widows and twenty adoptees at Ste Anne's Hospital", G Ritchie); Upper Canada, Kingston (65), Ottawa Branch: 200, Toronto: two hundred (2013, 174 members), Pacific: (2013, 98 members). Montreal vets Bruce Ducat and Reggie Daigle, past presidents of the Montreal Branch key worked diligently to keep Montreal Association vibrant as members retired to homes or moved away. The general advanced age of members means all Assn numbers will plummet further by 2015. See: BWA. Association Minutes; Minutes of the Association Presidents' Meeting November 5/11 (Carlisle); A Kerr, BW Data Archivist/RJJ 25 November 2013: "… some are tagged in more than one branch. FYI, we have a total database of 3237 [as at November 2013]." Data from W Carlisle; correspondence RJJ 2–3 December 2013. Hereafter, Carlisle.

180. Carlisle, Ibid.

181. GMAC Boire/RJJ 2 December 2013. When Bill Carlisle became president there were six hundred members. Carlisle: "The Lt Governor of Ontario was a HT Guest many times, the Chief of Police Draper, General Wavell, General Sir Neil Ritchie was Hon President. Sir William Mulock donated a camp to us in Wabashene which we had until 1978." Over the years TBWA donated a significant amount of money to the RHC; notably $6,000 to the museum in circa 1987; the Leopard Skin for the RHC Base Drummer in the '80's etc. See also, PP Hutchison, Canada's Black Watch, 165. Carlisle invited Colonel SF Angus to become "Patron" of TBWA before the 150th Anniversary of TBWA – that new position enabled him to ask Lt Col L Ferdon and Maj GMAC Boire to become Honorary President and VP. Previously, Angus had been appointed Honorary VP of TBWA in 1973, under W Leonard and then J Kemp, then H/President in 1990. SFA/RJJ, 2 June 14.

182. Royal Highlanders of Canada (RHC), Black Watch of Canada Foundation, and Regimental Secretary Reports and Minutes. RHC is composed of the Advisory Board and others elected to the corporation. It supports the operations of the Regimental family, for example, The Red Hackle Magazine, publications, the Kit Shop, Museum and Archives, communications, and the website. The Black Watch of Canada Foundation holds the Regiment's interests in the armoury, owns most of the artifacts of the museum and archives, manages the investment fund, and supports the components of the Regimental family through donations. Financial support has been given to the Unit for Highland uniforms (not provided by DND), awards, memorials, and pipe band instruments. The Association Branches, the Cadet Corps, The BW Scottish Arts Society, and the Ladies' Division have benefitted from this support and the Regiment is involved in community activities like those of the St. Andrew's Society of Montreal, such as the Montreal Highland Games.

183. The 5th Royal Highlanders Armoury Association [RHC] held the rights to 39.6 percent of Bleury Street armoury, now transferred to the Foundation.

184. The museum was re-opened to the public in December 2012.

185. Chapman, 4.

186. Both discovered by the Author during research – RJJ notified Colonel SF Angus. BW responded: Lt Col Bolton contacted Westmount High Principal Michael Cristofaro (a fellow elder at St Andrew and St Paul) to secure

Fisher for BW Museum. Next, on behalf of Board, he bid for Bundy's painting, securing it a year before the grand opening.

187. Col George L Logan OMM CD died suddenly 23 Dec 2013. Col SF Angus: "We have lost a loyal member of the Regiment." Logan graduated Royal Roads Military College (RRMC) / RMC 1957; commissioned into 2 RHC: "Infantry cadets in their fourth year at RMC had to apply for a regiment. No guarantee they would get what they asked for. Maj (as he then was) Gordon Sellar was the Army Staff Officer at RMC … 'recruited' me for The Black Watch. I couldn't have been more lucky!" Logan/RJJ 26 Oct 2012. In 1967, Col Logan returned to Royal Roads Military College as Commandant; after retirement, he was instrumental in raising the Upper Canada Branch of The Black Watch Association and was its first president.

188. Sewell recalls BW efforts led to good natured retorts: "Our campaign was so successful that when Jonathan Birks happened to be talking to the head of Canada Post he was bluntly told that if the Regiment got any more individuals to ask, he personally would cancel our getting a stamp!"

189. W Carlisle/RJJ, 3 December 2013: The Coin project was introduced at the original 2011 meeting of the Association Presidents. It was based on a business plan of self-financing in that each branch and RHC Inc tabled their anticipated purchase quantity. Gordon Ritchie, Keith O'Brien and Bill Carlisle went through design mods in conjunction with the other Branches. Although RHC Inc wrote-off a number of coins and distributed them free to the troops but they did not write-off the cost of the complete project; 75 percent of the coins went to the Association Branches who paid for them in full.

190. S Falconer, *An Illustrated History of the Regular Force Battalions, 1951–1970* (Fredericton: 2008); EJ Chapman, *Canada's Black Watch 1862–2012 – Legacies of Gallantry & Service* (Montreal: 2012); Tina June Caron et al, *Black Watch Historical Calendar 2012*.

191. The Black Watch Foundation and Associations supported a series of 150th Anniversary Projects: 1. Regular Force History (Falconer). 2. Publications: This History; pamphlet's and "Legacy" book by E Chapman; Women's Division *150th Anniversary Calendar*. 3. *Pipe Band CD*. 4. *The 73rd Battalion CEF History*, a CD PDF version of the unpublished manuscript by Colonel Paul Hutchison; financed by the Montreal Association. 5. The *Regimental Coin* – written off; coins given to RHC soldiers. 6. *Anniversary Portrait/Print*: Carlisle Syndicate financed the whole project (not including personal expenses and travel). Breakeven required sales of 110 mixed prints (mixed canvas and photorag); a total of eighty-four were sold. Gross profit to the Syndicate, "net loss absorbed by the syndicate members. Carlisle/RJJ 3 December 2013. 7. *Trooping of the Colours* – RHC Inc paid. 8. *Bronze colour-resin plaque* atop Hill 67 at St Martin, Normandy, overlooking Verrières Ridge. Designed by Terry Copp in consultation with BW Association. Cost split BW Association and The Canadian Battle of Normandy Foundation. 9. Support to The Montreal and Toronto Association Pipe Bands – since inception. 10. All other projects: self-financing, like the BBQ/Tattoo and the Remembrance Dinner. The unrealized bronze casting was priced by Artist "for two bronze statues and about half that for one." Colonel D O'Connor.

192. Scenes portrayed: Great War kilted BW soldiers advancing across No Man's Land; the Second World War, the campaign in the Scheldt Estuary; an inspection by the Colonel-in-Chief, Queen Elizabeth; Korea, soldiers standing at the 38th parallel marker, Peacekeeping operations in Cyprus; Balkans represented by UN blue headdress; Cold War images of manoeuvres in West Germany; culminating with a patrol scene in Afghanistan. Regimental landmarks: Armoury, Camp Gagetown, New Brunswick. The print in the Junior Ranks' Mess was presented by the Second World War veteran William Davis.

193. *MacDonald of Kinlochmoidart's Salute*, Pibroch; in memory of Donald MacDonald of Kinlochmoidart, executed for supporting Prince Charles Edward circa 1746.

194. Carlisle/RJJ, 25 November 2013.

195. Distinguished guests and Regimental family included: Mr Jacobson, US Ambassador to Canada; Patrick Holdrich, British Consul General; Andrew Parker, US Consul General; Senator Colin Kenny; Senator David Angus; Colonel Stephen and Pamela Angus; Dick Pound, former vice-president of the International Olympic Committee, and Hon Colonel CGG; BGen Richard Giguère OMM MSM; Colonel Dan O'Connor; Dr Steve MacLean, President Canadian Space Agency; Lionel Chetwynd; Colonel M Richard.

196. Jubilee Medals: Colonel Angus, Lt Cols Bolton, Plourde; and the 5 BW Assn Presidents: Carlisle, Leslie, Ritchie, Seaver, and Snow.

197. Bolton/RJJ 23 January 2014. The combined band included the Unit Pipe Band, Cadet Pipe Band, Lachute Cadet Corps P&D, and the Montreal and Toronto Association Pipe Bands.

198. Kennedy's service: The Black Watch, The Airborne Regiment, The Royal Canadian Regiment, and The Princess of Wales' Own Regiment in Kingston Ontario. Kennedy joined RHC Advisory Board in 2011.

199. Lt Col W Sewell/RJJ, 1 March 2014. Key organizers were organized by Michael Boire, Bill Carlisle, and Bruce Bolton, supported by Association Presidents Gord Ritchie, Art Snow, Terry Seaver, and Dave. P/Maj Stevens was the coordinator for all the Bands – active, MBWA & TBWA. "Each branch Prez organized transport options for their own gang." The event was coordinated by Lt Col Bill Sewell. Mike Boire secured the Base Kingston Senior NCO's Mess on base. Lt Col Bolton then suggested tying in with the tattoo at Fort Henry.

200. At Vimy the Piper's Lament was replaced completely by an aboriginal who recited a prayer and performed a Métis chant in lieu.

201. RH. RJ Jarymowycz, 29 October, "2011 Black Watch Repeats Triumph in Brigade March and Shoot Competition"; also, *Canada's Red Hackle* no. 18, Winter 2012.

202. The team was led by Sergeant Alexandre Sicard; their competitors were Canadian Grenadiers Guards (CGG), Les Fusiliers Mont-Royal, (FMR), 4e Battalion, Royal 22e Régiment (Chateauguay), the 6e Battalion, Royal 22e Régiment (the Van Doos), The Royal Montreal Regiment (RMR), and Le Régiment de Maisonneuve (RdeM). Weapons: 2x C9 machine guns, 2x C7 rifles with M203 grenade launchers and 4x C7s; in addition to the section radio, navigation equipment, rations, GPS and standard gear.

203. RSS WO PS Brasseur, Sgt D Batchelor and the RSM plus dozen senior and junior NCOs like Sgts Dittmar (one tour), Anderson (two) and Snoddon (with Bosnia and three tours in Afghanistan), MCpl Ramsey, Selika one each.

204. The recce and traces were conducted by WO Brasseur and Lt Baumans, who was engaged in completing his Masters in Political Science at l'Université de Montréal. Exercise *GP2* (19–21 October 2012) part of Operation *Hurricane*.

205. Baumans/RJJ, BWA 12 October, 6 May 2013.

206. Ibid.

207. Ibid.

208. Ibid., Captains L Baumans and D Farnham/RJJ, BWA 12 October 2012.

209. Plourde/RJJ 17 December 2013: "Following my initial visit in 2011 with HCol O'Connor, the CO 1-111th Lt Col Mike Wegscheider and I agreed to plan a reciprocal joint training between our units …"

210. WO PS Brasseur/RJJ 26 July 2013; twenty-four BW, three officers: Lts LM Baumans, JK Hinkson, H Maghakian.

211. Plourde/RJJ 20 September 2012.

212. See detailed articles on each March and Shoot competition 2011, 2012 in Red Hackles of same year. Batchelor had been mainly responsible for crafting the previous 2012 Brigade competition.

213. See RH, *Third Year in a row*: "A Hat trick" 2013; Intvw Sgt Batchelor 25 February 2013.BW team comprised MCpls Best, Ursine, Ciccone, Ptes Ghuniem, Lezet, Guenole, Kanaan, and three "spares"; of whom 2 went to Farnham and were key in providing replenishment and dry clothing at the end of the initial event.

214. Batchelor, Ibid. " We were the only unpenalized team … At the end we were completely bagged but with a little bit of a push, we ran most of the last leg to finish line. The guys were on the edge of puking – I staggered the run/walk rate. It worked: I'd pick a reference and say, *next tree or next pole as interim objectives*; not just the finish line … Managing guys on move. Everyone sucked it up but we had to ensure we finished at same rate and together. MCpl Best was the 2ic."

215. Teams: 6 teams: all Inf units and 4 Van Doos [BW, FMR, RdeMais, RMR, CGG, 6 R22R]Order of finish: BW, FMR, CGG [RMR last] Difficult for militia unit; who will volunteer after Sgt Batchelor leaves. No reps cus no other COs present – this year none. "We should change the name of trophy …" Lt Col Langlais, RMR "Practice, visualizing , managing and max effort by team". The veterans noticed something else: "Frankly our infantry skills had diminished just two years after Afghanistan … but we were well-rounded, and practised."

216. "The Hippopotamus Song" by Flanders and Swann, 1958.

217. Canadian Public Safety Minister, the Honourable Vic Toews, Montreal 10 January 2013.

218. Greg Gransden, Samantha Fornari, "The Black Watch in Afghanistan" a collection of interviews with Black Watch veterans; unpublished, 2013. Hereafter, Gransden. Sgt Bjorn Dittmar/Greg Gransden Interview, aural history, *The BW in Afghanistan*; Dittmar, 72.

219. Regular forces arrived in Kandahar during January–February 2002. In March 2002, three PPCLI snipers fought alongside US Army units during Op *Anaconda* – first time since Korea that Canadian soldiers relieved US

troops in combat. Canadian forces also undertook Ops *Harpoon, Mountain Thrust* and fought in the Battle of Panjwai'i. The Canadian BG came under NATO command at the end of July, and the 1 RCR Battle Group replaced the PPCLI. Canadians launched the complex Op *Medusa* in September 2006.

220. MacKay/RJJ 31 October 2012.

221. Ibid.

222. Ibid. "No one in the Regular Force loses a job, forced out the door at the end of an assignment; that's what happens when you say goodbye to Class B call-outs. No rent cheque, bills unpaid … of course they realize the risk – still, it is a hardship. It is traumatic at times to be a reservist employed by the CF."

223. Colonel P Kelly MSM, CD Dir Reserves Canada, correspondence RJJ 5–8 November 2013. Hereafter, Kelly.

224. Ibid.

225. Kelly, Ibid. "… CIMIC/PSYOPS, the All Source Intelligence Centre (ASIC) and Convoy Escort Troop were the nucleus of organizations that were Reserve heavy. I know of at least 2 rotations where the Convoy Escort Troop (Platoon if it was Inf heavy) were 100 percent Reserve … The Senior Reserve Officers in theatre were BGen's serving in ISAF/NTM-A on various rotations … at the Colonel level 50 percent of the Colonel positions were filled by Reservists largely as Advisors and Div HQ staff in multi-national staffs. The team teaching at the Command and Staff College in Kabul was 100 percent Reserve."

226. For example, WO Collins, Sgt Desy and Cpl Maillet all served in the same section in Bosnia; WO Snoddon, Sgt Batchelor, Sgt Dittmar found it easier to get back to work, though not necessarily with a "militia mindset".

227. MacKay, 29 October 2013.

228. BW Assn Presidents G Ritchie, W Carlisle, A Snow and, RSM Unger interviews/RJJ, November– February 2012–2013. Ritchie: "We set up a rota – every association sent a package to every soldier in theatre, even the East Coast Branch got involved. Every six weeks … each group was taken care of. We created a fund and kept those monies only for troops in the field." *Carlisle Report*: "… it is my pleasure to advise that your shipment of seven comfort packages to each of these soldiers in Afghanistan went out today [before Xmas]. Each package included energy bars, sun screen, lip balm, cookies, candy, gum, *handi-wipes*, a paperback book and the inevitable rolls of toilet paper."

229. Kelly and the CO's older brother, Andrew MacKay had a history of service in the Black Watch: "As the Colour Casing NCO for the Queen Mother's Parade in 1987 I was responsible to handle the colours before they were unfurled on parade. In the lead-up practice MCpl Quesnel and I decided to work over the Colour Officers who were practising with grey blankets … [before practice] We soaked the blankets in water which significantly increased their weight. Imagine the look of concern on young Lt Andrew MacKay's face when he realized he would be practising a Royal Salute with a blanket that now weighed in excess of 20lbs … young Lt MacKay shook uncontrollably during the march past with the colours lowered, it took days for the muscles in his arm to loosen up. All's well that ends well – we eventually stood up on behalf of each other at our respective weddings." Kelly/RJJ, 12 December 2012.

230. MacKay: "It was my good fortune to spend threeyears in Ottawa rebuilding my reputation." His main project was a praised study: "Examine and Rationalize the Number of Reservists working in the Army"; responsible with coordinating all activities of Army and Police with NATO. He was given the temp rank of full colonel and worked out of the *KAIA North ISAF Military Facility* directly beside King Abdulaziz International Airport (KAIA). About 950 Canadians were deployed as part of the International Security Assistance Force (ISAF). PM Harper announced at the NATO Summit that he would terminate the CF's combat role in 2012 but advised that an undisclosed cadre would remain in Afghanistan to assist training and mentorship programmes for Afghan National Army until 2014.

231. Maj Gen David Fraser, BG Commander in 2006, Regional Command, Southern Afghanistan, correspondence/ RJJ 1 November 2013. "The banter before any mission is the same; however, demanding and progressive training weeds out the unfit in both camps leaving one force ready for the challenges of the mission. During the mission, any mission, there are no regiments or corps in combat." Hereafter, MGen Fraser.

232. BWA. Bolton Papers 2002. Cowan was an original RHC officer cadet, graduated to Lt before joining Reg Force. Glenn would not have had any RHC soldiers in his PPCLI platoon in Afghanistan in 2002 (probably did not have any Reservists at all). He did serve as an instructor at the Infantry School in Gagetown where he was Course Officer to a few RHC officers (some of whom he had recruited himself before departing RHC for the Reg Force).

233. MGen D Fraser, Ibid.

234. Rudyard Kipling, Departmental Ditties and Other Verses (London: 1886).

235. Colonel David Patterson, Dir Army Reserves/RJJ, 3 November 2013.

236. MGen D Fraser, Ibid.

237. Lt Gen LD Holder, US Army/RJJ 2008. The theatre was full of ARMS (autonomous robot military systems); UGCV (unmanned ground combat vehicle); SWORD (special weapons observation reconnaissance detection system).

238. Two Canadian soldiers (Corporal Jason Warren RHC; Cpl Frank Gomez PPCLI) were killed, eight wounded.

239. MGen Fraser, Ibid.

240. War CAS: 158 Canadian soldiers died in the Afghanistan war. 2,047 were wounded. Of the KIA: 123 were due to hostile circumstances, including ninety-five due to IED or landmines, twenty-one due to Rocket Propelled Grenade (RPG), small arms or mortar fire, eleven due to suicide bomb attacks, and one died falling from a high ground position on a cliff during a firefight. The CF lost over thirty-four vehicles and 359 were damaged in Afghanistan. The Army lost thirteen LAV III APCs and another 159 were damaged by roadside bombs or enemy fires. At least three Leopard C2 tanks were destroyed and fifteen were damaged; a dozen unspecified trucks were damaged and seven were destroyed. A number of trailers were destroyed during various rocket attacks against Kandahar International Airport.

241. BWA Adj 3000-1 (Ops) 29 July 2006; "Funeral and Interment, Cpl Warren JP V43921011"Gazette 3–5 August 2006. Cpl Leroux from NB was killed with 1 RHC circa 1964–69 Cyprus – Jason Warren was first battle cas since the Second World War. Dr Topping: "I imagine how the 1st Battalion felt during the Second World War – when dozens were lost … Maj Phare was wonderful with [Warren] family in a very trying time." MacKay: "The BOR learned key lessons, wills, clear indication of death benefits proved to be important items." See also, Gazette 3–5 August 2006.

242. MacKay, 29 October 2013: "They were quite emotional … ignored the CDS when he called them over … I had to intervene to get them to go and listen to Gen Hillier. I don't think they were deliberate … they were simply caught up in their grief for their friend."

243. Capt D Farnham, 128. As adjutant, and not yet a veteran he was quickly made aware: "…one of them [BW soldiers] came to me one day and they said 'they got Corporal Warren' who I'd never met. I realized this was the friend of one of my instructors. I was [suddenly] very cognizant of how serious the situation was."

244. Capt D Farnham/RJJ, 7 November 2013; Farnham was also responsible for the CIMIC activities in and around KAF. This involved working with the RAF who controlled the area around the airfield; he was the CIMIC operator in Maywand District for his final month. "I caught the 'watermelon man' and saved Canada $1000 … it's a long story."

245. Capt Rod DeCastro/RJJ, 21 November 2013

246. Plourde/RJJ, 12 November 2013. "The nature of the international community involvement in Afghanistan was also a source of endless "turf war". ANSF (in my case, police) training … programmes fm UN, US (State department and Enduring Freedom), Specific yet uncoordinated national programmes for each province (Canada – Kandahar; UK – Helmand; Netherlands – Uruzgan). [They] often competed with each other. Same with the development projects."

247. WO Snoddon.

248. South Afghanistan: US, UK, NL, CA, RO, Denmark; UN or national/international NGO.

249. The Afghan National Army (ANA) National Military Command Centre; The Afghan Ground Forces Command; The National Police Coordination Centre; and The Kabul City Police Centre. Approx. 120 military and civilian pers from seven different nations including Canada, US, Italy, Spain, Germany, Croatia and Turkey.

250. MacKay/RJJ, 3 November 2013.

251. "A mountain never meets a mountain, but a man meets a man"; Ceud mìle fàilte: A hundred thousand welcomes!

252. Colonel David Patterson, Director Army Reserve, Army HQ/RJJ, 3 November 2013. Patterson, who commanded a Militia Artillery Regiment, served as Director Reserve Training CACSC, Kingston; then appointed Commander Task Force Addis Ababa, Op AUGURAL IN Ethiopia, and The Sudan; later appointed Executive Officer to Deputy Commanding General – Ops, 10th Mtn Div (Light), 2010–2011 at Kandahar. He well understands both sides of the Canadian Army. He added: "Of course, the [Regular–Reserve] relationship evolved over the ten year commitment and particularly after 2006 and the Kandahar deployment."

253. MCpl Matthew Ramsay; Sgt Brian Hill; Cpl Matthew Anderton.

254. The Imperials: Regimental uniforms worn by pipe bands but now a singular band uniform is being introduced. All soldiers wear same uniforms in Regiment of Scotland; only Balmorals tell them apart; Hackle only in combat uniform with the Balmoral, Glengarry worn with Trews; Kilts: 3rd Scots wear the Government No #1A Tartan vs Govt #1 in Cda, it is lighter than the RHC Black Watch Tartan. Pipe Maj Stevens as at 6 February 2013.

255. Title: The Black Watch, 3rd Battalion, The Royal Regiment of Scotland (3 SCOTS). The Battalion Headquarters, The Royal Regiment of Scotland HQ is in Inverness at Fort George. The 7th Battalion, The Royal Regiment of Scotland is located at Queen's Barracks, Dunkeld Road, Perth. In 2014 The Black Watch Museum at Balhousie Castle was renamed The Black Watch Castle and Museum.

256. MCpl (Sgt) D Batchelor/RJJ, 2–4 November 2013; 1 December 2013.

257. Ibid.

258. Ibid.

259. Ibid. "My team was outstanding. I had a good friend of mine from the RMR as my 2IC and another friend from the R de MAIS. These two guys had previous Afghanistan tours which gave us an outstanding experience level when it came to our jobs. We also had a Cpl from the FUS de SHER that was a young kid with little experience but he sure learned a lot on that tour." 2009 Tour: Sgt Bjorn Dittmar (RHC), MCpl Devin Batchelor (RHC), Cpl Tom Meisner (RHC), Cpl Lennard Maillet (RHC), Cpl Etienne Comtois (R de MAIS).

260. 2011 Tour: Sgt Devin Batchelor, MCpl Brent McNair (RMR), Cpl Piotr Burcew (R de MAIS), Cpl Ian Luc-Turgeon (SHER FUS).

261. WO MM Snoddon/RJJ, 3 November 2013. Tours: Kandahar, Afghanistan July 2007 – March 2008. Task Force 03–07. Task Force Kandahar Psychological Operation Unit. Tactical PSYOPS Team 2ic; Kandahar, Afghanistan March 2009 – October 2009; Task Force 01–09. Task Force Kandahar Psychological Operation Unit. Tactical PSYOPS Team Leader; Kandahar, Afghanistan November 2010 – July 2011. Task Force 03–10. Task Force Kandahar Civil Military Cooperation (CIMIC) Unit. Tactical CIMIC Operator.

262. Snoddon / RJJ 6 December 2013

263. Snoddon, Ibid. Two years after his last tour in Kandahar WO Snoddon found himself in another distant barren spot, Mauritania in Western Sahara working for Canadian engineering giant SNC-Lavalin. In 2014, Snoddon was commissioned as a Black Watch officer.

264. WO S Cyr/RJJ, 5 November 2013. Cyr joined BW in December 1998. Five tours: NATO Bosnia 2001; NATO Afghanistan 2001; UN Congo 2003; NATO Bosnia 2004; NATO Afghanistan 2008. CDS Commendation 2008 and 2011. Posted, USMC trg school at Twenty-nine Palms, California 2011–2014. Her goal: "breaking down the barrier of gender stereotypes."

265. Sgt KEJ Anderson/RJJ Correspondence 6–7 December 2013.

266. Anderson, Ibid. In 2013 Sgt Anderson left the Black Watch and transferred to the Regular Force, reverting to the rank of Corporal, posted to New Brunswick, CFB Gagetown where she graduated from the Canadian Forces School of Military Engineering as a Water, Fuel, Environment Technician (WFE Tech).

267. Colonel D Patterson, Director Army Reserve Army HQ, 2 November 2013.

268. The Prime Minister's Office – Communications/RHC, 9 May 2014. Process for the creation of Theatre Honours is the same for all types of Battle Honours – CF began determined battle nomenclature (theatres, campaigns, battles, etc.) in order to create the specific Battle Honours for specific conflicts. Afterward, the eligibility criteria for awarding each of those honours was determined. Each step required approval by the Chief of the Defence Staff, then the Governor General, the final authority for the creation of Battle Honours and the eligibility criteria for each. The third step in the process is the allocation of the Battle Honours to individual Canadian Armed Forces units by the Chief of the Defence Staff. Afghanistan involved twelve years, more than forty thousand soldiers, sailors, airmen and airwomen served in the South-West Asia region in the largest deployment of Canadian troops since the Second World War.

269. Save for the initial deployment of PPLCI in November 2001. The Army Reserve, along with the Air and NAVRES comprised approximately 20 percent of each rotation through Afghanistan in every manner of unit and HQ as well as individual augmentees.

270. Kelly, Ibid.

271. Lt Col B Plourde interview RJJ, Montreal, 30 April 2013. Hereafter, Plourde.

272. Ibid., "Afghanistan was my coming of age, [although] after Bosnia I felt confident I could deploy in an operational environment and be respected, not considered an untrained reservist. Could I work in a war zone and do a professional job? After Bosnia and Congo, I was confident I could – and proved it."

273. Including the US Meritorious Service Medal (MSM); BWA. "U.S. Awards to foreign military personnel", 11 December 2006, para 1–38. <u>Plourde decorations</u>: CD2; Peacekeeping medal; NATO (Ex Yugoslavia); UN: DR Congo; GCS-SWA (Afghanistan) et al. <u>Operational Deployments</u>: Op Unique (1991/1992) – CFB Goose Bay Airfield Security Cyo 2 I/C vs (Canadian aboriginal protest vs NATO low level flying training over Labrador); Op Palladium 11 (2001/2002);- Bosnia Herzegovina – Joint Military affairs Branch, Snr Ln O BiH Armed Forces, South West Bosnia; Op Crocodile (2004/2005) , DR Congo – Chief of staff Sector 2 (Orientale & Maniema Provinces); Op Athena (2008/2009) ISAF Regional Command South, DComd RPAC South (Op Enduring Freedom).

274. Plourde, Ibid. In his Farnham office Plourde displayed the Regimental Saltire from Bosnia to the Congo: "The Van Doos are not the only unit in this province."

275. Glencross, Ibid., Plourde recalled: "I was able to establish a good relationship with the commander: we were a Highland unit but we also spoke French – I invited BGen Barabé for a dinner of BW Honoraries … Tom MacKay was CO (he had been having *difficulties* [sic] with Barabé of the time) … H/Lt Col Vic Chartier sat next to the Brigadier." The piping was inspired: 9 pipers and drummers in No1 uniform with feather bonnets.

276. Lt Col B Plourde/RJJ, 6 November 2013.

277. Plourde: "This Regiment is a monster of compartementization [sic] – all of a sudden we have young families, kids, I wanted to bring in more families to events, to dinners … My sons wore Highland formal wear at the 2012 Highland Dinner."

278. Kelly, Ibid.

279. Plourde, Ibid.

280. "I had been told from day-one he was a delegator, that was his reputation in the Regular Force RHC..[but] He was decisive when required – he was clever, sly, yet diplomatic … he had a talent to use those around him." Bolton, Ibid. Also, Buzz Burdon, "Lt Gen D McAlpine", Special to *The Globe and Mail*, March 24, 2010.

281. BWA. McAlpine Pers File; also, Interview McAlpine/RJJ April 2009. SF Angus/RJJ, 25 Feb 2014: " Even though he was failing fast, especially after Bonnie died, and he died just after agreeing to be renewed for a third term, it was a good decision and he was good for the Regiment."

282. Bolton and Burdon, Ibid.

283. The *Last Post Fund Organization* was founded in 1909. Its mission is to bury Canadian veterans who are indigent with a dignified funeral and burial. The millennium definition of "Veteran" by DND is <u>anyone</u> completing <u>basic training</u> and honourably discharged.

284. Lt Col CN McCabe: NNS Highlanders; 28th Light Anti-Aircraft Regt; The Pictou Highlanders/Nova Scotia Highlanders. Black Watch: 1st, 2nd Battalions and Depot; 2 RCR October Crisis; DCO, 3 RCR Cyprus; Staff, SSF HQ; War Plans Offr G3 Div, Central Army Gp HQ, Heidelberg 1979; NDHQ 1982; transfer to Reserve Force, Class "B" as Commandant, Connaught Ranges; Class B service 1992–1997. Hon Lt Col RHC 2011.

285. Capt Rev R Topping/RJJ Interviews/Correspondence 23 October 2012; 5, 30 November 2012.

286. Ibid., and, BWA. Pers File, Capt Rev E Cecil Royle, 6 February 1945. Topping: "All these intersections in cultural Montreal … A measure of Scottish modesty, it is unseemly to brag from the John Knox tradition, John Calvin who was buried without a marker at his request."

287. Ibid. Despite a bilingual CF Headquarters, "All the meetings were in French; they asked if I understood. I said 'No'. They carried on regardless … They could have made life easier …"

288. Mackay, Ibid.

289. Ibid. "John [Barron] cared little re saluting etc.; at the internment of Cpl Jason Warren, the CDS Gen Hillier was there, the RSM blew by, no salute."

290. Bolton/RJJ, 2 January 2013.

291. CWO R Unger/RJJ July 2013, Hereafter, Unger.

292. Ibid.

293. See preface: James Laver, *British Military Uniforms* (Penguin:1948)

294. Kaulbach, 8 Jan 14. "Dress was standardized in 1965 Dress Instructions so that all Regular Army units wore one-inch pips with light puttees and kilt but dark puttees with battle dress trousers."

295. Ibid.

296. RSM Unger and P/Maj Stevens noted: "Everyone wears Greens in Montreal; The Grenadier Guards had to borrow Reds from the Ceremonial Guard at Parliament Hill to complete a full parade." The average Canadian militia unit sometimes manages to put members of the colour guard into their own particular unit garb.

297. DeCastro, Ibid.

298. BGen Cox, Ibid.

299. By the end of the century, a Hair Sporran ("a dying art") cost £140; a Leather Sporran £27. Silk Sashes were £150 in 1986, by 1996 they varied from £300 to £220 [$985 to $725 in 2013 C$]. Green Coatees were $1000, Trews $200, by the millennium, kilts started at £350 [$1,100 2013 C$] but soon "went through the roof as wool, and everything else multiplied in cost".

300. By 2015, this reserve trove had dwindled to approximately fifty sets "but these no longer fit 2015 sized soldiers." Lt Col B Bolton, 7 November 2015.

301. Uniform Purchases for the Presentation of Colours in November of 2009: $46,604.65; Uniform Purchases for the 150th Anniversary $121,871.80 and of course, on-going.

302. From top to bottom: Glengarry, Blue Balmoral, Fawn Balmoral, Coatee, Waistcoat, Mess Jacket (Scarlet and White for summer), sweater, dirk belt, cloth boards and *Pips*, badges, buttons, buckles, white gloves, shirt, wing collar, black box tie, Sash, cross Belt, white waist belt and buckle, gold tassels, kilt rosettes, stable belt, sporrans (hair and leather), Trews, Kilt, garter flashes, diced hose, lovat hose, hosetops, spats, brogues, evening shoes; Skean Dhu, Claymore. Garrison dress included options for CF shirts, and a complete variation of CF gear for dry, wet and winter weather, including gym dress, shoes and combat boots. Exercises required helmets, rucksacks and (usually used temporarily from the QM) parkas, artic gloves, mukluks and snow shoes. Accessories included scarves, gloves, under items, socks, and *Balaclava*. And the sine qua non of Black Watch dress – a Red Hackle!

303. The Cantlie tartan dates to the Great War when the 42nd found itself without BW Government Sett. Cantlie had Patton's mills in Sherbrooke produce the hunting tartan for kilts and glengarries. Lt Col Sewell/RJJ 30 November 2013: "The 16oz fabric came from the Imperials … the RHC used fabric mills in Sherbrooke, probably Patton, Clyen & Tinker or a company owned by a chap called Pick." See also, A Kellett, *Canadian Army Messes*, Ibid., *passim*.

304. BWA. HSB XII, circa 192.

305. Lt Col Bill Sewell recalls: "Dan, Vic and I strongly recommended a simple parade … we then found out it was to be a Trooping. Our mouths dropped." Parade 29 September 2012, Fletchers Field. Sewell/RJJ 12 September 2013.

306. Plourde/ BW BOR records as at 25 November 2013 re 150th Anniversary Trooping, 29 September 2012: Total eighty-eight troops; twenty-six Pipes & Drums: 114. BW Veterans fm Associations mainly (Mtl and Ont) were about seventy-five; pipes and drums were augmented by Toronto & Mtl Association pipes and drums (twenty); *la musique des FMR* (thirty). Plourde: "Cadets were limited but present. … around fifty from all cadets corps; I think that it safe to [est] a 350-ish attendance on parade, all included."

307. Sewell: "As I watched the Trooping I thought 'Well, Bruno's luck has finally run out' – then I saw the evening TV news and thought, 'Gee, I guess it hasn't.'"

308. Guest of honour, Brigadier General JR Giguère, OMM, MSM, CD; Commander Land Force Quebec Area.

309. DHH. Correspondence Ibid., Plourde/DHH 2011–2012; and, Ken Reynolds / RJJ Sept 2012; 13 March 2014. On 28 May 1812, new Bns created when Prevost ordered the draft of two thousand militia; chosen by "Draw", singles eighteen to thirty year olds. See, Volume 1, Part 1 Battle of Chateauguay / First Honours.

310. Lt Col John Fletcher, Ibid, (see: Parts 1 and 3) re the Montreal Volunteers Rifles and the Highland Rifle Company. The 2012 St Andrew's Ball celebrated 177 years of Scottish heritage in Montreal; the Society counting back to 1835.

311. See *Ottawa Citizen*, 12 August 2013, "DND Officials Resisted Extending Battle Honours System to the War of 1812" – the final historical awards/connections (and rationale) were confusing to regimental historians.

312. *Examine the past, examine the present, examine the future.*

313. In the fall of 2013, Lt Col Plourde was appointed CO of 2e *Groupe de Patrouille des Rangers Canadiens* (2 CRPG). The 2 Canadian Rangers Patrol Gp is responsible for Northern Quebec, providing patrols for national-security and public-safety missions in sparsely populated northern / isolated parts of Quebec – areas not conveniently covered by other parts of CF. Many of the younger Canadian Rangers are fluently bilingual or trilingual (Inuktitut, French, English, Cree; Montagnais) and assist their elders in communicating with visitors from the south.

314. Plourde was one of the few who could stand up to visiting staff officers, often skeptical re the ability of reservist COs: "What have you done operationally Lt Col?" Plourde would counter: "I've deployed into Bosnia and

the Congo and got shot at in Afghanistan, so have my soldiers – do you have that experience?" As an example of the Black Watch "Village legacy", in 1939–41, seventy-six men from a 5x3 city block area of Point St Charles joined RHC.

315. Who has not served cannot command.
316. General Walter John Natynczyk CMM, MSC, CD, former CDS was the popular GoH at the HCol's Dining-In on the night before. November 2013: Lt Col Phare's first St Andrew's Ball as CO featured: Ms Karyn Brooks, senior vice-president of Bell – the first woman guest of honour for the Ball in history! The Black Watch Officers filled three tables. "The night's best photo was five former and current CO's: O'Connor, Bolton, MacKay, Plourde and Chris Phare." MacKay/RJJ, 1 December 2013.
317. Phare/RJJ, May 2013. "Some of our junior officers were scoundrels and terrors yet beloved by the men. The CO's door still has indents from *BB* pellets after a subbies' dinner. Realizing what they had done, the culprits tried to disguise it with tooth paste and brown felt markers." Re London: Phare: The *Tor Scots* may have changed their name to 'Queen Mother's Own' shortly after."
318. Lt Col Phare retired as CO 1 May 2016. He was succeeded by Lt Col Tom MacKay who returned for a second tour. Tom, still working in NDHQ Ottawa, and now a proud father, would commute to command the battalion.
319. Michel Boyer, *Remembrance Day at McGill*: CJAD News, 11 November 2013, *CJAD Radio Blog*; reported on air.
320. *What I have written, I have written*; Pilate, John 19:22. There is a tradition in Scotland that Pontius Pilate was born in Fortingall, a small village in the Perthshire Highlands.
321. Readers are introduced to Lieutenant Colonel Phare and his command earlier in this book. The treatment of his time as CO here does not aim to repeat this, but rather to expand on elements that were beyond the scope and time frame of Lieutenant Colonel Jarymowycz's writing.
322. Lieutenant Colonel Phare interview with Alexander McGuckin, 27 January 2021
323. Ibid.
324. "BW O Plan, 2014-2015" Document provided by Lieutenant Colonel Phare to the Alexander McGuckin.
325. Lt Col Phare interview with Alexander McGuckin, 27 January 2021
326. Ibid.
327. Ibid.
328. Ibid.
329. Ibid.
330. Ibid.
331. Ibid.
332. *Canada's Red Hackle*, Fall 2013, 7.
333. *Canada's Red Hackle*, Spring 2014, 31
334. Lt Col Phare interview with Alexander McGuckin, 27 January 2021
335. Ibid.
336. *Canada's Red Hackle*, July 2016, 14–15.
337. Ibid.
338. Ibid.
339. The first was Lt Col Bruce D. Bolton, MMM, CD; the third would be Lt Col Bruno Plourde, CD, whose second term would follow Lt Col MacKay.
340. Col MacKay, interview with Alexander McGuckin, 25 January 2021.
341. Ibid.
342. Ibid.
343. *Canada's Red Hackle*, March 2017, pp. 7.
344. Col MacKay, interview with Alexander McGuckin, 25 January 2021
345. Ibid.
346. Ibid.
347. Ibid.
348. *Canada's Red Hackle*, July 2017, 12–13
349. City of Montreal Report on Floods, 10.
350. Col Mackay interview with Alexander McGuckin, 25 January 2021
351. Ibid.

352. Ibid.

353. Ibid.

354. Photos of the parade were featured in 45e Nord, a military-friendly publication, and circulated widely on social media.

355. *Canada's Red Hackle*, July 2017, 26.

356. Ibid.

357. Ibid.

358. Col MacKay interview with Alexander McGuckin

359. Col Mackay later became the Commander of 33 Brigade in Ottawa.

360. Lt Col Plourde correspondence with Alexander McGuckin, January 2021

361. *Canada's Red Hackle*, March 2019, 7.

362. Lt Col Plourde correspondence with Alexander McGuckin, January 2021

363. Lt Col Plourde interview with Alexander McGuckin, 25 January 2021

364. *Canada's Red Hackle*, March 2019, 7.

365. Government of Canada Op Lentus Overview, https://www.canada.ca/en/department-national-defence/services/operations/military-operations/current-operations/operation-lentus.html

366. Lt Col Plourde interview with Alexander McGuckin, 25 January 2021

367. *Canada's Red Hackle*, August 2018, 6.

368. Col Bolton interview with Alexander McGuckin, 12 February 2021

369. Ibid.

370. *Canada's Red Hackle*, January 2020, 35.

371. *Montreal Gazette*, 30 April 2020. https://montrealgazette.com/news/local-news/100-per-cent-infection-rate-at-laval-long-term-care-residence

372. *Canada's Red Hackle*, December 2020, 17. Note: They did return, in September 2021, visiting staff and residents.

373. Lt-Col Plourde, correspondence with Alexander McGuckin, January 2021

374. Ibid.

375. Ibid.

Part VI

Illustrations

St Hubert Air Base, June 1974. The Queen Mother as Col-in-Chief presents the new Queen's Colour to RHC.

Top left: HM inspects with LCol Len Ferdon, passing a row of officers that includes Majors A Malashenko and Hal Klepak (3rd and 2nd from right).

Top right, HM presents the Queen's Colour before a large "invitation only" crowd.

Above: CDS, war hero, General Jacques Dextraze CC CMM CBE DSO CD affectionately known to his soldiers first as "JADEX" guest at the Reunion Dinner, 1974. L to R: LCol L Ferdon, Col J Bourne, CDS, Lt Col JW Sharp and the dauphin, Major Bill Sewell.

Left: S/Sgt John Mitchell (left), a Regimental stalwart famous for his delightful humour. Drummer Sgt Everett McIntosh (right).

The Grizzly was available to Black Watch for training circa 1980s but never enough. Weekend exercises were a smorgasbord of what was available.

A mini Combat Team gathers at CFB Valcartier: Royal Canadian Hussars in Cougars, Black Watch in M113s, all borrowed from Regular stocks.

The Watch in more traditional style. Capt Brent Cowan's Tac CP as his company digs in beside the Route Cadieux in Valcartier.

A rifle platoon pauses in CFB Petawawa during a route march. The yellow appendages on weapons are *BFA*s ("Blank Firing Attachments") designed to allow a little realism ... or at least fun into weekend manoeuvres.

Right: The Queen Mum chats with a Black Watch soldier on her 8 July 1989 visit to Queen's Park, Toronto. The composite guard combined RHC and The Toronto Scottish. On the Queen Mum's left is the guard commander, Capt Gordon Lusk CD.

Below: Freedom of the City 1992; the Regiment parades through the centre of Montreal carrying the City Flag, escorted by soldiers in Great War and WWII uniforms.

Top left: Pipers right to left. Eric Booth, Dean Newton, and Ken Whitehall (who would become a Regular Force pipe-major).

Middle left: Natty summer togs: Pipe-Major Bruce Bolton MMM, Cpl Rob McLellan, Pipers Tim Mundy, Eric Booth, Dean Mitchell and Pipe-Sergeants Dan Smith and Andrew Kerr in Kentville, Nova Scotia, summer 1983.

Bottom: 5 July 1981, Fort York, Toronto.

Seated: Capt M Darney, Maj A Malashenko, Col T Price, LCol H Klepak, HM The Queen Mother, Col J Bourne, Maj A Ruthven, Maj P Chaput, Capt the Rev W Russell.

Standing: Ocdt L Beloin, Lt G Eberth, Lt R Clarke, Lt L Benn, Maj B Lloyd, Capt V Chartier, Capt J Conway, Capt H Bailey, Capt V Knowlton, Lt P McElroy, 2/Lt P Hindo, Lt C Mather, 2/Lt A von Hahn, 2/Lt J Hannah, 2/Lt G Lusk, Capt BA Jones.

Twin Pipers:

Left: Ewen Booth, at Regimental exercise in Fort Drum, NY, summer, 1980.

Right: His brother, MCpl Eric Booth, at Vimy Ridge 1994.

Below: Black Watch at Fort York Toronto, 5 July 1981. Pipe Band passes Ft York Guard of re-enactors. Regt greeted its Colonel-in-Chief with a 100-man Royal guard of honour commanded by Major A Ruthven, with CSM Labrèche as Guard Sergeant-Major. The band also played for Her Majesty at the state dinner given by the Province of Ontario in her honour.

Left: The officers' mess in summer 1981; Lt Col Klepak, beaming in centre.

Below right: H/Col Tom Price with Calgary Highlander raconteur Gordon Atkinson, well known broadcaster and H/Col of Fraser Highlanders. Left is BW vet, Lt Frank Rooney, 1995.

Above: The Regimental Tug of War team at the annual Glengarry Highland Games in Maxville, Ont, 2 Aug 2009. Team captain is Chris Phare urging the lads against the Camerons. BW won the championship in 2011.

Below left: The 2009 version of the ever-present Black Watch Floor Hockey team.

Below right: The Rugby Team, in stronger days.

Pte KA Sutcliffe, Farnham, 1972. First female graduate Black Watch *Leading Infantryman Course.*

Betty Ann Jones, left, was the second enrolled Black Watch female officer and the first to graduate from Staff College, Fort Frontenac, Kingston.

MCpl Katrina Anne (Sherry) Duplessis, Veteran UN Peacekeeper and Black Watch soldier. Served in Egypt and countless exercises with the Regiment.

Regimental Portrait June 1987, Officers, The Black Watch HRH with Colonel-in–Chief,
taken atop Mount Royal at the chalet that overlooks the city.
Front row: Capt G Lusk; Capt J Conway; Maj B Lloyd; Lt Col TE Price; Lt Col V Chartier;
HM the Col-in-Chief; Col J Bourne; Maj D O'Connor; Capt B Bolton; Capt G Fraser MD.
Back row: Capt R Ferguson, RSS; Lt M Mackisoc, BWCC; 2Lt G Lowe; 2Lt H Dimock; Lt J Galipeau;
Capt P Hindo; Capt B-A Malashenko; Capt B Gardner, CO BWCC; Capt the Rev JSS Armour;
Capt B Cowan; Capt M Delaney; Lt A Bissonnette; Lt D Jones; 2Lt A MacKay.

Above: RHC Pipers at St. Andrew's Ball: Booth, Mundy, Mitchell.

Right: Piped into the Regimental Ball at the Queen Elizabeth Hotel, a dazzling Queen Mother arrives to the enthusiastic applause of a delighted crowd. Col Bourne on the left.

The Trooping of 6 June 1987 also celebrated the Regiment's 125th anniversary – it was the last great Highland parade in Montreal of the century and millennium. HM Queen Elizabeth, the Queen Mother reprised her 1962 visit to Molson Stadium in a memorable parade.

Above: HM the Col-in-Chief of the Black Watch inspects Her regiment, escorted by Lt Col Victor Chartier OMM CD.

Below: the first guard marches past. Pipes and Drums play and an enthusiastic crowd fills the stadium.

Black Watch in London – The new millennium

London, August 2000, The Queen Mother's 100 Birthday Parade: marching off from Horse Guards Parade, the Black Watch contingent, led by Lt Col Gordon Lusk CD, is centre, between the Australian and Toronto Scottish colour parties.

Two years later, a sad return for HM Queen Elizabeth, the Queen Mother's funeral in London, on 09 Apr 2002. She was Colonel-in-Chief to a pride of Highland and Commonwealth Regiments. The state funeral (OP Taybridge) included the full schedule, and the regiments permitted to attend. Major Tom MacKay led the official RHC contingent, which was selected by LCol Bolton and included RSM CWO P Gannon. Photo (l to r): MCpl Kevin Camire (who had been awarded the Proven Cup as RHC Best Soldier), LCol Bruce Bolton MMM CD (CO), and Maj Thomas MacKay CD.

Right: West Coast BW veterans gather in Port Moody BC, 2007. Standing (l to r): Derek Warner, Bud Freeston, Lew Green, Frank Anselmo, John Calderwood Kneeling: R: Frank Huber, David Leslie, Dick Kidd.

Below: October 2009 at the statue in front of the Juno Beach Centre Museum. Left to right: Phil Scott, Harold (Bud) Freeston, Michael Brunner, William James Wilkinson, Frank Conlon, Gordon Betts, William (Bill) Ludlow, & Robert (Bob) Duplessis.

Atlantic Branch BW Association marching through Aldershot NS in 2011: Grant Payne is out front, Cecil Hiscock is carrying the Union Jack, Dave Miller the Canadian flag, Roy Boudreau the UN flag, Gordie Howe, the NS flag, and Melvin Chalk the Newfoundland flag.

BW Association in Montreal marching along Sherbrooke St after 2012 Church parade. Front file left to right is CWO (ret'd) Peter Gannon, MCPL (ret'd) Wallace Todorov and MWO (ret'd) Rolland Labreche. The second file is CWO (ret'd) Tom Miles, Capt Kevin O'Connor & MWO (ret'd) Richard Cartmel.

The always dapper Lt Col IA (Ike) Kennedy OMM CD, retired having served a hockeysockful of regiments from RCA, to RHC, RCR, Airborne Commando and finally, winning deserved recognition as CO of the Princess of Wales' Own Regiment in Kingston, which he resurrected to a prize winning battalion in 18 months

Right: Second World War veteran and esteemed Honorary Colonel, Lt General Duncan McAlpine CMM CD, taking the salute in front of Cantlie House Hotel. His devoted wife, Bonnie, is on the right. Behind him is Col Stephen Angus; his grandfather's house originally stood on this site and was the preferred reviewing stand for post-war RHC parades.

Left: Colonel Stephen Angus CD, former CO 3 RHC, Honorary Colonel, and Patron of The Black Watch – ever loyal to his beloved Regiment. As Chairman of the Advisory Board, he directed it with affectionate determination – an iron fist in a velvet glove. Photo taken at his farm, July 2010.

Below: RHC 150th Anniversary Celebration taking place at Fort Henry in Kingston, June 2012. One exhibit was a demonstration of Regimental uniforms through BW history (l to r): Chris Furlotte – WW1; Eric Booth - WW2; Dan Moreau – Korea; Mark Paine – UN Peacekeeping; and a current private in RHC. They appeared with the Historical Guard, which came out with the Pipes and Drums and were inspected by Lt Gen Sir Alistair Irwin KCB CBE, Royal Highland Regiment.

Above: On 25 July 2002, the Regiment's veterans returned to Normandy, at the "Hill 67 Memorial," overlooking Verrières Ridge, north of St Martin and St André. L to r: LCol Bruce Bolton, William Booth, Jim Wilkinson, Bruce Ducat (with cane), Piper Brian MacKenzie, French Councillor St-Martin, Capt Andy Kerr.

Left: Gordon Betts standing behind Lt Col SST Cantlie's headstone.

Below: In the 2009 Regimental battlefield tour, the veterans gather before the infamous Walcheren Causeway in the Scheldt. 1st November at the new location of the Walcheren causeway monument. L to R: Harold (Bud) Freeston, William James Wilkinson, Gordon Betts, Robert (Bob) Duplessis, Michael Brunner, Phil Scott, Frank Conlon and William (Bill) Ludlow.

Above left: Sergeants conduct annual Rabbie Burns Dinner, January 2012. The Haggis Party comprises: MWO D Cochrane CD, Sgt W Wong CD, Sgt A Wilson, Sgt G Rizzi, Sgt R Larman CD, WO P Brasseur CD.

Above right: Reunion Dinner 2012. Lt Cols Vic Chartier, Bruno Plourde, seated on the left is William James Wilkinson and Gordon Betts.

Sgt Bill Carlisle, President, Toronto BW Association.

Gordon Ritchie, President, Montreal BW Association.

Art Snow, President, Atlantic Branch, presenting a trophy, c 2013.

Above: Veterans at Work. The Toronto BW Association Pipe Band soldiers in good infantry weather. LCol Len Ferdon, far right, completely non-plussed, marches intent on eventually reaching The Trout Club.

Left: an international ambassador, Bill Davis, charms Air Cadets from 745 Sqn; he has spoken across Europe in memorial ceremonies. In 2014 Mr Davis was selected to represent the Regiment at the 70th commemoration of the Normandy Campaign at Juno Beach on 6 June, along with a great host of Canadian veterans.

Highland Winter: Montreal and Quebec in more familiar bunting. Five months of snow and ice is a common ingredient to Black Watch training, parades and range qualifications – not unbearable on sunny days.

The Pipers of course. play throughout, sans gloves, mittens, ear muffs or thermal underwear.

1st Bn, 111th US Infantry, Recce Platoon Training with Black Watch in CFB Valcartier, March 2012 "Ex Highland Yankee" – one of several exchanges between the two regiments. This is the first tactical exercise by the two units. LCols Plourde and LTC Mike Weg Scheider commanded the respective units.

RHC soldiers & members of 1-111th Infantry HHC Company during EX Highland Associator at Fort Indiantown Gap, Pennsylvania, 23 June – 3 July 2013.

Mike Reshitnyk 2006

Cpl Jason Patrick Warren, 29, was killed in Afghanistan when his convoy was hit by the first of two suicide bombings near Kandahar City. Corporal Warren had seen service in Bosnia in 2002. Above left, Cpl Warrens parents, below left, his decorations – the ISAF badge worn by all soldiers in Afghanistan. The Regimental funeral was conducted at The Church of St Andrew and St Paul in Montreal.

BW in Afghanistan 2004–2013

Above left: Lieutenant Loic Baumans and Sgt Snoddon at the Afghan front c. 2013. Baumans served with 1st Van Doos and the headquarters of 2nd Battalion R22eR. Snoddon is a Militia veteran, having served in Bosnia and completed three tours in Afghanistan.

Above right: Baumans with Sgt Enrique Munizaga CD … pleased as *Machine Gunners Punch*. Having joined the Black Watch Cadets in 1974 and the unit in 1977, Sgt. Enrique Munizaga is an example of Regimental and Forces' dedication. From 1977 to 1995, and then from 2003 to retirement in 2018, he served in the Reserves, on numerous military missions while being a constable with the Montreal Police force. As a police officer he served in Guatemala, Columbia and in Afghanistan where he worked as a Canadian with the US Army on police mentoring teams. He met many of his Black Watch buddies there while serving as a policeman.

Below left: As a police officer, BWC Sgt. Munizaga, with his American translator, Levi, meets farmers near Belanday, Kandahar.

Below right: Black Watch alumni, l. to r.: Corporals M. George, L. Maillet, and T. Meisner, Masum Ghar 2009.

Above: Cpl Michael Astudillo, Jun 2011, receiving his Afghan medal from General Bouchard. Below left: MCpl Nikolas AE Mouriopoulos CCTM-A ROTO 4-12 OP ATTENTION Kabul, Afghanistan 21 October 2012 – 7 July 2013. Below right: Corporal Dainium Sileik, 2009.

Left: Sergeant Kimberly Anderson CD on patrol. Anderson worked out of Kandahar during 2011 as a tactical CIMIC. She has also served in the Arctic, the Middle East and in Guli, in Northern Uganda.

Above: Looking slightly gruff but fatherly, LCol Plourde with American chum makes friends.

Below: Settled in his HumVee, Plourde makes ready to go out on patrol.

WO RM Unger MMM CD, deployed to Afghanistan in July 2006 as PSYOPS cell operations warrant officer. Like Plourde, he grew a great beard to relax the locals. Here he leads a patrol through an Afghan village, friendly, but cautious with the children.

Black Watch Afghan Chums, Lt Benoit (Ben) Leveille and Lt Derrick Farnham, September 2007, Kandahar Air Field. Their joy is prompted by high scores on the rifle range qualifications. Farnham returned to Montreal and became Adjutant.

WO Cam Stevens MMM CD, the Regimental Pipe Major, was selected to play 11 November 2011 lament for MTTF Roto 11 Operation Athena Kandahar Airfield (KAF) – MTTF being Mission Transition Task Force. This was the final Canadian Armistice Day ceremony at KAF.

Above: Sgt Bjorn Dittmar and MCpl Maillet while on OP TORA ARWA with 3 Scots.

Left: Sgt Dittmar's Mentioned in Dispatches certificate.

On behalf of THE QUEEN,
the Governor General and Commander-in-Chief of Canada
has given orders for the name of

Sergeant Bjorn Ivo Dittmar

to be published in the Canada Gazette as having been
Mentioned in Dispatches in recognition of gallant and
distinguished service.

On 10 June 2009, while Sergeant Dittmar's platoon was involved in a firefight in Afghanistan, a soldier in a separate element triggered an improvised explosive device, causing two casualties. Despite heavy enemy fire, Sergeant Dittmar crossed open ground to reach the blast site where he coordinated the fire support necessary to treat and extract the casualties. With the enemy firing from three sides and attempting to surround them, Sergeant Dittmar displayed great leadership and composure, which were critical to saving lives.

*I am charged to record
Her Majesty's high appreciation.*

1 October 2010

Chief of the Defence Staff

Above: PSYOPS Team 98 Bravo.
L. to r.: MCpl D. Batchelor, Habib (interpreter),
Sgt B. Dittmar, Cpl E. Courtois, Cpl L. Maillet, and
Cpl T. Meisner.

Right: Looking more like weary trench infantry. The
Cdn CADPAT uniform was popular and copied by
most NATO armies. Afghan opponents (who wore
their normal clothes) confirmed the old rule about
camouflage: shape, size, shadow and mainly, *don't
move*. Sgt Mathew Snoddon is 4th from left.

Left: Col MacKay with his HQ, 2013. From
l to r: Sgt Steve Manardi (US Army), MBdr
Desy Desrosiers-Ouellette (5e RALC),
Ahmed (his translator), MacKay, Capt Jean-
Francois (Jeff) Rancourt (12e RBC), LCol
Darrell Green (US Army), Master-Sergeant
Roger Marrko.

Seven Samurai. Afghanistan 2011. Black Watch members on a Canadian patrol with PSYOPS members after mission (l to r): Cpl Brent McNair CD – RMR, Sgt Devin Batchelor CD – BW, Sgt Mathew Snoddon CD – BW, Cpl Jean-François Belzil SMV CD – R22eR, Capt Loic Baumans CD - BW, Sgt Piotr Burcew MB CD - R de Mais (Burcew's insouciant middle finger rampant detracts from his Medal for Bravery awarded in 2006), and, Cpl Ian Luc-Turgeon CD - Fus de Sher. This all-Quebec group, very much Montreal and Black Watch, demonstrate the impedimenta modern soldiers carry.

Sgt Hill, 5 April 2009 on a clearing operation around the town of Sanjaray. "I was with the BG of the 2eR22eR B Coy 2 Pl as LAV Sgt/ Wpns det commander."

RHC with 3rd SCOTS; the Black Watch reunited in Afghanistan. Behind the Saltire: Cpl Lennard Maillet CD, Sgt Devin Batchelor (centre) and Sgt Bjorn Dittmar. Kandahar Airfield, August 2009.

Sgt Brian Hill CD and Cpl D'alesio CD propping up the Black Watch international reputation.

The presentation of Regimental Colours by the Colonel-in-Chief,
His Royal Highness Prince Charles, took place on 10 Nov 2009.

Above: A family portrait – Charles and Camilla with Cols MacKay and McAlpine pose with Black Watch officers and sergeants. On the right wall, the original road marker from the Ypres battlefield, 1915

Below left: Prince Charles chats with WO Martin Prince CD, a recent Afghanistan veteran.

Below right: Colonel-in-Chief and his wife, the Duchess of Cornwall, inscribe Regimental chronicles. .

To commemorate the 150th anniversary of the first Regimental Colours, military artist Katherine Taylor was commissioned to capture the spirit of RHC history. The centrepiece of this montage is the Canadian Black Watch Soldier, in full dress uniform representing the embodiment of today's Black Watch soldier. The project was initiated by the Toronto BW Association, led by its president, Sgt Bill Carlisle.

Another memorial was the anniversary stamp petitioned by the Regimental Advisory Board. The handsome result shows the 5th Royal Scots and BW in battle. Two soldiers posed for the stamp: Pipe-Cpl Alexandre Leger (left) and Cpl Ryan Clattenburg (right).

Stamp: © 2012 Canada Post. Reprinted with permission.

Hat Trick – The Black Watch won the Brigade tactical trophy "The March and Shoot Competition" three years in a row.

Top left – First Year victory (l to r): Cpl Vivian, Sgt Batchelor, Cpl Sileika, Cpl Qualizza, Cpl Clattenburg, Cpl Rizzi.

Above left – 2nd Year: BW team led by Sgt Devin Batchelor included: MCpls Best, Ursini, Ciccone, Ptes Ghuniem, Lezetc, Guenole, Kanaan, and three "spares"; of whom 2 went to Farnham and were key in administrative support.

Above right – 3rd Year: Team organized and trained by Sgt Batchelor and RSS WO Pierre Brasseur CD. Back, L to R: Ptes Thompson, Lezetc, Mazzocchi, MCpl Best, Cpl Ursini, Sgt Batchelor, Cpl Lees, Pte Ghuniem, Cpl Kanaan. Front LtoR: Cpl Guenole, Cpl Ciccone.

GPMG C6 Course Grads c. 1999: Cpls K Anderson, Daoust, Varelas, Firth, Leduc, George and Sgt M Estrada.

The Black Watch again won the Dubuc Trophy in 2012 as best unit of 34 GBC.
Left to right: CWO Alain Deslauriers, Sergeant Major 34 GBC. CWO R Unger,
LCol Bruno Plourde, Col Marc Richard, Commander 34th Brigade.

MCpl Francis Mamen, as president, presents a
certificate of appreciation from the members
of the Red Hackle Club (the BW soldiers' mess)
to LCol Bruce Bolton just before his (first)
retirement in 2003. It reads: "It has been an
honour and a pleasure to serve with you, sir."

9 June 2012, RHC at Brigade dining in on the occasion of the Regiment winning the Dubuc Trophy in 2012 as best unit of 34th Brigade. Left to right: PM(MWO) C Stevens, CWO R Unger, Lt H Maghakian, MWO D Cochrane, Maj M Walker, LCol B Plourde, Capt P Turcotte-Tremblay, Col(H) DF O'Connor.

Black Watch with Veterans, Remembrance Day Parade, November 2012. McGill Campus. LCol Phare CD, stands before the Regimental Guard, flanked by the Canadian Grenadier Guards.

Luis M Astudillo / Services Conseils AIGS Inc.

Bishop's College School leave armoury behind their Colours, Church Parade May 2000.

Below: The 150th Anniversary Parade. The Governor General, His Excellency, the Right Honourable, David L Johnston, CC CMM COM CD in the BW Armoury with parade guard and band members.

Luis M Astudillo / Services Conseils AIGS Inc.

Above left: Perth, Scotland – RHC contingent for Laying up of Colours of 1 BW (3rd SCOTS), 23 June 2012 (l to r): P/M Cameron Stevens, WO Mamen, Lt Chris Leone, H/Col O'Connor, LCol Bruno Plourde (CO), CWO Robert Unger (RSM), Cpl Moralis-Simms, Sgt Wilson (Pipe Sgt). Posed in front of UK 51st Division Memorial in North Inch Park where the laying up ceremony just concluded.

Above right: Handing over command of the Regiment. LCol Bruno Plourde and LCol CR Phare, 5 May 2013. The colonels stand before the Regimental Colours inside the Armoury. The north wall displays some of the new mahogany plaques erected by Plourde.

Affiliated Cadet Corps: King's-Edgehill School, April 2012.
Note senior cadets resplendent in Black Watch livery and kilts.

Above: Bishop's College School, May 2011, LCol Plourde inspects the BCS Cadet Corps and, on the special occasion celebrating the 75th Anniversary of the Corps formal association with the Watch, Plourde presents Red Hackles to Cadet Major Samantha Ewing. The objective was that when Cadets achieve the rank of Sergeant they are allowed to wear the Balmorals and Hackle. Compare with the RMC style pill box hat worn previously (left).

Left: Church Parade 1963, LCol Redpath, the Black Watch and Bishop's College School colour parties kneel.

Below: BCS Cadets march along Sherbrooke St with the Regiment in the May Church Parade 2009. The unique BCS Colours, awarded during Fenian Raids, centre.

Pipe Band at work: Remembrance Day Parade and, below, the annual St Patrick's Day Parade (the oldest in North America) in March 2007 in typical weather – though snow would not be unusual. L to R: P/Maj C Stevens CD (RHC), P/Maj AB Clark CD (The Cameron Highlanders of Ottawa), P/Maj DJ Smith CD (RCAF, CFB Shearwater), P/Sgt K Johnstone CD (RHC).

Pipes and Drums marching through the The Roddick Memorial Gates at McGill, Remembrance Day Parade, November 2012. L to R: Cpl T McLaren, Cpl A Leger, MCpl Langevin, MCpl Wilson, A Hislop, Cpl Marcianesi, Pte Bowes-Lyon.

BW Change of Command 1 May 2016. Lt Col Tom MacKay CD succeeded Lt Col Christopher Phare CD as CO Black Watch. MacKay returned for his second tour as commanding officer; his initial period was 2005–2009. Photograph shows the signing of documents on the Armoury parade square. Left to Right: Colonel Dan O'Connor, CD – Honourary Colonel, The Black Watch RHC; Lt Colonel Christopher Phare CD, Lt Col TEC MacKay CD and, Colonel Dan Chafaï CD – Commander 34 Brigade.

Cartoons by Smokey (A/Cpl D.M. Grosart) depicting 1 RHC scenes, incidents and caricatures during the campaign in Holland (October–November 1944). These were added to the 1 RHC War Diary and the Battalion newspaper. LAC and BWA

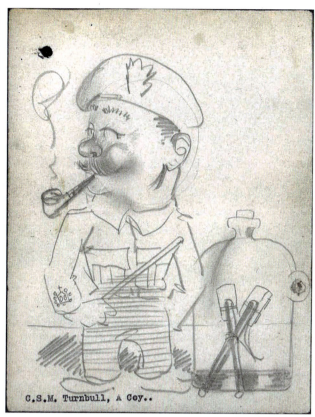

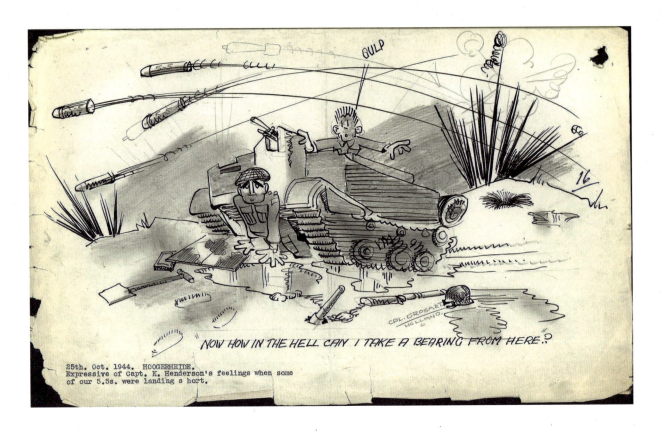

25th. Oct. 1944. HOOGERHEIDE.
Expressive of Capt. K. Henderson's feelings when some
of our 5.5s. were landing short.

The ex-Jock: "Remember 1967, when were both in The Black Watch?"

Perhaps the most popular piece from the book of cartoons, RV 81, which commemorated the first large Army manoeuvres to take place since the Cold War began. The Canadian brigades gathered in Gagetown, New Brunswick for war games and competitions. The formed Division included: "the Army of the West", The Airborne from Petawawa, the Quebec Brigade from Valcartier, and the regiments in CFB Gagetown. It was the first real reunion for Black Watch soldiers scattered across Canada since 1970.

The Dragoon: "This is the spot where we chased those dumb bears ..."

From RV 81. Gagetown bears were common and at times a nuisance. The Black Watch seemed to get on better with The Black Bear than other regiments.

RHC Red Hackle Cartoons

Black Watch RHC 2012

Germany, c 1950s

Black Watch in Afghanistan

Above, left, and opposite top: Urban Operations structure built on the armoury floor.

Right: The Afghanistan Battle Honour is added to the other monumental plaques of Battle Honours on the east wall of the armoury.

Above and left: OP LENTUS – Black Watch soldiers fighting floods in the Montreal area in 2017 (left) and again in 2019 (top).

Above: As the COVID-19 pandemic was surging in 2020, Sgt. Devon Best served in OP CALUMET in the Sinai Peninsula, Canada's contribution to a Multinational Force and Observers. He supervised a section of 7 soldiers in camera operations – monitoring major routes. He was also the main training NCO, shown here on the ranges supervising members of the multinational force. Below left: Sgt. Best (second from the left) on a patrol with soldiers from the Fijian, US and Australian Armed forces. Below center and right: Sgt. Jimmy Ray Thompson, a Montreal firefighter by profession and boxer when not in uniform, shown here as a Helicopter Door Gunner during OP IMPACT in Iraq.

The RHC contingent at the Prince of Wales' 70th Birthday Patronage Celebation of our Colonel-in-Chief, HRH Prince Charles at Buckingham Palace on 22 May 2018. The event recognized all the organizations for which Prince Charles is a Patron.

With the Prince having moved on to the next guests, Camilla, The Duchess of Cornwall, is seen here talking with Linda Campbell, the RSM's wife. On the left is Chantale Ménard, LCol Plourde's wife, and just visible between Camilla and the security guard is Lorraine McCabe, LCol McCabe's wife.

Above: The meeting with the Colonel-in-Chief at Clarence House on 14 March 2019. From left to right: Mr. Jock Green-Armytage, LCol Bruno Plourde, His Royal Highness, HCol Dan O'Connor, Sgt. Devon Best, and HLCol Bruce Bolton.

Right: HCol Dan O'Connor presents a walking stick to HRH – the Regiment's gift to mark his 70th birthday. The stick, with a loon head, was created from yellow birch by Quebec sculptor Tony Fortin.

Finale scene of the 75th Anniversary of the Battle for Vimy Tattoo produced by the Regiment at the Bell Centre, Montreal.

The combined CAF pipe band in the town square of Mons, Belgium, on 11 November 2018 marking the 100th anniversary of the end of World War I. Front rank, third from the left is WO Adam Wilson and seventh is Pipe-Major Dan Smith.

On 11 November 2018, a recreation of the 42nd Bn Pipe Band marches down the same street (above) that the original 42nd Bn Pipe Band did 100 years earlier to the day to mark the liberation of the town of Mons, Belgium (below). The 2018 pipe band was led by former Pipe-Major Andrew Kerr and the members came from across Canada, the USA, and Britain. These volunteers participated in a number of remembrance ceremonies in the area to mark the 100th anniversary of the end of the Great War.

The pipe bands of 3rd Bn (BW) The Royal Regiment of Scotland and of The Black Watch (RHR) of Canada at the Edinburgh Tattoo 2019.

OP LASER, the CAF operation for the COVID-19 pandemic in 2020, saw two platoons of Black Watch soldiers deployed to long term care homes for seniors.

Above: the departure ceremony held on 9 June 2020 at the St. Andrew's Home in Montreal after weeks of assisting the overwhelmed staff. The soldiers were considered godsends.

Left: Piper Robert Kerr plays his bagpipes.

Change of Command ceremony for the Commanding Officer and Regimental Sergeant-Major under COVID-19 restrictions, 12 September 2020. From left to right: CWO Francois Mamen, incoming RSM; HCol Bruce Bolton; LCol Francis Roy, incoming CO; Col. Michael Canavan, 34 Brigade Commander; WO Adam Wilson, Pipe-Major; CWO Alain Marcil, 34 Brigade Sergeant-Major; LCol Bruno Plourde, outgoing CO; HLCol H. Jonathan Birks; and CWO Stephen Campbell, outgoing RSM.

APPENDIX A

BLACK WATCH REGIMENTAL APPOINTMENTS 1950–2022

Colonels–in–Chief, The Colonel in Chief, appointed by the Crown

Her Majesty, Queen Elizabeth, The Queen Mother	1937–2003	[1937 Imperials, 1947 for RHC]
HRH Prince Charles, Duke of Rothesay	2005 to date	

Colonel of the Regiment, appointed by the Minister of Defence

Brigadier KG Blackader CBE DSO MC ED CD	1958–1963
Colonel JW Knox MBE ED CD	1963–1968
Colonel JG Bourne CVO ED CD	1968–1970

Honorary Colonels of the Regiment

Colonel Sir H Montagu Allan CVO ED	1920–1951	
Colonel GS Cantlie DSO VD CD	1951–1956	
Brigadier KG Blackader CBE DSO MC ED CD	1956–1958	(RHC appoints Col of Regt)
Colonel JG Bourne CVO ED CD	1970–1987	(RHC reverts to Hon Col in 1970)
Colonel TE Price CD	1987–1996	
Colonel SF Angus CD	1996–2000	
Lieutenant General DA McAlpine CMM CD	2000–2010	
Colonel DF O'Connor CD	2011–2020	
Colonel BD Bolton MMM, CD	2020 to date	

Honorary Lieutenant Colonels 1st Battalion RHC

[The Regular Bns did not appoint Hon Lt Cols]

Lieutenant Colonel GS Cantlie DSO VD	1920–1951
Brigadier KG Blackader CBE DSO MC ED CD	1951–1953

Honorary Lieutenant Colonels 2nd Battalion RHC

Lieutenant Colonel Herbert Molson CMG MC	1920–1938
Major–General GE McCuaig CMG DSO VD	1940–1946

Honorary Lieutenant Colonels 3 RHC / Montreal Battalion

LCol WH Clark–Kennedy VC CMG DSO ED	1940–1946	[during Second World War]
Brig KG Blackader CBE DSO MC ED CD	1953–1956	[Created upon estb Reg Bns 1/2 RHC]
Colonel WSM McTier DSO OBE MC VD	1957–1960	
Colonel HM Wallis DSO OBE MC VD	1961–1964	
Lieutenant Colonel JW Sharp CD	1964–1980	
Lieutenant Colonel TE Price CD	1980–1987	
Lieutenant Colonel SF Angus CD	1987–1996	
Lieutenant General DA McAlpine CMM CD	1996–2000	
Lieutenant Colonel VG Chartier OMM CD AdeC	2000–2009	
Lieutenant Colonel DF O'Connor CD	2009–2011	
Lieutenant Colonel CN McCabe OMM CD	2011–2017	
Lieutenant Colonel BD Bolton MMM CD	2017–2020	
Lieutenant Colonel HJ Birks	2020 to date	

APPENDIX B

THE BLACK WATCH COMMAND LIST – 1945–2022

1 CHB / 1 RHC 1951–1970

Commanding Officers

Lt Col RL Rutherford OBE CD	1951–1952
Lt Col HA Parker OBE CD	1952–1954
Lt Col WH Seamark CD	1954 1956
Lt Col JME Clarkson MC CD	1956 1959
Lt Col DS MacLennan CD	1959 1960
Lt Col WA Teed CD	1960
Lt Col WA Teed CD	1960 1963
Lt Col GH Sellar CD	1963 1966
Lt Col WJ Newlands CD	1966 1968
Lt Col GS Morrison CD	1968 1970

Battalion Sergeants Major

WO1 AWL Watson CD	1951–1952
WO1 RH Finnie	1952–1953
WO1 C McAfferty	1953–1954
WO1 RH Finnie CD	1954–1962
WO1 RH Finnie CD	1954–1962
WO1 RH Finnie CD	
WO1 VI Lawson CD	1962–1965
WO1 H Firby CD[2]	1965–1966
WO1 R Blackwell CD	1966–1967
CWO G Pyatt CD	1967–1970

Battalion Chaplains

Capt Rev N Sharkey	
Capt Rev R Cunningham 1954–	
Capt Rev R Cunningham 1956–1959	
Capt Fr Kennedy 1958–59	
Capt Fr RPJ Bouillard OMI 1959–1962[1]	
Capt Rev VH Johnson 1959–1962	
Capt Rev George Davidson 1967–	
Capt Rev G Davidson 1967–Cyprus	
Capt Rev George Davidson 1967–69	

Pipe Majors 1 CHB / 1 RHC

P/Maj W Magennis CD	1954–1967
P/Maj DM Carrigan CD	1967–1970
P/Maj J. Patterson CD	1967–1968
P/Maj DM Carrigan CD	1968–1970

2 CHB / 2 RHC 1952–1970

Commanding Officers

Lt Col RM Ross OBE[3] CD	1952–1955
Lt Col WdeN Watson DSO MC CD	1955–1959
Lt Col CHE Askwith CD	1959–1960
Lt Col WC Leonard MBE CD	1961–1963
Lt Col DA McAlpine CD	1963–1966
Lt Col HJ Harkes MC CD	1966–1968
Lt Col WB MacLeod OMM CD	1968–1970

Battalion Sergeants Major

WO1 FE Blakeney MM BEM CD	1952–1961
WO1 FE Blakeney MM BEM CD	1952–1961
WO1 FE Blakeney MM BEM CD	1952–1961
WO1 TF Charters CD	1961–1964
WO1 EF Cain CD	1964–1965
CWO CW Beacon CD	1965–1966
CWO DB Reekie MMM CD	1966–1970

Battalion Chaplains

Capt Rev R W Pierce 1953–55	
Capt Rev JGEA Travers 1959	
Capt Fr M Labrie 1961	
Capt Rev J Farmer 1964	
Capt R White 1965–68 Cyprus	
Capt Fr R Plourde 1966 Cyprus	
Capt Fr J Richard/Capt Rev F Jenkins[4]	
Maj Rev P DeLong, Cyprus Sept 1969	

Pipe Majors 2 CHB / 2 RHC

P/Maj D. Rankin CD	1953–1959
P/Maj JD Stewart CD	1959–1963
P/Maj WJL Gilmour CD	1963–1966
P/Maj PF Hogg CD	1966–1967
P/Maj WJL Gilmour CD	1967–1970

THE MONTREAL BATTALION (3 RHC) 1945–2022

Commanding officer		Regimental Sergeant Major		Regimental Chaplain
Lt Col IL Ibbotson ED	1945–46	WO1 E Bleasdale	1945–46	Capt Rev RJ Berlis (1946)[5]
Lt Col FM Mitchell ED	1946–47	WO1 R Diplock MBE	1946	Capt Rev RJ Berlis
Lt Col VE Traversy	1947–49	WO1 AF Turnbull DCM	1947–49	Capt Rev RJ Berlis
Lt Col JW Knox MBE ED CD	1949–52	WO1 Ralph Dynes MBE[6]	1949–52	Maj RJ Berlis CD
Lt Col JG Bourne CVO ED CD	1952–53 [55][7]	WO1 R Ablett	1952–55	Maj RJ Berlis CD
Lt Col JG Bourne CVO ED CD	1953–55	WO1 R Ablett	1952–55	Maj RJ Berlis CD
Lt Col IR McDougall CD	1955–58	WO1 T Turley CD	1955–58	Maj RJ Berlis CD
Lt Col WA Wood CD	1958–59	WO1 JR Jackson	1959–60	Maj RJ Berlis CD
Lt Col DJ McGovern CD	1959–62	WO1 JR Jackson	1960	Maj RJ Berlis CD
Lt Col WB Redpath CD	1962–65	WO1 M Gurevitch CD	1960–65	Maj RJ Berlis CD
Lt Col TE Price CD	1965–67	WO1 Ivor Watkins CD	1965–68	Capt Rev SA Hayes 1966
Lt Col JIB MacFarlane CD	1967–70	CWO GA McElheron MMM CD	1968–1970	Capt Rev SA Hayes
Lt Col SF Angus CD	1970–72[8]	CWO AD Rodgers CD	1970–72	Capt Rev SA Hayes[9]
Lt Col LN Ferdon CD	1972–74	CWO R Poirier CD	1972–74	Hayes 1973 / Capt Rev WR Russell
Lt Col LN Ferdon CD	1972–74	CWO AD Rodgers (HRH Col-in-Chief's Parade: Summer, 1974)		
Lt Col WR Sewell CD	1974–77	CWO VG Chartier OMM CD	1974–78	Capt Rev WR Russell
Lt Col GD Robertson CD	1977–80	CWO BD Bolton MMM CD	1978–80	Capt Rev WR Russell
Lt Col HP Klepak CD	1980–83	CWO GA McElheron MMM CD	1980–83	Russell 1983 / Capt Rev JSS Armour
Lt Col JC Stothers CD	1983–86	CWO DI Paull CD	1983–87	Capt Rev JSS Armour
Lt Col VG Chartier OMM CD[10]	1986–89	CWO MRG Kelly MMM CD	1987–90	Armour 1987 / Capt Rev B Glencross 1988
Lt Col DF O'Connor CD	1989–93	CWO J Rodger CD	1990–94	Capt Rev B Glencross
Lt Col IM McCulloch CD	1993–96	CWO T Miles CD	1994–98	Capt Rev B Glencross
Lt Col GT Lusk CD	1996–2000	CWO T Miles CD	1996–98	Capt Rev B Glencross
Lt Col BD Bolton MMM CD	2000–03	CWO P Gannon CD	1998–2001	Capt Rev B Glencross
Lt Col J Potter MC	2003	CWO C Hamel CD	2001–06	Capt Rev B Glencross
Lt Col BD Bolton MMM CD	2003–05	CWO C Hamel CD	2001–06	Capt Rev B Glencross CD
Lt Col TEC MacKay CD	2005–09[11]	CWO C Hamel CD	2001–06	Glencross 2008/Capt Rev RR Topping
Lt Col B Plourde CD	2009–	CWO JC Barron CD	2006–10	Capt Rev Topping 2009 [Rev JP Vaudry]
Lt Col B Plourde CD	2009–13	CWO R Unger MMM CD	2010–13	[Rev J Veenstra / Capt Rev David Godkin][12]
Lt Col CR Phare CD	2013–16	CWO M Carmosino CD	2013–16	Capt Rev David Godkin
Lt Col TEC MacKay CD	2016–17	CWO M Carmosino CD	2016–17	Capt Rev Alain Brosseau
Lt Col B Plourde CD	2017–20	CWO S Campbell CD	2017–20	Capt Rev Gary Karamoukian
Lt Col F. Roy CD	2020–	CWO F Mamen CD	2020–	

Pipe Majors 3 RHC 1945–2012

Pipe Major E Peden	1945 (1 RHC)
Pipe Major R Hannah	1939–1946
Pipe Major FG Hinton	1947–1951
Pipe Major WJ Hannah CD	1951–1967
Pipe Major G Grieg CD	1967–1968
Pipe Major H Brown CD	1968–1972
Pipe Major TI MacIntosh CD	1972–1973
Pipe Major BD Bolton CD	1973–1978
Pipe Major G McRae CD	1979
Pipe Major AS Dickson CD	1979–1980
Pipe Major BD Bolton MMM CD	1980–1983
Pipe Major AGM Kerr CD	1983–1993
Pipe Major BS MacKenzie CD	1993–1997
Pipe Major JD Anderson CD	1997–2000
Pipe Major CW Stevens MMM CD	2000–2017
Pipe Major DJ Smith, CD	2017–2019
Pipe Major AWJ Wilson, CD	2019–2022
Pipe Major RW Kerr	2022 to date

Canadian Highland Depot / The Black Watch Depot

Commanding Officers	*Depot Sergeants Major*
Major JEJ Caryi CD (RCA) 1953	WO 1 RH Finnie 1953–1954
Major JR Stobo MC CD 1953	
Major WJ MacDougall CD 1953–1958	WO 1 BH Smith 1954–1960
Major RO Porter CD 1958–1960	
Major GD Cochrane CD 1960–1963	WO 1 GW Wooten CD 1960–1964
Major LA Watling MC CD 1963–1967	WO 1 GW Wooten CD 1960–1964
Major BE Harper CD 1967–1968	CWO TF Charters CD 1964–1966
Major JW Cummings CD 1968	CWO CW Beacon CD 1966–1968

Depot Pipe Major[13]

P/Maj G Ogilvie CD

The Black Watch (RHR) of Canada Regimental Band[14]

Director of Music	1955–1961	Lt DV Start
	1961–1969	Lt/Capt HC Eagles
Band Sergeant Major (WO I)	1955–1961	WO I A MacCullough
	1961–1964	WO I REJ Milne
	1964–1969	WO I VNP Taylor
Band Sergeant Major (WO II)	1955–1965	WO II JBTitterton
	1965–1969	WO II BD Ford

APPENDIX C

REGIMENTAL BAGPIPE TUNES

ROUTINE CALLS

Johnnie Cope	REVEILLE
Brose and Butter	MEAL CALL
The Bugle Horn	5 MINUTE WARNING CALL (DINNER)
Any 4/4 March	5 MINUTE WARNING – INSPECTION – (COMPANYS)*
Any 6/8 March	5 MINUTE WARNING – DISMISSAL – (COMPANYS)*
A Man's A Man For A' That	COMMANDING OFFICERS' ORDERS (5 MINUTE WARNING)*
A Man's A Man For A' That	DEFAULTERS PARADE
Donald Blue	LIGHTS OUT

DUTY TUNES

Highland Laddie	REGIMENTAL MARCH PAST
The Red Hackle / My Home	REGIMENTAL SLOW MARCH
Bonnie Dundee	'A' COMPANY MARCH PAST
Blue Bonnets Over the Border	'B' COMPANY MARCH PAST
Wha Saw the 42nd	'HQ' COMPANY MARCH PAST
Scotland the Brave	ADVANCE
The Black Bear	DISMISSAL
Highland Laddie (8 Bars)	SALUTE
Mallorca	ROYAL SALUTE
Vice Regal	MALLORCA – O CANADA ENDING
Auld Lang Syne	MARCH OFF OF COLOURS FOR THE LAST TIME
Green Hills of Tyrol	RETREAT
Flowers of the Forest	FUNERAL MARCH
Lochaber No More	LAMENT

COMMEMORATION TUNES

1st Battalion The Black Watch of Canada's Farewell to Canada, by PM Donald Sutherland, WWII*

Bonnie McAlpine, by PM William Gilmour (1964)

Colonel Duncan McAlpine, by PM William Gilmour

Colonel G S (Scotty) Morrison, by PM Donald Carrigan, 1 RHC*

Colonel John G Bourne, CVO, ED, CD, by PM Andrew Kerr in 1986*

John F Kennedy, by PM William Gilmour*

Pipe Major DM Carrigan, by Pipe Major William Gilmour

Salute to the Saint Andrew's Society of Montreal, by PM Cameron W. Stevens, MMM, CD for the 175th Anniversary of the Society*

Sesquicentennial March, by PM Andrew Kerr for the 150th Anniversary of the St. Andrew's Society of Montreal, 1985

The Black Watch of Canada, by PM Duncan Rankine*

The Colonel in Chief, by Sgt T.E. White for the presentation of Colours in 1974*

The Red Hackle (Regimental Slow March), by PM Donald Sutherland WWII Pipe-Major 1940–43*

*Published in A Collection of Pipe Music of the Black Watch (Royal Highland Regiment), Balhousie Publications Ltd., Perth, Scotland 2012

APPENDIX D

FINAL PARADE:
OFFICERS OF THE BLACK WATCH (RHR) OF CANADA, BASE GAGETOWN – 1 APRIL 1970

Officers 1st Bn RHC

Lt Col GS Morrison CD, *Commanding Officer*

Majors

DA Fraser CD	JA Pugh CD
CN McCabe CD	JR Wigmore CD

Captains

PS Bury	WM Leonard
RL Fillman	DA Mills CD
J Fuller	AG Millar
LR Joudrey	

Lieutenants

DC Bondurant	DG Jack
AC Bonnycastle	RD MacKay
GW Carter	MJ Smith
JS Cox	AR Turpin
FM Fisher	JD Beavis
2/Lt KK Johnson	

Officers 2nd Bn RHC

Lt Col WB MacLeod CD, *Commanding Officer*

Majors

WH Eastwood CD	JS MacAulay CD
IS Fraser CD	JR MacPherson CD
GN Laird CD	

Captains

RP Alden	BV Johnson
RM MacAlpine	P Goldie CD
DS Martin	JE Patten
RM Gray	TPA Power
JD Harris	GW Garfoth-Bles, 1 BW

Lieutenants

EM Anderssen	AL Maitland
MS Campbell	HWG Mowat
WS Habington	MR Newman
JFI Jamieson	GP Nichols
WA Leavey	RC Wen
DM Mair	KL White

Regimental Adjutant
Captain D Fisher CD

APPENDIX E

3 SCOTS, AFFILIATIONS AND CADET CORPS

The Imperial Watch: 3 SCOTS and Commonwealth Regiments

Under a plan devised by Lt General Sir Alistair Irwin KCB (who began his service in the British Army commissioned into the Black Watch) and approved by General Sir Michael "Mike" Jackson GCB, CBE DSO (from the Parachute Regiment and then Chief of the General Staff of the British Army) on 16 December 2004, it was announced that the Black Watch was to join with five other Scottish regiments – the Royal Scots, the King's Own Scottish Borderers, the Royal Highland Fusiliers, The Highlanders and the Argyll and Sutherland Highlanders to form the Royal Regiment of Scotland, a single regiment consisting of five regular and two territorial battalions.

On 28 March 2006, The Black Watch (Royal Highland Regiment) was reduced from regimental status to a battalion, now titled: ***3rd Battalion Royal Regiment of Scotland (Black Watch)*** [3 SCOTS]. The Red Hackle grew to a ubiquitous *burning bush*. The Imperial Black Watch was sometimes referred to as "the Allied Regiment" or "the Parent Regiment" – officially abbreviated as "BW". The RHC remained on cordial terms with other Commonwealth regiments allied to the Parent Regiment:

- The Transvaal Scottish Regiment, South Africa, allied 1927
- The Lanark and Renfrew Scottish Regiment, Perth Ontario, allied 1928
- The Prince Edward Island Highlanders, Charlottetown, PEI, allied 1928 (disbanded 1945)
- The Tyneside Scottish Regiment, Newcastle-on-Tyne, England, affiliated 1939
- The New Zealand Scottish Regiment, New Zealand, allied 1942
- The Royal New South Wales Regiment, Sydney, Australia, allied 1963
- The Royal Queensland Regiment, Townsville, North Queensland, Australia, allied 1963

The Black Watch Cadet Corps

The 1st Battalion RHC officially perpetuated the 13th Battalion RHC (CEF) and the 2nd Battalion RHC officially perpetuated the 42nd Battalion (CEF) while the 3rd Battalion RHC perpetuated the 73rd Battalion (CEF). The Regimental establishment now included a Regimental Headquarters and a Colonel of the Regiment – appointed by the Minister of National Defence (usually based on the recommendation of the Regiment). In 1962 The Black Watch Cadet Corps had increased to six affiliated corps; by 2013 the Black Watch had four affiliated Cadet Corps:

No. 2   **Bishop's College School Cadet Corps**, Lennoxville, QC – Affiliated 22 Apr 1936 (Active)

No. 4   **Highland Cadet Battalion** (1899–1963); Affiliated 5th Royal Scots/RHC; D Company redesig 24 Feb 1965 as Lachute Cadet Corps. Re-affiliated RHC, 1 January 2000 (Active)

No. 153   Lachine High School Cadet Corps, Lachine QC – Affiliated 1 May 1958

No. 254   **King's-Edgehill School Cadet Corps**, Windsor, NS – Affiliated 1 January 1961 (Active)

No. 2647   Oromocto High School Cadet Corps, Oromocto, NB – Affiliated 1 March 1961

No. 130   The Rothesay Collegiate School Cadet Corps, Rothesay, NB – Affiliated 1 Nov 1962

No. 2497   **The Black Watch Cadet Corps**, Montreal – Affiliated 3 October 1953 (Active)

The Black Watch (Royal Highland Regiment) of Canada Cadet Corps 2497, 1953–2022

The Commanding Officers

1953–1956	Captain Ralph Dynes MBE
1956–1958	Captain Harry A Robertson
1958–1970	Major John T Gibson CD
1970–1972	Major Henry A "Mick" Darney CD
1972–1972	Major Larry Kavanaugh ED CD
1972–1974	Major John T Gibson CD (2 tours; longest serving, 14 years)
1974–1978	Major A.A. "Sandy" Campbell CD
1978–1981	Captain Michael H Darney CD
1981–1985	Captain Victor M Knowlton CD
1985–1988	Captain William H Gardner CD MStJ
1988–1991	Captain Robert F Clarke CD
1991–1994	Captain Mark E Mackisoc
1994–1998	Captain Vanessa J Royal
1998–1999	Captain Jennifer Lafrenière
1999–2004	Captain Robert F Clarke CD MStJ
2004–2005	Major Suzanne Bergeron CD
2005–2009	Captain Victor M Knowlton OStJ CD A de C
2009–2012	Captain Charles R Tawa CD
2012–2013	Captain Karl O Morel CD
2013–2014	Captain Wayne J Dover CD
2014–2018	Captain Andrew Baddeley, CD
2018–2022	Major Felix Macia, CD
2022 to date	Captain Frederic Bertrand, CD

APPENDIX F

Dates for Regimental Parades, Memorials, Annual Meetings and Social Occasions

- Regimental *Levée* – Hogmanay, January 1
- Regimental Birthday Parade, January 31
- Robbie Burns Dinner, WOs & Sgts Mess, January
- The Burns Shoot – annual Officers/NCO competition, January/February
- The Highland Dinner – February, before St Patrick's Parade
- The Battle of Ypres Parade – April
- Cadet Inspections, April / May
- Annual Parents and Cadets Banquet, Cadet Corps, Spring
- Montreal Black Watch Reunion – every second year either in Spring or the Fall.
- Advisory Board, Association Annual Meetings – May, and, November
- Honorary Colonel's Dining In, May, preceding Church Parade
- Regimental Church Parade, May
- Field of Honour, Pointe-Claire – June
- Scottish Day – Fort Ticonderoga, New York, June
- Upper Canada Association Barbeque – Closest Sunday to Regimental Day
- Regimental Day, June 9
- The Toronto Black Watch Association Barbeque – end of July
- The Battle of Dieppe Parade – August
- Montreal Black Watch Association BBQ – ever second year in August
- Maxville Games beginning of August
- Montreal Highland Games beginning of August – day after Maxville Highland Games

- Atlantic Branch Black Watch Reunion – September of every year.

- Scottish Country Dancing Rehearsals 6 Mondays before St Andrew's Ball in October and November

- Annual Reunion Dinner for officers, first Saturday in November

- Remembrance Day Parade, 11 November

- St Andrew's Ball, the last weekend in November – considered "a parade"

- The Sherry Luncheon – commencement of Christmas Festive season – first Friday of December

- Annual Unit visit to St. Anne's Hospital – first Sunday in December

- Red Hackle Club (Junior Ranks' Mess) Annual Dinner, first Saturday in December

- Children's' Christmas Party, mid-December

Scottish-Canadian affiliations, associations: Montreal Pistol Club; St Andrews Society, Highland Games Society, 78th Fraser Highlanders, Assoc Franco-Ecossaise etc

APPENDIX G

THE CAPTAIN GEORGE FRASER DINNER

Captain George "Doc" Fraser was the penultimate Regimental Medical Officer and "was able to touch everyone he met with kind words and a special interest in everything that went on around him." Doc Fraser was passionate about the Black Watch. His father, for whom he was named and who he never knew, was a fighting company commander: Major George C Fraser, killed in action with 1 RHC at Ifs, 21 July 1944. George joined himself in 1984 when he was 43 years old. His great uncle's name is on the brass plate beneath "the Waterloo Pipes" donated to the Mess in memory of Fraser's father. His own death, some ten years after he retired from the Regiment, left a void in the Officers' Mess. When Major Brent Cowan prepared for George Fraser's burial, he discovered a corner of the 1912 Colours, burned by the 1950 armoury fire, in the archival fonds. He decided it was an omen.

After he retired, Cowan was instrumental in organizing a dinner in Fraser's memory. This was possible because Doctor Fraser was both well remembered and much loved by the McGill University medical community, who sought to commemorate his service as "Teacher, Clinician, Friend of Patients."[15] The George Fraser Dinner was held in the Black Watch Officers' Mess from 2004–2011. It was held annually around George's February birthday – coincidentally, and appropriately, February is also Heart Month. Major Cowan recorded the history:

> George was an honorary life member of the Sergeants' Mess (named so shortly before his death in May 2002). For that reason ... the then RSM, CWO Claude Hamel and George's cousin, Peter Webster, who financed the acquisition, placed a cabinet in the Sergeants' Mess. The George Fraser cabinet held seven quaich cups representing the seven institutions George held dear: The Black Watch, the 78th Fraser Highlanders, Clan Fraser, St Mary's Hospital, The Royal Victoria Hospital, McGill University, and Lower Canada College.

> The first George Fraser Dinner was initially a buffet dinner held at the Royal Victoria Hospital in January 2003 following the first *George Fraser Lecture*. That spring I invited Dr Jacques Genest, head of McGill Cardiology, and his wife to the Hon Col's Dinning In. The aim was to introduce him to the Mess so that he might

come aboard the concept of moving the dinner here. He was won over. The next eight dinners were held in the Officers' Mess with preliminary cocktails in the Sergeants' Mess. Beyond its ostensible purpose to raise money for the George Fraser Memorial Fund, my aim was to bring prominent Montrealers into the Regiment and have them mix with military people. I thought the cross-pollination of experiences and ideas would benefit both communities. However, despite the occasional attendance of the Honorary Colonels and some regimental officers ... after the ninth dinner the joint dinner idea fizzled [further McGill administrators wished to return the dinner to the campus]. But the George Fraser cabinet is still in the Sergeants' Mess with the trays and quaichs – and could always be resurrected at some point ... There was a bottle of single malt whisky left over from the first George Fraser Dinner that had been placed in the cabinet. I have since removed it and will maintain custody until such time as the dinner is revived in whatever form ... or there arises a suitable occasion to consume it.[16]

APPENDIX H

PRESENTATION OF NEW COLOURS PARADE 2009

Lt Col MacKay reports the Regiment to HRH, Prince Charles.

Presentation of New Colours Parade – OP BLEURY,10 November 2009

CO, LCol TEC MacKay CD; DCO, LCol B Plourde CD; RSM, CWO J Barron CD; Adjutant, 2Lt J Vavasour-Williams

OC 1 Guard, Maj CR Phare CD ; SM 1 Gd , MWO R Unger CD;

OC 2 Guard, Capt Antoine Tardiff; SM 2 Gd, MWO M Carmosino CD;

OC 3 Guard, Capt Derric Bowes-Lyon, SM 3 Gd, MWO S Campbell CD;

OC 4 Guard, Capt D Farnham, SM 4 Gd, WO F Mamen CD.

Retiring Colours: Senior Colour Officer, Lt M Jonasz, Junior Colour Officer, 2Lt Loic Baumans; Colour WO, Retiring Colours, WO Fuller CD; Senior Colour Escort, Sgt James Quesnel CD; Junior Colour Escort, Sgt Donald Desy CD

New Colours: Senior Colour Officer, New Colours, 2Lt C Leone; Junior Colour Officer, 2Lt J Hinkson; Colour WO, WO Lawton CD ;

Senior Colour Escort, Sgt Hugh Lawson CD; Junior Colour Escort, Sgt Milton Estrada CD

Colour Orderly #1 Ocdt J Tremblay; Colour Orderly #2 Ocdt H Maghakian;

Presentations Officer, Ocdt C Leong; and, Pde Master of Ceremonies, Major Michael Boire, CD.

Lt B Leveille, Parade Administration.

APPENDIX I

3 RHC STRENGTH 1955–2014
AS PER ANNUAL HIST REPORTS

CO RHC	Date	Offrs	Sr/Jr NCOs	ORs	Total	Notes
Lt Col Bourne	1955	43	11/43	190	287	
Lt Col McDougall	1956	38	10/38	260	346	Philadelphia
Lt Col McDougall	1957	33	11/32	159	235	
Lt Col McDougall	1958	31	12/30	170	243	Philadelphia
Lt Col Wood	1959	29	10/25	145	209	
Lt Col McGovern	1960	29	7/39	191	266	
Lt Col McGovern	1961	30	7/35	136	208	National Survival Trg effects
Lt Col McGovern	1962	28	9/38	242	317	Presentation of Colours
Lt Col Redpath	1963	30	8/35	219	292	
Lt Col Redpath	1964	No Report Found				
Lt Col Redpath	1965	28	7/28	156	219	
Lt Col T Price	1966	No Report Found			217	AVG 10 ten years: 31 Offrs, 186 OR – Avg: 217
Lt Col T Price	1967	No Report Found				Centennial; Queen Mother Pde 3 Bns BW
Lt Col J MacFarlane	1968	No Report Found				
Lt Col J MacFarlane	1969	No Report Found				SSEP starts 1969 Camp Dube, CFB Valcartier
Lt Col J MacFarlane/Angus	1970	No Report Found				October Crisis; SSEP 2 Fd, Lacomb Armoury
Lt Col SF Angus	1971[17]	15	119		134	SSEP at RdeMais BW inclu 3 CWAC; 90 Avg Str
Lt Col SF Angus	1972	No statistics found			97[18]	SSEP at BW, 15% F; 1st trg F in BW
Lt Col LN Ferdon	1973	No statistics found[19]			106	All Ranks Pde Str; SSEP
Lt Col LN Ferdon	1974	19	11	165[20]	195	Presentation Queen's Colour St Hubert

CO RHC	Date	Offrs	Sr/Jr NCOs	ORs	Total	Notes
Lt Col WR Sewell	1975	13	9	126	148	
Lt Col WR Sewell	1976	12	20	88	120[21]	
Lt Col GD Robertson	1977	13	16	87	116	
Lt Col GD Robertson	1978	No report found			79	
Lt Col GD Robertson	1979	No report found			71	71 all ranks at Final Pde Dec '79: x100 Gd Hon TO; SYEP[22]
Lt Col GD Robertson	1980	20	17	122	159	SYEP; ColrPty Royal Tourney London 20–28 Jul
Lt Col HP Klepak	1981	23	20	116	159	SYEP
Lt Col HP Klepak	1982	21	34	130	185	SYEP; AVG Exercise, *Grizzly*
Lt Col JC Stothers	1983	23	23	102	148	*Highland Winter*, 3 units; SYEP
Lt Col JC Stothers	1984	26	28	106	160	SYEP Trg / Battlefield Tour Europe
Lt Col VG Chartier	1986	29	21	91	141	NB half unit are Offrs and Sr NCOs
Lt Col VG Chartier	1987	22	37	139	230[23]	Total includes Band – Trooping Colour; Queen Mother
Lt Col VG Chartier	1988	22	37	139	230	Total includes Band; 140 pending release
Lt Col DF O'Connor	1989	22	28	102	143	Total includes Band
Lt Col DF O'Connor	1990	24	22	144	190	
Lt Col DF O'Connor	1991	24	22	144	190[24]	
Lt Col DF O'Connor	1992	23	11	95	129[25]	Freedom of City Montreal; Scottish Festival
Lt Col IM McCulloch	1993	no report found				
Lt Col IM McCulloch	1994	20	24	129	173	placed 3rd in *Mary Otter Competition* #1 Dist[26]
Lt Col IM McCulloch	1995	23	19	110	167[27]	with Band
Lt Col GT Lusk	1996	15	20	122	157[28]	
Lt Col GT Lusk	1997	15	20	112	157[29]	Freedom of City Ormstown
Lt Col GT Lusk	1998	15	11	69	132[30]	Freedom of City Huntingdon
Lt Col GT Lusk	1999	16	21	74	111[31]	Ex *Verglas*; Freedom of City Verdun
Lt Col BD Bolton	2000	16	21	91	128[32]	
Lt Col BD Bolton	2001	20	20	77	117[33]	
Lt Col BD Bolton	2002	20	20	79	119	
Lt Col J Potter/Bolton	2003	18	25	79	122[34]	Freedom of City Mega City Montreal
Lt Col BD Bolton	2004	9	13 WO/Sgt	70	159[35]	
Lt Col TEC MacKay	2005	11	12 WO/Sgt	76	163[36]	
Lt Col TEC MacKay	2006	10	9 WO/Sgt	48	154[37]	
Lt Col TEC MacKay	2007	8	8 WO/Sgt	48	170[38]	
Lt Col TEC MacKay	2008	10	17 WO/Sgt	80	151[39]	
Lt Cols MacKay/Plourde	2009	stat annex not found			200 est[40]	143 On Pde, Pres Colours, HRH Prince Charles
Lt Col B Plourde	2010	stat annex not found			200 est	
Lt Col B Plourde	2011	18	25 WO/Sgt	114	222[41]	
Lt Col B Plourde	2012	19	9 WO/16 Sgt	111	209[42]	150th Anniversary, Fltchrs Fd Pde, Gov Gen Cda
Lt Col CR Phare	2013					

Note: All numbers from 1986–2012 are as listed in the Annual Historical Report filed with NDHQ by the Regiment.

Notes on Regimental Strengths, 3rd Bn:

1950–1970 avg str 241	mix WW2 era soldiers and recruits, few actual war veterans
1970–1980 avg str 136	*October Crisis, Unification,* loss of Regular Bns, "counter-culture"
1980–1990 avg str 174	Reagan resurgence vs *The Threat* in NATO, military rises in popularity
1990–2000 avg str 173	Rebuilding
2000–2008 avg str 160	Afghan War, Army increased popularity, callout/budget/trg
2008–2013 avg str 210	BW "Golden Age" created by Afghan War, Army v popular, call-out opportunity, budget/trg, effect returned war vets

"Effective Strength" (soldiers on Parade for exercises and training) was usually about 1/2 to 2/3 of the "paper strength" on official rolls. For a nominal roll total of 180, ninety on a regular parade was considered pretty good. The average attendance on weekend exercises and armoury drills averaged about one hundred, but it was not unusual to see fifty on an exercise. "In the Reserves you really cannot order attendance on exercise, for an accurate number of soldiers on exercise, you count who gets on the bus on Friday night. Same for Tuesday or Church Parade – see who forms up on the square. People work, study, have exams, family commitments or simply, they are burned out. Volunteer training takes its toll." (LCol Bruno Plourde).

The effects of war, Presentation of Colours and the effects of rebuilding (Bolton/MacKay) offered Lieutenant Colonel Plourde a first rate unit. His unique position (war veteran, considerable staff experience, and, executive position in the top echelon of Area HQ with access to powerful contacts within "the system") permitted the BW to enjoy "a golden age" circa 2008–2013.

In the last thirty years, battalion strength depended much on (1) Successful recruiting and, (2) The allotted budget which affected unit strength. Lieutenant Colonel Bruce Bolton: "Don't forget, the Brigade HQ rebalanced budgets to redistribute around its units, the old *bang bang bullet bullet* days [in lieu of training munitions] – we felt perhaps a little bit of favouritism showed to some units – but not overwhelming though. Ammunition allotment was inevitably based on whom you knew … one day an anchor chain arrived in front of the BW armoury – *the Squirrel* [Maj Lloyd, Rgtl RQM] could order anything through the system, he knew everyone."[43]

Notes to Appendices

1. Maj RP Bouillard, Chaplain with 1st then 2nd Bn RHC for four years. An Oblate Father, born in Belfort France. Served as missionary in the Canadian Arctic, joined Army in 1947; served across Canada and Korea. He retired to an Oblate Monastery in 1964.
2. Lt Col Newlands: "WO1 Firby served under my comd until Nov or Dec 1966. WO1 Blackwell succeeded Firby and served until 12 July 1967; succeeded by WO1 Pyatt to the end of my command and into Lt Col Morrison's command."
3. Not to be confused with Lt Col NH Ross DSO (Queen's Own Cameron Highlanders of Canada) listed in error on RHC Armoury memorial boards.
4. Both in Cyprus; padres at RHC services: Rev Capt G Davidson, Maj SM Malefont.
5. Rev Berlis, WIA in Normandy, later served with the Forestry Corps and Corps HQ in Europe before returning to RHC. Interview Rev Hayes 31 December 2012.
6. Later, CFR'd: Capt Dynes and head of BW Cadet Corps
7. Regular battalions formed; Montreal battalion becomes 3 RHC; Bourne first CO 3 RHC.
8. Lt Col Angus last CO 3 RHC, Regular battalions disbanded, Montreal battalion become RHC.
9. Rev Stephen Hayes took over as Padre when Rev Rod Berlis retired at fifty-five. JSS Armour: "Stephen took over rather than let the chaplaincy leave the church. He was chaplain for he thinks 3–4 years … his most notable service was the laying up of the colours of disbanded battalions. They were entrained to Montreal – masses of soldiers bedded down at the Armouries – church packed, Kildonan Hall overflowing (TV feed) and hundreds outside." JSSA 30 December 2012.
10. Stothers to Chartier 25 May 1986.
11. MacKay-Plourde: 14 November 2009.
12. Minister of The Church of St Andrew and St Paul, not BW Chaplain. No BW official chaplain since 2002; Rev Vaudrey was helping out after Topping. Rev J Veenstra filled in as well. As minister of the regimental church, he conducted the church parade and 150th Celebration for Reverend Captain Godkin, who was sworn in as chaplain in January 2013. Interestingly enough, Rev Godkin is a Lutheran pastor.
13. P/Maj Ogilvie attached to Depot for a short period prior to his retirement from the CF. "The Depot was not established for a Pipe Major... it would be incorrect to refer to him as the Depot Pipe Major". McCabe/RJJ 16 June 2014.
14. The Regimental Band was raised in Europe in 1955 and initially was stationed in Windsor Park, Halifax; moved in 1958 to Camp Gagetown, NB and co-located with 2 RHC. The Band remained under command GOC Eastern Command and had no command relationship with Second Battalion. In 1962, 2 RHC replaced 1 RHC in Fort St. Louis (Werl) Germany and simultaneously the RHC Regimental Band replaced the RCD Regimental Band in Fort York (Soest) Germany. Again, there was no command relationship – both functioned as separate units under Commander, 4CIBG. In 1965, the RHC Regimental Band was replaced in Fort York by the Band of the Royal Canadian Ordnance Corps and relocated to Long Pointe where it remained until its disbandment in 1969. Ibid.
15. A plaque with this inscription was placed on a wall in St Mary's Hospital Cardiology Ward on the occasion of his being presented with the prestigious William Hingston Award.
16. Brent Cowan/RJJ, [2, 13 May 2013
17. When the 2nd Bn BW converted to 2 RCR the strength, in the NAC Hist Report was [as at 1 January 1970 – 30 June 1970] was: 38 officers, 100 WOs and Sr NCOs, 542 Jr NCOs and 94 privates. Lt Col GS Morrison became CO 2nd Bn, The Royal Canadian Regiment. DHH. Annual Historical Report 5 April 1971.
18. BWA Unit Annual Historical Report (UAHR) 1 January 72 – 31 December 72 RHC. 5 July 1973. Lt Col LN Ferdon.
19. BWA UAHR 21 February 1974

20. BWA UAHR 25 March 1975. Parade strength 110; Reunion Dinner Gen JA Dextraze; St Hubert Queens Colour June, no summer trg; old colours laid up; twenty RHC on call-out Germany and Mid East on Class C Svc.

21. BWA UAHR 31 December 1976; UAHR 76–85 (sporadic).

22. MGen R Rohmer guest of honour at Reunion Dinner.

23. On Parade at Molson Stadium Trooping 1987: 14 Offrs, 128 NCO/ORs; 30 Band. Given previous year's numbers, RHC str 1987 likely 26 Offrs; 28 NCOs; 120 ORs; 35 Band for est total: 209 All Ranks. Large numbers during preparatory trg but Lt Col Chartier ordered to release them from regimental rolls – they were forbidden to march in the parade. Close scrutiny by senior HQs prompted by the gender discrimination complaint. Dozens from 3 BW Bns travelled to Mtl to parade before Queen Mother at own expense. RHC numbered close to 250 in May 1987.

24. DHH. Annual Historical Report 1991. Retirement Dinner held for MGen Christie; initially appointed member BW Advisory Board. BW placed 2nd in Secteur CIOR Competition1987.

25. Ibid., AHR 1992.

26. 1994, Lt Col McCulloch; RSS Officer Capt Harris Ivor Silver, DCO Maj Bolton, RSM CWO Miles; 1994, Lt Col McCulloch; on strength 193, Adverts in newspapers "Part Time Work". 28 Jan 1997 Regtl B'Day 135th Anniversary, Drumhead Ceremony. Padre Capt Glencross. 1 CO, 2 Maj, RSM; 5 capts, 1 RSS Capt; 4 lts.

27. DHH. AHR 1995. Proven Trophy: Sgt McLellan. UNPROFOR Medal: Ptes Camire, Ronalds, Weaver. 13 Trg Exercises.

28. Final numbers reflect "clearing deadwood from the nom rolls" and final releases; successful recruiting campaign; budget restrictions limited numbers trained on LI course.

29. DHH Annual Historical Report; 1997. Proven Trophy: Cpl BJ Miller. Decorations: 2 Yugoslavia; 7 Haiti.

30. Ibid., 1998; Cpl Marchand winner Proven Trophy; Medal Yugoslavia.

31. Ibid., 1999: enrolled 17; released 38.; Proven Trophy: Cpl Thompson; 3 x Yugoslavia Medals.

32. Ibid; 2000. Enrolled 26 vs 22 rel;Proven: MCpl Jonasz; 4 Yugoslavia Medals; the 11 training exercises included Ex with other units. Avg for BW during decade was 11–12 weekend exercise per trg year.

33. Ibid., Proven: MCpl Camire; 2 Yugoslavia Medals; 11 trg erxercise and, 10 Special Parade – Ticonderoga Tatto; Mtl Highland Games; Loon Mtn, NH; Church Parade; St Andrews' Levee; Regtl Birthday; Remembrance Day – average for a normal trg year. Special Pdes/Ceremonies include most of the Pipes and Drums.

34. DHH Ibid., Proven: Maj T MacKay; 4 Jubilee Medals; Dubuc Trophy, best unit 34 Bde.

35. BWA. 1325-1. Annual Hist Report 13 Dec 2004. Total 159, les pers on Release or Att working outside RHC reduced "Active" Bn strength to 95 All Ranks (2 H/Cols (McAlpine, Chartier), 1 LCol (Bolton), 1 Maj (DCO, Mackay), 2 Capt, 2 Lt, 3 2/Lt, 5 WOs, 9 Sgts, 39 MCpl/Cpl, 31 Privates. Producing a hundred or more for an important parade made trying to get soldiers release temporarily from postings. Difficult if they were out-of-province. Proven Trophy 2004, Cpl Daoust. Detached from BW, Major Phare (Jamaican Def College), Capt Kerr (West NSR), Lts Ward (London Scottish), Lt Evans (LFCA), 4 x Sgts. Exercises x15; Regt Pdes x2: Church Pde 79, Rem Day 65.

36. BWA 1325-1. Annual Hist Report 2005: 13 Offrs (Tom Mackay CO, inclu 2 H/Col), 13, 12 Sr NCOs, 5 MCpl, 40 Cpls, 31 Ptes. Active Total 101; "On Str" Total 163. Recruits 31; Released 7, Transfers (Reg Force) 26. Proven Trophy, Sgt Lawton. Adj/RSS, Capt Peter Radman. 10x Exercise, 2 Regtl Pdes (Church Pde x64; 11 Nov x61. Pipe Band had 28 Musical Engagements inclu Pdes, Mess Dinners, Alberta Centennary Tattoo, Highland Games, 2x Concerts. Avg 16–20 musicians. Church Pde and Change of Cmd band numbered 35.

37. BWA 1325-1. Annual Hist Report 2006. 12 Offrs, 3 WOs, 6 Sgts, 5 MCpl, 25 Cpl, 23 Ptes. Active Total 73. Total 154. Recruits 33, Releases 11, Trans 3. Course taken 55: avg 1–4, DP1 Inf 14,; Proven Trophy BW Soldier of the Year: Padre, Capt Glencross. KIA. Cpl JP Warren, Afghanistan 23 Jul 06. 13 Exercises; 8 Ceremonies, 2 Pdes: Church Pde x69; 11 Nov x 73.

38. BWA 1325-1. Annual Hist Report 2007. 10 Offrs (inclu 2 H/Col): 1 LCol, 1 Maj, 2 Capt, 4 Lts; 2 WO, 6 Sgts, 8 MCpl, 21 Cpl, 27 pte. Recruits 30, Releases 12, Transf 4. X 42 Course and Taskings (Instructors): avg 1–3; DP1 X13, Proven Trophy, Maj C Phare, 12 Unit exercises, Avg turn-out: 27 All Ranks; Range Weekend: 52. 13 Ceremonies/Pdes. Church Pde x69; 11 Nov x65. Band hand 79 engagements inclu Quebec City, Valleyfield, Dieppe, Vimy, Ypres.

39. BWA 1325-1. Annual Hist Report 2008. 12 Offrs (Inclu 2x HCols), 7 WOs, 10 Sgt, 11 MCpl, 44 Cpl, 25 Pte. Active Strength 109. Total Official Str 151; 14 Recruits; 13 Released. Course and Taskings (Instructors) x40; Church Pde 32; 11 Nov 73; Band x53 engagements, Mess Dinners, Parades. X32 at Church Pde, x33 at Regimental At-Home Mess Dinner.

40. *Presentation of Colours* (10 Nov 2009) saw 143 All Ranks on parade, this included soldiers on call-out and just returned from Afghanistan.

41. BWA 1325-1. Annual Hist Report 2011. Effective Strength 159. X37 Pdes and Ceremonies. x20 Courses; x9 Exercises.

42. BWA 1325-1. Annual Hist Report 2012. 21 Offrs (inclu 2 H/Cols), 9 WOs, 16 Sgts, 16 MCpl, 65 Cpl, 29 Pte. Band Engagements: x85; x40 at HRH visit Toronto, x35 St patricks Pde, x40 Church Parade, x30 Regtl B'Day Pde Jan; 30 11 Nov. Regtl Courses / Taskings 26+53 (Avg 1–3). Major Unit Exercises: x5 (Avg attendance: 44).

43. B Bolton 27 Jul 13 RHC Armoury.

Index to Volume III

Numbers in italics refer to photos or maps.

The ranks given for individuals are the highest they were
known to have held within the timeframe of this book.

Ablett, RSM WO 1 RA, 43, 48, 189, *241*
aboriginal peoples. *See* First Nations Peoples
Academy Award (movies), 104
Ace High (exercise) (1965–66), 113
ACE Mobile Force. *See* Allied Command Europe
    (ACE) Mobile Force
Acting While So Employed (AWSE) (rank), 345
Adamsville (Quebec), 79
Addy, Major Gen Paul G, 193; quoted as epigraph, 192
Advisory Board. *See* Black Watch Regimental
    Advisory Board
Afghan Air Force, 345, *430*
Afghan gong (award), *427*
Afghan National Army, 347
Afghan national police (ANP), 344
Afghan National Security Forces (ANSF), 340, 344, 345
Afghanistan Star (medal), 349
'Afghanistan' Theatre Honour, 303, 340, 350, 370, *453*
Afghanistan War (2001–14). *see* Battles and
    campaigns, Afghanistan War (2001–14)
Africa, 344; North Africa, 62, 94; East Africa, 281. *See*
    also specific countries
Agents Orange and *Purple*: testing at Camp
    Gagetown, 114–15
air forces: Canada (Royal Canadian Air Force), 42,
    67, 74, 107–08, 110, 113, 132, 186, 192, *442*;
    United Kingdom (Royal Air Force), 17, 77; NATO,
    173; United States Air Force, 22, 113, 132.
    Afghanistan (Afghan Air Force), 345, *430*. *See*
    also unification of Canadian Armed Forces

aircraft carrier: *Bonaventure*, 110. *See also* boats and
    ships
Aird, Capt Alastair, 146
Aird, 2Lt AR, *264*
Alabama Highland Games (US), 96
Alden, Brig Gen Robert ('Bob'), 134, 143, 147
Aldershot (Nova Scotia), 27, 29, *418*. *See also* Camp
    Aldershot (Nova Scotia)
Aldershot (UK), 69. *See also* Camp Aldershot (UK)
Alexander, Gen Sir Harold, Field Marshal Viscount,
    Earl Alexander of Tunis, Governor General
    1946–52, 33, 77, 255
Alexander, Lt/Capt, 43
Algeria, 97
All the Blue Bonnets are over the Border (song), 310
Allan, C Kennedy, 9–10
Allan, Col John B, 53
Allan, Col Sir Montagu, 7, 47, 194
Allard, Brig Gen Jean Victor, 26, 71, 105
Allen, Pte KA, *261*
Allen, Col C Kennedy, 52
Allied Command Europe (ACE) Mobile Force (AMF),
    110, 163, *257*; UN Cyprus deployment, including
    Winter Express (exercise), 110, 113–14, *257*; Allied
    Mobile Force North (AMFL North), 113
Allied Regiment. *See* Imperial Black Watch
Allmand, Hon Warren, 276, 277
Almelo Christian Male Chorus (Almelo Christelijk
    Mannenkoor) (Holland), 288
Alphand, Hervé, 52

Amazing Grace (song) 327–28

ambulances and ambulance units: *Régiment* de St John's Ambulance instruction, 61, 251; 51 Field Ambulance, 361

AMF. *See* Allied Command Europe (ACE) Mobile Force

AMFL North. *See* Allied Command Europe (ACE) Mobile Force

Anderson, Lt Gen WAB, 103, 128, 129; quoted as epigraph 128

Anderson, Pipe Major Jordon ('Jeordie'), 293, 295

Anderson, Sgt Kimberly Ellen Jane ('Kim'), 349, *428*, *436*; quoted as epigraph, 348

Anderton, Corporal Matthew, 346

Angus Yards (Quebec), 154

Angus, Allan, 154

Angus, Forbes, 154

Angus, Lt/Capt/Major/Lt Col/Col/Hon Col Stephen Frederick ('Steve'), 56, 60, 84, 89, 101, 153, 155, 164, *238*, *264–65*, 292, 377, *419*; quoted as epigraph, 29, 276, 304; Iroquois Reservation exercise, 63; appointment as company commander, 81; biographical description, 154–55; relationship with Malashenko, 156; October Crisis, 157–58; relationship with 2 R22eR, 159; relationship with District HQ, 159; transfer and relinquishment of command, 161–62, 164; as honorary lieutenant colonel and colonel, 198–99, 283, 300; reception with Queen Mother, 199; creation of Regimental Foundation, 274; appraisal of Jim Armour, 294; patron of the BW Foundation, 318–19; Advisory Board chairman, 323–14; death, 377

Angus, Meredith, 154

Angus, Molson, 154

Angus, Pamela, 63

Angus, Richard Bladworth, 60, 154, 312

Annapolis Valley (Nova Scotia), 27; Hurricane Edna (1954), 29

Anne, Princess Royal, 172

Anselmo, Frank, *417*

Arabia (Saudi Arabia), 306

'Arabian Sea' Theatre Honour, 350

Arabic (language), 179

Arbuthnott, Col Hon David, 198

Arbuthnott, Lt Col/Col JF, 113, 188

Arbuthnott, Major Gen Viscount of, 87

Archibald, Brig Gen Bruce, 273

Area Headquarters, 5; becomes Total Force Area Headquarters, 282. *See also* National Defence Headquarters

Arithmetic on the Frontiers (poem) (Kipling), 341

Armed Forces Centennial Tattoo, 106, 123–24 *passim*, 148, 160, *266*

Armed Forces Day: infantry parade (1968), 131–32

Armed Forces Staff College (US), 123

Armour, Dr Rev Capt Jim SS, 190, 191, 197, *245*, 280, 288, 300, 329, *414*; becomes padre, 169, 186; retirement, 190, 203, 294

armouries, general, 307; training, including officers, 12, 57, 247; recruitment, 56; Militia officers training (Plan B Training), 57; Special Militia Training Programme, 62; FLQ Westmount armouries attacks, 97; October Crisis, 157, 158; Royal 22nd Regiment occupation, 158; closing, 281–82. *See also* armoury (Fusiliers Mont-Royal Armoury); armoury (Grenadier Guards); armoury (Régiment de Maisonneuve); armoury (2nd Field Artillery Regiment); armoury (17th Duke of York's Hussars); armoury (62e Régiment d'artillerie de campagne); armoury (Victoria Rifles of Canada); Craig Street Armouries, including Drill Hall; Fort York Armoury; Spring City Armoury

armoury (2nd Field Artillery Regiment) (Lacombe Armoury) (Quebec): 1970 Summer Student Training Programme, 160

armoury (62e Régiment d'artillerie de campagne): FLQ raid, 97–98

armoury (BW) (Bleury Street) (Quebec), 5, 43, 49, 201, 204, 205, 278, 295, 297, 345, 351, 365, 366, 371–72; training, including Cadets, 20, 44, 106, 151, 160–61, 313, 334, 337; drills, 347; officers' mess, 31, 92, 119, 147, 170, 359; veteran post-war participation, 6; display cabinets, 7; fire, 8; refurbishment, 8, 9–10; artifacts, 28, 66, 359, 365; paintings, 28, 92, 119; trophies, 28; Philadelphia flag, 49; snuff mulls, 50; Gothic windows, 63; children's Christmas party, 79; Metro station establishment, 79; 1960s activities, 79–80; 1962 Royal Visit, 81, 84; sandblasted, 81; Band Room flood, 89–90; 1964 FLQ bomb explosion, 97; twice-weekly parades, 99; 1964 St Andrew's Ball, 104; Cadieux 1968 visit, 134–35; Good as member, 136; 1969 reunion dinner, 141–42; 1969 St Andrew's Ball, 142; 1970 Laying-Up the Colours, 147; 1970 reunion dinners, 150, 158–59; 75 mm Recoilless Rifles retention, 152; hours in 1970s, 153; quartermaster's stores, 155, 169; Alexei Malashenko as armoury worker, 156; October Crisis, 157–58; 1972 Summer Student Training Programme, 160–61; Ferdon's appointment ceremony, 161–62; *Recapture of Sanctuary Wood by The Black Watch, June 1916* (painting) presentation, 119; 1975 Imperial Black Watch visit, 173; Montreal Indoor Highland Games, 173–74; building of, 174; urban warfare exercise, 185, 187–88; Fraser as regular presence, 187; Drumhead Ceremony, 191; geographical location, including isolation, 193, 194, 198, 322; visit of Elizabeth II, 194–95; 2009 Presentation of Colours, 198, 361; 1992 Freedom of the City Parade, 205–06; Scottish Festival receptions, 206; repairs, 206; archives establishment, 279; 1996 parade, 283; Ormstown flag, 293; Quebec Thistle Council resolution, 296; as Scottish Community Centre, 296; atmosphere during Afghanistan War, 303; band practise, 310; informal Friday meetings, 312; 2006 Church Parade, 317; 2009 visit of Prince Charles, 318–21 *passim*; as fortress, 323; post-11 November parade receptions, 322, 324; Canadian Heritage Site declaration, 325; 150th Anniversary Dining-In, 328; death of Jason Warren, 342–43, 370; 2011 Remembrance Day Parade, 357; 2011 Trooping the Colour, 358; combat clothing etiquette, 360; 2012 Remembrance Day Dinner, 362; Regimental Boards unveiling, 362–63; exhibits, 363; 2016 change of command ceremony, 364

armoury (Fusiliers Mont-Royal): FLQ raid, 97, 98
armoury (Grenadier Guards) (Quebec), 361
armoury (Régiment de Maisonneuve) (Quebec): assumption of Victoria Rifles of Canada armoury, 107; 1971 Summer Student Training Programme, 160–61
armoury (Victoria Rifles of Canada) (Quebec): BW training, 8; Régiment de Maisonneuve occupation, 107, 160
Army Cadet League, 161, 313
Army Commander's Commendation, 340, 347
Army Headquarters. *See* Force Mobile Command
Army Meet (rifle competition), 78
Army Staff College (Camberley) (UK), 207
Arnhem, Battle of (Holland) (1944), 129
Ashbury College School (Ontario), 94
Askwith, Lt Col Charles Hopewell English, 36, 68, 75, *236*; biographical description, 37–38
Astudillo, Cpl Michael, *427*
Atlantic (Maritime) Black Watch Association (New Brunswick), 150, 324–25, *418*, *421*; publication of BW history, 326; 2012 Advisory Board meeting, 329. *See also* Black Watch Branch Associations
Atlantic Tri-Service (softball championship), 112
Auld Alliance, 159, 204–05, 295, 351
Auld Lang Syne (song), 197
awards and honours, 5, 33, 36, 116, 334, 340, 352, *418*; Member of the Order of the British Empire (MBE), 5, 7, 38, 91, 91, 167, 189, 236, 241, 241, 246, 268; Military Cross (MC), 4, 9, 28, 32, 33, 36, 42, 43, 50, 51, 75, 87, 121, *235–36*, *239*, *246*, *258*, *267*, 299, 305; Order of the British Empire (OBE), 13, 14, 19, 21, 22, 48, 75, 91, 95, 103–04, 134, 141, 191, *235–37 passim*, *248*, 288; Victoria Cross (VC), 59, 66, 80, 86, 87, 130, 136, 83–84, 325; Efficiency Trophy, 118; Mentioned in Despatches (MID), *passim*, 5, 21, 36, 59, 76, 94, 121, *241*, 305, 337, 346, 347; *Croix de Guerre*, 38, 135; Distinguished Service Order (DSO), *passim*, 4, 7, 9, 13, 21, 26, 32, 33, 36, 46–51 *passim*, 58–59, 59, 71, 79, 87, 91, 92, 103–04, 110, 134, 135, 142, 167, 197, *236*, *246*, 330, *407*; Distinguished Conduct Medal (DCM), 5, 13, 15, 67, 80, 241; Military Medal (MM), 20, 33, 198; Pulitzer Prize (literature), 7, 104; 13th, 42nd and 73rd Battalions commemorative plaques, 8, 9; Transvaal Cup (rifle competition), 9; British Empire Medal, 33; boxing championship (Eastern Command), 39, 75,
112; Canadian Amateur Championships (boxing), 39; rifle championship (Eastern Command), 39, 67, 68–69, 75, 112; Canadian Army championship (soccer), 43; Knockout Cup (rifle competition), 43–44; Canadian Forces Decoration (CD), 46–47; Freedom of the City parades, 49, 145–46, 204–06, 293–94, 304, *409*; Eastern Canadian Military fastball championship, 63; Garrison Cup (baseball), 63; Hamilton Gault Trophy (rifle shooting), 67, 140, 143, 149, *261*; Letson Gold Trophy (rifle championship), 67; softball championship, including Atlantic Tri-Service and Eastern Command, 67, 77, 112; Waterloo Trophy (weaponry), 67; Hamilton-Leigh Trophy (rifle shooting), 70; Bronze Star, 71; Donald MacLennan's *Moro* attack award, 71; Bantam Novice Crown (boxing), 74; Welter Open Championship (boxing), 74; volleyball championship, 75; British National 'B' championship, 77; Southern New Brunswick Senior League Championship (hockey), 77; Army Meet (rifle competition), 78; brigade championship (hockey), 78, 82, 91, 118–19, 142, 153, 308; Tri-Service championship (boxing), 78, 112; Grey Cup (football), 79, 330; hockey championship (Eastern Command), 91; Lord Strathcona Medal (cadet achievement), 95; Burns Trophy (rifle shooting), 96; Second Oldest Member Present (gathering prize), 101; Youngest Grandfather Present (gathering prize), 101; Academy Award (movies), 104; welterweight boxing championship (Eastern Command), 111; Kinnaird Trophy (game shooting), 112; Canadian Tank Trophy (NATO), 116; General Crerar Marches (piping), 118; Maple Leaf Marches (NATO infantry competition), 118; Skill-At-Arms competition (infantry), 118; Wakefield Sword (judo), 118; Drumming Competition, 119; Massachusetts state piping championships, 119; Novice Piping, 119; Royal Scottish Piping Society special award, 119; Maritime Tri-Service Trophy (hockey), 123; Order of Military Merit (OMM), 124, 133, 148, 163, 189, *236*, *239*, *258*, 266, 290, 326, 327, 329, 358, *415*, 354–55, *427*; engraved cups presentation (1968), 135; Perth Quaich (cup), 135, 164, 167; St-André-sur-Orne statue presentation, 135; Maritime Region championship (hockey), 144; Mary Otter Trophy (first aid), 144, 144, *261*, 281; Worthington Trophy (rifle shooting), 171; Dubuc Trophy (training), 172, 302–03, 294, 296, *419–20*; General Waters Trophy (rifle shooting), 175; Highland Winter I cup (exercise), 183; Military Merit (MMM), 190, *239*, *242*, *243*, 297, 298, 306, 330, 335, *410*, *416*, *428*, *429*, *442*; Duke of Edinburgh's Award, 194–95; Proven Cup (training), 198, 203, 293, 302, 356, *416*; United Nations service, 203; Sword of Honour (cadet achievement award) (Royal Military College of Canada), 207; recovered pipes commendation,

278; stolen medals (BW Regimental Museum), 279; cairn to 1758 assault, 288; Queen's Medal for Championship Shot, 290; 1998 commendation, 294; Vimy Award (defence and security), 294; G1 and G6 assessments, 299; Canadian Peacekeeping Service Medal (CPSM), 300; Hill 67 memorial plaque, 302; 'Afghanistan' Theatre Honour, 303, 340, 350, 370; hockey brigade championship (field hockey), 308; Diamond Jubilee Medal, 328; March and Shoot Competition, 330, *436*; infantry skills trophies, 334; Commendation for Bravery, 336; Army Commander's Commendation, 340, 347; General Campaign Star, 347; Afghanistan Star (medal), 349; Cyr's commendations, 349; 'Arabian Sea' Theatre Honour, 350; 'Kandahar', (honour), 350; 'Zhari-Panjwai'I' (honour), 350; Desert Storm (Operation) decoration, 352; Châteauguay 1812 (battle honour), 362; War of 1812 (honour), 362; tug of war championship, *412*; Afghan gong, *427*; Medal for Bravery, *432*; Bishop's College School (BCS) Colours, *442*

AWSE (Acting While So Employed) (rank), 345

Baddeley, Lt Andrew W, 314
Baden CF base (Germany), 208
Baffin Island (Nunavut): exercise (1973), 164
bagpipes. *See* pipes and drums
Bailey, Capt Harvey, 180–81, *410*
Baker, Brig HC, 102
Balhousie Castle (UK), 176, 188
Ballad of the Blue Berets (song), 122–23
Ballantrae, Baron, 173
balls: St Andrew's Ball, 6, 79, 87, 94–95, 103–04, 106, 142, 176, 181, 198–99, 295, 304, 306–07, 327; 1962 Royal Ball, 83; 1963 US military ball, 89; 1963 Trooping the Colour Ball, 91; 1963 Tri-Service Ball, 96; 1970 Camp Gagetown ball, 145; 1992 World Scottish Festival Tartan Ball, 206; 1987 Regimental Ball, *414*
balmorals, including blue balmorals, 335; 1954 permission to wear, 31, 45; 1974 Trooping the Colour, 170; blue balmoral continued wearing, 290; fawn balmoral, 290; khaki balmorals, 290; funeral of Queen Mother, 302; indicative of distinction between Reservist and Regular, 350; 1987 quantity, 359; cadets, *441*. *See also* green coatees; Red Hackles
bands, 1953 tattoos, 24; Black Watch Cadet Pipe Band, 44, 107, 297; Canadian Guards, 45; Regimental Military Band, 74–75, 101, 151–52, 162, 166, 195, 313; 1962 Presentation of Colours, 84; Halifax Massed Bands Concert, 86; Royal Canadian Dragoons Band, 111; Canadian Armed Forces Centennial Tattoo, 124–25; Camp Gagetown reunion, 126–26; 1987 Trooping the Colour, 195; Royal Canadian Artillery band, 195; Royal Military College of Canada Pipe Band, 201; 48th Highlanders Pipe Band, 277; 400th anniversary of Quebec City, 318; BW Association

bands, 328; CD production, 328; Fusiliers Mont-Royal instrumental band, 361, 42nd Bn Pipe Band, *458*, 3rd Bn (BW) The Royal Regiment of Scotland, *460. See also* pipes and drums
Banff (Alberta), 106–07
Bangkok (Thailand), 74
Bantam Novice Crown (boxing), 74
BAOR. *See* Units and Formations, Other, British Army of the Rhine
Barabé, Brig Gen JGJ Christian, 318, 351–52
Baril, Lt Gen J Maurice G, 285, 286, 289; quoted as epigraph, 286
Barlow, Lt/Capt Charles, 205, 275, 289
Barnett, Brig Garry C, 288
Barnum, PT, 52
Barrie (Ontario), 124
Barron, CWO John C, 205, *243*, 275, 321; biographical description, 314, 356
Barrow, Col Basil, 359
Barry, Corporal Sebastian: quoted as epigraph, 330
Base Gagetown. *See* Camp Gagetown
baseball and softball: Eastern Canadian Military fastball championship, 63; Garrison Cup (baseball), 63; softball championships, including Atlantic Tri-Service and Eastern Command, 67, 112
Batchelor, Sgt Devin, 334, *414–15*, *418*; biographical description, 345–46; deployment with 3 SCOTS, 347
Bathurst (New Brunswick), 136
Battalion Orderly Room (BOR), 106, 117, 181, 191, 320; Jimmy Evans's service, 99; allocation of clerks, 191; B Company (BW rifle company), 192
Battle of Châteauguay (Quebec): 150th Anniversary, 362
Battle of Normandy Museum (France), 188
Battles and Campaigns, First World War; Hill 70 (France), 9, 161; *Hundred Days*, 4, 80, 309; Cambrai, including Tilloy Hill, 309; Hangard Wood, 136; Mount Sorrel (battle) (1916), 76, 119; Somme, 59, 191; mock training attack (1992), 208; Vimy Ridge, Battle of (1917) (France), 150, 296, 309, 373, 377–78, *411*; BW grave crosses, 9, 161; three BW battalions, 126; 1984 visit, 188; and Camp Gagetown concentration, 208; memorial, including Remembrance Ceremonies (1960), *259*; pipes and drums ceremonies, 311; commemoration ceremony (2012), 330; Afghanistan War cartoon, *432;* 13th Battalion, 296; specific veterans, 4, 51, 80, 91, 105, 184, 191; long-term effect, 296; status within BW, 51, 296; road marker, *434. See also* First World War

BATTLES AND CAMPAIGNS, SECOND WORLD WAR; Battle of Britain, including *Blitz* (1940): 124

BATTLES AND CAMPAIGNS, DIEPPE, OPERATION JUBILEE, Mortar Platoon, 188, 330; Puys Beach, *passim*, 83; Edward Force (assault wave), 83; C Company (BW rifle company), 83; 20th Anniversary, 83; Richard Ross's performance, 21; *Web Foot* (exercise) compared, 132; 1984 memorial visit, 188; A Company (BW rifle company), 188; memorial pipes and drums, 311; 70th anniversary, 330;

BATTLES AND CAMPAIGNS, ITALY AND THE MEDITERRANEAN; Crete, 129; Hitler Line, 33; Lamone River, 75; Ortona, 36, 81, 331–32; San Lorenzo (Winter Line), 33–34. *See also* Italy;

BATTLES AND CAMPAIGNS, NORMANDY, OVERLORD (OPERATION), 103–04, 117, 186, 297; D Day, 132; 3rd Canadian Infantry Division, 38; 25th anniversary, 144; 40th Anniversary, 188; *In Desperate Battle* (television documentary episode), 204; ATLANTIC (OPERATION), as pinnacle of BW European success, 3; BURON, 38; CAEN, 25th Anniversary of battles south, 135; D-DAY (6 JUNE 1944), 3, 132; 3rd Canadian Infantry Division, 38; 25th anniversary, 144; 40th Anniversary, 188; GOODWOOD (OPERATION), veterans' return (2001), 302; MAY-SUR-ORNE: OPERATION SPRING, painting of 25 July 1944 attack, 8; Richard Rutherford wounded, 13; veterans' return (2001), 302. *See also* Motzfeldt Report; SPRING (OPERATION): casualties, including wounded, and fatalities percentage, *passim*, 13–14, 188; painting of 25 July 1944 attack, 8; Victor Foam, 9; Cameron Highlanders of Canada battle in St-André, 13–14; 25th Anniversary, 135; Verrières Ridge anniversary, 302, *420. See also Atlantic* (Operation); awards and honours; *specific individuals, locations, military units, and military tools and weapons;* ST-ANDRÉ-SUR-ORNE: summation of Cameron Highlanders of Canada's battle to secure, 13–14; 1969 veterans' return, 135; 1973 veterans' return, 164; 1984 veterans' return, 188; 2002 veterans' return, 302; ST-MARTIN-DE-FONTENAY, 2002 veterans' return, 302, *420*

BATTLES AND CAMPAIGNS, SCHELDT, 14, 110, 328; 'Black Friday' Hoogerheide–Woensdrecht attack, 121; Operation *Market Garden*, 3–4, 109; ARNHEM, 129; HOOGERHEIDE–WOENSDRECHT: 'Black Friday' attack (13 October 1944) 121; WALCHEREN CAUSEWAY, 110, *420;* WALCHEREN ISLAND, 110

BATTLES AND CAMPAIGNS, RHINELAND; Hochwald Campaign, 121

BATTLES AND CAMPAIGNS, NETHERLANDS; Hoogeveen, 118. *See also* Holland

BATTLES AND CAMPAIGNS, BOSNIAN CONFLICT (Third Balkan War) (Bosnia and Herzegovina, former Yugoslavia) (1992–95), including Bosnian peacekeeping, 284, 340; James Weir, 274; post-traumatic stress disorder, 279, 281; casualties, 280, *425*; description of BW participation, 280; Phare, including Phare as commander, 280, 314, 363; Royal 22nd Regiment ('*Van Doos*'), 280; Medak Pocket battle, 281; veterans, 281, 314; reserve forces proportional contribution, 284–85; Canadian Peacekeeping Service Medal, 300; funeral of Queen Mother, 302; battle groups personnel restrictions, 338–39; unit life reintegration, 339; Cyr, 349; Bruno Plourde, 351; Jason Warren, *425*; Snodden, *426*; Balkans: Balkan occupation (1941–44), 35, 36; Third Balkan War (1991–2001), 280, 281; Croatian War (1991–95), 274, 284–85

BATTLES AND CAMPAIGNS, IRAQ WAR, 331, 338, 346; Basra, 346; *Desert Storm* (Operation) (1991), 305, 352

BATTLES AND CAMPAIGNS, AFGHANISTAN WAR (2001–14), 318, 355, 363, 361, 368, 370, 371; veterans, general, 58, 159, 319, 322, 350–52 *passim*, 365; training, including training exercises, 194, 307–08, 313–14, 316, 331–32, 337, 353; specific veterans, 198, 294, 303, 316, 322, 331, 349–54 *passim*, 356, 357, *426–34*; first deployment, 303; honours and decorations, 303, 340, 349, 350, *425, 427*; Psychological Operations (PSYOPS) 307, 337–39 *passim*, 346–51 *passim*, 356, *428, 431–32*; pipes, 311, 313–14; safety of soldiers, 320; BW 150th Anniversary stamp, 325, 326, *435*; redeployment into Kandahar, 337; Canadian support groups, 338; need for reservists, 338–39; post-war retention of soldiers, 339–40; adjustment to modern combat, 340–41; as cyber-war, 341–42; relationship to traditional combat, 342; deaths of soldiers, 342–43, 348, *425*; staff officers, 343–44; colonel, 344–45; Afghanistan military culture, 345; Imperial BW (3 SCOTS) deployment, 346–47; Robinson (combat outpost), 349; conclusion, 350, 364; 'Force Generators', 350; Kandahar Battle Group, 352; repatriation ceremony, 355–56; expected officer performance, 359; CADPAT uniform, *449*; clearing operation, *432*; cartoons, *432. See also* Kabul; Kandahar. *See also* Kabul, Kandahar, Ma'Sum Ghar, Mushan; ATHENA (OPERATION) (2003–11), *429, 442;* ATTENTION (OPERATION) (2011–14), 345, *427;* TELIC (OPERATION) (2003–11), 346; ZHARI DISTRICT (AFGHANISTAN), 347

Baumans, Lt/Capt Loic Maxim, 331, 332, *426*
Beacon, WO 1/CWO CW ('Tiny'), 122, 127, *240*
Beare, Lt Gen Stuart: quoted as epigraph, 323
Beaver Club (Quebec), 190
Bedford (Quebec), 79
Bedford Ranges (Nova Scotia), 39

beer, 16; German, 116–17; Canadian, including Molson's, 86, 293

Belgium, 116; Allied entry and fighting, 19, 21, 66; guns and rifles, 77–78. *See also specific battles and locations*

Bell, Cpl J, *261*

Beloin, OCdt L, *410*

Belzil, Cpl (R22R) Jean Francois, *432*

Belzile, Lt Gen Charles H, 282

Benn, Lt L, *410*

Bennett, Capt/Major Edwin Ronald ('Ron') ('Ronnie'), *446*; relationship with Richard Rutherford, 13

Berlis, Capt Rev/Major RJ ('Rod'), 50, 62, 85, 103, 105–06, 147, 203, *245*; wounded, 66; sermons, 50, 103; church involvement with military, 146; retirement, 169

Bernard, Private JPE, 143

Bernatchez, Major Gen/Brig J Paul E, 46, 70, 134

Best, MCpl/Sgt, 376, 377, *436, 455, 457*

Betts, Sgt Gordie, 312, *417, 420–21*

Beverly Hills (US), *229*

Biafra, 171

Biddell, Lt JW, *264*

Biddle, AJ Drexel, Jr, 53

Birks, GD, 134

Birks, Henry Gifford, 55

Birks, HLCol H. Jonathan, 379, *462*

Bishop's College School (BCS) (Quebec): graduates, *passim*, 12, 94, 95, 154, 167–68, 198, 199, 314; Cadet Corps (School), 43, 95, 96–97, 106, 162, 172, 312–13, 321, *441*; Church Parades, *439, 441*

Bishop's University (Quebec), 95

Bisley (UK): rifle competition: 1952, 9; Private Pearson 1952 qualification, 44; James Ross as commander, 48; 1960, 69–70; Cadet team, 106–07; 1965, 112, *261*; 1996, 290. *See also* guns and rifles, including machine guns

Bissonnette, Lt A, *414*

Black Bear (exercise) (1965–66), 112–13

Black Bear (tune), 72, 85, 145–46, 196, 201, 378

Black Hussar (exercise), 165

Black Watch Archives (BWA), 279–80, 310, 355; proposed, 7

Black Watch Association, 55, 322; socials, 103; 1970 Ste Anne's Military Hospital visit, 159; visits to ailing soldiers, 159; 1974 Presentations of Colours, 166; 1987 Trooping the Colour, 194, 195; bands, 277, 310, 328; Henley as participant, 290; *Canadian Red Hackle* (magazine), 301, 369, 371, 376, 381, 382; *The Red Hackle Express*, 382; 2002 Normandy veterans' return, 302; BW relationship with Queen Mother, 319; 2009 Presentation of Colours, 320. *See also* Black Watch Branch Associations

Black Watch Avenue (New Brunswick), 326

Black Watch Branch Associations, 323–25; emergence, 6; Toronto Association (TBWA) ('Toronto Branch'); 6, 78, 150, 312, 324, 328, *421, 422, 435*; Montreal Regimental Association, 51, 312, 324, 327, *418*,

421; Atlantic (Maritime) Association, 150, 324–25, 326, 329, *418, 421*; 1987 Trooping the Colour, 195; *Canadian Red Hackle* (magazine), 301; Pacific Association, 324; Upper Canada/Ottawa Association, 324; Afghanistan War, 339. *See also* Black Watch Association

Black Watch Business Council, 274–75

Black Watch Cadet Corps, 278, 313, 314; 1954 parade, 43; part of 1 RHC, 96; Canadian Centennial, 106–07; relationship with Canadian Armed Forces, 107; recruitment advantage, 151; meeting with Queen Elizabeth, 194–95; Pipe Band, 44, 107, 277, 297, 310, 328; meeting with Prince Charles, 321

Black Watch Cadet Pipe Band, 297; formation, 44; performance locations, 107; combination with regimental band, 277; cadet programme, 310; CD production, 328. *See also* bands; Black Watch Cadet Corps; pipes and drums

Black Watch Canada Foundation, 274–75

Black Watch of Scotland. *See* Imperial Black Watch

Black Watch Regimental Advisory Board, 89; Neil Ritchie joins, 22; redesignation as BW, 23; Maritimes recruitment, 28; battalion representation, 58; luncheons, 59–60, 164; Blackader becomes chairman and John Bourne becomes vice-chairman, 92; Bourne's management style, 133; reduction to nil strength, 136, 138–39; difficulty in locating officers, 174; Sewell's contribution, 174; 1987 Trooping the Colour, 194; Stavert's contribution, 200; 1962, *262*; establishment of Regimental Foundation, 274–75; Regimental Headquarters as adjunct, 287–88; selection of khaki tam o'shanter pattern, 290; Bruce Bolton's relationship with, 298–99, 308; Stephen Angus as chairman, 300, 318–19, 323–24, *419*; Potter's relationship with, 306; discussions concerning 150th Anniversary, 324; relationship with BW Associations, 324–25; 2012 meeting, 329; Isaac Kennedy's contribution, 368; O'Connor's contribution, 354; 150th Anniversary stamp, *435*

Black Watch Regimental Museum: opening, 7; spared in fire, 8; 'The Road to Pittsburgh' (painting), 9–10; Jackson-Hall as curator, 51; 13th Battalion wooden crosses, 161; Korea and peacekeeping exhibits added, 279; security, 279; refurbishment, 281; reopening, 325, *439*; publication of *Canada's Black Watch 1862–2012*, 326

Black, Master Corporal Don, 170

Blackader, Lt Col/Col/Brig Gen Kenneth Gault ('Ken'), 3, 19, 51, 199, *246*; biographical description, 92; presentation of battle pennant, 12; 1940 BW church parade, 20; conversion of 1st and 2nd CHB, 23; relationship with William Watson, 37; 1954 State Dinner, 45; 1956 Regimental Parade, 46–47; description of George Cantlie, 47, 154; 1957 church parade, 51; relinquishment as honorary lieutenant colonel, 51; appointment as

Colonel-of-the-Regiment, 58; functions of the 5th Royal Highlanders; 58; 1968 reunion dinner, 59; 1 RHC in 1959 NATO brigade, 69; 1962 Denmark inspection, 82; 1962 visit of Queen Mother, 84; Vanier telegraph, 84; 1962 parade, 84; final six months as Regiment colonel, 90, 91, *260*; 1963 Trooping the Colour, 91, *260*; *Canada's Black Watch*, 92; retirement, 92; Advisory Board, 92, *262*; death, 130; 1962 Gagetown Depot inspection, 137

Blackwell, WO 1 Robert, 103, 123, *250*

Blaikie, Hon Bill, 277

Blakeney, RSM WO 1 Frederick Edward ('Fred'), 20, 33–34, 39, 69, *240*

Blazevic, WO V, 184

Bleasdale, RSM WO 1 E, 5, *241*

Bleury Street armoury. *See* armoury (BW)

Blissville airfield (New Brunswick), 46, *253*. *See also* Camp Gagetown

Blitzkrieg (*Vernichtungsschlacht*) (1940), 70; objectives and tactics, 18

blue balmorals. *See* balmorals, including blue balmorals. *See also* green coatees; Red Hackles

Blue Train, 124

Boat Cloak (exercise) (1963), 110. *See also* boats and ships

boats and ships: Lake Superior Regiment (Motor) (infantry regiment), 19; *Cornwallis* (patrol boat), 39; *Shearwater* (patrol boat), 39, 72, *424*; *Stadacona* (patrol boat), 39, 111; *Bonaventure* (aircraft carrier), 110; *Boat Cloak* (exercise), 110; *Donnaconna* (reserve ship), 282

Boer War (Second) (1899–1902), 160

Bogart, Major Gen FJ, 83–84

Bogisch, Lt GVM, 111

Boire, Major Michael, 158, 160, 161, 162, 321, 322, 326

Bolton, Pamela Margaret, 154

Bolton, Pipe Major/Capt/Lt Col/Col Bruce Douglas, 168, 186, 188, 206, *239*, *242*; 274, 282, 284, 370, 377, 379–80, *410, 457, 462*; 1974 Trooping the Colour, 166; Montreal Indoor Highland Games, 174; qualification as RSM, 176, 298; eightieth birthday of Queen Mother, 176; retirement, 180; 1992 Freedom of the City, 205; *The Way Ahead* proposal, 207; description of O'Connor, 207; creation of BW Business Council 275; quoted as epigraph, 276, 297, 307, 356; 1997 Hong Kong parade, 288; *Escort Patrol*, 293; appointment as colonel, 296, 298; biographical description, 297–98, 308; awarded MMM, 298; Black Watch Advisory Board, 298–99; relationship with brigade HQ, 299; relationship with regimental church, 300; launching of *Canadian Red Hackle*, 300; 100th birthday of Queen Mother, 301; funeral of Queen Mother, 301–02, *416*; Operation *Spring* anniversary, 302, *420*; Dubuc trophy, 303; Afghanistan War, 303; first retirement, 304–05, *437*; resumption as CO, 306; 2003 St Andrew's Ball, 306–07; second retirement, 308; composition of *Lieutenant Colonel Bruce D Bolton, MMM*, 308; work in retirement for pipes and drums, 310, 311, 313; approach to governance, 317; 2009 presentation of Colours, 320; Regimental Museum, 325; 2012 church parade, 328–29; function of officers, 356; 1987 Trooping the Colour, *414*

Bolton, Richard, 154–55

Bolton, WO2 CSM Charles Wilfred ('Charlie'), 297; wounded, 188

Bombardier Cadet Corps, 313

Bonaventure (aircraft carrier), 110. *See also* boats and ships

Bonnie McAlpine (tune), 100

Bonny McAlpine (march), 120

Bonnycastle, Lt AC, 145

Booth, Eric, *410, 411, 419*

Booth, Ewen, *411*

Booth, Private William Tripp ('Bill'), 96

Boran, Joseph, 310

Bosnia (former Yugoslavia). *See* Battles and campaigns, Bosnian Conflict

Boswell, Capt WC, *264*

Boswell, Major Allan Paterson, 12, 19, 247

Bouillard, Capt Rev R, *244*

Bourassa, Hon Robert, Liberal Premier of Quebec 1970–76, 1985–94, 157

Bourdon, Sgt B, 205; quoted as epigraph, 109

Bourne, A/Capt/Major/Lt Col/Col/Hon Col John Gilbert ('Johnny'), 52, 186, 203, 207, *237, 246, 414*, Selwyn House, 314; Special Service Force command, 42; relationship with Parker, 27; BW dress and custom, 28, 30–31; disciplinary incidents, 29; biographical description, 42–43, 133, 304; appointment as CO, 43; relationship with Queen Mother, 43, 198, 199, 292, 304; 1954 State Dinner, 45; promotions during tour, 48; 1957 church parade, 51; 1968 reunion dinner, 60; appointment as board vice chairman, 92; appointment as Colonel of the Regiment, 133, 135; 1968 reunion dinner, 134; BW disbandment, 136, 138–39, 140, 141–42; quoted as epigraph, 138, 194; communication with Trudeau, 139, 142; 1969 reunion dinner, 141–42; 1970 BW reception at Windsor Castle, 145; communication with Queen Mother, 146; reappointment as Honorary Colonel, 147; 1970–72 reunion dinners, 150, 159, 164, *407*; meeting with William Russell, 169; 1974 Trooping the Colour, 170; extension of Honorary Colonel position, 171; 1977 reunion dinner, 171; problems with Advisory Board, 174; relationship with Klepak, 180, 186; audience with Colonel-in-Chief, 188; appointment as CO, 189; appraisal of Chartier, 190; capabilities at raising funds, 190; 1987 Trooping the Colour, 194, 195, 196; name for pipe band tune, 196, 300, 311; 1987 church parade, 197; retirement, 198–99; relationship with Stavert, 199–200; Cyprus tour, 200, *258*; 1989 reunion dinner, 202; 1962 Advisory Board,

262; McCulloch employment interview, 273–74; eightieth birthday, 292–93; visits to RHQ, 298; relationship with Bruce Bolton, 298–99; death, 304; Queen Mother 1981 visit, *410*

Bourne, Dr Wesley, 42

Bovington (UK), 201

Bowes-Lyon, Pte, *442*

boxing: I RHC dominance (1955), 24; boxing championship (Eastern Command), 39, 75, 112; BW as boxing bastion, 39; Canadian Amateur Championships, 39; 2 RHC championship (1958), 67; in 1959, 69; Bantam Novice Crown, 74; team champions, including Welter Open Championship (1958–59), 74, *254*; victories under Leonard, 75; 2 RHC Tri-Service championship (1960), 78; championship (1963), 91, *254*; competition victories against Navy (1963–64), 111–12; Brasseur's skills as boxer, 354

Boy Scouts: Germany, 73; Canada, 94

Boyd, Capt Rob, 274

Boyd, Lt Col John, 274

Boyle, Corporal Kieran, 276, 278

Bradeen, Capt CS, *264*

Brasseur, WO Pierre Serge, 332, 361, 369, *421, 436*; biographical description, 353–54

Bray-Dunes (commune) (France), 14

Breau, Lance Corporal JJ, 70

Bretteville-sur-Laize (France): Canadian War Cemetery, 188

British Empire Medal, 33

British National 'B' championship (hockey), 77

Brockville (Ontario), 27

Bromont (Quebec), 172

Bronze Star, 71

Brown, Pipe Major Harry H, 106, 142, 159

Brunette, André, 293

Brunner, Michael, *417, 420*

Buchanan, Erskine, 134

Bundy, Edgar, 119, 325–26

Burcew, Sgt (R de Mais) Piotr, *432*

Burke, Hon James, 89

Burma, 12, 173

Burns Trophy (rifle shooting), 96

Burns, Robert ('Robbie'), 115; quoted as epigraph, 48, 285

Buron (France), battles of (1944): 38

Burpee, 2Lt LD, *264*

Burrows, Corporal Bert, 144

Bush, Stan ('Fender Bender'), 12–13

Bushy Run, Battle of (US) (1763): painting, 9–10, 52

'But we will carry on' (poem) (Lenathen), 143

Butcher, Capt Tony, 168

Butts, Private Joe, 111

Byrne, S/Sgt Jim Y, 75, 91

Caccia, Sir Harold, 52

Cadet Pipe Band. *See* Black Watch Cadet Pipe Band. *See also* bands; pipes and drums

Cadet Services, 99

cadets, including cadet-officers, 127, 189, 298, 301; officer cadets, 96–97; Bishop's College School Cadet Corps, 43, 95, 96–97, 162, 172, 312–13, 321, *441*; Highland Cadet Battalion, 312–13, 321; Royal Military College of Canada, 46, 207; Sea-Cadets, 192; 1953 foundation, 43, 44, 107, 312–13; Pipe Band, including BW, 44, 107, 297, 313; Regimental Military Band cadet training, 44; summer camp, 45; 1957 parade, 50–51; officer cadet badge use, 57; Rothesay Collegiate School Cadet Corps, 79, 96–97, 313; Lord Strathcona Medal, 95; King's College School, 96–97; Lachine High School Cadet Corps, 96–97; Oromocto High School Cadet Corps, 96–97, 313; Cadet Services, 99, differing treatment of COTC and Regular Officer Training Plan (ROTP) cadets, 100; Loyola COTC officer cadets, 100–01; Camp Gagetown eastern corps, 106; Bisley rifle competition, 106–07; National Cadet Camp, 106–07; relationship with Canadian Armed Forces, 107; 1967 Royal Parade, 127; 1970 Laying-Up the Colours, 147; 'Cadet Leader Instructor' certificate, 151; participation advantage, 151; specific BW Corps graduates, 154, 160, 274, 278, 312; Darney as BW commander, 161; Army Cadet League, including admission of girls and young women, 161, 313; 1974 Presentations of Colours, 166; Imperial Black Watch, 170; King's-Edgehill School Cadet Corps, 170, 313, 321, *440*; Collège militaire royal de Saint-Jean (CMR), 183, 357, *357*, 362, 364; 1987 Trooping the Colour, 194, *195*; Duke of Edinburgh's Award, 194–95; Cotie as Queen Elizabeth II duty piper, 195; West Nova Scotia Regiment Cadets, 201; *Black Bear* (exercise), 201; Sword of Honour (award) (Royal Military College of Canada), 207; Camp Gagetown graduation, 293; Cadet Corps, affiliated, 301; BW general history, 312–14; Bombardier Cadet Corps, 313; Mick Darney as BW training officer, 313; BW exercises' description, 313; BW history, 313–14; BW shooting team, 313–14; 2006 Church Parade, 317; 2009 Presentation of Colours, 321; 2012 Church Parade, 328–29; 2011 Remembrance Day Parade, 357; 451 Squadron Air Cadets, *422*

Cadieux, Hon Léo, Liberal Minister of Defence, 1967–70, 134–35, 138–39; quoted as epigraph, 138

CADPAT (uniform), 342, 352, *431*

Cain, WO1 EF, *240*

Cain, Private RD, 15

Cairo (Egypt), 170

Calderwood, John, *417*

Camberley (UK): Staff College, 207

Cambridge University (UK): 'Oxbridge', 80

Cameron, Col AC, 174; quoted as epigraph, 16

Cameron, Col Peter, 170, 171, 175, 176, 190

Cameron, Lt Ian, 176

Camilla, Duchess of Cornwall, 118, 318, *434, 456*

Camire, Master Corporal/Sgt Kevin, 302, 308, *416*

Camolese, Lt EDR, 161

camouflage, 348; CADPAT, 342, 352, *431*; rule, *431*; Princess Margaret parade at Camp Gagetown, 67–68

Camp Aldershot (Nova Scotia), 22, 29, 200–01, *250*, 298, 358; church parade, 20; description, 20, 27; 2 RHC marshalled, 20; Korean War deployment anticipation, 29; fire, 32; training, 38, 117, 132–33, 298; 1 RHC soccer team, 43; 1 RHC George Cantlie parade representation, 46; vacation of temporary summer camps, 65; rifle competitions, 69; Scott Morrison posting, 131; 2 RHC return, 138; uniform, 358; Maritime BW Association march, *418*

Camp Aldershot (UK), 45; Gagetown compared, 45

Camp Borden (Ontario), 200–01, 310; Royal Canadian School of Infantry (Infantry School), 46, 207

Camp Bouchard (Quebec), 158

Camp Dubé (Quebec), 160. *See also* Camp Valcartier

Camp Farnham (Quebec), 42–43, 331, *431*, *436*; training, 6, 63, 106; exercises, 79, 168, 184, 204, 335, 347, 354; inspection incident, 117; officers' mess, 181; 2012 March and Shoot competition, 330

Camp Gagetown (Base Gagetown) (New Brunswick), 32, 81, 87, 143, 175, 200–01, 326, 340; 1st Canadian Division concentration location, 32, 35; garrison duties, 38–39; construction, 45; subaltern qualification course, 57; description, 65–66, 125; St Andrew's Barracks, 66, 110, 125; opening, 66–67; summer training, 82, 86; 1963 Trooping the Colour, 91, 92, *260*; training exercises, 103, *251*; eastern Cadet Corps, 106; boxing competition, 111–12; rifle ranges and rifle championships, 112; *Ace High* (exercise), 113; pipers, 114; *Agents Orange* and *Purple* testing, 114–15; character, 116, 125–26; 1967 reunion, 126–27; 1967 Trooping the Colour, 127–28; 1968 Trooping the Colour, 130–31; Regimental Depot closure, 132–33; Knox's retirement ceremony, 134; orientation to Cyprus deployment, 136–37; absence of Quebec soldiers, 137; disbandment, 140–41, 146, 147, 149; hockey training and games, 142–43, 144; 1970 Trooping the Colour, 144–46; becomes Base Gagetown, 144; 3 RHC 1966 visit, 152; 1967 Trooping the Colour, 96, 162, 165, *267*, 312; RV 81, 184; *EnGarde 90* (exercise), 202; 1992 summer concentration, 207–08; as 'ghost camp', *251*; march on Blissville airfield, *253*; St Andrew statue, *253*; Royal Canadian School of Infantry (Infantry School), 275, 291, 298, 363; Phase 2 Infantry graduation, 293; Afghanistan War training, 337; Combat Arms School, 341; uniforms, 359

Camp Lejeune (US), 331

Camp Longue-Pointe (Long Point Garrison) (Quebec), 193, 194, 361; as Long Point Garrison, 152

Camp Maple Leaf (Cyprus), 144

Camp Nathan Smith (Afghanistan), 346

Camp Petawawa (Canadian Forces Base Petawawa) (Ontario), 29, 163, 182, 200–01, *408*

Camp St Bruno (Quebec), 313–14

Camp Sussex (New Brunswick), 29, 67

Camp Valcartier (Quebec), 95, 162, 328; exercises, 6, 160, 184, 187, 200, 291, 292, 331–32, 333, 335, 337, 354, *408*, *424*; clan gatherings, 15; subaltern qualification course, 57; boxing championships, 91; brigade evaluation, 145; Junior Leaders Course, 160–61; militia weekends, 182; Eastern Area Battle School, 335; Combat Team, *408*; Tactical Command Post (Tac CP), *408*; 1981 RV 81 participation, *448*

Camp Wainwright (Alberta), 187, 188, 372

Campaign Star (award), 347

Campbell, Capt Bob, 136

Campbell, Capt/Major Alexander ('Sandy'), 174, 207, 311, 313, *407*

Campbell, Douglas, 150, 151

Campbell, Linda, *456*

Campbell, Major DC, 102

Campbell, MWO/CWO SD ('Steve'), *243*, 281, 374, 375, 382, *462*

Camrose (Alberta), 39

Canada Day (Dominion Day), 71, 131

Canada's Red Hackle (journal), 301, 369, 371, 376, 381, 382

Canadian Air/Sea Transportable (CAST): brigade, 172

Canadian Amateur Championships (boxing), 39

Canadian Armed Forces, 302, 322; relationship with BW Cadet Corps, 107; Centennial Tattoo, 106, 123–25 passim, 148, 160, 266; reorganization and BW disbandment, 36, 128–29, 138–41, 146–49 passim, 151, 159, 363; first aid supremacy, 144; Red Hackles, 154; shift to gender-free, 193. *See also* Units and Formations

Canadian Armoured Corps, 98, 101, 129, 315

Canadian Army Command and Staff College. *See* Canadian Land Forces Command and Staff College

Canadian Army Headquarters. *See* Force Mobile Command

Canadian Army Reserve Force, 42

Canadian Army Staff College. *See* Canadian Land Forces Command and Staff College

Canadian Bible Society, 169

Canadian Charter of Rights and Freedoms (1982), 284

Canadian Force Europe, 75, 118

Canadian Forces Base Cornwallis (CFB Cornwallis) Recruit School (Nova Scotia), 132, 148

Canadian Forces Base Kingston (CFB Kingston) (Ontario): Eastern Command boxing championship, 39, 75; Militia Command and Staff College, 74, 147, 164, 185, 275, 279, 298, *431*

Canadian Forces Base Petawawa. *See* Camp Petawawa

Canadian Forces Base Shearwater (Nova Scotia), *442*

Canadian Forces College (Ontario), 352

Canadian Forces Decoration (CD), 46–47

Canadian Forces Military College. *See* Collège militaire royal de Saint-Jean

Canadian Forces Sports Hall of Fame, 290

Canadian Guards: pipe band, 45. *See also* 27th Canadian Infantry Brigade

Canadian Human Rights Commission, 192, 193

Canadian Land Forces Command and Staff College (later Canadian Army Command and Staff College) (Canadian Army Staff College) (Ontario), 352; Fire Power Demonstrations, 132; tactical demonstrations, 140

Canadian Military Policemen (MPs): Korean War, 25–26

Canadian Military Training Team: service in Ghana, 109

Canadian Officers' Training Corps (COTC), 57; McGill University, including graduates, 100, 147, 134; Loyola College, 46, 100–01, 134, 160; Sir George Williams University, 46, 100; university contingents, general, 46; Université de Montréal, 100; Dalhousie University, 131; 1968 disbandment, 173. *See also* recruitment; training

Canadian Patrol Concentration (CPC), 372, 376

Canadian Peacekeeping Service Medal (CPSM), 300

Canadian Provost Corps, 112

Canadian Red Hackle (magazine), 369, 371, 376, 381, 382; launched, 296, 300–01. *See also Red Hackle* (Canada) (vols 1–2); *Red Hackle* (UK)

Canadian School of Infantry. *See* Royal Canadian School of Infantry

Canadian Special Operations Forces, 350

Canadian Tank Trophy (NATO), 116

Canadian War Cemetery: in Brettevillesur-Laize (France), 188

Canadian War Museum (Ottawa), 161, 294

Canadian Women's Army Corps (CWAC), 191

Canavan, Col Michael, *462*

Cannon, Fred T, 159

Cantin, WO Y, 299

Cantlie Tartan (uniform), 30, 360

Cantlie, Capt/Major/Lt Col Stuart Stephen Tuffnel, 154, 348–49; Operation *Spring*, 85, 184; appraisal of Blackader, 37; headstone, *420*

Cantlie, Col George Stephen, 27, 81, 82, 129, 133, 155, 311, 360–61; Great War, 47, 13; 1949 reunion dinner, 7; death, 46, 47; special regimental parade, 46–47; awarded CD and DSO, 47; biographical description, 47; 1912 Trooping the Colour, 85, 361, quoted as epigraph, 154; christened The Father of the Regiment, 154

Cantlie, Lt Col James Alexander, Jr, 13

Cantlie, Lt Col/Col Stephen Douglas ('Steve'), 154

Cape Breton (Nova Scotia), 12–13, 110, 148

Cardinal Newman High School (Quebec), 313

Carleton University, 273

Carlisle, Corporal/Sgt William James ('Bill'), 127, 312, *421*; BW instructor, including SEEP, 156,

160–61, 192; biographical description, 160; 2009 presentation of Colours, 321; BW 150th anniversary, 324; Katherine Taylor anniversary painting, 326, 327, *435*; *Operation Santa 2012*, 339

Carlisle, Margaret McGiverin, 312, 326

Carmosino, CWO M, *43*, 363, 370, 374

Carozza, Sgt/WO Gio, 176, 205

Cartmel, MWO Richard, 171, *418*

Castle Ehreshoven (Germany), 91

Caughnawaga Indians, 63. *See also* First Nations Peoples

Caverhill, Lt Col Frank, 56

CD (Canadian Forces Decoration), 46–47

Centennial (Canada) (1967), 36, 359; Trooping the Colour, 96, 162, 165, *267*, 312; Canadian Armed Forces Tattoo, 106, 123–28 passim, 148, 160, *266*; Centennial kilt parachute jump, 131. *See also Expo 67*

Chafi, Col Dan, Commander 34 Brigade, *443*

Chambers, Egan E, 43

Champagne, Lt JAG, 291

Chapdelaine, Lt Col G, 322

Chapman, Earl, 326

Chaput, Maj P, *410*

Charest, Jean, 326

Charles, Prince of Wales 1958–present, 198, 318, 320, 321–22, 356, 377, *456*, *457*, *479*; presentation of Colours to BW, 118, 316, 319, 334, 347, *434*; becomes Colonel-in-Chief, 301–02, 316

Charlottetown Conference (1864), 98

Charters, WO 1 TF, 80, *240*, *263*

Chartier, Sgt/WO 2/RSM WO 1/Capt/Major/Lt Col/ Hon Col Victor Girard ('Vic'), 91, 180, 186, 191, 203, *239*, *242*, 280, 296, 297, 308, 370, *410*, *414–15*, *421*; promotion to WO 2, 100; promotion to RSM, 168, 189; promotion to Capt, 176; commander of guard of honour, 187; appointment as CO, 189; quoted as epigraph, 189, 198; biographical description, 189–90, 300; 1987 Trooping the Colour, 193–96 passim; 1988 brigade exercises, 200; regimental secretary, 275, 301; honorary lieutenant colonel, 300, 315; 2009 presentation of Colours, 319; death, 370

Châteauguay (Quebec), 185, 353

Châteauguay (battle honour), 362

Chateauguay Valley (Quebec), 289

Châteauguay, Battle of the (Quebec): 150th Anniversary, 362

Cher, Cpl Mike, 100, 312

Cher, Sgt John, 100

Chetwynd, Corporal Lionel, 311

China, 10–11, 25, 288. *See also* Hong Kong

Chouinard, Brig, 159

Christie, Col Jack, 102

Christie, Major Gen/Lt Col/Brig Gen Andrew G, 39, 162–63

Christmas, Private Mike, 39

Church of St Andrew and St Paul (BW regimental church) (Quebec), 47, 103, 139, 154–55, 190, 198–99, 294, 355; Church Parades, 5–6, 50–51, 85, 288, 293, 302, 305, 314, 363; BW Centennial Parade (1962), 85; 3rd Battalion Laying Up of Colours (1962), 88; 1970 Laying-Up the Colours, 146–47, 139, 146, 147; stonework, 154–55; 1962 Laying-Up the Colours, 167; funeral of Thomas Price, 283; Board of Trustees chairmanship, 300; strengthening of BW relationship, 300; Montreal memorial service for Queen Mother, 302; traditional parade route, 317; funeral of Jason Warren, 343, 370, *425*

Churchill, Sir Winston, UK Prime Minister 1940–45, 1951–55, 10

Ciccone, MCpl, *436*

Civian, Cpl, *436*

civil-military co-operation (CIMIC): need to enhance, 307; in Afghanistan, 338, 343, 349, 350, 352, *428*. *See also* Psychological Operations

Clarence House (UK), 98; BW visits with Queen Mother, 60, 83, 90, 95, 133, 176, 188, 199, 283; with Prince Charles, 319

Clark, Lt/Capt Robert F ('Bob'), 183, 184, 313

Clark, P/Maj (CHofO) AB, *442*

Clarke, CSM 'Nobby,' 39

Clarke, Lt/Capt RF, 176, 287–88, *410*

Clarke, Private RA, 119

Clark-Kennedy, Lt Col Hew, 80, 87

Clarkson, Lt Col John Michael Elliott, 37, 38; 39, *235*; biographical description, 36, 40; relinquishment of command, 40; relationship with Archibald Wood, 51–52; training for UN Force in Cyprus, 113

Clattenburg, Cpl Ryan, *435–36*

Claxton, Brooke, Liberal Minister of Defence 1946–54, 11, 16, 45

Clements, Pte SW, *261*

Clemson University (US), 168

coatees (green coatees), 31, 45, 357. *See also* balmorals, including blue balmorals; Red Hackles

Cobourg (Ontario), 169

Cochrane, Major GD ('Tex'), 78, *262*

Cochrane, MWO D, *421*, *438*

Cock of the North (tune), 309

Coderre, Denis, Mayor of Montreal, 373

Coffie, Private MH, 111

Cohen, Lt Myer, 85

coins, regimental dome (BW), 326

Collège militaire royal de Saint-Jean (CMR St-Jean) (Quebec), 162, 179, 180, 364; Combat Arms Club, 182–83, 184, cadets, 357, 362

Collenette, Hon David M, Liberal Minister of National Defence 1993–96, 276, 282, 284, 285

Collingwood (Ontario), 122

Colonel Johnny Bourne (tune), 196, 311

Colour Party: 1962 Presentation of Colours (Montreal), 82–83, 84; 1987 Trooping the Colour (Montreal), 195; 1992 Freedom of the City (Montreal), 205; 1997 Freedom of the City (Ormstown), 289; 2006 Church Parade (Montreal), 317; 400th anniversary of Quebec City, 318; 2011 Trooping the Colour (Montreal), 358; 2012 Remembrance Day Parade (Montreal), 362. *See also* Presentation of Colours

Colours Presentation. *See* Presentation of Colours

Combat Arms Club (Quebec), 182–83, 184. *See also* Collège militaire royal de Saint-Jean

Combat Arms School (New Brunswick), 341. *See also* Camp Gagetown

Combat Related Employment of Women (CREW), 192

Combat Training Centre (New Brunswick), 175

Commendation for Bravery, 336

commissions (government): Dickson (Canada) (1995), 282, 284, 294; Suttie (Canada) (1964), 93–94, 107; Independent International Commission on Decommissioning (UK) (1997–2010), 304

competitions. *See* awards and honours

Comtois, Corporal Etienne, 346

Confederation (1867), 98, 125, 284

Congo, the, 171, 349, 351

Conlon, Frank, *417*, *420*

Connaught Ranges (Ontario), 165, 184, 186, 290, 355

Connaught, Prince Arthur and Duke of, Governor General 1911–16, 85, 91, 360–61

Connolly, Senator Joseph, 129

Conway, Private/Lt James, 98–99, 176, *410*, *414*

Cook, Major W, 155

Copenhagen (Denmark), 130; tattoo (1953), 24

Copp, Terry, 279; quoted as epigraph, 278

Coppold, Leslie, 7

Cornut, Private, 164

Cornwall, Duchess of, 118, 318, 322, 377, *434*

Cornwallis (patrol boat), 39. *See also* boats and ships

Côte St Paul (Quebec), 160

Côté, Robert, 287

Cotie, Pipe Major Neil, 195

Cotton, Lt Murray, 166–67

Coughlin, Capt Bing, 103

COVID-19 Pandemic, 455, 379–81, 383, *461*, 462

Cowan, Lt Glenn, 293, 303; quoted as epigraph, 340

Cowan, Lt/Major Brent, 184, 205, 206, 364, *408*, *414*

Cowansville (Quebec), 79

Cox, Brig Gen James S, 163, 359

CPSM (Canadian Peacekeeping Service Medal), 300

Craig Street Armouries and Drill Hall (Quebec), 4, 54

Craig, Major Gen Wesley E, 333

Crawford, Lt Col JD, 56

CREW (Combat Related Employment of Women), 192

Croak, Private JB, 136

Croix de Guerre (award), 38, 135

Cross, James, 157

Cuba, 179–80

Cuthbertson, Major Brian, 117, 326; quoted as epigraph, 65

CWAC (Canadian Women's Army Corps), 191

Cyprus, 147, 171; United Nations Peacekeeping Force in Cyprus (UNFICYP), 113, 122–24 *passim*, 130, 136, 137, 139–44 *passim*, 156, 200, *258*, 340, 361; description, 120, 122; Canadian Peacekeeping Service Medal, 300

Cyr, WO Marie Danielle Stephanie, 349

D'Alesio, Corporal Ryan, 346, *433*

Dagenais, Daniel, 310

Dalhousie University (Nova Scotia), Canadian Officers' Training Corps (COTC), 131

Dallaire, Major Gen Romeo, 282

Danyluk, Lt Peter, 206

Daoust, Cpl, *436*

Darney, Capt Mike, 313, *410*

Darney, Major HA, 161

Darney, Major Mick, 313

Darwin, Charles: quoted as epigraph, 93

Davidson, Capt Rev G, *244*

Davidson-Houston, Aubrey, 92

Davis, William, 326, *422*

De Chastelain, Gen AJGD, 304

Dé Sousa, Col Luis, 364

Death March (exercise) (1969), 152

Debison, S/Sgt John, 39

DeCastro, Capt Rod: quoted as epigraph, 343–44, 359

Decca records: pipes and drums recording, 119

Delaney, Capt M, *414*

Demarcation Line (Korean War), 24, 25

Demers, André, 206

Denmark: Copenhagen, 24, 130; tattoos, 24; NATO manoeuvres, 82

Department of Manpower and Immigration (Canada), 160

Department of National Defence (DND) (Canada), 134, 315; responsibilities of 5th Royal Highlanders of Canada Armoury Association, 58; introduction of Militia civil defence role, 61; FLQ armouries raids, 97–98; St-Hubert Air Base closing, 103; relationship to pipers, 115; October Crisis, 158; Summer Student Training Programme administration, 160; BW designation as *mechanized infantry*, 182; implementation of gender-free uniforms, 193; reduction in militia pipe bands, 273, 277; development of operational envy, 280; amendments to National Defence Act, 284; Operation *Jubilee* (Dieppe) 70th anniversary, 330. *See also* Area Headquarters; National Defence Headquarters

Deslauriers, CWO Alain Sgt-Maj 34th Brigade, *437*

Desrosiers-Ouellette, MBdr Desy, *430*

destroyers (ships): *Boat Cloak* (exercise), 110; *Web Foot* (exercise), 132. *See also* boats and ships

Desy, Sgt Donald ('Don'), 281

Dextraze, Lt Gen/Gen Jacques Alfred, 162, 167, *407*

Diamond Jubilee Medal (2012), 328

Diana, Princess, 329

Dickson Commission (1995), 282, 284, 294

Dickson, Rt Hon Brian, 282

Diefenbaker, John George, Conservative Prime Minister 1957–63, 62, 83

Dietz, Sgt Henry, 124

Dill, Private Stan, 111

Dilworth, Richardson, Philadelphia Mayor 1956–62, 49

Dimock, 2Lt H, *414*

Dinesen, Lt Thomas Fasti ('Tom'), 348–49; as recipient of VC, 83–84, 86, 130; reception for Queen Mother, 83–84, later visits to Regiment, 130

Dingwell, Cadet Ken, 106–07

Diplock, CSM/WO 1 Ralph N, 5, 81, *241*

Director Steps Up (tune), 308

Directorate of History & Heritage (DHH) (Canada), 283, 318

disbandments: 2nd Battalion (1943), 5–6; regimental headquarters (1946), 5; Regular BW Battalions (1970), 36, 128–29, 138–41, 146–49 *passim*, 151, 159, 363; Canadian Army Reserve Force (1953), 42; Suttie Commission, 93–94, 107; Princess Patricia's Canadian Light Infantry (PPCLI) and Royal 22nd Regiment (R22eR) at BW 1970 disbandment, 147; Gagetown 3rd Brigade (1969), 140–41, 146, 147, 149; Canadian Officers' Training Corps (COTC) (1968), 173; Canadian Airborne Regiment (1995), 281, 287; BW proposed disbandment and rescindment (1996), 285–87, 289; 22nd Armoured Regiment (Canadian Grenadier Guards) and Royal Montreal Regiment proposed disbandment, 285; regular battalions (1970), 292–93, 313, 324, 359; piping schools, 310; Rothesay Collegiate School Cadet Corps (1995), 313

Distinguished Conduct Medal (DCM), William Frost, 13; Turnbull, 5, 80, *241*; Richardson, 15; Colin Forrest, 67, 80. *See also* awards and honours

Distinguished Service Order (DSO), Bartlett McLennan, 110; Blackader, 51, 58, 92, *246*; Hugh Johnston, 4; George Cantlie, 7, 13, 47; Eric McCuaig, 7, 51; Fergusson, 9, 142; Neil Ritchie, 9, 134; Richard Ross (recommended), 21; Allard, 26; Ross, 32, 33; William Watson, 32, 36, 135, *236*; Logan, 36; Rockingham, 46, 79; Forster, 48; Vokes, 48; Lovat, 50; IMR Sinclair, 51; Andrew Gault, 58–59; Pearkes, 59; Rhodes, 71; Viscount of Arbuthnott, 87; Vanier, 87; Wallis, 91, 134; Moncel, 103–04; Bernatchez, 134; Topp, 134; Dextraze, 167, *407*; Bartlett McLellan, 197; Stevens's uncle as non-recipient, 330. *See also* awards and honours

District Headquarters (District 1 HQ), 63, 89, 169, 174, 175, 284; BW recruitment and training, 159; disorganization, 3; draconian directives, 181; summer BW budgets and staff, 156; Mitchell's acceptance of position, 164; McElheron transference to BW, 180; reaction to highland uniform, 200, 206; Montérégie Region exercise, 275; G1 and G6 assessments, 299

Dittmar, Sgt Bjorn, *268*, 339, 346, *433*; quoted as
epigraph, 337; awarded MID, 347
DND. *See* Department of National Defence
Dominion Day (Canada Day), 71, 131
Dominion of Canada Rifle Association, 290
Donaldson, Major GA, 20, *248*
Donnaconna (reserve ship), 282
Dorval Airport (Trudeau Airport), 82, 83, 166, 197
Doucet, Lt Col/Brig Gen Herbert Emile Theodore
('Herb') ('Pot'), 34–35, 69; awarded MID and OBE,
35, 134
Dover, Capt Wayne, 314
Dover, Major/DCO Gary Donald, 205, 206–08, 274,
282, 284; appointment as Gurkha, 162; quoted as
epigraph, 207, 208
Downey, Major Don, 56
Downey, Private Bob, 111
Drapeau, Jean, Mayor of Montreal 1954–57, 1960–86,
83, 157
Draper, Johann, 56, *264*
Drew, George, 77
Drill Hall (armoury) (Quebec), 4
Drone (attack aircraft), 341
Drum Head ceremony (2001), 300
drums. *See* pipes and drums
Dubuc Trophy (training, including musketry):
instigation, 172; BW awarded, 302–03, 294, 296,
437–38
Ducat, Lance Corporal Bruce, 164, *420*
Duffield, A/Capt/Major Ernest Stanley ('Stan'), 62
Duke of Edinburgh's Award, 194–95, 304
Duma, Capt Zach, 380
Dunkirk (France), 14
Dunn, Brig Gen John, 171
Duplessis, Sgt Robert ('Bob'), *417, 420*
Duplessis-Hummell, Corporal Sherry. *See* Hummell
(Duplessis-Hummell), Corporal Sherry
Dupplin, Viscount and Viscountess, 304
Dynes, WO 1/Capt Ralph A, 43, 44, 189, *241*

Eagles, Lt HC, 74
Early Thaw (exercise) (2013), 331
East Germany (German Democratic Republic), 10. *See
also* Germany
Eastern Command, 29, 260; rifle championship,
39, 67, 68–69, 75, 112; boxing championship,
39, 75, 112; hockey championship, 91; *Boat
Cloak* (exercise), 110; Headquarters (HQ), 110,
113; welterweight championship, 111; softball
championship, 112; *Winter Express* (exercise),
113–14
Eastern Townships (later Montérégie Region)
(Quebec), 94, 321; 1961 concentration, 79,
defensive exercise, 168; *Quick Sword* (exercise),
185; Huntingdon exercise, 275; 34th Brigade
March and Shoot competition, 330. *See also* Camp
Farnham
Eberth, Lt EG, 183, *410*

'Ed Sullivan Show, The' (television program) 44
Edinburgh (UK), 80, 188, 273–74; tattoo, 24, *460*
Edward VII, King 1901–10, 87
Efficiency Trophy, 118
Eggleton, Art, Liberal Minister of Defence 1997–2000,
294
Egypt, deployment: United Nations, including UN
Emergency Force (UNEF), 156, 170–71, 203,
413; and Canadian Peacekeeping Service Medal
(CPSM), 300
Ehrhardt, Lt/Major Ross, 165, 168, 170
Eisenhower, Gen Dwight David ('Ike'), US President
1953–61, 16, 37, 50
Elizabeth II, Queen 1952–present, formerly
Princess Elizabeth, 50; 1951; inspection of
48th Highlanders and the North Nova Scotia
regiments, 15; coronation parade, 22; 1954 1 RHC
royal guard, 29; BW 1957 performance in US,
37; 1967 Centennial visit to Quebec City, 98;
Centennial performance, 107; 1970 invitation to
luncheon, 145; 1976 Montreal Olympics, 172
Elizabeth, the Queen Mother: relationship with
BW, 301–02; 1939 Coronation, 197; named BW
Colonel-in-Chief, 7; 1950 luncheon with Knox
and Traversy, 9; birthday parade in Hanover,
16; 1954 1 RHC royal guard, 29; relationship
with John Bourne, 43, 198, 199, 292, 304; 1954
Union of the United States dinner, 44–45; 1962
visit and presentation of Colours, 80–85 *passim*,
87, 99, 101, 165, 189, *262–63, 265, 415*; 1963
presentation of Colours, 89, 90; portrait, 92,
264, 319; relationship with Thomas Price, 95,
283; photograph request, 98; presentation of
claymore, 53; favourite dinner food, 60; audience
with Donald MacLennan, 74; 1967 parade and
Trooping the Colour, 96, 126, 127–28, *267*;
audience with Scott Morrison and Bentley
MacLeod, 133; text of 1968 note to Knox, 135;
BW disbandment, 142; Laying-Up of Colours and
Final Parade, 146, 147; 1974 Trooping the Colour,
166–68 *passim, 407*; reception of CO, 176; 1981
visit and Ontario state dinner, 183; 1985 visit and
guard of honour, 187; 1987 visit and Trooping
the Colour, 188–89, 192–98 *passim*, 202, *359,
414–15*; BW Advisory Board, *262*; reception with
McCulloch, 283; description by Lusk, 301; death
and funeral, 301–02, 318, *416*; relationship with
Betts, 312; ninetieth birthday, 314, 315; August
2000 Birthday Parade, 363, *416*; 1989 visit, *409*;
1981 visit, *410*
Emo, Sgt Jimmy, 159
EnGarde 90 (exercise) (1990), 202
England, 33, 48, 74, 174; Robertson visit, 176;
highland dress suppliers, 359, 360. *See also
specific battles, competitions, institutions,
locations, and operations*
English (language), 196; English-Speaking Union
of the United States, 44–45; Quebec schools,

103; infantry units as political football, 108; and Quebec separation movement, 157; elimination as Quebec business language, 172; Quebec English-speaking farmers, 289

English-Speaking Union of the United States, 44–45

Erin (Ontario), 311–12

Estada, Sgt, *436*

Ethier, Corporal Stéphane, 277–78

Evans, Corporal/WO 2/Major Jimmy AB ('Jim'), 99, 155, 166, 167, 168

Ewing, Cadet Major Samantha, *441*

Ewing, Sgt/Capt Major William ('Bill'), 312

exercises, 86, 180, 208, 315–16, 355, 363; Camp Valcartier, including near, 6, 160, 184, 187, 200, 291, 292, 331, 333, 335, 337, 354, *408*, *424*, *448*; immediate post-war period, 6; *Spitfire* (1957), 35; *Little Korea* (1952), 44; *Rising Star* (1954), 45–46; cancelled Iroquois Nation exercise (1960), 63; Camp Gagetown opening (1958), 66–67; demonstration before Princess Margaret, 68; part of training cycle, 68; locations, 69; mock counterstrike to Soviet nuclear attack, 73; 4th Canadian Infantry Brigade German exercises, 76; Camp Farnham (1961); 79; *Tyro 2* (1961), 79; Soltau exercises (1962), 82; Gurevitch at exercises, 87; in 1962, 91; quality by 1964, 95; in Newfoundland (1963), 96–97; monitored, 98; weekend, 99; Camp Gagetown (1965), 103; *Boat Cloak* (1963), 110; *Winter Express* (1964), 110, 113–14, *257*; *Black Bear* (1965–66), 112–13; *Ace High* (1965–66), 113; *Morning Star* (1965), 119–20; Camp Gagetown (1965), 126; *New Broom* (1968), 131; *Panzer Partners* (1968), 131; *Naked Sword* (1968), 131–32; *Nautical Ranger* (1968), 131–32; *Web Foot* (1968), 132; *Pibroch Patrol* (1967), 136–37; quality of cadres, 152; *Death March* (1969), 152; weaponry, 152; minutiae required, 155; increase in participant work, 156; in Baffin Island (1973), 164; *Patrouille Nocturne* (1972), 164; *Pleine Neige* (1973), 164; *Black Hussar* (1973), 165; support of A Squadron Royal Canadian Hussars, 165; Camp Franham (1974), 168; quality of tanks, 172–73; *Pet Hackle* (1981), 182–83; *Highland Winter I, II, III* (1982–83), 183, 184, 186, *423*; cross-training with Pennsylvania National Guard, 184, 369, 370, 376; with Royal Military Combat Arms Club, 184; Camp Valcartier (including 1982–83, 1985), 184, 187; *Quick Sword* (1983), 185; urban warfare exercise, 185; Camp Wainwright, 187; *Urban Assault* (1985), 187; immediately prior and after 125th Anniversary Trooping (1987, 1988), 200; *EnGarde 90* (1990), 202; Camp Farnham (1990), 204; Camp Gagetown (1992), 207–08; in Huntingdon (Quebec) (1994), 275; in early-1990s, 276; part of regimental training, 278, 283; *Frozen Hackle* (1998), 292; *Tambour Roulant 98* (1998), 293; Y2K preparation, 303; 2003 cancellation because of Afghanistan War, 307;

cadet exercises, 313; Kenyan exercise, 315; *Early Thaw* (2013), 331; *Guerrier Nordique* (2013), 331; *Highland Yankee* (2013), 331, 333, *424*; *Noble Guerrier* (2013), 331; effect of Afghanistan War, 331–32; difficulties creating, 332; FIBUA doctrine incorporation (2009–12), 332; Mirabel Airport, 332; Camp Valcartier (2012), 333; attendance, 333; with 111th US Army National Guard (2012), 333; *Highland Associator* (2013), 333, *424*; 2013 training, 334–35; Camps Farnham and Valcartier (2013), 335; Snoddon at Camp Farnham, 347; Kimberly Anderson on exercise, 349; Brasseur's management, 353–54; with Americans, 354. *See also* manoeuvres; training

Expo 67 (Quebec) (1967), 162; guards of honour call-outs, 106, 123; pipes and drums, 107, 148; Canadian Armed Forces Centennial Tattoo, 106, 123–25 *passim*, 148, 160, *266*; effect of job opportunities, 165. *See also* Centennial (Canada)

Eyre, General Wayne, 382

Fairlie, Rev William ('Bill') ('Colonel Bill'), 280, 311

Farnham (Quebec), 156. *See also* Camp Farnham

Farnham, Capt/Adjutant Derrick, 314, 318, 320, *429*; biographical description, 316, 343–44

Farwell, Brig Father Murray, 307

Feggelen, B/Sgt Carol van, 74

Fenian Raids (1866–71), *442*

Ferbie, Herbert ('Herbie Ferbie'), 103

Ferdon, Capt/Major/Lt Col Leonard ('Len'), 84, 154, 155, *238*, *264*, 312, *407*, *422*; biographical description, 56, 161–62; BW interview and training, 56–57; promotion to field officer, 101; October Crisis, 157; inspection of Bishop's College School Cadet Corps, 162; appointment as lieutenant colonel, 164; exercise program, 164; Connaught Ranges accident, 165; 1974 Trooping the Colour, 166, *407*; relinquishment of command, 167

Ferguson, Capt PJ, 67

Ferguson, Capt R (RSS), *414*

Fergusson, Lt Col/Col/Brig Sir Bernard Edward, 142, 173, 9, 17

Fetherstonhaugh, Harold Lea, 154–55

Fetherstonhaugh, Robert Collier, 155

Fettes College (UK), 273–74

Fielding, B/Sgt Henry, 74

Fighting In Built-Up Areas (FIBUA) (doctrine), 331–32

Finnie, WO 2/WO 1/SM RH ('Ron'), 14, 29, 70, 80, 82, 91, 170, *240*, *263*; biographical description, 18; appointment to senior RSM, 38; direction of pipes, 72; retirement, 112

Firby, WO 1 EH, 123, *240*, *250*, *260*

Firstbrook, Lt IS, *248*

First Nations Peoples (aboriginal peoples): Special Militia Training Programme, 62; Indians of Caughnawaga, 63; Oka Crisis (1990), 203–04

First World War (Great War) (1914–18): BW Second

World War compared, 3–4; Memorial Museum section, 7; doggerel tradition, 75–76; helmet, 77; foreign Troopings, 91; Mons anniversary, 92, 377–78, *458*; Montreal Canadian Officers' Training Corps (COTC) traditions, 100; employment of women, 191, 339; statuette, 327; care packages, 339. *See also* paintings; reunions; *specific awards, battalions, battles, individuals, memorials, and weapons*

Firth, Corporal, *436*

Fischer, Sgt Carl, 170

Fisher, Corporal Frederick, VC, 325

Fisher, Lt FM, 145

Fisher, Sgt/Capt Donald, 145, *248*

Fisher, SSgt Donald, *248*

Fitzpatrick, Private PPJ, *261*

flags: St Andrews, 352; regimental, 8; 1 RHC battalion, 28; Philadelphia, 49; Canadian Maple Leaf, 139, 166; Union Jack, 166, *418*; Montreal, 205, 293; New Brunswick, *418*; Newfoundland, *418*; Nova Scotia, *418*; United Nations, *418*

Fleming, Col Andrew, *262*

Fletcher's Field (Parc Jeanne-Mance) (Quebec), 194, 360–61, 364; 1912 parade, 85; 2012 Trooping the Colour (150th Anniversary), 325

Fleury, Major Gen Frank, 83–84, 100

Floods, see Operation LENTUS

Flora MacDonald (regimental goat), 309, 378

Florida (US), 175, 354

Foam, RSM Charles, 8–9

FOB (Forward Operating Base) (Afghanistan), 346, 348

Foley, Private Joe, 111

Fontenay-le-Marmion (France), 447

football, 44, 52, 53; college and university, 109, 168; Grey Cup, 79, 330

Forand, Major Gen Alain, 285, 286; quoted as epigraph, 285

'Force Generators': Afghanistan War, 350

Force Mobile Command (formerly Army Headquarters) (FMC), 129; as Canadian Army Headquarters, general, 31; becomes Force Mobile Command, 186; as FMC Headquarters, 207, 208, 273, 286; as Army Headquarters (St-Hubert, Quebec), 284; as Canadian Army Headquarters (Ottawa, Ontario), 339–40

Forrest, John, *269*

Forrest, Major Colin G, 67, 80

Forrest, Private, 81

Fort Bragg (US), 131

Fort Drum (US), 171–72, 293, 303, 354, *411*

Fort Duquesne (later City of Pittsburgh) (US), 10, 52

Fort Frontenac (Ontario), 163, *413*

Fort Henry (Old Fort Henry) (Ontario), 330, *419*

Fort Île Ste Hélène (Old Fort) (Quebec), 107

Fort Indiantown Gap (US), 333, *424*

Fort Montgomery (Lake Champlain) (US), 288

Fort Myers (US), 37

Fort Pickett (US), 354

Fort Pitt (later City of Pittsburgh) (US), 10, 52

Fort St Louis (West Germany), 65, 86, 116, 117; description, 69, 70; BW inauguration, 69–70; Roman Catholic (RC) Chapel, *253*

Fort Ticonderoga (US), 52; Ticonderoga, 288, 295

Fort York Armoury (Old Fort York) (Ontario), 183, *410–11*

Fortin, Tony, 457

Forward Operating Base (FOB) (Afghanistan), 346, 348

Fox, Lt Gen James A, 195, 198

Frampton, Aloysius ('Wish'), 12–13, *418*

France, 14, 21, 104, 180, *426*; Normandy Campaign, 3; initial attack through France, 19; 42nd Battalion, 55, 91; 73rd Battalion, 55, 149, 150; Camp Gagetown compared, 66; 1963 reunion, 82–83, 91; Front de libération nationale (FLN), 97; Royal Regiment of Canada, 117; Auld Alliance, 204–05; 1960 Remembrance Day, including Vimy Ridge memorial, *259*. *See also specific awards, battles, locations, memorials, and operations*

Franklin, Benjamin, 50, 52

Fraser, Alistair, Lieutenant Governor of Nova Scotia 1952–58, 28

Fraser, Capt Dr Derek George, 186–87, 202, *414*

Fraser, Hon John Allen, 296

Fraser, John, MP, 277

Fraser, Major Doug, *269*

Fraser, Major Gen David, 341; quoted as epigraph, 340

Fraser, Major George Climie ('Pudge'), 187

Fraser, Major/Col Ian Simon, 122, 124–25, 141, 266, *269*

Fredericton (New Brunswick), 66, 113, 127, 174, 323; opening of provincial legislature, 143; opening of Princess Margaret Bridge, 67; brigade parade (1959), 72

Freedom of the City parades (honour): Philadelphia (US) (1956), 49; Saint John and Oromocto (New Brunswick) (1970), 145–46; petition, 204–05; Montreal (Quebec) (1990, 1992), 204–06, *409*; Huntingdon (Quebec) (1998), 293–94; (1990), Verdun (Ypres Parade) (Quebec) (1999), 295–96; 2002, 304

Freeston, Capt Harold ('Bud'), *417, 420*

Freestone, Harry, 119

French (language): specific speakers, 179–80, 196; and BW relationship with Montreal, 204–05; Regular Force French-speaking regiments, 331

Front de libération du Québec (FLQ), 97–98, 101, 102; armory raids, 97–98; October Crisis, 156–58, 162, 166, 172, 287

Front de libération nationale (FLN) (France), 97

Frost, CSM William Leslie, 13

Frozen Hackle (exercise) (1998), 292

Fuller, WO Keith, 281

Fulton, WO Robert ('Bob'), 311

Furlotte, Chris, *419*

Gagetown Warriors (hockey team), 142

Gale, Gen Sir Richard, 73

Galipeau, Lt J, *414*

game shooting: Kinnaird Trophy, 112

Gannon, MWO/CWO Peter M, *243*, 293, 302, *416*, *418*; biographical description, 299

Gardner, Capt B, *414*

Gardner, Capt WH, 195

Garneau, Major Charles, 158

Garrison Cup (baseball), 63

Gault, Brig Andrew Hamilton, 7, 58–59, 163

Gault, Brig Andrew Hamilton, Mrs, 140

Gauthier, André D, 327

Gazeley, Lt John, 39

Gelston, Lt Robert C, 89, *264*

Gemmill, Lt AW, 20–21

General Campaign Star (award), 347

General Crerar Marches (piping award): 1963 and 1964, 118

General Waters Trophy (rifle shooting), 175

George, Cpl, *436*

George V, King 1910–36, 87, 301–02

George VI, King 1936–52, 43

German (language), 117, 179

Germany, 20, 147, 148, 200–01, 305, 314; as Russian enemy, 10; BW entry and attack description, 4; East Germany, 10; 1st Highland Battalion, 20; pipes and drums, 24, 27; 1963 Trooping the Colour, 86, 90–91; 4th British Division, 123; 1 CHB, *248*; arrival of BW family, *249*; 1 RHC march, *252*; 4th Canadian Infantry Brigade, including Group Trophy, *255*; St Andrew's stained-glass window, 281; Black Watch Claymores, 360; cartoon, *449*. *See also* navy (Germany); North Atlantic Treaty Organization; *specific awards, battles, locations, memorials and operations*

Gervais, Arthur, 159

Gervais, Col/Brig Gen Jean, 206, 208, 286

Gettysburg (US): battlefield, 278

Ghana, 109

Ghuniem, Pte/Cpl, *436*

Gibb-Carsley, Major John ('Jack'), 43, 54

Gibson, Major JT, 161, 313

Giguère, Brig Gen, 333

Gilday, Col Thomas, 293

Giles, WO1 D (1BW), *263*

Gilmore, Pipe Major WJL ('Bill'), 119, 120, 300

Glace Bay (Nova Scotia), 124, 125

Glamis Castle (UK), 301

Glasgow (UK), 57, 305

Glen, Lt, 43

Glencross, Sgt/Capt Rev Canon R Bruce, 171, 190, *245*, 288, 300, 307, 343, 352; quoted as epigraph, 203; biographical description, 203, 280–81

Glickman, Lt Toby, 165

Gloin, Private, 164

Godkin, Capt Rev David, *245*, 356

Golan Heights (Israeli Occupied Territory): UN deployment, 170, 171; Canadian Peacekeeping Service Medal, 300

Gomez, Corporal Francisco ('Frank'), 342–43

Good, Lance Sgt Herman, 130, 136

Goodison, Sgt TJ, 118

Gosman, Corporal M, 299, 320

Granatstein, Dr Jack L, 282, 294

Grand Ceilidh (Scottish Festival) (1992), 206

Granger, Sgt John, 17

'Granger's Rangers' (27th Canadian Infantry Brigade sniper group), 17

Gray, Lt Col/Col Richard M, 111, *260*

Great Britain. *See* United Kingdom

Great War. *See* First World War

Green-Armytage, Jock, *457*

green coatees, 31, 45, 357. *See also* balmorals, including blue balmorals; Red Hackles

Green, LCol (US Army) Darrell, *430*

Green, Lew, *417*

Green, Sgt Norm, 124

Gregg, Col/Brig Hon Milton F, 130, 134, 136

Greig, Pipe Major George, 106

Grey Cup (football), 330, 79

Griffin, Major Frederick Philip ('Phil'), docudrama *In Desperate Battle*, 204

Guay, Capt Roger, 328, 353, 361

Guenole, Pte/Cpl, *436*

Guerrier Nordique (exercise) (2013), 331

Gulf War One (1991), 274

gunships, 279, 341

Gurevitch, WO 1 Moe, 80, 81, 88–89, 91, 95–96, 100, *241*, *263*; biographical description, 87

Gurkhas (Nepal): pipers, 24. *See also* 2nd Battalion King Edward VII's Own Gurkha Rifles

Habington, S, 145

hackles. *See* Red Hackles

haggis, 50; *To a Haggis* (R. Burns), 285; *Toast to the Haggis*, 327; Haggis Party, *421*

Hainse, WO, 353

hair sporrans, 15, 29, 31, 127, 143, 359

Haiti, 316; earthquake (2010), 336

Halifax (Nova Scotia), 101, 131, 273, 323; RHC departure, 20; Bedford Ranges, 39; boxing competitions, 39, 111; Windsor Park, 74; Massed Bands Concert, 86; *Boat Cloak* (exercise), 110

Halifax Citadel Guard (Nova Scotia), 37

Hall-Humpherson, Major P, 120, *249*

Halpenny, Capt Drew, 180–81, 185

Hamel, CWO Claude, *205*, 243, 299, *305*

Hamilton (Bermuda): Tattoo (1956), 29, *268*

Hamilton (Ontario), 185, 278

Hamilton (UK), 305

Hamilton Gault Trophy (rifle shooting), 67, 140, 143, 149, *261*

Hamilton, ('Pull-Through'), 12–13

Hamilton, Joe, 159

Hamilton, Major Bill, 120

Hamilton-Leigh Trophy (rifle shooting), 70

Hampstead (Quebec), 313

Hangard Wood (France), 136

Hannah, Pipe Major Robert, 24, 106, 310–11

Hannah, Pipe Major William John ('Bill') ('Willie'),
45, 49, 50, 80, 195, 310–11, *410*; biographical
description, 106; assumption of control of pipes
and drums, 48

Hannah, 2Lt J, *410*

Harkes, Capt/Lt Col Harold J ('Harry'), 26, 36,
118, 123, 126, 127, 134, 135, *236*, *267*; quoted
as epigraph, 121; biographical description,
120, 121–22; becomes Exercise director, 136;
relinquishment of command, 131; Cyprus, 258

Harmon Air Force Base (USAF), Stephenville,
Newfoundland, 113

Harper, Capt/Major BE, 135, *267*; quoted as epigraph,
38

Harper, Stephen, Conservative Prime Minister
2006–15, 350

Hartnell, CWO Stu, 379

Harvey, Corporal W, 119

Hasek, Lt/Major John, 180, *260*

Hasty Pudding Club (Harvard University), 104–05

Hauschild, Capt Herbert F ('Herb'), 155

Hayes, Capt Rev Stephen A, 105–06, 147, 169, *245*

Hellyer, Hon Paul, Liberal Minister of Defence
1963–67, 107, 114, 115, 123, 128, 129

Hemisfair '68 (World's Fair) (US), 106. *See also*
World's Fairs

Henley, Corporal Roy, 290

Herzegovina (former Yugoslavia). *See* Bosnian Conflict

Highland Associator (exercise) (2013), 333, *424*. *See
also Highland Yankee*

Highland Cadet Battalion (HCB) (Quebec), 312–13,
321. *See also* cadets, including cadet-officers

Highland Laddie (tune), 72, 73, 84, 201, 296, 321, 378

Highland Rifle Company (Highland Rifles) (Canada
West), 362

Highland Winter I, II, III (exercises) (1982–83), 183,
184, 186, *423*

Highland Yankee (exercise) (2013), 331, 333, *424*. *See
also Highland Associator*

Highlanders (UK): becomes part of Royal Regiment of
Scotland, 346

Hill, Lt Sean, 293

Hill, Sgt Brian, 346, *432*, *433*

Hillier, Lt Gen/Gen RJ, 307, 343

Hindo, Capt/HCol of the Canadian Army Paul, 195,
379, *410*, *414*

Hinkson, Capt Jay, 369, 374

Hippopotamus Song, 335

Hiscock, Cicel, *418*

Hislop, MCpl A, *442*

Hockett, Corporal Charles E, 112

hockey, 32, 109, *255*, 309, 339, *412*; BW teams, 16,
40, 56, 24, 63, 67, 69, 72, 75, 112, 144; British

National 'B' championship participation (1961),
77; Southern NB Senior League Championship,
77; brigade championship (1961, 1962, 1962,
1964, 1969, 2004, 2005), 78, 82, 91, 118–19, 142,
153, 308; Maritime Tri-Service Trophy (1967),
123; Maritime Region championship, 144

Hogg, Pipe Corporal/Pipe Major Peter, 118, 124

Hogmanay (UK): 1963, 89; 1974, 165; 1977, 174

Holdam, MWO WCA ('Wilf'), 166, *250*

Holland (Netherlands), recapture, 4, 297, *444*;
veterans at McGill University parade (1962),
84–85, competition, 118; 1987 Church Parade and
indebtedness to BW, 288; Afghanistan War, 344.
See also specific locations

Hong Kong (formerly UK), 70, 74, 95; battle and fall
(1941), 21; reversion to Chinese control, 288, 346.
See also China

Hooper, Private, 124

Horace: quoted as epigraph, 278

Horse Guards Parade: 1978, 176; 2000, *416*

House of Commons (Canada), 165, 273, 296; armed
forces unification, 129; reduction in paid Reserve
pipers, 276, 277

House of Commons (UK), 59

Howard, Col Andrew T, 191, *262*

Howe, Gordie, *418*

Howson, Capt JDL, *244*

Howick (Quebec), 185

Hubbard, Private LPE, *261*

Huber, Frank, *417*

Huggett, Lt G, 18

Hughes, Sam, Conservative Minister of Militia and
Defence 1911–16, 47, 129

Hughes, SSgt JW, *260*

Hummell (Duplessis-Hummell), Cpl/MCpl Sherry,
165, 171, 181, 312, *413*

Hummell, MCpl Rick, 165

Huntingdon (Quebec): training base, 275; Freedom of
the City (1998), 293

Hurricane Edna (1954), 29

Hutchison, Lt Col/Col Paul P, 5, 116, 315; quoted
as epigraph, 20; relinquishment of command,
5; Regimental Museum and Archives, 7; Camp
Aldershot as permanent training centre, 20;
1 RHC opening of Nova Scotia legislature, 28–29;
ram's head snuff mull, 29; 1957 church parade,
51; commemoration of BW Seven Years' War
assault, 52; appraisal of Kenneth Gault, 59; as
BW historian, 80, 89, 92, 101, 167; 1963 reunion
dinner, 92; 1966 reunion dinner, 101; Hasty
Pudding Club dinner, 104; Duncan McAlpine's
2 RHC posting, 117; 1968 reunion dinner, 134;
1970 Trooping the Colour, 146; BW disbandment,
149; 1970 reunion dinner, 150; absence of working
daily staff, 153; 1974 reunion dinner, 167;
described manner of, 199; 1962 Advisory Board,
262; description of BW, 365

Hutchison, Right Rev Andrew S, 302

Ibbotson, Lt Col/Col Ivan Leonard, 51, 101–02, 105, *237, 262*; biographical description, 5; assumption of command, 5

Ice Storm (Operation *Verglas* or *Recuperation*) (Quebec) (1998), 292, 294, 374

Île Ste Hélène (Quebec), Old Fort: 107

Imjin River (Korea), 25

Imperial 42nd Regiment (UK), 66; 'The Road to Pittsburgh' (painting), 9–10, 52

Imperial War Museum (UK), 119, 188

Improvised Explosive Device (IED), 340, 344, 347, 348, 349

In Desperate Battle (documentary episode), 204

Inchon (South Korea), 24

Independent International Commission on Decommissioning (UK) (1997–2010), 304

India, 12, 74, 343. *See also* Pakistan

Indian Army Staff College, 131

Indian Defence Services Staff College, 124

Infantry School. *See* Royal Canadian School of Infantry

infantrymen: Group 1, 68, 99–100; Camp Valcartier Junior Leaders Course, 160–61. *See also* training; *specific battalions and infantry*

Intelligence Corps (UK Army), 155, 156, 207

Internal Security (training program), 156–57

International Commission for Supervision and Control (ICSC) for Indo-China, 143

International Firearms (Quebec) 98

International Security Assistance Force (ISAF), 338, 351; Joint Command HQ, 345, 351, 352; badge, *425*

Ireland, 24. *See also* Northern Ireland

Irvine, Sgt, 205

Irwin, Lt Gen Sir Alistair, 327, 330, *419*

ISAF. *See* International Security Assistance Force

Island of Madam (Nova Scotia), 110

Ismailia Canal (Egypt), 170

Israel, including Palestine, 328; United Nations Emergency Force (UNEF), 123, 203

Italian Alpini (warfare corps), 201

Italy, including BW actions and achievements in, *passim*, 4, 5, 33–34, 70, 103, 117, 133; battalion reinforcements, 6; Villa Rogatti capture, 33; 48th Highlanders, 36; Ian McDougall's reconnaissances, 48; William Wood promoted to staff officer, 51; Nesbitt as commander, 55; Hastings and Prince Edward Regiment, 62; Leonard's service, 75; *Winter Express* participation (NATO exercise) (1966), 114; Italian Alpini training, 201; John Bourne's service, 293. *See also specific locations*

Jackson, JR, 62, *241*

Jackson-Hall, Sgt, 51

Jacobs, Private, 63

Jacobson, David Cary, 328

Jamaican Defence College, 363

Jamaican Military Tattoo (1968), 131

Japan, 10, 23, 26, 118; prisoner of war camps, 21, 95; operations against, 70–71

Jarvis, Major G, 51

Jarymowycz, Roman Johann, 367–68

Javornik, Col George, 206, 285

Jean, Michaëlle, Governor General 2005–10, 355–56

Jette, Ppr S, *268*

Johnny Cope (tune), 18, 42–43, 50

Johnson, Lt Col Brian, 290

Johnson, Lyndon, US President 1963–69, 107

Johnston, Major/Lt Col Hugh A, 5–6, 4

Johnston, RSM MF, 89

Johnston, Rt Hon David, Governor General 2010–present, 325, *439*

Johnstone, P/Sgt K, *442*

Jolly Beggars, The (poem) (Burns), 115

Jones, Capt Betty Ann, 123; as Capt Betty Ann Jones Malashenko, 177, 192, *410, 413, 414*

Jones, Lt D, *414*

Jones, Rev James Peter, 307

Jongers, Alphonse, 47

Joseph, Corporal Raymond, 198

Joudrey, Capt Laurie, *260*

Jubilee Medal (2012), 328

judo: Wakefield Sword championship (1964): 118

Junior Leaders Course (Camp Valcartier) (Quebec), 160–61

Juno Beach (France), 96

Juno Beach Centre Museum (France), *417*

Kabul (Afghanistan), 340, 345, *427, 430*; international airport, 345. *See also* Afghanistan War

KAIA–North (Afghan Air Force base), 345

Kanaan, Pte/Cpl, *418*

Kandahar (Afghanistan), 303, 316, 319, 320, 346–49 *passim*, 303; stand-down ceremony, 311; deployment, 337; growth of battle group, 338; BW fatality, 342; Provincial Reconstruction Team, 343, 346, 350; suicide attack, 344. *See also* Afghanistan War

'Kandahar' (honour), 350

Kandahar Air Field (KAF), 344, 348, 349, *429, 442*. *See also* Afghanistan War

Kansas Line (Korean War), 25

KATCOMS (Korean Attached Commonwealth Division), 25, *248*. *See also* Korean War

Kaulbach, Lt Col Thurston ('Tud'), 290; quoted as epigraph, 137, 358

Kavanagh, Cadet Major, 106–07

Kelly, Capt/Col Patrick, 282, 340

Kelly, CWO Mike RG, 190, 205, *242*, 335–36; death 335

Kelly, Lt Michael U ('Mike'), 118

Kemp, Capt/Major John PG, appraisal of Richard Rutherford, 13; selected as second-in-command, 43; retirement, 48

Kennedy Board (1953), 42

Kennedy, Capt JW, *244*

Kennedy, Lt/Lt Col Isaac Allen ('Ike'), 111, 134, 329, *418*; quoted as epigraph, 65

Kennedy, Major Gen Howard K, 42

Kenny, Senator Colin, 328

Kent, Hon Peter, Conservative Minister of the Environment 2011–13, 325

Kentville (Nova Scotia), 20, 24, 65, *410*

Kenya, 186, 315

Kerr, Pipe Major/Capt Andrew GM ('Andy'), 169, 176, 287–88, 298, 302, 311, *410, 420, 458, 461*; strengths as pipe major, 195; Regiment *Webmaster*, 290; *Colonel John (Johnny) Bourne* march composer, 300, 311; as ball chairman, 306

Kettle, Dr Brig Gen David, 322

Kidd, Dick, *417*

kilts, 15, 16, 23, 28, 30–31, 32, 104, 108, 132, 141, 163, 179, 273–74, 309, 312, 358–59, 365, *440*; pipe band, 55; parades, 16–17, 305, 348, 357; opening of Maritime legislatures, 29, 143; 5th Royal Scots, 29; Troubadours, 74; perceived as archaic, 116; in parachute jump, 131; uniform changes, 136, 139, 193, 202; when worn by girls and women, 161, 191; under, 169; unfortunate incident photographed, 187; National Defence Headquarters review and dress issues, 192, 269, 294; Royal Stewart, 277

King's College School (Nova Scotia), 96–97

King's-Edgehill School (Nova Scotia), Cadet Corps: 170, 313, 321, *440*

Kinghorn (UK), 313

Kingston (Jamaica): Military Tattoo, 131

Kingston (Ontario), 123, 293, 330; National Defence College (NDC) (Ontario), 163; BW clan gathering (2012), 330; Old Fort Henry, 330, *419*; Land Forces Doctrine and Training System HQ, 335; Peace Support Training Centre, 338. *See also* Canadian Forces Base Kingston; Princess of Wales' Own Regiment; Royal Military College of Canada

Kingston Staff College (Ontario), 275, 279

Kinnaird Trophy (game shooting), 112

Kinnear, Major JD ('Jock'), 123, *260*

Kipling, Rudyard, 329; quoted as epigraph, 341

Klepak, Lt Col Harold ('Hal'), 158, 166, 179–81, 184, 190, *238*, 279, 288, *410, 412*; quoted as epigraph, 54, 191; teacher at CMR, 162, 179, 182–83; graduate education, 174, 176, 179; implementation of *Highland Winter*, 183; creation of mega TEWT, 185; relinquishment of command, 185, 186; Operation *Spring* guide of tour, 188; master of 1987 Trooping the Colour, 196

Knockout Cup (rifle competition), 43–44

Knorr, Lt EM, 37

Knowlton, Capt Victor ('Vic'), 313, *410*

Knox, Major/Lt Col James W ('Jim') ('Gander Neck'), 43, 48, 51, 104, 111, 119, 127, 142, 167, 173, 189, 199, *237, 246*, 273; conductor of 1949 reunion dinner, 7; as director of rescue of artifacts and records, 8; visit of 1 RHC in Berlin, 9; delineation of Colonel-in-Chief position, 58; reunion dinner in honour, 91; becomes colonel, 92; quoted as

epigraph, 109; visits fourth regimental command, 126; possible BW disbandment, 128; reaction to proposed airborne regiment, 129; 1968 regimental birthday, 131; steps down as colonel, 133–35 *passim*; relationship with John Bourne, 169; part of advisory board, *262*, 298–99; part of Centennial Trooping the Colour, *267*; drive to create Regimental Foundation, 274

Korean Attached Commonwealth Division (KATCOMS), 25, 248. *See also* Korean War

Korean War (1950–53), 134, 148; and Toronto memberships, 6; causes, 10, 11; 25th Canadian Infantry Brigade initial deployment, 11, 12; unpopularity, 12; initial composite battalions, 12; A Company, 12–13, *247*; training, 14–15, 25–26; 2nd Battalion ordered to, 22; departure for Korea, 23; deployment within Korea, 24–25, 27; Korean Augmentation Troops, 25; inspection by Louis St Laurent, 25–26; deaths of soldiers, 26; departure, 26, 138; cancelled 1 RHC deployment post-war, 29–30; 'The Ladies from Hell' (documentary), 141; service of specific officers, 45, 71, 110, 122, 123, 131, 168; veterans, 147, 152, 158, 159, 290; *Death March* (exercise), 152; veterans in 2 Royal 22e Regiment, 158; B Company, *248*; Regimental Museum, 279; Afghanistan War participation compared, 303, 337, 364; uniform, *419*

Kouprie, B/Sgt Martin, 74

Kyrenia (Cyprus), 137, 143

La Macaza (Quebec), 102

Labrèche, CSM/WO Roland ('Rolly') ('Skunky'), 170, 176, 183, 192, *411, 418*; quality as instructor, 313

Lachance, Col Jacques, 308

Lachine High School Cadet Corps (Quebec), 96–97

Lacombe Armoury (2nd Field Artillery Regiment): 1970 Summer Student Training Programme, 160. *See also* 2nd Field Artillery Regiment

Ladies Badminton Club, 312

Laframboise, Private Clifford, 26

Lahr CF base (Germany), 208

Laird, Major GN, 145

Lamontagne, Hon Gilles, Lieutenant Governor of Quebec 1984–90, 195

Land Forces Command (Canada), 132, 163

Land Forces Doctrine and Training System HQ (Ontario), 335

Landing of the First Canadian Division at Saint-Nazaire (painting), 119

Langevin, MCpl, *442*

Langille, Private Ken, 124

Lanno, Drum Major Michael, 321

Lanthier, General Jean Marc, 379

Laos, 74

Laporte, Hon Pierre, Quebec Liberal Minister of Labour 1970, 157

Larman, Sgt Ross, *268*, 311, *421*

Larochelle, Capt Gaetan, 328

Last Post (bugle call), 150–51

Last Post Fund, 354
Latin (language), 318. *See also* maxims, mottos, and
    sayings
Laurin, Hon Camille, Quebec PQ Minister of State for
    Cultural Development 1976–80, 169
Laver, James: quoted as epigraph, 358
Lavigne, Corporal R, 118
Lawson, Lt Col Rhett, 155, 167
Lawson, Piper S, *268*
Lawson, R RSM Vic I ('Bull'), 91, *260*
Lawton, WO John, 281
Layden, Major Patrick, 176
LCC. *See* Lower Canada College
Leach, Lt Gen William, 335–36
Lebanon, 171
Ledwon, Corporal George, 144
Lee, Pipe Major Keith, 14, 24
Lees, Cpl, *436*
Leigh, Drum Major CA, 166
Legault, François, Quebec Premier, 380
Leger, Cpl Debbie, 196
Leger, Pte/Cpl/Pipe Cpl A, 268, *435*, *442*
Leja, RSM Walter ('Rocky'), 97
Lenathen, M/Corporal: quoted as epigraph, 143
Leonard, Major Gen/Lt Col William Clark ('Bill'),
    36, 76, 78, 82, 83, 84, 134, *236*, *262*; becomes
    CO of 2 RHC, 38; biographical description, 75;
    relinquishment of command, 117
Leone, Lt Chris, *440*
Lerue, Private JA, 143
Leslie, David ('Dave'), 324, *417*
Lessard, Lt Col Guy, 159
Letson Gold Trophy (rifle championship), 67
Leveille, Lt Benoit ('Ben'), *429*
Levesque, CWO Chuck, 160
Lezet, Private, *418*
Lieutenant Colonel Bruce D Bolton, MMM (tune), 308
Lindsay (Ontario), 200
Lipscombe, Corporal Gerry, 156, 160
Listowel (Ontario), 121
Little Korea (exercise) (1952), 44
Lloyd, Major Brian, 206, *410*, *414*
LOB. *See Left Out of Battle*
Lochaber No More (tune), 142
Logan, Lt-Col George McLean, 20, 35–36, 134, 326
London (Ontario), 274
London (UK), 130, 176, 180; tailors, 54, 329; Clarence
    House, 83, 90, 95, 134, 188; rediscovery of
    Recapture of Sanctuary Wood (painting), 119;
    birthdays of Queen Mother, 176, 314, 363, *416*;
    Imperial War Museum, 188; funeral of Queen
    Mother, 301, *416*. *See also* Canadian Military
    Headquarters London; Clarence House; Imperial
    War Museum
Long Armour–Infantry Course, 201
Long Point Garrison. *See* Camp Longue-Pointe
Longstop Hill, Battle of (1943), 94
Loomis, Major Gen Sir Frederick, 91, 325–26, 348–49
Lord Lovat's Lament (tune), 50

Lord Strathcona Medal (cadet achievement), 95
Lord, Capt Catherine, 313
Loudon, Lt Col Alasdair, 288
Lovat, Brig Lord, 50
Lowe, Lt Greg, 205, *414*
Lower Canada College (LCC) (Quebec): graduates, 51,
    86, 186, 199
Loyola College: graduates, 207; Canadian Officers'
    Training Corps (COTC), 46, 100–01, 134, 160
Luc-Turgeon, Cpl Ian (Fus de Sher), *432*
Ludlow, Bill, *417*, *420*
Ludlow, Lt/Capt Don P, 69, 136–37, *260*, *420*
Lüneberg (German training area). *See* Soltau
Lusk, Capt/Major/Lt Col Gordon T ('Gord'), 191,
    206, *239*, 274, 275, 282, *410*, *414*; 1987 parade
    adjutant, 195; biographical description, 283–84,
    296; BW disbandment and rescindment, 285, 286;
    BW viability appraisal, 287; US excursion, 288;
    granted Freedom of municipality of Ormstown,
    289; 1998 Ice Storm, 292, 294; Phase 2 Infantry
    graduation, 293; Freedoms of the City, 293, 295;
    quoted as epigraph, 295; Dubuc Trophy, 296,
    303; relinquishment of command, 296; *Canadian
    Red Hackle*, 300–01; Queen Mother, including
    Birthday Parade, 301, *409*, *416*

Ma'Sum Ghar (Afghanistan), 346, 348
Maarko, Master Sergeant (US Army) Roger, *430*
MacArthur, Gen Douglas, 10–11, 70–71
MacAulay, Capt/Major JS ('Stu'), 107, 145, *269*
Macaulay, Maj Ian, 264
MacDonald, Capt RF, *257*
MacDonald of Kinlochmoidart's Salute (tune), 327
Macdonald Stewart Museum (Montreal Military and
    Maritime Museum) (Quebec), 297, 308
MacDonald, Donald, Liberal Minister of National
    Defence 1970–72, 159
MacDonnell of Keppoch, Alice: quoted as epigraph, 30
MacDonnell, 26
MacDougall, Ian, 79
MacDougall, Major JE, 42–43
MacEachern, Bud, *269*
Macfarlane, Lt Col John Ibbotson Buchanan, 95, 106,
    145, 153, 165, *238*, *268*; Loyola COTC, 100–01;
    biographical description, 105; relinquishment of
    command, 154
Macfarlane, Major Jim, 49, 50
Macfarlane, Major/Lt Col Walter E, 105
Macintyre, Lt John LC, *264*
MacIntyre, Mark, 206
MacIntyre, Private D, 119
MacKay, Andrew, 314
MacKay, Drum Major WM, 111
MacKay, Lt Col Dan, 183
MacKay, Lt/Capt/Major/Lt Col/Col Thomas Edward
    Charles ('Tom'), 203, *239*, 364, 370, 371–75 *414*,
    416; as platoon leader, 274; Huntington field
    exercises, 275; quoted as epigraph, 283, 316,
    342, 355; possibility of BW disbandment, 287;

command of test platoon, 291; 1998 Ice Storm, 292; as operational company commander, 299; funeral of Queen Mother, 302; resignation of Potter, 306; preparations for command, 307; biographical description, 314, 339–40; relationship with Duncan McAlpine, 315; training, 316–17, 318, 353; 2006 church parade, 317; 2008 Quebec City founding anniversary, 318; 2009 presentation of Colours, 319, 320, 322, *434*; relinquishment of command, 322; ties with 111th US Infantry, 333, 337–38; Afghanistan war, including Operation *Attention*, 338–39, 340, 344, 345, 352, *430*; Bosnian conflict, 338–39; death of Jason Warren, 342, 343, 370; appraisal of Phare, 355; reappointment as CO, 364, *425*

MacKay, 2Lt A, *414*

MacKenzie, Pipe Major/Major Brian, 302, 306, 310, 313, *420*; transition to volunteers, 276; bagpipes theft investigation, 278

Mackisoc, Capt Mark (BWCC), 194–95, *414*

MacLean, ('Hoodlum') ('Hooch'), 12–13

MacLean, Lt AW, *264*

MacLean, CSM Cluie Louis, 25

MacLennan, Bartlett ('Bart'), 109, 110

MacLennan, Lt Col/Col/Brig Gen Donald Samuel ('Don'), 36, 40, 161, *235*; relationship between Montreal and Atlantic BW battalions, 30; biographical description, 70–73; quoted as epigraph, 70, 187; reception with Queen Mother, 74; relinquishment of command, 74

MacLeod, Corporal RA, 119

MacLeod, Major Lt Col/Col W Bentley, 131, *236*; proposed BW disbandment, 36; BW boxing, 91, 254; appraisal of Sellar, 112–13; reception with Queen Mother, 133; Cyprus tours, 137, 141–42, 144, *258*; actual BW disbandment, 140; 1969 reunion, 141–42; *Yeltneb*, 144, *258*; luncheon with Queen, 145; 1970 Trooping the Colour, 145; posting to Staff College, 147

MacPherson, RJ, 145

MacTier, Col WSM ('Bill'), 1957 church parade, 51; biographical description and assumption of command, 51; presentation of 'MacTier Dirk', 53; relinquishment of command as honorary colonel, 78–79; chairmanship of Centennial Committee, 80; 1972 reunion dinner, 164; death, 184; 1962 Advisory Board, *262*

Magennis, Pipe Major W, 24, 80, 111

Maghakian, Lt/Capt H, *438*

Maillet, Corporal Leonard ('Len'), 293, 346, 347, *433*

Malashenko, Capt Betty Ann Jones, 177, 192, *413*, *414*

Malashenko, Lt/Major Alexei ('Alex'), 161, 176, 186, 202, *407*, *410*; transfer from Intelligence Corps, 155, 156; biographical description, 156; marriage, 177; field exercises, 180, 185; relationship with Chartier, 190; death, 191

Malbeuf, Peter ('Moose'), 16

Mamen, MCpl/WO/CWO Francis, *437*, *382*, *440*, *462*

Manardi, Sgt (US Army) Steve, *430*

Manila (Philippines), 70–71

manoeuvres, Lüneburg Heath (Germany) (1952), 16; NATO (near Denmark) (1962), 82; *RV 81* (New Brunswick), 184, *448*; *RV 83* (Alberta), 188; militia summer manoeuvres (MILCON), 205, 206, 281, 284; in Camp Petawawa (Ontario), *408*. See also exercises; training

Maple Leaf (tartan), 274

Maple Leaf Forever (song), 309

Maple Leaf Marches (NATO infantry competition) (1964), 118

Maple Leaf, The (newspaper), 103

March and Shoot Competition, 330, *436*

Marcianesi, Cadet Corporal Alex, 194–95, *442*

Marcil, CWO Alain, *462*

Marestan, Georges Savarin de, 52

Margaret, Princess, 67–68

Maritime (Atlantic) Black Watch Association. *See* Atlantic (Maritime) Black Watch Association

Maritime Region championship (hockey), 144

Maritime Tri-Service Trophy (hockey), 123

Marr, CWO John, 336

Marr, Private AT, *261*

Marshall, ('Beekie'), 12–13

Martin, Sgt François, 320

Mary Otter Trophy (first aid), 144, 281

mascots: of 1st Canadian Infantry Battalion (Indian), 15; *Yeltneb* (donkey), 144, *258*

Mason, Private Daniel, 374

Mason, Sgt Les, 39

Massachusetts (US): state piping championships, 119

Massed Bands Concert (Nova Scotia), 86

Massey, Vincent, Governor General 1952–59, 44–45

Mather, Lt C, *410*

Matheson, AH: quoted as epigraph, 27

Mathewson, Major/ Lt Col/Col/ Stanton, 76

Matta, Sgt George J, 89

Mauduit, M, 135

maxims, mottos and sayings: *Nemo Pee Impune Cesspit* (pipe band), 146; *Unite* (Cameron Highlanders of Canada), 14–15; *He was the kind of a guy the padre would like to punch in the mouth*, 25; controversies concerning banners, 31; *Freicudan Du* (US Air Force 59 Fighter Interceptor Squadron), 113; *Ne Obliviscaris – Never Forget* (5th Royal Scots), 146; *Twelve highlanders and a bagpipe make a rebellion*, 141; *You just can't have war vets junior to rookies* (3rd Battalion), 151; *When you wear this Red hackle, it makes you stand a foot taller or so* (BW), 360

Maxville Highland Games. *See* North American Highland Games

Mazzocchi, Private, *436*

MBE. *See* Member of the Order of the British Empire

MC. *See* Military Cross

McAlpine, Donald Ian, 117

McAlpine, Major/Lt Col/Brig Gen/Hon Col Duncan Ian A ('Snuffy') ('the Dunc'), 36, 175, 201, *236*, 308, 316, *419*; assumption of command, 19;

NATO battalion, 90; 1963 reunion dinner, 91; quoted as epigraph, 116; Leonard's funeral, 117; posting to 2 RHC, 117; commander, Canadian Forces Europe, 118; 2 RHC, 118; 2009 Trooping the Colour, 118; Exercise *Morning Star*, 119–20; relinquishment of 2 RHC command, 120; appointment as honorary colonel and lieutenant general, 120, 300; commander of *National Training Centre*, 141; Cyprus tour, 144, *258*; appointment as honorary lieutenant colonel, 283; BW disbandment, 285; 1997 reunion dinner, 289; millennium Watch, 315; 2009 presentation of colours, 321, *434*; Bleury Street armoury as historic site, 325; relationship with Bruno Plourde, 353; death, 354

McAuslan, Peter, 327

McCabe, Lorraine, *456*

McCabe, Lt Col Charles ('Chuck'), *269*, 290, 354–55

McCarthy, Master Corporal Jeffrey, *268*, 308

McConnell, Capt/Major Ronald, 120, 329

McConnell, Drill Sgt-Major, 29

McCuaig, Brig Gen/Hon Col/Major Gen Eric: 2 RHC disbandment, 6; Regimental Museum fundraising, 7; 1957 memorial service, 51

McCulloch, Dmr A, *268*

McCulloch, Lt Col Ian Macpherson, *239*, 282, 338; assumption of command, 208; biographical description, 273–74, 279; quoted as epigraph, 273; Regimental Foundation, 274–75; Advanced Reconnaissance Course, 275; BW rear guard, 277; Gettysburg visit, 278; PTSD seminar, 279; BW archives, 279; visit with Queen Mother, 283; relinquishment of command, 283

McDougall, Capt GS, 48

McDougall, Lt Col Ian Roydon, 37, *237*, *262*; biographical description, 48–49; BW recruitment and US visit, 49, 50, 52, 288; relinquishment of command, 51

McEachran, Major DCA, 4

McElheron, RSM WO1/CWO GA ('Gerry'), 106, 155, 180, 186, *242*

McElroy, Lt P, *410*

McGill University (Quebec), 325; Canadian Officers' Training Corps (COTC), including COTC graduates, 100, 147, 134; graduates and students, general, 38, 42, 46, 55, 56, 154, 179, 180, 185, 186, 190, 199, 201, 203, 279, 297, 311, 349; campus ceremony (1945), 4; invention of Canadian football rules, 53; parades, 84–86 *passim*, 104, 147, 198, 322, 357, 362, 364, *439*, *442*; Afghanistan War cartoon, 432

McGovern, Major/Lt Col D'Arcy J, 52, 78, 79, 84, 100, *237*, *262*, *264*; as leader of Philadelphia contingent, 53; biographical description, 62; marriage, 82; steps down as CO, 86

McGuckin, Ppr A, *268*

McInnis, Sgt Bill, 124, 132

McIntosh, Sgt Everett, *407*

McKay, Private Henry ('Hawk'), 112

McLaren, Corporal T, *424*

McLellan, Corporal Rob, *410*

McLellan, Corporal/Capt Brenda, 187, 192

McLellan, Lt Col Bartlett, 197

McLellan, WO Ross, 299, 320

McLeod Piper/Corporal Carolyn, 276

McNair, Cpl (RMR) Brent, *432*

McNeil, Private JM, 74, 254

McQueen, Major George, 90

Medal for Bravery, *432*

medals. *See* awards and honours

'Mega City' (Quebec): parade, 304–05

Megill, Brig JW, 26

Meisner, Corporal Tom, 343, 346

Member of the Order of the British Empire (MBE), awarded to or held by: Diplock, 5, 241; Leonard, 38, 91, 236; Knox, 7, 91, 167, 246, 268; Dynes, 189, 241. *See also* awards and honours

Memorial Day (US): parade (1963), 89

Memorial Museum. *See* Black Watch Regimental Museum

Ménard, Chantale, *456*

Mentioned in Despatches (MID), awarded to or held by: Paul Ibbotson, 5; Diplock, *241*, 337; Richard Ross, 21; Clarkson, 36; Andrew Gault, 59; Teed, 76; Sharp, 94; Harkes, 121; Potter, 305; Dittmar, 346, 347. *See also* awards and honours

Mentiply, 2Lt Sidney, *264*

Mercer, Officer-Cadet Jay, 183

Michener, Right Hon Roland, Governor General 1967–74, 127, 164

MID. *See* Mentioned in Despatches

MILCON. *See* militia summer manoeuvres

Miles, CWO Thomas, *243*, 274, 289, 293, *418*

Miles, Sgt Bob, 125

Miles, WO2 Bobby, 91–92

military bands. *See* bands

Military Cross (MC), awarded to or held by: Hugh Johnston, 4; Macfarlane, 4; Blackader, *246*; Ritchie, 9; Fraser, 28; William Watson, 32, 33, *236*; Clarkson, 36, *235*; Howard Kennedy, 42; Chambers, 43; Lovat, 50; Sinclair, 51; Leonard (recommended), 75; Vanier, 87; Viscount of Arbuthnott, 87; Harkes, 121, *236*, *258*, *267*; Potter, *239*, 299, 305. *See also* awards and honours

Military Medal (MM), awarded to or held by: Blakeney, 20, 33; Proven, 198. *See also* awards and honours

Military Merit (MMM), 298, *416*; Mike Kelly, 190, *242*, 335; Bruce Bolton, *239*, *242*, 297, 298, 306, *410*, *416*; Chartier, *242*; McElheron, *242*; Unger, *243*, *428*; Cameron Stevens, 330, *429*, *442*. *See also* awards and honours

Militia Command and Staff College (CFB Kingston). *See* Canadian Forces Base Kingston

Militia Districts: Western Militia District, 134; proposed replacement with Militia brigade groups, 282

Militia Group Headquarters, 42, 93–94

Militia Monitor, The (journal), 284

militia summer manoeuvres (MILCON) (New Brunswick), 205, 206, 281, 284. *See also* manoeuvres

Miller, Capt TM, 155, *243*

Miller, Maj RE, *291*

Mills, Col Arthur LS, *262*

Mills, GN, 81

Mills, Lt Col/Col Andrew LS, 51, *262*

Mirabel Airport (Quebec), 332

Mitchell, Capt/Lt Col Francis Murray ('Frank'), 51, *237*; relationship with Megill, 26; appointment as CO of Montreal Battalion, 5; 1972 reunion dinner, 164; 1962 Advisory Board, *262*

Mitchell, Lt M, 167

Mitchell, Piper Dean, *410*

Mitchell, S/Sgt John, *407*

MM. *See* Military Medal

MMM. *See* Military Merit

Molnar, Capt WJ ('Bill'), 112, 290

Molson Stadium. *See* Percival Molson Stadium

Molson, Col John Herbert, 104

Molson, Major Walter, 7

Molson, Major/Lt Col John Henry, 134

Molson, Senator Hartland, 48, 129

Moncel, Lt Gen RW, 103–05

Mons, 100th Anniversary of end of Great War, 377–78, *458*

Montcalm, Marquis de, 52

monteith bowl (vessel), 202, *264*, 319

Monteith, Brig/Col JC, 176

Montérégie Region. *See* Eastern Townships

Montgomery, Gen/Field Marshal Sir Bernard LM ('Monty'), 36; control through submarines, 134

Montreal (Quebec), 328, *423*; recruitment, 90; elite as officers, 134, 154, 275; Operation *Spring* failure, 4; post-war, 8; NATO and Korean War training, 12; relationship with George Cantlie, 46–47; economic status on 3rd Battalion, 48, 56, 106; tailors, 54; air raid sirens, 60; drivers, 70; in 1962, 79; Quiet Revolution (*Révolution tranquille*), 86; *The Main*, 87; *youth counter-culture*, 90; and Front de libération du Québec, 97–98, 101, 102, 156–58, 287; number of infantry units, 108; *Expo 67* (World's Fair), 106, 107, 123–25 *passim*, 148, 162, 165; western migration from, 150; relationship to BW, 153, 277, 295, 306–07, 309, 317, 353, 362, 364–65; rise of Quebec separatism, 153, 157; 1976 Quebec election, 157; demotion to second-rate city, 157, 172; 1976 Olympics, 172, 173–74; roads and service stations, 182; Anglophone community, 196, 286–87, 295; Oka Crisis (1990), 203–04, 374; Freedom of the City parades (1990, 1992), 204–06, *409*; Ice Storm (1998), 292, 294, 374; St-Jean-Baptiste Society (*Société Saint-Jean-Baptiste*), 295; relationship to Verdun, 296; 'Mega City' creation (2002), 304–05; relationship to military, 332; *Highland Dinner* (2012), 353; highland dress suppliers, 359; 1987 and 2012 Trooping the Colour, 361, *415*; *Châteauguay* 1812 (battle honour) (2012), 362. *See also* Quebec; floods, see Op LENTUS; *specific institutions and locations*

Montreal Gazette (newspaper), 61, 115, 145, 380; George Cantlie eulogy, 47; BW front page, 187

Montreal Highland dinner (Quebec), 327

Montreal Indoor Highland Games (later Montreal Highland Games) (Quebec), 173–74, 293

Montreal Light Infantry (Quebec), 362

Montreal Military and Maritime Museum (Macdonald Stewart Museum) (Quebec), 297, 308

Montreal Olympics (1976) (Quebec), 172, 173–74

Montreal Pistol Club (Quebec), 79, 157

Montreal Regimental Association (Quebec), *418*, *421*; veterans' services, 51; pipe band combined with Toronto Branch, 312; relationship to Toronto Black Watch Association, 324; regimental whisky, 327. *See also* Black Watch Branch Associations

Montrouge, Lt/Capt Jean Lucien Duchastel de. *See* Duchastel, Lt/Capt Jean Lucien ('John')

Moosehead Lament, The (song), 125

Moralis-Simms, Cpl, *440*

Moreau, Dan, *419*

Morel, Capt Karl, 314

Morgan, Col, 101

Morgan, HW, 102

Morgan, Major Henry, 54, 164

Morley, Sgt Brian, 74

Morning Star (exercise) (1965), 119–20

Morris, Lt Col JM, 117

Morrison, Lt Col Gilbert Scott ('Scotty'), 36, 131, 145, 147, *235*, *269*; biographical description, 131, 133; quoted as epigraph, 136, 138, 140; demise of 1 and 2 RHC, 140; Trooping the Colour, 144; move from 1 to 2 RHC, 147; John Bourne, 292–93

Morton, Capt JD, 24

Morton, Desmond, 279, 287

Morton, Major Gen ROG, 13

mottos. *See* maxims, mottos and sayings

Motzfeldt, Major/Lt Col Eric, death, 130

Mount Bruno (Quebec), 14; Ranges, 12, 171, 172

Mount Royal Club (Quebec), 60, 273

Mountbatten, Philip (Prince Philip, Duke of Edinburgh), 98, 172

Mouriopoulos, MCpl Nikolas AE, *427*

Mowat, Lt HWG, 145

MPs (Military Policemen): Korean War, 25–26

Mulligan, Corporal Dave M, 22

Mundy, Piper Tim, *410*

Munizaga, Sgt Enrique, 205, *426*

Munroe, Bandmaster R, 166

Murison, Major Gen CAP, 146

Murray, Lance Corporal W, 43

Murray, Major David, 24

museums: BW Regimental Museum (Memorial Museum), 7–10 *passim*, 51, 161, 279, 281, 325, 326, *421*; Ticonderoga Museum, 52; Imperial

War Museum, 119, 188; Centennial Tattoo use of European museums, 125; Canadian War Museum, 161, 294; Battle of Normandy Museum, 188; Macdonald Stewart Museum (Montreal Military and Maritime Museum), 297, 308; Isaac Kennedy's unofficial artifacts museum, 329; Juno Beach Centre Museum, *417*

Mushan (Afghanistan), 349

Naked Sword (exercise) (1968), 131–32
Nalgham (Afghanistan), 347
National Archives (Ottawa), 279
National Cadet Camp (Alberta), 106–07
National Council of the Duke of Edinburgh's Award Scheme, 304
National Defence Act (Canada), 284
National Defence College (NDC) (Ontario), 163
National Defence Headquarters (NDHQ): ckilts and dress issues, 192, 269, 294; Area Headquarters, 5; Ibbotson's responsibilities, 5; Regimental Depot, location planning 20; textile purchase, 30; document description shift, 101; 1960s attitude towards highland regiments, 116; request for new Queen's Colours, 136; BW presence at Headquarters 1980s, 148, 154; marksmanship programme, 183; BW advancement of women, 192; 1987 Trooping the Colour, 194; 1992 Freedom of the City, 205; attitude towards pipes and drums, 276; Area Headquarters becomes Total Force Area Headquarters, 282; efficiency planning and Militia funding, 284; BW pipes and drums at gala memorial, 311; Princess of Wales' Own Regiment rifle competition success, 329; Mike Kelly becomes chief warrant, 336; attitude toward Afghanistan War reservists, 345; MacKay as liaison, 364. *See also* Department of National Defence; Regimental Depot (BW)
National Film Board of Canada: *Valour and the Horror, The* (television documentary series): *In Desperate Battle* (episode), 204
National Historic Sites, 325, 327
National Survival Training, 165, 166, *251. See also* training
National Training Centre, 141
NATO. *See* North Atlantic Treaty Organization
Nautical Ranger (exercise) (1968), 131–32
naval transport: *Marine Lynx)*, 23. *See also* boats and ships
navy (Canada). *See* Royal Canadian Navy
navy (Japan), 71
navy (UK) (Royal Navy), 70, 179
navy (US), 179; naval transport (*Marine Lynx*), 23; Navy Yard, 50
Nechin (France), 91
Nesbitt, Capt James Aird, 134, 174; biographical description, 55
Netherlands. *See* Holland
New Broom (exercise) (1968), 131
New Brunswick, 38, 65–66, 74, 90, 110, 136, 142, 143,

205, *448. See also specific camps, locations, and regiments*
New Orleans (US), 106, 107
New York World's Fair (1964–65), 96, 148. *See also* World's Fairs
New Zealand, 24, 142, 173
Newfoundland, 12–13, 72; 1 RHC in War, 32; description of BW performance, 70; exercise (1963), 96–97; *Ace High* (exercise), 113; USAF base, 113; part of *Winter Express* (NATO exercise), 113–14; *Screech*, 125
Newlands, Lt Col William J, 36, 114, 126, 131, 134, 135, *235, 267*; biographical description, 123; quoted as epigraph, 27; Cyprus tour, 137, 258, 361; Fletcher's Field Parade, 361–62
Newton, Dean, *410*
Niagara Falls (Ontario), 175, 176
Nicholson, Major J Duncan ('Dunc'), 145, 153, 155–56
Nisbet, B/S/Sgt Jock, 74
Nixon, Lt/Capt Jose Alexander Banfield ('Joe'), 328
Noble Guerrier (exercise) (2013), 331
non-commissioned members (NCMs), 351, 357; training, 335; creation of senior Canadian Forces appointment, 336
Normandy Campaign. *See* Battles, Second World War, *Overlord* (Operation)
Norris, Len, 139
North American Highland Games (Maxville Highland Games) (Ontario): 1967, 107; 1968, 131; 1998, 293; 2009, *412*
North Atlantic Treaty Organization (NATO), 126, 134, 358; creation, 10; in Korea, 12; 1 CHB joint training, 16–19; Camp Aldershot (Nova Scotia), 65; 1 RHC and 2 RHC tours, 69–70; Germany, including rotations, 12, 20, 22, 27, 30, 38, 69–70, 73–74, 76–77, 79, 84, 116–18 *passim*, 123, 131, 136, 173, 185, 187, *249, 252, 449*; shooting brigade competition, 78; 1962 wargames, 82; General Crerar Forced March competition, 90; *Americanisation* of, 102; Arctic Circle mobile reserve, 110; *Winter Express* (exercise), 110, 113–14, *257*; Canadian Tank Trophy donation, 116; setting of 1960s standard, 116; Maple Leaf Marches (infantry competition), 118; battalion Combat Team Commander's Courses, 143; Allied Command Europe (ACE) Mobile Force (AMF), 163; 3 (Mechanized) Commando position, 163; Canadian Air/Sea Transportable (CAST) brigade, 172; US in 1970s, 172; Norwegian mission (1976), 172–73; Peacekeeping exhibit, 281; *Leopard* 2A6M CAN tank, 342; Afghanistan War, 344; CADPAT uniform, *431*; 1990s budget, 207
North Sydney (Nova Scotia), 33
Northern Ireland, 157, 172, 207, 305, 352; peace process, 304. *See also* Ireland
Norway, 110; *Winter Express* (NATO exercise), 110, 113–14, *257*; NATO mission (1976), 172–73
Notre-Dame-de-Grâce (NDG) (Quebec), 310
Nova Scotia, 27, 138; legislature, 27; Scottish

settlement, 88. *See also specific camps, institutions, and locations*
NTM-A (North Atlantic Treaty Organization Training Mission–Afghanistan), 338. *See also* North Atlantic Treaty Organization

O'Brien, Brig Gen Gary, 333
O'Connor, Kevin, *418*
O'Connor, Major/Lt Col/Hon Lt Col Daniel ('Dan'), 206, *239, 377, 379, 457*; appointment as DCO, 190; creation of gender-free uniforms, 193; 1987 Trooping the Colour, 195, *414*; quoted as epigraph, 200; biographical description, 200–01, 207, 208; BW in 1989, 201–02; 1990 and 1992 concentrations, 202; relationship with Glencross, 203; docudrama *In Desperate Battle*, 204; 1992 Freedom of the City, 204, 205–06; relinquishment of command, 208; 2003 St Andrew's Ball, 306; 2009 presentation of Colours, 319, 320–21; 150th anniversary BW whisky, 327; appointment as honorary colonel, 354; Dubuc trophy reception, *438*; 2012 Trooping the Colour, *440*; 2016 Change of Command, *443*
O'Neil, Johanna, 279
O'Neil, Lance Corporal HE, 67, 69, 70
OBE. *See* Order of the British Empire
October Crisis (1970), 156–58, 162, 166, 172, 287, 374. *See also* Front de libération du Québec
Ogilvie, Lt Col GL, *262*, 164
Ogilvie, Major William Watson ('Bill'), 4
Ogilvy, James A, 174
Ogilvy's (retail store) (Quebec), 55
Oka Crisis (1990), 203–04, 374
Oklahoma State University (US), 175
Oktoberfest (US), 296
Olav V (Norway), 114
Olav V, King of Norway 1957–91, 114
Old Fort Henry (Ontario), 330, *419*
Old Fort York (Ontario), 183
Old Fort, Île Ste Hélène (Quebec), 107
OMM. *See* Order of Military Merit
Ontario, Scottish settlers' achievement, 88; presence at Camp Gagetown inspection, 137; 1970 Laying-Up the Colours, 146; 1981 state dinner, 183, *411*; Quebec Ice Storm (1998), 292, 374. *See also specific camps, institutions, and locations*
operations: Jubilee (Dieppe) (1942), 21, 83, 132, 188, 311, 330; Atlantic (1944), 3; Verglas or Recuperation (1998), 292, 294; Taybridge (2000), 301–02, 318, *416*; Desert Storm (1991), 305, 352; Palladium (2002), 342; Attention (2011–14), 345, *427*; Telic (2003–11), 346; Athena (2003–11) *429, 442*; Lentus (2017, 2019), 373–76, 381, , *454*; Calumet (2020), *455*, Laser (2020), *461*; Impact (Iraq), 376; Reassurance (Latvia), 376; Univer (Ukraine), 376, Presence (Senegal/Mali), 376. See also Battles and campaigns
Operation *Santa 2012* (Christmas project), 339
Order of Military Merit (OMM), awarded to or held

by: Ian Fraser, 124, 266; W MacLeod, 133, *236, 258*; Alden, 148; Cox, 163; Chartier, 189, *239, 415*; Kaulbach, 290; McCabe, 290, 354–55; Logan, 326; Gauthier, 327; Isaac Kennedy, 329, *418*; Cameron Stevens, 358; Unger, 358; Juneau, *427*. *See also* awards and honours
Order of the British Empire (OBE), awarded to or held by: James Weir, 134; Somerville, 33; Doucet, 134; Richard Rutherford, 13, 14, 22, 141, *235, 248*; Parker, 19, *235*; Richard Ross, 21, *236*; McDougall, 48; Leonard, 75; Wallis, 91; JH Price, 95, 134; Moncel, 103–04; Howard, 191; Knox, *237*; Barnett, 288. *See also* awards and honours
Ordnance Depot (Quebec), 182
Ormstown (Quebec), 289
Oromocto (NB), 144–45; Black Watch Avenue, 326
Oromocto High School Cadet Corps (NB), 96–97, 313
Orsogna (Italy), 81
Osprey (attack aircraft), 341
Ostola, Dr Larry, 325, 327
Ottawa (Ontario), 29, 162, 167, 187, 199; *Highland Winter II* (exercise), 184; Remembrance Day (2009), 322
Ottawa/Upper Canada Black Watch Association (Ontario), 324. *See also* Black Watch Branch Associations
Oxford University (UK), 311; 'Oxbridge', 80; Wycliffe Hall, 203

Pacific Black Watch Association (British Columbia), 324. *See also* Black Watch Branch Associations
Page, RSM James, 83
Paine, Mark, *419*
paintings: destroyed, 8; in BW Armoury, 28; of Blackader, *246*; of attack on May-sur-Orn, 8; *The Road to Pittsburgh* (Battle of Bushy Run), 9–10, 52; *Landing of the First Canadian Division at Saint-Nazaire* (Bundy), 119; *Recapture of Sanctuary Wood by The Black Watch, June 1916* (Wollen), 119; *Portrait of Major General Sir Frederick Oscar Warren Loomis* (Bundy), 325–26; BW history print (K. Taylor), 326–27
Paisley, Lt/Maj DS, 26, *260*
Pakistan, 24, 337, 359, 360. *See also* India
Palestine, including Israel, 123, 203
Paley, Piper Gerry, 106
Palladium (Operation) (2002), 342
Pangman, Major/Brig JEC, 19
Panzer Partners (exercise) (1968), 131
parachutes and parachuting, proposed training program, 129; Centennial kilt jump, 131; Hazek, 180; O'Connor, 201, 208; Edmonton airborne parachute depot, 206; artifacts museum, 329; British Parachute Regiment, 343–44; Brasseur, 353–54
parades, 15–16, 32, 61, 148, 208, *250*, 349, 354; Verdun, 6; before Queen Mother, 16–17, 29, 81, 87, 88, 96, 106, 165, 166–67, 170, 183, 187, 190, 192, 267, 314, 363, *416*; church, 5–6, 12, 20, 26,

43, 50–51, 62, 84–86 *passim*, 94, 103, 105, 106, 127–28, 139, 146–47, 161, 162, 189, 190, 288, 193–94 *passim*, 247, 277, 283, 293–94, 296, 305, 307, 308, 314, 316, 317, 328–29, 333, 334, 358, 362–63, *442*; training, including parade drills, 81–82, 99, 162; Montreal victory parade, 4; Reserve Battalion, 6; uniforms, including kilts, 16–17, 29, 305, 348, 357–59 passim; Aldershot (UK), 20; Queen Elizabeth coronation, 22; on deck to Montreal, 24; pay parades, 25, 37; before Queen Elizabeth, 29; BW Centennial, 36; Canadian Centennial, 36, 162; Halifax Citadel Guard, 37; Washington, DC, 37, 50; Bishop's College School Cadet Corps, 43, 162; BW Cadet Corps, 43; 1st Canadian Infantry Division, 46; George Cantlie parade, 46–47; parade strength, 49, 152; Philadelphia, 49, 53; 1960 and 1961 summer camps, 63; Remembrance Day, 63, 289–90, 295, 322, 324, 357, 362, 364, *439*, *442*; Camp Gagetown, 66, 67–68, 87, 89, 92, 144, 145–46, 253, 267, 312; before Princess Margaret, 67; Canada Day (Dominion Day), 72; Dorval Airport (Trudeau Airport), 82; 1962 Trooping the Colour, 82, 101, 194, 199; McGill University, 84–86 passim, 104, 147, 189, 194–96 passim, 206, 312, 318, 198, 322, 357, 362, 364, *439*, *442*; Church of St Andrew and St Paul Centennial, 85; Fletcher's Field (1912), 85; 1963 (Germany), 86, 90–91; US Memorial Day, 89; 1963 (New Brunswick) (two), 91, 92, *260*; Balls compared, 104; Ypres Day, 106, 295–96; 1965 Trooping the Colour, 110–11, *260*; Canadian Armed Forces Centennial Tattoo compared, 124–25; 1967 Trooping the Colour, 126, 127–28, 96, 162, 165, *267*, 312; 1st, 2nd and 3rd Battalions together, 126–28; Beacon as Parade Regimental Sergeant Major, 127; M-181 armoured personnel carriers 'roll past', 130–31; 1968 Trooping the Colour, 130–31; 1968 Armed Forces Day infantry, 131–32; final Regimental (1970), 139, 146–47; 1970 Trooping the Colour, 141, 142, 144–46 *passim*; Scotland in winter, 143; 1970 Oromocto Freedom of the City, 145–46; 1970 Saint John Freedom of the City, 145–46; 1970 Laying-Up The Colours, 146–47, 139; 1919 Trooping the Colour (two) (France and Germany), 91; 1970 Ste Anne's Military Hospital, 159; girls, 161; 1972 Summer Student Training Programme, 161; 1974 Trooping the Colour, 165–67 *passim*; in song (*Glenwhorple*) 165; 1974 Presentation of Colours, 166–68 *passim*; St-Hubert Air Base, 166–67; Change of Command, 167; Imperial Black Watch, 170; 1978 UK Trooping the Colour, 176; Horse Guards, 176, *416*; advancement of women, 187, 192–93; 1987 Trooping the Colour, 188–89, 193–95 *passim*, 198–200 *passim*, 359, *415*; first Colours 125th Anniversary, 190; announcement of Lusk's death, 191; Alexei Malashenko commemorative parade, 191; Human Rights Commission complaint, 192–93; Montreal Freedom of the City (1990

and 1992), 204–06, *409*; cadet march-offs, 201; Glencross on parade, 203; 1992 Montreal Freedom of the City, 204–06; Gary Dover on parade, 207; early-1990s, 281; 1996 armoury, 283; Hong Kong, 288; Ticonderoga, 288; 1997 Ormstown Freedom of the City, 289; 1998 and 2002 Huntingdon Freedom of the City, 293–95, 304; St Patrick's Day, 294, 295, *424*; Santa Claus, 295; St-Jean-Baptiste Day, 295; perceived surfeit, 295–96; Drum Head, 300; 'Mega City'; Bruce Bolton's centenary, 301; 304–05; in 2012, 310; relationship to piping, 311; Queen Mother birthday party, 314; in *Montreal Gazette*, 317; traditional parade route, 317; Quebec City 106th anniversary, 318; Prince Charles visit, 318–22 *passim*, 356, 361; 2012 Trooping the Colour, 325, 358, 360–61, 364; 2009 Presentation of Colours, 347; Snoddon on parade, 347, 348; Topping's reaction, 355; 1912 Trooping the Colour, 360–61; Bishop's College School Church, *439*, *441*. See also pipes and drums; tattoos; training
paratroopers, 15, 329
Parc Jeanne-Mance. See Fletcher's Field
Paris (France), 188, 274; 1966 NATO meeting, 114
Parker, Lt Col H Hugh Alexander ('Harry'), 28, 235; biographical description, 19; relinquishment of command, 27, 28; orders of dress, 30–31
Parnell, Sgt A, 9
Parti Québécois, 172
Passchendaele (Belgium): battle of, 309
Paton, Hugh, 29, 30
Patrick, Lt AJ, 166
Patrick, Major John ('Jack'), 55–56, 180
patrol boats: Cornwallis, 39; Shearwater, 39, 72, *442*; *Stadacona*, 39, 111. *See also* boats and ships
Patrol Competition (1983), 184
Patrouille Nocturne (exercise) (1972), 164
Patterson, Captain Dick, *260*
Patterson, Col David: quoted as epigraph, 345
Patton, Gen George S, 200, 307, 329
Paull, Corporal/Sgt/WO David I ('Dave'), 165, 170, 186, 195, *242*; biographical description, 186, 190
Pauls, Corporal Bud: quoted as epigraph, 11
Payne, Grant, *418*
Peace Support Training Centre (Ontario), 338
Pearkes trophy (soccer), 112
Pearkes, Major Gen George, Conservative Minister of Defence 1957–60, 59, 66
Pearson, Lester Bowles, Liberal Prime Minister 1963–68, 90, 93, 139
Pearson, Private, 44
Peden, Pipe Major E ('Torchy'), 4
PPennington, Maura, 279
Percival Molson Stadium (Quebec), 198; parades, including tattoos, 84, 86, 189, 195–96, 206, 312, 318; descriptions, 184, 194; 1962 and 1987 Trooping the Colour, *265*, *415*. *See also* McGill University
Percival, Capt Jackie, 171, 192

Perkin, Corporal VJ, 143

Perth (UK), *440*; Imperial BW Depot, 30, 45; Balhousie Castle, 176, 188; Imperial BW barracks, 325

Perth Quaich (Perth Quaich Cup), 135, 164, 167

Pet Hackle (exercise) (1981), 182–83

Petch, Capt/Lt Col Charles ('Charlie'), Jr, 48

Petras, BGen Herb, 336

Pettipas, Major Bill, 132

Phare, Capt/Major Christopher ('Chris'), *239*, 274, 343, 355, 368–71, *412*; Advanced Reconnaissance Course, 275; Bosnia, 280, 363–64; second-in-command to Thomas MacKay, 314; biographical description, 363–64; relinquishment of command, 364, *440*, *443*; 2013 Remembrance Day Parade, 364, *439*

Phase 2, including Infantry, 274, 293, 303

Phelan, Drum Major Michael, 24, 34–35, 148

Philadelphia (US), 9–10, 49–53 *passim*, 86, 295, 333; Navy Yard, 50

Philip, Prince (Philip Mountbatten, Duke of Edinburgh), 98, 172

Pibroch (Piobaireachd) (musical form), 114, 115, 311, 330

Pibroch Patrol (exercise) (1967), 136–37

Pilkie, Lance Corporal HS, 70

Pinard, Officer Cadet, 194–89

Piobaireachd (Pibroch) (musical form), 114, 115, 311, 330

pipes and drums, 368, 369, 372, 374, 377–79, *410*: Verdun parade, 296; Sherwood's visit, 7; Lee's responsibilities and achievements, 14, 24; 1st Canadian Infantry Battalion training, 15; 1 CHB NATO training, 17, 18; Hanover to Munsterlager march, 17; *Johnny Cope*, 18, 42–43, 50; *Reveille*, 18, 150–51; Rankine as pipe major, 20–21; Edinburgh Castle and British Military tattoos, 24, 377–79; military drills, 25; Korean War, 26; destitution, 27; pipe tunes determination, 28; Hamilton (Bermuda) tattoo, 29, *268*; 1954 visit of Queen Mother, 29; Phelan as drum major, 34; Queen Elizabeth Washington, DC reception, 37; duty piper, 42–43, 50, 104, 195; Black Watch Boys' pipes and drums, 44; 'Ed Sullivan Show', 44; New York visit of Queen Mother, 44–45; Ottawa State dinner, 45; Camp Gagetown, 46, 67, 126–27, 143, 208; William Hannah's assumption of command, 48; Philadelphia visits, 49–50, 53; *Lochaber No More*, 50; 1956 reunion dinner, 50; Fort Ticonderoga, 52; Ogilvy's, 55; regional highland games, 67; *The Black Bear*, 72; *Shearwater* (patrol boat), 39, 72, *424*; before Boy Scouts, 73; German rotations, 73; Maritime tours, 74–75; BW Centennial, 80; 1962 parade, 84, 85; *The Black Bear*, 85; Seattle World's Fair, 86, 148; Royal Highlanders' Canadian visit, 89; Alabama Highland Games, 96; Macfarlane's piper, 100; within older BW structures, 101, 151–52, 155, 357; 1968 reunion dinner, 104, 135; Greig's assumption of command, 106;

Hemisfair '68 (World's Fair), 106; New Orleans, 106, 107; 1967 Ypres Day Parade, 106; *Expo 67* (World's Fair), 107, 124, 148, 266; Cadet Pipes and Drums (Cadet Pipe Band), 44, 107, 277, 297, 310, 313, 328; Île Ste Hélène Old Fort, 107; Maxwell Highland Games, 107, 131; Trooping the Colour, including 1987 Queen Mother visit, 111, 195, 196, 358, *414*; *Winter Express* (NATO exercise), 114; winter operations, 114; government classification of pipers, 115; British Army of the Rhine competition, 119; Decca records recording, 119; Massachusetts state piping championships, 119; Centennial Tattoo, including *Blue Train* and *Red Train*, 124, *266*; 1967 Royal Parade, 127–28; retraining, 141; 1969 reunion dinner, 142; 1970 Laying-Up the Colours, 146–47; 1971 First World War commemoration, 150–51; 3 RHC reinforcement, 155; bagpipes' effect on soldiers, 159; Ste Anne's Military Hospital, 159; final performance with Regimental Military Band, 161–62; 1972 reunion dinner, 164; *Glenwhorple* (song), 165; Presentations of Colours, 166, 321; Bruce Bolton as major, 168, 176, 180, 186, 274, 296–99 *passim*, 302, 308; 1974 visit of Queen Mother, 169; Montreal Olympics (1976), 174; Betty Ann Jones's reaction, 177; Waterloo bagpipes, 186; Kerr as major, 195, 298; 3rd Battalion, 195, 311; Stone Mountain Highland Games, 198; O'Connor as RMC Pipe Band major, 200, 201; 1992 Freedom of the City, 204; 1992 Scottish Festival, 206; proposed systemizing of operations, 207; 1992 summer concentration, 208; Beverly Hills, *269*; militia band reduction, 273; McCulloch's experience, 273–74; first female piper, 276; National Defence Headquarters (NDHQ) attitude towards, 276; quota cut and new later structures, 276–77, 357; 48th Highlanders Pipe Band strength retention, 277; stolen, 277–78; 1995 reunion dinner, 282; planned elimination, 285; Lake Champlain, 288; Ormstown parade, 289; Maxville competition, 293; Montreal Highland Games, 293; St Patrick's Day Parade, 294, 295, *442*; Montreal's relationship with, 295; Remembrance Day Parade, 295, 322, 362, *442*; Santa Claus Parade, 295; St-Jean-Baptiste Day Parade, 295; Rhode Island Oktoberfest, 296; St Andrew's Society Learner's Programme, 297; Stevens as major, including instructor, 299, 301, 302, 310, 330, 357, 358; Gilmore plays Duncan McAlpine; 300; De Chastelain as piper, 304; funeral of John Bourne, 304; 'Mega City' parade, 304–05; psychological importance, 309–10, 323; BW embodiment of BW, 309–11; general history, 309–11; BW school, 310; Afghanistan War (pipes), 311, 313–14; NDHQ gala memorial, 311; pipe majors' retention, 311; annual BBQ, 311–14; Church Parade, 317, *442*; Toronto Branch, 324, *422*; BW 150th Anniversary stamp, 325, 326, *435*; Montreal Highland dinner,

327–28, 353; CD production, 328; 2012 concerts, 328; *Sea of Hackles*, 328–29; Fort Henry Guard, 330; Operation *Jubilee* (Dieppe) 70th anniversary, 330; Camps Valcartier, Camp Farnham, and Fort Pickett, 354; Fort Drum, 365, *411*; international status, 365; Fort York, *411*; Vimy Ridge, 373, 377–78, *411*; during military training, *423*; montage, *435*. *See also* bands; parades; songs and tunes

Pitts, Private LM, *261*

Pleine Neige (exercise) (1973), 164

Plourde, Father Romeo, 122

Plourde, Lt Col/Col Bruno, 53, 189, *239*, 318, 327, 331, 356, 361–62, 364, 368, 375–82, *421*, *428*, *437–38*, *440–41, 457, 462*; as incoming CO, 319; assumption of BW command, 322; Highland tradition, 328; 75th anniversary Dieppe Raid, 330; quoted as epigraph, 332; BW relationship with 111th US Regiment, 332–33; Afghanistan war, 344–45, 351–53; biographical description, 351–53, 363; appointment of Guay, 353; BW 150th anniversary, 357–58; reforms to BW, 362–63; command of technical exercise, *424*

Plow, Major Gen EC, 29

poems, 294; *So weave well the black threads* (A MacDonell of Keppoch), 30; *In years gone past* (B Harper), 38; *In years gone past I was the class of every major exercise* (Clarkson), 40; *Epitaph on My Own Friend and My Father's Friend* (R Burns), 48; *If you can look onto the seeds of time* (Shakespeare), 56; *But Black Watch marksmanship must improve* (Ludlow), 69; *The rink was dim and foggy* (anonymous), 75–76; *Patrols, and not Survival* (anonymous), 78; *The Jolly Beggars* (R Burns), 115; *But we will carry on* (Lenathen), 143; *Eheu! Fugaces, Posthume, Posthume* (Horace), 278; *To a Haggis* (R Burns), 285; *Blow, winds, and crack your cheeks! rage! blow!* (Shakespeare), 292; *The Image of Irelande* (Derrick), 309; *Arithmetic on the Frontiers* (Kipling), 341; *The poppy* (anonymous), 357. *See also* songs and tunes

Pointe-Claire (Quebec): hospital evacuation exercise (2001), 303

Pointe-St-Charles (Quebec), 312

Poirier, CWO Ron, 162, 166, *242*

Poland, 8, 74

Pollock, WO George, 144

Portrait of Major General Sir Frederick Oscar Warren Loomis (painting), 325–26

post-traumatic stress disorder (PTSD), 279, 281, 355

POTS. *See* Provisional Officers Training School of the Regiment

Potter, Lt Col John, *239*, 299, 308, 352; biographical description, 305–06

Powers, Private, 164

Poxon, Dmr M, *268*

Préfontaine, Brig Gen Marc A, 308

Presentation of Colours: 1912, 360–61; 1962, 80,

82–84, *passim*, 89, *265*; 2009, 118, 316, 318, 320–22 passim, 334, 347; 352, 356, 361; 1974, 166, 168, 169

Price, Brig/Col JH, 95, 134

Price, CSM NW, awarded *Croix de Guerre*, 38

Price, Lt Col/Col Thomas Even ('Tom'), 60, 104, 126, 162, 181, *238, 267, 410, 412, 414*; guard of honour for Queen Mother, 83; appointment as CO, 94; biographical description, 94–96; relieved of command, 105; absent from New Year's Levee, 191; appointment as honorary colonel, 198; reception with Queen Mother, 199; McCulloch employment interview, 273; Regimental Foundation, 274; biographical description, 283; relationship with Charles MacKay, 314

Prince Edward Island, 133

Prince, WO Martin, *416*

Prisoner of War (PW) camps: *passim*, 328; Japanese, 21, 95

Proven Cup (BW training award), 203, *416*; 1987, 198; 1998, 293; 2002, 302, *416*; 2010, 356

Proven, Major AB, 198

Provincial Reconstruction Team (PRT) (Afghanistan), 343, 346, 350

Provisional Officers Training School of the Regiment (POTS): attitude of Militia headquarters towards, 3; graduates, 19

Pryde, Capt AR, *264*

Psychological Operations (PSYOPS): Afghanistan War, 338, *431*; introduction, 307; work with local Afghan populations, 337; Dittmar's detachment, 339, 346–47; Batchelor as Section member, including as commander, 347, *432*; Snoddon as Tactical Team member, including as Leader, 347–48, *432*; dangers to patrols, 349; as platoons attached to battle group, 350–51; Unger attached to cells, 356, *428*. *See also* civil-military co-operation

PSYOPS. *See* Psychological Operations

PTSD (post-traumatic stress disorder), 279, 281, 355

Pugh, Lance Corporal AW, 138; quoted as epigraph, 6

Pulitzer Prize (literature), 7, 104

Purple Network (padres), 203

Puys Beach (Blue Beach) (France): Operation *Jubilee* (Dieppe), *passim*, 83

PW camps. *See* Prisoner of War (PW) camps

Pyatt, WO1 G, 133

QR&O (Queen's Regulations and Orders), 284

Quaich Cup (Perth Quaich Cup), 135, 164, 167

Qualizza, Cpl, *436*

Quebec (province), *423*; Quiet Revolution (*Révolution tranquille*), 90; separatism, 97, 157, 172, 173, 285, 295, 304; dearth of soldiers in Gagetown battalions, 137; first female infantry soldiers, 192; shift to unilingual nationalist state, 153, 172; economic effect of 1976 election, 157; affiliation of French-Canadians and Scots, 159; Oka Crisis (1990), 203–04, 374; Auld Alliance significance,

205; Ice Storm (1998), 292, 294, 374; fatality in Afghanistan War, 342–43; and importance of BW as Montreal icon, 353; BW support for cultural values, 354; Psychological Operations (PSYOPS) team, *432. See also specific camps, institutions, and locations*

Quebec City (Quebec), 69, 100, 189, 319, 342, *413*; Quebec Conference Centennial, 98; boxing championships, 111; 106th anniversary, 318

Quebec District Number 1 Headquarters, 335

Quebec Thistle Council, 296

Queen Elizabeth Hotel (Quebec), 83–84, 104, 196–97, *414*

Queen Mary Veterans' Hospital (Quebec), 51

Queen's Medal for Championship Shot, 290

Queen's Regulations and Orders (QR&O), 284

Queen's University (Ontario), 123, 349

Quetta (War College) (India, later Pakistan), 337

Quick Sword (exercise) (1983), 185

Quiet Revolution (*Révolution tranquille*), 86, 90

Quincy (US), 89

Quinn, Brig Gen Kenneth, 335

Radio Engineer Products (company), 49

radios (wireless), 89; Camp Gagetown training, 35–36; 1962 Royal Visit broadcasts, 83; *Web Foot* (exercise), 132

Radman, Capt Peter, 287, 299, 303, 314, 343; appointment as staff officer, 287; biographical description, 315–16

Ramsay, Master Corporal/Sgt Matthew, *268*, 346, 374

Rancourt, Capt Jean-Francois ('Jeff'), *430*

Rankine, Pipe Major/WO Duncan, 20–21, 24, 37

Reay, Gen Gordie, 274

Recapture of Sanctuary Wood by The Black Watch, June 1916 (painting), 119

Recruit School (Nova Scotia), 148. *See also* training

Recruit Training Programme, 105. *See also* training

recruitment, 92, 101, 126; specific difficulties at start of War, 11; post-war and Cold War, 6, 12; abilities of 48th Highlanders and the North Nova Scotia, 15; Maritimes, 28, 39; difficulties in producing sufficient recruits, 41; strong increase, 44; need to jump-start post-Korean War, 49; 1956 improvement, 50; Andrew Gault's assistance, 59; Recruit Training Syllabus, 61; Special Militia Training Programme, 62; in new Montreal suburbs, 79; by First World War Royal Highlanders in US cities, 89; 1960s *youth counter-culture* effect, 90; *Reorganization of Reserves* effect, 96; Recruit Training Programme (BW), 105; 1970 revitalization, 155; Quebec English-speaking population as recruitment base, 157; difficulties in 1970s recruitment, 159, 162, 175; of second BW female officer, 177; bureaucratic aspect of promotion, 187; female infantry soldiers, 192; early 1999s, 194, 198; early-1950s recruitment and training of single companies, 247; 2nd Ypres recruitment posters, 304;

revamped at start of millennium, 299; difficulties by 2012, 332; Afghanistan War, 352. *See also* training

Recuperation or *Verglas* (Quebec Ice Storm) (Operation) (1998), 292, 294, 374

Red Cross Organization, 380

Red Deer (Alberta), 355

Red Hackle (magazine) (UK): quoted as epigraph, 46. *See also Canadian Red Hackle*

Red Hackle (vol. 1) (magazine) (Canada), 150. *See also Canadian Red Hackle*

Red Hackle (vol. 2) (magazine) (Canada): quoted as epigraph, 154. *See also Canadian Red Hackle*

Red Hackle Club (soldiers' mess) (Quebec), 196, 321, *437*

Red Hackles, 23, 29, 79, 87, 148, 154, 182–83, 290, 302, 309, 336, 340, 351; care and BW catechetics, 28; 1954 opening of Nova Scotia legislature, 28; in cartoons, 32, *448–49*; 1954 permission to wear, 45; Church Parades, 50, 328–29, 334; Presentation of Colours, 85, 321; New Orleans, 107; absence in Cyprus, 122; Operation *Spring* 25th Anniversary, 135; 1974 Trooping the Colour, 170; women's uniforms, 192, 193, 202; 1992 Concentration, 202; Army Bisley Team, *261*; funeral of Queen Mother, 302; Imperial Black Watch, 302, 346; indicative of distinction between Reservist and Regular, 350; bestowal ceremony, 354; 2011 Remembrance Day Parade, 357; uniqueness of uniform, 358–59; 1987 quantity, 359; quantity, 360; 2012 Trooping the Colour, 365; 150th Anniversary montage and stamp, *435*; cadets, *441*; objective, *441. See also* balmorals, including blue balmorals; green coatees; *specific photographs*

Red Train, 124

Redpath, Major/Lt Col William Bradford ('Bill'), 79, 91, *238*, *264*, *441*; becomes 3 RHC second-in-command, 62; assumption of full command, 86; biographical description, 86; appraisal of Gurevitch, 87; 1963 Memorial Day Parade, 89; relinquishment of command, 94

Reekie, WO 1 Don B, 127, 133, 141, *240*; quoted as epigraph, 122; biographical description, 122, 145

Regimental Advisory Board. *See* Black Watch Regimental Advisory Board

regimental church. *See* Church of St Andrew and St Paul

Regimental Depot (BW) (New Brunswick), 81, 82, 87, 91, 135; establishment proposed, 20; 1958 Sussex March, 32; 1968 reunion dinner, 59; Recruit Training Syllabus modification, 61, *251*; Sussex closure, 67; Cochrane as commander, 78; 1962 Presentation of Colours, 80; Watling as commander, 91, 104, 126; training standards, 129, 133; closure, 132–33; recruits' geographical composition, 138–39; Bleury Street armoury exhibits, 363

Regimental Depot (Imperial Black Watch) (UK), 30; closure, 45

Regimental Dress Committee, 359, 360. *See also* uniforms

Regimental Foundation: establishment, 207, 274–75; contributions to historical projects, 326; and K. Taylor's BW history print, 326

Regimental Lament (tune), 302

Regimental Military Band: British embassy in Washington, DC, 37; cadet training, 44; tours, including Germany, 74–75; 1962 Presentation of Colours, 84; within BW organizational structure, 101, 151–52; 1967 Royal Parade, 127–28; size, 151–52; with pipes and drums, 162; 1974 Presentation of Colours, 166; 1987 Trooping the Colour, 195. *See also* bands; pipes and drums

Regimental Museum. *See* Black Watch Regimental Museum

Regimental Support Staff (RSS), 287, 316, *414*, *436*; Butcher's experience, 168; Klepak's appraisal of Halpenny, 180–81; Stothers's experience, 185; Tactical Exercise Without Troops, 185; Radman's experience, 303, 315–16; Larochelle's experience, 328; Farnham as interim officer, 343; Guay's experience, 353, 361; 2010 Trooping the Colour, 361

Regional Battle Group (South): Afghanistan War, 346

Regular Officer Training Plan (ROTP), 100, 174–75

Reid, Corporal Alexander, *268*, 346

Reid, Major Mac, 14

Reinforcement Training School Canada, 94

Remembrance Day (11 November), 328, *429*; dinners and parades, 295, 324; 1960, 63; 1997, 289–90; 2009, 322; 2010, *442*; 2011, 357; 2012, 362, *443*; 2013, 364, *439*; 2016, *442*

Reserve Entry Scheme Officer (RESO): entrance tests, 291

Reserve Officer University Training Plan (ROUTP), 173

reserve ships. *See* boats and ships

Reserves 2000 (lobbyist group), 285

retention: as main concern, 129, 162, 187, 287, 331; Afghanistan soldiers, 339–40

reunions, including reunion dinners, 101, 149, 282, 325, 359; 1945, 5; 1949, 6–7; 1950, 9–10; 1954, 50; 1959, 59; 1961, 78–79; 1962, 86, 87; 1963, 91–92; 1964, 103–04; 1965, 102; 1966, 103–04, 123; 1967, 105, 126; 1968, 133–35; 1969, 141–42; 1970, 149–50, 158–59; 1971, 150–51, 159; 1972, 151; 1972, 164; 1973, 151; 1974, 167, *407*; 1975, 171; 1980, 181; 1987, 198–99; 1990, 204; 1992, 202; 1994, 281–82; 1996, 287; 1997, 289; 1998, 294; 1999, 296; 2000, 300; 2002, 304; 2003, 306; 2012 (BW 150th Anniversary), 333, 362, *421*; 13th Battalion, 150; 42nd Battalion, 150; 73rd Battalion CEF, 149–50; barbeque-reunion (2012), 330

Reveille (bugle call), 18, 150–51

Révolution tranquille (Quiet Revolution), 86, 90

Rhode Island (US), 296

Rhodes, Major Dusty, 71

Richard, Col Marc Commander 34th Brigade, *437*

Richardson, Lt William, 380

Richardson, Sgt John Henry, 15

Rickets, Private T, 119

Rising Star (exercise) (1954), 45–46

Ritchie, Col/Gen Sir Neil Methuen: quoted as epigraph, 9; 1950 regimental function, 9; 1951 company inspection, 13; relinquishment of command, 22; 1961 reunion dinner, 78; 1962 presentation of Colours, 83–84; 1968 reunion dinner, 134; 1969 reunion dinner, 141–42; 1972 reunion dinner, 164; BW Advisory Board, *262*; presentation of Ritchie Tiger, 314

Ritchie, Corporal/WO Gordon Scott ('Gord'), 162, *421*; quoted as epigraph, 193; Egypt deployment, 170; 1967 Olympics, 172; awarded Proven Cup, 198; 150th Association committee, 324; regimental dome coins, 326; 150th regimental whisky, 327; Operation *Santa 2012*, 339

Rivière-des-Prairies (Quebec), 286

Rizzi, Cpl/Sgt G, *421*, *436*

'Road to Pittsburgh, The' (painting), 9–10

Robert, Corporal Lucette, 187

Roberts, B/Sgt Cecil, 74

Roberts, Capt Ian, 264

Robertson, Capt/Major/Lt Col Graham Douglas ('Doug'), 133, 174–75, 176–77, 180, 190, *238*, 279, 283–84, 298; quoted as epigraph, 54; biographical description, 174–75; visit to Colonel-in-Chief, 176; departure, 177

Robichaud, Hédard, Lieutenant Governor of New Brunswick 1971–81, 175

Robinson (combat outpost) (COP) (Afghanistan), 349

Robinson, John, *418*

Robinson, Lt Col Colin, 318

Rockingham, Lt Col/Major Gen/Gen John ('Rocky'), 46, 59, 79; conflict with Logan, 35–36

Roderick, George H, 53

Rodger, CWO John, 202, *243*

Rodgers, CWO AD ('Al'), 155, 162, 166, 168, 189, *242*

Roe, Sgt Jack ('The Voice'), 103

Roger, Corporal, 176

Rommel, Field Marshal Erwin ('Desert Fox'), 22, 78, 82

Rooney, Lt (ret'd) Frank, *412*

Roosevelt, Franklin D., US President 1933–45, 7, 104

Roper, Capt Gordon, 281

Rose, Lt Col David, 25

Roslyn School (Quebec), 56

Ross, Lt Col/Brig Gen Richard Montgomery ('Dick'), 38, 45, 159, *236*; quoted as epigraph, 21, 24; biographical description, 21–22, 25; declaration of BW, 23; becomes acting brigade commander, 26; relinquishment of command, 32

Ross, Major Gen James, 47–48

Rothesay Collegiate School Cadet Corps (No. 130) (New Brunswick): 79, 96–97, 313

ROTP (Regular Officer Training Plan), 100, 174–75

Routledge, Maj Jim C, 6

ROUTP (Reserve Officer University Training Plan), 173

Roy, Commander Armand, 277

Roy, Francis, LCol, 380, 382–83, *462*

Roy, Sgt Don, 24

Royal Air Force (RAF) (UK), 77; 1 CHB's sniper section raid, 17

Royal Canadian Air Force (RCAF), 42, 377, *442*; sports competition, 67, 74; popularity in 1960s, 107–08; *Boat Cloak* (exercise), 110; *Ace High* (exercise), 113; B Company Fire Power Demonstrations, 132; St-Hubert station, 186; restrictions on women employment, 192; Afghanistan War, 350; Canadian Forces Base Shearwater (Nova Scotia), *442*

Royal Canadian Mounted Police (RCMP): Fort Pitt 195th anniversary, 52; FLQ bombings, 102; 1962 Regimental Dinner, 196; 2009 and 2012 Trooping the Colour, 320, 361

Royal Canadian Navy (RCN), 96; boxing competitions, 39, 111; post-war association with BW, 72; armed forces unification, 94, 102, 122, 128–29; *Nautical Ranger* (exercise), 131–32; *Web Foot* (exercise), 132; Combat Related Employment of Women (CREW) trials, 192; Afghanistan War, 350; 2012 Remembrance Dinner, 362; 2013 Remembrance Day service, 364

Royal Canadian School of Infantry (Canadian Infantry School), 112; Highland Light Infantry of Canada, 46, 207; Camp Gagetown, 275, 291, 298, 363

Royal Military College of Canada (RMC) (Ontario), 273; graduates, 12, 46, 109, 121, 137, 185, 201, 204, 273, 279, 283, 331; Parker as staff instructor, 19; training, including cadets, 46, 57, 100; billeting of lieutenant colonel candidates, 164; Klepak as instructor, 179; Strategic Studies Programme, 180; Pipe Band, 201; proximity to Old Fort Henry, 330; uniform, *441*

Royal Military College of Science (UK), 207

Royal Military College Sandhurst (RMA Sandhurst) (UK), 121, 173, 207

Royal Scottish Piping Society (UK), 119

Royal Thames Yacht Club (UK), 180

Royal Victoria Hospital (Quebec), 55, 194

Royle, H/Capt Rev E Cecil, 355

Rue de Royal Black Watch (street) (France), 135, 188

Rue des Canadiens (street) (France), 164

rugby, 180, *412*

Russell, G Home, 325

Russell, Rev William R, 168–69, *245*, *410*

Russia (Soviet Union): development of Cold War, 10, 11; Korean War, 10; possibility of attack on Germany, 16; possibility of nuclear attack, 60; in Trench song, 41; preparations for attack by, 73; possibility of attack on Europe, 172; occupation of Afghanistan, 345

Rust, Major Grant, 201, 206

Rutherford, Lt Col Richard L ('Dickie'), 15, 21, 141–42, *235*, *248*; biographical description, 13–14; appointment as brigade major, 14

Rutherford, Sgt, 345

Ruthven, Major Alasdair, 168, 183, *410*, *411*

RV 81 (manoeuvres), 184; cartoons, *448*

RV 83 (manoeuvres), 188

Rwanda, 282

Saint John (New Brunswick), 127, 128, 145

Saint-Chrysostome (Quebec), 185

Saltire (St Andrew's Cross), 354, *433*

San Antonio (US), 106

Sangster, Private, 120

Sasebo (Japan), 24

Saskatchewan, 138

Saudi Arabia (Arabia), 306

sayings. *See* maxims, mottos and sayings

Scotland (UK), 19, 74, 85, 104, 273, 313; BW kilt parade, 16–17; 1st Gordons, 87; BW tweed, 30; Gagetown settlement, 66; conditions of winter parades, 143; 1974 Trooping the Colour, 170; Auld Alliance, 204–05; Montreal heraldic shield, 205; *Canadian Red Hackle* (magazine), 300; 22nd Armoured Regiment (Canadian Grenadier Guards) lamp gift, 325; whisky industry, 327; highland dress suppliers, 359, 360; BW at Imperial Black Watch 2012 Laying Up of Colours, *422*. *See also* Imperial Black Watch

Scotland the Brave (song), 309

Scott, Corporal, 124

Scott, MWO Gordon, 160

Scott, Phil, *417*, *420*

Scottish Festival (Quebec) (1992), 204–06; Tartan Ball, 206

Scullion, Corporal, 124

Seamark, Lt Col WH ('Bill'), 29, 36, 45, 51–52, *235*; biographical description, 27; standardization of BW dress, 28, 30–31

Seattle (US), 22–23; World's Fair (1962), 82, 86, 124, 148

Seaver, Terry, 324

Second Oldest Member Present (gathering prize), 101

Secteur du Québec de la force terrestre (SQFT) (later 2nd Canadian Division) (Quebec), 286, 340, 343; becomes 2nd Canadian Division (Quebec), 284; Lusk appointed area commander, 285; communication with Bruce Bolton, 308; collective style, 317; appointments given to Bruno Plourde, 351, 352; Topping appointed padre, 355

Sécurité Interne Programme D'Entrainement—Counter-terrorist, 145

Sedbergh School (Quebec), 57

Select Embodied Militia: 5th Battalion, 362

Sellar, Lt Col Gordon Harper, 36, 91, 104, 110, *235*; presentation of Queen Mother portrait, 92; Newfoundland exercise, 96; biographical description, 109–10; Exercise *Winter Express*, 110, 114, 257; 1965 Trooping the Colour, 110, 260; Newfoundland Winter Warfare training, 112–13; Bentley MacLeod's appraisal, 112–13; relinquishment of command, 114, 123; *Agent Orange* and subsequent death, 115

Selwyn House School (Quebec): graduates, 86, 94, 314
Sennelager (Germany), 118
451 Squadron (451 Sqn): Air Cadets, *422*
Serapins, Lt David, 369
Seven Years' War (1756–63), 52, 288
78th Fraser Highlanders (historical re-enactment group), 297–98
73rd Battalion Association, 54
Sewell, Major/Lt Col WR ('Bill'), 155, 162, 172, 190, *238*; promotion to field officer status, 101; 1970s political and social shifts, 162; qualification as lieutenant colonel, 164; 1974 Trooping the Colour, 166; assumption of command, 167, 189; quoted as epigraph, 167; biographical description, 167–68; appointment of Chartier, 168; officers' mess, 170; women and 1975 reunion dinner, 171; shortage of officers, 174, 175, 177; relinquishment of command, 174; regimental secretary, 320, 326; commemorative stamp, 326; 150th anniversary regimental whisky, 327; 1974 reunion dinner, *407*
Shakespeare, William: quoted as epigraph, 56, 292
Sharkey, Norm, 14
Sharp, Lt Col John Wemyss ('Jake'), 104, 134, 164, 190, 191, *407*; biographical description, 94, retirement, 181
Shaw, WO Chad, 320
Shawinigan (Quebec), 97–98
Shearwater (patrol boat), 39, 72, *442. See also* boats and ships
Sherwood, Robert E, 7, 44, 104–05
ships. *See* boats and ships
Shoot to Kill (marksmanship programme): renamed *Shoot to Live*, 183
Sinai Peninsula, *455*
Signal Section, *258*
Siket, Sgt George, 291, 292
Sileika, Cpl, *436*
Simonds, Lt Gen/Gen Guy Granville, formation of composite battalions, 12; conversion of 1st and 2nd CHB to BW, 23; reorganization of reserve units, 41, 42; 1st Canadian Infantry Division, parade, 46
Simpson, Corporal Ernest, 170
Sinclair, Lt Col IMR, 50–51
Sinclair, Major Jock, 359
Sir George Williams University (Quebec), 162; Canadian Officers' Training Corps (COTC), 46, 100
Skill-At-Arms (infantry competition) (1963), 118
Smiley, Corporal, 124
Smith, Pipe Major (RCAF) DJ, *442, 458*
Smith, Pipe Sergeant Dan, 374, 378, *410*
Smith, Sergeant RD, *261*
SMTP (Special Militia Training Programme), 62. *See also* training
Smythe, WO Frank, 51
snipers, including sniper fire, 309; 1 CHB sniper section, 17; Korean War, 26; Afghanistan War, 342

Snoddon, Sgt/WO Mathew Mark, 280; appraisal of Bruno Plourde, 344–45; Kandahar deployments, 347–48, *426–28, 431–32*; rank qualifications, 356–57; Brigade tactical trophy, *436*
Snow, Corporal Art, 111–12, 324, *421*
soccer, 77, 112; Canadian Army championship, 43
Société Saint-Jean-Baptiste (St Jean-Baptiste Society), 295
Soest (Germany), 24, 81
softball. *See* baseball and softball
62e Régiment d'artillerie de campagne (Quebec): FLQ armoury raid, 97–98
Solomon, Private Nelson, 111
Soltau (Lüneburg or Lüneburg Heath) (German training area), 16 17, 73, 76, 82
Somalia Affair (1993), 281
Sommerville, GR, 134
songs and tunes, 28, 125, 142, 282, 309. trench song, including adapted version, 41; *Lament, 442; Auld Lang Syne*, 197; instruction, 14, 72; *Johnny Cope*, 18, 42–43, 50; *Reveille*, 18, 150–51; *Lord Lovat's Lament*, 50; *Black Bear*, 72, 85, 145–46, 196, 201, 378; *Highland Laddie*, 72, 73, 84, 201, 296, 321, 378; *Squid Jiggin Ground*, 72; *Bonnie McAlpine*, 100; Pibroch (Piobaireachd) (musical form), 114, 115, 311, 330; *Ballad of the Blue Berets*, 122–23; *Zorba the Greek*, 123; *Moosehead Lament, The*, 125; *Scotland the Brave*, 127, 327–28; *Lochaber No More*, 142; *tunes of glory*, 147; *It's a lie, it's a lie! Oh you know you're telling a lie*, 149; *Glenwhorple*, 165; *Colonel Johnny Bourne (Colonel Bourne)*, 196, 311; *Will ye no come back again*, 197; *Regimental Lament*, 302; *Director Steps Up*, 308; *Lieutenant Colonel Bruce D Bolton, MMM*, 308; *Cock of the North*, 309; *Maple Leaf Forever*, 309; *Vive la Canadienne*, 309; *All the Blue Bonnets are over the Border*, 310; *MacDonald of Kinlochmoidart's Salute*, 327; *Amazing Grace*, 327–28; *Hippopotamus Song*, 335. *See also* pipes and drums; poems
South Africa, 24, 59, 168
Southern New Brunswick Senior League Championship (hockey), 77
Southward, 2Lt RM, *264*
Soviet Union. *See* Russia
Special Militia Training Programme (SMTP), 62. *See also* training
Speidel, Gen Hans, 82
Spence, Cpl Dave, 100
Spitfire (exercise) (1957), 35
sporrans. *See* hair sporrans
sports. *See specific sports*
Spring City Armoury (US), 278
Springhill (Nova Scotia): 1958 mine disaster, 68
SQFT. *See Secteur du Québec de la force terrestre*
Squid Jiggin Ground (tune), 72
SSEP and SSEP2 (Summer Student Training Programmes), 160, 161, 164

St Andrew's (stained-glass window), 281

St Andrew's Ball, 94–95, 181; 1949, 6; 1961, 79; 1962, 87; 1964, 103–04; 1966, 104; 1967, 106; 1969, 142; 1978, 176; 1987, 198–99; 1999, 295; 2002, 304; 2003, 306; 2003, 306–07; 2011, 327

St Andrew's Barracks (New Brunswick), 66, 110, 125. *See also* Camp Gagetown

St Andrew's Church (Quebec), 293–94

St Andrew's Cross (Saltire), 354, *433*

St Andrew's Day, 115; Mess Dinner, 143

St Andrew's Hall (British Columbia), 356

St Andrew's Society (Quebec), 44, 354; Learner's Programme, 297

St James Club (Quebec), 60, 128, 169, 171; Regimental Advisory Board meetings, 138, 164

St John's Ambulance: instruction, 61, 251

St Lambert (Quebec), 356

St Laurent, Louis, Liberal Prime Minister 1948–57, 25

St Louis, Col Gilbert, 174

St Margaret's Bay (Nova Scotia), 132

St Patrick's Day Parade (Quebec), 295; 1999, 294; 2007, *442*

Stadacona (patrol boat), 39, 111. *See also* boats and ships

Staff College, Camberley (Army Staff College) (UK), 207

stamp: BW 150th Anniversary, 325, 326, *435*

Stars and Stripes (newspaper), 200–01

Start, Lt DV, 74

Starzynski, Capt/Major RF ('Bob'), 155, 166, 168, 170

Stavert, Major William Ewart ('Bill'), 199–200, *264*, 274; quoted as epigraph, 58

Ste Anne's Military Hospital (Quebec), 51, 159, 324

Steacy, Sgt/WO Gerald P ('Gerry'), 26, 67, 69, 70, 78, 144–45; quoted as epigraph, 69

Steeves, Corporal Vince, 277

Stephen, Col, 311–12

Stephen, Frank, 60

Stephen, Lord Mount, 60, 154

Stevens, Pipe Major/WO Cameron ('Cam') ('Pipey'), *268*, 314, 357, 374; appointment as head, 299; mustering of new musicians, 309–10; BW piping school, 310; Afghanistan stand-down ceremony, 311, *429*, *424*; 2009 Trooping the Colours, 321; 2011 Highland Dinner, 327–28; 75th anniversary Dieppe Raid, 330; 2012 Trooping the Colours, 358; awarded OMM, 358; Dubuc Trophy, *438*; Scotland 2012 Laying up of Colours, *440*; 2007 Remembrance Day Parade, *442*

Stewart, Anne, 279, 325

Stewart, Mrs David M, 204

Stewart, Pipe Major J, 80

Stewart, Pipe Sgt John, 124

Stewart, Sgt James, 278

St-Hubert Air Base (Quebec), as Force Mobile Command HQ, 103, 129, 284; parade and presentation of new Queen's Colour, 166–67, *407*; becomes Canadian Forces functional command, 186; eliminated, 208; reserve helicopter sqdn, 293

Stikeman, John, 134

St-Jean Air Base (Quebec), 180

St-Jean-Baptiste Society (*Société Saint-Jean-Baptiste*), 295

Stone Mountain Highland Games (US), 198

Stonewall, Harry ('Stone Blind'), 12–13

Stothers, Lt Col John Charles, 186–89, 190, 201, *238*, 298; quoted as epigraph, 185; biographical description, 185–86

Strathcona Medal (cadet achievement), 95

Stuart, Capt Campbell Lewis, 1582; wounded, 135; awarded MID and *Croix de Guerre*, 38; St-André Operation *Spring* anniversary, 135

Stuart, Okill, 288

Stubbert, Private WGR, 74, *254*

submarines, including submarine warfare: Soviet fleet, 134

Sudbury (Ontario), 283–84

Suffield Training Camp (Alberta), 198

Sullivan, Ed, 44

Sullivan, Private Wilfrid, 18

Summer Student Training Programmes (SSEP and SSEP2), 160, 161, 164

Summer Youth Employment Programme (SYEP), 183, 186

Sun Life Building (Quebec), 289

support companies: early-1950s Regular Force, 155

Sussex (New Brunswick), 32, 67; Camp Sussex, 29, 132–33, 67

Sutcliffe, Private/Corporal Karen, 192, *413*; quoted as epigraph, 191

Suttie Commission (1964), 93–94, 107

Suttie, Brig ER, 93

Sweeney, Corporal Rod, 144

Sweet, Ward, 156

Switzerland, 48, 273

Sword of Honour (cadet achievement award): Royal Military College Sandhurst (US), 207

SYEP (Summer Youth Employment Programme), 183, 186

Tactical Exercise Without Troops (TEWT), 185

Taliban, 343, 352; and deployment to Kandahar, 303, 337; suicide bomber attack, 342; BW strategy against, 346; attack on B COY, 347; attack in Talukan Panjwai'I; 349

Talukan Panjwai'I (Talukan) (Afghanistan), 349

Tambour Roulant 98 (exercise) (1998), 293

tartans, 309; 1st Canadian Highland Battalion, 14–15, 28; 2nd Canadian Highland Battalion, 22, 28; *Cantlie*, 30, 360; BW, 127; Elliot, 142; Glenwhorple, 165; BW skirts, including proposed, 171, 193; World Scottish Festival Tartan Ball (1992), 206; Maple Leaf, 274; mess kit vest, 359; Royal Stewart, 378

tattoos, 148: Copenhagen (Denmark) (1953), 24; Edinburgh (UK) (Edinburgh Castle) (1953), 24; Hamilton (Bermuda) (1956), 29, *268*; Centennial (Canada) (1967), general, 106, 160, *266*; Armed

Forces (Canada) (1967), 106, 123–25 *passim*, 148, 160, *266*; Montreal (Quebec) (World's Fair) (1967), 123–25, 148, 160, 266; Seattle (US) (World's Fair) (1962), 124; Victoria (BC) (1967), 124, 266; Kingston (Jamaica) (Jamaican Military) (1968), 131; Montreal (Scottish Festival) (1992), 206; Kingston (Ont.) (Fort Henry Guard) (2012), 330; Montreal (Highland Tattoo) (2016), 364; Bell Centre, Montreal (2017), 372–73; Edinburgh (2019), 377–79. *See also* parades; pipes and drums; Trooping the Colour

Tawa, Capt Charles, 313

Taybridge (Operation) (funeral of Queen Mother) (2000), 301–02, 318, *416*

Taylor, Katherine, 326; painting by, *435*

TBWA. *See* Toronto Black Watch Association

Teed, Lt Col William Arthur ('Bill'), 36, 78, 82, 84, *235*, *262*; assumption of 1 RHC command, 74; biographical description, 76; relinquishment of command, 109; 1960 Remembrance Ceremony, 259

terrorism: Sécurité Interne Programme D'Entrainement—Counter-terrorist, 145; anti-terrorism operations, 305. *See also* Front de libération du Québec

Third Balkan War. *See* Bosnian Conflict

Thompson, Private, *436*

Thompson, Sgt Jimmy Ray, 380, *455*

Ticonderoga (US), 288, 295; Fort Ticonderoga, 52

Ticonderoga Museum (US), 52

Timmons, Corporal Jim, 160

Todorov, Wallace, *418*

Topp, Brig CP Beresford, 134, 150

Topping, Capt Rev Richard R, *245*, 300, 343, 355–56

Toronto, 15, 43, 127, 183, 301, *422*; Toronto BW Association clubhouses, 6, 324; regimental drift towards, 180; challenges of physical distance, 323, 330; *Red Hackle Dinner*, 328; *Highland Dinner*, 353; Queen's Park Queen Mother visit, *409*; Fort York, *410*–11. *See also specific institutions*

Toronto Black Watch Association (TBWA) ('Toronto Branch'), 6, 78, 150, 324, 328; pipe band combined with Montreal Branch, 312; relationship to Montreal Regimental Association, 324; William Carlisle as President, *421*, *435*; Pipe Band soldiers, *422*; BW 150th Anniversary stamp, *435*

Total Force Area Headquarters, 282; as Area Headquarters, 5

Tracey, Capt Kitch, 20

Training Militia Programme, 105. *See also* training

training, 278, 283, 331–32; Provisional Officers Training School of the Regiment, 3, 19; Canadian Officers' Training Corps (COTC), 46, 57, 100–01, 131, 134, 147, 160, 173; District Headquarters (District 1 HQ) BW recruitment and training, 159; Bishop's University, 95; Huntingdon training base, 275; Royal Military College of Canada, 12, 19, 46, 57, 100, 109, 121, 137, 164, 179, 180, 185, 201, 204, 273, 279, 283, 330, 331, *441*; Camp Farnham, 6, 63, 106; Victoria Rifles of Canada,

8; Korean War, 14–15, 25–26; Soltau, 16, 17, 73, 76, 82; radio, 35–36; Loyola College, 46, 100–01, 134, 160; Regimental Depot Recruit Training, 61, 129, 133, *251*; First Nations Peoples Special Militia Training Programme, 62; Special Militia Training Programme, 62; Camp Gagetown, 82, 86, 103, 142–44 *passim*, 207–08, *251*, 337; Reinforcement Training School Canada, 94; Junior NCO Course, 99; *Leading Infantryman Group 1* and Trade Tests, 68, 99; Regular Officer Training Plan, 100, 174–75; Université de Montréal, 100; General Military Training, 105; Recruit Training Programme, including Syllabus, 61, 105; Training Militia Programme, 105; Canadian Military Training Team service in Ghana, 109; Recruit School, 148; Internal Security, 156–57; Junior Leaders Course, 160–61; Régiment de Maisonneuve, 160–61, 334; Summer Student Training Programmes, 160–61, 164; Dubuc Trophy 172, 302–03, 294, 296, *437–38*; Reserve Officer University Training Plan, 173; Combat Training Centre, 175; Pennsylvania National Guard cross-training, 184, 369, 370, 376; Leading Infantryman Course, 192, *413*; Afghanistan War, 194, 303, 307–08, 313–14, 316, 331–32, 337, 353; Proven Cup, 198, 203, 293, 302, 356, *416*; Suffield Training Camp, 198; Italian Alpini, 201; parachutes and parachuting, 38, 206; 1992 Regina Trench mock training attack, 208; early-1950s recruitment and training of single companies, 247; 1996–97 winter, 287; training program viability, 287; allotted training days, 289; General Purpose Machine Gun, 291; 1996–97 collective training evaluations, 291; Reserve Entry Scheme Officer entrance tests, 291; 22nd Armoured Regiment (Royal 22nd), 291, 334; Basic Military Training Courses, 299; pipes and drums, 310; Fusiliers Mont-Royal, 334; Royal Montreal Regiment, 334; 2013 infantry competition, 334–35; Land Forces Doctrine and Training System HQ, 335; non-commissioned members, 335; Peace Support Training Centre, 338; guns and rifles, general, *423*, *424*. *See also* exercises; manoeuvres; recruitment

Transvaal Cup (rifle competition), 9

Travers, Capt Rev JGEA, *244*

Traversy, Capt/Lt Col Valmore Eric ('Val'), 183, *237*; BW return to Montreal, 4; Cold War, 5; relinquishment of command, 7; proposal of Regimental Museum, 7; armoury fire, 8; luncheon with Queen Mother and visit with 1 RHC, 9; appointment as Vice Chair of advisory board, 58; decline of further appointment, 92; 1968 reunion dinner, 134; 1972 reunion dinner, 164; 1962 Advisory Board, *262*

Traversy, Mrs Val, 183

Tremblay, Gérald, 304–05

Trenholme, Major CR, 325

Tri-Service Ball (Quebec): 1963 Ball, 96

Tri-Service championships: boxing, 78; softball, 112

Trooping the Colour: 1919 (Germany), 91; 1919
(France), 91; 1962 (Canadian BW Centennial)
(UK), 82, 101, 194, 199; 1963 (Germany), 86,
90–91; 1963 (New Brunswick) (two), 91, 92, *260*;
1965 (New Brunswick), 110–11, *260*; 1967 (New
Brunswick), 126, 127–28, 96, 162, 165, *267*,
312; 1968 (New Brunswick), 130–31; 1970 (New
Brunswick), 141, 142, 144–46; 1970 (Quebec),
145–47; 1974 (Quebec), 165–67 *passim*; 1974
(Imperial Black Watch) (UK), 170; 1978 (Horse
Guards Parade) (UK), 176; 1987 (BW 125th
Anniversary) (Quebec), 188–89, 193–95 *passim*,
198–200 *passim*, 359, *415*; 2000 (Queen Mother
birthday parade) (UK), 363; 2012 (BW 150th
Anniversary) (Quebec), 325, 358, 360–61, 364;
1912 Trooping the Colour (Quebec), 360–61. *See
also* parades; tattoos

trophies. *See* awards and honours

Trudeau Airport. *See* Dorval Airport

Trudeau, Justin, Liberal Prime Minister, 377–78

Trudeau, Pierre Elliott, Liberal Prime Minister
1968–79, 1980–84, 90, 139, 142

tug of war: championship (2009), *412*

tunes of glory, 147. *See also* songs and tunes

Tunisia, 94

Turcot, Major/ Lt Gen GA, 111, 159, *260*

Turcotte-Tremblay, Capt P, *438*

Turley, RSM WO1 T, 48, *241*

Turnbull, Private Ralph, 26

Turnbull, RSM WO Alan F, 5, *241*

Tyro 2 (exercise) (1961), 79

Uganda, 349, *428*

UNAMIR (United Nations Assistance Mission for
Rwanda), 282

UNEF (UN Emergency Force), 156, 170–71, 203, *413*

UNFICYP. *See* United Nations Peacekeeping Force in
Cyprus

Unger, RSM CWO/Capt Robert M, *243*, 362, 364,
428, *437*, *438*, *440*; biographical description, 356;
appointment as MWO, 356–57; awarded OMM,
358

unification of Canadian Armed Forces, 122, 94,
128–29; placement under Mobile Command, 102

UNITS AND FORMATIONS

THE BLACK WATCH (ROYAL HIGHLAND
REGIMENT) OF CANADA: *passim*, 13–14,
188; Edward Force, 83; Woensdrecht attack,
121; Battle of Walcheren Causeway, *420*;
analysis of Second World War contribution,
3–4; Montreal victory parade, 4; post-war
and Cold War recruitment, 6, 12; Archives,
7, 279–80, 310, 355; armoury fire, 8; Korean
War training, 14–15, 25–26; NATO 1 CHB
joint training in Germany, 16–19; BW
redesignation, 22–23; deployment within
Korea, 24–25, 27; Regular Force battalions
and Cold War army restructuring, 11–16

passim, 20; 1950s customs and dress, 28–32
passim; shift in reserves' function, 41–36;
Philadelphia visits, 49–53 *passim*, 86, 295,
333; pre-Millennium Montreal relationship,
54–56; professional officers' vetting pre-
Millennium, 56–57; civil defence role
establishment, 60–62; cancelled Iroquois
Nation exercise, 63; 1 RHC and 2 RHC
NATO tours, 69–70, 73–74; Regimental
Military Band, 74–75, 101, 151–52, 162,
166, 195, 313; BW Centennial, including
specific celebrations, 82–88, 101, 194, 199;
Suttie Commission, 93–94, 107; FLQ armory
raids, 97–98; Hasty Pudding Club, 104–05;
threats to militia continuation, 107–08;
Allied Command Europe (ACE) Mobile Force,
110, 163, *257*; 1st Battalion conversion to
Armoured Personnel Carrier (APC) role, 111;
Allied Mobile Force North (AMFL North),
113; *Agents Orange* and *Purple* testing, 114–
15; Canadian Armed Forces unification, 122,
94, 128–29; retention, 129, 162, 187, 287, 331,
339–40; Operation *Spring* 25th Anniversary,
135; demographics, 136–38; reduction to nil
strength, 136, 138–40; 1970 disbandment,
140–41, 146, 147, 149; in early- and mid-
1970s, 151–53, 155–56; Egypt deployment,
including veterans, 156, 170–71, 203, 300,
413; October Crisis, 156–58, 162, 166, 172,
287; Summer Student Training Programmes
(SSEP and SSEP2), 160, 161, 164; Golan
Heights deployment, 170, 171, 300; Norway
NATO mission, 172–73; Armoured Vehicle
General Purpose (AVGP) Grizzly, 182,
184, 186, *408*; designated as mechanized
infantry, 182; 1970s and 1980s recruitment,
187; Oka Crisis, 203–04, 374; *In Desperate
Battle* (television documentary episode), 204;
Scottish Festival, 204–06; 1996 proposed
disbandment and rescindment, 285–87,
289; khaki pattern tam adoption, 290; Unit
Viability Assessment, 291; *Canadian Red
Hackle* launching, 300; current uniform, 358–
60. *See also* Afghanistan War; armoury (BW);
awards and honours; Black Watch Cadet
Corps; Black Watch Regimental Museum;
Bosnian Conflict; Canadian Officers' Training
Corps; Centennial (Canada); Church of St
Andrew and St Paul; exercises; Cyprus; 5th
Canadian Infantry Brigade, 2nd Canadian
Infantry Division; Force Mobile Command;
parades; pipes and drums; Presentation
of Colours; Psychological Operations;
Regimental Depot (BW); reunions; Trooping
the Colour; 27th Canadian Infantry Brigade;
women in BW; *specific associations, battles,
camps, countries, individuals, institutions,
locations, memorials, military units,
operations, sports, and wars*

A COMPANY (BW rifle company), 20, 151–52; training, 110; Donaldson as commander, 20; William Watson as platoon commander, 35; awarded 4th Canadian Infantry Brigade 'Skill at Arms Competition' trophy, 90; Harkes's assumption of command, 122; Third Platoon part of Centennial Tattoo, 124; awarded sports day regimental trophy, 131; Starzynski as commander, 155; Gordon Scott as CSM, 160; component of women to efficiency, 181; *Pet Hackle* (exercise), 182–83; Operation *Jubilee* (Dieppe) memorial visit, 188; O'Connor as commander, 201; 1982 concentration, 207–08; in 1951, *247*; Korean War, *247*; Patrick Kelly's assumption of command, 282; Quebec Ice Storm (1998), 292, 294, 374; Psychological Operations (PSYOPS) team, 346. *See also Spring* (Operation)

B COMPANY (BW rifle company), 151–52; Gibb-Carsley's assumption of command, 43; Royal Canadian Air Force Fire Power Demonstrations, 132; dubbed 'the Depot', 152, 312; W Cook as commander, 155; *Pet Hackle* (exercise), 182–83; urban assault exercise, 188; Battalion Orderly Room (BOR), 192; Korean War Korean Attached Commonwealth Divisions (KATCOMs), *248*; Potter's assumption of command, 305; Taliban, 343, 352

C COMPANY (BW rifle company), 151–52; Korean War fatality, 26; size reduction, 189

D COMPANY (BW rifle company), 151–52; George Climie Fraser as commander, 186; Victor Foam in Operation *Spring*, 9; Korean War patrol capture, 25

SUPPORT COMPANY (BW), *passim*, 330; 1970s company, 152; Nicholson as commander, 155–56

MORTAR PLATOON (BW), Operation *Jubilee*, third wave assault, 330; ,

5TH ROYAL SCOTS (later BW), 5, 47–48, 85, 150, 163, 174; kilts, 29; traditional officer vetting, 56; motto, 146; ignorance concerning parent regiment, 358; 150th Anniversary stamp, *435*

42ND BATTALION CEF, 365, 378–79; veterans, 55, 76, 83, 104, 106, 130, 159; Topp as Battalion historian, 150, 164; reunion dinners, 6–7, 150; commemorative plaques, 8, 9, 197; George Cantlie as commander, 47; Camp Gagetown, 66; Church of St Andrew and St Paul window, 85; 1963 Trooping the Colour, 91; Mons victory commemoration, 92, 377–78, *458*; status, 101; Bartlett MacLennan as commander, 110; Victoria Cross recipients, 130; McCulloch as Battalion historian, 279

73RD BATTALION CEF, 365; veterans, 7, 51, 54, 55, 130; Third Battle of Ypres, including 1971 memorial service, 150; commemorative plaques, 8, 9; 1957 Memorial Service, 51; Association, 54; 50th Anniversary, 101–02; Worthington's relationship, 102, 130; song, 149; CEF Battalions reunions, including 1970, 149–50; *Canadian Red Hackle* (magazine), 150, 300; 1972 reunion dinner, 164

CANADIAN INFANTRY DIVISIONS

1ST CANADIAN INFANTRY DIVISION: Rockingham as commander, 35, 46; 1954 Camp Gagetown militia parade, 46; *Landing of the First Canadian Division at Saint-Nazaire* (painting), 119

3RD CANADIAN INFANTRY DIVISION: Blackader as General Officer Commanding, 92; Cameron Highlanders of Ottawa appointment as machine-gun battalion, 21

4TH CANADIAN ARMOURED DIVISION, 102

CANADIAN INFANTRY BRIGADES (CDN INF BDE GPS)

1st Canadian Infantry Brigade, 48.

3rd Canadian Infantry Brigade, 136–37, 143; 3 CIBG sports meet, 67.

4th Canadian Infantry Brigade, 74, 76, 77, 90, 116, 118

5th Canadian Infantry Brigade, 38

6th Canadian Infantry Brigade, 14

7th Canadian Infantry Brigade, 3rd Canadian Infantry Division (7 CIB), 279

9th Canadian Infantry Brigade, 38.

25th Canadian Infantry Brigade, 11, 12, 22–23

27th Canadian Infantry Brigade, 32; NATO missions in Germany, 6, 12, 16–17; proposed, 11; Reserve Army used to create, 12; 'Granger's Rangers' (sniper group), 17; Pangman's assumption of command, 19; Queen Elizabeth coronation parade, 22

34th Canadian Brigade Group (34e Groupe-brigade du Canada), 372, 383, *437, 443*; BW joins, 284; Camp Valcartier training exercise, 291; Dubuc Trophy, 294, 302–03, *438*; Potter as deputy commander, 306; Lachance as commander, 308; 2005 Church Parade, 308; March and Shoot competition, 330; Battle Group, 331; *Noble Guerrier* (exercise), 331; creation of new Group, 335; death of Jason Warren, 342–43, 370; De Sousa as commander, 364

CANADIAN MECHANIZED BRIGADE GROUPS

3 Canadian Mechanized Brigade Group, 67, 143; *Pibroch Patrol* (exercise), 136–37

4 Canadian Mechanized Brigade Group, 74, 77; NATO, including Germany, 116–17; German hockey championship, 77, *255*

CANADIAN ARMOURED REGIMENTS

8th Canadian Hussars, 175

17th Duke of York's Royal Canadian Hussars, 174

Governor General's Foot Guards, 203

Grenadier Guards (22nd Armoured Regiment), 108, 325, 336, 372; proposed disbandment, 285; becomes rifle company in Royal 22nd Regiment, 285–86; and BW parade route, 317; 2009 Presentation of Colours, 334; 2012 Remembrance Day, 362; 2013 Remembrance Day, *439*

Royal Canadian Dragoons, 45, 126, 174, 175, 315; Band, 111

Royal Canadian Hussars, 164, 181, 185, 315, 372, *408*; 17th Duke of York's Royal Canadian Hussars, 174; A Squadron, 165

Three Rivers (Tank) Regiment (later 12e RBC), 162, 167

CANADIAN INFANTRY REGIMENTS

Algonquin Regiment, mascot, 15–16; part of composite battalion, 18–19

Calgary Highlanders, *412*; Mac Reid's transfer from, 14; Sellar's accomplishment within, 109

Cameron Highlanders of Canada, summation of battle to secure St-André, 13–14; motto (*Unite*), 14–15; appointed 3rd Canadian Infantry Division machine gun battalion, 21; Richard Ross as member and commanding officer, 21; *Black Hussar* (exercise), 165; *Highland Winter II* (exercise), 184, *423*; 2009 Glengarry Highland Games, *412*

Cameron Highlanders of Ottawa, 20–21, 340; *Highland Winter I, II, III* (exercises), 183, 184, 186; 2007 St. Patrick's Day Parade, *442*

Canadian Airborne Regiment, 124, 163, 172, 185; creation, 129; disbandment, 281, 287

Cape Breton Highlanders (CBH) (formerly 85th Battalion), 20, 55, 122, 377–78

Carleton and York Regiment, 117–18

48th Highlanders, 14, 15, 19, 105, 170, 185, 201, 284; formation as B Company, 14; strength in recruitment, 15; in Italy, 36; baseball competitions with BW, 43; Pipe Band, 277. *See also* 1st Canadian Infantry Brigade, 1st Canadian Infantry Division

Fusiliers Mont-Royal: FLQ FMR Armoury raid, 97, 98; as Montreal active reserve battalion, 277; *Tambour Roulant* (exercise), 293; infantry competitions, 334; instrumental band, 361. *See also* 5th Canadian Infantry Brigade; 6th Canadian Infantry Brigade, 2nd Canadian Infantry Division

Grey & Simcoe Foresters, 122

Hastings and Prince Edward Regiment, 62

Highland Light Infantry of Canada, 24

Irish Regiment of Canada, 43, 75

Lake Superior Regiment (Motor), 19

Lorne Scots (Peel, Dufferin and Halton Regiment), 1st, 3rd, 6th and 7th Canadian Infantry Brigades, 1st, 2nd and 3rd Canadian Infantry Divisions, 121.

North Nova Scotia Highlanders (North Novas) (NNS), 377–78; contributor to Support Company, 14; strength in recruitment, 15; contributor to 2nd Battalion, 20

North Shore (New Brunswick) Regiment, 33, 76

Peel, Dufferin and Halton Regiment (Lorne Scots), 121

Princess Louise Fusiliers (MG) Regiment, 131

Princess of Wales' Own Regiment, 329, *418*

Princess Patricia's Canadian Light Infantry, 15, 59, 110, 274, 342, 353; founding, 158; and post-war Regular Force, 11; 3rd Battalion (3 PPCLI) (3rd Bn PPCLI), 22, 163, 341; William Watson joins, 32; A Company, 33; Gault's participation, 59; inability to provide reinforcements, 137; retention, 138; BW choice at disbandment, 147; Vernon's appointment, 163; first Canadian regular female soldier, 192; 2nd Battalion, 281; Afghanistan War, 303, 342; as Militia integrators, 338; death of Gomez, 342; BW acquirement of Anglophone RSS officers, 353. *See also* 25th Canadian Infantry Brigade

Queen's Own Cameron Highlanders of Canada. *See* Cameron Highlanders of Canada

Queen's Own Rifles of Canada, 26, 29, 137;

Régiment de la Chaudière, Le, 351

Régiment de Maisonneuve, Le, 186, 346, 372; proposed elimination, 107; assumption of Victoria Rifles of Canada armoury, 107; Summer Student Training Programme, 160; relationship with District Headquarters, 181; 2013 infantry competition, 334; Afghanistan War, *432*

Regina Rifle Regiment (Regina Rifles), 18–19

Royal 22nd Regiment (Royal 22e Régiment), 134, 317; post-war Canadian Army structure, 11; music at 1958 Fort Ticonderoga reunion, 52; NATO mission in Germany, 69, 76–77; 1959 Canada Day (Dominion Day), 72; *The Hundred Days* (1918), 87; 1968 reunion dinner, 133; retention, 138; in song, 143; BW members posted to, 147; B Company (2 R22eR), 157, 158, 346; October Crisis, 157, 158; city regiment armouries as garrisons, 158; relationship with BW, 158; 1970 BW reunion, 158–59; *Pleine Neige* (exercise), 164; 1974 Presentation of the Queen's Colour, 166; German NATO tour, 185; specific veterans, 185, 186, 206, 286, 328, 343–43, 346, 351, 353, *426*, *432*; 1992 exercise, 207–08; Bosnian Conflict, 280; part of 4th Battalion, 285–86; 1998 training, 291; Ice Storm (1998), 292, 374; French-speaking officers, 331; recruitment, 331; 6 R22eR, 334; A Company (A Coy) (1 R22eR), 347; 2012 Trooping the Colour, 361; Afghan War, 331, 338, 344, 346, 347, *426*, *432*; 2013 infantry competition, 334

Royal Canadian Regiment, 80, 123, 163, 273, 130, 136, 279, *418*; post-war Canadian Army composition, 11; Battle of Ortona, 81; Ian

Fraser's 2nd Battalion command, 124, 141; perception of Gregg, 130; 1st Battalion in Korean War, 131; First World War, 136; inability to provide reinforcements, 137; service in 4CMBC, 137; 1969 retention decision, 138; conversion to 2nd Battalion, 140–41, 147–48; in song, 143; 1st Battalion Cyprus deployment, 144; regimental property disposal, 144; *Yeltneb* donation to 1st Battalion, 144, *258*; Morrison's shift from 1st Battalion to 2nd Battalion commanding officer, 147; operational tasks assigned, 158; Halpenny as RSS Officer, 180; Bailey's appointment from 3rd Battalion, 180–81; O'Connor's appointment, 301; 2nd Battalion in Oka Crisis (1990), 203–04; 2nd Battalion members at 1970 dinner, *269*; McCulloch's appointment into Regiment, 273; Home Station, 274; Radman's appointment to 2nd Battalion, 287, 315; 2nd Battalion assumption of Oromocto Corps, 313; Radman's departure, 316; Bachelor's appointment as 2nd Battalion corporal, 335; as home front integrator, 338; ease of BW obtaining Anglophone RCR officers, 353

Royal Montreal Regiment, 206, 282, 293, 318; designation as bilingual unit, 108; Strike Company, 145, 155; competition for BW recruits, 155; anti-tank platoon exercise, 165; strengthening of BW ties, 181; proposed later disbandment, 285; conversion to Royal 22nd Regiment rifle company, 285–86; commanding officers' collective style, 317; 2009 Presentation of Colours, 321; infantry competitions, 334; 2012 Trooping the Colour, 361; Afghanistan War, *432*

Royal New Brunswick Regiment: 1st Bn, 175

Royal Regiment of Canada, 117; Harkes as platoon commander, 121; Hochwald, 121

Royal Rifles of Canada, 95

Seaforth Highlanders, 14, 356

Stormont, Dundas and Glengarry Highlanders, 377–78, 14, 184, 186

Toronto Scottish Regiment: Fort York walkabout, 183; composite guard with BW, 301, *409*; 2000 Queen Mother birthday parade, 363, *416*

Victoria Rifles of Canada, BW training, 8; Cathcart Street armoury, 8, 107, 160

West Nova Scotia Regiment, 20; A Company, 33–34; Cadets, 201

CANADIAN – OTHER

2nd Field Artillery Regiment (Lacombe Armoury), 181, 372; 1970 Summer Student Training Programme, 160; *Black Hussar* (exercise), 165; 2011 Remembrance Day Parade, 357

3 Service Battalion: United Nations Peacekeeping Force in Cyprus (UNFICYP), 113; *Winter Express* (NATO exercise), *257*

3 Signals Squadron, 113, 257

3rd Field Engineers, 286

4th Regiment, Royal Canadian Horse Artillery, 113, *257.*

51 Field Ambulance (Quebec), 361

438 ETAH (helicopter squadron), 293

Arctic Response Company Group (ARGC), 383

First Special Service Force ('The Devil's Brigade), 42, 133

Joint Task Force 2, 369

Royal Canadian Air Force, 377–78

Royal Canadian Army Medical Corps, 144

Royal Canadian Artillery: band, 195

Royal Canadian Engineers: *Winter Express* (NATO exercise) (1964), 113, *257*

Royal Canadian Horse Artillery, 67; 4th Regiment, 113, *257*

Service Battalion, 182, 317; 3 Service Battalion, 113, 257

OTHER – GENERAL

ANP (Afghan national police), 344

ANSF (Afghan National Security Forces), 340, 344, 345

IJC (ISAF Joint Command), 338, 345

OTHER – BRITISH

1 Royal Scots Battle Group: Operation *Desert Storm*, 305

2nd Battalion King Edward VII's Own Gurkha Rifles (Sirmoor Rifles) (Royal Gurkha Regiment), 162, 207, 348

4th British Infantry Division, 123

5th Battalion (Royal Irish Regiment), 305

8th Punjab Regiment, 24

51st Highland Volunteers: amalgamation of Imperial Black Watch battalions, 346

Argyll and Sutherland Highlanders, 8th in North Africa, 94; becomes part of Royal Regiment of Scotland, 346

British Army Intelligence Corps, 207

British Army of the Rhine (BAOR), 16, 43–44, 70, 119

British Parachute Regiment, 343–44

Imperial Black Watch (Allied Regiment) (Black Watch of Scotland) (1 BW) (3 SCOTS), 141–42, 162, 198, 207, 379; First Battalion Black Watch, 149, 288; Berlin, 6; Korean War, 25; blue balmoral with Red Hackle, 45; reduction to one battalion, 45; 111th Infantry Regiment of Pennsylvania National Guard, 50, 52, 369, 370, 376; Fort Ticonderoga, 52, 288; presentation to Queen Mother, 53; 42nd Regiment and Camp Gagetown, 66; pipes and drums recordings, 75; centenary of BW, including gift, 84, 87; 1965 reunion dinner, 102; becomes 3rd Battalion, Royal Regiment of Scotland (3 SCOTS), 141, 142, 346; cadets, 170; Fergusson as Aide-De-Camp, 173; Waterloo bagpipes, 186; Ypres Parade,

295; *Canadian Red Hackle* launching, 300; funeral of Queen Mother, 301, 302; strength reduction and loss of regimental status, 302; Territorial battalions amalgamation, 346; Afghanistan War, 346–47; A Company (A Coy), 347; 2012 Trooping the Colour, 360; BW at 2012 Laying Up of Colours, *440*

King's Own Scottish Borderers: becomes part of Royal Regiment of Scotland, 346

Royal Gurkha Regiment (2nd Battalion King Edward VII's Own Gurkha Rifles) (Sirmoor Rifles), 162, 207, 348

Royal Highland Fusiliers, 305; becomes part of Royal Regiment of Scotland, 346

Royal Irish Regiment: 5th Battalion, 305

Royal Regiment of Fusiliers, 315

Royal Regiment of Scotland: formation, 346. *See also* Imperial Black Watch

Royal Scots: becomes part of Royal Regiment of Scotland, 346

Royal Scots Greys, 24

Sirmoor Rifles (2nd Battalion King Edward VII's Own Gurkha Rifles) (Royal Gurkha Regiment) (UK), 162, 207, 348

South Wales Borders, 131

OTHER – GERMAN

272nd Wehrmacht Infantry Division, Cameron Highlanders of Canada battle in St-André, 13–14

Afrika Korps, *431*

panzer-grenadiers, 73, 131

OTHER – US

41st Infantry Division, 70–71

163rd Infantry Regiment, 70–71

Pennsylvania National Guard, 53, 333. 111th Infantry Regiment, 50, 369, 370, 376; 104th US Armored Cavalry Squadron, 184

Union Jack (flag) (UK), 166, 167, *267*, *418*

United Kingdom (UK) (Great Britain). *See also* England; Northern Ireland; Scotland*; specific battles, competitions, institutions, locations, and operations*

United Nations (UN), 20, 65, 134, 192, 305. Korean War, 10–11, 12; Security Council, 10; Peacekeeping Force in Cyprus (UNFICYP), 113, 120, 122–23, 130, 136–37, 139, 140, 141–42, 143–45, 147, 156, *158*, 171, 200, 201, 340, 361; Palestine deployment, including Israel, 123, 203; Germany, 126; Egypt deployment, including veterans, 156, 170–71, 203, 300, *413*; Emergency Force (UNEF), 156, 170–71, 203, *413*; Golan Heights deployment, 170, 171, 300; Bosnia and Herzegovina (former Yugoslavia), including veterans, 274, 279–81 *passim*, 284–85, 300, 302, 314, 338–40 *passim*, 349, 351, 363, 284, 338–39, *425–26*; Protection Force (UNPROFOR), 280; Assistance Mission for Rwanda (UNAMIR), 282; Canadian Peacekeeping Service Medal (CPSM),

300; Haiti, 316; flag, *418*; Peacekeeping outfit, *419*. *See also* Bosnian Conflict; Cyprus; *specific countries and veterans*

United Nations Peacekeeping Force in Cyprus (UNFICYP), 120, 122–23, 147, 171, 340; BW assumption of command (1963), 113; description, 120, 122; *Ballad of the Blue Berets* (song), 122–23; first 2 RHC tour (1966), 123, 136; reunion (1966), 123; 1 RHC (1967–68), 124, 130, 361; *Pibroch Patrol* (exercise), 136–37; Cyprus Establishment' creation, 137; second 2 RHC tour (1969–70), 139–44 *passim*; included in televised account, 141; deaths of BW soldiers, 143; third tour, 144; opportunity for Call-Outs, 156; John Bourne's excursion, 200, *258*; BW Signal Section, *258*; tours, general, *258*; Canadian Peacekeeping Service Medal (CPSM), 300

United Services Club (Quebec), 181

United States (US) Army Staff College, 123

United States (US), 49, 52, 89, 175, 328; as NATO participant, 10, 172; Korean War instigation, 10–11; Queen Elizabeth 1957 visit, 37; 1987 Trooping the Colour, 194; military technological renaissance, 279; exercises, 354. *See also specific competitions, exercises, institutions, locations, operations, tattoos, and wars*

United States Air Force (USAF): Globemaster (aircraft), 22; Airforce Base (Newfoundland), 113; 59 Fighter Interceptor Squadron, 113; uniform style, 132

United States Marine Corps (USMC), 50; University, 352

Université de Montréal (Quebec), Canadian Officers' Training Corps (COTC), 100

University of British Columbia, St Andrew's Hall, 356

University of Glasgow (UK), 186

University of London (UK), 179

University of Nairobi (Kenya), 186

University of New Brunswick, 175, 283–84

University of Toronto (Ontario), 36; Trinity College, 19

UNPROFOR (United Nations Protection Force), 280

Upper Canada/Ottawa Black Watch Association (Ontario), 324. *See also* Black Watch Branch Associations

Urban Assault (exercise) (1985), 187

Ursine, MCpl, *436*

US Army Staff College, 123

USAF. See United States Air Force

USMC (United States Marine Corps), 50; University, 352

Vachon, Lt Commander Gord, 199

Valour and the Horror, The (television documentary series): 204

Vancouver (BC), 4, 62, 124, 146, 164, 323

Vanden Abeele, Cpl H, *268*

Vanier, Georges-Philéas, Governor General 1959–67, 80, 83, 87, 130; quoted as epigraph, 84, 86; unnamed, 88

Varelas, Cpl, *436*

Vaudry, Rev John P, 322

Veenstra, Rev Jeff, 329

Verdun (Quebec), 4, 18, 81, 160; as source of BW soldiers, 12; recruitment, 6; Ypres Day Parades, 106, 295–96; description, 296

Verglas or *Recuperation* (Operation) (Quebec Ice Storm) (1998), 292, 294, 374

Vernon, Major Gen Brian, 163

Veterans' Company (BW): formation (1962), 81. *See also* 42nd Reserve Veterans' Company; Reserve Veterans' Company

Victoria (British Columbia), 124, 125

Victoria Cross (VC): Gregg, 136; Dinesen, 83–84, 86; Pearkes, 59, 66; Clark-Kennedy, 80, 87; holders in Canadian Centennial year, 130; Croak, 136; Good, 136; Frederick Fisher, 325. *See also* awards and honours

Vietnam, 171; Vietnam War, including anti-War movement, 90, 161, 172

Villa Rogatti (crossing point) (Italy): Italian Campaign (1943), 33

Vimy Award (defence and security): 1998, 294

Vimy, Battle of, Tattoo (1992), *458*

Vimy, Battle of, Tattoo (2017), 372–73

Vive la Canadienne (song), 309

Vivian, Corporal Brook, 369

Vokes, Major-Gen Chris, 48

volleyball: championship, 75

von Hahn, Lt A, *410*

Wakefield Sword (judo award), 118

Walker, Major Mike, 314, 343, *438*; 2010 Haiti earthquake, 316, 336

Wallis, Col/Hon Lt Col Hugh M, 1957 church parade, 51; 1968 reunion dinner, 134, 135; 1972 reunion dinner, 164; 1962 Advisory Board, *262*; 1963 reunion dinner, 91; 1965 church parade and retirement, 94; 1961 reunion dinner, 78; 1964 reunion dinner, 104

Walsh, Brig Geoffrey, 19

Walsh, Piper A, *268*

War Diary (BW): journey to Inchon (15 October 1953 entry), 23; cartoons, 1944 Holland campaign, *444*

War of 1812 (1812–14), 48, 53, 205, 364; Battle of the Châteauguay 150th Anniversary, 362

War of 1812 (honour), 362

Warren, Corporal Jason Patrick, 342–43, 348, 370, *425*

Warren, Gerry, 343

Warsaw Pact (1955), 172, 280

Washington, DC (US), 9, 37, 102, 328

Washington, George, US President 1789–97, 50

Waterloo (Belgium), 186

Waterloo Highlander, The (statuette), 87

Waterloo Trophy (weaponry), 67

Watkins, WO 2/WO 1/Corporal/Sgt/Capt Ivor Eugene ('Junior'), 88, 95–96, 106, 195, *242*

Watling, Major LA, 91, 104, 126

Watson, Lt Col William de Norban, 37, 38, 51–52, 67, *236*; biographical description, 32–36; quoted as epigraph, 35; relinquishment of command, 68; Operation *Spring* anniversary, 135

Watson, RSM A, 14

Waugh, Evelyn, 297

Wavell, Field Marshal Lord, Viceroy of India 1943–47, 7–8, 142, 173

Way Ahead, The (proposal), 207

WEAPONS

aircraft; A10 (air support aircraft), 198; Globemaster (United States Air Force aircraft), 22; Messerschmitt (aircraft), 279; Centennial Tattoo, 124

Armoured Combat Vehicles (ACVs): Coyote and LAV III, 342

Armoured Personnel Carriers (APCs), 131, 172; M113A1, 70; 1st Battalion as APC role, 111; M113, 111, 116, 126, 130–31, 256, *408*; New Broom and Panzer Partners (exercises), 131; performances and demonstrations, 136

Armoured Vehicle General Purpose (AVGP): Grizzly, 182, 186, *408*; exercises, 184

artillery, anti-aircraft, field and anti-tank, anti-aircraft guns, general, 22

17-pounder (17-pdr) (anti-tank gun), 17

50-calibre (machine gun), 25

20-pounder (tank gun), 116

25-pounder (87.6mm) (howitzer) (gun), Lake Superior Regiment (Motor), 19

50-calibre (machine gun), 25

75 mm Recoilless Rifles (RR), 152

105 mm howitzer (Russian) (tank gun), 116

106 mm Recoilless Rifle (RR) (anti-tank gun), 152, 165, 256

Claymore broadsword, 360

Coyote, 342

grenades: FLQ Fusiliers Mont-Royal Armoury raid, 97

helicopters, 129, 200; Kiowa, 113; Voyageur, 113; 438 ETAH (squadron), 293; Chinook, 347, 349; Mi-17, *430*

Humvee, *428*

LAV III, 342

M-181 (APC), 116; M113A1, 70; and BW APC role, 111; course and introduction to, 126; Armed Forces Day infantry parade (1968), 130–31; on manoeuvres, 256; at Camp Valcartier, *408*

missiles, including missile defence, 107, 129: intercontinental, 11; Soviet submarine fleet long-range ballistic, 134; SS-11 ATGMs (anti-tank), 116; anti-tank, general, 256

mortar fire, German, Villa Rogatti, 33; Hitler Line, 33; Ortona, 36

PIAT (Projector, Infantry, Anti-Tank) (anti-tank weapon), obsolete, 17

Recoilless Rifle (RR) (anti-tank gun): 75 mm, 152; 106 mm, 152, 165, 256 rifles and machine guns, 22, 97–98; Bisley rifle competition, 9, 44; 48, 69–70, 106–07, 112, 261, 290; Transvaal Cup (rifle competition), 9; Knockout Cup (rifle competition), 43–44; Hamilton Gault Trophy (rifle shooting), 67, 140, 143, 149, 261; Letson Gold Trophy (rifle championship), 67; Hamilton-Leigh Trophy (rifle shooting), 70; Army Meet (rifle competition), 78; Burns Trophy (rifle shooting), 96; and FLQ armouries raids, 97–98; Dubuc Trophy (training, including musketry), 172, 302–03, 294, 296, *419*–20; General Waters Trophy (rifle shooting), 175; part of Korean War, general, 247, 249; in trophy championship, general, 261; Blank Firing Attachments (BFAs), 313, *408*; part of 1990 Freedom of the City, *409*; part of 150th Anniversary, including commemorative stamp, *419*, *435*; in training, general, *423*, *424*; part of Afghanistan War, general, *426*, *428*, *430*, *433*, 432; in Blitzkrieg and Afrika Korps PSYOPS, *431*–32; in March and Shoot Competition, *436*; cartoons, *444*, *447*–48, *432*–33

Bren LMG (light machine gun), 251; replacement by FN C2, 77–78; Fusiliers Mont-Royal Armoury FLQ raid, 97; competition, 189.

C7 (rifle), 345

Chinese Burp Gun (submachine gun), 26

FN C1 (7.62mm) and C2 Assault Rifles, 78–79, 97–98, *455*, 313; Belgian FN, 116

General Purpose Machine Gun (GPMG) (30-calibre), 152; Korean War, 25; training exercise (1998), 291

Lee Enfield (.303) rifle, 17, 251

Sten (submachine gun), 26

Stirling 1 (9mm) Submachine Gun, 78–79

rocket launchers, 97; 3.5-inch, 17

tanks, , 13–14, 19, 36, 68, 73, 136, 152, 154, 162, 172–73, 182, 256, 315; Soviet, 17

Centurion, 45, 73; tank-guns, 66, 116; trophy model, 116, Mk II, 172–73

Leopard 2A6M CAN, 342, *431*

M1A1/2 Abrams, 279

Tiger I, Ritchie Tiger, 314

SS-11 ATGMs (anti-tank guided missiles), 116

Warner, Derek, *417*

Web Foot (exercise) (1968), 132

Webb, Lt Peter A, *264*

Wegscheider, LTC (111th) Mike, 332, *424*

Weir, Capt Pat, 274

Weir, RSM/Major/Col/Brig James G Buchanan ('Jim'), assumption of BW command, 5; 1968 reunion dinner, 134; 1972 reunion dinner, 164

Welter Open Championship (boxing), 74

West Germany. *See* Germany

West Indies, 148, 179

Western Militia District, 134

Westmount (Quebec), 41, 56, 286, 97; Roslyn School, 56; armouries, 97

Westmount Academy (Westmount High School) (Quebec): graduates, 48, 174–75, 325

Westmount High School. *See* Westmount Academy

whisky, 54, 118; ration, 80; 1963 Trooping the Colour, 91; German, 116; 1969 reunion, 142; 1961 reunion, 78; 1992 Freedom of the City parade, 205–06; 1999 St Jean Baptiste Parade, 295; 150th Anniversary regimental, 327

White, Col, 53

Whitehall, Corporal Allan ('Al'), 160, 198

Whitehall, Ken, *410*

Wigmore, Major John R, 143, 145

Wilgar, Lt SA, *264*

Wilkinson, Corporal William James ('Jim'), *417*, *420–1*

Will ye no come back again (song), 197

Willard, WO David ('Dave'), 301, 326

Williams, WT, 159

Wilson, Barbara, 279

Wilson, Cpl Doug, *255*

Wilson, 2Lt WH, *264*

Wilson, MCpl/Sgt/WO Adam, *268*, 378–79, 380, *421*, *440*, *442*, *458*, *462*

Wilson, Sgt Drum Major Calvin C ('Cal'), *259*, 311

Windsor Park (CFB Halifax) (Nova Scotia), 74

Windsor, Sgt Mel, 170, 172

Winnipeg (Manitoba), 13, 70, 151, 184

Winter Express (NATO exercise) (1964), 110, 113–14, *257*

wireless. *See* radios

Withers, Gen Ramsey, 139

Woensdrecht–Hoogerheide. *See* Hoogerheide–Woensdrecht

Wollen, William Barnes, 119

women in BW: Women's Division, 326, 339; absence at reunion dinners, 59; Women's Auxiliary, 159; Army Cadet League, 160; Summer Student Training Programme, 161; Percival as first woman officer, 171; Golan Heights female detachment, 171; Betty Ann Jones (Malashenko) as second woman officer, 177, 192, *431*; importance to efficiency, 181; at 1985 Queen Mother parade, 187; Canadian Women's Army Corps, 191; Sutcliffe as first BW woman infantry soldier, 191, 192, *431*; expansion since First World War, 191–92; Combat Related Employment of Women, 192; 1987 Queen Mother parade complaint, 192; uniforms, 192–93, 202; Leger in 1987 Trooping the Colour, 195; Carolyn McLeod as first piper, 276; advantages in Afghanistan, 350

Women's Auxiliary, 159

Women's Division, 326, 339

Wood, Lt William McKenzie, 328

Wood, Lt Col William Archibald, Jr ('Billy'), 51–52, 62, *237*, *262*, 288

Wood, Sgt W, *421*

Wooten, WO1 GW, 80, *263*
World Scottish Festival (Quebec) (1992), 204–06; Tartan Ball, 206
World's Fairs: Seattle (1962), 82, 86, 124, 148; New York (1964–65), 96, 148; *Hemisfair '68* (San Antonio), 106. *See also Expo 67*
Worthington Trophy (rifle shooting), 171
Worthington, Major Gen Frederick Franklin ('Fearless Frank') ('Worthy'), biographical description, 101–02; death, 130
Wycliffe Hall (Oxford University) (UK), 203
Wyoming Line (Korean War), 25

Yeltneb (donkey mascot), 144, *258*
Young, Cpl/WO/CSM Gary Wayne Patrick, 100, 176, 187, 312
Young, Sgt Hal, 20–21
Young, WO, 176
Young, WO/Brig HA, 205
Youngest Grandfather Present (gathering prize), 101
Ypres Day Parade (Quebec), 1967, 106; 1999, 295–96
Yugoslavia, former. *See* Bosnian Conflict

'Zhari-Panjwai'I' (honour), 350
Zorba the Greek (tune), 123